Contents

Section 3 *Glasgow*

Scot land the Best

PETER IRVINE

Collins

HarperCollins Publishers
77-85 Fulham Palace Road
London W6 8JB

www.collins.co.uk

Collins is a registered trademark of
HarperCollins Publishers Ltd.

Text © Pete Irvine 2009
Maps © Collins Bartholomew Ltd 2009

Pete Irvine asserts his moral right to be identified as the author of this work

12 11 10

10 9 8 7 6 5 4 3 2 1

First published in Great Britain in 1993 by Mainstream Publishing Company (Edinburgh) Ltd

First published by HarperCollins Publishers in 1997

This edition published in 2009

A catalogue record for this book is available from the British Library.

ISBN-13 978 000 731965-7

Collins uses papers that are natural, renewable and recyclable products made from wood grown in sustainable forests. The manufacturing processes conform to the environmental regulations of the country of origin.

Produced by **The Printer's Devil, Glasgow**

Printed in Germany by Bercker

Section 4   *Regional Hotels & Restaurants*

Section 5 *Particular Places to Eat and Stay in Scotland*

Section 6 *Good Food & Drink*

Section 7 *Outdoor Places*

Section 8   *Historical Places*

Section 9   *Strolls, Walks and Hikes*

Section 10   *Outdoor Activities*

Introduction

I can't believe I've finished it again, never mind that this is the 10th edition of *Scotland the Best*. It's published every two years (though it was consecutive in the first three) so this 10th edition happily falls in 2010. To mark the event, there's a new section, 'My Top 10 for 2010', and a new email address so you can contact me directly (see below).

Ten editions is a fair length of time to observe and record both the changes in the Scotland that we live in and the experience we offer visitors. Most things have improved immeasurably (although we won't talk about the traffic). Where once good food was a rarity outside the city, there has been a marked proliferation in restaurants and hotels that are worth recommending at all levels. Once again, I like to think I've found them all. Everything from fish and chips to twee tearooms have come a long way from the days of lard and boiled-ham sandwiches. And though in Scotland we debate this endlessly, we have moved on from the less-than-welcoming, 'you'll have had your tea' attitude that once prevailed. Having covered the country from the far north beaches to the Solway coast, I honestly believe that Scotland, as in so many things, punches well above its weight. When it comes to accessible opening hours, local sourcing of ingredients and creative home cookery, we do excel.

Since the first edition I've tried to convey the many ways of appreciating a landscape: looking at it, driving through it, walking, swimming outdoors, watching birds, wild camping. In many ways, Scotland has led the way in the development of eco-tourism from those very first days when ospreys appeared at Loch Garten in 1954. Now there are more ways than ever of enjoying the outdoors. These categories, like all the others, have been updated for this edition.

New readers should know that this is not a book about all the options – it only registers and commends the best of what there is. We don't venture into the mediocre even if that's all there is. Yet no matter how I strive to raise the bar in each edition, there is more rather than less that demands to be included. I try to be completely comprehensive and embrace and include anywhere that deserves recognition. But the book is big enough already and it's supposed to be something that you can carry easily with you in your car or in your backpack so in this edition I've removed a couple of categories that I think people don't use as much.

Clearly more and more people get the information they need from the internet and their mobile phone. I don't think (and I hope I'm right) that this makes a guidebook like this redundant. Indeed, it complements all the other forms of instant information; it is a complete and personal guide. However, it is time to allow a more direct communication with readers who want to offer feedback so there's now an email address to write to and I hope you'll use it. From the volume of old-fashioned letters that I currently get, I know this will unleash a deluge of responses from people who like a particular place and think I should know about it or have had a rubbish dinner at somewhere I've recommended and want to complain. That will be great but please don't expect me to reply to all. Everything will be logged and checked and in two year's time I will be going everywhere in Scotland again armed with all your information.

In the meantime, if you're a new reader, thanks for joining us; and to the hundreds and thousands of others, thanks for coming back. We travel together. Enjoy this Scotland in a new decade.

Pete Irvine
Edinburgh
December 2009

stb@lumison.co.uk

How To Use This Book

There are three ways to find things in this book:

1. There's an index at the back.
2. The book can be used by category, e.g. you can look up the best restaurants in the Borders or the best scenic routes in the whole of Scotland. Each entry has an item number in the outside margin. These are in numerical order and allow easy cross-referencing.
3. You can start with the maps and see how individual items are located, how they are grouped together and how much there is that's worth seeing or doing in any particular area. Then just look up the item numbers. If you are travelling around Scotland, I would urge you to use the maps and this method of finding the best of what an area or town has to offer.

Top tip: as a general guide and when searching by using the maps, items numbered below 1500 generally refer to places to eat and stay.

All items have a code which gives (1) the specific item number; (2) the map on which it can be found; and (3) the map co-ordinates. For space reasons, items in Glasgow and Edinburgh are not marked on Maps 1 and 2, although they do have co-ordinates in the margin to give you a rough idea of location. A typical entry is shown below, identifying the various elements that make it up:

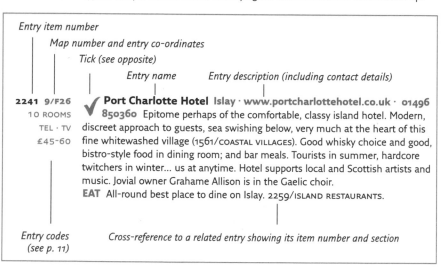

Entry item number

  Map number and entry co-ordinates

    Tick (see opposite)

      Entry name   *Entry description (including contact details)*

2241 9/F26 ✓ **Port Charlotte Hotel** Islay · www.portcharlottehotel.co.uk · 01496
10 ROOMS   850360 Epitome perhaps of the comfortable, classy island hotel. Modern,
TEL · TV   discreet approach to guests, sea swishing below, very much at the heart of this
£45-60   fine whitewashed village (1561/COASTAL VILLAGES). Good whisky choice and good,
         bistro-style food in dining room; and bar meals. Tourists in summer, hardcore
         twitchers in winter... us at anytime. Hotel supports local and Scottish artists and
         music. Jovial owner Grahame Allison is in the Gaelic choir.
         EAT All-round best place to dine on Islay. 2259/ISLAND RESTAURANTS.

Entry codes   *Cross-reference to a related entry showing its item number and section*
(see p. 11)

A Note On Categories

Edinburgh and Glasgow, the destinations of most visitors and the nearest cities to more than half of the population, are covered in the substantial Sections 2 and 3. You will probably need a city map to get around, although Maps 1 and 2 should give you the rough layout.

For the purposes of maps, and particularly in Section 4 (Regional Hotels & Restaurants), I have used a combination of the subdivision of Scotland based on current standard political regions and on historical ones, eg Argyll, Clyde Valley. Section 4 is meant to give a comprehensive and concise guide to the best of the major Scottish towns in each area. Some recommended hotels and restaurants will be amongst the best in the region (or even amongst the best in Scotland) and have been selected because they are the best there is in the town or the immediate area.

From Sections 5 to 11, the categories are based on activities, interests and geography and are Scotland-wide. Section 12 covers the islands, with a page-by-page guide to the larger ones.

There are some categories like Bed and Breakfasts, Fishing Beats, Antique Shops that haven't been included because at TGP (time of going to press) they are impracticable to assess (there are too many of them, are too small, etc). However, if there are categories that you would like to see in future editions, please let us know at **stb@lumison.co.uk** (see p. 431).

Ticks For The Best There Is

Although everything listed in the book is notable and remarkable in some way, there are places that are outstanding even in this superlative company. Instead of marking them with a rosette or a star, they have been 'awarded' a tick.

 Amongst the very best in Scotland

 Amongst the best (of its type) in the UK

 A particular commendation for Andrew Fairlie and Martin Wishart, acknowledged as two of the top chefs in Scotland and the UK

Amongst the best (of its type) in the world, or simply unique

Listings generally are not in an order of merit although if there is one outstanding item it will always be at the top of the page and this obviously includes anything which has been given a tick. Hotels and restaurants are also grouped according to price and this is why a cross-marked place may appear further down the page (ticks also indicate exceptional value for money).

The Codes

1. The Item Code
At the left-hand margin of every item is a code which will enable you to find it on a map. Thus **2389 9/F26** should be read as follows: **2389** is the item number, listed in simple consecutive order; **9** identifies the particular map at the back of the book; **F26** is the map co-ordinate, to help pinpoint the item's location on the map grid. A co-ordinate such as **xA5** indicates that the item can be reached by leaving the map at grid reference **A5**.

2. The Accommodation Code
Beside each recommended accommodation or property is a series of codes as follows:

16 ROOMS	NO KIDS
MAR-DEC	NO PETS
TEL · TV	ECO
NO C/CARDS	GF
DA	HS/NTS
ATMOS	£45-60
☕	

ROOMS indicates the number of bedrooms in total. No differentiation is made as to the type of room. Most hotels will offer twin rooms as singles or put extra beds in doubles if required.
MAR-DEC shows when the accommodation is open. No dates means it is open all year.
TEL · TV refers to the facilities: **TEL** means there are direct-dial phones in the bedrooms while **TV** means there are TVs in the bedrooms.

NO C/CARDS means the establishment does not accept credit cards.
DA denotes a place that accepts dogs, although often with conditions. Check in advance.
ATMOS indicates a place whose special atmosphere is an attraction in itself.
NO KIDS does not necessarily mean children are unwelcome, only that special provisions are not usually made; ask in advance. In other cases, children are welcome, often with special rates.
NO PETS indicates that the hotel does not generally accept pets.
ECO denotes a place with an active 'green' agenda (eg, energy-saving policies, organic food).
GF denotes a place that has no issue with gay clients and their partners.
HS or **NTS** denotes a place in the care of Historic Scotland or the National Trust for Scotland.
⌣ indicates a property with an exceptional tearoom.
£45-60 indicates the price band of the accommodation, based on per person per night. They are worked out by halving the published average rate for a twin room in high season and should be used only to give an impression of cost. They are based on 2009 prices. Add between £2 to £5 per year, though the band should stay the same unless the hotel undergoes improvements.

3. The Dining Codes

The price code marked against eateries refers to the price of an average dinner per person with a starter, a main course and dessert. It doesn't include wine, coffee or extras. Prices are based on 2009 rates. Where a hotel is notable also for its restaurant, this is identified by **EAT** on a separate line below the main accommodation description, with details following.

LO means last orders at the kitchen. Some close earlier if they are quiet and go later on request.

10pm/10.30pm means usually 10pm Mon-Fri, 10.30pm at weekends. It is very common, especially for city restaurants, to open later at weekends, particularly in Edinburgh during the Festival (Aug).

4. The Walk Code

Beside each of the many walks in the book is a series of codes as follows:

3-10KM   BIKES/ XBIKES/ MTBIKES
CIRC/ XCIRC   1-A-1

3-10KM means the walk(s) described may vary in length between the distances shown.
CIRC means the walk can be circular, while **XCIRC** shows the walk is not circular and you must return more or less the way you came.
BIKES indicates the walk has a path which is suitable for ordinary bikes. **XBIKES** means the walk is not suitable for, or does not permit, cycling. **MTBIKES** means the track is suitable for mountain or all-terrain bikes.

The **1-A-1** Code:
First number (**1, 2** or **3**) indicates how easy the walk is.
1 the walk is easy.
2 medium difficulty, eg standard hillwalking, not dangerous nor requiring special knowledge or equipment.
3 difficult: care and preparation and a map are needed.
The letters (**A, B** or **C**) indicate how easy it is to find the path.
A the route is easy to find. The way is either marked or otherwise obvious.
B the route is not very obvious, but you'll get there.
C you will need a map and preparation or a guide.
The last number (**1, 2** or **3**) indicates what to wear on your feet.
1 ordinary outdoor shoes, including trainers, are probably okay unless the ground is very wet.
2 you will need walking boots.
3 you will need serious walking or hiking boots.
Apart from designated walks, the 1-A-1 code is employed wherever there is more than a short stroll required to get to somewhere, eg a waterfall or a monument.

My Top 10 For 2010

A special selection of
top places for the 10th edition of
Scotland the Best

scotland the best

Top 10 Edinburgh Restaurants

1 Martin Wishart 123/FINE DINING One of only 2 restaurants with more than 2 ticks in *StB*. Coz it's the best. Handily, a stone's throw from my office in Leith.

2 Number 1 Princes Street 124/FINE DINING Here No. 1 is not just an address. It is dear but damned fine.

3 Urban Angel 136/BISTROS Two easy-to-love café/bistros in the city centre. Manage to be both urban in atmos and angelic in their approach to food.

4 Amore Dogs 179/ITALIAN RESTAURANTS The Italian version of the expanding litter of 'Dogs' diners. Great value and noise.

5 Redwood 143/BISTROS Fresh from California in old St Stephen Street where they still remember the Grateful Dead. Sunny, simple, light food. Scottish ingredients; pacific time.

6 Iris 145/BISTROS The 2010 secret spot in midtown. Iris just lowers her eyes when we say we adore to dine with her.

7 La Cucina 180/ITALIAN RESTAURANTS Bold and brash Missoni style, the rock 'n' roll ristorante at the tacky end of the Royal Mile. Perfect if pricey pasta.

8 Tail End 216/FISH & CHIPS The mid-Leith Walk caff and takeaway with the lighter, fresher touch. You wait but you want to.

9 Café Marlayne 168/FRENCH RESTAURANTS In a city with more French restaurants than any other in the UK, this tiny bistro is simply *sans pareil*.

10 Loopy Lorna's 275/TEAROOMS Taking the tearoom into a new realm in the Miss Jean Brodie end of town, LL gets a VG++ from me

Top 10 Glasgow Restaurants

1 Ubiquitous Chip 489/FINE DINING The longest-established restaurant on this page by a margin. As Glasgow's bastion of fine dining, the UC would be on anybody's top 10 list.

2 Martin Wishart at Cameron House 491/FINE DINING Edinburgh's top and Michelin chef overseeing the elegant serene dining room of De Vere's remodeled Cameron House on Loch Lomond, outside the city.

3 Bistro Du Vin 490/FINE DINING Compared to 'The Chip' this is a recent arrival, replacing previous restaurants in Glasgow's original boutique hotel. Effortlessly stylish.

4 Cafézique 497/BISTROS Neighbourhood café/bistro that's the offshoot of the West End's most simpatico deli. Casual meet-and-eat doesn't come cooler than this.

5 Guy's 498/BISTROS Underestimated and my favourite Merchant City caff for eclectic eats. Lengthy menu; all good.

6 La Vallée Blanche 540/FRENCH RESTAURANTS Heart of Byres Road area, an upstairs room with great atmosphere and French flair.

7 The Two Figs 503/BISTROS New fig on the Byres Road block where there are many food-stops to choose from. Casual, contemporary caff and bistro; born to be loved.

8 Stravaigin 518/GASTROPUBS All Stravaigins are tops but the street-level pub above the main restaurant excels for gastrogrub value and vibe.

9 City Merchant 542/SCOTTISH RESTAURANTS The defining Merchant City restaurant. Family-run, sound Scottish sourcing; totally reliable. Best choice near George Square.

10 Crabshakk 588/SEAFOOD RESTAURANTS The seafood shack that arrived in Glasgow's emerging foodie district west of west to immediate acclaim. And mine. Kill for a table!

Top 10 Individual Hotels With Great Service

1 **Prestonfield, Edinburgh** 82/EDINBURGH BOUTIQUE HOTELS The only 3-tick hotel in *StB* (apart from Gleneagles, the resort) because there's simply nothing like it anywhere.

2 **The Bonham, Edinburgh** 87/EDINBURGH BOUTIQUE HOTELS Discreet boutique town-house hotel so perfectly West End. Service attentive but unobtrusive. Smart dining.

3 **Airds, Port Appin** 744/ARGYLL HOTELS Landmark hotel in the north, the epitome of hushed hospitality. Top service and beautiful food at your table with the view.

4 **Glenapp Castle, Girvan** 1117/COUNTRY-HOUSE HOTELS No corporate in sight in this lavishly serviced, highly individual hotel where there are as many gardeners as chefs.

5 **Knockinaam, Portpatrick** 780/SOUTH WEST HOTELS A faraway country house by the sea where service is as good as a London luvvy hotel but much friendlier. Dinner a highpoint.

6 **Monachyle Mhor, Balquhidder** 1181/GET-AWAY HOTELS Sex and the countryside!

7 **Ardeonaig, Loch Tay** 877/PERTHSHIRE HOTELS Half way along the busy road to nowhere, this country inn combines rustic charm with safari-lodge chic.

8 **Boath House, Nairn** 991/HIGHLAND HOTELS Small, beautiful; elegance abounding. Dinner is perfectly pitched. The polar opposite of any hotel in Dubai.

9 **Rocpool Reserve, Inverness** 993/HIGHLAND HOTELS 'Boutique' is exactly the right word to describe this modern, sexy townhouse hotel. And discounted Albert Roux.

10 **The House Over-By, Skye** 1161/ROADSIDE INNS The Spiers spearheaded contemporary rooms in the Highlands. Their Three Chimneys still raises the roof.

Top 10 Best-Value Hotels

1 **10 Hill Place, Edinburgh** 95/EDINBURGH BOUTIQUE HOTELS Not found in the style guides but this cool hotel on a quiet square by the university is a real find for you.

2 **Six St Mary's Place, Edinburgh** 101/EDINBURGH LODGINGS Friendly, 'ethical' B&B in boho Stockbridge. No frills but refreshingly realistic rates.

3 **George Hotel, Inverary** 747/ARGYLL HOTELS Old, family-run. Rooms quite chic; atmos-pheric bar, famous for food – all at no'-bad prices.

4 **Ship Inn, Gatehouse of Fleet** 782/SOUTH WEST HOTELS Renovated pub with rooms in charming GoF. Great base for Galloway gallivantings.

5 **Royal Hotel, Comrie** 881/PERTHSHIRE HOTELS Town hotel of canny wee Comrie in the best bit of Perthshire for walk 'n' thought. Stylish. Good food; local bar.

6 **Craigatin House, Pitlochry** 882/PERTHSHIRE HOTELS Contemporary and comfy guest house at end of the strip in this tourist town. *Muy ambiente.*

7 **Fortingall House, Aberfeldy** 886/PERTHSHIRE HOTELS Country-estate hospitality and style near one of Scotland's grandest glens.

8 **Lovat Arms, Fort Augustus** 1014/HIGHLAND HOTELS Family-run contemporary hotel at foot of Loch Ness. Tourists go past – you should linger.

9 **The Globe Inn, Aberdeen** 952/ABERDEEN HOTELS Inexpensive, pleasant rooms above a great pub in a city centre where deals are few.

10 **Glenfinnan House** 1226/SCOTTISH HOTELS Highland atmosphere, friendly people, a country house on Loch Shiel: the real hospitality.

Top 10 Pubs With ATMOS

1 Drover's Inn, Inverarnan   1264/BLOODY GOOD PUBS   The classic roadside hostelry seems unchanged since 1705 – dark, firelit, raucous: real.

2 Castlebay Hotel Bar, Barra   1268/BLOODY GOOD PUBS   Overlooking the said castle and bay. Great craic for islanders and visitors alike.

3 The Mishnish, Mull   1265/BLOODY GOOD PUBS   Legendary Tobermory quayside bar in same family forever. All things to a' folks. Drink the atmos.

4 The Ceilidh Place, Ullapool   1009/HIGHLAND HOTELS   One of the most sociable, creative and life-affirming, all-purpose places in these Highlands.

5 Clachaig Inn, Glencoe   1267/BLOODY GOOD PUBS   Deep in the glen, the definitive after-the-hill spot to descend on: crowded, universal, vital.

6 The Ship Inn, Elie   1293/GASTROPUBS   Great for grub but much more. Hub of the village with outside terrace on tranquil Elie beach and lagoon.

7 Scotia Bar, Glasgow   652/UNIQUE PUBS   Intimate, historic, city-centre pub, a den of drinking, music, craic and culture since yon times.

8 Òran Mór, Glasgow   647/UNIQUE PUBS   Converted church on a prominent corner of the West End; pubs/theatre/club/bistros, all celebrating Glasgow life.

9 Café Royal, Edinburgh   336/UNIQUE PUBS   Classic, lofty, Victorian watering hole and oyster bar; atmos built in with the mirrors and tiles.

10 Port o' Leith, Edinburgh   332/UNIQUE PUBS   Created in recent memory by one Mary Moriarty; the epitome of a worldly yet neighbourhood tavern.

Top 10 Best-Value Restaurants

1 Sangster's, Elie   871/FIFE RESTAURANTS   Michelin chef Bruce Sangster's bijou bistro is top value for this standard of cuisine.

2 Braidwoods, Dalry   775/AYRSHIRE RESTAURANTS   For a long time the rural fine-dining (without the fuss or cost) choice in the South West.

3 The Plumed Horse, Edinburgh   126/EDINBURGH FINE DINING   Michelin-starred and inspired cooking that's great value in a tucked-away Leith bistro.

4 Chez Pierre, Edinburgh   173/EDINBURGH FRENCH RESTAURANTS   Exceptional value, the back-to-basics creation of serial restauranteur Pierre Levicky.

5 Eat on the Green, Udny Green   945/NORTH EAST RESTAURANTS   Small rooms in small village but big value for the best cooking in a big county.

6 The Glass House, Grantown   1039/HIGHLAND RESTAURANTS   The only top place to eat in this bit of Speyside is also a steal of a meal.

7 Russell's, Spean Bridge   1046/HIGHLAND RESTAURANTS   Wide-ranging, accessible menu and a bill that goes with it on the road to the west.

8 Carron Restaurant, Strathcarron   1036/HIGHLAND RESTAURANTS   Long in the family: conscientious cooking in a roadside caff that you should make the journey for.

9 Osso, Peebles   830/BORDERS RESTAURANTS   Changing menus all day but great pricing throughout in loveable main street bistro.

10 The But 'n' Ben, Auchmithie   902/PERTHSHIRE RESTAURANTS   Cottage-on-the-coast tearoom and bistro and legendary destination for aeons.

Top 10 Romantic Hideaways

1 The Howard, Edinburgh   86/EDINBURGH BOUTIQUE HOTELS   Central *gentil* Georgian townhouse hotel; the epitome of understated elegance.

2 Inner Sanctum, Edinburgh   97/EDINBURGH MOST EXCELLENT LODGINGS   The heart of the Old Town. Deliciously decadent for both dirty and purifying weekends.

3 Crinan Hotel, Crinan   745/ARGYLL HOTELS   Divine spot at the end of the Crinan road and canal. Sunset dinner doesn't get more romantic than this.

4 Roman Camp, Callander   800/CENTRAL HOTELS   Behind busy main street, another world. You are enveloped in good taste and atmosphere.

5 Monachyle Mhor, Balquhidder   799/CENTRAL HOTELS   Top boutique hotel far away above the loch but only a short drive from the traffic of life.

6 Lake Hotel, Port of Menteith   803/CENTRAL HOTELS   A placid place in the heart of the Trossachs, Scotland's most romantic landscape. Walk or just gaze across the water.

7 Ardeonaig, Loch Tay   877/PERTHSHIRE HOTELS   Road and lochside inn now the apogee of a retreat with comfort, style and service.

8 Dalmunzie House, Spittal o' Glenshee   883/PERTHSHIRE HOTELS   Funky, inexpensive country-house hotel at the end of a Grampian glen.

9 Ardanaiseig, Loch Awe   1121/COUNTRY-HOUSE HOTELS   End of the road – a remote corner of the noble loch: house with antiques and glorious grounds.

10 Eilean Iarmain, Skye   1225/SCOTTISH HOTELS   Quintessential is a long and oft-used word in this book; this is quintessentially the quintessential island inn.

Top 10 Places For Contemplation

1 Pluscarden Abbey, Elgin   1888/ABBEYS, 1229/RETREATS   Medieval Benedictine monastery in inspiring spot. You can stay or simply attend their many services.

2 Angus's Garden, Taynuilt   1516/GARDENS   Extensive, partly wild private garden around a loch in memory of a lost son. A calm contemplative corner of Argyll.

3 Loch an Eilean, Rothiemurchus   1617/LOCHS   Perfect Highland loch. By no means a secret but large enough in circumference for meditative meanderings.

4 Iona Abbey   1887/ABBEYS   The ancient cradle of Christianity on tiny Iona where it is always mild. An active community but built for personal enlightenments.

5 Jura House Gardens, Jura   1511/GARDENS   Amongst the many gardens in Scotland, this is so remote you may have it to yourself; an island on an island of perfect tranquillity.

6 Graveyards in Edinburgh   1876/GRAVEYARDS   There are many and not just in the Old Town where one can wander and ponder on the history of an ancient influential city.

7 The Angus Glens   1594/GLENS   There are three, all with different characters but easy to find yourself in. Strolls, hikes and views aplenty. A civilised back-of-beyond.

8 Castle Tioram & Ardnamurchan   1783/RUINS   The enigmatic ruin in a dreamy spot but the whole of this peninsula, from bare hills to ancient woodlands, is balm for the soul.

9 The Brown and White Caterhuns, Edzell   1810/PREHISTORIC SITES   Iron Age remains on hillocks that look into prehistory and the Highlands where one can sense our place in it all.

10 The Commando Monument, Spean Bridge   1845/MONUMENTS   A prominent and much-visited crossroads. Consider the nobility and the sacrifice of a soldier's life in all wars.

Top 10 Away Days With Kids

1 **Crieff Hydro** 1122/KIDS' HOTELS Scotland's favourite family hotel resort where everyone can play. Prodigious menu of distractions.

2 **Calgary Farmhouse Hotel, Mull** 1129/KIDS' HOTELS Laid-back hotel/gallery/bistro in rare woods with art/adventure trail.

3 **Drumlanrig, Thornhill** 1533/COUNTRY PARKS House with art and courtyard of things but also huge grounds to explore, especially by bike.

4 **Cromarty, Black Isle** 1558/COASTAL VILLAGES Seaside village perfect for kids with walks and caffs and usually dolphins.

5 **Auchrannie, Arran** 1123/KIDS' HOTELS Extensive hotel annex built for families for day or stay. Pools and ploys and outdoors, there's Arran.

6 **Falls of Bruar, Blair Atholl** 1602/WATERFALLS Waterfall and woodland walks away from the supershop emporium on the A9. Relief from retail.

7 **Edinburgh Zoo, Edinburgh** 1691/KIDS Your kids and their animals staring at each other in wonder... A world-class family attraction.

8 **Cream o' Galloway, Rainton** 1703/KIDS An eco-activity-and-adventure park based on the irresistible allure of their ice cream.

9 **Kelburn, Largs** 1696/KIDS Attraction-stuffed grounds of mansion near Largs; Millport and Cumbrae a wee ferry away. Nardini's ice cream on the way home

10 **Loch Insh, Kincraig** 1718/KIDS Lochside centre (stay or visit) in scenic Rothiemurchus with range of cool activities on and off water.

Top 10 Romantic & Bittersweet Scotland

1 **Glencoe** 1627/ROUTES Few roads anywhere are as dramatic as the A82 through the most impressive of glens: history and geography, the ridge and the mountains.

2 **Rosslyn Chapel, Roslin** 1853/CHURCHES A church so steeped in human mystery and romance that it can be hard to even think of God.

3 **Dryburgh Abbey** 1891/ABBEYS Of all the Border abbeys with their history of glory and gore, this remains in its stones and situation the epitome of romance.

4 **Culloden** 1895/BATTLES A battleground and story veiled in tears powerfully demonstrates the enduring fascination of that doomed cause.

5 **Kildrummy Castle, Alford** 1785/RUINS The most evocative of Highland castle ruins with a gorgeful of gardens besides.

6 **The Italian Chapel, Orkney** 1855/CHURCHES Hard to leave without a tear in the eye. A touching statement of faith made so far from home.

7 **Dunvegan Castle, Skye** 1771/CASTLES The location, the Fairy Flag and the gardens to the mystic shore all combine to fuel our romantic imagination.

8 **Grave of Flora Macdonald, Skye** 1837/MONUMENTS Scotland's most romantic heroine whose mass funeral here showed she was a Di of her day.

9 **Balquhidder Churchyard** 1884/GRAVEYARDS Not just Rob Roy's grave but the whole setting and the viewpoint above suffuse you with Scottishness.

10 **The Road to the Isles** 1641/ROUTES The A830 between Glenfinnan and Mallaig takes you through the magnificent heart of Bonnie Prince Charlie country.

Section 1

Wha's Like Us?

Famously Big Attractions

Among the 'top 10' (paid admission) and the 'top 10' (free) visitor attractions, these are the ones *really worth seeing*. Find them under their item numbers.

Edinburgh Castle; **Holyrood Palace**; **Edinburgh Zoo**; **The National Gallery**; **Our Dynamic Earth** 397/400/399/406/405/MAIN ATTRACTIONS.
The People's Palace, Glasgow; **The Burrell Collection**; **Kelvingrove** 688/686/685/MAIN ATTRACTIONS.
The Museum of Transport; **The Glasgow Botanic Gardens**; **The Gallery of Modern Art** 692/693/694/OTHER ATTRACTIONS.
The Edinburgh Botanics 410/OTHER ATTRACTIONS.
Culzean Castle; **Stirling Castle**; **Castle of Mey** 1762/1759/1764/BEST CASTLES.
Mount Stuart; **Manderston** 1823/1824/COUNTRY HOUSES.
Skara Brae; **The Callanish Stones** 1800/1802/PREHISTORIC SITES.
Rosslyn Chapel 1853/CHURCHES.

OTHER UNMISSABLES ARE:

1 9/L25 ✓ ✓ ✓ **Loch Lomond** Approach via Stirling and A811 to Drymen or from Glasgow, the A82 Dumbarton road to Balloch. Britain's largest inland waterway and a traditional playground, especially for Glaswegians; jet-skis, show-off boats. **Lomond Shores** at Balloch is the heavily retail gateway to the loch (including Jenners) and the **Loch Lomond National Park** which covers a vast area. Orientate and shop here.

The west bank between Balloch and Tarbert is most developed: marinas, cruises, ferry to Inchmurrin Island. Luss is tweeville, like a movie set (it was used in the Scottish TV soap, *High Road*) but has an OK tearoom (1401/TEAROOMS). The road is more picturesque beyond Tarbert to Ardlui; see 1264/BLOODY GOOD PUBS for the non-tourist/real Scots experience of the Drover's Inn at Inverarnan.

The east is more natural, wooded; good lochside and hill walks (1960/MUNROS). The road is winding but picturesque beyond Balmaha towards Ben Lomond. Hire a rowboat at Balmaha to Inchcailloch Island: lovely woodland walks (2010/WALKS).

2 7/G19 ✓ ✓ ✓ **The Cuillin Mountains** Skye This hugely impressive east range in the south of Skye, often shrouded in cloud or rain, is the romantic heartland of the Islands and was 'sold' in 2003 to a combination of public agencies so... it's ours now! The Red Cuillin are smoother and nearer the Portree-Broadford road; the Black Cuillin gather behind and are best approached from Glen Brittle (1979/SERIOUS WALKS; 1605/WATERFALLS). This classic, untameable mountain scenery has attracted walkers, climbers and artists for centuries. It still claims lives regularly. For best views apart from Glen Brittle, see 1634/SCENIC ROUTES; 1654/VIEWS. Vast range of walks and scrambles (see also 1669/PICNICS).

3 7/M18 ✓ ✓ ✓ **Loch Ness** Most visits start from Inverness at the north end via the River Ness. Fort Augustus is at the other end, 56km to the south. Loch Ness is part of the still-navigable Caledonian Canal linking to the west coast at Fort William. Many small boats line the shores of the River Ness; one of the best ways to see the loch is on a cruise from Inverness (Jacobite Cruises 01463 233999 1-6 hours, several options). Other cruise operators from Fort Augustus (01320 366277) and the small, friendly Nessie Hunter from Drumnadrochit (01456 450395). Most tourist traffic uses the main A82 north bank road converging on Drumnadrochit where the Loch Ness Monster industry gobbles up your money. If you must, the 'official' Loch Ness Monster Exhibition is the one to choose. On the A82 you can't miss Urquhart Castle (1797/RUINS). But the two best things about

Loch Ness are: the south road (B862) from Fort Augustus back to Inverness (1639/SCENIC ROUTES; 1614/WATERFALLS); and the detour from Drumnadrochit to Cannich to Glen Affric (20-30km) (1589/GLENS; 1986/GLEN & RIVER WALKS; 1601/WATERFALLS). Best bet to eat (and stay) is the Loch Ness Inn at Drumnadrochit (1016/HIGHLAND HOTELS).

4 10/N25 ✓✓ **Falkirk Wheel** 08700 500 208 · **Falkirk** Tamfourhill, half-way between Edinburgh and Glasgow, signed from the M9, M80 and locally. The splendid and deliberately dramatic massive boat-lift at the convergence of the (Millennium-funded) reinstated Union and Forth & Clyde canals – the world's first coast-to-coast ship canal (to wander or plooter along). The 35-metre lift is impressive to watch and great to go on. Boats leave the Visitor Centre every 30 minutes for the 45-minute journey. Great network of paths to walk and cycle from here.

Favourite Scottish Journeys

5 9/K25 **Wemyss Bay-Rothesay Ferry** www.calmac.co.uk · 01475 650100 The glass-roofed station at Wemyss Bay, the railhead from Glasgow (60km by road on the A78), is redolent of an age-old terminus. The frequent (CalMac) ferry has all the Scottish traits and treats you can handle, and Rothesay (with its period seaside mansions) appears out of blood-smeared sunsets and rain-sodden mornings alike, a gentle watercolour from summer holidays past. Visit the (Victorian) toilet when you get there and Mount Stuart (1911/HOUSES) on beautiful Bute.

6 9/J22 **Loch Etive Cruises** 01866 822430 From Taynuilt (Oban 20km) through the long narrow waters of one of Scotland's most atmospheric lochs, 2- or 3-hour journeys in a small cruiser with indoor and outdoor seating. The pier is 2km from main Taynuilt crossroads on the A85. Easter-mid Oct. Leaves 12noon and 2pm (not Sat). Booking not essential. Also **Loch Shiel Cruises, 01687 470322**. From near Glenfinnan House Hotel (1226/SCOTTISH HOTELS) on the Road to the Isles, A830. A 1-2-stop cruise on glorious Loch Shiel. Various trips available Easter-Oct.

7 7/H19 **Glenelg-Kylerhea** www.skyeferry.co.uk · 01599 522273 The shorter of the 2 remaining ferry journeys to Skye and definitely the best way to get there if you're not pushed for time. The drive to Glenelg from the A87 is spectacular (1628/SCENIC ROUTES) and so is this 5-minute crossing of the deep Narrows of Kylerhea. Apr-Oct (frequent) 9am-6pm (7pm in summer) and Sun in summer (9am-6pm). The ferry is run by and very much a part of the local community around Glenelg. Cute wee shack to visit before departure. The ferry is worth supporting. There's an otter-watch hide at Kylerhea.

8 9/J21 **Corran Ferry** 01855 841243 Runs from Ardgour on A861 to Nether Lochaber on the A82 across the narrows of Loch Linnhe. A convenient 5-minute crossing which can save time to points south of Mallaig and takes you to the wildernesses of Moidart and Ardnamurchan. A charming and fondly regarded journey in its own right. New people '09 likely to improve the Corran Inn. Runs continuously till 8.50pm in summer, 9.30pm in winter.

9 10/P25 **The Maid of the Forth Cruise to Inchcolm Island** 0131 331 4857 The wee boat (though they say it holds 225 people) which leaves every day at different times (phone for details) from Hawes Pier in South Queensferry (15km Central Edinburgh via A90) opposite the Hawes Inn, just under the famous railway bridge (398/MAIN ATTRACTIONS). 45-minute trips under the bridge and on to Inchcolm, an attractive island with walks and an impressive ruined abbey. Much birdlife and also many seals to be seen. 1 hour 30 minutes ashore. Tickets at pier. Mar-Oct.

10 2   The *Waverley* 0845 130 4647   See the Clyde, see the world! It's a party. Jul/Aug and other times. Report: 701/OTHER GLASGOW ATTRACTIONS.

11 9/J21   The West Highland Line 08457 484950   One of the most picturesque railway journeys in Europe and quite the best way to get to Skye from the south. Travel to Fort William from Glasgow, then relax and watch the stunning scenery, the Bonnie Prince Charlie country (MARY, CHARLIE & BOB, p. 331) and much that is close to a railwayman's heart go past the window. Viaducts (including the Harry Potter one) and tunnels over loch and down dale. It's also possible to make the same journey (from Fort William to Mallaig and/or return) by steam train from mid May to mid Oct (details 01524 737751). There's a museum in the restored station at Glenfinnan with a tearoom and bunk accommodation. Trains for Mallaig leave from Glasgow Queen St, 3 times a day and take about 5 hours. The Fort William-Mallaig steam train gets very busy.

12 7/M18   From Inverness 08457 484950   Two less-celebrated but mesmerising rail journeys start from Inverness. The journey to Kyle of Lochalsh no longer has an observation car in the summer months, so get a window seat and take a map; the last section through Glen Carron and around the coast at Loch Carron is especially fine. There are 3 trains a day and it takes 2 hours 30 minutes. Inverness to Wick is a 3 hour 50 minute journey. The section skirting the east coast from Lairg-Helmsdale is full of drama, followed by the transfixing monotony of the Flow Country. 3 trains a day in summer.

13 5/C20   The Plane to Barra 0871 700 2000   Most of the island plane journeys pass over many smaller islands (eg Glasgow-Tiree, Glasgow-Stornoway, Wick-Orkney) and are fascinating on a clear day, but the daily flight from Glasgow to Barra is doubly special because the island's airport is on Cockleshell Beach in the north of the island (11 km from Castlebay) after a splendid approach. The 12-seater Otter leaves and lands on the beach according to the tide.

14 7/G19   Elgol, Isle of Skye 0871 700 2000   Trips on either the *Bella Jane* (0800 731 3089) or the *Misty Isle* (01471 866288) on Loch Coruisk to see the whales, dolphins, basking sharks and of course the famous view (1654/VIEWS). Other sea and wildlife cruises – see pp. 303-06.

Great Ways To Get Around

15 By Seaplane www.lochlomond.seaplanes.com · 0870 242 1457 See Scotland from the air, landing on land and water in the remoter parts other transport can't reach. From Glasgow Science Centre to Oban and Tobermory and other, mainly West Coast destinations. Routes can be customised. You can reach Loch Lomond in 20 minutes. Operates Mar-Oct.

16 By VW Campervan www.scoobycampers.com · Scoobycampers Edinburgh-based company offers VW microbuses and campervans on a self-drive rental basis to see Scotland at a gentle pace and save on accommodation. All vehicles are the classic version, converted with contemporary comforts. Microbuses take 6 people comfortably, but you can't really sleep overnight (hire the company's camping equipment). Campervans take 4 – best suited to 2 adults/2 kids. Vehicles have CD radios/DVD players and satnav. There are 7 options, each with its own name. They look really cool and you'll find that everyone's delighted to see you. About £90 a day.

17 By Classic Car www.caledonianclassics.co.uk · 01259 742476 · Caledonian Classic Car Rental Choose a fabulous motor and take off round the by-roads, experiencing that old forgotten joy of motoring. Packages are customised, but there's unlimited mileage and free delivery/collection locally for hire of 2 days or more. Short trips come with a complimentary picnic hamper. Cars include Jaguar E-type, Porche 912, MGB Roadster, Austin Healey, Morgan 4/4, Triumph TR6 and Beetle Convertible. Prices from £140 per day/£1000 per week at TGP. They have their own 4-star B&B in Dollar (a good place to start).

18 By Motorbike www.scotlandbybike.com · 07515 851876 · Scotlandbybike Biking your way around Scotland offers a freedom often absent from driving today. Scotlandbybike organises a range of tours and packages that combine accommodation, insurance and hire of BMW, Triumph, Yamaha and Suzuki, including some for smaller riders – or just bring your own. There's even tuition if you want to improve your bike-riding skills en route. Tours are from 5-10 days; check for rates.

19 By Kayak www.seafreedomkayak.co.uk · 01631 710173 · Seafreedom Kayaks Great way to see parts of Scotland from the sea is by kayak. Of course you can bring your own but for instruction, guidance and finding spectacular routes you couldn't do better than first finding Seafreedom Kayaks at Connel. The coastline here offers all kinds of sea and loch possibilities including Loch Etive and the island of Seil. Tony Hammoch and his wife Olga can also offer accommodation at their B&B situated on the A85 overlooking the Falls of Connel, and Olga does evening meals about 4 times a week. Just about anyone can do this after basic training; Tony keeps his groups small.

20 By Traditional Fishing Boat www.themajesticline.co.uk · 0131 623 5012 · The Majestic Line Unique, all-inclusive holidays on 1 of 2 traditional, wooden, 85-foot fishing boats which have been sensitively converted to a high standard. The Majestic Line operates various itineraries of 3- to 6-night cruises leaving Dunoon and taking in Bute and Arran or departing Oban for Mull and Iona. 6 ensuite double cabins. This is cruising, nay, coasting from a different perspective. Operates Apr-Oct.

The Best Events

Most of these events have websites. Go Google.

21
JAN
Up-Helly-Aa 01595 693434 · Lerwick Traditionally on the 24th day after Christmas, but now always the last Tue in Jan. A mid-winter fire festival based on Viking lore where 'the Guizers' haul a galley through the streets of Lerwick and burn it in the park; and the night goes on.

22
JAN
Celtic Connections www.celticconnections.com · 0141 353 8000 · Glasgow A huge, 3-week festival of Celtic music from round the world held in the Royal Concert Hall and other city venues . Concerts, ceilidhs, workshops. Craic.

23
25 JAN
Burns Night The National Bard celebrated with supper. Increasing number of local and family celebrations following the '09 Year of Homecoming, which took Burns as its major theme.

24
MAR
Borders Potato Day 08700 505152 · Galashiels Curious, but for some hundreds of people a vital event that celebrates the enduring appeal of the tattie or spud. 250 varieties on sale here (for growing). Go early to scoop the specials. Run by Borders Organic Growers (BOG) at Borders College.

25
APR
Glasgow Art Fair www.glasgowartfair.com · 0141 552 6027 · Glasgow Britain's most significant commercial art fair outside London held in mid-Apr in tented pavilions in George Sq with selected galleries from Scotland and the UK.

26
MID-APR
Glasgow International www.glasgowinternational.org · Glasgow Biennial ('10, '12) festival presenting contemporary visual art in main venues and unusual or found space throughout the city centre, celebrating Glasgow's significance as a source of important contemporary artists.

27
APR
Melrose Sevens www.melrose7s.com · 0870 608 0404 · Melrose This Border town is completely taken over by tournament in their small-is-beautiful rugby ground. 7-a-side teams from all over including overseas. Lots of big lads!

28
APR
Fife Point-To-Point www.fifedirect.org.uk · 01333 360229 · Leven Major 'society', ie county set, get-together at Balcormo Mains Farm. Sort of Scottish equivalent of Henley with horses organised by Fife Fox and Hounds. Range Rovers, hampers, Hermès and what's left of the Tories in Scotland.

29
MAY
Paps of Jura Hill Race www.jurafellrace.org.uk · 01496 820243 · Jura The amazing hill race up and down the 3 Paps (total of 7 hills altogether) on this large, remote island (2207/MAGICAL ISLANDS). About 150 runners take on the 16-mile challenge from the distillery in Craighouse, the village. Winner does it in 3 hours!

30
MAY
Big in Falkirk www.biginfalkirk.com · 0141 552 6027 · Falkirk Held mainly in Callander Park outside town centre so a delightful, almost rural setting for 'Scotland's International Street Arts Festival'. Street theatre usually including one big finale show with fireworks. Hugely popular. First weekend in May.

31
MAY-JUL
Common Ridings 0870 608 0404 · Border Towns The Border town festivals. Similar formats over different weeks with 'ride-outs' (on horseback to outlying villages, etc), 'shows', dances and games, culminating on the Fri and Sat. Total local involvement. Hawick is first, then Selkirk, Peebles/Melrose, Gala, Jedburgh, Kelso and Lauder at the end of Jul. All authentic and truly local.

32
MAY
Ten Under The Ben 01397 772899 · Fort William A 10-hour mountain-bike endurance event around Ben Nevis. Good fun, though. Run by No Fuss Events (others in the SW and Moray in '09).

33
MAY OR JUN
RockNess Dores Open-air nedfest in beautiful setting looking over Loch Ness at the tiny village of Dores which is besieged for the weekend. Scotland's second-biggest music festival.

34
JUN &
EARLY AUG
Flower Shows Edinburgh · 0131 333 0969 · & Ayr Many Scottish towns hold flower shows, mainly in autumn, but the big spring show at Gardening Scotland at the Royal Highland Centre (Ingliston) is well worth a look. Meanwhile the annual Ayr show in Aug is huge! Check local tourist information for details.

35
JUN
Royal Highland Show 0131 335 6200 · Ingliston Showground, Edinburgh The premier agricultural show (over 4 days) in Scotland and for the farming world, the event of the year. Animals, machinery, food, crafts, shopping. 150,000 attend.

36
JUN
Mountain Bike World Cup 01397 703781 · Fort William Held at Nevis Range 5K run, around the ski gondola. Awesome course with international competitors over 2 days. Evening events in town. Date varies.

37
MID JUN
The Caledonian Challenge 0131 524 0350 · Fort William A very big (80k) walk run by the Scottish Community Foundation through various 'check points' in Lochaber, using parts of the West Highland Way.

38
EARLY JUL
Scottish Traditional Boat Festival 01261 842951 · Portsoy Perfect little festival in perfect little Moray coast town over a weekend in early Jul. Old boats in old and new harbours, open-air ceilidhs plus a great atmosphere.

39
LATE JUN
Edinburgh International Film Festival www.edfilmfest.org.uk · 0131 228 4051 Various screens and other locations in Edinburgh city centre. One of the world's oldest film festivals and the most important in the UK. 10 days of film and movie matters. To discover.

40
LATE JUN
St Magnus Festival www.stmagnusfestival.com · 01856 871445 · Kirkwall, Orkney Midsummer celebration of the arts has attracted big names over the years. More highbrow than hoi polloi; the cathedral figures. The days are very long.

41
END JUN
Mendelssohn on Mull www.mullfest.org.uk · 01688 812377 Classical music festival in various halls and venues around the island that celebrates the connection between the composer and this rocky far-flung part of the world. Nice idea, and a great time to be here (see 2282/MULL).

42
JUL
Scottish Game Conservancy Fair www.scottishfair.com · 01620 850577 · Perth Held in the rural and historical setting of Scone Palace, a major Perthshire day out and gathering for the hunting, shooting, fishing and shopping brigade.

43
JUL
T in the Park www.tinthepark.com · Balado Airfield, near Kinross Scotland's highly successful pop festival now owned, like almost everything else, by Live Nation. The T stands for Tennents, the sponsors who are much in evidence. Not lifestyle-affirming like Glastonbury, but among the best festivals in the UK.

44 **Hebridean Celtic Festival** www.hebceltfest.com · 01851 621234 ·
MID-JUL **Stornoway** Folk-rock format festival under canvas on faraway Lewis. Celebrated 14th year in '09 with Sharon Shannon and once, the Proclaimers. Music and craic.

45 **The Great Kindrochit Quadrathlon** www.artemisgreatkindrochit.com ·
MID-JUL 01567 820409 · **Loch Tay** The toughest one-day sporting event – swim 1.6km across loch, run 24km (including 7 Munros), canoe 11km and cycle 54km. Then slice a melon with a sword. Jings!

46 **Wickerman Festival** www.thewickermanfestival.co.uk · 01738 449430 ·
END JUL **near Gatehouse Of Fleet** Annual music fest for the South West in fields on the A755 between Gatehouse and Kirkcudbright. Under wide skies on a cool coast. They burn a huge effigy at midnight on the Sat. Audience slow and loose.

47 **Black Isle Show** www.blackisleshow.info · **Muir of Ord** Notable agricultural
EARLY AUG show and countryside gathering for the Northeast Highlands. A big family day out.

48 **Art Week** www.pittenweemartsfestival.co.uk · 01333 312168 · **Pitten-**
AUG **weem** Remarkable local event where the whole of Pittenweem in Fife becomes a gallery. Over 70 venues show work, including public building and people's houses. The quality is not strained. Other events include fireworks. First full week of Aug.

49 **Traquair Fair** www.traquair.co.uk · 01896 830323 · **near Innerleithen** In
EARLY AUG the grounds of Traquair House (1825/COUNTRY HOUSES), a mini Glastonbury with music, comedy and crafts. A respite from the Festival up the road in Edinburgh.

50 **Belladrum 'Tartan Heart' Festival** www.tartanheartfestival.co.uk ·
AUG 01463 741366 · **near Kiltarlity** Off A862 Beauly road west of Inverness. Friendly, 2-day music fest with a loyal local following in terraced grounds. Good for families.

51 **Edinburgh International Festival** www.eif.co.uk · 0131 473 2000 ·
AUG **Edinburgh** A major programme of music, drama and dance with the **Bank of Scotland Fireworks** on the final Sun. In Aug Edinburgh hosts the biggest arts festival in the world, including the **International Military Tattoo,** www.edintattoo.co.uk; **The Fringe,** www.edfringe.com with hundreds of events every night; the **Jazz Festival,** www.edinburghjazz festival.co.uk and (mainly for delegates on a bit of a jolly) the TV festival. This is the best place to be in the world if you're into the arts. See 426/EDINBURGH BEST FESTIVALS.

52 **Edinburgh International Book Festival** www.edbookfest.co.uk · 0131 718
AUG 5666 · **Edinburgh** A tented village in Charlotte Sq gardens. Same time as the above but deserving of a separate entry as it is so uniquely good. See 426/EDIN-BURGH BEST FESTIVALS.

53 **The World Pipe Band Championships** www.theworlds.co.uk · 0141 564
AUG 4242 · **Glasgow** Unbelievable numbers (3,000-4,000) of pipers from all over the world competing and seriously attuned on Glasgow Green.

54 **Cowal Highland Gathering** www.cowalgathering.com · 01369 703206 ·
AUG **Dunoon** One of many Highland games but this, along with Luss and Loch Lomond Games and Inverness in Jul, and Braemar (below) are the main events in the calendar that extends from May to Sep. Expect heavy events (very big lads only), dancing, pipe bands, field and track events and much drinking and chat.

55 **Braemar Gathering** www.braemargathering.org · 01339 741098 ·
EARLY **Braemar** Another of many Highland games (Aboyne early Aug, Ballater mid Aug
SEP on Deeside alone) up north but this is where the royals gather and probably local
laird Billy Connolly and Hollywood A-list. Go ogle.

56 **Blas** www.blas-festival.com · 01463 783447 · **Highlands** Across the
SEP Highlands in a variety of venues. A rapidly expanding celebration of traditional and
Gaelic music with an eclectic line up. It's a long week.

57 **Leuchars Air Show** www.airshow.co.uk · 08700 130877 · **near St Andrews**
SEP Major airshow held over one day in RAF airfield with flying displays, exhibitions,
classic cars, etc.

58 **The Ben Nevis Race** Fort William The race over 100 years old up Britain's
SEP highest mountain and back. The record is 1 hour 25 minutes which seems
amazing. 500 runners though curiously little national, even local interest. Starts
2pm at Claggan Park off Glen Nevis roundabout.

59 **The Pedal for Scotland Glasgow-to-Edinburgh Bike Ride** 01695 682020
SEP Fun, charity fund-raiser annual bike event. From Glasgow Green to Victoria Park
with a pasta party at the halfway point.

60 **Loch Ness Marathon** www.lochnessmarathon.com · 0870 127 8000 One
EARLY of the UK's top marathons, starting midway along the southeast shore of the loch
OCT and finishing in Inverness. Also 10ks and kids' events.

61 **Tiree Wave Classic** www.tireewaveclassic.com · 01879 220399 · Isle of
EARLY **Tiree** Windsurfing heaven of the faraway island (2213/MAGICAL ISLANDS) where
OCT beaches offer challenging wind conditions and islanders offer warm hospitality.

62 **Tour of Mull Rally** www.2300club.org · 01254 826564 · Isle of Mull The
OCT highlight of the national rally calendar is this raging around Mull weekend. Though
drivers enter from all over the world, the overall winner has often been a local man
(well plenty time for practice). There's usually a waiting list for accommodation,
but the camping is OK and locals put you up.

63 **Glasgay** www.glasgay.co.uk · 0141 552 7575 · **Glasgow** Annual, month-long
OCT-NOV celebration of queer culture in different venues in the city centre: film, music, performance, club nights. It is for everybody.

64 **St Andrews Night** Increasingly a bigger deal than before, with government-
NOV sponsored events. National holiday, anyone?

65 **Stonehaven Hogmanay** Stonehaven Celebrated since 1910, a traditional fire
31 festival that probably wouldn't get started nowadays for 'health and safety'
DEC reasons. 40 fireballers throw the fireballs around in the streets before processing
to the harbour and heaving them in. We watch. Arrive early.

66 **Edinburgh's Hogmanay** www.edinburghshogmanay.org · 0131 651 3380 ·
DEC-JAN **Edinburgh** Everywhere gets booked up but call the tourist information centre for
accommodation. There are Hogmanays in other cities but this is one of the world's
major winter events. Launched with a **Torchlight Procession** through the city
centre. Main event is the **Street Party** on 31st. Be part of a huge, good-natured
crowd and experience the Scots at their best!

Hidden Places We Should Love More

67 6/P15 Helmsdale The wee town on the A9 between Inverness and Wick that you might hurtle through. We should stop more often! Though not an old town, built in the 1880s, it charmingly and subtly reveals the ancient spirit and recent history of this northern coast and the strath behind it. This is conveyed effectively in Timespan, a brilliant all-purpose museum, gallery, coffee shop and performance space with a terrace by the river and a geology and herb garden that are perfectly pleasant.

For a small place, it's well served for accommodation (the **Bridge Hotel** 1019/HIGHLAND HOTELS) and food: the hotel, the **Mirage** (1045/HIGHLAND RESTAURANTS), a legendary caff and **Gilbert's**, an emporium and coffee shop-restaurant (10am-ish-5pm; till 8pm Fri & 9pm Sat). The latter two have great home baking and they're all in the main street. The Telford Bridge and the sentinel church (with chiming bells) are lit at night and there are great walks along the river and the coast. Once there was a gold rush in Kildonan here but there's never been a tourist rush – it deserves our attention and anywhere with the Bohemian Bar on one corner and the Bannockburn Bar on the other has got to be interesting.

68 9/H25 Knapdale For a start, hardly anyone knows where Knapdale is – it seems like it should be in the Lake District. But it's the north bit of the Kintyre peninsula: the tongues of land bounded by Loch Fyne, the great sealoch to the east and the Sound of Jura in the west. Its location, in the midst of the most serrated of Scotland's coastline, with islands large and small visible from innumerable perspectives, means that from close up and afar it is immensely scenic, possibly the most pleasing place to the eye on the western seaboard.

The area loosely extends from Crinan in the north to Tarbert in the south, both places that are dearly loved, especially by yachties, and the **Crinan Hotel** has long been a bastion of good taste, good seafood and unforgettable views over dinner (745/ARGYLL HOTELS). Tayvallich also has its forever fans and now there's a passenger ferry to Jura (2280/ISLAY & JURA), there's another reason to go.

But it's the single-track road, the B8024 that follows the coast from Tarbert to Lochgilphead, that skirts and best encapsulates Knapdale (1643/SCENIC ROUTES). Bang in the middle is the excellent **Kilberry Inn** for food and shelter (1288/ GASTROPUBS; 1163/ROADSIDE INNS). 3km south towards Tarbert, a sign 'To the Coves' takes you 500m to the Kilberry Coves to watch otters and to swim in summer.

The unique and vital feature of Knapdale is the woodland. Thousands of acres of original, diverse, deciduous woodland – oak, birch, hazel and alder and the wildlife that lives there: owls, red squirrels, eagles and hedgerows and meadows of wild flowers. The Forestry Commission have a leaflet with many walks and cycle routes available locally and at their Interpretation Centre at Barnluasgan south of Crinan in the heart of the Caledonian Forest Reserve. These are the forests that once clothed Scotland. In Knapdale we rediscover our roots and branches.

69 9/J23 Loch Awe Lochs Lomond, Ness and Tay are the big ones in our imaginations and there are many we love to call our own (p. 285, The Lochs We Love) but though we may gaze on it on our way to Oban, somehow Loch Awe has gone unloved. I felt so too until one brilliant summer evening in 2009, roof of the car open, I drove over from Inveraray to meet the south Loch Awe road through Caledonian forest of oaks and birch, the loch glittering, Ben Cruachan above, and I realised how resplendent is this mighty body of water that stabs through the heart of Argyll.

A quick evaluation shows how many exceptional places are associated with it: places to stay at Kilchrenan, **Roineabhal**, **Taychreggan** and **Ardanaiseig** located on the water (754/ARGYLL HOTELS; 1121/COUNTRY-HOUSE HOTELS). The plethora of woodland walks on **Lochaweside** (2006/WOODLAND WALKS), others in the Forestry Commission pamphlet, *Loch Awe*. Fishing, cycling, picnicking – all that. The spirit of the loch itself seems to seep into the hallowed stones of **St Conan's Kirk**, one of the most atmospheric churches in the land (1854/CHURCHES) and you sense its power again at **Kilchurn Castle** (1792/RUINS) a short walk from the main A85.

From these perspectives and countless places on the south loch road, it becomes clear that Loch Awe is actually quite awesome.

70 **7/H16** **Pool House** Poolewe No apologies for a personal paean to this labour of love. This is a historic house and its transformation has been a remarkable venture for the Harrison Family who've been working to realise their vision for years. Once the home of Osgood Mackenzie who created **Inverewe** across the way and bay, its situation at the lochhead where the river comes in made it a wartime operations base and it has a special place in naval history. Loch Ewe is a deep anchorage still used by NATO so you might see a submarine or a battleship or a cruise liner from the terrace. Rooms in the house are named after ships and one is themed on the *Titanic*, whose captain was related to mum Margaret Harrison's grandfather.

All the rooms are presented with extraordinary attention to detail by daughter Liz and are hand-painted. The family work to create the garden which provides herbs and salad stuff and in 2010 they're constructing a new cottage, a specially imported Scandinavian BBQ pavilion (a first in the UK) and creating a new Chinese suite to complement the Indian one they have already (complete with maharajah bed and palatial bathroom; surely the most sumptuous single room in the land).

There are only 5 (soon to be 7) rooms. To relieve the pressure on old Pop and Mom Harrison the formal dinner is only at weekends (supper on other days); the whole homely yet exotic experience is outrageously inexpensive. One of the rooms is named after HMS *Opportune*. Take it! Go love this place as much as they do. Report: 990/HIGHLAND HOTELS.

71 **10/R27** **The Border Lands** As regular readers will know, I'm a Borders lad and like most people I'm easily drawn back to my roots. My home town Jedburgh doesn't feature a lot in *Scotland the Best* because, if I'm honest (and you know I am), I can't recommend any hotels or restaurants there, though **Jedburgh Abbey** (1890/ABBEYS) and **Mary, Queen of Scots' House** (1903/MARY, CHARLIE & BOB) are well worth visiting. Most visitors trundle past Jedburgh on the A68 as they do with most of the Border towns on the way to or from Edinburgh.

This is a pity! Though its high street seems forlorn, Jedburgh, the first town in Scotland, is picturesque and peaceful. Melrose is much admired and visited and is, in all actuality, the Borders' Food Town (see Borders Hotels & Restaurants, p. 155) but there are many villages and towns that invite exploration in the gentle green hills. They include Lilliesleaf, **Bowden** (1866/CHURCHES), Denholm (**Cross Keys**; 1292/GASTROPUBS), Newtown St Boswells and Kelso with its abbey and a couple of good places to eat: **Cobbles** (839/BORDERS RESTAURANTS) and **Under the Sun** (1376/TEAROOMS). I haven't included Hawick in this list though it now has a great deli/café in **Turnbulls** (1450/DELIS) and an intrepid tearoom, **Damascus Drum** (838/BORDERS RESTAURANTS). It's not what you'd call a pretty town and since all the valley communities of the Borders have an issue with the others (and I'm no exception), I find it hard to enthuse about Hawick.

But the best way to appreciate the Borders is to wander in it. There are many hills from which to take in its bucolic serenity: the **Eildons** (1956/HILLS), **Peniel Heugh** and **Smailholm Tower** (1839/1852/MONUMENTS). Other great views are the famous **Scott's View** and my own **Irvine's View** (1657/1649/VIEWS), the best panorama in southern Scotland. The first vista coming into Scotland is worth more than the usual stop you might make at a border (**Carter Bar**; 1668/VIEWS).

All Southern Scotland is perhaps a little neglected and we can't go everywhere, but on foot or by bike or just tootling in the car, a trip to the Borders is as soothing an antidote to the city and the stresses of life that you can get for almost nothing.

What The Scots Gave The Modern World...

Scotland's population has never been much over 5 million and yet we discovered, invented or manufactured for the first time the following quite important things.

The Advertising Film
Anaesthesia
Ante-Natal Clinics
Antiseptics
Artificial Ice
The Alpha Chip
The ATM
The Bank of England
The Bicycle
Bovril
The Bowling Green
The Bus
Colour Photographs
The Compass
The Decimal Point
The Documentary
Dolly, the Cloned Sheep
Electric Light
Encyclopaedia Britannica
The Fax Machine
Fingerprinting
The Flushing Toilet
The Fountain Pen
Gardenias
The Gas Mask
Geology
Golf Clubs
The Golf Course
Helium
The Hypodermic Syringe
Insulin
Interferon
The Kaleidoscope
Kinetic Energy

The Lawnmower
Life Insurance
The Locomotive
Logarithms
The Mackintosh
Marmalade
Motor Insurance
The Modern Road Surface
Morphine
Neon
The Overdraft
Paraffin˜
Penicillin
The Photocopier
The Pneumatic Tyre
Postage Stamps
Postcards
Radar
The Steam Engine
Street Lighting
Stocks and Shares
The Telegraph
The Telephone
Television
Tennis Courts
The Thermometer
The Threshing Machine
Typhoid Vaccine
The Theory of Combustion
The Vacuum Flask
Video
Wave Power
Writing Paper

and *Auld Lang Syne*

Section 2

Edinburgh

The Major Hotels

72 1/D3
168 ROOMS
20 SUITES
TEL · TV
£85+

✓ ✓ **The Balmoral** www.thebalmoralhotel.com · 0131 556 2414 ·
Princes Street At east end above Waverley Station. Capital landmark
with its clock always 2 minutes fast (except at Hogmanay); so you don't miss your
train. The old pile dear to owner Sir Rocco Forte's heart. Expensive for a mere
tourist but if you can't afford to stay there's always the fabulous afternoon tea in
the piano-tinkling Palm Court. Few hotels anywhere are so much in the heart of
things. Good business centre, some sports facilities (though pool small); luxurious
and distinctive, mainly traditional rooms have ethereal views of the city (some
don't and you pay for the 'Castle view').
EAT Main restaurant, Number One Princes Street (124/BEST RESTAURANTS), is tops
and less formal brasserie, Hadrian's (good power breakfast venue).
Even the non-pretentious bar, NB, works (occasionally has music and open till
1am). Top Rooms: the 3 'Royal' suites: Balmoral, Glamis and Scone & Crombie.

73 1/A4
254 ROOMS
TEL · TV
NO PETS
£85+

✓ **The Caledonian Hilton** www.hilton.co.uk/caledonian · 0131 222
8888 · Princes Street Edinburgh institution at the West End of Princes St:
former station hotel built in 1903. Constant refurbishment under the Hilton group
continues to reinforce 5-star status of Edinburgh's other landmark hotel. Good
business hotel with all facilities you'd expect (though not in all rooms). 'Living
Well' spa with not large pool. Endearing lack of uniformity in the rooms. Executive
rooms on fifth floor (and deluxe rooms elsewhere) have great views. Capital kind of
place in every respect. Main restaurant, The Pompadour, for fine and très formal
dining in ornate and elegant setting does lack the glamour and gourmet cred of
days gone by but Chisholm's on the ground floor is perfectly serviceable. The Cally
(whisky) bar is a famous rendezvous with impressive whisky selection. Top Room:
The 'Sean (Connery) Suite'.

74 1/D2
187 ROOMS
TEL · TV
£60-85+

✓ **Apex Waterloo Place** www.apexhotels.co.uk · 0845 365 0000 ·
23 Waterloo Place As with all hotels in this emerging Edinburgh-based
chain (also in London and Dundee: 911/DUNDEE HOTELS), a central location and a
very contemporary look. This, the new flagship (see others, below), opened '09
after a major, almost miraculous conversion of the council offices where you used
to pay your council tax. Bedrooms may want for a view and public areas (bar and
restaurant) not immediately impressive, but this is a well-run, modern business
hotel a stone's throw from the station.

75 1/XE1
100 ROOMS
TEL · TV
£60-85

✓ **The Malmaison** www.malmaison-edinburgh.com · 0131 468 5000 ·
Tower Place, Leith At the dock gates. This was the first Malmaison all those
design-led years ago but it wears well. All facilities that we who were once smart
and young expect eg internet, 24-hour service, DVD players in each chambre (bor-
row product from reception). Some 'superior' rooms have harbour views and 4-
poster beds. Brasserie and café-bar have stylish ambience too. Pity about the flats
out front but Leith, even in the recession, is still onwards and upwards. (Pity those
off-plan and off-yer-heid folk who paid what they asked for a boxy flat with a glint
of the sea and a purposeless balcony.) Rant over. Enjoy the Malmaison.

76 1/B5
139 ROOMS
TEL · TV
£60-85+

✓ **The Point** www.point-hotel.co.uk · 0131 221 5555 · **34 Bread Street**
This used to be a Co-operative department store. Space and colour combina-
tions manage to look simultaneously rich and minimal; some castle views. Top
Rooms: the suites come with side-lit Jacuzzis. Once mentioned as one of the great
designery hotels in the world and on the cover of *Hotel Design*. Café-bar
Monboddo and restaurant have modern and spacious, mid-Euro feel. Good places

to meet Edinburgers though food and service can be less to the point. Conference Centre adjacent with great penthouse often used for cool Edinburgh launches and parties. (Try to get up there for a unique view of the city: 451/VIEWS.) Pay WiFi!

77 1/C4
116/162
ROOMS
TEL · TV
NO PETS
£85+

Apex City Hotel & Apex International www.apexhotels.co.uk · 0845 365 0000 Both in the middle of the Grassmarket, the picturesque but rowdy Saturday night city centre. Modern, *soi-disant* – but close to castle, club life and other bits of essential Edinburgh. More cool to roam from than in, though. Restaurants called Aqua and Metro on street level are decent and you can usually get a table in the otherwise busy Grassmarket. Heights restaurant on 5th floor of International has great view of the Castle but you can't sit on the terrace. Some castle views (4th-floor rooms at International have balconies). Shared pool and facilities are minimal. There's another, travel-lodgy Apex beyond the West End (106/ECONOMY HOTELS).

78 1/A4
260 ROOMS
TEL · TV
£85+

The Sheraton Grand www.sheratonedinburgh.co.uk · 0131 229 9131 · **Festival Square** On Lothian Rd and Conference Sq, this city-centre business hotel won no prizes for architecture when it opened late 1980s between Edinburgh's 2 most recently created squares: Festival Sq (now with BBC screen – to watch the Olympics etc) and Conference Sq behind, which always seems forlorn. This is a fairly reliable stopover at the heart of the financial district, with excellent service but in need of a good refurbishment now (bedrooms to be done 2010). Larger rooms and castle views carry premiums, but make big difference. Terrace restaurant only adequate. Santini round the back is better (187/BEST ITALIANS). But the superlative feature of the Sheraton is the health club 'One', routinely identified as one of the best spas in the UK, with great half-outdoor pool (1240/SPAS).

79 1/D4
236 ROOMS
TEL · TV
£85+

Radisson SAS www.edinburgh.radissonsas.com · 0131 557 9797 · **80 High Street** Modern but sympathetic building on the Royal Mile, handy for everything (especially during the Festival) and typical Radisson contemporary smart feel. Good facilities but some say service lacking. Thin walls, not great views. Leisure facilities include tiny, subterranean pool and gym. 'Itchycoo' bar/brasserie and many choices nearby. Adjacent parking handy in a hotel so central.

80 1/B3
244 ROOMS
TEL · TV
£85+

The George www.edinburghgeorgehotel.co.uk · 0131 225 1251 · **George Street** Between Hanover St and St Andrew Sq. Refurbished by Principal Hotel Group with new extension adding 50 rooms. Robert Adam-designed and dating back to the late 18th century. Views of the Forth (or the Castle) only from the de luxe rooms in the older part. It's all a bit pricey, but you pay for the location and the Georgian niceties. Busy on-street bar. Good Festival and Hogmanay hotel close to the heart of things (taken over by luvvies during TV Festival). The George has successfully shrugged off its staid, traditional image fitting in to George St's more progressive and opportunistic present.
EAT Impressive brasserie restaurant **Tempus** (one of the best dining rooms in town to be in though food not so remarkable.) Dinner LO 9.45pm.

81 1/F2
94 ROOMS
13 SUITES
TEL · TV
NO PETS
£85+

Royal Terrace www.primahotels.co.uk/royal-terrace.html · 0131 557 3222 · **18 Royal Terrace** Discreet multi-townhouse hotel along elegant terrace backing on to Calton Hill. Multi-level terraced garden out back, deceptively large number of rooms and townhouse décor a tad on the Baroque side make this fabulous for some, merely a good business bet for others. Bar/restaurant not so notable among the natives but we love the garden in summer.

The Best Individual & Boutique Hotels

82 1/XE5
24 ROOMS
TEL · TV
NO KIDS
ATMOS
£85+

✓ ✓ ✓ Prestonfield House www.prestonfield.com · 0131 668 3346 · **off Priestfield Road** 3km south of city centre. I admit that the last 3 editions of *StB* have been launched at Prestonfield and I like many others have enjoyed the lavish hospitalities of owner James Thomson but Prestonfield gets 3 ticks because there's simply nothing like it anywhere else in the world. The Heilan' cattle in the 14-acre grounds tell you this isn't your average urban bed for the night. A romantic, almost other-worldly 17th-century building with period features still intact. In 2003 James, Edinburgh's most notable restauranteur of The Tower (129/BEST RESTAURANTS) and The Witchery (130/BEST RESTAURANTS), turned this old bastion of Edinburgh sensibilities into Scotland's most sumptuous hotel. The architecture and the detail is exceptional and romantic. All rooms are highly individualistic with hand-picked antiques and artefacts, flat screens, DVDs and WiFi. Prestonfield probably hosts more awards dinners and accommodates more celebrity guests than anywhere else in town and it itself wins more awards, especially as a 'Romantic' or Individual Hotel. In summer the nightly Scottish cabaret (in the stable block) is hugely popular.
EAT House restaurant Rhubarb: a memorable experience (131/BEST RESTAURANTS).

83 1/C2
33 ROOMS
TEL · TV
NO PETS
£85+

✓ ✓ Tigerlily www.tigerlilyedinburgh.co.uk · 0131 225 5005 · **125 George Street** Edinburgh's designtastic hotel on style boulevard by Montpellier Group who have Rick's nearby which also has (much cheaper) rooms (96/INDIVIDUAL HOTELS). This surprisingly large hotel sits atop the never-other-than-rammed Tigerlily bar and restaurant. Rooms fairly fab from '07 design catalogue with metal and pale wood and glass. Not cheap for this, possibly the most fashion-conscious lodging in town. Top Rooms: The Georgian Suites.
EAT Fair to say food ain't the main event – the people are – but it's fun and fast and probably better than it has to be. Excellent service!

84 1/D5
47 ROOMS
TEL · TV
£60-85+

✓ ✓ Hotel du Vin www.hotelduvin.com · 0131 247 4900 · **11 Bristo Place** One of the latest in the expanding chain of hotels (467/GLASGOW HOTELS) created by imaginative and sympatico conversion of city-centre, often historic buildings – in this case, the Lunatic Asylum and Infirmary where Robert Fergusson, one of Scotland's iconic poets and revered by Robert Burns, died in 1774. So this place was old! The hotel however, enclosing a courtyard (with 'cigar bothy') and making maximum use of the up-and-down labyrinthine space, is comfortable and modern. Rooms in 4 categories are all different but have the same look. Monsoon showers in all but standard rooms. All, including suites, are well priced. Bar, a whisky snug (250 to try) and 2-level bistro (138/BISTROS). As with other H du V, there's much to-do about wine. In busy quarter near university and museum.

85 1/D3
79 ROOMS
TEL · TV
NO PETS
ATMOS
£85+

✓ ✓ The Scotsman www.thescotsmanhotel.co.uk · 0131 556 5565 · **North Bridge** Deluxe boutique hotel (Eton hotel group) in landmark building (the old offices of *The Scotsman* newspaper group) converted into chic, highly individual accommodation with every modern facility: internet, flat-screen TV, privacy locker in all rooms. Labyrinthine lay-out (stairs and firedoors everywhere) and slow lifts apart, this is the convenient cool hotel in mid-town. Buzzy brasserie (147/BISTROS). Spa in beautiful ground-floor Escape has a beautiful, low-lit, steel pool.

86 1/C1
18 ROOMS
TEL · TV
NO PETS
NO KIDS
£85+

The Howard www.thehoward.com · 0131 315 2220 · **34 Great King Street** In the heart of the Georgian New Town, 3 townhouses in splendid street imbued with quiet elegance though only 5 minutes from Princes Street. No bar but restful drawing room. 15 spacious individual rooms, sympatico with architecture and 3 suites downstairs with own entrances for discreet liaisons or just convenience and own drawing room for entertaining. 24-hour room service. Athol restaurant for breakfast or dinner; and a delightful afternoon tea. Cute garden. No leisure facilities. A very Edinburgh accommodation.

87 1/XA3
50 ROOMS
TEL · TV
NO KIDS · GF
£85+

The Bonham www.thebonham.com · 0131 226 6050 · **35 Drumsheugh Gardens** Discreet townhouse in quiet West End crescent. Cosmopolitan service and ambience a stroll from Princes St. Much favoured by visiting celebs and writers at the Book Festival. Owned by same people as the Howard (above) and Channings (below). Rooms stylish and individual (with some bold colour schemes). Great views out back over Dean Village and New Town from floors 2 and up. One room for doggies. No bar.
EAT Elegant dining in calm, spacious restaurant (especially the end table by back window). Chef Michel Bouyer forges a foody Auld Alliance of top Scottish ingredients and French flair. No-nonsense, simple 4/5 choices described in plain English. Popular 'boozy snoozy' lunch at weekends: 4 people, 2 bottles of wine for £80.

88 1/C4
138 ROOMS
TEL · TV
NO PETS
£85+

Hotel Missoni www.hotelmissoni.com · 0131 240 1666 · **1 George IV Bridge** Converted from an old eyesore council building and opened summer '09, this is the first Missoni hotel in the UK and to some extent they were still sucking it to see at TGP. But the design statement has been made from the start; all Italian retro and moderno and either you like that stuff or you don't. 'The Look' is in every room: 'Missoni', 'Maggiori' and the 5th-floor suites, categories determined by size and view. It's on a busy corner of the Royal Mile with its tourist tide, but rooms are quiet. Cucina is rather better than Pizza Express slotted into the same building, somewhat clouding the image of the chic fashion brand adjacent and the prices it commands. Nice uniforms, though! And cool bar.
EAT Great Italian food and smart dining at a price. 180/ITALIAN RESTAURANTS.

89 1/XA3
41 ROOMS
TEL · TV
NO PETS
£85+

Channings www.townhousecompany.com · 0131 315 2226 · **South Learmonth Gardens** Parallel to Queensferry Rd after Dean Bridge. Tasteful alternative to big-chain hospitality. 5 period townhouses joined to form a quietly elegant West End hotel. Efficient and individual service including 24-hour room service. Great views from top-floor rooms. Top Rooms: The Shackleton Suites - 5 on the top floor with great views and fabulous bathrooms. The polar explorer once lived here and pictures of his expedition adorn the walls. Restaurant under chef Karen Mackay with pleasant wine bar and garden terrace and deck. A discerning and discreet corner of the West End.

90 1/A3
12 ROOMS
TEL · TV
NO PETS
NO KIDS
£60-85+

The Rutland Hotel www.therutlandhotel.com · 0131 229 3402 · **1 Rutland Street** Corner at the West End of Princes St. Opposite (in every respect) to the staid old Cally (the landmark Caledonian Hotel; 73/MAJOR HOTELS). This brash arriviste is designed from top to (probably black) painted toe and if you like shiny modern chic, this is for you. Rooms individual but all on-message, some views; no lift. Buzzy street-level bar.
EAT Wrap-around first-floor restaurant with great city perspective and seriously sourced menu winning plaudits and many punters.

91 1/B3
18 ROOMS
TEL · TV
NO PETS
NO KIDS
£60-85+

✓ **Le Monde** www.lemondehotel.co.uk · 0131 270 3900 · **16 George Street** New in '06, well-defined boutique hotel on Edinburgh's emerging designer dressed street. Part of megabar/restaurant all themed on the world on our doorstep. Highly individual rooms are named after cities and designed accordingly: Havana, Rome, New York, even Dublin (no Glasgow!). Serious attention to detail and very rock 'n' roll. All a tad OTT (the bar not the coolest in town) but the theme does work and beds/bathrooms/facilities are excellent.

92 1/E2
65 ROOMS
TEL · TV
NO PETS
£85+

✓ **The Glasshouse** www.e-travelguide.info/glasshouse · 0131 525 8200 · **2 Greenside Place** Between Playhouse Theatre and the Omnicentre. It's built above the multiplex (rooms on 2 floors) and the restaurants in the mall below. Surprisingly large and labyrinthine. Part of Eton Hotels, as The Scotsman (85/INDIVIDUAL HOTELS). Main feature is extensive lawned garden on roof on to which about half the rooms look out – with patios (non-private) including their standard 'deluxe doubles'. No restaurant (breakfast in room or 'the Observatory'), honesty bar. The Mall below is a disappointment; the restaurants within are all High Street staples, but guests can use Virgin Active health facilities and spa (including 25m pool).

93 1/XA3
29 ROOMS
TEL · TV
NO PETS
£85+

✓ **Edinburgh Residence** www.theedinburghresidence.com · 0131 226 3380 · **7 Rothesay Terrace** Your home in the city on extravagant scale. 3 Victorian townhouses have been joined into an elegant apartment hotel by the Townhouse Group who own the Howard and the Bonham (above). Only in-room dining but the Bonham do breakfasts and 24-hour and concièrge room service, so a discreet and distinctive stopover in 3 different levels of suite. Big bathrooms, views of Dean Village. Drawing room if you're feeling lonely in this quiet West End retreat but nightlife and shops a stroll away.

94 1/A3
31 ROOMS
TEL · TV
NO PETS
NO KIDS
£38-60

✓ **The Hudson Hotel** 0131 247 7000 · **9-11 Hope Street** Near corner of Charlotte Sq. Unashamedly paying homage to North America or more specifically NYC, this '06 addition to the city's boutique portfolio captured some urbanity but not the humanity of its papa and no yellow cab on the kerb. It does have style uniformity throughout and is not as expensive as others; often good walk-in rates. Café-bar on street level a little too cool and dark for its own good, has never attracted the crowds of nearby George St but is a convenient rendezvous.

95 1/E4
78 ROOMS
TEL · TV
NO PETS
£45-60

✓ **10 Hill Place** 0131 662 2080 Address as title on surprising and secret square on South Side near the university, only 100m from busy Nicolson St. Unlikely and surprising departure for the Royal College of Surgeons (412/OTHER ATTRACTIONS) who occupy the nearby imposing neoclassical building complex which fronts onto Nicolson St, and who built this unfussy, utilitarian, very modern hotel that's probably the best-value boutique hotel in town. Masculine, clean elegance in uniform design in 3 categories of rooms depending on size and view. Small restaurant and bar.

96 1/B2
10 ROOMS
TEL · TV
NO PETS
NO KIDS
£60-85

Rick's www.ricksedinburgh.co.uk · 0131 622 7800 · **55 Frederick Street** Very city centre hotel and bar/restaurant in downtown location a stone's throw from George St. By same people who have indigo (yard) and nearby Opal Lounge (383/COOL BARS) so the bar is full-on especially late. Restaurant (165/GASTROPUBS) has (loud) contemporary dining. Rooms upstairs surprisingly quiet. Modern, urban feel and recently refurbished. Book well in advance. Don't let the rooms above the bar thing put you off but get as high as you can!

Most Excellent Lodgings

97 1/C4
2 + 6 APTS
TEL · TV
NO PETS
NO KIDS · GF
ATMOS
£85+

✓ ✓ **Inner Sanctum** and the **Old Rectory** at the **Witchery** www.thewitchery.com · 0131 225 5613 · Castlehill 2 gorgeous rooms and an apartment above the Witchery Restaurant (130/BEST RESTAURANTS) at the top of the Royal Mile and 5 sumptuous apartments across the street that put class into classic Old Town. A stone's throw from the castle, few accommodations anywhere are as emphatically *mise en place* as this. Probably the most exceptional and atmospheric in town – designed by owner James Thomson and Mark Rowley – fairly camp/theatrical, OTT and very sexy. Breakfast and everything else you need en suite including champagne. Weekends booked far ahead.

98 1/E2
4 ROOMS
TEL · TV
NO PETS
£85+

✓ **21212** www.21212restaurant.co.uk · 0845 22 21212 · 3 Royal Terrace Mainly a restaurant with rooms above, all quite lavish and urban and now. 4 rooms only up Georgian staircase (no lift), comfortable and sexy with views to the cruisy gardens opposite and lush, leafy Calton Hill at the back. No leisure facilities to work off your gorgeous dinner (132/FINE-DINING RESTAURANTS) but the bedrooms are made for activities not provided for in the gym.

99 1/XE5
8 ROOMS
TEL · TV
NO PETS · GF
£38-60

Southside www.southsideguesthouse.co.uk · 0131 668 4422 · 8 Newington Road On main street in South Side where indifferent hotels and guesthouses stretch halfway to Dalkeith, this a surprisingly civilised haven. Attention to decor and detail and excellent breakfast. Nice prints, rugs, books and DVDs. Some traffic noise, but upstairs rooms double-glazed. There are 2 4-poster rooms. Parking nearby.

100 1/XE1
5 ROOMS · TV
GF
£38-45

Ardmor House www.ardmorhouse.com · 0131 554 4944 · 74 Pilrig Street Off Leith Walk with lots of other B&Bs but this the top spot. Individual, contemporary and relaxed. There's a gorgeous wee dog called Lola. Proprietors also have 2 lovely New Town apartments for short lets.

101 1/A1
8 ROOMS
TEL · TV
NO PETS · GF
£38-45

Six St Mary's Place www.sixmarysplace.co.uk · 0131 332 8965 Vegetarian-friendly, award-winning guest house on main street of Stockbridge (St Mary's Pl, part of Raeburn Pl) and busy main road out of town for Forth Road Bridge and north, this is a tastefully converted Georgian townhouse. Informal, friendly, well-cared-for accommodation popular with academics and people we like. Vegetarian breakfast in conservatory overlooking garden.

102 1/C2
3 ROOMS
TEL · TV
NO PETS
NO KIDS
£45-60

24 Northumberland Street www.ingrams.co.uk · 0131 556 8140 A definitive New Town B&B. Georgian townhouse in mid-New Town (owner a notable antique dealer). Only 3 rooms (one overlooks garden) so often booked; they can sleep 7. Has become a Wolsey Lodge but no dinner is served (there are many great restaurants nearby).

103 1/XF5
7 ROOMS
TEL · TV
NO PETS · GF
£45-60

94DR www.94dr.com · 0131 662 9265 · 94 Dalkeith Road As Southside (above), this boutique guest house is one of many on the main road south from the city centre. But here they definitely try harder to please and accommodate in individually furnished and decorated rooms (though all have that no-frills modern feel). A real chef cooks breakfast. Some parking.

The Best Economy Hotels

104 1/D4
99 ROOMS
TEL · TV
£30-45

✓ **Ibis** www.ibishotel.com · 0131 240 7000 · **Hunter Square** First in Scotland of the Euro budget chain (one other in Glasgow, 476/TRAVEL LODGES). Dead central behind the Tron. Serviceable and efficient. For tourists doing the sights, this is the best bedbox for location but it's crowded and a bit crazy outside (stag party central). Rates vary hugely.

105 1/XE1
10 ROOMS
TV
£30-45

The Port Inn www.portinn.co.uk · 0131 467 1807 · **48-50 Constitution Street** Rooms above a pub (and round a courtyard) in the heart of Leith (both geographically and passionately) next to the legendary Port o' Leith (332/UNIQUE PUBS). Simple, serviceable rooms. Friendly folk and breakfast. Home-made pub grub on the go but many food choices nearby. Eilidh Moriarty (daughter of Saint Mary of Leith) watches over you.

106 1/XA4
234 ROOMS
TEL · TV
NO PETS
£60-85

Apex European www.apexhotels.co.uk/hotels/edinburgh-european · 0131 474 3456 · **90 Haymarket Terrace** The western, more bedbox version of the Apex collection. Apex Waterloo Place the grooviest (74/MAJOR HOTELS); the other Apexes (77/MAJJOR HOTELS) are in the Grassmarket. The European is the cheaper, not-so-central option (on the way out of town towards the airport).

107 1/E2
160 ROOMS
TEL · TV
NO PETS
£45-60

Holiday Inn Express www.hieedinburgh.co.uk · 0131 558 2300/0800 434040 · **16 Picardy Place** Not unpleasant conversion of several New Town houses in exceptionally convenient location opposite the Playhouse Theatre. Rooms all same standard (twin or double). Bar, no restaurant but area awash with options. This is a very clever Holiday Inn. There are 3 others in town.

108 1/C5
180 ROOMS
TEL · TV
NO PETS
£45-60

Novotel Edinburgh Centre www.novotel.com · 0131 656 3500 · **80 Lauriston Place** New build near Tollcross and university. No charm but functional and reasonably contemporary. Small pool, bar and contemporary-like brasserie. Good beds and facilities. But Premier Travel Inn adjacent is half the price (see below).

109 1/C4
44/42
ROOMS
TEL · TV
NO PETS
£38-45

Grassmarket Hotel www.festival-inns.co.uk · 0131 220 2299 · **94-96 Grassmarket** Basic and boisterously located accommodation next to Biddy Mulligan's which is open till 1am, but levels 4/5 at the back are best. The Grassmarket is often full-on (though the City is making attempts to civilise it), so good for party-animal business types on a budget – stags rut here. The same people have the similarly party-on **Tailors Hall** (0131 622 6800) on Cowgate, around and above the 3 Sisters pub.

110 1/E4
193 ROOMS
TEL · TV
NO PETS
£30-38

Travel Lodge www.travelodge.co.uk · 0131 557 6281/08700 850 950/ 08719 848484 · **33 St Mary's Street** Edinburgh's most central version of national (often roadside) chain. All usual, formulaic facilities but inexpensive and near Royal Mile (Holyrood end) and Cowgate for late-night action. Expect stag and hen groups being disgusting.

111 1/C5
1/XA4
1/XE1
£30-38

Premier Travel Inn Chain www.premiertravelinn.co.uk 7 (and counting) in Edinburgh area. All much of a less-ness. Most handy for Old Town is at 82 Lauriston Place (0870 990 6610) near university. 1 Morrison Link (0870 238 3319) is near Haymarket Station. The best one in Newhaven/Leith (taxi/bus) (08701 977 093) is near the bars and restaurants of Leith with Loch Fyne (213/SEAFOOD) adjacent and David Lloyd health club (helpfully not available to guests). 30 rooms have surprising views of sea and sunset. Other Inns are suburban.

The Best Hostels

112 1/XE1
71 ROOMS
24 HOURS
£15-50

✓✓ **SY Edinburgh Central** www.syha.org.uk · 0131 524 2090 · **9 Haddington Place** Central it is in a good part of town though perhaps unobvious to casual visitors, ie it's not in the Old Town area. Haddington Pl is part of Leith Walk (corner of Annandale St) near theatres/bars/restaurants and gay quarter and on way to Leith. Converted from office block with café, internet and every hostel facility. Clean, efficient; rooms from singles to family 4-8 beds. Run by the Scottish Youth Hostels Association.

113 1/E4
630 ROOMS
24 HOURS
£20-90

✓✓ **Smartcity Hostels** 0870 892 3000 · 50 Blackfriars Street Building is enormous so also opens on to Cowgate. £10 million made this place as hotel-like as you get without completely losing the hostel vibe. Self-service restaurant, extensive bar, facilities including roof terrace (with heaters and sometimes BBQ), self-catering kitchens and hordes of staying-up/out-late people. Massive number of rooms (630) round interior courtyard, varying from 2-12 occupancy. Students stay here in term time. Good location and well smart.

114 1/C4
24 HOURS
£30 OR LESS

✓ **Royal Mile Backpackers** www.royalmilebackpackers.com · 0131 557 6120 · 105 High Street On the Royal Mile, near the Cowgate with its late-night bars. Ideal central cheap 24-hour crash-out dormitory accommodation with all the facilities itinerant youth on a budget might look for. Original hostel in the group: **The High Street Hostel**, 8 Blackfriars St (0131 557 3984), and the **Castle Rock**, 15 Johnston Terrace (0131 225 9666) in the old Council Environmental Health HQ. Is huge (190 beds in various dorms; 6 'private' rooms book up fast) and some great views across the Grassmarket or to the castle which is just over there. Same folk also have hostels in Fort William, Inverness, Oban, Pitlochry and Skye, and Mac Backpacker tours so expect to be sold a trip to the Highlands.

115 1/XB3
£30 OR LESS

✓ **Argyle Backpackers Hotel** www.sol.co.uk/a/argyle · 0131 667 9991 · 14 Argyle Place Quiet area though in Marchmont there are great bars eg the Earl of Marchmont (390/COOL BARS) and interesting shops nearby. 1km to centre across the Meadows (not advised for women at night). This is a bit like living in a student flat and there are tenements full of them all around. But it's homely with kitchen, internet, lounge, conservatory and garden. Own key.

116 1/XA3
£30 OR LESS

✓ **Globetrotter Inn** www.globetrotterinn.com · 0131 336 1030 · Marine Drive, Cramond Large mansion-house hostel in exceptional setting and with great facilities. Huge number of bunks (400), spa, gym, internet, cinema and shop. Only drawback is distance from downtown (half hour) but hostel runs own hourly service (till 11pm). Lawns and trees and riverside view do compensate. Continental breakfast included or cooked possible at weekends.

117 1/D3
29 ROOMS
NO PETS
£20-60

✓ **St Christopher Inn** www.st-christophers.co.uk · 0207 407 1856 · 9-13 Market Street Couldn't be handier for the station or city centre. This (with branches in London and other Euro cultural cities) a hostel rather than hotel with bunk rooms though there are single and double rooms. As always, price depends on number sharing. Belushi's café-bar on ground floor open till 1am. A very central option, better than most other hostels (facilities are ensuite) but not so cheap. Provides linen. Internet access.

The Best Hotels Outside Town

118 10/P25
16 ROOMS
TEL · TV
NO PETS
£85+

✓✓ **Champany Inn** www.champany.com · 01506 834532 · near Linlithgow On A904, 3km Linlithgow on road to Forth Road Bridge and South Queensferry. Exemplary restaurant with rooms, some overlooking garden. Legendary steaks and seafood; ambience and service. Breakfast in cosy dining kitchen is excellent (nice bacon, of course!). Extraordinary wine list and cellar shop for take home (daily 12-10pm). But veggies best not to venture here.
EAT Superb. 261/BURGERS & STEAKS.

119 10/P25
132 ROOMS
TEL · TV
NO PETS
£85+

✓✓ **Dakota** www.dakotahotels.co.uk · 0870 423 4293 · South Queensferry Two ticks for a very different kind of hotel from the above. Pioneer in emerging chain by the people who brought us the Malmaisons and before that, 1 Devonshire Gardens (now Hotel du Vin; 467/GLASGOW HOTELS). A bold concept from design statement of the black metropolis-type block to the locations – in this case a car park serving the mini mall of Tesco etc on the edge of South Queensferry but on main carriageway north from Edinburgh by the Forth Road Bridge. As a businesslike bedblock it's superb, a designer (Amanda Rosa) world away from anonymous others of the ilk. No frills but far from basic. Amanda also does Gleneagles. This is the stripped-down version but rooms are calm and whisper 'understated chic'. The Grill restaurant a destination in itself (guests should book when they make a room reservation). Ken McCulloch's vision and restless energy. Unceasing! See also 483/HOTELS OUTSIDE GLASGOW.
EAT Brasserie-type daily-changing menu in setting reminiscent of a Malmaison. Spotlights, dark woods, brick and slats everywhere. Seafood, including 3 varieties of oyster. A destination restaurant from Edinburgh and Fife.

120 10/P25
83 ROOMS
TEL · TV
NO PETS
£60-85+

✓✓ **Norton House** www.handpickedhotels.co.uk · 0131 333 1275 · Ingliston Off A8 near the airport, 10km west of city centre. Victorian country house in 55 acres of greenery, surprisingly woody and pastoral so close to city. Highly regarded Hand-Picked Hotel group. 'Executive' rooms have countryside views. Labyrinthine layout with good conference/function facilities. Brasserie and small internal restaurant. Good contemporary (the bedrooms) and traditional (public rooms) mix. Some rooms quite swish. Gorgeous new spa with pool etc.

121 10/Q26
10 ROOMS
MAR-DEC
TEL
£85+

✓ **Borthwick Castle** www.borthwickcastle.com · 01875 820514 · North Middleton On B6367, 3km off the A7, 18km bypass, 26km southeast of centre. A real Border castle with walls 30m high. This magnificent tower house knocks you off your horse with its authenticity – Mary Queen of Scots was blockaded here once and at night you expect to see her swishing up the (narrow, unavoidable) spiral stairs. 8 rooms in castle, 2 in gatehouse. The banqueting hall is impressive but you came for the days gone by, not the dinner to come.

122 10/P25
18 ROOMS
TEL · TV
NO PETS
£45-60

✓ **Orocco Pier** www.oroccopier.co.uk · 0131 331 1298 · Main Street, South Queensferry A buzzy restaurant and boutique style hotel, in often tourist-thronged South Q with great views of the Forth and the bridge (398/MAIN ATTRACTIONS). From Edinburgh take first turnoff from dual carriageway. Formerly Queensferry Arms, substantial makeover has created a cool bistro and contemporary rooms above and beside (not all have views). Food in bar, restaurant or terrace (LO 10pm). Event programme and they do conferences, weddings, etc. Parking tricky, but a great outside-town option.

Open Arms Hotel Dirleton Report: 845/LOTHIANS.

Tweedale Arms Gifford Report: 846/LOTHIANS.

The Best Fine-Dining Restaurants

123 1/XE1
£32+

✓ ✓+ **Martin Wishart** www.martin-wishart.co.uk · 0131 553 3557 ·
54 The Shore Discreet waterside frontage for Edinburgh's most
notable cookery and the standard by which other fine-dining menus in Edinburgh
and Glasgow can be judged. Room designed on simple lines; uncomplicated menu
and wine list (no cheap plonk). Michelin-star chef Martin and a clutch of awards
raise expectation, but preparation, cooking and presentation are demonstrably a
cut above the rest even now that there are other Michelin stars nearby. Great
vegetarian menu. Unobtrusive service. No nonsense, only the best meal in town.
Martin has a cook school round the corner and is executive chef at Cameron
House, Loch Lomond (482/HOTELS OUTSIDE GLASGOW). MW gets one of 2 ticks-plus
in this book – in the UK frontrunners. Lunch Tue-Fri, Dinner Tue-Sat. LO 9.30pm.

124 1/D3
£32+

✓ ✓ **Number One Princes Street** www.thebalmoralhotel.com · 0131
556 2414 Not many Edinburgers perhaps venture below stairs at the
Balmoral, the landmark hotel they pass every day on Princes St. They're missing
one of the best dining experiences in foodtown. Subterranean opulence with only
opaque light from the windows on Waverley Steps (shadowy figures pass) and perhaps less ritzy than once was but the calm, cosmopolitan ambience perfectly complements confident cuisine. Michelin starred since 2003, Jeff Bland is executive
chef and Craig Sandle delivers the simple-to-follow à la carte and tasting menus.
Attentive, not-too-fussing-over-you staff: knowledgeable sommelier and 'cheesel-
lier' can talk you through the impressive list and board. But none of this is cheap.
7 days. Dinner only LO 10pm. **Hadrian's Brasserie,** a pastel lounge at street
level (grills and light choices among the mains), complements well. Closed Sat/Sun
lunch. LO 9.45pm.

125 1/B4
£32+

✓ **The Atrium** www.atriumrestaurant.co.uk · 0131 228 8882 · Cambridge
Street Foyer of the Traverse Theatre, Lothian Rd. Solid since 1993, Andrew
and Lisa Radford's understated restaurant is still the best non-fussy or -fussed-
over food in town. Michelin Bib Gourmand chef Neil Forbes has a confident and
magic touch and ingredients are seriously sourced. Cooking contemporary and
slow, service attentive and smart, the Atrium never pretends with an ambience
that gently accommodates both business and romance. A la carte and a tasting
menu. Often easier to get a table here than the more glam foody locations. After
all these years I'd still rate the Atrium as Edinburgh's most classily casual: fine dining without the fripperies. Lunch Mon-Fri. Dinner LO 10pm. Closed Sun.

126 1/XE1
£32+

✓ **Plumed Horse** 0131 554 5556 · 50 Henderson Street On a corner in a
backstreet location between Great Junction St and the Shore, this is nevertheless a destination for the inspired and understated cookery of Michelin-starred
chef Tony Borthwick. I imagine Tony gets a tad irritated when critics suggest the
decor lacks the finesse of the food and I had a go myself about the art, but this is
largely beside the point. In a town of many Michelin would-be stars, a meal from
his unpretentious à la carte is a meal to remember, especially what you paid for it.
This is the best fine-dining value in town. Fixed price includes canapés. Lunch and
LO 9pm. Tue-Sat.

127 1/B4
£32+

✓ **Abstract** 0131 229 1222 · 33 Castle Terrace Near Usher Hall and Traverse
Theatre. Rare event of a notable Scottish restaurant moving to, rather than
from Edinburgh. Abstract also in Inverness at owner Barry Larsen's Glenmoriston
Hotel (1066/BEST INVERNESS). Here as there, very contemporary dining with excellent service. Seemed a tad overdesigned when it opened but like a good haircut,
it's lived-in and now and it all seems to work effortlessly. Many of the original

Inverness staff are now seem to be here, a great team and the menu is imaginative and full of tasty twists from chef Geoffrey Malmedy. Piano player at weekends. A la carte, 'market' and tasting menus. Lunch and LO 9.30pm. Closed Sun/Mon.

128 1/XE1
£32+

✔ **The Kitchin** www.thekitchin.com · 0131 555 1755 · **78 Commercial Quay, Leith** In the row of restaurants in front of the Scottish Government offices, Tom Kitchin's brilliant, busy kitchen looks out on the calm, urbane restaurant which has received so much attention and awards since it opened in '06, including an early Michelin star. Though Tom is a fixture on the foodfest circuit (especially with his new book '09, *From Nature to Plate*), he seems omnipresent in the kitchen keeping an eye on us as well as what we eat. Good-value lunch menu (set and à la carte), additional tasting (6-course) and 'celebration of the season' menus in the evening; so lots of choice but all driven by impeccable and serious sourcing of local and market ingredients. Not a large room, you get lots of attention. Wine list as you would expect, superb and the sommelier will guide you through it (many suggestions already on the menu). Good value at this standard, TK is often booked out even as the waves of recession lap. Lunch and dinner. LO 10pm. Closed Sun/Mon.

129 1/D4
£32+

✔ **The Tower** www.tower-restaurant.co.uk · 0131 225 3003 · **Chambers Street** At George IV Bridge above the Museum of Scotland. Restaurant supremo James Thomson's celebrated and celebrity-strewn restaurant atop the distinctive 'tower' on the corner of the sandstone museum building benefits from the much-admired grand design and detail of Gordon Benson's architectural vision. The long, narrow room with terrace tables and banquettes could be in any sophisticated urban setting, except you're looking over Edinburgh rooftops and to the castle. Great private dining room in the tower itself. Kitchens far below in 'Prehistoric Scotland', but food everything one would expect – Scottish slant on modern British. Great starters, great steaks. Best to book. Lunch and dinner LO 11pm. 7 days.

130 1/C4
ATMOS
£32+

✔ **The Witchery** www.thewitchery.com · 0131 225 5613 · **Castlehill** At the top of the Royal Mile where the tourists throng, maybe unaware that this is one of the city's most stylishly atmospheric restaurants. 2 salons, the upper more 'witchery'; and in the 'secret garden' downstairs, a converted school playground, James Thomson has created a more spacious ambience for the (same) elegant Scottish menu. Locals on a treat, many regulars and visiting celebs pack this place out, and although they do turn round the tables, you should book. The Witchery Apartments encapsulate this remarkable ambience (104/LODGINGS). The wine list is exceptional, the atmosphere *sans pareil*. Lunch and dinner. LO a very civilised 11.30pm. See 298/LATE-NIGHT RESTAURANTS.

131 1/XE5
ATMOS
£32+

✔ **Rhubarb @ Prestonfield** www.prestonfield.com · 0131 668 3346 A little out of town but the restaurant of fabulous Prestonfield (82/HOTELS) makes 3 in a row of great restaurants for James Thomson (see above). And as above it's the whole dining experience rather than Michelin-minded menus that drives their success. Rhubarb the most gorgeously decadent in opulent Regency rooms at the heart of the hotel; the public rooms adjacent for before and après are superb, especially the upstairs drawing rooms. An evening of rich romance awaits. And you get your (rhubarb) desserts.

132 1/E2
£32+

21212 www.21212restaurant.co.uk · 0845 22 21212 · **3 Royal Terrace** The name of this place which shimmied onto the city's gastromap in '09 is a bit of a memory-fxxx but it refers to the menu régime of 2 choices for starters, mains and puds with bouche bits in between; so betwixt à la carte and tasting. Michelin star (was and contender) chef/owner Paul Kitching also stars in the beautiful and very visible kitchen where a well-lit team attends your food as if it were a patient in an operating theatre. Every dish brims with unusual, sometimes amusing ingredients, so you are on a food trip. The wine list is surpringly good value, the room is fab; no expense spared. And you can fall upstairs. 98/EXCELLENT LODGINGS.

133 1/B3 **Oloroso** www.oloroso.co.uk · 0131 226 7614 · 33 Castle Street Unassuming
£32+ entrance and lift to this rooftop restaurant renowned for its terrace with views of the castle, the New Town and Fife. Bar snacks are a great deal – can't go wrong with 'curry of the day'. Chef/prop Tony Singh excels especially with the meatier dishes and in the main dining room, light and spacious and spilling on to the terrace, steaks are rightly popular though there are many imaginative dishes with fish and that. Has always been a fashionable, foody room at the top. Many ladies lunch. Excellent for evening cocktails and a top private dining space. Lunch and dinner LO 10pm. 7 days. Bar till 1am.

 Champany's 01506 834532 · near Linlithgow 22km from town. Report: 261/BURGERS & STEAKS.

The Best Bistros & Brasseries

134 1/D2
£22-32+ ✓ ✓ **Forth Floor, Harvey Nichols** www.harveynichols.com · 0131 524 8350 · **St Andrews Square** On the fourth floor (through deli and furnishings and HN souvenirs) and you see the Forth from the balcony (superb outside dining on rare summer days, though somewhat in a row). Store and restaurant for ladies who lunch and the chic supper crowd; food and service reliably spot-on. You can partake of cheaper brasserie or more expensive (but similar) Modern British comfort-food menus either side of the bar. Estimable chef Stuart Muir with HN since it opened. Nice just to come for cocktails! Lunch 7 days, dinner Tue-Sat LO 10.30pm.

135 1/C2
ATMOS
£15-22 ✓ ✓ **The Dogs** www.thedogsonline.co.uk · 0131 220 1208 · **110 Hanover St** Upstairs on busy Hanover St, this was *the* must-visit foodie destination when it opened in '08 in spite (and most likely because) of the legendary brusque charm (or rudeness) of inimitable owner Dave Ramsden. Lofty, busy main and smaller back room always rammed (and you are rammed in). Old-fashioned, simple, robust food at giveaway prices. Wine ditto. 7 days lunch and LO 10pm (bar 11pm). Must book. We loved it a lot so then came **Amore Dogs** downstairs (179/ITALIAN RESTAURANTS).

136 1/C2
£15-22 ✓ ✓ **Urban Angel** www.urban-angel.co.uk · 0131 225 6215 · **121 Hanover Street** & 0131 556 6323 · **1 Forth Street** In a basement near Queen St and the East Village version. Contemporary, relaxed, great value and, not surprisingly, packed from breakfast to suppertime. Organic where sensible and free trade (lots). Food is wholesome British but with a light touch and a great pastry chef supplying both places. Takeaway counter and great Sun brunch rendezvous (308/SUNDAY BREAKFAST). 7 days breakfast, lunch and dinner. LO 9.45pm (Sun 5pm).

137 1/D4
ATMOS
£15-22 ✓ ✓ **The Outsider** 0131 226 3131 · **15 George IV Bridge** The downtown dining room of The Apartment (below). Notoriously rude owner Malcolm Innes once again created a sexy, contemporary and inexpensive restaurant which even in a recession is always full. Minimalist design with surprising view of the castle. Innovative menu contrasts. Big helpings, pretty people. 7 days, lunch and LO 10.30pm.

138 1/D5
£22-32 ✓ **Bistro du Vin** www.hotelduvin.com · 0131 247 4900 · **11 Bristo Place** Near the university area. The restaurant of the Hotel du Vin (84/BOUTIQUE HOTELS), entered through the sprawling and tightly fitting courtyard and reception of the conversion that transformed Bedlam into a bistro bar and a comfy bed for the night. Though a chain, there's nothing uniform in sight or on the menu which offers classic French bistro fare in a room that's been designed to buzz. Opinions differ as to whether the food is fab or just not fab enough, and though spacious it's always busy, so best book. 7 days lunch and LO 10.30pm.

139 1/XA4
£15-22 ✓ **First Coast** www.first-coast.co.uk · 0131 313 4404 · **99 Dalry Road** Named after a place in the far north where chef/proprietor Hector McRae used to go on his holidays, this cool urban restaurant is also on the edge of the known world – well, Dalry Rd. Food here is superb value and full of integrity. Straight-talking menu with no bamboozling choices. It's also a great choice if you're at Cineworld, the multiplex used by the Film Festival. Mon-Sat lunch and LO 10.30pm.

140 1/XE5
£15-22
✓ **Home Bistro** 0131 667 7010 · 41 West Nicolson Street Comfort food heaven in tiny living-room bistro on South Side near university. Rowland Thomson and chef Richard Logan's formula of simple, reassuring modern and traditional British grub. Home-made everything from bread to bread-and-butter pudding. Great value and precious simplicity. Lunch Tue-Fri, dinner Tue-Sat.

141 1/E3
£15-22
✓ **Monteith's** www.monteithsbar.co.uk · 0131 557 0330 · 57 High Street Down a fairy-lit close at the tartan-clad centre of the Royal Mile, a cool, woody and clubby bar/restaurant with great food, drinkies and smart service. The gastropub-style menu is quite meaty. Lunch goes through to 5pm then à la carte. 7 days LO 10/10.30pm. Bar 1am.

142 1/B4
£15-22
✓ **blue bar café** www.bluescotland.co.uk · 0131 221 1222 · Cambridge Street Upstairs in Traverse Theatre. From the makers of the Atrium (125/ BEST RESTAURANTS), a lighter, more informal menu. Went from blue to brown in '07 but remains cool and fresh. Still the best drop-in diner in town; convenient for West End entertainments. The menu changes every 6 weeks and is mix 'n' match with 'light blue' snackier options and a 'slow food' ethos. Sound levels high; people do talk. 12noon-3pm, 6pm-10.30pm daily. Bar to midnight (1am Fri/Sat). Closed Sun.

143 1/A1
✓ **Redwood** www.redwood-restaurant.co.uk · 0131 225 8342 · 33 St Stephen Street Basement bistro in the middle of once 'trendy' St Stephen St at the heart of Stockbridge. Annette Spraghe's take on Californian cuisine means lovely, light food with lots going on on the plate. Simple, seasonal menu. Great salads and vegetarian choice. A wee gem and we do mean 'wee', so best book. Lunch Wed-Sun, dinner Wed-Sat. Closed Mon/Tue.

144 1/XB5
£15-22
✓ **The Apartment** 0131 228 6456 · 7 Barclay Place The first of Malcolm Innes's hugely popular contemporary eating-out experiences (see also The Outsider, above), undergoing a major makeover at TGP after 10 years as a Bruntsfield food destination and fixture. So watch this space. 7 days dinner; LO 11pm. Sat/Sun from noon.

145 1/B2
£15-22
✓ **Iris** www.irisedinburgh.co.uk · 0131 220 2111 · 47 Thistle Street Sweet little Iris tucked away in the middle of Thistle St punches above her weight. Elegant, modern rooms, well judged Modern British menu and excellent service – what's not to like? An urban-chic retreat for those that know. 7 days noon-10pm.

146 1/XE1
ATMOS
£22-32
✓ **The Vintners Rooms** www.thevintnersrooms.com · 0131 554 6767 · The Vaults, 87 Giles Street Off a courtyard in a Leith backstreet, this long-established bar/restaurant in 'the vaults' below what is now the Malt Whisky Society offers one of the most atmospheric dinners in town. Imaginative Mediterranean-style cooking from chef Patrice Ginestière with a top wine list. Food in bar (also at lunch) and more formally in the 18th-century dining room lit by candlelight. Lunch and LO 9.45pm. Closed Sun/Mon.

147 1/D3
£22-32
✓ **North Bridge** www.northbridgebrasserie.com · 0131 622 2900 · 20 North Bridge The brasserie of the Scotsman Hotel (85/INDIVIDUAL HOTELS) with separate entrance directly on to main road. Formerly the foyer and public counter of *The Scotsman* newspaper converted into excellent bar/brasserie. Surrounding balcony reached by rather intrusive metal staircase, but overall very sympathetic ambience for exemplary brasserie-type menu with seasonal variations; emphasis on North British, ie Scottish, ingredients. Toilets are a find when you find them. 7 days, all day LO 10pm/10.30pm. Bar midnight (1am Fri/Sat).

148 1/B2 ✓ **Tony's Table** www.tonystable.co.uk · 0131 226 6743 · 58 North Castle Street A long-established restaurant site now in the capable and ambitious hands of Tony Singh who has Oloroso (133/FINE DINING) – you can see the terrace from here. Decor unchanged at TGP (never Tony's strong point) but the eclectic menu with an interesting take on Scottish comfort food does work. This no-fuss bistro even has a large communal table. Lunch and LO 10pm. Closed Sun/Mon.

149 1/XB5 ✓ **Sweet Melinda's** www.sweetmelindas.co.uk · 0131 229 7953 · 11 £22-32 Roseneath Street Owner-chef Kevin O'Connor's living-room restaurant in deepest Marchmont catering for the neighbourhood (not short of a bob) clientele but famous across the city. Mainly fish (from estimable Eddie's over the road), but 1 meat and 1 vegetarian. Everything made from scratch. Great touches, good wines and fizz. Lunch (not Mon) and LO 10pm. Closed Sun. BYO Tue £3.

150 1/XA5 ✓ **Shapes** 0131 453 2666 · Bankhead Avenue, Sighthill On edge of the city £22-32 in highly unlikely setting of an industrial estate. But this is home to Shapes furniture and auctioneers; this 100-capacity restaurant was formerly a work's canteen. Now it's more like a top showroom: the floor is Italian marble, there's darkwood and gilt and opulence wherever you look. Food's not bad either in an extensive menu and the wine list is a revelation. Mon-Sat 9am-4pm. Dinner Sat only.

151 1/D1 **Olive Branch** www.theolivebranchscotland.co.uk · 0131 557 8589 · 91 £15-22 Broughton Street On the corner with Broghton Pl; also at 46 George IV Bridge (0131 226 4155) and 19 Colinton Rd (0131 452 8453). Remarkably successful small bistro chain that has taken over failing sites and turned them around, mainly coz they do straightforward food we like at great prices. Lunch and LO 10pm. Broughton St open all day and great for breakfast (313/SUNDAY BREAKFAST).

152 1/XE5 **Blonde** www.blonderestaurant.com · 0131 668 2917 · 75 St Leonard's £15-22 Street Tucked away in the South Side; you must be good to survive here. Conscientious owner-chef Andy Macgregor so deserves to and he has. Food and ambience relaxed, it's inexpensive and simply good. Handily near Queens Hall and Pleasance (in Fringe time). Pale wood, spartan ie blonde rooms and easy-eat food with quaffable wine (several house wines under £13). Easy Andy! Lunch (not Mon) and LO 10pm. 7 days.

153 1/A1 **Stockbridge Restaurant** 0131 226 6766 · 54 St Stephen Street Basement £15-22 on boho-chic street and one of the New Town's reliable bistros, with carefully sourced ingredients served in classic Modern British dishes. Intimate, so good à deux. Often 'offers', eg BYOB on Sun. Lunch Fri/Sat, dinner Tue-Sun. LO 9.30pm.

154 1/E5 **Pink Olive** www.ilovepinkolive.co.uk · 0131 662 4493 · 55-57 West ECO Nicolson Street Corner of West Nicolson St and the university whence comes much of the clientele. Airy, clean lines, bistro candlelit at night. Simple, not fussed and actually quite scrumptious food with good vegetarian choice. Lunch and LO 9.30/10.30. Sun 10.30-4pm. Closed Mon.

155 1/B2 **Iglu** 0131 476 5333 · 2b Jamaica Street Tiny upstairs bistro of Iglu, the New ECO Town bar (393/COOL BARS). Organic approach to ingredients. Scottish/local and quite meaty menu. Nice accompaniments include sourdough bread. You fit in tight. Book at weekends. Lunch Fri-Sun, dinner 7 days. LO 10pm, bar 1am.

Gastropubs

156 1/XB5
£15-22

✓ **The New Bell** www.thenewbell.com · 0131 668 2868 · 233
Causewayside Way down Causewayside in the South Side, the New Bell is upstairs from the Old Bell; you may walk through the pub to find it. Worn now a bit round the edges but a woody, warm, pubby atmosphere; nice rugs, etc. Richard and Michelle Heller have got the room and the Modern British menu just right. They've opened a new place nearby, **Hellers Kitchen** (0131 667 4654), so they're not always here (though it is still the best). Food and very decent vino well-priced for the quality and the smart delivery. Excellent steaks and puds. Sun lunch. Dinner only Tue-Sun. LO 10.30pm.

157 1/XE1
ATMOS
£22-32

✓ **The Shore** www.theshore.biz · 0131 553 5080 · 3 The Shore, Leith
Long established as a gastropub; an *StB* favourite. The people from Fishers next door (208/BEST SEAFOOD) have given The Shore a fresh look and menu. Real fire and large windows looking out to the quayside – strewn with bods on summer nights coz when it's sunny we head to The Shore. Modern British menu in cosy-in-winter, woody bar (live music Tue-Thu & Sun) or quieter restaurant room. 7 days lunch and LO 10pm, bar till 12.

158 1/XE1
£15-22

✓ **King's Wark** 0131 554 9260 · 36 The Shore On the corner of Bernard St. Woody, candlelit, stone-walled and comfortable – a classic gastropub, ie the emphasis is on food. Bar and bistro dining room. Pub-food classics and more adventurous evening menu. Though traditional and dark rather than pale, light and modern, this has long been one of the best bets in Leith. Chef Mike Greig was Scottish Gastropub Chef of the Year '09. Scottish slant on the menu, with excellent fish including famous beer batter and chips. Lunch and LO 9.45pm. Bar open to 11pm, 12midnight Fri-Sat.

159 1/XE1
£15-22

✓ **The Ship on the Shore** 0131 555 0409 · 24 The Shore And midway between The Shore bar and the King's Wark (above) arrived a new ship on the Shore '08, or at least its reputation as a great quayside bistro/gastropub, especially for seafood. Good ingredient sourcing and wine list (top by-the-glass selection, including champagnes). Excellent fruits de mer and the right ambience to enjoy them. 7 days 12noon-10pm. Bar 11pm.

160 1/XA5
£15-22

✓ **Caley Sample Room** www.thecaleysampleroom.co.uk · 0131 337 7204 · 58 Angle Park Terrace The CSR sells all the expected Caledonian real ales from nearby brewery and a couple of guests besides. Run by the people who have the Cambridge Bar (below) and Wannaburger (276/BURGERS) so great burgers and steaks but eclectic and full menu with daily specials. Nice, woody ambience. Loadsa wine by the glass. Out-of-the-way location but this is *the* west-of-the-city destination for great pub grub. 7 days LO 9pm, 10pm Fri/Sat. Bar much later.

161 1/B3
£15-22

✓ **Cambridge Bar** www.thecambridgebar.co.uk · 0131 226 2120 · 20 Young Street On the west extension of Thistle St. Discreet doorway to Edinburgh institution. Sporty in a rugger kind of way and more recently notable for its gastroburgers, thought by many to be the best in town. Huge in size and huge choice including vegetarian (bean burgers); Mackie's estimable ice-cream to follow. Sadly only a handful of tables but same folk (and same menu) have Wannaburger (265/BURGERS). Food 12noon-8.45pm. Bar 11pm/12midnight and 1am Fri/Sat.

162 1/XC1 ✓**The Orchard** www.theorchardbar.co.uk · 0131 550 0850 · 1 Howard
£15 OR LESS **Place** At Inverleith Row near the Botanics. Pub that's been here forever and
which has seriously upped its game foodwise in the last couple of years. So for
those in the know; a find for others. Light, airy and as you'd expect, pubby. Light
touch in the kitchen too from chef James Fletcher. Seasonal, well-thought-out
menu. The same people have **Avoca** at 4 Dean St off Stockbridge main street.
Expect developments '10. 7 days, 12noon to 8.30pm.

163 1/XB5 **The Canny Man** 0131 447 1484 · 237 Morningside Road Aka The Volunteer
ATMOS Arms on the A702 via Tollcross, 7km from centre. Idiosyncratic renowned eaterie
£15-22 with a certain hauteur and a true, original gastropub. Carries a complement of
malts as long as your arm and a serious wine list. Smorrebrod lunches (12noon-
3pm) and evenings (6.30-9.30pm) seem dated now but we go for the atmosphere,
not the food. No loonies or undesirables welcome nor mobile phones, cameras or
backpackers, so a grumpy but civilised pub; a labyrinth of good taste and a nice
garden. Till 11pm Sun-Thu, 1am Fri, 12midnight Sat. 359/REAL-ALE PUBS.

164 1/XB5 **Montpeliers** www.montpeliersedinburgh.co.uk · 0131 229 3115 ·
£15-22 159 Bruntsfield Place They call it 'Montpeliers of Bruntsfield' and it is almost an
institution now south of the Meadows. Same ownership as Rick's (below) and similar buzz and noise levels, but more accent on food. From breakfast menu to late
supper, they've thought of everything. All the contemporary faves. Sunday roasts.
Gets very busy. 7 days 9am-10pm. LO 10pm. Bar till 1am.

165 1/B2 **Rick's** www.ricksedinburgh.co.uk · 0131 622 7800 · 55a Frederick Street
£22-32 Basement bar/restaurant of Rick's Hotel (96/INDIVIDUAL HOTELS) by same people
as indigo (yard), Montpeliers (above), Opal Lounge and Tigerlily (83/INDIVIDUAL
HOTELS). Drinking is the main activity here but they do have a well thought-out
café-bar-type menu. Later on probably too noisy to enjoy food, so choose time and
table carefully. Inner courtyard best for dining. Up-for-it crowd enjoy champagne,
cocktails and shouting. 7 days all day. LO 10pm (11pm weekends). Bar 1am. Also
open for breakfast from 7am.

166 1/XE1 **A Room In Leith** www.aroomin.co.uk · 0131 554 7427 · 1c Dock Place
ATMOS Long-established wine bar in this foody corner of the waterfront now joined to
£15-22 Skippers (207/SEAFOOD RESTAURANTS) and spilling over the quayside renamed
'Teuchter's Landing'. The conservatory overlooks the backwater dock. Scottish-
slanted bistro menu with half- or full-pint 'Mug' menu to eat in or out. Excellent
wine and malt selection. 7 days, lunch and LO 9.30/10pm. Bar 12midnight/1am.

The Best French Restaurants

167 1/D3
£22-32
✓✓**La Garrigue** www.lagarrigue.co.uk · 0131 557 3032 · 31 Jeffrey
Street Airy yet intimate restaurant near Royal Mile. Chef/proprietor Jean
Michel Gauffre brings warm Languedoc to your plate. Simple food with flair and
unusual touches. Veggies may flounder between the leggy langoustines and les
lapins but meat eaters and Francophiles are très content here. Mon-Sat lunch and
LO 9pm. Closed Sun.

168 1/B2
£15-22
✓✓**Café Marlayne** 0131 226 2230 · 76 Thistle Street The first in the
triumvirate of excellent and authentic French eateries within 100m of
another (Café St Honoré, La P'tite Folie; below), this is a wee gem (we do mean
wee). Personal, intimate and very, very French. Food generally fab (though not
great for veggies). Isla Fraser' in the kitchen. This really is like a place you find in
rural France on your hols and Marlayne never fails to please! Lunch and LO 10pm.

169 1/D4
£15-22
✓**(The Old Town) Café Marlayne** 0131 225 3838 · Old Fishmarket Close
Off 190 High St just below the cathedral. Down a wynd in the tourist-
thronged Royal Mile and definitely one of the best food options. As Café Marlayne
above, authentic, homely French cooking (Isla's brother Jeff on the stove). Slim
outside terrace in summer. Good value. Lunch and LO 10pm. Closed Sun/Mon.

170 1/B2
ATMOS
£22-32
✓**Café Saint Honoré** www.cafesthonore.com · 0131 226 2211 · 34
Thistle Street Lane Between Frederick and Hanover Sts. Suits aplenty, New
Town regulars and occasional lunching ladies are the loyal following (after a management change '08) for this shiny bistro-cum-restaurant which oozes and even
smells like Paris. Scottish sourcing listed. Meat dishes are especially good; minimal
vegetarian choice. Backroom is a little forlorn, quarters are cramped but a great
bistro atmosphere. Lunch Mon-Fri, LO 10pm.

171 1/C4
£15-22
✓**Petit Paris** www.petitparis-restaurant.co.uk · 0131 226 2442 · 40
Grassmarket On busy north side of street below the castle; teems on weekend nights – get an outside table and watch: this could be Montmartre apart from
the general inebriation and bad behaviour. Good atmosphere and value with très
typical menu. BYOB (not weekends); corkage £3.50. 7 days lunch and LO 10pm.

172 1/B2
£15-22
✓**La P'tite Folie** www.laptitefolie.co.uk · 0131 225 7983 · 61 Frederick
Street & Randolph Place Best word for it: 'unpretentious'; maybe 'ambi-
ente'. Mismatched furniture, inexpensive French plat du jour. Relaxed dining in sin-
gle New Town room or the two-floor Tudoresque 'maison' in West End cul de sac.
Both great value. LO 10pm (10.45pm weekends). Both closed Sun. In Randolph Pl,
La Di-Vin adjacent is a large, lofty wine bar and a surprise find behind the bistro.
Great wine list and atmosphere.

173 1/XD1
£15-22
✓**Chez Pierre** www.pierrelevicky.co.uk · 0131 556 0006 · 18 Eyre Place
The irrepressible Pierre Levicky bounced back in '08 from self-imposed exile in
France after his famously cheap Pierre Victoire chain went belly-up. Once again
with a winning formula of great-value, authentic French country cooking, this
place was packed from the start. It's the deal as well as the feel that packs them in
with lunch for £6.90 at TGP and £10 dinners. 7 days lunch and LO 10pm.

174 1/A3
£15-22
✓**Petit Paris** 0131 226 1890 · Queensferry Street at Alva Street Upstairs
bistro once associated with Petit Paris above, but now à deux with L'Escargot
below. Popular with a loyal following who like the authentic, lively atmosphere and
the inexpensive food and fine wines. Lunch and LO 10/10.30pm. Closed Sun.

175 1/D1
£15-22

✓ **L'Escargot Bleu** www.lescargotbleu.co.uk · 0131 557 1600 · **56 Broughton Street** In a strong French field in this city, another authentic Auld Alliance bistro popped up in '09 – this one en famille with Petit Paris in Queensferry St, so expect Buccleuch beef and black pudding and other named-source ingredients in their fine French cooking. Friendly atmosphere, great cheese selection. Cute épicerie downstairs. Lunch and LO 10pm. Closed Sun.

176 1/C4
£15-22

Maison Bleue www.maisonbleuerestaurant.com · 0131 226 1900 · **36 Victoria Street** Cosy, very Edinburgh café-bistro with a similar convivial ambiance. French and North African mezze approach, building a meal from small-ish dishes they call bouchées. 7 days lunch and LO 10pm/11pm weekends.

177 1/XE1
£15-22

Daniel's www.daniels-bistro.co.uk · 0131 553 5933 · **88 Commercial Quay** Versatile, hard-working (open all day) café, takeaway and bistro. Main eaterie is housed in conservatory at back of old bonded warehouse off Dock Pl in Leith's 'restaurant row'. Clean lines, modern look; popular. Offers rustic French menu from breakfast to evening brasserie staples with Alsace and external influences we like, especially tartiflette, tarte flambé, casseroles and classic crème brulée (196/PIZZAS). Also tables by the water 7 days, 10am-10pm.

 Restaurant Martin Wishart 54 The Shore French influence on finest dining. Report: 123/BEST RESTAURANTS.

The Best Italian Restaurants

178 1/D1
£15-22

✓ **Bella Mbriana** 0131 558 9581 · 7 East London Street On the roundabout at the bottom of Broughton St. The triumphantly slimmed-down chef/pro-prietor Rosario Sartore continues his homage to native Napoli in this modern Italian eaterie, winning good reviews (many posted) and plaudits along the way (Scottish Italian Restaurant of the Year '09). It's all down to the right ingredients and great home cooking (you need to have Rosario on the stove). Buzzes upstairs and down. Nice table in the wine cellar. Lunch and LO 11pm. Closed Sun.

179 1/C2

✓ **Amore Dogs** www.amoredogs.co.uk · 0131 220 5155 · 104 Hanover Street Named after the hugely successful bistro upstairs (135/BISTROS), itself named after the 'dog' of somewhat eccentric proprietor Dave Ramsden, this Italian version is also to love. It's got all the staples of a British tratt and though some have referred to the cuisine as 'a dog's dinner', the light Med menu is easy to take and to like, especially on the wallet. Hallmark buzzing atmosphere in the main room and mezzanine. Goes like Italy. 7 days lunch and LO 10pm.

180 1/C4
£32+

✓ **La Cucina @ Hotel Missoni** 0131 240 1666 · 1 George IV Bridge Corner with the Royal Mile. The upstairs Italian kitchen of the first Missoni hotel (88/INDIVIDUAL HOTELS) where fashion, ie the brand comes first. But the food here is excellent and not at all fancified. Ambience relaxed, chic and sexy, like the trousers. Smart, solicitous service; good sommelier. Cheap it ain't. Breakfast, lunch and dinner LO 10pm/11pm.

181 1/XA4
£15-22

✓ **La Bruschetta** www.labruschetta.co.uk · 0131 467 7464 · 13 Clifton Terrace Extension of Shandwick Pl opposite Haymarket Station. Giovanni Cariello's Italian kitchen and tiny dining room in the West End. A modest restorante with impeccable pedigree and a big following; so book. The space does not cramp their style nor the excellent service. Lunch and LO 10.30pm. Closed Sun/Mon.

182 1/E1
£22-32

✓ **Valvona & Crolla** www.valvonacrolla.co.uk · 0131 556 6066 · 19 Elm Row First caff of the empire which spread to Multrees Walk (see below) and to London, this one discreetly buzzing away at the back of the legendary deli (324/DELIS). An Alexander McCall Smith kind of café much favoured by ladies who lunch. First-class ingredients and great Italian domestic cooking. Own bakery. One of the best and healthiest breakfasts in town (till 11.15am), fabuloso lunch and afternoon tea (from 3pm). Can BYOB from shop (£3 corkage). Mon-Sat 8am-5pm, Sun 10.30am-4.30pm. VC also do Jenners' food hall.

183 1/B3
ATMOS
£15-22

✓ **Centotre** www.centotre.com · 0131 225 1550 · 103 George Street Fabulous conversion of lofty, pillared Georgian room towards west end of the street by Victor and Carina Contini into the most stylish Italian joint in town. Passion for food and good service always evident: ubiquitous (though they've got Zanzero below, to deal with too) and never letting it slip. Bar and central pizza oven, unexpected combos in a straightforward. oft-changing menu. Great people-watching strip of tables on the street. 8am till LO 10pm (10.30pm Fri/Sat), 11am-5pm Sun. Bar open later.

184 1/A1
£15-22

✓ **Zanzero** 0131 220 0333 · 15 North West Circus Place On main road leading from the centre (Frederick and Howe Sts) to Stockbridge, the ubiquitous and unceasing V&C family (see above) have done something completely fresh and different. This contemporary bright and buzzy café/restaurant complements Centotre and owners Victor and Carina somehow juggle themselves, their family and these two very different menus and rooms and not shred like spaghetti. Healthy, sexy variations on the pasta/pizza theme with home baking (lovely cakes), so a caff that works from breakfast to late supper with big, colourful cocktails in between. 7 days 8am-11pm. They also deliver.

185 1/D2
£15-22

✓ **Vin Caffe** www.valvonacrolla.co.uk · 0131 557 0088 · Multrees Walk The downtown smart eaterie of the Valvona & Crolla dynasty (see above) in the posh-shop passage beside Harvey Nix. Café counter downstairs, restaurant above. Interesting pastas, pizzas and other lovely creations. It's always busy downstairs for authentic espresso and fast snacks. Upstairs can be quite star-studded, both on-screen (Italian classics projected) and at the end table (we ate with Nigella; Sean goes too) under the Leon Morocco. A dolce vita kind of place. 7 days 8am-9.15/10.15pm, Sun 11-5.30pm.

186 1/XE1
£15-22

✓ **La Favorita** www.la-favorita.com · 0131 554 2430 · 325 Leith Walk Tony Crolla's (of Vittoria; 188/TRATTS) upmarket pizzeria halfway down the Walk where the trams will come one day (you'll be happier then, Tony). From the twin, specially imported, wood-fired ovens, Tony was determined to produce 'the best pizza in Scotland' and in '09 he won 'best in the UK', so there (193/PIZZAS)! Gluten-free available and a menu of fancy pastas. Family-friendly, especially on Sunday. This is many folks' favorita. 7 days 12noon-11pm.

187 1/A4
£15-32

Santini www.santiniedinburgh.co.uk · 0131 221 7788 · Conference Square Back of the Sheraton (of which it's a part, below their excellent health club). Business-like Italian restaurant and bistro created by a Mr Santini himself who brought the same clean lines and stylish eating-out experience as in London and Milan though now run by the hotel. Waiters and ingredients very Italia. Casual dining looking out on a usually people-less piazza. Lunch and dinner LO 10.30pm. Closed Sun.

The Trusty Tratts

188 1/E1 ✓✓**Vittoria** www.vittoriarestaurant.com · 0131 556 6171 · **Brunswick**
1/D4 **Street** The original on the corner of Leith Walk and also at **19 George**
£15-22 **IV Bridge**(0131 225 1740). For over 30 years Tony Crolla has provided one of the best, least pretentious Scottish-Italian café-restaurants in town. Uptown branch near the university equally full-on. Full Italian menu with classic and contemporary pastas. In Leith the outside tables on an interesting corner are always packed when the sun's out. Nice for kids (186/KID-FRIENDLY) and for breakfast (porridge, omelettes). Pizzeria/ristorante further down the Walk (La Favorita 196/ITALIAN RESTAURANTS). 7 days. 10am-11pm.

189 1/XA4 ✓**La Partenhope** 0131 347 8880 · **96 Dalry Road** A corner and cucina of
£15-22 Naples halfway up Dalry Rd (about 200m from Haymarket) where chef Paolo Tersigni presides over what has long been one of the most loved tratts in town. Menu changes weekly with daily specials from market produce. Fish specials are tops. Even the most basic aglio e olio shows how it should be done. This place fills up fast – book weekends. 7 days. Lunch Tue-Sat, dinner LO 10.45pm. Closed Sun.

190 1/A3 ✓**Bar Roma** www.bar-roma.co.uk · 0131 226 2977 · **39 Queensferry**
£15-22 **Street** One of Edinburgh's long-standing fave Italians, revamped so it almost looks like a Pizza Express from the outside. Inside it's massive and always bustling (this includes the menu) with Italian rudeboy waiters as the floor show. We love their chat; they love football. 7 days, all day. LO 11pm (later weekends).

191 1/D2 ✓**Giuliano's** www.giulianos.co.uk · 0131 556 6590 · **18 Union Place** Top
£15-22 of Leith Walk near the main roundabout, opposite Playhouse Theatre. Giuli's has a new Al Fresco restaurant down the street after the takeaway counter but it's the original that rocks and it feeds the Playhouse opposite. It's just pasta and pizza but it's what we like. The food is great, the wine list has some superb moments, the din is loud and it's always somebody's birthday. Lunch and LO 2am daily. **Giuliano's On The Shore** (0131 554 5272) on the corner of the bridge in Leith Central has recently had a makeover but it's the same, reliable tratt menu. Especially good for kids (269/KID-FRIENDLY). Also 7 days, LO 10.30/11pm.

192 1/C2 **La Lanterna** 0131 226 3090 · **83 Hanover Street** One of several tratts sub
£15-22 street level in this block, all family-owned. But this gets our vote. For over 20 years the Zaino family have produced a straight-down-the-line Italian menu from their open kitchen at the back of their long, low, no-frills restaurant. Most of their customers are regulars and wouldn't go anywhere else. Well chosen wines. Lunch and LO 10pm. Closed Sun.

The Best Pizza

193 1/XE1 ✓**La Favorita** www.la-favorita.com · 0131 554 2430 · **325 Leith Walk**
£15-22   They say it's 'the best' and in '09 the rest of the UK agreed: the 'award'. Huge variety, great mozza; takeaway and home delivery and now on the road at festivals. This pizza has travelled! Report: 186/ITALIAN RESTAURANTS.

194 1/B1 **Anima** 0131 558 2918 · **11 Henderson Row** The takeaway pizza section of the
£15 OR LESS   estimable fish 'n' chip shop L'Alba D'Oro next door (217/FISH & CHIPS). Definitely a slice above the rest. 3 sizes (including individual 7-inch) and infinite toppings to go. Not thin but crispy and crunchy. Also pasta, great wine to go, olive oils, Luca's ice cream and fresh OJ. This is no ordinary takeaway (see 315/TAKEAWAY)! 7 days lunch and LO 11pm.

195 1/C4 **Mamma's** www.mammaspizza.co.uk · 0131 225 6464 · **30 Grassmarket**
£15 OR LESS   Busy, inexpensive American-style pizza. Some alternatives, eg nachos, but you come to mix 'n' match – haggis, calamari and BBQ sauce and 40 other toppings piled deep with quite chunky crust. Outside tables on revamped Grassmarket. Stag and hen parties are not welcomed here (hurrah!). 7 days till 11pm/12midnight.

196 1/XE1 **Daniel's Bistro** www.daniels-bistro.co.uk · 0131 553 5933 · **88 Commercial**
£15-22   **Street** On 'restaurant row' in Leith. Great for the Tarte Flambé – very like a thin pizza made from milk-bread dough topped with onions, crème fraîche and lardons – an Alsace and house speciality. There are other thin pizzas too (177/FRENCH RESTAURANTS). 7 days 10am-10pm.

197 1/E1 **Jolly's** 0131 556 1588 · **9 Elm Row** On the part of Leith Walk near Valvona &
£15-22   Crolla 324/DELIS). Long-established (over 40 years!) tratt/ristorante well known locally for their thinner-than-usual wood-fired pizza and Vito the owner who's always waiting for you to come in. Over 40 varieties. Good family spot. Also takeaway. 7 days. Lunch and LO 10.30pm. Closed Sun lunch.

198 1/XF2 **Caprice 2 Go** 0131 665 2991 · **198 High Street, Musselburgh** Near the
£15-22   bridge. The number is for their takeaway joint round the corner which delivers to this eastern suburb of the city and other nearby East Lothian towns. The adjacent restaurant serves the same wood-fired pizza and the usual Italian fare. Ask them to crisp it but pizza here still lighter than most. 7 days lunch and till 11pm.

214 1/E1
£15-22

✓ **Café Fish** www.cafefish.net · 0131 538 6131 · 6o Henderson Street In deepest Leith behind Gt Junction St. Richard Muir's elegant, airy neighbourhood bistro keeps it simple with a menu that's sussed and sustainable. He knows exactly where everything comes from and it's all avowedly good value. A cool addition ('09) to Edinburgh's dock of good restaurants. Lunch Tue-Sun, dinner Tue-Sat.

215 1/D2
£22-32

✓ **Café Royal Oyster Bar** www.thespiritgroup.com · 0131 556 1884 · 17 West Register Street On the corner between St Andrews Square and Burger King at the East End of Princes St. Long-standing – and we do mean 'long': a classic Victorian oyster bar. Decor is unchanged so the marble, dark wood, tiles and glass partition are all major reasons for coming here. Food has been up and down and often an also-ran over the years and this is a Punch Tavern, but under Valerie Graham the classic seafood menu has improved remarkably. The Oyster Bar is back and winning awards again! 7 days lunch and LO 9.30pm. The bar through the partition is also a classic (336/UNIQUE BARS).

The Best Fish & Chips

216 1/XE1

✓ **The Tail End Restaurant & Fish Bar** 0131 555 3577 · 14 Albert Place On the right-hand side of Leith Walk going down. Opened '08 in the middle of tram construction chaos. Unpretentious caff where you can often get a table (only 10) though the menu, from starters to simple-choice puds, is all good stuff. Menu of fish du jour, battered, grilled and with a variety of sauces. Caff and counter cook to order, so fresh as it comes. A drop-in favourite! 7 days 11.30am-10pm.

217 1/B1

✓ **L'Alba D'Oro** Henderson Row Near corner with Dundas St. Large selection of deep-fried goodies, including many vegetarian savouries. Since 1975 Filippo Crolla's chipper has been way above the ordinary – as several plaques on the wall attest (including *StB!*) and the pasta/pizza counter Anima next door is also a winner (194/PIZZAS, 315/TAKEAWAY). Surprising and notable wine selection (including fine wines and champagne), olive oils, Luca's ice cream. Open 5pm-11pm (12midnight weekends); pizza 10pm (11pm weekends).

218 1/E2

✓ **The Deep Sea** Leith Walk Opposite Playhouse Theatre. Open late and often has queues but these are quickly dispatched. The haddock has to be 'of a certain size' and is famously fresh (via Something Fishy in Broughton St nearby). Traditional menu and 'fried chocolate'. Still one of the best fish suppers with which to feed a hangover (there's also a pharmacy of pills alongside the Irn Bru). Open till 2am (-ish) (3am Fri-Sat).

219 1/E1

✓ **The Montgomery** Montgomery Street Just off Leith Walk and midway between the Tail End and the Deep Sea, there are those that swear this place is the chipper to choose. Sit in the friendly, very traditional caff adjacent or take away. Closed Sun.

220 1/D2

Caffe Piccante Broughton Street Takeaway and café with tables on the black 'n' white tiles. Near the Playhouse Theatre, this is the clubbers' chippy with unhealthy lads purveying delicious unhealthy food to the flotsam of the Pink Triangle and club world. Including deep-fried Mars Bars (you'd need to be well out of it). You can sit in. Open till 2am (3am weekends).

Ye Old Peacock Inn Newhaven Road Report: 271/KID-FRIENDLY
King's Wark 36 The Shore Report: 158/GASTROPUBS.

The Best Vegetarian Restaurants

221 1/E5   ✓✓ **David Bann's** www.davidbann.com · 0131 556 5888 · St Mary's
£15-22   **Street** Bottom of the street off Royal Mile – a bit off the beaten track,
but always a busy restaurant and not only with non-meaters, because this is one of
the best restaurants in the city: mood lighting, non-moody staff and no dodgy
stodge. A creative take on round-the-world dishes. Light meal selection; lovely
tartlets and 'parcels'. Not a huge vegan selection and no ostentatious 'organics' –
just honest-to-goodness good. 7 days, lunch and LO 10pm.

222 1/XC1   ✓✓ **L'Artichaut** www.lartichaut.co.uuk · 0131 558 1608 · 14 Eyre Place
£15-22   North-east edge of New Town near Canonmills and adjacent Chez Pierre
(173/FRENCH) so two notable restauranteurs are neighbours in this quiet neighbourhood. This superb vegetarian restaurant with chef Belinda Woollett comes
from Jean Michel Gauffre of top French restaurant La Garrigue (167/FRENCH).
Unlikely though it is for a Frenchman to go vegetarian, this has a plethora of
choice, perfectly balanced menu and hardly any goat's cheese in sight. Room
needs cosifying at TGP but this is a notable addition to Edinburgh's extraordinary
vegetarian collection. Lunch and dinner, Tue-Sat. LO 9pm.

223 1/E5   ✓✓ **Kalpna** www.kalpnarestaurant.com · 0131 667 9890 ·
£15-22   2-3 St Patrick Square They say 'you do not have to eat meat to be
strong and wise' and they are of course right. Maxim taken seriously in this long-
established Indian restaurant on the South Side for over 25 years, one of the best
vegetarian menus in the UK and ever-dependable, vegetarian or not. Thali gives a
good overview. Lovely, light and long may it prevail. Mon-Sat, lunch and LO
10.30pm. Open Sun in summer. Report: 238/INDIAN RESTAURANTS.

224 1/C2   ✓✓ **Henderson's** www.hendersonsofedinburgh.co.uk · 0131 225 2131 ·
ATMOS   94 Hanover Street Edinburgh's original and trail-blazing basement
15 OR LESS   vegetarian self-serve café-cum-wine bar. Canteen seating to the left, candles and
live piano or guitar downstairs to the right (pine interior is retro-perfect). Happy
wee wine list and organic real ales. Those salads, hot main dishes and famous puds
will go on forever. 7.30am-10pm. Closed Sun (though open during the Festival).
Farm Shop upstairs with a deli and takeaway and, round the corner in Thistle St,
the cosier **Henderson's Bistro** with waiter service (open 7 days, LO 8.30pm,
9.30pm weekends). Oh, and there's the 'Gallery' upstairs. An all-round Henderson
way of life. And Henderson's (organic) oatcakes are *the* best.

225 1/E5   ✓ **Susie's Diner** 0131 667 8729 · 51-53 West Nicolson Street Cosy,
£15 OR LESS   neighbourhood (the university) self-service diner. Nice people behind and in
front of the self-service counter. Mexican and Middle-Eastern dishes. Lotsa choice
menu includes excellent coffee. Susie's has been here a long time now with its
laid-back Californian vibe, but actually it just gets better. Licensed, also BYOB.
9am-9pm. Closed 8pm Sun/Mon.

226 1/E5   ✓ **Ann Purna** 0131 662 1807 · 45 St Patrick Square Excellent vegetarian
£15-22   restaurant near Edinburgh University with genuine Gujarati cuisine. Good
atmosphere – old customers are greeted like friends by Mr and Mrs Pandya. Indian
beer, some suitable wines. 7 days, lunch and LO 10.30pm. Report: 242/INDIAN
RESTAURANTS.

227 1/XE5   ✓ **Engine Shed Café** www.engineshed.org.uk · 0131 662 0040 ·
£15 OR LESS   19 St Leonard's Lane Hidden away off St Leonard's St, this is a lunch-
oriented vegetarian café where much of the work is done by adults with learning

difficulties on training placements. It's worth supporting and it's light, airy and a good place to hang out. Simple, decent food and great bread – baked on premises, for sale separately and found all over town. Nice stopping-off point after a tramp over Arthur's Seat. 10am-3.30pm. Closed Sun.

228 1/D4
£15 OR LESS
Black Bo's 0131 557 6136 · 57 Blackfriars Street Long-established, laid-back vegetarian restaurant with some unpredictable, often inspired vegetarian ideas and combos. Lots of nuts in the mix. Intimate and woody and boho. Adjacent bar has been cool for years – lots of nutters in this mix too. Dinner only. LO 9.30/10.30pm. Closed Sun. Bar 1am.

229 1/A3
£15 OR LESS
Cornerstone Café 0131 229 0212 · Princes Street At Lothian Rd underneath St John's Church at the corner. Very central and PC self-service coffee shop in church vaults. Home-baking and hot dishes at lunchtime. Some seats outside in summer (in graveyard!) and market stalls during the Festival. One World Shop adjacent is full of Third World-type crafts and very good for presents. A respite from the fast-food frenzy of Princes St. Open 10am-5pm (later in Festival). Closed Sun.

230 1/D5
ATMOS
£15 OR LESS
The Forest www.theforest.org.uk · 0131 220 4538 · 3 Bristo Place Gimme Shelter off-campus eaterie. On one hand hippy-dippy dreadlock city; on the other, refreshingly non-designery retro-sixties chic. Junk furniture, cool noticeboard and people strewn around the room. Decent veggie (and vegan) global menu whevever the mainly volunteer staff are on it. 'Total Kunst' art space, monthly 'Free Shop'. Performance most nights. Home to the 'Free Fringe'. 7 days, 12noon-late.

✓ ✓+ **Restaurant Martin Wishart** 0131 553 3557 · 54 The Shore Not of course a vegetarian restaurant, but does have a vegetarian menu. Food, ingredients and presentation are taken seriously here, so this is where to go for *the best* vegetarian food in Scotland. Report: 123/BEST RESTAURANTS.

The Best Scottish Restaurants

231 1/D3
£22-32
✓ **Dubh Prais** www.dubhpraisrestaurant.com · 0131 557 5732 · 123b High Street Slap bang (but downstairs) on the Royal Mile opposite the Radisson. Only 24 covers and a miniature galley kitchen from which proprietor/chef James McWilliams and his team have produced a remarkably reliable and easy-to-take à la carte menu and specials from sound and sometimes surprising Scottish ingredients (haggis is panfried, smoked haddock comes with Ayrshire bacon) for over 20 years. Atholl Brose is as good as it gets. Very regular clientele and lucked-out tourists in this outpost of culinary integrity on the High St. Closed Sun/Mon. Lunch and LO 10pm. Pronounced 'Du Prash'.

232 1/C4
ATMOS
£22-32
✓ **The Grain Store** www.grainstore-restaurant.co.uk · 0131 225 7635 · 30 Victoria Street Long-established, revered bistro in interesting street near Royal Mile. Regulars and discriminating tourists climb the stairs for the excellent-value grazing lunch menu or innovative à la carte at night. A laid-back first-floor eaterie in a welcoming stone-walled labyrinth. Good for groups. Perhaps more Modern British than simply Scottish. Chef/proprietor Carlo Coxon here for 20 years and the team work damned hard to deliver quality. Hunting/shooting/fishing ingredients like roe deer, woodcock along with your usual oysters. 7 days lunch and LO 10pm (11pm Fri/Sat).

233 1/D1
£22-32
Haldane's www.haldanesrestaurant.com · 0131 556 8407 · 39 Albany Street Michelle and George Kelso's basement restaurant overlooking the wee garden of the boutique-style Albany Hotel. Fine dining near Broughton St and probably the best proper meal in the area. Scottish by nature rather than hype. Everything done in a country-house style, though menu unpretentious and room not overly sumptuous. A reliably good and discreet rendezvous. Lunch and LO 9.30pm. Closed Sun/Mon.

234 1/B4
£22-32
Stac Polly www.stacpolly.com · 0131 229 5405 · 8a Grindlay Street Opposite Lyceum Theatre. Dark-wood and tartan-touched interior is business-like and smart; service, too. Scottish beef, salmon, game well sourced. Haggis filo parcels a house fave. Cheeses from Iain Mellis; black pudding from Stornoway, naturally. There are others below-stairs at 29-33 Dublin Street (0131 556 2231) and at 38 St Mary's Street near the Royal Mile (0131 557 5754), even more intimate and informal and BYOB. Lunch Mon-Fri. Dinner 7 days LO 10pm.

235 1/B2
£15-22
A Room In The Town www.aroomin.co.uk · 0131 225 8204 · 18 Howe Street Corner of Jamaica St. The room is in the New Town for these lads (Peter Knight and John Tindal) originally from the Highlands and reflects something of that legendary hospitality. So good value, friendly service; you can BYOB (£3 corkage at all their branches). Mainly Scottish menu with twists. Expect haggis, game, salmon. Beers and malts (and loadsa corks!). Same folk have **A Room in Leith** (166/GASTROPUBS) and **A Room In The West End** (226 1036) in William St with upstairs bar **Teuchters** (Scots word for northern, rural folk with no manners: these guys love to be outsiders) and the restaurant downstairs. Similar menu. 7 days lunch and LO 10pm. All these Rooms are reliably good and popular; best book!

✓ **The Witchery** 0131 225 5613 Top restaurant that really couldn't be anywhere else but Scotland. Report: 130/BEST RESTAURANTS.

The Best Mexican Restaurant

236 1/D3
£15 22
✓ **Viva Mexico** www.viva-mexico.co.uk · 0131 226 5145 · Anchor Close, Cockburn Street Since 1984 the pre-eminent and only decent Mexican bistro in town. Judy Gonzalez's menu still innovates, although all the expected dishes are here. Genuine originals, famously good calamares and fajitas; lovely salad sides. Lots of seafood. Reliable venue for those times when nothing else fits the mood but proper fajitas and limey lager. 2 floors; nice atmosphere downstairs. Lunch (not Sun) and LO 10.30pm (Sun 10pm).

The Best Japanese Restaurant

237 1/E5
£15-22
✓ **Bonsai** www.bonsaibarbistro.co.uk · 0131 668 3847 · 4 West Richmond Street On discreet street on South Side, a Jap café/bistro (good to graze) where Andrew and Noriko Ramage show a deft hand in the kitchen. Freshly made sushi/yakitori and teppanyaki. No conveyor belt in sight, just superb value in downbeat neighbourhood café setting. Teriyaki steaks, salads and crème brûlée – actually, great crème brûlée (and green tea cake)! 7 days 12noon-10pm (not Sun lunch). Can BYOB (£5). Still no better taste of Tokyo in this town.

The Best Indian Restaurants

238 1/E5
£15-22
✓✓ **Kalpna** www.kalpnarestaurant.com · 0131 667 9890 · St Patrick Square The original Edinburgh Indian veggie restaurant, still very much the business. Favourites remain on the Gujarati menu and the thalis are famous but also unique dishes and dosas to die for. Report 223/VEGETARIAN RESTAURANTS.

239 1/E4
✓✓ **Mother India Café** 0131 524 9801 · 3 Infirmary Street Off South Bridge. That rare thing: a restaurant successfully transferred from Glasgow (551/GLASGOW INDIAN RESTAURANTS), this the eastern outpost in a growing empire. Has all the things that made it work in Glasgow's West End: neighbourhood feel, great value, small tapas-like dishes to share (40 to choose from), some specials; great service. Mother couldn't fail. 7 days 12noon-10/10.30pm.

240 1/B3
£22-32
✓ **Roti** www.roti.uk.com · 0131 221 9998 · 73 Morrison Street Near Conference Centre, in a corner by Scottish Widows building. Has often seemed a forlorn corner but people have been beating a path to the discreet door of this spacious room since it was turned into Roti by Tony Singh (133/BEST RESTAURANTS). Cousin Ryari runs it now but crucially chef Anand Sehgal still brings his light, imaginative touch to North and South Indian food. Decor may lack but service is as subtle as the fare. Good vegetarian. Tue-Sat, dinner only LO 11pm.

241 1/E5
£15 OR LESS
✓ **Khushi's Diner** www.khushisdiner.com · 0131 667 4871 · 32b West Nicolson Street Go downstairs on busy-with-restaurants, off-campus street to a big and unusually busy restaurant, the latest home of Edinburgh's legendary Khushi's, started so long ago nearby in Drummond St. Sons of Khushi, Islam and Riaz moved here '09 after a huge fire destroyed their pride and joy in Victoria St and their loyal clientele have followed. The room is fresh and contemporary and the Punjabi-driven menu is full of the usual and the unusual flavas. Fast service. No alcohol but BYO is free. 7 days, no Sun lunch.

242 1/E5
£15-22
✓ **Ann Purna** 0131 662 1807 · 45 St Patrick Square Friendly and family-run Gujarati veggie restaurant with seriously value-for-money business lunch and harmonious food at all times. Report: 226/VEGETARIAN RESTAURANTS.

243 1/D5
£15 OR LESS
✓ **Kebab Mahal** www.kebab-mahal.co.uk · 0131 667 5214 · 7 Nicolson Square Near Edinburgh University and Festival Theatre. Since 1979 Zahid Khan's slightly misnamed Indian diner (kebabs figure only slightly on a mainly curry menu) has been a word-of-mouth winner. As a no-frills Indo-Pakistani halal café it attracts Asian families as well as students and others who know. Great takeaway selection of pakoras, samosas, etc. One of Edinburgh's most cosmopolitan restaurants. And it's open late! 7 days 12noon-12midnight (2am Fri/Sat). Prayers on Fri (1-2pm). No-alcohol zone.

244 1/D4
£15-22
Saffrani 0131 667 1597 · 11 South College Street Off South Bridge and behind the Old Quad of the university. Small, tucked-away, personally run Indian bistro. Once again, no prizes for decor but conscientious, delicious and quite the real thing. North Indian menu and good for seafood. 7 days lunch and LO 11pm.

245 1/D5
£15-22
Namaste Kathmandu 0131 225 2000 · 17 Forest Road Big windows, big room but the weird chairs much loved by Indian/Chinese restaurateurs seem a wasted opportunity in the aesthetics department. However, it's the food with its Nepalese influence that we like. Chef Bimal Basnet's lovingly prepared North Indian and Nepalese dishes bring back the gap-year daze. Certainly this curry house stands out from others in the area. 7 days, LO 11pm.

246 1/XA4
£15-22
The Khukuri www.thekhukuri.co.uk · 0131 228 2085 · **8 West Maitland Street** The western extension of Princes St and Shandwick Pl before Haymarket Station. This unassuming Nepalese restaurant is a quiet secret. Costumed, endlessly polite Nepali waiters. Chef Dharam Maharjan routinely wins awards and 'brings the herbs himself' from the mountains of Nepal. Despite massive menu and mellow atmosphere, meat-eaters (lamb and chicken only) will be happiest here (there are prawns). 7 days lunch and LO 11pm (closed Sun lunch).

247 1/D2
9 Cellars www.9cellars.co.uk · 0131 557 9899 · **3 York Place** This small basement restaurant tucked away on busy York Pl is an Indian food lover's secret. Chef PC Thakur from Shimla ensures that this is one of the most authentic and unpretentious Indian meals in mid-town. Lunch (not Sun/Mon) and LO 10.30pm.

248 1/XA4
£15-22
Indian Cavalry Club www.indiancavalryclub.co.uk · 0131 228 3282 · **22 Coates Crescent** Off the main Glasgow road between Haymarket and Princes St. More upmarket than many on this page: with smart waiters and linen cloths, the CC has always attracted the suits, especially at lunchtime. Good buzz here and food always pukka. An unlikely carry-out place, but they do, and it's one of the best to your door. Lunch and LO including 'pakora bar' till 10.45pm.

✓ **In Delhi** Nicolson Street Near Nicolson Square. Sweet little Indian caff/ chai shop on busy street near the university. Cool spot. Report: 291/CAFÉS.

▮▮▮ The Best Thai Restaurants

249 1/C2
£22-32
✓✓ **Dusit** www.dusit.co.uk · 0131 220 6846 · **49 Thistle Street** In the continuing proliferation of Thai restaurants in Edinburgh, this one still gets the gold orchid. Elegant interior, excellent service and food that's good in any language but just happens to be exquisite Thai cuisine. Tantalising combinations with atypical Scottish ingredients; strong signature dishes. Decent wine list. Lunch and LO 10.30pm.

250 1/XB5
£15-22
✓ **Leven's** 0131 229 8988 · **30 Leven Street** Near the Cameo Cinema (and best nearby food). Almost gave this contemporary Thai restaurant 2 ticks coz it's so different to the others below. Owned by the same people who have Thai Lemongrass (and many others) but here Bangkok chef Nat Kowitwattana does something innovative and unique with the cuisine so you'll find pasta and potatoes with your exquisite vegetable curry. The fusion does work for once and the service is excellent. 7 days lunch and LO 10.45pm.

251 1/XB5
£15-22
✓ **Thai Lemongrass** 0131 229 2225 · **40 Bruntsfield Place** Smart but intimate, not too tiddlythai eatery by the people who have the estimable Jasmine (255/BEST CHINESE) and a few other Thais to boot. This one has a nice, solid, woody ambience, charming waitresses (Thai and Chinese) and food that's well good enough for Euro/Thai afficionados. Can BYOB (hefty £6 corkage) though has good wine list. Lunch Fri-Sun. Dinner 7 days, LO 11pm.

252 1/E1
£15-22
Phuket Pavilion 0131 556 4323 · **8 Union Street** Near Playhouse Theatre and Omni Cinemaplex. When other restaurants in this busy area are full, you can often get a table at this roomy, unpretentious Thai place that never lets you down. Friendly Thai staff. Bit of a local secret, just the right touch of holy basil and the rest. 7 days. LO 10.30pm.

The Best Chinese Restaurants

253 1/B1
£22-32
✓ **Kweilin** www.kweilin.co.uk · 0131 557 1875 · **19 Dundas Street** Though recent new owners, after 25 years this is still the New Town choice for imaginative Cantonese cooking (and other regions). Very good seafood and genuine dim sum in pleasant though somewhat uninspired setting. Excellent wine list. No kids allowed in the evening, so somewhere for grown-ups to eat their quail and especially good seafood in peace. You may have to book. LO 10.45pm (11.30pm Fri/Sat). Closed Mon & Sun lunch.

254 1/XA5
ATMOS
£15 OR LESS
✓ **Chop Chop** 0131 221 1155 · **248 Morrison Street** Haymarket Station end of street. Authenticity and simplicity are the watchwords in Madame Wang's stripped-back Chinese diner that's been packing us in since '06. Company makes dumplings wholsale and supplies Sainsbury's so they're de rigeur here; there's a vast selection. As with everything else. All comes in small dishes when ready. Full of people and brisk like China. Lunch Tue-Fri, dinner Tue-Sun. LO 10.30pm.

255 1/B4
£15-22
✓ **Jasmine** 0131 229 5757 · **32 Grindlay Street** Opposite Lyceum Theatre. Very Chinesey restaurant with big following. The only Chinese restaurant of the Chinese owners of an expanding Thai chain (Thai Lemongrass, above, and the one next door in Grindlay St). Pre- and post-theatre menus and good service to match (though it can be brusque). Seafood a speciality (Cantonese style). May need to book or queue in tiny doorway. Some memorable dishes await. Mon-Fri lunch. Dinner 7 days, LO 11.30/12midnight.

256 1/B2
£15-22
✓ **Wok & Wine** www.wokandwine.com · 0131 225 2382 · **57a Frederick Street** Next to Rick's (96/INDIVIDUAL HOTELS). Find this discreet basement restaurant refreshed a couple of years back. It's one of the best contemporary eastern restaurants in town, using all the right suppliers for meat and fish and other carefully sourced ingredients. Wok bites allow a tapas approach but this is a proper eating-out experience, not a drop-in as the name may suggest. And everything looks good – it's Edinburgh's chilled-out Chinese. 7 days 5.30pm-11pm.

257 1/A5
£15-22
✓ **Rainbow Arch** 0131 221 1288 · **8 Morrison Street** Unprepossessing but those who know go here and it's certainly the best real food choice adjacent Lothian Rd. Authentic menu, especially dim sum (dedicated chef). This is... well, proper Chinese cuisine. Open extraordinarily late. 7 days noon-3am (Thu closes at 12midnight).

258 1/XB1
£15-22
Loon Fung 0131 556 1781 · **2 Warriston Place, Canonmills** This place has been a destination diner since 1972. The famous lemon chicken and crispy duck signature dishes of this traditional neighbourhood restaurant specialising in Cantonese food. Good dim sum. Mon-Thu 12noon-11pm, weekends 2pm-12midnight.

259 1/XE1
ATMOS
£15 OR LESS
The Golden Bridge 0131 467 5441 · **16 Henderson Street** Backstreet Leith; easy to miss. This back-to-basics diner makes up for the 70s decor (including wax tablecloths and plastic ivy) with excellent authentic Chinese soulfood and charming service from Sue the fastidious owner. Loyal and avid following, no longer a well-kept secret. Evenings only, LO 10.30/11.30pm. No licence; BYO. No credit cards.

260 1/XF5
£15-22
Karen Wong's 0131 622 0777 · **107 St Leonard's Street** Two front rooms on the South Side; Ms Wong is always there to welcome you, smile and advise in her charming Sino-South Side accent. Mr Wong in the kitchen turning out the usual and an unusual dizzying array of dishes. Daily 4-11pm. Closed Tue. Takeaway.

The Best Burgers & Steaks

261 10/P25
ATMOS
£22-32+

✓ ✓ **Champany's** www.champany.com · 01506 834532 On A904, Linlithgow to South Queensferry road (3km Linlithgow) near M9 at junction 3. Accolade-laden restaurant (and 'Chop and Ale House') different from others below because it's out of town (and out of some pockets). Superbly surf 'n' turf. Live lobsters. The best Aberdeen Angus beef hung 3 weeks and butchered on premises. Good service, huge helpings (Americans may feel at home). Top wine list (and wine cellar shop). Chop House also has great home-made sausages. 7 days, from noon onwards at weekends; lunch and LO 10pm. Restaurant lunch (not Sat) and LO 10pm. Closed Sun. Hotel rooms adjacent (118/HOTELS OUTSIDE TOWN).

262 1/A1
£15-22

✓ **Bell's Diner** 0131 225 8116 · 7 St Stephen Street Edinburgh's small, but celebrated burger joint, the antithesis of the posh nosh. Nothing has changed in over 30 years except the annual paint job and (with an unusually low turnover) the gorgeous staff. Some people go to Bill Allen's Bell's *every* week in life and why? For perfect burgers, steaks, shakes and coincidentally, the best veggie (nut) burger in town. Bill's pushing on now but both he and his diner were born to run and run. Sun-Fri 6-10.30pm, Sat 12noon-10.30pm.

263 1/D3
£15-22

✓ **Buffalo Grill** www.buffalogrill.co.uk · 0131 667 7427 · 12-14 Chapel Street & 0131 332 3846 · 1 Raeburn Place Opposite Appleton Tower on the university campus. Over 25 years in burgerland, this diner trades on its reputation for steaks and such-like (Scotch beef natch) but there are some Mexican and Southern US variants and some concessions to veggies. Both great spots for easy-going nights out with chums; not large so book. BYOB (corkage only £1). Lunch Mon-Fri, LO 10.15pm (Sun 10pm).

264 1/D1
1/XE1
£15-22

Smoke Stack www.smokestack.org.uk · 0131 556 6032 · 53-55 Broughton Street From the makers of The Basement (338/UNIQUE EDINBURGH PUBS) came something equally groovy across the road – though that was a long time ago now. Loads of burgers (Scottish beef or vegetarian), seared salmon, blackened tuna; all jollied along by a great staff. Looking a little wasted now (the caff, not the staff) but this menu could go on forever. Lunch Mon-Sat, dinner 7 days, LO 10.30pm.

265 1/D4
1/A3
£15-22

Wannaburger www.wannaburger.com · 0131 225 8770 · 217 High Street & 7 Queensferry Street · 0131 220 0036 The first is bang in the middle of the Royal Mile below the Cathedral; the second a large West End window-watching room. Emphatically (gastro) burger joint with no starters and limited desserts (though Mackie's ice cream and milkshakes). Towering burgers in huge variety (13 vegetarian versions) and top toppings. Queensferry St great for breakfast from 8am (Sun 10am). Same people (and similar menu) have the Cambridge Bar (161/GAS-TROPUBS). 7 days all day, LO 9.30pm.

Kid-Friendly Places

266 1/XB5
£15-22

✓ **Luca's** www.s-luca.co.uk · 0131 446 0233 · 16 Morningside Road The ice cream kings (1434/ICE CREAM) from Musselburgh opened this modern ice creamerie and café where kids with dads will enjoy their spag and their sundae Sundays. Big cups of capp. Crowded and clamouring upstairs especially on weekends. Excellent for daytime snacks, family evening meals and gorgeous ice-cream at all times. BYOB. 9am-10pm. 7 days.

267 1/XF2
£15 OR LESS
✓ **Reds** 0131 669 5558 · 254 High Street, Portobello In main street, a much-welcomed, purposefully kid-friendly café (Derek and Louise have 4 kids themselves). A camera projects the rear playing/climbing area to a plasma screen in front. Regulation rather than inspired kids' food though all freshly and conscientiously prepared. Reopens as local bistro on weekend nights. 10am-4.30pm, weekends till 3.30pm then 5.30-9pm.

268 1/E1
✓ **Vittoria** www.vittoriarestaurant.com · 0131 556 6171 · Corner of Brunswick Street & Leith Walk Excellent Italian all-rounder that can seat 200 people including outside on the pavement on a people-watching corner. Kids eat for £1 which is donated to a kids' charity. And they get a balloon and crayons and stuff. Now that's friendly. Report: 188/ TRUSTY TRATTS.

269 1/XE1
£15-22
✓ **Giuliano's on the Shore** www.giulianos.co.uk · 0131 554 5272 · 1 Commercial Street By the bridge, the Leith version of 'Giuli's' (191/TRUSTY TRATTS) has all the traditional Italian trappings especially through the back (with a more contemporary feeling front-end; same food throughout). Cheerful pizza/pasta and waiters. Kids can make their own pizzas. For grown-ups nice antipasto, fish specials and a decent wine list. Always a birthday party happening at weekends. Luca's ice-cream (see above). 12noon-10.15/10.45pm. 7 days.

270 1/C4
£15-22
Café Hub www.thehub-edinburgh.com · 0131 473 2067 · Castlehill Top of Royal Mile, so tourist central. Roomy restaurant for adults that caters in a superior way for kids. This café is in the International Festival Centre, so busy busy in Aug. Outside terrace a child-friendly zone (370/DRINKING OUTDOORS) and the kids' menu has real food and nice touches: sautéd potatoes, not chips with the home-made burger. All kids' stuff under £3. 7 days Sun-Thu 11am-6pm (later in Festival), Fri/Sat 11am-10pm.

271 1/XB1
£15 OR LESS
Ye Olde Peacock Inn 0131 552 8707 · Newhaven Road Near the harbour. One of Edinburgh's unsung all-round family eateries for years – take gran as well as bairns. The fish really is fresh and the menu more adventurous than you'd think with lots that wee kids and we kids like. High tea is a treat. Pud list is a classic Scots dietary disaster, but irresistible. Lunch and LO 9.45pm. Bar till 11pm. 7 days.

OUTSIDE TOWN

272 10/Q26
£15-22
Cramond Brig www.cramondbrig.com · 0131 339 4350 · Cramond At the River Almond as you hit Edinburgh on the dual carriageway from the Forth Road Bridge. Outside there's a play area by the old brig itself and a river walk. Kids' menu and half portions available from the à la carte. Lunch and LO 9pm, 7 days. Weekends 12noon onwards. At the other end of the Almond river walk at Cramond itself, **The Cramond Inn** (0131 336 2035) has a very decent pub-grub menu (famously good chips) and is family-friendly and laid-back. Outside is the prom and the island (429/WALKS IN THE CITY).

273 10/R25
£15-22
Goblin Ha' www.goblinha.com · 01620 810244 · Gifford 35km from town in neat East Lothian village. One of two hotels, this has the pub grub cornered. Lunch and supper (6-9pm, 9.30pm Fri-Sat). The garden, busy in summer, is nice for kids.

274 10/P25
£15-22
Bridge Inn www.bridgeinn.com · 0131 333 1320· Ratho 16km west of centre via A71, turning right opposite Dalmahoy Golf Club. Large choice of comforting food in canalside setting. Has won various awards, including for its kids' menu. Restaurant, traditional and basic bar food and canal cruises with nosh (minimum booking is 20). Pop Inn restaurant 12noon-9pm daily. Children not after 8pm. Restaurant lunch daily and LO 9pm Mon-Sat. Bar till 11pm, 12midnight Fri-Sat.

The Best Tearooms & Coffee Shops

275 1/XB5
ATMOS

✓✓ **Loopy Lorna's Teahouse** www.loopylornas.com · 0131 447 9217 · **370 Morningside Road** At the end on the corner with Maxwell St. If you're into tea, cakes or top snacks, LL's is the real deal. You might have to kill for a table because some of those gals just want to linger longer. Mad selection of tea and cakes as you might expect plus lunch dishes, savoury tarts, etc. High level of chat and teapot envy. Not licensed at TGP (though you can bring your own champagne). 7 days 9am-6pm.

276 1/XB5
ATMOS

✓✓ **Falko Konditorei** www.falko.co.uk · 0131 656 0763 · **185 Bruntsfield Place** At the other (town) end of Morningside to LL's above, another exquisite teashop – some would say the Morningside matrons are too well served but Falko (who are also in Gullane; 1382/TEASHOPS) is baking at its best (from the 'Meiterhand'). Well known for their artisan bread (at the Farmers Market), the tortes are exceptional (Black Forest especially). Great tea list; soup at lunchtime. Daytime only. Closed Mon/Tue.

277 1/XD5

✓ **Peter's Yard** www.petersyard.com · 0131 228 5876 · **Quartermile** Actually located on Middle Meadow Walk, the pedestrian path through the Meadows, part of the new- (and old-) build Quartermile project that was once the Edinburgh Royal Infirmary. Light, airy bakery/deli/café that feels not like Edinburgh. Soup, salads, artisan bread and non-cream-laden cakes: big on baking. Nice, outside, people-watching patio. 7am-6pm (from 9am Sat/Sun). 'Pizza and wine' on Thu nights in summer.

278 1/XA3

✓ **Gallery (Of Modern Art) Café** www.nationalgalleries.org · **Belford Road** Unbeatable on a fine day when you can sit out on the patio on the lawn, with sculptures around, have some wine and a plate of Scottish cheese and oatcakes. Hot dishes are good – always 2 soups, meat/fish/vegetarian dish. Coffee and cake whenever. Art upstairs may provoke; this snack break is always welcome. 7 days 10am-4.30pm (413/OTHER ATTRACTIONS). Lunch dishes usually gone by 2.30pm. **Café Newton** at the Dean Gallery (414/OTHER ATTRACTIONS) across the road and the gardens from GOMA (above) is a smaller, more interior café by the same people. Soup, sandwiches and 2 hot lunch dishes. Coffee from mega machine. Same hours as GOMA.

279 1/D3

✓ **Fruitmarket Café** www.fruitmarket.co.uk · 0131 226 1843 · **45 Market Street** Attached to the Fruitmarket Gallery, a cool, spacious place for coffee, pastries or a light lunch. Big salads, home cookin', deli-plates and 2 daily specials. Some imaginative and surprising combos. Mhairi and Roy work harder than ever (1464/FARM SHOPS) and now they have a coffee shop in the crypt of **St Giles' Cathedral** (416/ATTRACTIONS) which has a similar set-up without the big windows. Both attract a mix of tourists, Edinburgh faithfuls and people who meet to eat. Fruitmarket: Mon-Sat 11.30am-4pm, Sun 12noon-4.30pm. Open till 5.30pm for coffee and cakes. St Giles 9am-4pm, Sun 12.30-4pm.

280 1/C2

✓ **G&T (Glass & Thompson)** 0131 557 0909 · **2 Dundas Street** Patrician New Town coffee shop and deli with a chef and a food attitude. Many 'ladies who latte', a phrase coined by Alexander McCall Smith whom you'd expect to see with a notepad in a corner seat. Great *antipasti*, soups, salads, sandwiches to go; and very fine cakes that you won't find anywhere else (cake doyenne Sue Lawrence uses their recipes). 9am-5.45pm, Sun 10.30am-4.15pm. See 316/TAKEAWAYS.

281 1/F3 ✓ **Clarinda's** 0131 557 1888 · **69 Canongate** Near the bottom of the Royal Mile near the Palace and Parliament building. Small but despite frilly touches, has total tearoom integrity. With hot dishes and snacks worth the sit-down stop on the tourist trail and some of the best home baking in town (especially the apple pie). Inexpensive; run by good Edinburgh folk (Marion Thomson and team) who work that tiny kitchen. Takeaways possible. Outside tables overlook the garden. 7 days 8.30am-4.45pm (from 9.30am Sun).

282 1/XB1 **Circle Coffee Shop** 0131 624 4666 · **Canonmills** Near the clock. Barry Bryson's cute deli/takeaway counter and lovely café in the back. Hot meals, salads, soups, ciabattas all made to order. Nice place to read the papers or linger for Sunday breakfast; this is a very New Town rendezvous. 7 days 8.30am-4.30pm. Sun 9am-4pm.

283 1/XD5 **Toast** 0131 446 9873 · **146 Marchmont Road** Converted bank and popular hangout on the Marchmont fringes. Brill brunch spot with home-made just about everything. Breakfast till 3pm. Damned good dinner and famously good puds. 7 days 10am-9.30pm (Sun till 6pm).

284 1/D4 **Black Medicine Coffee Shop** 0131 622 7209 · **2 Nicolson Street & 108 Marchmont Road** Corner of Drummond St. Funky American-style coffee shop on busy South Side corner opposite Festival Theatre and university Old Quad. Good place to take your book from Blackwells! Good smell. Big bagels, cookies and smoothies. 7 days 8am-6pm, Sun 10am-6pm. Also at **108 Marchmont Rd** in student land. 7 days 8am-5pm (till 6pm weekends), Sun 10am-6pm.

285 1/D4 **The Elephant House** www.elephant-house.co.uk · 0131 220 5355 · **21 George IV Bridge** Near libraries and Edinburgh University, a rather self-conscious but elephantine and well-run coffee shop with light snacks and big choice. J.K. Rowling (1921/LITERARY PLACES) once sat here: they say 'the birthplace of Harry Potter'. Counter during day, waitress service evenings. Cakes/pastries are bought in but can be taken out. View of graveyard and castle to dream away a student life in Edinburgh. 7 days 9am-10pm (7pm in winter).

286 1/XB1 **Botanic Gardens Cafeteria** www.rbge.org.uk By 'the House' (where there are regular exhibitions) within the gardens (410/OTHER ATTRACTIONS). For café only, enter by Arboretum Place. Catering-style food operation is better than it was. The outside tables and view of the city are why we come. And the cheeky, not-red squirrels. 10am-5pm.

287 1/C3 **Police Box Coffee Bars** 0131 228 5001 Kiosks not caffs! Rose Street (behind Jenners), Morningside Park, Hope Park Crescent (east of Meadows), top of Middle Meadow Walk (opposite Forrest Road) and outside John Lewis department store and St Andrew's Cathedral. Caffeine kiosks in former police boxes. Similar fare to Starbucks and Costas but these are home-grown and have, in their way, reclaimed the streets. Hours vary but early-late. Great coffee to go.

The Best Caffs

Also see Best Takeaway Places, p. 70.

288 1/XB5 ✓ **Zulu Lounge** www.thezululounge.com · 0131 466 8337 · 366 **Morningside Road** Way at the end of Morningside Rd. Tiny, tucked-away South African tea shack run by brother-and-sister team Chris and Kim Wedge. Soups, sandwiches, great home-made muffins. Miele bread and biltong and their signature espresso made from red Rooibos tea which they are rolling round the country. Cool spot (might be hotter closer to town). Open early-5/6pm.

289 1/D4 ✓ **Spoon** 0131 556 6922 · 15 **Blackfriars Street** Off the Royal Mile opposite High Street Hostel (114/BEST HOSTELS). Richard and Moira's friendly, off-high-street, almost neighbourhood but modern, minimalist café. Counter service for snacks and imaginative hot dishes made with more TLC than usual in open kitchen. Big bowls of soup, nice coffee. 9am-5pm, Sat from 10am. Open for supper Fri/Sat. Closed Sun.

290 1/E1 ✓ **Café Renroc** 0131 556 0432 · 91 **Montgomery Street** Billy and Jane Ross's neighbourhood cool caff on the corner ('renroc' backwards) with outside tables and more downstairs where there are, curiously, massage and treatment rooms. Popular hangout. Breakfasts, ciabattas, stromboli, nice coffee, fresh OJ. 7 days 8am-9pm.

291 1/E5 ✓ **In Delhi Nicolson Street** Near Nicolson Sq and the university. A maharajah's tent on the South Side, homage to Bollywood (movies on TV) and sweet memories of India. Chai and chatpatta (savoury snacks), naan rolls and sweetmeats. Chilled vibe, nice people. 7 days 10am-10pm.

292 1/XB5 ✓ **Luca's** www.s-luca.co.uk · 0131 446 0233 · 16 **Morningside Road** In-town version of legendary ice cream parlour in Musselburgh (1434/ICE CREAM). Ice cream and snacks downstairs, more family food parlour up. Cheap and cheerful. Great for kids. 7 days. Report: 266/KIDS.

293 1/A1 ✓ **Sprio** 0131 226 7533 · 37 **St Stephen Street** Tiny, authentic Italian coffee shop – a splash of Milano style in old St Stephen St. Few tables but you can take away. Paninis, piadines (unleavened bread), cured meats, cakes and the *best* espresso – oh, and the cioccolatissima (a hot-choc addiction). 7 days. Mon-Sat 8.30am-5.30pm, Sun 10.30am-5pm.

294 1/D1 **Blue Moon Café** www.bluemooncafe.co.uk · 0131 557 0911 · 1 **Barony Street** Longest-established gay café in Scotland (1090/GAY EDINBURGH). Straight-friendly and a good place to hang out from breakfast to late. All-day breakfast. Female staff efficient, boys more spacey. Nachos-and-burgers kind of menu. 7 days 10am-10pm. Food till 10pm, bar till 11pm. Juice bar **Sejuiced** is attached (enter from Broughton St).

295 1/D5 **Monster Mash** 0131 225 7069 · 4 **Forrest Road** Near the university. Comfort-food café capitalising on the mash comeback with properly sourced big sausages and gravy; shepherd's pie, steak pie, etc. Great British puds are similarly retro. Vegetarian options. Nice idea, no frills. 7 days 8am-10pm (Sat 9am, Sun 10am).

296 1/D4 **Always Sunday** www.alwayssunday.co.uk · 0131 622 0667 · 170 **High Street** A café on the Royal Mile that tries to please with home cooking and baking. Deli-style counter offering 'healthy' breakfasts through lunch to afternoon 'treats'. Hot specials and soups. 7 days 8am-6pm (Sat/Sun from 9am).

297 1/XE1 **Diner 7** 0131 553 0624 · **7 Commercial Street** Along from the bridge at the shore in Leith. Sliver of local diner/restaurant on a busy road. Burger/steaks and more adventurous dishes with fish and vegetarian all at cheapo prices make this a popular, casual and local diner. 9.30am-10pm, 7 days.

Kebab Mahal 7 Nicolson Square Report: 243/INDIAN.

The Best Late-Night Restaurants

298 1/C4
ATMOS
£22-32

✓**The Witchery** www.thewitchery.com · 0131 225 5613 · **Castlehill** Top of Royal Mile near the castle. Excellent value menu post- (and pre-) theatre menu from one of the city's best restaurants which means there's somewhere good to go late that's not Italian or Chinese. 2 courses only £12.99 at TGP. Worth it for the atmosphere alone. (130/BEST RESTAURANTS). 7 days, lunch and **LO 11.30pm**.

299 1/D5
£15-22

✓**Negociants** 0131 225 6313 · **45 Lothian Street** Near the university, a long-established all-day and late-night hangout. Chairs outside in summer. Food of the 'popular' variety ain't the strongest point but it is probably as good as it gets this late. Good mix of people. DJs in Medina downstairs at weekends. **Till 11.30pm & 2am Fri-Sat.**

300 1/E2
£15-22

✓**Giuliano's** www.giulianos.co.uk · 0131 556 6590 · **18 Union Place** Leith Walk opposite Playhouse. Buzzing Italian tratt day and night. Report 191/TRUSTY TRATTS. **Till 2am (2.30am weekends).**

301 1/A5
£15-22

✓**Rainbow Arch** 0131 221 1288 · **8 Morrison Street** **7 days 12noon-3am.** Authentic Chinese food of high standard. Report: 257/CHINESE.

302 1/B3
£15-22

The George Street Chains The **Living Room** (0131 226 0880) is the best of many for eats on 'stylish' George St and open later than others, especially at weekends. Like everywhere else on this street, it's part of a chain. Full-on bar at front; surprisingly large dining area at back. Modern British menu with food better than you'd expect. Very noisy and music too loud at weekends, but service is excellent. This ain't a bad 'product'. **7 days LO 11pm, 12midnight weekends**. The other 3 late-ish eateries on George St (all at the west end) are **Gourmet Burger Kitchen** (0131 260 9896) till **10.45pm; Gusto** (0131 225 2555) with the best makeover, till **11.15pm**; and **Browns** (0131 225 4442), comfort-food central, till **11pm**.

303 1/D5
£22-32

Favorit 0131 220 6880 · **20 Teviot Place** New York diner-type café/restaurant – salads, pasta, wraps, Ben & Jerry's. Food not so favourite these days but a useful nightowl/nighthawk spot. **7 days till midnight, Fri/Sat 2.30am.**

304 1/A3
£15-22

Bar Roma www.bar-roma.co.uk · 0131 226 2977 · **39a Queensferry Street** An Edinburgh institution, buzzing day and night. The old standbys snappily served and lots of late-night Italian jive. The best wine list you'll find in West End after ordinary hours (see 190/TRUSTY TRATTS). **12noon-11pm Sun-Thu; midnight Fri-Sat.**

305 1/C4
£15-22

Mamma's www.mammaspizza.co.uk · 0131 225 6464 · **30 Grassmarket** Open **till 11pm always & 12midnight** if you're lucky. Report: 195/PIZZAS.

Good Places For Sunday Breakfast

306 1/D3 ✓**Hadrian's** www.thebalmoralhotel.com · 0131 557 5000 · 2 North Bridge At the corner and brasseries restaurant of Balmoral (79/HOTELS). Good daily (power) brunch place, but also Sun. **From 7am (Sun 7.30am)**. Not cheap, but light (or lavish) and laid-back.

307 1/B2 ✓**Rick's** www.ricksedinburgh.co.uk · 0131 622 7800 · 55a Frederick Street The cool café-bar (391/COOL BARS) with rooms (96/INDIVIDUAL HOTELS) opens early as well as late; an excellent spot for laid-back or power breakfast brunch 7 days, including unusually early start on Suns. Eclectic, contemporary menu. **Open 7 days from 7am**.

308 1/C2 ✓**Urban Angel** www.urban-angel.co.uk · 0131 225 6215 · 121 Hanover Street & 1 Forth Street · 0131 556 6323 Convivial, contemporary breakfast from eggs benedict to honey and waffles. Freshly made croissants and the potato scones (136/BISTROS)! Full of bright people that can still remember their Saturday night. **From 9am Forth St, 10am Hanover St**.

309 1/D4 **City Café** 131 220 0125 · Blair Street It's been here so long, it's easy to take for granted… but for that 'BIG' breakfast (carnivore or veggie), few places in the city beat it for content or American diner atmosphere. Not open early; most of the clientele have been up very late. **From 11am**.

310 1/XE1 **King's Wark** 0131 554 9260 · 36 The Shore On busy corner for traffic, but calm and comforting inside. Dining room or bar. No early start (**11am**), but a civilised brunch on the waterfront.

311 1/D4 **Elephant House** www.elephant-house.co.uk · 0131 220 5355 · 21 George IV Bridge Another (this time extensive) coffee-house near the university that's open early for caffeine and sustenance. 285/COFFEE SHOPS. **From 9am**.

312 1/D1 **The Broughton Street Breakfast** There's lots of choice in the main street of Edinburgh's East Village. From the top down: **Mather's** the no-compromise drinking den does a traditional fry-up from **12noon**, as does **The Outhouse** down the lane but with veggie variants and until 4pm Including their famous BBQs out the back once a month. Lovely-looking **Treacle** kicks in from **10am** with upmarket gastropub choices. **The Basement** also does Tex-Mex brex from **12noon** and regulars attest to its ability to hit the spot. Further down on corner with people-watching windows is **The Barony** with breakfast and papers from **12.30-3.30pm** (great live music Sun evenings); and last but not least:

313 1/D1 **The Olive Branch** www.theolivebranchscotland.co.uk · 0131 557 8589 · Corner of Broughton Street & Broughton Place The definitive Broughton St breakfast: big windows, outside tables. Med menu and breakfast fry-ups. This place is routinely packed. On Suns you pray for a table. **From 10am**.

The Globe 23 Henderson Row Report: 322/TAKEAWAY.

The Best Takeaway Places

314 1/B2 ✓ **Appetite @ Rowland's** www.appetitedirect.com · 0131 225 3711 · **42 Howe Street** Great home-made food for takeaway, parties or just for your own supper/picnic, etc. Nearest thing in Edinburgh to a traiteur. Daily soups/curry/quiche/pizza and specials. Good vegetarian and salads. Best in the Stockbridge quarter; just possibly the best in town. Mon-Fri 8.30am-6pm.

315 1/B1 ✓ **Anima** 0131 558 2918 · **11 Henderson Row** Adjacent and part of L'Alba D'Oro (217/FISH & CHIPS). Smart, busy Italian hot 'n' cold takeaway. 'Italian soul food' includes great pizza, freshly prepared pastas made to order. Excellent wine selection, some desserts. A welcome expansion from chips – our soul food – to theirs. 7 days. Lunch and 5pm-10pm LO (11pm weekends). Closed Sun lunch.

316 1/C2 ✓ **G&T (Glass & Thompson)** 0131 557 0909 · **2 Dundas Street** Deli and coffee shop offering takeaway sandwiches/rolls in infinite formats using their drool-making selection of quality ingredients. Very fine cakes. Take to office, dinner party or gardens. Sit-in area and small terrace with New Townies and their chat. Mon-Sat 8am-5.45pm, Sun 10.30am-4.15pm. Report: 280/BEST TEAROOMS.

317 1/XF1 **Shapla** www.shaplatakeaway.co.uk · **87 Easter Road** Bangladeshi takeaway with growing reputation though chef Kabir has been cooking up the spices for 30 years. Menu features North Indian and Kashmiri dishes. Can order online. 7 days 5-11pm.

318 1/XA5 **Jaspers** 0131 229 8944 · **Grove Street** Bottom of the street, round corner of Morrison St near Haymarket. Small, simple café/takeaway with home-made quiches/tartlets as well as soups/sandwiches, etc. They do a nice omelette and stovies. 7.30am-3pm (Sat 8.30am). Closed Sun.

319 1/E5 **Kebab Mahal** 0131 667 5214 · **7 Nicolson Square** For 30 years this unassuming but cosmopolitan Indian diner and takeaway has occupied a fond place on the edge of the university quarter for snacks, curries, babas, kulfi and lassis. Open late. 12noon-12midnight, till 2am Fri/Sat.

320 1/XF1 **The Manna House** 0131 652 2349 · **22 Easter Road** Unlikely spot for relatively genuine French pâtisserie. Cakes to covet, artisan bread and baps; some tables and a quiche/salad/sandwich menu. Bakery through back. 8am-6pm. Closed Sun.

321 1/XE1 **Embo** 0131 652 3880 · **29 Haddington Place** Halfway down Leith Walk and a reason for going that far. Mike Marshall's neighbourhood hangout and takeaway is just better than the rest. Bespoke sandwiches, wraps, etc. Excellent coffee and smoothies. Few seats in and a couple of tables outside the door. Nice cakes. This place is good to know. Mon-Fri 8am-4pm, from 9am Sat. 10am-3pm Sun.

322 1/D1 **The Globe** 0131 558 3837 · **42 Broughton Street** A bright spot on the corner in the East Village. Open all day till 3/4pm for sandwiches, rolls and focaccia. Big window for people-watching. Branches at 23 Henderson Row and Bernard St, Leith (another busy shop on the corner). Henderson Row branch the best for real breakfast and newspaper reading, especially on Suns (outside tables).

323 1/XB1 **Eastern Spices** 0131 558 3609 · **2 Canonmills** Bridge by the clock. Long on the grapevine, this place is simply better than most – phone in your order or turn up and wait. Also home delivery in a 5-mile radius. Full Indian menu from pakora to pasanda and meals for one. 5-11.30pm. 7 days.

The Best Delis

324 1/E1
ATMOS
✓ ✓ ✓ **Valvona & Crolla** www.valvonacrolla.com · **19 Elm Row**
Near top of Leith Walk. Since 1934 an Edinburgh institution, the shop you show visitors. Full of smells, genial, knowledgeable staff and a floor-to-ceiling range of cheese, meats, oils, wines and other good things in life. Superlative fresh produce, irresistible cheese counter, on-premises bakery, great café/bar (182/ITALIAN RESTAURANTS). Demos, tastings and a Fringe venue, Valvona's is an Edinburgh landmark and a national treasure. 8am-6.30pm (Sun 11am-5pm).

325 1/C4
✓ ✓ **I.J. Mellis** www.mellischeese.co.uk · **Victoria Street, Morningside Road & Baker's Place, Stockbridge** Started out as the cheese guy, now more of a very select deli for food that's good and 'slow'. Coffees, hams, sausages, olives and seasonal stuff like apples and mushrooms (branches vary), so smells mingle. Branches also in Glasgow (642/GLASGOW DELIS) and St Andrews (1446/REALLY GOOD DELIS). 7 days though times vary. See also 1473/CHEESES.

326 1/XD5
✓ **Earthy 33 Ratcliffe Terrace** Tucked-away kitchen, garden and lifestyle emporium on South Side on road out of centre via Causewayside. Enter (via car park) an ambitious 2-floor shop and café (that feels like a market) with plants outside. Kind of co-op of like-minded gardeners and growers passionate about food, so all suppliers are hand-picked along with most of the fruit and veg. Local, organic, freetrade and seasonal are the watchwords here. Initially not easy to find, but you'll be back. 10am-7pm (6pm Sun). Café 10am-5pm.

327 1/C2
✓ **G&T (Glass & Thompson) 2 Dundas Street** Exemplary, contemporary provisioner. A choice of Mediterranean-style goodies to eat or take away and bread/pâtisserie; the New Town DP (dinner party to you). Report: 280/TEAROOMS.

328 1/A1
✓ **Herbie 1 North West Circus Place, 66 Raeburn Place & 7 William Street (takeaway)** Notable originally for cheese (that Brie!) and other cold-counter irresistibles (1474/CHEESES), Herbie's expanded. The original under new management does what it does best (cheese, olives), the bigger version on NW Circus Pl is mainly a takeaway and coffee shop. Nice bread and scrumptious munchies. There's also a takeaway on William St. Mon-Sat till 6pm. Closed Sun.

329 1/D1
✓ **Broughton Delicatessen 7 Barony Street** 2 doors from Broughton St corner but busy through reputation and loyal clientele. Some tables. Mainly a coffee shop but with a selection of good products: salads, quiche, hot dishes and home-made cakes to stay or to go. 9am-6pm (Sat 5pm), Sun 11am-5pm.

330 1/XA1
✓ **The Store 0131 315 0030 · 13 Comely Bank Road** At the end of main street in Stockbridge. Beautifully presented deli selling produce from the home farm (1462/FARM SHOPS), especially meats and all good things besides. Ready meals, homegrown fruits, good, dirty carrots. All you need for the Stockbridge dinner party. 7 days. Till 6.30pm Mon-Thu, till 6pm Sat, 5pm Sun.

331 1/XB5
✓ **Clarks** www.clarksfoods.co.uk · **0131 656 0500 · 202 Bruntsfield Place** Small, carefully run provisioner at the foody corner of Bruntsfield. Artisan bread (from AU Gourmand), fruit and veg and excellent selection of UK and especially Scottish cheeses. 7 days 10am-6pm (Sat till 5pm, Sun 12-4pm).

Unique Edinburgh Pubs

332 1/XE1
ATMOS
DA
✓ **Port o' Leith** 58 Constitution Street The legendary Leith bar on the busy road to what used to be the docks. (Saint) Mary Moriarty has 'retired' (we'll see if she can keep away). This pub was her creation: a remarkable woman of warmth and with an understanding of the human condition, a pub where all sorts and sods were welcome, from sailors and old Leithers to young dudes and tourists looking for Irvine Welsh. This pub makes us all feel better. Since '09 she ain't been there – let's see how it fares.

333 1/XB5
ATMOS
✓ **Bennet's** Leven Street By King's Theatre. Just stand at the back and watch light stream through the stained glass on a sunny day as it always did. Same era as Café Royal and similar ambience, mirrors and tiles. Decent food at lunch and early evening (368/PUB FOOD). Till 12.30am Mon-Fri, 1am Sat, 11pm Sun.

334 1/XE1
DA
✓ **The Pond** 0131 467 3815 · 2 Bath Road, Leith Cool Edinburgh bar off Seafield Road on the edge of dead dockland. They don't make 'em as understated or laid-back as this anymore. Funky fishtanks and al fresco bit out the back. Poker on Mon, quiz on Thu. Till 1am. (392/COOL BARS).

335 1/D5
ATMOS
✓ **Sandy Bells** 0131 225 2751 · Forrest Road Near the university and Greyfriars Kirk and seems like it's been there as long. Mainly known as a folky/traditional music haven (live 7 nights), it reeks (and we do mean reeks) of atmosphere. Should be given a dispensation from the smoking ban. Long may it... 7 days till 1am (Sun 11pm).

336 1/D2
ATMOS
✓ **Café Royal** West Register Street Behind Burger King at the east end of Princes Street, one of Edinburgh's longest-celebrated pubs. Unrelated to the London version, though there is a similar Victorian/Baroque elegance. Through the partition is the Oyster Bar (good atmosphere and food improved of late; 215/SEAFOOD). Central counter and often standing room only. Open to 11pm (later at weekends). Bar food till 9.45pm.

337 1/D1
Barony Bar 81 Broughton Street East Village venue with a mixed clientele and good vibe. Belgian and guest beers. Newspapers to browse over a Sun afternoon breakfast or a (big) lunchtime pie. Bert's band and others on Sun afternoons/evenings one of the best pub nights in town. Till 12midnight Mon-Thu, 12.30am Fri-Sat, 11pm Sun.

338 1/D1
The Basement www.thebasement.org.uk · 109 Broughton Street Much-imitated, still crucial, this is a chunky, happening sort of, er, basement with perennially popular Mex-style food served by laaarvely staff in Hawaiian shirts. At night, the punters are well up for it – late, loud and still alive. Till 1am daily.

339 1/B2
ATMOS
Kay's Bar 39 Jamaica Street The New Town – including Jamaica St – sometimes gives the impression that it's populated by people who were around in the late 18th century. It's an Edinburgh thing (mainly male). They care for the beer (360/REAL-ALE PUBS) and do nice grub at lunchtime. Until 11.45pm (11pm Sun).

340 1/A3
Mather's 1 Queensferry Street Edinburgh's West End has a complement of 'smart' bars that cater for people with tight trousers and tight agendas. The alternative is here – a stand-up space for old-fashioned pubbery, slack coiffure and idle talk (352/'UNSPOILT' PUBS). Wimmin rarely venture. Till 12midnight Mon-Thu, 1am Fri-Sat, 11pm Sun.

341 1/E1 **Sofi/Boda/Joseph Pearce/Victoria** Leith 4 pubs listed roughly in the order that they opened in the last few years in the Leith area where swingin' Swedes Anna and Mike Christopherson have built a funky little empire that could only happen in Edinburgh. All have been transformed from old, defunct pubs and are fresh, quirky, laid-back, mix 'n' match and full of individual touches. Sofi is the smallest, in a Leith backstreet (Henderson St); JP the largest on a busy corner (Elm Row) at the top of Leith Walk (with good pub-grub menu and outside tables); the others are on corners on The Walk. All till 12midnight/1am.

342 1/XE1 **Robbie's** Leith Walk On the corner with Iona St. Some bars on Leith Walk are downright scary and there are many new, fluffier ones of late but Robbie's stays real. Good range of beer, TV will have the football on (or not). Magi-mix of Trainspotters, locals and the odd dodgy character (350/'UNSPOILT' PUBS). Till 12midnight Mon-Sat, 11pm Sun.

343 1/D4 **City Café** 0131 220 0127 · **19 Blair Street** Seems ancient, but 20 years on, the retro Americana chic has aged gracefully. Always-occupied pool tables, all-day food, decent coffee. A hip Edinburgh bar that has stood the test of mind-altering time. Music downstairs weekends courtesy of guest DJs (309/SUNDAY BREAKFAST). 11am-1am daily.

344 1/C2 **The Dome** www.thedomeedinburgh.com · **0131 624 8624** · **14 George Street** Edinburgh's first megabar but not a chain. Former bank and grandiose in a way that only a converted temple to Mammon could be. The main part sits 15m under an elegant domed roof with island bar and raised platform at back for determined diners. Big chandeliers, big flower arrangements: you come for the surroundings more than the victuals perhaps. Adjacent and separate Club Room is more intimate, more clubby, better for a blether. 'Garden' patio bar at back (in good weather) – enter via Rose Street. Final bit, downstairs: Why Not? – a nightclub for over-25s still lookin' for lurvv (Fri/Sat). Main bar Sun-Thu till 11.30pm, Fri-Sat till 1am. Food till 10pm.

345 1/D3 **The Doric** www.the-doric.com · **0131 225 1084** · **15 Market Street** More a bistro than a mere pub, but the smaller room by the bar is Edinburgh in a nutshell. The window tables upstairs looking over the town to the Balmoral offer one of the defining views of the city.

■ The Best Old 'Unspoilt' Pubs

Of course it's not necessarily the case that when a pub's done up, it's spoiled, or that all old pubs are worth preserving, but some have resisted change and that's part of their appeal. Money and effort are often spent to 'oldify' bars and contrive an atmosphere. The following places don't have to try.

346 1/XA4 ✓ **The Diggers** 1 **Angle Park Terrace** (Officially the Athletic Arms.) Jambo pub *par excellence*, stowed with the Tynecastle faithful before and after games. Still keeps a great pint of locally brewed 80/-. The food is basic, ie pies at lunchtime (from local baker's, Morrison's). Till 11pm/12midnight Mon-Sat, 11pm Sun.

347 1/D4 ✓ **The Royal Oak** www.royal-oak-folk.com · **Infirmary Street** Tiny
ATMOS upstairs and not much bigger down. During the day, pensioners sip their pints (couple of real ales) while the cellar opens till 2am. Has surprisingly survived the

smoking ban. Mainly known as a folk-music stronghold (live music every night for 50 years!), they definitely don't make 'em like this any more. Gold-carat pubness.

348 1/XA4 ✓ **Roseburn Bar** 1 **Roseburn Terrace** On main Glasgow road out west from Haymarket and one of the nearest pubs to Murrayfield Stadium. Wood and grandeur and red leather, bonny wee snug, fine pint of McEwan's and wall-to-wall rugby, of course. Heaving before internationals. Till 11pm (12midnight weekends).

349 1/C2 ✓ **Clark's** 142 **Dundas Street** A couple of snug snugs, red leather, brewery mirrors and decidedly no frills. Good McEwan's. Habitués grow old here, hand on pint, eye on telly, but this is a local to love. Till 11pm (11.30pm Thu-Sat).

350 1/XE1 **Robbie's** Leith Walk On the corner of Iona St. Real ales and new lagers in a neighbourhood howff that takes all sorts. More rough than smooth of course, but with the footy on the box, a pint and a packet of Hula Hoops – this is a bar to save or savour life. Till 12midnight Mon-Sat, 11pm Sun. Report: 342/UNIQUE EDINBURGH PUBS.

351 1/B3 **Oxford Bar** www.oxfordbar.com · 8 Young Street Downhill from George Street. No time machine needed – just step in the door to see an Edinburgh that hasn't changed since yon times. Careful what you say; this is an off-duty cop shop possibly including Inspector Rebus (and Ian Rankin fans from far and wide). Be prepared to be scrutinised when you come in. Some real ales but they're as beside the point as the pies. Till 1am (12midnight Sun).

352 1/A3 **Mather's** 1 **Queensferry Street** Not only a reasonable real-ale pub but almost worth visiting just to look at the ornate fixtures and fittings – frieze and bar especially. Unreconstructed in every sense since 1903. Pies all day. Till 12midnight Mon-Thu, 1am Fri-Sat, 11pm Sun. Report: 340/UNIQUE PUBS. There's another, unrelated, **Mather's** in Broughton St which is managing to keep its head in the city's grooviest thoroughfare by remaining pub-like and unpretentious. Football telly.

▇▇▇ The Best Real-Ale Pubs

353 1/C1 DA ✓ **The Cumberland Bar** www.cumberlandbar.co.uk · Cumberland Street Corner of Dundonald St. After work this New Town bar attracts its share of suits, but later the locals (and recently droves of posh students) claim it. CAMRA (Campaign for Real Ale) supporters seek it out too. Average of 8 real ales on tap. Nicely appointed, decent pub lunches, unexpected beer garden (375/DRINK OUTDOORS). 7 days till 1am.

354 1/C4 DA ✓ **The Bow Bar** 80 West Bow Halfway down Victoria St. They know how to treat drink in this excellent wee bar. Huge selection ales and whiskies – no cocktails! One of the few places in the Grassmarket area an over 25-year-old might not feel out of place. Pie 'n' pint at lunch. Till 11.30pm Mon-Sat, 11pm Sun.

355 1/B5 ✓ **Cloisters** 26 Brougham Street, Tollcross This is a drinker's paradise: 9 real ales on tap, 70 whiskies with 35ml measures and 9 wines by the glass in this simple and unfussy bar with its wooden floors and laid-back approach. Same owners as the Bow Bar (above). Good pub grub; times vary and not Mon or Fri. Bar closes 12midnight (12.30am Fri-Sat).

356 1/D2 ✓ **The Guildford Arms** www.guildfordarms.com · 1 West Register Street Behind Burger King at east end of Princes St on same block as the Café Royal (336/UNIQUE PUBS). Forever in the same family. Lofty, ornate Victorian hostelry with loadsa good ales, typically 7 Scottish, 3 English (and 16 wines by the glass). There are some you won't find anywhere else in the city. Pub grub available on 'gallery' floor as well as bar. Mingin' carpet, by the way! Sun-Wed till 11pm, Thu-Sat till 12midnight.

357 1/B5 ✓ **Blue Blazer** 2 Spittal Street Opposite Point Hotel (76/MAJOR HOTELS). No frills, no pretensions, just wooden fixtures and fittings, pies and toasties in this fine howff that carries a huge range of real ales. Regularly a CAMRA pub of the year with 8 ales on tap. Extraordinary rum and gin list and then the malts. More soul than its competitors nearby even after recent refurbishment. 7 days till 1am.

358 1/XA4 **Bert's** 29 William Street Rare ales as well as house IPA and 80/-, suits as well as casual crowd in this *faux* Edwardian bar. Decent pies for carnivores or veggies alike all day, with other good pub-grub lunch till 8pm. Good range of up to 8 guest ales. Till 11pm Sun-Thu, 12midnight Fri-Sat.

359 1/XB5 **The Canny Man** 237 Morningside Road Officially known as the Volunteer Arms, everybody calls it the Canny Man. Smorrebrod at lunch time and evenings (163/GASTROPUBS), a wide range of real ales and myriad malts. Casual visitors may feel that management have an attitude (problem) – there's a list of dos and don'ts on the door – but this much-loved family fiefdom is a Morningside must.

360 1/B2 **Kay's Bar** 39 Jamaica Street Off India St in the New Town. Go on an afternoon when gentlemen of a certain age talk politics, history and rugby over pints of porter. The knowledgeable barman patiently serves. All red and black and vaguely distinguished with a tiny snug: the Library. Comfort food simmers in the window (lunch only). Till 12midnight (11pm Sun). (339/UNIQUE PUBS.)

361 1/XB1 **Starbank Inn** www.starbankinn.co.uk · 64 Laverockbank Road, Newhaven On the seafront road west of Newhaven Harbour. Handful of different ales on offer. Great place to sit with pint in hand and watch the sun sink over the Forth. The food is fine (till 9pm). Bar till 11pm Sun-Wed, 12midnight Thu-Sat.

362 1/D1 **Cask & Barrel** www.broughtonstreet.co.uk/cask&.htm · 115 Broughton Street Wall-to-wall distressed wood, great selection of real ales and a mixed crowd at the foot of groovy Broughton St. Here they prefer a good pint and the football. Till 12.30am Sun-Wed, 1am Thu-Sat. Outside tables.

Pubs With Good Food

Also see Gastropubs, p. 47. These below are not so high-falutin' foodwise, but nevertheless are worth going to for food as well as drink.

363 1/XE1 ✓ **The Compass** 0131 554 1979 · 44 Queen Charlotte Street Corner of Constitution St opposite Leith Police Station. This 'Bar & Grill' is a popular Leith haunt, maybe missed by uptown grazers. Stone and woody look with mix-match furniture; food better and more ambitious than you might first think. Staple fare. Bar kicks in later. 7 days, lunch and LO 9pm.

364 1/XE5 ✓ **Sheep's Heid** www.sheepheid.co.uk · 0131 656 6951 · Causeway, ATMOS Duddingston 18th-century inn 6km from centre behind Arthur's Seat and reached most easily through the Queen's Park. OK grub including alfresco dining when possible and comfy upstairs room at weekends. Village and nearby wildfowl loch should be strolled around if you have time. Great atmosphere; food improving. Lunch and 6.30-8pm, LO 7.45pm. Bar till 11pm/12midnight. Book weekends.

365 1/XF1 ✓ **The Espy** www.the-espy.com · 0131 669 0082 · 62 Bath Street, Portobello At the end of the said 'Esplanade'. The place for pub grub in Porty (the Portobello seaside suburb) with comfy couches in the lounge area and a fair few tables (including in the window, with a view of the espy, the beach and the sea), usually full. Food all fresh and cooked to order; good burgers. Occasional live music. 7 days 12noon-9.45pm. Bar 1am.

366 1/D3 **Ecco Vino** www.eccovinoedinburgh.com · 0131 225 1441 · 19 Cockburn Street Discreet frontage in street strewn with pierced youth. A narrow room where wines are supped. Mediterranean menu from the world's smallest kitchen, with imaginative soups, spags and tarts. You can eat small or large. Food 12noon-10pm, bar till 12midnight, 1am Fri/Sat.

367 1/XE1 **Guilty Lily** 0131 554 5824 · 284 Bonnington Road The back road to Leith. A moribund pub taken over by the same people who have the Espy (above) and transformed with great pub food into a new destination '09. Simple menu (lotsa burgers) but all freshly and conscientiously done, from daily meze to crumbles. Book weekends. 11am-10pm (Sun 8.30pm). Bar 12midnight/1am.

368 1/XB5 **Bennet's** 0131 229 5143 · 8 Leven Street Next to the King's Theatre. An ATMOS Edinburgh standby, listed for several reasons (333/UNIQUE PUBS), not least its honest-to-goodness (and cheap) pub lunch. A la carte (stovies, steak pie, etc.) and daily specials under the enormous mirrors. Lunch and till 8.30pm (not Sun).

369 1/C3 **The Abbotsford** www.theabbotsford.com · 0131 225 5276 · 3 Rose Street A doughty remnant of Rose St drinking days of yore, and still the best pub lunch near Princes St. Fancier than it used to be but still grills and bread-and-butter pudding. Huge portions. Restaurant upstairs more cuisine. Lunch and LO 9.45pm. Bar till 11pm/12midnight. Closed Sun.

The Best Places To Drink Outdoors

370 1/C4   **The (Café) Hub**   www.thehub-edinburgh.com · 0131 473 2067 · Castlehill
The café-bar of the International Festival Centre much improved for food and with a great enclosed terrace for people-watching. Brollies and heaters extend the possibilities. Ok for kids. 7 days 9.30am-10pm (till 6.30pm Sun).

371 1/XE1   **The Shore**   www.theshore.biz · 0131 553 5080 · 3 The Shore, Leith   Excellent place to eat (157/GASTROPUBS), some tables just outside the door, but it's fine to wander over to the quayside and sit with your legs over the edge. Do try not to fall in. From 11am daily.

372 1/XE1   **Teuchter's Landing**   www.aroomin.co.uk · 0131 554 7427 · 1c Dock Place
Another very good Leith eaterie (166/GASTROPUBS) but with waterside tables and spread over adjacent pontoons. Mugs of prawns, stovies, etc in half- or full-pint portions. Great wine list – 20 by the glass. From 12noon Mon-Sat, 12.30pm Sun.

373 1/D5   **Pear Tree**   0131 667 7533 · 38 West Nicholson Street   Adjacent to parts of Edinburgh University so real student style with big beer garden. Serried ranks of tables, refectory-style food. Stage for occasional live music, and BBQ. Good malt list. From 12noon Mon-Sat, 12.30pm Sun.

374 1/D2   **The Outhouse**   0131 557 6668 · 12a Broughton Street Lane   Large enclosed patio out back, home to summer Sun afternoon barbecues once a month. No view except of other people. Report: 387/COOL BARS.

375 1/B1   **The Cumberland Bar**   0131 558 3134 · Cumberland Street   Some tables by the door slightly raised above street level but more space in the beer garden below. Packed on summer evenings (till 9pm). Report: 353/REAL ALE.

376 1/E4   **The Pleasance**   www.pleasance.co.uk · The Pleasance & George Square Gardens   Both open during the Festival only, these are major Fringe venues, one a large, open courtyard and the other in the heart of the university and the new south-centred Fringe. If you're here, you're on the Fringe, so to speak.

377 1/A5   **Cargo**   0131 659 7880 · 129 Fountainbridge   At the so-called 'Edinburgh Quay'. Lofty emporium pub with over-ambitious menu, mainly distinguished by outdoor seating (in ranks of tables) on the basin of the Caledonian Canal – a surprising waterside spot in the city centre.

378 1/D2   **The Street**   0131 556 4272 · Corner of Picardy Place & Broughton Street
Great people-watching potential on busy corner. See 389/COOL BARS.

General locations: **Greenside Place** (**Theatre Royal** and **Café Habana**), bars in **The Grassmarket**, and **Negociants** and **Assembly** on **Lothian Street**. All rise (or sit down) to pavement café culture when the sun's out.

Cool Bars

Depends what you mean by 'cool', of course. On this page there's the ultra-contemporary, style bar ethos of Tigerlily/Opal Lounge/Rick's and the funkier, not-trying-so-hard ambience of 99 Hanover/Villager/Outhouse/Pond, etc. It may depend on whether it's looks you like, or feels.

379 1/B4 ✓ ✓ **Dragonfly** www.dragonflycocktailbar.com · 0131 228 4543 · **West Port** On the western extension of the Grassmarket. Discreet frontage but you enter a more beautiful, more stylish world where alcohol is treated like food in a fine-dining restaurant and cocktails are king. Lofty room with mezzanine. Not too many distractions from the aesthetic. Same people have the Voodoo Rooms and the Villager (see below). 7 days till 1am.

380 1/C2 ✓ ✓ **Bramble** 0131 226 6343 · **Queen Street** At Hanover St. A discreet, hidden-away corner basement but cool as, especially for cocktails. Discerning drinkers' haven so great gins, voddies, whiskies, etc. Nice Gen X (and Y and Z) people in the mix and non-compromising soundtrack rather than fluffy lounge music. Evenings only; till 1am.

381 1/XD2 ✓ ✓ **The Voodoo Rooms** www.thevoodoorooms.com · 0131 556 7060 · **West Register Street** Between St Andrews Square and the east end of Princes St. Opulent Victorian rooms above the Café Royal (336/UNIQUE PUBS, 215/SEAFOOD RESTAURANTS) transformed into a very contemporary, very happening group of salons for drinking, eating, carousing. Major Edinburgh live-music venue for interesting new bands. Food Scottish with a Cajun twist (till 9.45pm). Bars 1am.

382 1/C2 ✓ **Tigerlily** 0131 225 5005 · 125 George Street Some will revel in it, others go 'yuck' to this style-blinding bar/restaurant/hotel. Opened '06 in the middle of all the other style bars on George St and immediately became 'it'. Every design feature of the times with great attention to detail. A destination for the smart and ambitious and those with nice hair and teeth. 7 days till 1am.

383 1/B3 ✓ **Opal Lounge** www.opallounge.co.uk · 0131 226 2275 · 51a George Street Basement in Edinburgh's fashion mile for ambitious 'lifestyle' project from the indigo (yard) stable (see below). Sunken and sexy lounges including dancefloor and restaurant (fusion menu though not what they do best). Great staff know how to serve cocktails. Big door presence. Wills with St Andrews mates was famously once a regular. Admission and queue after 10pm. Open till 3am 7 days (food till 10pm).

384 1/C3 ✓ **99 Hanover Street** 0131 225 8200 Address as is. Unlikely up-the-town location but a civilised, draped and candlelit world with chabby-chic, pic-n-mix furniture, cool clientele and excellent music. It rocks. Till 1am.

385 1/D4 ✓ **The Jazz Bar** 0131 220 4298 · Chambers Street Down long stairs to the basement, this is not an obvious 'cool' bar unless you like good music and then it's very cool. No 'live band' tokenism here. Funk, hip-hop, ambient... and jazz. Great ambiance, interesting people. Mostly free but occasional name-band nights. An Edinburgh treasure chest. 7 days 5pm-3am (2am Mon). Go groove!

386 1/D4 **Villager** www.villager-e.com · 0131 226 2781 · 50 George IV Bridge Near university and National Library, a funked-up, laid-back place to hang out. DJs (Fri/Sat), reasonable pub food till 9.30 but mainly the right faces in a photo from the early days of the 21st century. Bar till 1am.

387 1/D2   **The Outhouse** 0131 557 6668 · 12a Broughton Street Lane Happily mixed and unobtrusive modern bar off Broughton Street 'in the lane'. Regular Sun barbecue on the patio. Till 1am.

388 1/D2   **Hawke & Hunter** 0131 557 0952 · 12 Picardy Place Across from the Playhouse Theatre near the top of Broughton St. In a 4-floor townhouse customised to be a private club, H&H has finally made it work. Restaurant on ground floor, main bar with DJs, pool room and whisky bar up top, but the garden bar (no real plants), **The Green Room** next door is also theirs. It's big! reached by the back staircase, is the coolest place to lounge. Popular though H&H is, inclusion in the *Observer*'s World's Top 50 Hip Places '09 was perhaps pushing it too far. 7 days till 1am.

389 1/D2   **The Street** 0131 556 4272 · 2 Picardy Place Corner glass box at the top of Broughton Street at central crossroads in the Pink Triangle; gay friendly. Great people-watching spot (outside tables) and pre-club venue. DJs weekends. Madame (Trendy) Wendy and gals manage the groove. 7 days till 1am.

390 1/C5   **Earl of Marchmont** 0131 667 1398 · 22 Marchmont Crescent Corner with Roseneath St in the heart of studentmont. Definitive bar of the area by the people who have cool caff Renroc (290/CAFFS). Pub grub all day, nice wines, outside tables, live music, DJs. Plus good vibe; it works. 7 days till 1am (Sun 12midnight).

391 1/B2   **Rick's** www.ricksedinburgh.co.uk · 0131 622 7800 · 55a Frederick Street New Town café-bar-restaurant with rooms (96/MAJOR HOTELS). Same problem with the eating experience here as the others in the group (Indigo Yard, Opal Lounge, etc), viz too much noise from the bar, though you come for cool, not calm. Bar service good and they know how to make cocktails. Rocks from 10pm onwards.

392 1/XE1   **The Pond** Bath Road & Salamander Street, Leith Turn right at foot of Constitution St past the warehouses. This anti-style bar is a long way from George St. Originally from the people who had clubs like Soft, Edinburgh Beige Cricket Team and the fanzine, *Shavers Weekly*, the Pond is where you'll find folk who don't want to be cool; they want to watch fish, play poker (Mon) and smoke in the garden. Till 12midnight/1am.

393 1/B2   **Iglu** www.theiglu.com · Jamaica Street Off Howe St in the New Town. Surprisingly cool bar in conservative territory. Handily open late (depending how busy). Small upstairs garret is a well-regarded bistro (155/BISTROS). Very Edinburgh, kind of lovely! 4pm-1am (Fri/Sat from 12noon).

394 1/E4   **Brass Monkey** 0131 556 1961 · 14 Drummond Street Student, Gen X and funky South Side pub with backroom Bedouin boudoir full of cushions to lounge and big screen (movies at 3pm daily); can hire for private functions. 7 days. LO 12.45am.

395 1/D4   **City Café** www.thecitycafe.co.uk · 0131 220 0127 · 19 Blair Street A true original that went from *the* hippest, to nowhere and back again with cool and crazy people and all tomorrow's parties. Buzzing at the weekend, downstairs the DJs play all kinds depending on the night. Pool tables never stop. 11am-1am daily. Then Sunday: 309/SUNDAY BREAKFAST.

396 1/XE1   **The Tourmalet** Iona & Buchanan Streets, Leith Named after a mountain in the Pyrenées, a stage in the Tour de France cycle race, this pub opening at TGP is something to do with cycling, fish tanks and train sets but mainly about the quirks and passions of owner Murray McKean who made the Pond (above). Vive la différence! Traditional opening hours.

397 **1/B4**
HS
ADMISSION

✓ ✓ ✓ **Edinburgh Castle** www.historic-scotland.gov.uk · 0131 225 9846 Go to Princes St and look up. Extremely busy all year round and yet the city's must-see main attraction does not disappoint. St Margaret's 12th-century chapel is simple and beautiful, the rolling history lesson that leads up to the display of Scotland's crown jewels is fascinating; the Stone of Destiny is a big deal to the Scots (though others may not see why). And, ultimately, the Scottish National War Memorial is one of the most genuinely affecting places in the country – a simple, dignified testament to shared pain and loss. The Esplanade is a major concert venue just before the International Tattoo in July, a major event of the Festival in August. Last ticket 45 minutes before closing. Apr-Oct 9.30am-6pm, Nov-Mar 9.30am-5pm.

398 **10/P25**

✓ ✓ ✓ **The Forth Bridge** www.forthbridges.org.uk · South Queensferry 20km west of Edinburgh via A90. First turning for South Queensferry from dual carriageway; don't confuse with signs for road bridge. Or train from Waverley to Dalmeny, and walk 1km. Knocking on now and seeming to be permanently under shrouds, the bridge was 100 in 1990. But still... Can't see too many private finance initiative wallahs rushing in to do anything of similar scope these days. And who would have the vision? An international symbol of Scotland, it should be seen, but go to the north side, South Queensferry's very crowded and sadly, very tacky these days (shame on Tesco for spoiling the view from the road bridge approach and well done the Dakota for dramatising it; 119/HOTELS OUTSIDE TOWN). There is also a good hotel restaurant in South Queensferry (122/HOTELS OUTSIDE TOWN) with views of the bridge.

399 **1/XA4**
ADMISSION

✓ ✓ ✓ **Edinburgh Zoo** www.edinburghzoo.org.uk · 0131 334 9171 · Corstorphine Road 4km west of Princes St; buses from Princes St Gardens side. Whatever you think of zoos (see *Life of Pi*, the 2003 Booker prize winner), this one, born 1909, is highly respected and its serious zoology is still fun for kids (organised activities in Jul/Aug). Penguins parade at 2.15pm daily in summer months and there are many other old friends and favourites as well as new ones: the Sumatran tigers, the only UK koalas and the beavers – there are many animals here to love and cherish. Open all year 7 days, Apr-Sep 9am-6pm, Nov-Feb 9am-4.30pm, Mar & Oct 9am-5pm. (1776/KIDS)

400 **1/XF3**
HS
🖥
ADMISSION

✓ ✓ **Palace of Holyroodhouse** www.royalcollection.org.uk · 0131 556 5100 Foot of the Royal Mile, the Queen's North British timeshare – she's here for a wee while late June/early July. Large parts of the palace are dull (Duke of Hamilton's loo, Queen's wardrobes) and only a dozen or so rooms are open, most dating from the 17th century with a couple from the earlier 16th. Lovely cornices abound. Anomalous Stuart features, adjacent 12th-century abbey ruins quite interesting. Courtyard and conservation café one of the nicest in town. Apr-Oct: 9.30am-5pm (last ticket), daily. Nov-Mar: 9.30am-3.45pm (last ticket) daily. Also... **The Queen's Gallery** 0131 556 5100 Visually appealing addition opposite the Parliament building with separate entrance. By architect Ben Tindall (who also did the Hub at the top of the Royal Mile, though this is better). Beautiful, contemporary setting for changing exhibits from Royal Collection every 6 months which include art, ceramics, tapestries, etc. Shop stuffed with monarchist mementoes. Nice caff in courtyard. 7 days 9.30am-6pm (closed 4.30pm in winter).

401 1/C4
1/D4
1/D3
1/E3
1/F3
✓✓**The Royal Mile** www.edinburgh-royalmile.com The High Street, the medieval main thoroughfare of the capital following the trail from the volcanic crag of Castle Rock and connecting the 2 landmarks above. Heaving during the Festival but if on a winter's night you chance by with a frost settling on the cobbles and there's no one around, it's magical. Always interesting with its wynds and closes (Dunbar's Close, Whitehorse Close, the secret garden opposite Huntly House), but lots of tacky tartan shops too. Central block closed to traffic and during the Festival Fringe it's the best street performance space in UK. See the Mile on a walking tour: there are several especially at night (ghost/ghouls/witches, etc.). Mercat Tours (0131 225 5445), Witchery (0131 225 6745) and City of the Dead (0131 225 9044) are pretty good.
Mary King's Close is part of a medieval street actually under the Royal Mile. Tours daily 10am-9pm (last tour), till 4pm Nov-Mar. Enter through Warriston's Close near City Chambers. **Scottish Poetry Library** is in Crichton's Close on right between St Mary's Street and the Parliament. Great collections, lovely contemplative space. Endorses Edinburgh's status as City of Literature. Mon-Fri 11am-6pm, Sat 1-5pm. Closed Sun.

402 1/F3
ADMISSION
✓✓**The Scottish Parliament** www.scottish.parliament.uk · Royal Mile · 0131 348 5200 Adjacent Holyrood (above) and Our Dynamic Earth (below). Designed by Catalan architect Enric Morales who died long before it opened, this building has been mired in controversy since first First Minister Donald Dewar laid the first stone. Opened finally after huge cost overruns in 2004, it is loved and hated in equal measure but should not be missed. Guided tours and ticketed access to the Debating Chamber. Unquestionably the finest modern building in the city (in my view and others – it won the 2005 Stirling Prize, the UK's premier architectural award). Tour times vary; book in advance.

403 1/D4
FREE
✓✓**Royal Museum** www.nms.ac.uk · 0131 247 4422 · Chambers Street From the skeletons to archaeological artefacts, stuffed-animal habitats to all that we have done. Humankind and its interests encapsulated (and displayed) here. Building designed by Captain Francis Fowkes, Royal Engineers, and completed in 1888. Impressive galleried atrium (with coffee shop) often hosts dinners and parties. Reopening end 2011 after major renovation. 7 days 10am-5pm.

404 1/D4
FREE
✓✓**Museum of Scotland** www.nms.ac.uk · 0131 247 4422 · Chambers Street The story of Scotland from geological beginnings to 21st-century paraphernalia, all housed in a marvellous, honey-sandstone building by Gordon Benson and Alan Forsyth, a delight to wander in. World-class space with resonant treasures like St Filian's Crozier and the Monymusk Reliquary, said to contain bits of St Columba. Early peoples to famous recent ones. 7 days 10am-5pm. Tue open till 8pm. **Tower Restaurant** (own entrance) is on the top floor (129/BEST RESTAURANTS). Roof terrace reveals the city's skyline (452/VIEWS).

405 1/F3
ADMISSION
✓✓**Our Dynamic Earth** www.dynamicearth.co.uk · 0131 550 7800 · Holyrood Road Edinburgh's Millennium Dome, an interactive museum/visitor attraction, made with Millennium money and a huge success when it opened summer '99 though a little less dynamic than it was. Now within the orbit and campus of the Parliament building. Salisbury Crags rise above. Vast restaurant, and outside an amphitheatre. Apr-Oct 10am-6pm daily. Nov-Mar 10am-5pm, Wed-Sun. Last admission 1 hour 10 minutes before closing.

406 1/C3
FREE
✓✓**National Gallery of Scotland** www.nationalgalleries.org · 0131 624 6200 · The Mound Neoclassical buildings housing a superb Old Masters collection in a series of hushed salons. Many are world famous but you

don't emerge goggle-eyed as from the National in London – more quietly elevated. The building in front, the **Royal Scottish Academy**, often has blockbuster exhibitions. Daily 10am-5pm, Thu 7pm. Extended hours during Festival. Serviceable caff.

407 1/XE1
ADMISSION

✓ ✓ **Royal Yacht Britannia** www.royalyachtbritannia.co.uk · 0131 555 5566 · **Ocean Drive, Leith** In the docks, enter by Commercial St at end of Great Junction St. Berthed outside Conran's shopping mall, the Ocean Terminal. Done with ruling the waves, the royal yacht has found a permanent home as a tourist attraction (and prestigious corporate night out). Check out the new Royal Deck tearoom. Close up, the Art Deco lines are surprisingly attractive, while the interior was one of the sets for our best-ever soap opera. Apr-Oct 10am-4pm; Jan-Mar & Oct Dec 10am-3.30pm. Booking advised in Aug.

408 1/XE5

✓ **Royal Commonwealth Pool** www.edinburghleisure.co.uk · 0131 667 7211 · **Dalkeith Road** Hugely successful pool complex which includes a 50m main pool, a gym, sauna/steam room/suntan suites, children's pool and play area, crèche and a jungle of flumes. Closed for major refurbishment. Check the website for opening hours in 2011.

409 10/Q26
ATMOS
ADMISSION

✓ ✓ ✓ **Rosslyn Chapel, Roslin** www.rosslynchapel.org.uk · 0131 440 2159 The ancient chapel 12km south of city, made famous recently by the world bestseller, *The Da Vinci Code*. The huge conservation and site-improvement project should complete by July 2010. Apr-Oct Mon-Sat, 9.30am-6pm. Oct-Mar Sun only, 12noon-4.45pm. Report: 1853/CHURCHES.

■ The Other Attractions

410 1/XB1
⌨
ADMISSION
FOR
GLASSHOUSES;
OTHERWISE
FREE

✓ ✓ ✓ **Royal Botanic Garden** www.rbge.org.uk · 0131 552 7171 · **Inverleith Row** 3km Princes Street. Enter from Inverleith Row or the great new gateway in Arboretum Place. 70 acres of ornamental gardens, trees and walkways; a joy in every season. Tropical plant houses, landscaped rock and heath garden and space just to wander. Chinese Garden coming on nicely, precocious squirrels everywhere. The Botanics have talks, guided tours, events (info 0131 248 2968). They also look after other important outstanding gardens in Scotland. Gallery with occasional exhibitions and café with outdoor terrace for serene afternoon teas (286/BEST TEAROOMS). Total integrity and the natural high. Houses the National Biodiversity Interpretation Centre and Garden. Open 7 days Nov-Feb 10am-4pm, Mar & Oct 10-6pm, Apr-Sep 10am-7pm.

411 1/C2
ATMOS
⌨
FREE

✓ ✓ **Scottish National Portrait Gallery** www.nationalgalleries.org · 0131 624 6200 · **1 Queen Street** Sir Robert Rowand Anderson's fabulous and custom-built neo-Gothic pile holds paintings and photos of the good, great and merely famous. Alex Ferguson hangs out next to Queen Mum and Nasmyth's familiar Burns pic is here. Good venue for photo exhibitions, beautiful atrium with star-flecked ceiling and frieze of (mainly) men in Scottish history from a Stone-Age chief to Carlyle. Closed for a mega internal revamp. Scheduled to reopen Nov 2011 – should be glorious again!

412 1/E4

✓ ✓ **Surgeons' Hall Museum** www.museum.rcsed.ac.uk · 0131 527 1649 · **Nicolson Street** Housed in the landmark Playfair building (1832), this museum is the real deal, integrity writ large and full of fascinating stuff. For over 500 years the Royal College of Surgeons has set and tested the standards of their craft and this museum records the growth of scientific medicine and

Edinburgh's extraordinary contribution to it. Changing exhibitions but wonder and wince through the Pathology Museum and get your teeth into the Dentistry Collection, both the finest in the UK. Mon-Fri 12-4pm.

413 1/XA3 ✓ **Scottish National Gallery of Modern Art** www.nationalgalleries.org ·
🖥 0131 624 6200 · **Belford Road** Between Queensferry Rd and Dean Village
FREE (nice to walk through). Best to start from Palmerston Pl and keep left or see below (Dean Gallery). Former school with permanent collection from Impressionism to Hockney; the Scottish painters alongside. An intimate space where you can fall in love (with paintings or each other). Important temporary exhibitions. Excellent café (278/BEST TEAROOMS). Charles Jencks art in the landscape piece outside is stunning. Mon-Sat 10am-5pm, 7pm on Thu. Extended hours during Festival.

414 1/XA3 ✓ **Dean Gallery** www.nationalgalleries.org · 0131 624 6200 · Belford
🖥 Road Across (busy) road from GOMA. In spacious grounds, a mansion of inti-
FREE mate spaces. Cool coffee shop, gardens to wander. Superb 20th-century collection; many surreal moments. Great way to approach both galleries is by Water of Leith Walkway (427/WALKS IN THE CITY). Mon-Sat 10am-5pm, Thu 7pm.

415 1/E3 **Museum of Childhood** www.museumofchildhood.org.uk · 0131 529 4142 ·
FREE 42 High Street Local-authority-run shrine to the dreamstuff of tender days where you'll find everything from tin soldiers to Lady Penelope on video. Full of adults saying, 'I had one of them!' Child-size mannequins in upper gallery can be very spooky if you're up there alone. Mon-Sat 10am-5pm. Jul & Aug Sun 12noon-5pm.

416 1/D4 **St Giles' Cathedral** www.stgilescathedral.org.uk · 0131 225 9442 · Royal
🖥 Mile Not a cathedral really, though it was once: the High Kirk of Edinburgh,
FREE Church of Scotland central and heart of the city since the 9th century. Building is mainly medieval with Norman fragments encased in a Georgian exterior. Lorimer's oddly ornate chapel and the 'big new organ' are impressive. Simple, austere design and bronze of John Knox set the tone historically. Holy Communion daily; other regular services. Atmospheric coffee shop in the crypt by Mhairi and Roy (279/COFFEESHOPS). Mon-Fri 9am-7pm (till 5pm in winter), Sat 9am-5pm, Sun 1-5pm.

417 1/A3 **The Georgian House** www.nts.org.uk · 0131 225 2160 · 7 Charlotte Square
NTS Built in the 1790s, this townhouse is full of period furniture and fittings. Not many
ADMISSION rooms, but the dining room and kitchen are drop-dead gorgeous – you want to eat and cook there. Delightful ladies from the National Trust for Scotland answer your queries. Apr-Oct 10am-5pm (1 Jul-31 August 10am-6pm), Mar & Nov 11am-3pm. Closed Dec-Feb.

418 10/P25 **Lauriston Castle** www.cac.org.uk · 0131 336 2060 · Cramond Road South
ADMISSION 9km west of centre by A90, turn right for Cramond. Elegant architecture and gracious living. Largely Jacobean tower house set in tranquil grounds overlooking the Forth. The liveability of the house and preoccupations of the Reid family make you wish you could poke around but exquisite decorative pieces and furniture mean it's guided tours only. Continue to Cramond for the air (429/WALKS IN THE CITY). Apr-Oct 2pm. Closed Fri. Nov-Mar 2pm weekends only.

Arthur's Seat Report: 428/WALKS IN THE CITY.
The Pentlands Report: 431/WALKS OUTSIDE THE CITY.
The Scott Monument/Calton Hill Report: 453/449/BEST VIEWS.
Newhailes House Report: 1826/COUNTRY HOUSES.
Dr Neil's (Secret) Garden Report: 1517/GARDENS.

The Best Small Galleries

419 1/XF2 ✓ ✓ **Ingleby Gallery** www.inglebygallery.com · 0131 556 4441 · 6 Calton Road Fabulous, light, new premises behind Waverley Station for this important contemporary gallery. Shows work by significant UK artists and the Scots, eg Callum Innes and Alison Watt with a refreshing and innovative approach to the constantly changing exhibition programme.

420 1/D3 ✓ ✓ **The Fruitmarket Gallery** www.fruitmarket.co.uk · 0131 225 2383 · Market Street Opposite City Art Centre. Around for a while but very much on a roll these days, a 2-floor, warehousey gallery showing contemporary work, retrospectives, installations; this is the space to watch. Excellent bookshop. Always interesting. Café (279/BEST TEAROOMS) highly recommended for meeting and eating and watching the (art) world go by.

421 1/E1 ✓ ✓ **doggerfisher** www.doggerfisher.com · 0131 558 7110 · 11 Gayfield Square Susanna Beaumont's vital gallery in a converted garage in the East Village. Limited wall space but always challenging new work. Weekend viewing. She does Venice Biennale and Frieze and very good openings in old Edinburgh.

422 1/C2 ✓ **Open Eye Gallery** www.openeyegallery.co.uk · 0131 557 1020 & i2 0131 558 9872 · both at 34 Abercromby Place. Excellent 2 galleries in residential part of New Town. Always worth checking out for accessible contemporary painting and ceramics. Almost too accessible (take a cheque book) – Tom Wilson will know what you want (and probably sell it to you).

423 1/E1 ✓ **The Printmakers' Workshop & Gallery** 0131 557 2479 · 23 Union Street · www.edinburgh-printmakers.co.uk Off Leith Walk near London Rd roundabout. Workshops that you can look over. Exhibitions of work by contemporary printmakers and shop where prints from many of the notable names in Scotland are on sale at reasonable prices. Bit of a treasure.

424 1/D3 **The Collective Gallery** www.collectivegallery.net · 0131 220 1260 · 22 Cockburn Street Installations of Scottish and other young contemporary trailblazers. Members' work won't break the bank.

425 1/C2 **The Scottish Gallery** www.scottish-gallery.co.uk · 0131 558 1200 · 16 Dundas Street Guy Peploe's influential New Town gallery. Where to go to buy something painted, sculpted, thrown or crafted by up-and-comers or established names – everything from affordable jewellery to original Joan Eardleys. Or just look.

The Best Festivals

426 ✓ ✓ ✓ Edinburgh invented arts festivals (more than 50 years ago) and now can truly be called the Festival City. Most of those listed below are world leaders. Unless otherwise stated, they are in August.
Edinburgh International Festival www.eif.co.uk · 0131 473 2000
Edinburgh Festival Fringe www.edfringe.com · 0131 226 0026
Edinburgh International Book Festival www.edbookfest.co.uk · 0131 228 5444
Edinburgh Military Tattoo www.edintattoo.co.uk · 08707 5551188
Edinburgh International Jazz & Blues Festival 0131 467 5200 · www.edinburghjazzfestival.co.uk

Edinburgh International Film Festival www.edfilmfest.org.uk · 0131 229 2550 Mid-late Jun.
Edinburgh International Science Festival www.sciencefestival.co.uk · 0131 220 1882 1-2 weeks Apr.
Scottish International Children's Festival www.imaginate.org.uk · 0131 225 8050 1 week end May/beginning Jun.
Edinburgh Mela www.edinburgh-mela.co.uk · 0131 557 1400 2 days end Aug/early Sep.
Edinburgh's Hogmanay www.edinburghshogmanay.org · 0131 561 3380 4 days, end of Dec-1 Jan.

■ The Best Walks In The City

See p. 12 for walk codes.

427 1/XA2
1/A2
1/A1
1/XA1
1-15KM
XCIRC
BIKES
1-A-1

✔✔**Water Of Leith** www.waterofleith.org.uk The indefatigable wee river that runs from the Pentlands through the city and into the docks at Leith can be walked for most of its length. The longest section is from Balerno 12km outside the city, through Colinton Dell to the Dell Inn car park on Lanark Road (4km from city centre). The 'Dell' itself is a popular glen walk (1-2km). All in all a superb urban walk. The Water of Leith visitor centre is worth a look. (0131 455 7367). Open 7 days 10am-4pm all year round.
STARTS (A) A70 to Currie, Juniper Green, Balerno; park by High School.
(B) Dean Village to Stockbridge: enter through a marked gate opposite the hotel on Belford Road (combine with a visit to the art galleries) (413/414/ATTRACTIONS).
(C) Warriston, past the spooky old graveyard to the Shore in Leith (plenty of pubs to repair to). Enter by going to the end of the cul-de-sac at Warriston Crescent in Canonmills; climb up the bank and turn left. Most of the Walkway (A, B and C) is cinder track and good cycling.

428 1/XF3
1-8KM
CIRC
MTBIKES
(RESTRICTED
ACCESS)
2-B-2

✔✔**Arthur's Seat** Of many walks, a good circular one taking in the wilder bits, the lochs and great views (450/BEST VIEWS) starts from St Margaret's Loch at the far end of the park from Holyrood Palace. Leaving the car park, skirt the loch and head for the ruined chapel. After 250m in a dry valley, the buttress of the main summit rears above you on the right. Keeping it to the right, ascend over a saddle joining the main route from Dunsapie Loch which appears below on the left. Crow Hill is the other peak crowned by a triangular cairn – both can be slippery when wet. From Arthur's Seat head for and traverse the long steep incline of Salisbury Crags. Paths parallel to the edge lead back to the chapel. Just cross the road by the Palace and head up. No mountain bikes. For info on the Ranger service and special events through the year, call 0131 652 8150.
PARK There are car parks beside the loch and in front of the palace (paths start here too, across the road).
START Enter park at palace by the Parliament. Cross main road or follow it and find your path, eg via the ruined chapel.

429 1/XA1
1/3/8KM
XCIRC
BIKES
1-A-1

Cramond The charming village (though not the suburb) on the Forth at the mouth of the Almond with a variety of great walks. (A) To the right along the prom; the traditional seaside stroll. (B) Across the causeway at low tide to Cramond Island (1km). Best to follow the tide out; this allows 4 hours (tides are posted). People have been known to stay the night in summer, but this is discouraged. (C) Past the boathouse, up the River Almond Heritage Trail which goes eventually to the Cramond Brig Hotel on the A90 and thence to the old airport (3-8km).

Though it goes through suburbs and seems to be on the flight path of the London shuttle, the Almond is a real river with a charm and ecosystem of its own.
The Cramond Gallery Bistro (0131 312 6555) on the riverside is not a bad wee bistro – its great cakes await your return. 7 days. **Cramond Inn** is another great place to recharge with decent pub grub.
START Leave centre by Queensferry Road (A90), then right following signs for Cramond. Cramond Road North leads to Cramond Glebe Road; go to end.
PARK Large car park off Cramond Glebe Road to right. Walk 100m to sea.

430 1/XA4
1-7KM
CIRC
XBIKES
1-A-1
Corstorphine Hill www.corstorphinehill.org.uk West of centre, a knobbly hilly area of birch, beech and oak, criss-crossed by trails. A perfect place for the contemplation of life's little mysteries and mistakes. Or walking the dog. It has a radio mast, a ruined tower, a boundary with the wild plains of Africa (at the zoo) and a vast redundant nuclear shelter that nobody's supposed to know about. See how many you can spot. If it had a tearoom in an old pavilion, it would be perfect.
START Leave centre by Queensferry Road and 8km out turn left at lights, signed Clermiston. The hill is on your left for the next 2km.
PARK Park where safe, on or near this road (Clermiston Road).

Easy Walks Outside The City

431 10/P26
1-20KM
CAN BE CIRC
MTBIKES
2-B-2
✓ **The Pentlands** www.pentlandhills.org · 01968 677879 or 0131 445 3383 A serious range of hills rising to almost 600m, remote in parts and offering some fine walking. There are many paths up the various tops and round the lochs and reservoirs. (A) A good start in town is made by going off the bypass at Colinton, follow signs for Colinton Village, then the left fork up Woodhall Road. Go left (signed Pentland Hills Regional Park). Drive/walk as far as you can (2km) and park by the gate leading to the hill proper where there is a map showing routes. The path to Glencorse is one of the classic Pentland walks. (B) Most walks start from signposted gateways on the A702 Biggar Road. There are starts at Boghall (5km after Hillend ski slope); on the long straight stretch before Silverburn (a 10km path to Balerno); from Habbie's Howe about 18km from town; and from the village of Carlops, 22km from town. (C) The most popular start is probably from the visitor centre behind the Flotterstone Inn, also on the A702, 14km from town (decent pub lunch and 6-10pm, all day weekends); trailboard and ranger service. The remoter tops around Loganlea Reservoir are worth the extra mile.

432 10/Q25
1-4KM
CAN BE CIRC
XBIKES
1-A-1
Hermitage of Braid www.fohb.org Strictly speaking, still in town, but a real sense of being in a country glen and from the windy tops of the Braid Hills there are some marvellous views back over the city. Main track along the burn is easy to follow and you eventually come to Hermitage House info centre; any paths ascending to the right take you to the ridge of Blackford Hill. In snowy winters there's a great sledging place over the first bridge up to the left across the main road.
START Blackford Glen Road. Go south on Mayfield to main T-junction with Liberton Road, turn right (signed Penicuik) then hard right.

433 10/Q26
1-8KM
XCIRC
BIKES
1-A-1
Roslin Glen www.midlothian.gov.uk Spiritual, historical, enchanting, now very famous (thanks to *The Da Vinci Code*) with the chapel (1853/CHURCHES), a ruined castle and woodland walks along the River Esk.
START A701 from Mayfield, Newington or bypass: turnoff Penicuik, A702 then left at Gowkley roundabout and other signed roads). Park at chapel 500m from Main St/Manse Rd corner, or follow B7003 to Rosewell (also marked Rosslynlee Hospital) and 1km from village the main car park is to the left.

434 10/P25
2-8KM
XCIRC
BIKES
1-A-1

Almondell www.westlothian.gov.uk · 01506 882254 A country park west of city (18km) near Livingston. A deep, peaceful woody cleft with easy paths and riverine meadows. Fine for kids, lovers and dog walkers. Visitor centre with teashop. Trails marked. Event programme.
START From Edinburgh by A71 via Sighthill. After Wilkieston, turn right for Camps (B7015); follow signs. Or A89 to Broxburn; follow signs from Broxburn.

435 10/N25
2-8KM
CIRC
MTBIKES
1-A-1

Beecraigs & Cockleroy Hill www.beecraigs.com Another country park south of Linlithgow with trails and clearings in mixed woods, a deer farm and a fishing loch. Great adventure playground for kids. Best is the climb and extraordinary view from Cockleroy Hill, far better than you'd expect for the effort – from Ben Lomond to the Bass Rock; and the gunge of Grangemouth in the sky to the east. 01506 844516 for park and visitor centre opening times. The hill never closes.
START M90 to Linlithgow (26km), through town and left on Preston Rd. Go on 4km, park is signed, but for hill you don't need to take the left turn. The hill, and nearest car park to it, are on the right.

436 10/Q26
7KM
XCIRC
XBIKES
1-B-2

Borthwick & Crichton Castles www.borthwickcastle.com Takes in 2 impressive castles, the first a posh hotel (121/HOTELS OUTSIDE TOWN), the other an imposing ruin on a ridge overlooking the Tyne. Walk through dramatic Border country steeped in lore. From Borthwick follow the old railway line. From Crichton, start behind ruined chapel. In summer vegetation can be high and may defeat you.
START From Borthwick: A7 south for 16km, past Gorebridge, left at North Middleton; signed. From Crichton: A68 almost to Pathhead, signed then 3km past church. Park and walk 250m.

▓▓▓ Woodland Walks Near Edinburgh

437 10/P27
ADMISSION

✓ **Dawyck Gardens** www.rbge.org.uk · 01721 760254 · Near Stobo 10km west of Peebles on B712 Moffat road. Outstation of the Edinburgh Botanics. Tree planting here goes back 300 years. Sloping grounds around the Scrape Burn which trickles into the Tweed. Landscaped woody pathways for meditative walks. Famous for shrubs, fungi and blue Himalayan poppies. Visitor centre. Apr-Sep 10am-6pm, Mar & Oct 10am-5pm, Nov & Feb 10am-4pm. 7 days. Closed Dec-Jan.

438 10/Q25
ADMISSION

✓ **Dalkeith Country Park** www.dalkeithcountrypark.com · Dalkeith 15km SE by A68. The wooded policies of Dalkeith House; enter at end of Main Street. Along the river banks and under these stately deciduous trees, carpets of bluebells, daffs and snowdrops, primroses and wild garlic according to season. Most extensive preserved ancient oak forest in southern Scotland. Excellent adventure playground. Rangers 654 1666. Open 7 days 10am-5.30pm through summer.

439 10/R26

✓ **The Yester Estate** Gifford With the decease of opera impresario Minotti, the large estate surrounding his house has become more approachable and there are some beautiful woodland walks. Hard to find (and I won't tell you how) is the legendary **Goblin Ha'**, the bad-fairy place (the hotel in the village takes its name; 1314/GASTROPUBS). Can walk in from The Avenue in the village or better: 3km along the B6365 road, foot of steep tree-lined hill, on bend. Park by house and go through marked gate. 3km through to village, it's 2km to Goblin Ha' itself.

440 10/R26

Humbie Woods 25km SE by A68 turnoff at Fala; signed for church. Beech woods beyond car park. The churchyard is a reassuring place to be buried; if you're set on cremation, come and think of earth. Follow path from churchyard wall past cottage.

441 10/R25   **Smeaton Nursery & Gardens** www.eastlothian.gov.uk · 01620 860501 · East Linton 2km from village on North Berwick road (signed Smeaton). Up a drive in an old estate is this early-19th-century walled garden. An additional pleasure is the Lake Walk halfway down the drive through a small gate in the woods. A 1km stroll round a secret finger lake in magnificent woodland. Garden Centre hours Mon-Sat 9.30am-4.30pm, Sun from 10.30am; phone for winter hours. Nice tearoom 10.30am-4pm Wed-Sun (2204/GARDEN CENTRES). Lake walk 10am-dusk.

442 10/Q26   **Vogrie Country Park** www.midlothian.gov.uk · Near Gorebridge 25km south by A7 then B6372 6km from Gorebridge. Small country park well organised for 'recreational pursuits'. 9-hole golf course, tearoom and country ranger staff. 01875 821990 for events and opening times. Busy on Sun, but a spacious corral of countryside on the very edge of town. Open 7.30am-sunset.

443 10/Q27   **Cardrona Forest/Glentress** www.7stanes.gov.uk · Near Peebles 40km south to Peebles, 8km east on B7062 and similar distance on A72. Cardrona on same road as Kailzie Garden. Tearoom (Apr-Oct). Forestry Commission woodlands so mostly regimented firs, but Scots pine and deciduous trees up the burn. Glentress (on A72 to Innerleithen) has become a major destination for mountain bikers, but tracks also to walk. Consult at **The Hub** (01721 721736) by car park (1375/GREAT CAFÉS). See 2091/CYCLING.

The Best Beaches

444 10/R25   ✓ **Seacliff** The best: least crowded/littered; perfect for picnics, beachcombing and rock-pool gazing. Harbour good for swimming. 50km from Edinburgh off the A198 out of North Berwick, 3km after Tantallon Castle (1795/RUINS). At a bend in the road and a farm (Auldhame) is an unsigned road to the left. 2km on there's a barrier, costing £2 (2 x £1 coins) for cars. Car park 1km then walk. From A1, take East Linton turnoff, go through Whitekirk towards North Berwick, then same.

445 10/Q25   ✓ **Tyninghame Beach & St Baldred's Cradle** Also off A198: going towards North Berwick from the A1, it's the first (unmarked) turning on the right after Tyninghame village. 1km then park, walk to left through gate 1km, past log cabin on clifftop which you can hire for parties (like I have); great wild camping and the beach is magnificent. And nearer North Berwick just beyond the Glen Golf Club and on the A198 to Tantallon is gorgeous little Canty Bay.

446 10/Q25   **Portobello** Edinburgh's town beach, 8km from centre by London Rd. When sunny – chips, lager, bad ice cream and hordes of people, like Bondi, minus the surf. When miserable – soulful dog-walkers and the echo of summers past. Arcades, mini-funfair, long prom and pool. The Espy is great for a seaside drink and food and occasional music.

447 10/R25   **Yellowcraigs** Another East Lothian splendour 35km from town. A1 or bypass, then A198 coast road. Left outside Dirleton for 2km, park and walk 100m across links to fairly clean strand and sea. Gets busy, but big enough to share. Hardly anyone swims, but you can. Many a barbie has braved the indifferent breeze, but on summer evenings, the sea slips ashore like liquid gold. See also 1694/KIDS PLACES. Scenic. **Gullane Bents**, a sweep of beach, is nearby and reached from village main street. Connects westwards with **Aberlady Reserve**.

448 10/P25   **Silver Sands** Aberdour Over Forth Bridge on edge of charming Fife village (1564/COASTAL VILLAGES). Train from Edinburgh (nice station). Cliff walk.

449 1/E2 ✓✓ **Calton Hill** Great view of the city easily gained by walking up from east end of Princes Street by Waterloo Place, to the end of the buildings and then up stairs on the left. The City Observatory and the Greek-style folly lend an elegant backdrop to a panorama (unfolding as you walk round) where the view up Princes St and the sweep of the Forth estuary are particularly fine. At night, the city twinkles. Popular cruising area for gays – take care if you do.

450 1/XF3 ✓✓ **Arthur's Seat** East of city centre. Best approach through Holyrood Park from foot of Canongate by Holyrood Palace. The igneous core of an extinct volcano with the precipitous sill of Salisbury Crags presiding over the city and offering fine views for the fit. Top is 251m; on a clear day you can see 100km. Surprisingly wild considering proximity to city. Report: 428/WALKS IN THE CITY.

451 1/B5 **Penthouse of the Point Hotel** www.point-hotel.co.uk · 0131 221 5555 · **34 Bread Street** Unadvertised spot but the penthouse function space of the cool, design-driven Point Hotel (76/MAJOR HOTELS) offers a unique perspective of the city. They allow you up if there's nothing booked in. This room is where a group first met to 'rebrand' the city in a campaign where Edinburgh is now Edinburgh Inspiring Capital. This view is where the 'inspiration' came from.

452 1/D4 **Terrace of the Museum of Scotland** www.nms.ac.uk · 0131 247 4422 · **Chambers Street** 6th floor (by annoyingly slow lift) of the fabulous museum (404/ATTRACTIONS) has a beautiful terrace planted all round and offering revealing city-skyline views and a great castle perspective. Andy Goldsworthy sculptures.

453 1/C3 ADMISSION **Scott Monument** www.cac.org.uk · 0131 529 4068 · **Princes Street** Design inspiration for Thunderbird 3. This 1844 Gothic memorial to one of Scotland's best-kent literary sons (1919/LITERARY PLACES) rises 61.5m above the main drag and provides scope for the vertiginous to come to terms with their affliction. 287 steps mean it's no cakewalk; narrow stairwells weed out claustrophobics too. Those who make it to the top are rewarded with fine views. Underneath, a statue of the mournful Sir Walter gazes across at Jenners. Apr-Sep, Mon-Sat 9am-6pm, Sun 10am-6pm; Oct-Mar, Mon-Sat 9am-3pm, Sun 10am-3pm. Last entry 30 minutes before closing.

454 1/C4 ADMISSION **Camera Obscura** www.camera-obscura.co.uk · 0131 226 3709 · **Castlehill, Royal Mile** At very top of street near castle entrance, a tourist attraction that, surprisingly, has been there for over a century. You ascend through a shop, photography exhibitions and interactive gallery to the viewing area where a continuous stream of small groups are shown the effect of the giant revolving periscope thingie. All Edinburgh life is visible – amazing how much fun can be had from a pin-hole camera with a focal length of 8.6m. Apr-Oct 9.30am-6pm; later in high season. Nov-Mar 10am-5pm. 7 days.

455 10/R25 BOTH 1-A-1 **North Berwick Law** www.eastlothian.gov.uk The conical volcanic hill, a 170m-high beacon in the East Lothian landscape easily reached from downtown North Berwick. **Traprain Law** nearby is higher, tends to be frequented by rock-climbers, but has major prehistoric hill fort citadel of the Goddodin and a definite aura. Both are good family climbs. Allow 2-3 hours.

The Pentlands/Hermitage Report: 431/432/WALKS OUTSIDE CITY.
Edinburgh Castle Ramparts Report: 397/ATTRACTIONS.
Oloroso Terrace Report: 133/BEST RESTAURANTS.

Section 3

Glasgow

The Major Hotels

456 2/C2
247 ROOMS
TEL · TV
NO PETS
ECO
£85+

✓✓ **Radisson SAS** www.glasgow.radissonsas.com · 0141 204 3333 · **301 Argyle Street** Bold, brash relative newcomer in emerging west end of Argyle St. Frontage makes major modernist statement, lifts the coolest in town. Leaning to minimalism but rooms have all you need, though no great views; some face the internal 'garden'. All in all a sexy urban bed for the night. Good rendezvous bar in large, open foyer and restaurant, Collage. Fitness facilities c/o LA Leisure Club in basement include a pool. No parking.

457 2/B2
72 ROOMS
TEL · TV
NO PETS
£60-85

✓ **The Malmaison** www.malmaison-glasgow.com · 0141 572 1000 · **278 West George Street** Sister hotel of the one in Edinburgh and elsewhere and originally from the same stable and same team as One Devonshire (see Hotel du Vin above). This 'chain' of good design hotels has all the must-have features – well-proportioned rooms (though small), with DVDs, cable, etc. – though the location just off West End affords no great views. However this is reliable, stylish and discreet. Contemporary French menu sits well in the woody clubbiness of The Brasserie downstairs (541/FRENCH RESTAURANTS).

458 2/C2
63 ROOMS
TEL · TV
NO PETS
£45-60

✓ **Abode Glasgow** www.abodehotels.co.uk/glasgow · 0141 572 6000 · **129 Bath Street** Smart, contemporary townhouse hotel, formerly The Arthouse, with wide, tiled stairwell and funky lift to 3 floors of individual rooms (so size, views and noise levels vary a lot). Fab gold embossed wallpaper in the hallways, notable stained glass and nice pictures. Grill downstairs has Modern British dishes and bar ('Vibe Bar') where the vibe can sometimes be lacking.
EAT The restaurant, Michael Caines@Abode is one of Glasgow's best fine-dining experiences (496/BEST RESTAURANTS).

459 2/D2
100 ROOMS
TEL · TV
NO PETS
£85+

✓ **Park Inn** www.glasgow.parkinn.co.uk · 0141 333 1500 · **Port Dundas Place** Near the Concert Hall. Good-looking modern high-rise hotel with designs – the millennium-period decor is still wearing well. Glass tiles in internal bathroom wall and sunken beds (though very comfy) won't suit everybody. Satellite TV/DVD and Playstations in all rooms. Oshi restaurant on ground floor with oriental pretension (nice plates) and spa (no pool, but treatments). Top Rooms: Duplexes on first floor. Innovative late-checkout facility on Sun (you pay by the hour after noon). Parking 200m and drop-off a bit tricky, but a very central option close to Queen St Station.

460 2/D3
117 ROOMS
TEL · TV
£85+

✓ **The Millennium Hotel** www.millenniumhotels.com · 0141 332 6711 · **50 George Square** Situated on the square which is the municipal heart of the city and next to Queen St Station (trains to Edinburgh and points north), Glasgow will be going on all about you and there's a conservatory terrace, serving breakfast and afternoon tea, from which to watch. Bedrooms vary; best on front. No parking or leisure facilities.

461 2/B3
319 ROOMS
TEL · TV
£85+

✓ **Glasgow Hilton** www.hilton.co.uk/glasgow · 0141 204 5555 · **1 William Street** Approach from the M8 slip road or from city centre via Waterloo St. It has a forbidding Fritz Lang/Metropolis appearance and the entrance via the underground car park is grim. Though this hotel could be in any city anywhere, it is one of the top in town with good service and appointments. Japanese people made especially welcome. Huge atrium. 20 floors with top 3 'executive'. Views from here to north are stunning. Leisure facilities include pool. Cameron's, the hotel's main restaurant, is present and correct and highly Michelin-rated though it has never been starred. Minsky's bistro and Raffles bar are serviceable.

462 2/XA4
164 ROOMS
TEL · TV
NO PETS
NO KIDS
£60-85

✓ **City Inn** www.cityinn.com/glasgow · 0141 240 1002 · Finnieston Quay
Modern block by the big crane near the SECC makes most of its Clydeside
location with deck and views; rooms here are a cut above the usual though not
large. Uniformity throughout but thought out. City Café on ground floor takes itself
seriously as a restaurant. Gym facilities nearby. Part of small UK chain, price and
particularity elevate from the economy travel lodge to the designer (though not
quite boutique) hotel. The river's the thing.

463 2/D2
64 ROOMS
TEL · TV
NO PETS
£60-85

Carlton George www.carltonhotels.co.uk/george · 0141 353 6373 ·
44 West George Street By Queen St Station and George Sq, this is a smart and
discreet central option and apart from parking (a hike to car park behind the
station or at Buchanan Galleries, the nearby mall) a decent bet in the city centre
for the business traveller. It's more 'fun' than that though, with a huge Irish bar,
the bafflingly popular Waxy O'Connor's, downstairs and an airy 7th-floor restaurant, **Windows**, up top. Residents' lounge and drinks in room all on the house.
Good service and the usual comforts.

464 2/B3
302 ROOMS
TEL · TV
£85+

Glasgow Marriott www.marriott.com · 0141 226 5577 · 500 Argyle Street
Modern and functional business hotel on 12 floors near M8. Rooms do seem small.
Parking is a test for the nerves. Nevertheless, there's a calm, helpful attitude from
the staff inside; for further de-stressing you can hypnotise yourself by watching
the soundless traffic on the Kingston Bridge outside; or there's a wee pool to lap
and separate gym. Mediterraneo restaurant, called Source, ain't bad (but ain't good
either).

465 2/XA4
283 ROOMS
TEL · TV
£85+

Crown Plaza www.qmh-hotels.com · 0870 448 1691 · Congress Road
Beside the SECC, on the Clyde, this towering, glass monument to the 1980s feels
like it's in a constant state of 'siege readiness'. Science Centre and Tower gleam
and twinkle on the opposite bank near the new BBC HQ; there's a footbridge
across. Some good river views from the 16 floors (executive rooms on 15 and 16).
The One Restaurant in the lobby has a carvery and some ringside seating for river-
gazing. Somewhat removed from city centre (about 3km, you wouldn't want to
walk), it's especially handy for SECC and Armadillo goings-on.

The Best Individual & Boutique Hotels

466 2/E4
100 ROOMS
TEL · TV
£60-85+

✓✓ **Blythswood Square** www.blythswoodsquare.com · 0141 208 2458 ·
11 Blythswood Square Address as is along one side of one of
Glasgow's dear green places, in the city centre. A huge conversion of the historic
building that was home to the RAC Club so newly opened that we hadn't been
able to visit at TGP. We know that it will be very good because it's the meticulous
and classy Townhouse Company of Edinburgh who are doing it (87/89/EDINBURGH
INDIVIDUAL HOTELS) and it has taken a very long time. Expect impressive original
features, lofty rooms and every modern comfort. Spa augurs well in a city not so
well served and chef Daniel Hall is a real catch: a guy on the way up, constructing
both classic and contemporary menus. Unquestionably this will be the fashionable
address on gardens that have been quietly elegant forever.

467 2/C2
49 ROOMS
TEL · TV
ATMOS
£85+

✓✓ **Hotel du Vin** www.hotelduvin.com · 0141 339 2001 · 1 Devonshire
Gardens, off Great Western Road (A82) Long Glasgow's landmark
smart hotel (as One Devonshire Gardens, the first 'boutique hotel' in the UK), now
part of the small but beautiful Hotel/Bistro du Vin chain. Five townhouses, the
whole of a West End terrace integrated into an elegant and sumptuous retreat but

a world away from Glasgow's wilder West End (centred on Byres Rd). Even parking is easy. House 1 has the bistro, bar, etc, House 5 the function rooms, but each retains character with fabulous stained glass, staircases and own doors to the street (though enter by reception in House 3). Cosy sitting rooms everywhere. Rooms large, as are beds, bathrooms, drapes, etc. Great bar (especially late) with malt list and as you'd expect, well chosen wines. No spa, pool, etc but long after its original conception, this is still an enduring oasis of style.
EAT Chic dining in elegant salons with fastidious service and excellent wine list.

468 2/E3
22 ROOMS
TEL · TV
NO PETS
£45-60

✓ **The Brunswick Hotel** www.brunswickhotel.co.uk · 0141 552 0001 · **104-108 Brunswick Street** Contemporary, minimalist hotel which epitomised a Merchant City style that emerged back in the 90s. Time, perhaps, for titivation but rooms economically designed to make use of tight space. Bold colours. Good base for nocturnal forays into pub- and clubland. Restaurant till 10pm, breakfast pleasant, especially Sun. Penthouse suite often used for parties. No parking.

469 2/C2
103 ROOMS
TEL · TV
£45-60

✓ **Marks Hotel** www.markshotels.com · 0141 353 0800 · **110 Bath Street** In the downtown section of Bath St but near the style bars and designer restaurants, a bedblock with more taste and character than most. Contemporary, of course, with big wallpaper, free WiFi, fresh flowers and restaurant on Bath St itself: One Ten bar and grill. Very central location though parking not so close.

470 2/C3
51 ROOMS
TV
£38 OR LESS

✓ **Artto Hotel** www.arttohotel.com · 0141 248 2480 · **37 Hope Street** Surprising, boutique-ish hotel very centrally situated behind Central Station on busy-with-traffic Hope St, though its rooms are double-glazed and quiet. Facilities basic but this place is amazing value. Restaurant adjacent – Bombay Blue, which features an Indian buffet – where you have your tiffin.

471 2/B2
5 ROOMS
TEL · TV
NO PETS
NO KIDS
£45-60

St Jude's www.saintjudes.com · 0141 352 0220 · **190 Bath Street** Glasgow's first small boutique hotel began as a northern Groucho Club. Million-pound refurbishment in '07 freshened the rooms (all upstairs, no lift) with big wallpaper, plasmas, etc. Bathrooms retain a '90s chic. Penthouse suites if you want to impress. Free champagne/martinis. Basement bar/restaurant **Mamasan** does an Asian-fusion-tapas thing and is a cool rendezvous; mixology and tasty tunes. Bar 3am.

472 2/D1
8 ROOMS
TEL · TV
NO PETS
£30-45

The Pipers' Tryst Hotel www.thepipingcentre.co.uk · 0141 353 5551 · **McPhater Street** Opposite the top of Hope St and visible from dual carriageway near The Herald HQ at Cowcaddens. Hard to get to the street in a car. Hotel upstairs from café-bar of the adjacent piping centre and whole complex a nice conversion of an old church and manse. Centre has courses, conferences and a museum, so staying here is to get close to Highland culture. Small restaurant.

473 2/XF3
7 ROOMS
TEL · TV
£38-45

Cathedral House www.cathedralhousehotel.org · 0141 552 3519 · **Cathedral Square** Opposite Glasgow Cathedral. Rooms above the bar; their main appeal is the outlook to the edifice, ie Cathedral and Necropolis (1875/GRAVEYARDS). Functional and friendly though needs some attention. A walk to Merchant City.

474 2/F3
6 ROOMS
TEL
NO PETS
NO KIDS
£38-45

Babbity Bowster 0141 552 5055 · **16-18 Blackfriars Street** This 18th-century townhouse was pivotal in the redevelopment of the Merchant City and famous for its bar (666/REAL-ALE PUBS, 547/SCOTTISH RESTAURANTS) and beer garden, Schottische restaurant upstairs and rooms above with basic facilities. Bathrooms ensuite. No TV but nice books. A very Glasgow hostelry, popular so book ahead.

Travel Lodges

475 2/E2
2/B2
239/279
ROOMS
TEL · TV
NO PETS
£38-45

Premier Travel Inns www.premiertravelinn.co.uk Of 16 in Glasgow area, most convenient probably east on corner of Merchant City at **187 George Street** (0870 238 3320) and west at **10 Elmbank Gardens** (0870 990 6312) above Charing Cross Station. Latter once an office block, now a vast city-centre budget hotel with no frills or pretence, but a very adequate room for the night. Functionality, anonymity and urban melancholy may suit lonesome travellers or the families/mates packed into a room. George St in area of many restaurants, Charing Cross opposite the excellent Baby Grand (565/LATE-NIGHT RESTAURANTS).

476 2/B2
139/141
ROOMS
TEL · TV
£60-85/
£45 OR LESS

Novotel www.novotel.com · 0141 222 2775 · **181 Pitt Street** Branch of the French bedbox empire in quiet corner near the west end of Sauchiehall St. Nothing much to distinguish, but brasserie/restaurant is bright enough and Novotel beds are very good. Small bathrooms. The 2-star **Ibis** (0141 225 6000) is adjacent (as opposed to Novotel's 3). If it's merely a bed for the night you want, it's much cheaper and hard to see what difference a star makes. They're both pretty soulless but parent chain Accor due accord better than UK rivals.

477 2/D2
113/119
ROOMS
TEL · TV
NO PETS
£38-85

Holiday Inn, City Centre www.higlasgow.com · 0141 352 8300 · **161 West Nile Street** Another block off the old block. In the city centre near Concert Hall. Gym, but no pool; restaurant but not great shakes. Holiday Inn Express adjacent is better value (25% less). Room rates vary depending on occupancy. A lot of shopping goes on around you.

478 2/D5
128 ROOMS

Express by Holiday Inn www.hiexpressglasgow.co.uk · 0141 548 5000 · **Corner of Stockwell & Clyde Streets** Functional bedbox that's not a bad deal, but only 5 rooms on the river. All you do is sleep here. Near Merchant City so lots of restaurants, nightlife and other distractions, and curiously midway between 2 of Glasgow's oldest, funkiest bars, the Scotia and Victoria (652/651/UNIQUE PUBS). Another Express adjacent Holiday Inn, City Centre (above), but this one is best.

The Best Hostels

The SYHA is the Scottish Youth Hostel Association, of which you have to be a member (or a member of an affiliated organisation from another country) to stay in their many hostels round Scotland. Phone 01786 451181 for details, or contact any YHA hostel.

479 2/XA1
150 BEDS

✓ **SY Hostel** www.syha.org.uk · 0870 004 1119 · **8 Park Terrace** Oddly quiet and up-market location in an elegant terrace in posh West End near the university and Kelvingrove Park. This building was converted in 1992 from the Beacons Hotel, which was where rock 'n' roll bands used to stay in the 1980s. Dorms for 4-6 (some larger) and the public rooms are common rooms with TV, games, etc. Coffeeshop and breakfast room in the basement till 3pm (open Fri/Sat evenings at TGP). You must be a member of the SYHA. See above.

480 2/F2
70 BEDS

Murray Hall, Strathclyde University www.strath.ac.uk · 0141 548 3560 · **Cathedral Street** Modern but not sterile block of single rooms on edge of main campus and facing towards Cathedral. Part of large complex (also some student flats to rent by the week) with bar/shop/laundrette. Quite central, close to Merchant City bars. Vacations only. There's also Chancellors Hall adjacent, 218 rooms, same deal, same number.

481 2/C4
365 BEDS

Euro Hostel Glasgow www.euro-hostels.co.uk · 0141 222 2828 · **318 Clyde Street** A very central independent hostel block at the bottom of Union/Renfield St and almost overlooking the river. Mix of single, twin or dorm accommodation, but all ensuite and clean. Breakfast included in price. Kitchen and laundry. Games and TV room. The ground-floor bar, Osmosis, is open to the public. Not as cheap as some but well appointed. Open all year.

Note: Both Strathclyde and Glasgow Universities have several other halls of residence available for short-term accommodation in the summer months. Phone: Glasgow 0141 330 4116/2318 or Strathclyde 0141 553 4148 (central booking).

The Best Hotels Outside Town

482 9/L25
134 ROOMS
TEL · TV
NO PETS
£60-85

✓✓ **De Vere Cameron House Hotel** www.devere.co.uk · 01389 755565 · **Loch Lomond** A82 via West End or Erskine Bridge and M8. 45km from centre. International-standard mansion-house hotel complex with excellent leisure facilities in 100 acres of open grounds on the loch's bonny banks (and the new Carrick golf course and spa 5km along the lochside). Recent extensive refurbishments have improved immensely the hotel, the rooms, the public areas and especially the restaurants. Sports include 9-hole golf by the hotel ('the wee demon' – no booking) as well as the 18-hole Carrick, pool (with chutes for kids), tennis, snooker and lots to do on the loch including windsurfing and cruising (and you can arrive by seaplane). Casual dining at poolside or the estimable Cameron Grill and 'Martin Wishart' with the celebrated eponymous chef (though run by his team); 491/GLASGOW FINE DINING. Excellent whisky bar pre- and après. The Spa with a huge range of treatments and pamperings has outdoor deck and pool, bar/restaurant and not much they haven't thought of. All this ain't cheap, but as they say, 'this is the life': they're not wrong.
EAT 4 main restaurants to choose from including Michelin-star-chef Martin Wishart's make this probably the best dining-out prospect in the west.

483 10/M26
92 ROOMS
TEL · TV
NO PETS
£38-45

✓✓ **Dakota** www.dakotahotels.co.uk · 0870 220 8281 · **EuroCentral** 24km from centre on the M8. Like the South Queensferry version (119/HOTELS OUTSIDE EDINBURGH) this is a chip off the new (black granite, smoked glass) block and similarly situated overlooking the highway, in the spot of regenerating Lanarkshire they call EuroCentral. Behind the severe exterior is a design-driven roadhouse that is a paean to travel and elegantly rises to meet the requirements of modern travellers. Another hotel hit for the McCulloch/Rosa team.
EAT The Grill is superb: probably the best motorway caff in the UK.

484 9/L25
53 ROOMS
TEL · TV
NO PETS
£60-85

✓✓ **Mar Hall** www.marhall.com · 0141 812 9999 · **Earl of Mar Estate, Bishopton** M8 junction 28A/29, A726 then A8 into Bishopton. 5-star luxury 10 minutes to airport and 25 minutes to central Glasgow. Impressive conversion of imposing, *très elegant* baronial house with grand, slightly gloomy public spaces including the hall and rooms that vary (some huge) but all with 5-star niceties. (Aveda) spa/leisure club adjacent with 15m pool. The Cristal, with long windows on to the gardens, is the fine-dining restaurant under Jim Kerr (fusion Scottish); casual lunches in the hall! The new rock 'n' roll stopover for the city (Take That came and took that in '09).

485 9/L24 ✓ **The Lodge On Loch Lomond** www.lochlomondlodge.co.uk · 01436
47 ROOMS 860201 Edge of Luss on A82 north from Balloch; 40 minutes to Glasgow's
TEL · TV West End. In a linear arrangement that makes the most of a great lochside setting.
£38-45 This hotel, ignored by the posher guides, still punches well above its weight.
Wood-lined rooms (the 'Corbetts') overlook the bonny banks with balconies and
saunas, then there's the 'Grahams' and in the adjacent, newer block the 'Munros'
– it's a Scottish hill thing. Colquhoun's restaurant has the view and the terrace and
is surprisingly good; book at weekends. Rooms in Munro Lodge, back from
lochside, are more corporate. Spa and nice pool. Many weddings; some conferences. Bill Clinton once came by.

486 10/L26 ✓ **Ashtree House Hotel** www.ashtreehousehotel.com · 0141 848 6411 ·
14 ROOMS **Orr Square, Paisley** In the centre near the station which has frequent trains
£38-45 to Glasgow Central (9 minutes) and also only 15 minutes to Glasgow Airport so it's
handy to know and it's easy to like. A Regency townhouse with courtyard and
walled garden (all bedrooms overlook), this place has far more class and calm than
anything simlar in town and it's so reasonably priced. Restaurant opening 2010.

487 10/L25 **The Black Bull Hotel** www.blackbullhotel.com · 01360 550215 · 2 The
12 ROOMS **Square, Killearn** A81 towards Aberfoyle, take the right fork after Strathblane, and
TEL · TV the hotel is at the top end of the village next to the church. Urban values, design
£45-60 and comforts in this restaurant with rooms in quiet village situation. Clubby casual
bistro and bar meals and finer-dining conservatory restaurant.

488 10/M26 **Eglinton Arms Hotel** www.eglintonarms.co.uk · 01355 302631 ·
38 ROOMS **Eaglesham** Sprawling inn in a charming conservation village, a quiet contrast to
TEL · TV downtown Glasgow but a surprisingly close 10km to south city boundary. A differ-
£38-45 ent green world and gurgling brook besides. Very decent and locally popular
bar/grill restaurant, and refurbished rooms for less than any comparable city stay.

The Best Fine-Dining Restaurants

489 2/XA1
£22-32+
ATMOS

✓✓ **Ubiquitous Chip** www.ubiquitouschip.co.uk · 0141 334 5007 ·
12 Ashton Lane It's not easy to say anything new about this cornerstone of culinary Glasgow: a 2-storey, covered courtyard draped with vines, off a
bar-strewn cobbled lane in the heart of the West End and which has been here
longer than anyone else (a pioneer restaurant since 1971) even though there is
nothing stale or static about it. The main room is still one of the most atmospheric
of salons and Ian Brown's menu is exemplary – the best of Scottish seafood, game
and beef impeccably sourced and fine, original cooking. An outstanding wine list.
The Chip upstairs has a different, lighter brasserie menu and there's also a pub-
food menu though this may not be available on weekend nights. All in all, the Chip
is the long-standing destination restaurant in the West End. It is handily open later
than most. Daily lunch and 6.30-11pm.

490 2/XA1
£22-32

✓✓ **Bistro du Vin** 0141 339 2001 · 1 Devonshire Gardens, off Great
Western Road Glasgow's oldest boutique hotel (467/BEST HOTELS) has,
since it opened, had one of the city's classiest fine-dining salons. The dining rooms
in house 5 in this elegant row are now confidently established as an informal but
smart restaurant which Joanna Blythman once described as 'a masterpiece'. Posh
London club-like setting and a great chef Paul Tamburrini has restored Devonshire
Gardens as a must-eat destination in the West End. 7 days lunch and dinner
(closed Sun lunch). LO 9.30/10pm.

491 9/L25
£32+

✓✓ **Martin Wishart at Loch Lomond** www.devere.co.uk · 01389
755565 · Loch Lomond Michelin-star chef Martin Wishart (and to some
hand-wringing each year they're announced, there are none awarded to Glasgow
chefs) here at Cameron House (482/HOTELS OUTSIDE TOWN) from his base in
Edinburgh (123/EDINBURGH FINE DINING). Though the man himself is only here 2
weekends a month, the kitchen under Canadian Stewart Boyles, who's been with
Martin for 5 years, produces its 6-course tasting menu (and à la carte) with
expected purpose and panache. Fans of Martin, of which I am one, will love this
simply stylish room by the loch. 7 days dinner and Sun lunch. The hotel also has
the Cameron Grill which does what it says on the tin, though fabulously well.

492 2/C2
£22-32

✓ **Le Chardon D'Or** www.brianmaule.com · 0141 248 3801 · 176 West
Regent Street Brian Maule's (formerly head chef at the Roux brothers'
famed Le Gavroche) Golden Thistle in French with contemporary spin on Auld
Alliance as far as the food's concerned: impeccable ingredients, French influence in
preparation. A delightfully simple, unpretentious menu and a tranquil room in one
of Glasgow's temples to culinary excellence; eyebrows are raised annually when
it's bypassed again by Michelin. Excellent, well-priced wine list, especially French.
Artisan cheeses. The chef may grace your table after dinner. You can tell him how
much you adore his food. Lunch Mon-Fri, LO 9.30pm. Closed Sun.

493 2/A3
ATMOS
£32+

✓ **Two Fat Ladies At The Buttery** www.twofatladiesrestaurant.com ·
0141 221 8188 · 652 Argyle Street The quite-hard-to-find or even hard-to-
explain-how-to-find extension of Argyle St west of the M8: satnav or phone. Under
Ryan James and his team the Buttery, aeons ago *the* best restaurant in Glasgow, is
back. It was perhaps ambitious to extend the Fat Ladies to this hallowed turf
(587/SEAFOOD RESTAURANTS), but this is less fishy and more (given the sumptuous,
mahogany-encased surroundings) fine dining with a fin and many legs on. Melt-
in-the-mouth meats also. Won the Best Newcomer at the Scottish Restaurant
Awards '09. By the time you read this it won't be new any more but elegantly

established like its forebear. **Shandon Belles**, the Ladies' thinner sister downstairs is the bistro version, cosier and less costly. Both 7 days lunch and dinner LO 10/11pm.

494 2/XA1
ATMOS
£15-32

✓ **Stravaigin** www.stravaigin.com · 0141 334 2665 · 28-30 Gibson Street Ok, it's not fine dining you get at Stravaigin but it is fine and way better than a bistro. Much awarded and always rewarding to visit, this is one of Glasgow's most dependable restaurants with a constantly changing, innovative and consciously eclectic menu you don't tire of. Mixes cuisines, especially Asian and Pacific Rim: 'think global, eat local'. Excellent, affordable food without the foodie formalities and open later than most. The bar on street level has probably the best bar food in town, similarly eclectic and accomplished. Can be cramped but it buzzes brilliantly (518/GASTROPUBS). 7 days 11am-11pm; bar till 12midnight. Also **Stravaigin 2** which is different but awfy good too; 0141 334 7165 (see 546/BISTROS).

495 2/D3
ATMOS
£32+

Rogano www.roganoglasgow.com · 0141 248 4055 · 11 Exchange Place Between Buchanan and Queen Sts. A Glasgow institution since the 1930s. Decor replicating a Cunard ship, the *Queen Mary*, is the major attraction. It does seem to change hands a lot but it is always a flagship restaurant. Food has improved of late. Though the room is spacious and perennially fashionable, there's a sense of trading on fading glory, especially downstairs in 'Café Rogano', the cheaper alternative. Outdoor heated 'terrace' with fake hedges. Restaurant lunch and 6pm-10.30pm. Café Rogano 12noon-11pm (Sun until 10pm). Upstairs for seafood especially oysters (you may even venture the lobster thermidor); some glamour still lingers.

496 2/C2
£22-32

Michael Caines @ Abode www.michaelcaines.com · 0141 221 6789 · 129 Bath Street Ground-floor fine-dining restaurant of boutique hotel Abode (458/HOTELS) in the midst of restaurant-packed Bath St. This a cut above the rest. There are also Caines in Canterbury, Exeter and Manchester, and he is executive chef at 2-Michelin-star Gidleigh Park; though like other celebrity chefs he's rarely rattling the pans here. Recently elevated chef Craig Dunn is confidently in charge of the Modern British menu using sound Scottish ingredients especially in the hunting, shooting and fishing departments, and this smart restaurant is beginning to fulfil some of its earlier promise. The glass-walled wine cellar is à la mode, contents also. Lunch; LO 10pm. Closed Sun.

The Best Bistros & Brasseries

See also Best Scottish Restaurants, p. 106.

497 2/XA1
ATMOS
£15-22

✓✓ **Cafezique** 0141 339 7180 · **66 Hyndland Street** The original location for Mhairi Taylor's landmark deli (which moved 2 doors up: 640/DELIS) is now a definitive West End grazing spot and hugely popular (book at weekends). 'Convivial' is the word and though cramped, the ground floor and mezzanine buzz along nicely day and night. Light, easy food with top ingredients, Mediterranean with apple crumble. In every sense, a real West End winner! 7 days 9am-10.30pm.

498 2/E4
ATMOS

✓✓ **Guy's Restaurant & Bar** www.guysrestaurant.co.uk · 0141 552 1114 · **24 Candleriggs** This intimate and busy Merchant City restaurant does 'real food' really well and I've decided to elevate Guy's to two ticks because it is quite simply one of my favourites. Though the menu is long and diverse and you could eat for a month and never have the same thing twice, it never disappoints. In a welcoming old-style room, the eponymous Guy and his charming family serve you Scottish staples like mince 'n' tatties and prawn cocktail, sushi and particularly good pasta. Absolutely everything home made. Wines vary from good house to Crystal Rosé at £600 a bottle. Piano Fri/Sat, jazz Thu. 12noon-10.30/11.30pm. Closed Mon. Good for late suppers. He is some guy, by the way.

499 2/XA1
£15-22

✓ **Stravaigin 2** www.stravaigin.5pm.co.uk · 0141 334 7165 · **8 Ruthven Lane** Just off Byres Road through vennel opposite underground station. Off-shoot of **Stravaigin** (494/BEST RESTAURANTS), one of Glasgow's finest. Similar eclectic often inspirational but lighter menu somewhere between the upstairs bar and downstairs finer dining of the mothership. Distinctly different but still inviting us to 'think global, eat local'. Smallish rooms (upper brighter) and couple of tables in lane; book weekends. Famously good burgers (come in many meats). 7 days 11am/12noon-11pm.

500 2/XA1
£22-32

✓ **No. Sixteen** www.number16.co.uk · 0141 339 2544 · **16 Byres Road** The well-loved No. 16 at the unfashionable, Partick end of Byres Rd closed dramatically in early '09 like a visible victim of the recession and re-opened just as suddenly a couple of months later with the same name, layout and vibe but new owners. They used to work there so they know how it works. And it does, with lovely fresh, bistro food at great prices. *Plus ça change.* 7 days, lunch and LO 10pm.

501 2/C2
£22-32

✓ **Manna** www.mannarestaurant.co.uk · 0141 332 6678 · **104 Bath Street** A bistro in a basement among many (in Bath St) but as many Glaswegians know, food, service and wine list here have always been spot-on. Chef, menu and perhaps approach changed '09 with more popular dishes, steaks, etc figuring more effectively. Usual great service. A reliable repast. Lunch and LO 10/10.30pm. Closed Sun lunch.

502 2/XA1
£15-22

✓ **The Left Bank** www.theleftbank.co.uk · 0141 339 5969 · **33 Gibson Street** Laid-back, stylish, all-round eaterie in West End near university. From healthy, imaginative breakfast to great-value, prix-fixe menus and soup 'n' sandwich lunches, this is a grown-up Glasgow place to hang. It works when it's reading-the-papers quiet and when it's queue-for-a-table buzzing. Good vegetarian choices. 7 days 9am-10pm, Sun from 10am. Bar till midnight.

503 2/XA1

✓ **The Two Figs** www.twofigs.co.uk · 0141 334 7277 · **5 Byres Road** The unfashionable end became very cool '09 when No. 16 (above) reopened and then this, the new love-child of the Left Bank's (above) owners Catherine Hardy and Jacqueline Fennessy, sprang up in the stony soil. Great look and feel with carefully selected floor, walls (the wallpaper!) and furnishings. Specials and à la carte cosmopolitan menu overseen by chef Liz McGougan of LB. Or hang at the bar. 7 days 10am-10pm, bar later. Merchant City branch opening at TGP.

504 2/XA2
£15-22 ✓ **Fanny Trollopes** www.fannytrollopes.co.uk · 0141 564 6464 · **1066 Argyle Street** Discreet presence on this unlovely boulevard and a narrow room, but Fanny's has always been a dining destination. Unpretentious, great value and some flair in the kitchen from chef/patron Gary Bayless makes this a Glasgow fave night out. Franco-Scottish menu with lovely puds. Can BYO. No credit cards. Lunch and LO 9.30/10pm. Closed Sun/Mon.

505 2/C3
£15-22 ✓ **Fifi and Ally** www.fifiandally.com · 0141 226 2286 · **80 Wellington Street** Following the success of their luncheon and tearoom in Princes Sq (597/TEAROOMS), a much larger, more ambitious deli and restaurant opened in late '07 here on the edge of the financial district. Dark, chic interior which twinkles at night. Delicious food and delicious wine. Sandwiches, salads and Celtic/North African/Italian mix to mains. Famous meringues. Lunch and LO 10pm. Closed Sun.

506 2/XA1
ATMOS ✓ **Velvet Elvis** www.velvet-elvis.com · 0141 334 6677 · **566 Dumbarton Road** With Pintxo (578/SPANISH RESTAURANTS) next door and others in the neighbourhood, this distant extension of Partick is becoming a culinary highway. Elvis is a treasure trove of cool things and found objects from the golden age of music. Menus come in old LP covers, so lots of nostalgia but the food is modish with well-sourced ingredients and flair in the cooking. Like the furniture, its cuisine is mix-n-match but consistently good. Dining with a difference! 7 days 12-9/10pm.

507 2/XF3
£15-22 ✓ **Tibo** www.cafetibo.com · 0141 550 2050 · **443 Duke Street, Dennistoun** Neighbourhood cool caff/bistro. Kinda funky and kinda rustic-in-the-city. Full-on menu but can graze and great for breakfast. It's an East End thing! 7 days 10am-9pm (9.45pm Fri/Sat). Sun noon-11pm.

508 2/E4
£15-22 ✓ **Gramofon** 0141 552 7177 · **7 King Street** Just off the Trongate near the Tron. Cheery, busy urban bistro with art on the walls and owner-chef Garry MacArthur very visible in the tiny kitchen. Simple food with integrity. Open mic stuff downstairs. 10am-9pm, till 9.30pm Fri/Sat. Sun 11am-6pm. Closed Mon.

509 2/D3
£15-22 ✓ **The Grill Room At The Square** www.29glasgow.com · 0141 225 5615 · **29 Royal Exchange Square** Upstairs on the corner of the square, the restaurant of 29, a 'private members' club' (members only on Sat night). Big windows, big aspirations, big steaks (a 'secret glaze' seals in the flavour). Very Glasgow new money, their famous faces adorning the stairs. Sunday roasts; some live jazz. A beautiful room with a view. 7 days 12noon-10.30pm. Bar 3am.

510 2/D3
£22-32 ✓ **The Urban Bar & Brasserie** www.urbanbrasserie.co.uk · 0141 248 5636 · **23 St Vincent Place** Very central (off George Sq), urban as they say and a very Glasgow restaurant: 'brasserie' for once is used correctly. Proprietor Alan Tomkins (Gamba, 585/SEAFOOD and Manna, previous page) knows a thing or two about food and how to make a room work. Clubby atmosphere in different seating areas; outside terrace for people-watching. Bar and changing brazz menu with loads of interest and intention. Lunch and LO 10pm; 10.30pm Fri/Sat.

511 2/XA5
£15-22 ✓ **Dine** 0141 621 1903 · **205 Fenwick Road** Way out on the South Side but probably all the better for that with the feel of a laid-back but smart suburban restaurant where there's time to care about the customers and the food. Just 6

doors down from the Ivy (see below) so 2 decent dining rooms on the same far-away block. Small modern room and seasonal modern menu. The 'Grand Dessert' for sharing is gorgeous. Lunch and LO 9/9.30pm. Closed Mon.

512 2/XA1
£22-32

✓**An Lochan** 0141 338 6606 · 340 Crow Road West End borders (can approach via Hyndland Rd – Clarence Drive to bottom then right onto Crow Rd) but not so far to go for authentic, mainly seafood bistro that's more than just a neighbourhood place. The An Lochan 'brand' includes their hotel in Perthshire (880/PERTH HOTELS) and the estimable An Lochan in Tighnabruich (750/BEST ARGYLL). Many fishy ingredients come from the west (sourcing noted on menu). Lunch Tue-Sun; dinner Tue-Sat. Closed Mon.

513 2/XA5
£15-22

Merrylee Road Bar & Kitchen www.merryleeroad.com · 0141 637 5774 · 128 Merrylee Road In suburban South Side near Clarkston Rd junction. Proving again that you can't keep a good man down, serial restauranteur Gordon Yuill, having briefly disappeared from his Glasgow stamping ground, has reappeared with his most ambitious venture yet and a dream come true. This vast 'a' things to a' folk' cantina has everything a Weegie wants on a menu; there are both fat chips and skinny fries. Outside beer garden with herbs, vines and tomatoes growing around you and heading for your plate. This place wouldn't be out of place in a North American suburb except, of course, it's better. 7 days 12noon-9pm. Bar 11pm.

514 2/C2
£15-22

Red Onion www.red-onion.co.uk · 0141 221 6000 · 247 West Campbell Street Big reputation John Quigley confidently in command here of a good-value, eclectic menu featuring all the things we like from sound, safe choices to food with more flourish and Quigley flair. Though not so multi-layered, the Onion is informal, accessible and easy to drop in at any time. 7 days 12noon-10.30/11pm.

515 2/XA5
£15-22

The Giffnock Ivy 0141 620 1003 · 219 Fenwick Road, Giffnock Set in Glasgow's South Side and not London's West End, the joke may be lost but pop-stars and luvvies could graze here, too. Big local reputation and at weekends it may be just as difficult to get a table. Great bistro atmosphere in small, busy room; love the white linen. Modest menu with blackboard specials. Very Scottish and nicely refined. 7 days, lunch and LO 9.30pm. Closed Mon.

516 2/XA1
£15-22

Sisters Jordanhill www.thesisters.co.uk · 0141 434 1179 · 1a Ashwood Gardens, off Crow Road Out of the way and a little out of the ordinary, a great Scottish eaterie by sisters Pauline and Jacqueline O'Donnell. Great atmosphere, home cooking from fine ingredients. Loyal clientele. Seems like a bit of a find. If you've never been beyond the bright lights of Byres Rd, phone for directions. Tue-Sun lunch and dinner. LO 9.30pm.

517 2/XA1
£15-22

Sisters Kelvingrove www.thesisters.co.uk · 0141 564 1157 · 36 Kelvingrove Street From the same sisters as above though here on a busy West End corner in a (not large) more 'modern' room. Similar menu with Scottish-sourced ingredients and the signature puff-candy ice cream. Decent value for this standard of consci-entious cookery. Lunch and LO 9/9.30pm (Sun 8pm). Closed Mon.

✓✓**Café Gandolfi** Among the last but right up there with the best. Report: 594/BEST TEAROOMS.

✓✓**City Merchant** Long established Merchant City restaurant still has the edge over many newcomers. Report: 542/SCOTTISH RESTAURANTS.

✓**Firebird** Well-loved West End corner bistro, renowned for pizza. Report: 536/BEST PIZZA.

Gastropubs

518 2/XA1
ATMOS

✓ ✓ **Stravaigin** www.stravaigin.5pm.co.uk · 0141 334 2665 · 28-30 Gibson Street Excellent pub food upstairs from one of the best restaurants in town. Doors open on to sunny Gibson St and mezzanine gallery above. Often packed, but inspirational grub and no pretence. These must be the busiest, most exercised waiters in town. Nice wines to go with. 7 days all day and LO 10pm. Report: 494/BEST RESTAURANTS.

519 2/E4

✓ ✓ **Bar Gandolfi** www.cafegandolfi.com · 0141 552 6813 · 64 Albion Street Above Café Gandolfi (594/TEAROOMS). Bar Gandolfi and Stravaigin still head up this section where 'Glasgow' and 'gastropub' together never quite roll off the tongue. A foody pub with classy comfort food in a light, airy upstairs garret, served all day till 10pm. Bar later. Good veggie choice. Great macaroni cheese. Great rendezvous spot. 7 days 11am-9/10pm (Sun from 12noon).

520 2/XA1

✓ **Liquid Ship** www.stravaigin.com · 0141 331 1901 · 171 Great Western Road From the makers of Stravaigin (above), another congenial howff that's good to visit for many reasons (Mon quiz, Wed open mic, live bands downstairs), not least the innovative eclectic menu you'd expect from the Clydesdale camp. From Spain to the Ukraine with lots of Stravaigin touches. Food 10am-10pm then tapas menu till 11pm/12midnight. 7 days.

521 2/D3 **Sloans** 0141 221 8886 · Argyll Arcade, Argyle Street In the jewellery arcade that runs between Argyle and Buchanan Sts, one of Glasgow's most original, still-stylish eating parlours on 2 floors. Both offer authentic, early-20th century decor in wood and tiles and stained glass with an atmosphere that retro style bars can only dream of. Upstairs Crystal restaurant with beautiful snug (private use) open for dinner at weekends, whereas weekend market outside is a bit tacky. Downstairs an all-day pub and dining room with usual fare and daily specials. On the top floor there's a ballroom; guided tours; private hires are available. Bar 7 days. Food 12noon-10pm. Bar 12midnight.

522 2/XA1
ATMOS

Òran Mór www.oran-mor.co.uk · 0141 357 6200 · 731 Corner of Byres and Great Western Roads Converted church and reverence due for the scale of ambition here and the unflagging commitment, a paean to all things 'Scottish contemporary'. Every cloister and chapel has been turned into a den for drinking in and the din can be heaven or hell, depending on your proclivity. However 'The Conservatory' to one side has a very passable gastropub-style menu and 'The Brasserie' takes its grub more seriously. Lunch and LO 9pm.

 Babbity Bowsters Report: 547/SCOTTISH RESTAURANTS.

The Best Italian Restaurants

523 2/XA1
£22-32

✓ **La Parmigiana** www.laparmigiana.co.uk · 0141 334 0686 · 447 Great Western Road Long-established, top ristorante near Kelvin Bridge by the Giovanazzi brothers (Sandro here) who also have Paperino's (534/TRATTS). In most food guides including Michelin. No great surprises on the menu but reliably fine. Traditional, solicitous service, authentic ingredients and contemporary Italian cooking meld into a seamless performance. Carefully chosen wine list. Mon-Sat lunch and 6-10.30pm. Closed Sun.

524 2/D2
2/C2
ATMOS
£15-32

✓ **Fratelli Sarti** www.sarti.co.uk · 0141 248 2228 · 133 Wellington Street & 0141 204 0440 (best number for bookings) 121 Bath Street Glasgow's famed *emporio d'Italia* combining a deli/wine shop in Wellington St, wine shop in Bath St and bistro in each. Great bustling atmosphere. Eating upstairs in deli has more atmosphere. Both may have lunchtime queues. Good pizza, specials change every day, *dolci* and *gelati* in super-calorific abundance. 7 days 8am-10/11pm (Sun from noon) (539/PIZZA). The **Sarti** restaurant at **43 Renfield St** (corner of West George St; 0141 572 7000) is for finer Italian dining in an elegant room with exceptional marble tiling and wine list. Same menu as others, but more ristorante specials. 7 days 8am-10.30pm (Sat from 10am, Sun from 12noon).

525 10/N27
£22-32

✓ **La Vigna, Lanark** www.lavigna.co.uk · 01555 664320 · 40 Wellgate Not Glasgow, but downtown Lanark; worth a 40km drive for the authentic ristorante, family-run for over 20 years. 7 days, lunch and LO 10pm (Sun dinner only).

526 2/C2

Osteria Piero www.osteriapiero.co.uk · 0141 248 3471 · 111 West Regent Street In basement at the Wellington St corner. A restaurant/upmarket tratt by the former owner of Sarti (above). Great antipasti and hearty north Italian and Tuscan dishes supplement the pizza/pasta. Chunky, woody interior inherited from previous occupants. Smart, knowlegeable service; excellent wine selection. Open for breakfast from 7.45am (Sat 10am), lunch and LO 10.30pm. Sun 12noon-8pm.

527 2/D3
ATMOS
£22-32

L'Ariosto www.lariosto.com · 0141 221 0971 · 92 Mitchell Street An institution! Old-style ristorante set in an indoor courtyard. Full-blown Tuscan fare with flair and after 40 years still some passion; obliging staff. Notable for using only the right ingredients including wild mushrooms and many meats (veal, venison, etc). Dinner-dancing: this is old-style but real style. Great wine list with good house. A full night's entertainment. Mon-Sat. Lunch and LO 11pm. Closed Sun lunch.

528 2/F3

The Italian Caffe www.theitaliancaffe.co.uk · 0141 552 3186 · 92 Albion Street The Italian Caffe is far too sophisticated to see itself as a mere tratt but it's modelled on a traditional enoteca (a wine bar with small, tapas-like plates of food) and though one can dine seriously, it ain't a ristorante in the conventional sense. Good location and often packed. I never felt myself that it lived up to its hype. There's some flair and attention in the kitchen and a lotta risotto and other choices, but a fritatta is still a fritatta. Good wine selection. Lots of buzz. 7 days lunch and LO 10/10.30pm.

529 2/XA5
ATMOS
£22-32

La Fiorentina/Little Tuscany www.la-fiorentina.com · 0141 420 1585 · 2 Paisley Road West Not far from river and motorway over Kingston Bridge, but approach from Eglinton St (A77 Kilmarnock Rd). It's at the Y-junction with Govan Rd. Fiorentina has absorbed traditional tratt Little Tuscany from next door which is only open when they're very busy. Fabulous, old-style room and service, always buzzing. Usually seafood specials; lighter Tuscan menu. As Italian as you want it to be, enormous menu and wine list. Mon-Sat lunch and LO 10.30pm. Closed Sun.

The Trusty Tratts

Old-style family-run restaurants (real Italians) with familiar pasta/pizza staples and the rest. There are many of these in Glasgow as elsewhere; these are the best.

530 2/D2
£15-22
✓**Ristorante Caprese** 0141 332 3070 · 217 Buchanan Street The Buchanan St secret: basement café near the Concert Hall. Glaswegians (and footballers) love this place – see the wall-to-wall gallery of happy, smiling punters. It's a fave of ours, too. Checked tablecloths and crooning in the background create an authentic 'mamma mia' atmosphere. Friendly service, totally reliable pasta 'n' pizza. Everything made for you; ask about specials. LO 9/10pm. Closed Sun. Book at weekends.

531 2/XB5
£15-22
✓**Battlefield Rest** www.battlefieldrest.co.uk · 0141 636 6955 · 55 Battlefield Road On South Side near Victoria Park and opposite Infirmary in landmark pavilion building, former tram station. Calls itself a 'continental bistro'; what they mean is the continent of Italy. Family-run with great pasta list, home-made puds and lovely, thin bread. Small, with good daylight, this place unquestionably is still one of the most convivial places to eat on the South Side. 7 days 10am-10pm. Closed Sun.

532 2/XA5
£15-22
✓**Roma Mia** www.romamiaglasgow.co.uk · 0141 423 6694 · 164 Darnley Street Near the Tramway on the South Side and the best option pre-/post-theatre. Family-friendly tratt, members of 'Ciao Italia' (denoting a 'real' Italian restaurant). Out of the way, but this is a backstreet of Rome, not just Glasgow. Closed Sun lunch and Mon. LO 10pm.

533 2/XA5
£15-22
✓**Bella Napoli** 0141 632 4222 · 83 Kilmarnock Road Another family tratt on the main road of the South Side, this one a' things to a' body (meaning universal appeal). Big hams in the cold counter may amuse the kids. Bright presence on the street, inside the space goes on forever. Closed Mon/Tue lunch. LO 10.30pm.

534 2/B1
WE
£15-22
Paperino's www.paperinosglasgow.com · 0141 332 3800 · 283 Sauchiehall Street & 227 Byres Road · 0141 334 3811 Ordinary-looking though both are smart restaurants better than the rest; down to the Giovanazzi brothers who also own La Parmigiana (523/BEST ITALIAN RESTAURANTS) and The Big Blue (618/KID-FRIENDLY). Perfect pasta and good service. The newer Byres Rd version is vast but often packed. Attests to the endless attraction of straightforward Italian food done well. 7 days. LO 10.50pm.

535 2/XA5
£15 OR LESS
Buongiorno 0141 649 1029 · 1012 Pollokshaws Road Near Shawlands Cross. Ronaldo follows parents' footsteps and recipe book. Pasta/pizza straight-up. Some home-made desserts. Conveniently there are 3 good tratts within 100m of each other near these corners: **Di Maggio's**, the **Brooklyn** (606/CAFÉS) and this Buongiorno. All are often full, so it's good to have the choice. Takeaway menu. 7 days, lunch and LO 10/11pm.

✓**The Big Blue** Report: 538/PIZZA.

The Best Pizza

536 2/XA1
£15-22

✓ **Firebird** www.firebirdglasgow.com · 0141 334 0594 · 1321 Argyle
Street Big-windowed, spacious bistro at the far west end of Argyle St. Mixed modern menu and everything covered but notable for wood-smoked dishes, of which their light, imaginative pizzas are excellent. Firebird is a perennially popular hangout and a key spirit-of-Glasgow spot. 12noon-10/10.30pm (bar 12midnight/1am).

537 2/E3
£15-22

✓ **The Brunswick (Hotel Bar/Café)** www.brunswickhotel.co.uk · 0141
552 0001 · 104 Brunswick Street The not-large, usually bustling bar and restaurant of this hip-ish hotel in the Merchant City (468/BOUTIQUE HOTELS, 680/COOL BARS) has a big reputation for its 'brutti bread', a delicious, thin pizza – the star on a grazing/sharing menu turned out from a gantry kitchen. 7 days till 10pm.

538 2/XA1
£15-22

The Big Blue 0141 357 1038 · 445 Great Western Road On corner of Kelvin Bridge and with terrace overlooking the river. Bar and restaurant together so noise can obliterate meal and conversation later on. Lots of other dishes and morsels including spot-on pasta, but the big thin pizzas here are good – that's a well-known fact. 7 days lunch and LO 9.45pm (weekends 10.30pm).

539 2/C2
2/D2
£15-22

Fratelli Sarti www.sarti.co.uk · 0141 248 2228 · 133 Wellington Street,
121 Bath Street & 404 Sauchiehall Street Excellent, thin-crust pie, buffalo mozzarella and freshly made *pomodoro*. 7 days, hours vary. It's the ingredients that count here, the pizza dough a bit on the chunky side. Full report: 524/ITALIAN RESTAURANTS.

The Best French Restaurants

✓✓ **Le Chardon D'Or** www.brianmaule.com · 0141 248 3801 · 176
West Regent Street Two ticks as Glasgow's finest French. Report: 492/FINE DINING.

540 2/XA1
ATMOS
£22-32

✓ **La Vallée Blanche** www.lavalleeblanche.com · 0141 334 3333 ·
360 Byres Road Upstairs and small street presence. Straight-up brasserie-type menu using seasonal produce in a room that's woody and cosy and night and light during the day (prix-fixe lunch a great deal). Veal and rabbit with Peterhead halibut and some vegetarian choice. Welcoming and fastidious service. A salle nouvelle for Glasgow somewhat sans French cuisine. Lunch and LO 9.45pm. Closed Mon.

541 2/B2
£22-32

✓ **Malmaison** www.malmaison-glasgow.com · 0141 572 1001 · 278 West
George Street The brasserie in the basement of the hotel (457/MAJOR HOTELS) with the same setup as Edinburgh and elsewhere and a very similar menu – based on the classic Parisian brasseries like La Coupole. Excellent brasserie ambience in woody if dark salon. Seating layout and busy waiters mean lots of buzz; also private dining rooms and the adjacent Champagne Bar which serves lite bites (oysters, burgers, eggs Benedict) throughout the day. Declared sources. Scottish ingredients on their 'homegrown' and local menu. 7 days, breakfast, lunch and LO 10.30pm.

The Best Scottish Restaurants

Restaurants where there is a conscious effort to offer traditional or contemporary Scottish dishes using sourced Scottish seafood/beef/lamb, etc.

542 2/E3
£22-32

✓ ✓ **City Merchant** www.citymerchant.co.uk · 0141 553 1577 · **97 Candleriggs** Predating (here for 20 years) the Merchant City and still one of the first restaurants in the district. The Matteo family's love affair with Scotland has an enduring appeal. 'Seafood, game, steaks' focussing on quality Scottish produce with Italian flair. Lovely oysters; top fish platter, mince 'n' tatties. Daily and à la carte menus in warm bistro atmosphere. Good biz restaurant or intimate rendezvous. Lunch and dinner LO 10.30pm. Closed Sun.

543 2/XA1
£15-22

✓ **Roastit Bubbly Jocks** 0141 339 3355 · **450 Dumbarton Road** Far up in the West End but many beat their way to this Partick dining room where Mo Abdulla expanded his cosy wee empire from Fanny Trollopes (504/BISTROS). This is small and excellent value and very Scottish; ie it feels very Scottish. Risottos and Tuscan sausages with your mince 'n' tatties and other dishes your mammy made, like bread-n-butter pudding. Lunch (weekends only). LO 9.30pm. Can BYOB (£5).

544 2/F3
£15-22

✓ **Arisaig** www.arisaigrestaurant.co.uk · 0141 553 1010 · **1 Merchant Square** Relocated '09 to this warehousy mall in Candleriggs near the City Halls. Though the square itself has often seemed forlorn, the restaurants around it, all with outside terraces, are always busy and Arisaig raises the game. Downstairs brasserie, upstairs (Thu-Sat only) more formal dining in surprisingly spacious mezzanine terrace overlooking the square. Well-sourced Scottish and good value produce throughout. Smart and convivial. 7 days 11am-9.30/10.30pm.

545 2/XA1
£22-32

✓ **Cail Bruich** www.cailbruich.co.uk · 0141 334 6265 · **725 Great Western Road** The busy road west that runs past the end of Byres Rd. The name means 'eat well' and you do in this very small bistro with a nice, light ambience. Scottish take and produce as you might expect in simple, sensible menu. Good-value lunch. Lunch and LO 9.30pm (Sun 9pm). Closed Mon.

546 2/XA1
£15-22

✓ **Blas** 0141 357 4328 · **1397 Argyle Street** Opposite Kelvingrove Museum (685/ATTRACTIONS). A smart, modern café/restaurant with decidedly Scottish slant which means down-to-earth dishes and very good value: stovies, poshed-up haggis. Sound ingredients from named quality butchers, etc. Cheese from Ayrshire, ice cream is Mackie's, decor by Timorous Beasties. 12noon-10pm. Closed Mon.

547 2/F3

✓ **Babbity Bowster** 0141 552 5055 · **16 Blackfriars Street** Listed as a pub for real ale and as a hotel (there are rooms upstairs), the food is mentioned mainly for its Scottishness (haggis and stovies) and all-day availability. It's pleasant to eat outside on the patio/garden in summer. There is a restaurant upstairs called **Schottische** (dinner Tue-Sat): ok, I have never ventured. Also breakfast served from 8am (Sun 10am). Report: 666/REAL-ALE PUBS, 474/INDIVIDUAL HOTELS.

548 2/D3
ATMOS

✓ **The Horseshoe** 0141 204 4056 · **17 Drury Street** A classic pub to be recommended for all kinds of reasons, and on this page because it's the epitome of the Scottish pub 'bar lunch'. And it is a particularly good deal with 3 courses for £3.95, and old favourites on the menu like mushy peas, macaroni cheese, jelly and fruit. Lunch 12noon-2.30pm. Upstairs open all afternoon, then high tea till 7.45pm (not Sun). All Glasgow characters (and what they still love to eat) are here (especially in the upstairs karaoke nights after tea). Pub open daily till 12midnight. Report: 648/UNIQUE GLASGOW PUBS.

549 2/XA1
£15-22
✔ **Tattie Mac's** www.tattiemacs.co.uk · 0141 337 2282 · **61 Otago Street**
Decidedly neighbourhood bistro in a quiet street near the university, opened by notable chef Iain McMaster on a site that's seen a lot of tatties come and go over the years. This should work! A well-considered, comforting menu with sound Scottish produce; good steaks, tempting puds. And excellent value, which is surely the key. 7 days 11am-10pm.

550 2/XA1
£15-22
The Bothy 0141 334 4040 · **11 Ruthven Lane** Part of Stefan King's G1 Group's takeover of the West End, this tucked-away site has spawned other Bothys Perth and St Andrews. Contemporary-retro design and menu confidently conceived and presented. All Scottish fares and ingredients present and correct. A pleasant ambience; doesn't seem too contrived (even if it was). 7 days 12noon-9.45pm.

Òran Mór 522/GASTROPUBS, 647/UNIQUE PUBS.

The Best Indian Restaurants

551 2/XA1
ATMOS
£15-22
✔ ✔ **Mother India** 0141 221 1663 · **28 Westminster Terrace** Famously good Glasgow restaurant for Indian home-cooking in a 3-floor laid-back but stylish set up where the food rarely lets you down. The same, not absurdly long menu throughout, slightly different ambience in the ground-floor original, the cosy upstairs and the contemporary basement rooms. All buzz. Many faves and specialities by people who know how to work the flavours and textures. House wine and Kingfisher beer but for 2 quid corkage you can BYOB. Best to book. Lots of vegetarian choice. 7 days, lunch (not Sun-Tue) and LO 10.30/11pm. Takeaway too.

552 2/E3
£15-22
✔ **Dakhin** www.dakhin.com · 0141 553 2585 · **89 Candleriggs** Upstairs and out of sight but a must-find for lovers of Indian food (also found by Michelin). Same owners as The Dhabba (see the next page) but menu is a subcontinent away (ie south as opposed to north India). Lighter, saucier with coconut, ginger and chilli and selection of light-as-a-feather dosas make essential different to the tandoori/tikka-driven menus of most other restaurants in this category. Signature dish: the must-have paper dosa. 7 days. Lunch and LO 10/10.30pm.

553 2/XA1
£15 OR LESS
✔ **Mother India Café** 0141 339 9145 · **1355 Argyle Street** (Opposite Kelvingrove Museum; 685/ATTRACTIONS.) Rudely healthy progeny of Mother (above) and cousins to Wee Currys (next page); a distinctive twist here ensures another packed house at all times. Menu made up of 40 thali or tapas-like dishes (4/5 for a party of 2), so just as we always did, we get tastes of each other's choices - only it's cheaper! Fastidious waiters (do turn round the tables). Miraculous tiny kitchen. Can't book; you may wait! Lunch and LO 10/10.30pm.

554 2/XA1
ATMOS
£15 OR LESS
✔ **Banana Leaf** www.thebananaleaf.co.uk · 0141 334 4445 · **76 Old Dumbarton Road** Across Argyle St from Kelvingrove Museum, up Moray St, turn left. Discreet doorway to a tiny room: a south Indian living room in a Glasgow tenement. Some chicken and lamb dishes but mostly vegetarian and loadsa dosas. So authentic it hurts and cheap as... 7 days 11.30am-11pm. Sun 10am-11pm.

555 2/C1
2/XA1
£15 OR LESS
✓ **The Wee Curry Shop** www.weecurryshopglasgow.co.uk · 0141 353 0777 · 7 Buccleuch Street (near Concert Hall) & Ashton Lane · 0141 357 5280 & 41 Byres Road · 0141 339 1339 Tiny outposts of Mother India above, 3 neighbourhood home-style cooking curry shops, just as they say. Cheap, always cheerful. Stripped-down menu in small, if not micro rooms. Buccleuch St 6 tables, Byres Road maybe 8; Ashton Lane the biggest. House red and white and Kingfisher but can BYOB (wine only; £2.50 but not Byres Rd). Lunch and LO 10.30pm. Closed Sun lunch except Byres Rd. LO 10.30pm. No credit cards.

556 2/XA1
£15-22
✓ **Balbir's** www.balbirsrestaurants.co.uk · 0141 439 7711 · 7 Church Street At the bottom end of Byres Rd the grandee Glasgow proprietor Balbir Singh Sumal presides in a cavernous, contemporary, routinely packed restaurant. Both regular and innovative dishes from the Subcontinent that Glasgow has taken to its heart (though low-cholesterol rapeseed oil is used instead of ghee) and stomach. Closed lunch. LO 10.30/11pm. Balbir also has the more contemporary (although menus are indistinguishable) **Saffron Lounge** at 61 Kilmarnock Road (0141 632 8564) and **Tiffin Rooms** at 573 Sauchiehall St (0141 221 3696) west of the M8.

557 2/XA2
£15-22
Shish Mahal www.shishmahal.co.uk · 0141 339 8256 · 68 Park Road First-generation Indian restaurant that still, after 'only 44 years', remains one of the city's faves. Modernised some years back but not compromised and still feels like it's been here forever. Menu of epic size. Many different influences in the cooking, and total commitment to the Glasgow curry (and chips). The Shish Mahal's great claim to fame is that it invented chicken tikka masala. 7 days till 11pm/11.30.

558 2/A1
£15 OR LESS
Shish Mahal Café www.shishmahal.co.uk · 0141 332 2808 · 48 Woodlands Road Opened summer '09, perhaps taking a leaf out of the Mother India book. Open all day for a grazing curry/tapas menu. 7 days 10am-10/11pm.

559 2/XA1
£15-22
Ashoka Ashton Lane www.harlequinrestaurants.com · 0141 357 5904 · 19 Ashton Lane & Ashoka West End · 0141 339 0936 · 1284 Argyle Street Part of the Harlequin Restaurants chain, they have always been good, simple and dependable places to go for curry but have kept up with the times. Argyle St is *the* original. Nothing surprising about the menus, just sound Punjabi via Glasgow fare. Good takeaway service (0800 195 3 195). Lunch and LO 11.30pm (not Sun lunch Ashton Lane; West End evenings only at weekends). Open till 12midnight (West End even later).

560 2/E4
£15-22
The Dhabba www.thedhabba.com · 0141 553 1249 · 44 Candleriggs Mid-Merchant City curry house which presented itself as ground-breaking when it opened in '03. It is at least modern and enthusiastic. North Indian cuisine in big-window diner. Complemented by sister restaurant Dakhin (previous page) and often busy, the Dhabba is a decent Merchant City choice. 7 days 12noon-10.30pm.

561 2/XB5
£15-22
Ali Shan www.alishantandoori.co.uk · 0141 632 5294 · 250 Battlefield Road South Siders and many from further afield swear by this Indo-Pak restaurant that's especially good for veggie and other diets. It's been here for 20 years and hasn't changed much but honesty and integrity are in their mix of spices on a very long menu. 7 days from 5pm, LO 11pm (12midnight weekends).

THAI

562 2/D2
£22-32

✓ **Thai Lemongrass** 0141 331 1315 · 24 Renfrew Street Noticing perhaps that Glasgow has far fewer good Thai restaurants than Edinburgh (see p. 61), TL has opened up here, near the Concert Hall and opposite Cineworld and is possibly the best in town. Contemporary (those fans) while still cosy. It gives old Thai Fountain (below) a run for its baht. Good service and presentation of all the new Thai faves. 7 days lunch and LO 11pm.

563 2/A1
£22-32

Thai Fountain www.thai-fountain.com · 0141 332 2599 · 2 Woodside Crescent Near Charing Cross. Same ownership as Amber Regent (see below), this was for a long time Glasgow's best Asian restaurant; now there are many contenders. Genuinely Thai and not at all Chinese. Innovative dishes with great diversity of flavours and textures, so sharing several is best. Of course you will eat too much. Room very interior and rather dated now. 7 days. LO 11/11.30pm. Signature dish: weeping tiger beef.

564 2/XA2
£22-32

Thai Siam www.thaisiamglasgow.com · 0141 229 1191 · 1191 Argyle Street Traditional (those high-back chairs), low-lit atmosphere but a discerning clientele forgive the decor and get their heads down into fragrant curries et al. All-Thai staff maintain authenticity. What it lacks in style up front it makes up for in the kitchen. There's another Thai Siam in Paisley. Lunch and LO 11pm. Closed Sun lunch.

CHINESE

565 2/B1
ATMOS
£22-32

✓✓ **Loon Fung** 0141 332 1240 · 417 Sauchiehall Street Here since 1976 and just possibly Glasgow's most 'respected' Cantonese, the place where the local Chinese community meet for lunch on a Sun/Mon/Tue. The room is large, the pace is fast and friendly while the food is fresh and authentic. Great dim sum. Everybody on chopsticks. 2 of the 3 menus are in Chinese only. There's even a travel agency on site if Beijing beckons. Open very late. 7 days, 12noon-4am.

566 2/XA1
£15 OR LESS

✓ **Asia Style** 0141 332 8828 · 185 St George's Road Near Charing Cross. Discreet, authentic and exceptionally good value, this makes for an excellent late-night rendezvous though you'd have to love Chinese food. Bright canteen with banter to match. Traditional Chinese without MSG. Malaysian dishes (reputation for shellfish). 7 days, dinner only LO 2.30am. Cash only.

567 2/D1
£22-32

✓ **Dragon-i** www.dragon-i.co.uk · 0141 332 7728 · 311 Hope Street Refreshingly contemporary Chinese-pan-Asian opposite Theatre Royal. Thai/Malaysia and rice/noodle/tempura dishes with sound non-MSG, often unlikely Scottish ingredients make for fusion at its best. Proper puds. Chilled-out room and creative Chinese cuisine. Lunch Mon-Fri, dinner 7 days LO 12midnight (11pm Sun).

568 2/C2
£22-32

✓ **Amber Regent** www.amberregent.com · 0141 331 1655 · 50 West Regent Street Elegant Cantonese restaurant that prides itself on courteous service and the quality of its cuisine, especially seafood. Here over 20 years, its menu is traditional, as is the atmosphere. Influences from Mongolia to Malaysia. Creditable wine list, quite romantic at night and a good business-lunch spot. Only Glasgow Chinese restaurant regularly featured in AA and Michelin. Lunch, LO 10.30pm weekends 11/11.30pm. Closed Sat lunch and Sun.

569 2/XA1
£15-22

✓ **Chow** 0141 334 9818 · 98 Byres Road Away from other Chinese restaurants clustered downtown, this is the contemporary, smarter and buzzy West End version. Broad menu imaginative and different. Good vegetarian choice. Can be a tight squeeze down or up. Takeaway and delivery. Good value, especially lunch. 7 days lunch and dinner (Sun from 4.30pm). LO 11.30pm.

570 2/C2
£22-32
✓ **Peking Inn** 0141 332 8971 · 191 Hope Street For 25 years a smart, urban Chinese restaurant on busy corner (with West Regent St) but light, relaxing room. Famous for its spicy, Szechuan specials as well as Beijing cuisine via Hong Kong; and nights on town. Perennially popular. Lunch (not Sun), LO 10.30/11.30pm.

571 2/C4
£22-32
✓ **Ho Wong** www.ho-wong.com · 0141 221 3550 · 82 York Street Unlikely location for a discreet, urbane Pekinese/Cantonese restaurant which relies on its reputation and makes few compromises. Calm, quite chic room with mainly up-market clientele; roomful of suits at lunch and champagne list. Reassuringly expensive. Notable for seafood and duck. Lunch (not Sun) and LO 11/11.30pm.

572 2/B1
£15 OR LESS
Glasgow Noodle Bar 0141 333 1883 · 482 Sauchiehall Street Authentic, stripped-back Chinese-style noodle bar, 100m from Charing Cross. A fast-food joint with genuine, made-on-the-spot – in the wok – food late into the AM. Not the smartest diner hereabouts but quite groovy in a clubzone way. 7 days, 12noon-4am. 623/LATE-NIGHT RESTAURANTS.

JAPANESE

573 2/D2
£15-22
Wagamama www.wagamama.com · 0141 229 1468 · 97 West George Street Wagamama brand and formula here in midtown near the stations (also in Silverburn shopping mall). We don't do chains in *StB* but if you like fast Asian food that's good for you, you'll be a fan of their formula: big canteen tables, 'healthy' Japanese-based food made to order and brought when ready. Seems to work universally but the novelty does wear off. 7 days 12noon-11pm (Sun 12.30-10pm).

574 2/D3
WE
£15-22
Ichiban www.ichiban.co.uk · 0141 204 4200 · 50 Queen Street & 184 Dumbarton Road, Partick Noodle bar based loosely on the Wagamama formula. Fundamental food, egalitarian presentation, some technology. Ramen, udon, soba noodle dishes; also chow meins, tempuras and other Japanese snacks. Long tables, eat-as-it-comes 'methodology'. Light, calm, hip. Lunch and LO 10pm (weekends 11pm), Sun 1-10pm. The Partick Ichiban which is near Byres Rd is possibly better of the 2; a healthy option in the quarter.

FUSION

575 2/E3
£15-22
✓ **Rumours** www.rumourskopitiam.co.uk · 0141 353 0678 · 21 Bath Street From an elevated first-floor position at the corner of West Nile and Bath Sts, this Malysian caff eschews the style dictates of the restaurant/bar culture further along and is the better for it. Odd name but the word on the street is that this is the real deal: fusion/Malaysian which means Chinese/Thai and other influences in cooking that is fresh and authentic. 7 days 12noon-10pm.

577 2/XA4
£15-32
Yen www.yenrotunda.com · 0141 847 0110 · 28 Tunnel Street In the Rotunda near the SECC so often busy with pre- or après-concert audiences. Upstairs café has Cantonese/Japanese/Thai noodle vibe, ground floor has more expensive, more full-on teppanyaki restaurant with 8-course menus you watch being prepared on searing hobs. 7 days, lunch and LO 10.30pm (closed Sun lunch).

Other Ethnic Restaurants

SPANISH

578 2/XA1
£15 OR LESS

✓ **Pintxo** 0141 334 8886 · 562 Dumbarton Road It's a long way into Partick, almost a neighbourhood caff but folk are coming from way across town for top tapas and cooking which makes you think again about Spain. Though the name is Basque, the menu has highlights from all over as well as wines. Hard to know what to choose but this is food to share. 7 days. 5pm-10pm, Sat 1pm-10pm.

579 2/XA1
2/D3
£15 OR LESS

Café Andaluz www.cafeandaluz.com · 0141 339 1111 · 2 Cresswell Lane, off Byres Road & St Vincent Place · 0141 222 2255 The original is a basement on corner of Cresswell (the less heaving of the Byres Rd lanes) where folks gather of an evening. Nice atmosphere encased in ceramica with a wide choice of passable tapas and mains (including vegetarian). Owned by Di Maggio (Italian) chain. St Vincent Pl also busy but through location perhaps rather than as a destination. 7 days LO 10/10.30pm. Andaluz now in Edinburgh possibly best of the 3.

580 2/XB5

Tinto Tapas Bar 0141 636 6838 · 138 Battlefield Road On the South Side near the Victoria Infirmary. Sliver of a restaurant serving tapas and specials all day with good, inexpensive wine selection. 7 days 10.30am-9.45pm (10.30pm Fri-Sun).

MEXICAN

581 2/D5
£15-22

Salsa www.salsa.5pm.co.uk · 0141 420 6328 · 63 Carlton Place On the south bank of the river at end of Glasgow Bridge (pedestrian), an unlikely location perhaps since bright, spicy salsa lurks in a basement here. Bar with relatively small restaurant section but some of the best Mexican staples and imaginative mains in town. Some big tables, good for parties! This place deserves to do well – cross that bridge when you come to it! Lunch and LO 9.30/10pm (bar later).

GREEK

582 2/XA1
ATMOS
£15 OR LESS

✓ **Konaki** www.konakitaverna.co.uk · 0141 342 4010 · 920 Sauchiehall Street Far end of Sauchiehall St beyone the M8. Giorgios and Dimitri's mutual love affair with Glasgow and Crete. A down-to-earth taverna/deli that's great value and a lot of fun. Oregano and olive oil shipped over from their home village. All Greek faves are here, from mezze to honeyed puds and much melt-in-the-mouth meat between. Deli in front, surprisingly big room through the back. A Greek treat and no' that dear. 7 days, lunch and dinner (not Sun lunch). LO 11pm.

TURKISH

583 2/B1
£15 OR LESS

Alla Turca www.allaturca.co.uk · 0141 332 5300 · 192 Pitt Street Top, if not the only proper Turkish restaurant in town, reminding us that the kebab joints nearby do so little justice to an underestimated culinary tradition. Bigger than you think and contemporary room with cool lighting. Lotsa mezze in a big menu where fresh ingredients and slow-cooked dishes come as standard. Good vegetarian choice. And yes, kebabs! Soulful, atmospheric live music may accompany your supper. Lunch and LO 10/11pm.

NORTH AFRICAN

584 2/XA2
£15-22

Mzouda 0141 221 3910 · 141 Elderslie Street Behind the Mitchell Theatre, a worthy and worth-supporting airy eaterie named after a faraway village in the Atlas Mountains. Mix of Catalan and Moroccan 'country' cuisine. Menu somewhere between Berber and Basque is a refreshing change. Signature dish: Djas Harissa is... hot. Lunch and LO 9/10pm.

The Best Seafood & Fish

585 2/C2 ✓✓ **Gamba** www.gamba.co.uk · 0141 572 0899 · **225a West George**
£22-32 **Street** In basement at corner of West Campbell St, a seafood bistro
which for a long time now has been one of the best restaurants in the city.
Fashionable clientele enjoy uncluttered setting and snappy service. The excellent
maître d' has been here a long time too – a tenure that tells you something.
Similarly, chef Derek Marshall, back from ventures elsewhere, leads from the
front... well, the kitchen. Simple but imaginative dishes and presentation; always
impeccable. One meat, one vegetarian choice in a longish menu for a seafood
restaurant. Exemplary wine list. Gamba – a consistently cool port of call. Unlike
many, open on Mon (closed Sun). Lunch and LO 10.30pm.

586 2/E4 ✓✓ **Gandolfi Fish** www.cafegandolfi.com · 0141 552 9475 · **84 Albion**
£22-32 **Street** Once there was Café Gandolfi (594/TEAROOMS), then Bar Gandolfi
(519/GASTROPUBS) and only a couple of fish restaurants in all of Glasgow. Now
there's a shoal of them (the best are on this page). Adjacent the caff and bar, the
big-windowed bistro has a good location, stylish look (nice paintings by Lewis artist
Moira Maclean), good proprietorship (Seumas MacInnes) and a direct link to the
West Coast and Hebridean fishing grounds, especially Barra (where Seumas is from)
and fish supplier Jonathan Boyd. Lunch and LO 10.30pm (Sun till 9pm). Closed
Mon.

587 2/A3 ✓✓ **Two Fat Ladies** www.twofatladiesrestaurant.com · 0141 339 1944 ·
2/C2 **88 Dumbarton Road & 118 Blythswood Square** · 0141 847 0088
ATMOS The landmark West End restaurant and its 'city' extension. Everything selectively
£22-32 sourced; both tiny kitchens produce delicious dishes with a light touch for packed-
in discerning diners. Splendid puds. Similar, though not the same menus. 7 days
(not Sun lunch in West End). Lunch and LO 10/11pm. More ladies also at the
Buttery: 493/FINE DINING.

588 2/XA2 ✓✓ **Crabshakk** www.crabshakk.com · 0141 334 6127 · **1114 Argyle**
ATMOS **Street** Recent addition to seafood and funky, stylish dining in Glasgow,
£15-22 John Macleod's tiny, 3-floor caffshakk has been packed with appreciative foodies
and their fish-loving friends since it opened '09. Champagne and oysters to fab
fish 'n' chips, but most notably the meat of shell and claw in a drop-in, grab-a-
seat kind of atmosphere (though definitely best to book). 11am-10pm (Sun 12noon-
6pm). Bar till 12midnight. Closed Mon.

589 2/C2 ✓ **Mussel Inn** www.mussel-inn.com · 0141 572 1405 · **157 Hope Street**
£15-22 Downtown location for light, bright bistro (big windows) where seafood is serious, but fun. Mussels, scallops, oysters, catch-of-the-day-type blackboard specials
and vegetarian option, but mussels in variant concoctions and kilo pots are the
thing. As in Edinburgh (212/SEAFOOD), this formula is sound and the owners are to
be commended for keeping it real and for giving excellent value. 7 days. Lunch and
LO 10pm (not Sun lunch).

✓ **An Lochan** Report: 512/BISTROS.

Rogano Report: 495/BEST RESTAURANTS.

The Best Vegetarian Restaurants

590 2/C3
ATMOS
£15 OR LESS

✓ **Stereo** www.stereocafebar.com · 0141 222 2254 · 20 Renfield Lane
Unobtrusive in this lane off Renfield St near Central Station, Stereo neverthe-less happily occupies a notable building, the former *Daily Record* printing works designed by Charles Rennie Mackintosh (731/MACKINTOSH) and built in 1900. Sits above street level with a music venue downstairs and is crowded weekends. Menu is all vegetarian and basically organic. 'Small plates' an inexpensive way to graze; daily specials. Hand-made and delicious. 7 days 11am-8pm. Bar till 12midnight.

591 2/E4
£15 OR LESS

✓ **Mono** 0141 553 2400 · Kings Court In odd no-man's land between the Merchant City and East End behind Parnie St, a cool hangout in a forlorn mall. An alternative world! PC in a 'people's collective' kind of way; the antithesis of Glasgow's manufactured style. Great space with art, music (and a record store), occasional performance and interesting if utilitarian vegetarian food served with few frills by friendly staff. Organic ales/wines. 7 days 12noon-8/9pm (bar 12mid-night).

592 2/XF3
2/XA5
£15 OR LESS

Tapa Bakehouse www.tapabakehouse.com · 0141 554 9981 · 21 Whitehill Street, Dennistoun **Tapa Coffeehouse** 0141 423 9494 · 721 Pollokshaws Road Two organic caffs, the original in the East End producing their artisan bread and bakes and with a smattering of seats, the larger laid-back deli and proper café way down Pollokshaws Rd in the South Side. Soups and mezze sold here and cakes. Both dispense their 'best coffee in Glasgow' and good for breakfast. Both 8am-6pm. Sun 9am-5pm.

593 2/E4
£15 OR LESS

The 13th Note www.13thnote.co.uk · 0141 553 1638 · 50-60 King Street Old style veggie hangout – a good attitude/good vibes café-bar with live music downstairs. Menu unexceptional but honest, from vegeburgers to Indian, Greek meze dishes. All suitable for vegans. Organic booze on offer, but also normal Glasgow bevvy. 7 days, 12noon-12midnight. Food 8/9pm.

Tchai-Ovna www.tchaiovna.com · 0141 357 4524 · Otago Lane Old-style vegetarian caff for modern people; boasts best boho credentials. Report: 602/TEA-ROOMS.

Restaurants serving particularly good vegetarian food but not exclusively vegetarian:

The Ubiquitous Chip Report: 389/BEST RESTAURANTS.
Baby Grand Report: 621/LATE-NIGHT RESTAURANTS.
Arisaig Report: 544/BEST SCOTTISH RESTAURANTS.
Mother India, Dakhin Report: 551/552/INDIAN RESTAURANTS.
Café Gandolfi Report: 594/TEAROOMS.
Banana Leaf Report: 554/INDIAN RESTAURANTS.
Alla Turca Report: 583/OTHER ETHNIC RESTAURANTS.
Pakistani Café Report: 608/CAFÉS.

The Best Tearooms & Coffee Shops

594 2/E4
ATMOS
✓ ✓ **Café Gandolfi** www.cafegandolfi.com · 0141 552 6813 · **64 Albion Street** For well over 20 years Seumas MacInnes's definitive and landmark meeting/eating place. A bistro menu, but the casual, boho ambience of a tearoom or coffee shop. Long ago now the stained glass and heavy, over-sized wooden furniture created a unique ambience that has withstood the vagaries of Glasgow style. The food is light and imaginative and served all day. You may have to queue. 7 days, 9am-11.30pm, Sun from 12noon (628/SUNDAY BREAKFAST). The more recent Bar upstairs (519/GASTROPUBS) is different and just as congenial.

595 2/XA1
✓ ✓ **Kember & Jones** www.kemberandjones.co.uk · 0141 337 3851 · **134 Byres Road** They call it a 'Fine Food Emporium' and it is, though some would say 'at a price'. A deli with well-sourced nibbles and the stuff of the good life especially cheese and olives. Tables outside and on the mezzanine. Great sandwiches and the best tartes and tortes and quiche in town. Home baking to a high standard - how they do it all from that small kitchen is a triumph of cookery. 7 days, 8am-10pm (9am-10pm Sat, 9am-6pm Sun).

596 2/XA1
✓ **Sonny & Vito's** 0141 357 0640 · **52 Park Road** On an urban corner between Great Western Rd and Gibson St, a daytime deli-caff with excellent home baking, light menus and tartlettes to eat in or take away. Not many tables, always busy; those outside have interesting aspects (though not views). Nice for breakfast. 7 days 9am-6pm (5pm in winter).

597 2/D3
2/C3
✓ **Fifi and Ally** www.fifiandally.com · 0141 229 0386 · **Princes Square & 80 Wellington Street** · 0141 226 2286 More a lifestyle experience than a mere tearoom but this they do so uniquely well. Both have gift shop as part of mix and newer Wellington St unit has a deli and a restaurant/bar. Good for hot snacks, sandwiches and cakes, especially meringues. Many ladies lunch! Afternoon tea 2-5pm with the 3-tier treatment. Hours vary. Princes Square closed in evening. For Wellington St hours, see 505/BISTROS.

598 2/XA1
2/E3
Tinderbox 0141 339 3108 · **189 Byres Road & 14 Ingram Street** · 0141 552 6907 Stylish, shiny coffee shops. Snacks and Elektra, the good-looking coffee machine. Great people-watching potential inside and out. Better sandwiches and cakey things than others of this ilk. Daily soups, pies, etc (methinks hot food not so hot). Tinderbox has made the leap to London (Upper St, Islington). 7 days, 7.15am-10pm, 10.40pm Byres Rd. Both Sun from 7.45am.

599 2/XA1
North Star 0141 946 5365 · **108 Queen Margaret Drive** Portuguese/Iberian deli-cum-neighbourhood caff. Minimalist and boho approach to food and feel; very laid-back in rough-cosy surroundings. All home-made except (organic) bread. Daily specials on the tiles. Can BYOB. 7 days, Mon-Sat 8am-7/8pm. Sun 11am-5pm.

600 2/D1
Café Hula www.cafehula.co.uk · 0141 353 1660 · **321 Hope Street** Central, some say overlooked café opposite Theatre Royal by people who have North Star (above). Simple, imaginative menu with home-made appeal; good vegetarian choice. Anti-style, mix 'n' match – a downbeat atmosphere rare in this town. Famous brownies. 7 days 8.30am-10pm, Sun 11am-6pm.

601 2/XA1
Jelly Hill 0141 341 0055 · **195 Hyndland Road** On a prominent West End corner, very (quite posh) neighbourhood caff; a local landmark. Small, kinda quirky caff by day, wine bar of an evening. Crafty, woody decor; good terrace tables. Food brought in but home-made. 8am-10pm (till 12noon Thu-Sat, 9am-9pm Sun).

602 2/XA1 **Tchai-ovna** www.tchaiovna.com · 0141 357 4524 · 42 Otago Lane A 'house of tea' hidden away off Otago St on the banks of the Kelvin with verandah and garden terrace. A decidedly gap-year tearoom which could be Eastern Europe, North Africa or Kathmandu but the vibe mainly Middle Eastern. 70 kinds of tea, soup, organic sandwiches and cakes. Impromptu performances likely. A real find but suits and ladies who lunch may not be not comfortable here. 7 days 11am-11pm.

603 2/XA5 **Art Lover's Café** www.houseforanartlover.co.uk · 0141 353 4779 · 10 Dumbreck Road, Bellahouston Park On the ground floor of House for an Art Lover, a building based on drawings left by Mackintosh (734/MACKINTOSH). Bright room, crisp presentation and a counterpoint to wrought iron, purply, swirly Mockintosh caffs elsewhere. This is unfussy and elegant. Garden views. Soup 'n' sandwiches and à la carte all beautifully presented; a serious and aesthetically pleasing lunch spot. 7 days 10am-4pm.

▬▬ The Best Caffs

604 2/XA1
ATMOS
✓✓ **University Café** 87 Byres Road 'People have been coming here for generations to sit at the "kneesy" tables and share the salt and vinegar. Run by the Verecchia family who administer advice, sympathy and pie, beans and chips with equal aplomb.' These astute words of the late Graeme Kelling, describing a real Glasgow gem, still stand 5 editions of this book later. 6 booths only; it resists all change. BYOB; no corkage. Daily till 10pm (weekends till 10.30pm). Takeaway open later.

605 2/XF3
✓ **Coia's Café** www.coiascafe.co.uk · 0141 554 3822 · 473 Duke Street Since 1928, Coia's has been supplying this East End high street with ice cream, great-deal breakfasts and the kind of comforting lunch that any neighbourhood needs. A few years back a substantial makeover and expansion turned this caff into a full-blown food operation with deli counter, takeaway and restaurant. So now it's traditional grub and ice cream along with the olive-oil niceties. They still do the Havana cigars. 7 days. 7am-9pm; till 9.45pm Fri/Sat. Sun from 10am.

606 2/XA5
✓ **Brooklyn Café** 0141 632 3427 · 21 Minard Road Here just off Pollokshaws Rd for 70+ years, the kind of all-purpose caff any neighbourhood would be proud of. More tratt perhaps than caff, with pasta/pizza, 3 risottos, 6 salads, excellent puds and great ice cream. It will, of course, never die, like their Empire biscuits. 7 days 8am-9pm (weekends 10pm). Sun from 9am. Can BYO.

607 2/XA1
✓ **Café Pop** 657 Great Western Road Small, bright, poppy caff (and deli) with a '60s vibe but very au courant menu and delivery. Organic bread sandwiches 'n' soup, hot specials like chilli and broth, waffles and most especially home-made cakes of a traditional nature including dee-lish cup cakes (natch). All a bit of a groove, really. 7 days. 8am-5.50pm (9am-6pm Sat, 10am-5pm Sun).

608 2/XA5
ATMOS
✓ **The Pakistani Café** 0141 423 5791 · 607 Pollokshaws Road Jimshaed Sharif's quirky, homespun paean to Pakistan on the South Side has got personality written all over it. Cheap enough and discounts to asylum-seekers. Superb curries, good vegetarian, smooth lassis, all fresh to the table. 7 days 11am-8pm, Sun 12noon-8pm. BYOB.

609 2/C2   **Where The Monkey Sleeps** www.monkeysleeps.com · 0141 226 3406 · 182 West Regent Street Adjacent Compass Gallery and in basement below Chardon D'Or (492/BEST RESTAURANTS), its commercial and spiritual opposite. Exhibition space ie hanging as well as hanging out. Wall of menu (and sound). Big on breakfasts. Coffee, soups and picmix sandwiches, including their famous 'stoofa'. Art students and what they turn into (especially bike couriers). Eat in (on funky furnishings) or take away. 7am-5pm. Sat 10am-5pm. Closed Sun.

610 2/C2   **Bradfords** 245 Sauchiehall Street Since 1924 the coffee shop/restaurant upstairs from the flagship shop of this local and estimable bakery chain. Familiar wifie waitresses, the macaroni cheese is close to mum's and the cakes and pies from downstairs represent Scottish bakery at its figure-building best. The best strawberry tarts and pre-fashion cup cakes. Mon-Sat 9am-5.30pm.

611 2/XF3   **Olive** 0141 554 9404 · 27 Hillfoot Street, Dennistoun Off Duke St. Neighbourhood soup 'n' sandwich caff (and they say, deli) in the East End. Home bakes, all-day breakfast. Nothing flash or frenzied here, just a mellow vibe for slow days in the east (end). 9.30am-4pm, Sat 9-5, Sun 11-4. Closed Wed.

612 2/E4   **Trans-Europe Café** 0141 552 7999 · 25 Parnie Street Easygoing caff in emerging gallery quarter off the east end of Argyle St with neighbourhood atmosphere and home-made food individually prepared in a mad gantry kitchen. Light food, especially bespoke sandwiches and more meal-like at night (Thu-Sat only). A friendly vibe. 10am-5pm; take out (weekends till 10pm).

▮▮▮ Kid-Friendly Places

613 2/XA1   ✓**Rio Café** 0141 334 9909 · 27 Hyndland Street, Partick A kid-friendly caff that's cool, cool for parents that is with decent food and service for both. Here there's also DJs, the 'spoken word' jazz on Thursdays, poker on Sundays and sweeties. An all-round neighbourhood place for all Jock Tamson's bairns. 7 days 9am-7.30pm (bar 11pm/12midnight).

614 2/XA1   **Di Maggio's** www.dimaggios.co.uk · 0141 334 8560 · 61 Ruthven Lane off
    2/XA5   Byres Road & 1038 Pollokshaws Road · 0141 632 4194 & 21 Royal Exchange
    2/D3   Square · 0141 248 2111 'Our family serving your family' they say and they do. Bustling, friendly pizza joints with good Italian attitude to brats. There's a choice to defy the most finicky kid. High chairs, special menu. Handy outdoor section in Exchange Sq is best for runaround kids. 7 days.

615 2/XA1   **Jelly Hill** 0141 341 0055 · 195 Hyndland Street Prominent corner location with outside tables. Casual caff by day (more grown up by night) with cakes, pannini, etc; and sweeties and juice. 7 days from 8am.

616 2/XA5   **Tramway Café** 0141 422 2023 · 25 Albert Drive Caff at the back of Tramway arts venue on the South Side. Venue itself cavernous, contemporary with continuously changing programme always worth visiting. Caff well run with great grub and facing on to the Secret Garden (1531/GARDENS). Play area and healthy 'snack bag' options; nice for kids. 10am-8pm, Sun 12noon-6pm. Closed Mon.

617 2/XA5   **Brooklyn Café** 0141 632 3427 · 21 Minard Road The unassuming, long-established South Side (off Pollokshaws Rd) caff where families are very welcome for the carbo and the cones and the jars of sweeties on the shelf. Report: 606/CAFFS.

618 2/XA1 **The Big Blue** 0141 357 1038 · **445 Great Western Road** Downstairs on Kelvin Bridge corner. Accessible, Italian-led menu but main attraction is the family-friendly open-air terrace overlooking the river. 7 days lunch and dinner. More drink-driven later.

619 2/XA5 **Art Lover's Café** www.houseforanartlover.co.uk · 0141 353 4779 · **Dumbreck Road** Informal, light café with enough space for kids and parents not to feel confined. Report: 603/COFFEE SHOPS.

620 2/D3 **Princes Square** **Buchanan Street** Glasgow's smart downtown mall has many eateries with 'outside' tables and suitable kids' choices. Basement has mosaic area where kids can play. **Il Pavone** and **Darcy's** offer good family Italian fare.

Bella Napoli Family-run and run for families: a tratt with the standard Italian grub we've all loved ever since we could keep spaghetti on a spoon. Report: 533/TRUSTY TRATTS.

▇▇▇ The Best Late-Night Restaurants

621 2/A2
ATMOS
✓ **Baby Grand** www.babygrandglasgow.com · 0141 248 4942 · **Elmbank Gardens** It's not easy to find by Charing Cross Station and Premier Lodge skyscraper hotel behind King's Theatre, but persevere – this is a useful bar/diner at any time of day but comes into its own after 10pm when just about everywhere that's decent is closing. Chargrilled food and grazing contemporary menu. Piano player Wed-Sat; night-time people. **Daily till 12midnight, Fri/Sat 2am.**

622 2/XA1
ATMOS
✓ **Asia Style** 0141 332 8828 · **185 St George's Road** Simple, authentic Chinese and Malaysian café/canteen with familiar sweet 'n' sour, curry and satays, 4 kinds of noodle, exotic specials and 5 kinds of 'porridge'. Only open evenings. **7 days 5pm-3am** (may close 2am if quiet).

623 2/B1 **Glasgow Noodle Bar** 0141 333 1883 · **482 Sauchiehall Street** The stripped-down noodle bar in Sauchiehall St where and when you need it. Authentic, fast, no-frills Chinese (ticket service and eezee-kleen tables). The noodle is 'king'; but cooking *is* taken seriously. Report: 572/FAR-EASTERN RESTAURANTS. **7 days, 12noon-4am.**

624 2/XA1 **Stravaigin & Stravaigin 2** www.stravaigin.5pm.co.uk · 0141 334 2665 · **Gibson Street & 0141 334 7165 Ruthven Lane, off Byres Road** Worth remembering that both these excellent restaurants (494/FINE-DINING RESTAURANTS and 499/BISTROS) serve food **till 11pm**. It is later than most in 'cosmopolitan' Glasgow.

✓✓ **Ubiquitous Chip** www.ubiquitouschip.co.uk · 0141 334 5007 · **Ashton Lane** 489/FINE-DINING RESTAURANTS. **7 days till 11pm.** Best late choice in the West End.

✓✓ **Guy's Restaurant & Bar** 498/BISTROS. **11.30pm Fri/Sat.** Best late choice in the Merchant City.

Good Places For Sunday Breakfast

625 2/XA1
ATMOS
✓ ✓ **Cafézique** 0141 339 7180 · 66 Hyndland Street This award-winning, hard-to-fault, two-level bistro/caff opens at 9am every day for snacking or more ambitious breakfast. A very civilised start to the day; fills up quickly. **From 9am.**

626 2/XA1
✓ **The Left Bank** www.theleftbank.co.uk · 0141 339 5969 · 33 Gibson Street Classy and popular café-bar-restaurant in student and luvvyland. From great granola to eggs mornay and beans on toast. 502/BISTROS. From 9am weekdays, **10am Sun.**

627 2/F3
✓ **Babbity Bowster** 0141 552 5055 · 16 Blackfriars Street The seminal Merchant City bar/hotel recommended for many things (547/SCOTTISH RESTAURANTS, 672/DRINKING OUTDOORS), but worth remembering as one of the best and earliest spots for Sunday breakfast. **From 10am.**

628 2/E4
ATMOS
✓ **Café Gandolfi** www.cafegandolfi.com · 0141 552 6813 · 64 Albion Street Atmospheric room, with daylight filtering through stained glass and comforting, oversized wooden furniture. This is pleasant start to Sunday, that day of rest and more shopping made even better with pastrami, a pot of tea and the papers. 594/BEST TEAROOMS. Bar upstairs has all-day menu. **Both from 12noon.**

629 2/XA1
✓ **Sonny & Vito's** www.sonnyandvitosdeli.co.uk · 0141 357 0640 · 52 Park Road Much-loved West End brunch rendezvous. A deli-caff with home baking from scones and muffins to Mediterranean platefuls. Outside tables and takeaway. 596/BEST COFFEESHOPS. **From 9am.**

630 2/XF3
✓ **Coia's Café** 473 Duke Street They've been doing breakfast here for over 75 years. Goes like a fair and still damned good. The full-fry monty lasts all day (vegetarian too). The East End choice. 605/BEST CAFFS. **From 10am.**

631 2/XA1
✓ **Stravaigin** www.stravaigin.5pm.co.uk · 0141 334 2665 · 28 Gibson Street Same care and flair given to breakfast menu as the rest (494/BEST RESTAURANTS). Cramped maybe, but reflects appetite for Sunday breakfast from home-made granola to French toast, real Ayrshire bacon. Served till 5pm. **From 11am.**

632 2/XA1
Tinderbox 0141 339 3108 · 189 Byres Road · 14 Ingram Street · 0141 552 6907 Great café/diner open early to late. Probably the earliest decent breakfast for out-all-nighters. Porridge, muesli and cake. 598/COFFEE SHOPS. Weekdays from 7.15am. Weekends **from 7.45am.**

The Best Takeaway Places

633 2/XA1 ✓✓ **Heart Buchanan** www.heartbuchanan.co.uk · 0141 334 7626 · **380 Byres Road** Deli and takeaway with tables, adjacent 'traiteur' and adjacent caff: Fiona Buchanan endorses the French idea that excellent food can be pre-prepared to take home. Certainly an extraordinary and changing menu (every 2 weeks) is produced in the kitchens downstairs according to a published list. Lots of other selected goodies to go. Fiona puts her 'heart' into this place. Every urban neighbourhood should have a heart and Buchanan. Programme of cookery classes. 7 days 8.30am-9.30pm. Sun 10am-6pm.

634 2/XA1 ✓✓ **Delizique** www.delizique.co.uk · 0141 339 2000 · **70 Hyndland Street** Down from Cottier's and two doors up from their original corner, a larger, busy emporium serving the luvvies, loaded and long-term denizens of Hyndland and beyond. In-house bakery with top breads. Fruit/veg, cheese counter; the unusual alongside dinner-party essentials. Gorgeous food to go includes salads, tarts and scrumptious cakes. 7 days 9am-9pm (till 8pm Sat/Sun).

635 2/XA5 ✓ **Cherry and Heather** www.cherryandheather.co.uk · 0141 427 0272 · **7 North Gower Street, Cessnock** Near Bellahouston Post Office. Far on the Southwest Side, a perfect wee takeaway with integrity food and a great range of soups, casseroles and truly gourmet sandwiches. Artisan bread, unusual combos. A few stools. Delivery service. Just wish they were closer to town. 10am-5pm (Sat 11am-4pm). Closed Sun.

636 2/XA1 ✓ **Roots & Fruits** 0141 339 3077 · **Great Western Road** A row of wholefood provisioner shops near Kelvinbridge and at **351 Byres Rd**, famously where to go for fruit and veg in the West End. GW Rd branch has traiteur section and a couple of chairs by one of the windows, but the delicious home-made food (paellas, tortillas, salads) and bakery is mainly to take home. 7 days. 8.30/9am-6.30pm (7pm Thu/Fri).

637 2/E3 **Fressh** 0141 552 5532 · **51 Cochrane Street** A takeaway with integrity in the Merchant City, at George Sq along (in every sense) from Greggs. Hearty (and lite) healthy soups and famously good juices. Sandwiches made up or ready-to-go. Much vegetarian. All dolphin-friendly. 7 days 9am-5pm (Sun from 11am).

638 2/XA1 **Grassroots** www.grassrootsorganic.com · 0141 353 3278 · **20 Woodlands Road, Charing Cross** Food to go, but mainly big organic deli. Vegetarian ready meals, bespoke sandwiches. 7 days 8am-6/7pm, Sat 9-6pm, Sun 11-5pm.

Philadelphia Fish & Chicken Bar The West End standby! Report: 1353/FISH & CHIPS.

Where The Monkey Sleeps Report: 609/CAFFS.

639 2/XA1 ✓ ✓ **Grassroots Organic** 48 Woodlands Road Long-established (and long before anyone else used and abused the word 'organic') first-class vegetarian food and provisions store, everything chemically unaltered and environmentally friendly. Great breads and sandwiches for lunch and the best organic fruit/veg range in town. 7 days 8am-6pm (Thu/Fri till 7pm, Sun till 5pm).

640 2/XA1 ✓ ✓ **Delizique** 70 Hyndland Street Excellent neighbourhood deli for the affluent Hyndlanders and others who roam and graze round here. Counters, kitchen and bakery. Great prepared meals (in-house chef), tarts, pasta and gorgeous cakes. Other hand-picked goodies include oils, hams, flowers and Mellis cheeses. Open till 9pm Mon-Fri, till 8 weekends. 634/TAKEAWAY. Cafézique at number 66, the original location, is the top café-bistro in the west (497/BISTROS).

641 2/XA1 ✓ ✓ **Heart Buchanan** 380 Byres Road Great deli and first-rate takeaway. Report: 633/TAKEAWAY.

642 2/XA1 ✓ ✓ **I.J. Mellis** www.mellischeese.co.uk · 0141 339 8998 · 492 Great Western Road Started out as the cheese guy, now more of a very select deli for food that's good and 'slow'. Coffees, hams, sausages, olives and seasonal stuff like apples and mushrooms (branches vary), so smells mingle. Irresistible! Branches also in Edinburgh (324/EDINBURGH DELIS) and St Andrews (1446/REALLY GOOD DELIS). 7 days though times vary. See also 1473/CHEESES.

643 2/XA5 ✓ **Eat Deli** 0141 638 7123 · 16 Busby Road Way down south towards East Kilbride, a café-cum-deli and outside-catering outfit; essentially great home-cooked food to go. From antipasti to wholesome meals and sweet and savoury bakes. This is way better than M&S. 7 days 8am-7pm, Sun 11am-5pm.

644 2/XA5 ✓ **Gusto and Relish** www.gustoandrelish.com · 0141 424 1233 · 729 Pollokshaws Road More perhaps a caff than a deli. They cure their own ham, make sausages etc, so brill for breakfast. Other wholesome options and nice salads. All to go. 7 days 9.30am-6pm, Sat 10am-5pm, Sun from 10.30am.

645 2/XA5 ✓ **Deli 1901** www.deli1901.co.uk · 0141 632 1630 · 11 Skirving Street Just off Kilmarnock Rd at the Granary. South Side 'traiteur' with meals, pies and bakes to go. Lots for starters. Good cheese selection. Big on outside catering. 7 days 9am-7pm, Sun 10am-5pm.

646 2/XF3 **Eusebi Deli** 0141 763 0399 · 793 Shettleston Road Another gem in the ever-improving food range of the East End and customers travel here from way beyond the neighbourhood. Great Italian wine and beer selections, good deli ranges and imaginative take-home options that change according to the market today. Outside catering. Giovanna is passionate about good food and personally sources items from Italy. Tue-Sat 8.30am-5.30pm. Times approximate.

Unique Glasgow Pubs

647 2/XA1 ✓✓**Òran Mór** www.oran-mor.co.uk · **Corner of Byres & Great**
ATMOS   **Western Roads** This is the epitome of all the things you can do with a pub. A huge and hugely popular emporium of drink and divertissements in a converted church on a prominent West End corner, the always-evolving vision of Colin Beattie. Drinking on all levels (and outside) but also good pub food (522/GASTRO-PUBS) and separate brasserie, though not quite engendering that brasserie lightness and jollity. Big entertainment programme from DJs to comedy in the club and home of the brilliant 'A Play and a Pint'. They thought of everything. From lunch till very late, this is a happening hostelry. 7 days till 12midnight.

648 2/D3 ✓✓**The Horseshoe** 17 Drury Street A mighty pub since the 19th century
ATMOS   in the small street between West Nile and Renfield Sts near Central Station. Early example of this style of pub, dubbed 'gin palaces'. Island rather than horseshoe bar ('the longest in the UK'), impressive selection of alcohols and an upstairs lounge where they serve lunch and high tea. The food is amazing value (548/SCOTTISH RESTAURANTS). All kinds of folk. Daily till 12midnight.

649 2/E1 ✓**Corinthian** www.g1group.co.uk · 191 Ingram Street Mega makeover of impressive listed building to form cavernous bar/restaurant, 2 comfy lounge/cocktail bars and a restaurant serving top-end 'traditional Scottish food' in glorious surroundings. Near George Sq and Gallery of Modern Art. Awesome ceiling in main room, the 'Lite Bar', which is way better than megabars elsewhere. 7 days, till 12midnight. (Piano bar Thu-Sun.)

650 2/E4 ✓**Arta** www.arta.co.uk · Old Cheesemarket, Walls Street, Merchant City Near and same ownership as Corinthian (above) and similar scale of vision completely realised. Dated now but this massive, OTT bar/restaurant/club somewhere between old Madrid and new Barcelona could only happen in Glasgow at the end of the 20th century. 'Mediterranean' menu upstairs where paella meets pizza (till 11pm) and below, the full-on Glasgow drinking, dressing-up and chatting-up experience. Food: 5pm-9.30pm (11pm Fri-Sun). Closed Mon/Tue. Bar 3am. It's a long way out for a fag.

651 2/D5 ✓**Victoria Bar** 157 Bridgegate The Vicky is in the Briggait, one of Glasgow's oldest streets, near the Victoria Bridge over the Clyde. Once a pub for the fish-market and open odd hours, now it's a howff for all those who like an atmosphere that's old, friendly and uncontrived. Ales. Mon-Sat till 12midnight, Sun 11pm.

652 2/D5 ✓**Scotia Bar** 112 Stockwell Street Near the Victoria (above), established
ATMOS   1792, Tudor-style pub with a low-beamed ceiling and intimate, woody snug. Long the haunt of folk musicians, writers and raconteurs. Music and poetry sessions, folk and blues Wed-Sun. Open till 12midnight.

653 2/D5 ✓**Clutha Vaults** 167 Stockwell Street This and the pubs above are part of the same family of traditional Glasgow pubs. The Clutha (ancient name for the Clyde) has a Victorian-style interior and an even longer history. Known for live music (Wed-Sun). Mon-Sat till 12midnight, Sun till 11pm.

654 2/XA1   **The Halt Bar** 160 Woodlands Road Edwardian pub largely unspoiled and unchanged since at least the 1970s. Original counter and snug intact. Always great atmosphere – though may be a tad grungy for some. Live music and DJs Thu-Sun, football on the telly. Open mic nights. Open till 11pm/12midnight.

655 2/XA1 **Lismore** 206 Dumbarton Road Lismore/Lios mor named after the long island
ATMOS off Oban. Great neighbourhood (Partick) bar that welcomes all sorts. Gives good
atmosphere, succour and malts. Occasional music. Daily till 12midnight.

656 2/XA2 **Ben Nevis** 1147 Argyle Street Owned by the same people as Lismore and Òran
Mór (above) but run by others. An excellent makeover in contemporary but not
faux-Scottish style. Small and pubby, the Deuchars is spot-on and great malt list.
They have pie 'n' beans. Live music Thu/Sun.

Hummingbird 186 Bath Street 681/COOL BARS. Glasgow style loud and proud.

The Best Old 'Unspoilt' Pubs

✓ **Horseshoe** 17 Drury Street 648/UNIQUE PUBS.

✓ **Halt Bar** 160 Woodlands Road 654/UNIQUE PUBS.

✓ **Victoria Bar** 157 Bridgegate 651/UNIQUE PUBS.

✓ **Scotia Bar** 112 Stockwell Street 652/UNIQUE PUBS.

✓ **Clutha Vaults** 167 Stockwell Street 653/UNIQUE PUBS.

657 2/B2 **The Griffin (& The Griffiny & The Griffinette)** 266 Bath Street Corner of
Elmbank St near the King's Theatre. Built in 1903 to anticipate the completion of
the theatre and offer the patrons a pre-show drink. Stand at the Edwardian bar like
generations of Glaswegians. The main bar still retains its 'snug' with a posh,
etched-glass partition; booths have been added but the atmosphere, even with
new owners in '09, is still 'Old Glasgow'. Food till 6.30pm.

658 2/E3 **Steps** 66 Glassford Street Tiny pub and barely noticed but has the indelible
marks of better, by-gone days. In no way celebrated like Rogano (495/FINE-
DINING), but also refers to the *Queen Mary* with stained glass and great panelling.
Very typical, friendly Glasgow. Pies and often snacks on the house.

659 2/XA5 **M.J. Heraghty** 708 Pollokshaws Road More than a touch of the Irish here
and easily more authentic than the rash of imports. A local with loyal regulars
who'll make you welcome; old pub practices still hold in this howff in the sowff.
Ladies' loos introduced in 1996! Sun-Thu till 11pm, Fri-Sat till 12midnight.

660 2/XA5 **Brechin's** 803 Govan Road Near Paisley Road West junction and M8 over-
pass. Established in 1798 and, as they say, always in the same family. A former
shipyard pub close in heart and soul to Rangers FC. It's behind the statue of ship-
builder Sir William Pearce (which, covered in grime, was known as the 'Black Man')
and the feline rat-catcher on the roof makes it a listed building. Unaffected neighbourhood atmosphere, some flute-playing. 7 days till 11pm, Fri/Sat 12midnight.

661 2/XA5 **The Old Toll Bar** 1 Paisley Road West Opposite the site of the original
Parkhouse Toll, where monies were collected for use of the 'turnpikes' between
Glasgow and Greenock. Opened in 1874, the original interior is still intact; the *fin
de siècle* painted glass and magnificent old gantry preserved under order. A 'palace
pub' classic. Real ale and some single malts. 7 days till 11pm.

The Best Real-Ale Pubs

Pubs on other pages may purvey real ale; the following take it seriously. All open 7 days till 11pm (midnight weekends) unless stated.

662 2/A2 ✓ **Bon Accord** www.thebonaccord.com · **153 North Street** On a slip road of the motorway swathe near the Mitchell Library. One of the first real-ale pubs in Glasgow. Good selection of malts and up to 12 beers; always Theakstons, Deuchars and IPA plus many guest ales on hand pump. Food at lunchtime and till 7.45pm. Light, easy-going atmosphere here, but they do take their ale to heart; there's even a 'tour' of the cellars if you want it (and quiz on Wed, live band on Sat). Till 12midnight, Sun till 11pm.

663 2/XF5 ✓ **WEST** www.westbeer.com · **4 Binnie Place, Templeton Building, Glasgow Green** First find the People's Palace (688/MAIN ATTRACTIONS) then gaze at the fabulous exterior of the Templeton edifice where on the bottom corner the UK's only German brewery brews its award-winning beers. 5 in total in a beer-hall setting and garden overlooking the Green. St Mungo for starters and a massive selection of imports. 'Simple, hearty' food with a German slant. Decent wine list. 11am-11pm (Sat 12midnight, Sun 9pm).

664 2/B1 ✓ **The State** **148 Holland Street** Off Sauchiehall St at the West End. No-
ATMOS compromising, old-style pub, all wood and old pictures. 8 guest ales. No fancy extras. Will probably outlive the many makeovers around here. Food at lunchtime. Some music. 7 days till 12midnight.

665 2/XA1 **Tennent's** **191 Byres Road** Near the always-red traffic lights at University Ave, a big, booming watering-hole of a place where you're never far away from the horse-shoe bar and its dozen excellent hand-pumped ales, including up to 3 or 4 guests. 'Tennent's is an institution': some regulars do appear to live here. Basic bar meals including 'the steak pie' till 9pm. Till 12midnight at weekends.

666 2/F3 **Babbity Bowster** **16 Blackfriars Street** In a pedestrianised part of the Merchant City and just off the High St, a highly successful pub/restaurant/hotel (474/INDIVIDUAL HOTELS); but the pub comes first. Caledonian, Deuchars, IPA and well-chosen guests. Many malts and cask cider. Food all day (574/SCOTTISH RESTAURANTS), occasional folk music, outside patio (672/DRINK OUTDOORS).

667 2/D3 **The Horseshoe** **17 Drury Street** Great for lots of reasons (648/UNIQUE GLAS-GOW PUBS), not the least of which is its range of beers in exactly the right sur-roundings to drink them. Sky sports.

668 2/D5 **Victoria Bar** **157 Bridgegate** Another pub mentioned before (651/UNIQUE GLASGOW PUBS) where IPA, Maclays and others can be drunk in a dark woody atmosphere enlivened by traditional music (Tue & Fri-Sun).

Places To Drink Outdoors

669 2/XA1 **Lock 27** www.lock27.com · **1100 Crow Road** At the very north end of Crow Rd beyond Anniesland, an unusual boozer for Glasgow: a canalside pub on a lock of the Forth & Clyde Canal (703/WALKS IN THE CITY), a (very wee) touch English, where of a summer's day you can sit outside. Slightly worn around the edges but excel-lent bar food and always busy.

670 2/XA1 **Cottier's** www.thecottier.com · **93 Hyndland Street** First on the left after the swing park on Highburgh Road (going west) and the converted church is on your right, around the corner. Heart of West End location. Think: a cold beer on a hot day sitting in the leafy shade of a churchyard. Some barbeques – it's a Hyndland kind of life! Cottier's refurbished and rethought (again) at TGP.

671 2/XA1 **Bar Brel & others in Ashton Lane** www.brelbarrestaurant.com As soon as the sun comes out, so do the punters. With numerous watering holes, benches suddenly appear and Ashton Lane becomes a cobbled, alfresco pub. The nearest Glasgow gets to Euro or even Dublin drinking. Brel has a grassy bit out back.

672 2/F3 **Babbity Bowster** 16 Blackfriars Street Unique in the Merchant City for several reasons (666/REAL-ALE PUBS, 547/SCOTTISH RESTAURANTS), but in summer certainly for its napkin of garden in an area bereft of greenery. Though enclosed by surrounding streets, it's a concrete oasis. Could be somewhere else but it feels a lot like Glasgow and there's always good craic.

The Big Blue Outside terrace overlooks the murky Kelvin. 538/PIZZA.
The Goat Not the cleanest air but clear views from this corner all the way into town. 679/COOL BARS.

Pubs With Good Food

See also Gastropubs, p. 102.

673 2/XA1 ✓**McPhabbs** www.mcphabbs.com · **22 Sandyford Place** Sauchiehall St west of Charing Cross. Long-standing great Glasgow pub with loyal following. Tables in front garden and on back decks. Standard home-made pub-grub menu and great specials. Food till 9pm. Bar 11pm/12midnight. Bit of a West End secret.

674 2/C2 ✓**The Butterfly And The Pig** www.thebutterflyandthepig.com · **153 Bath Street** Among many style-heavy bars and eateries the BF&P arrived as quite the latest thing but neatly avoided the gastropub bandwagon by being more real than just recherché and cooler than merely contrived. Daft food descriptions but what comes is imaginative and fun to eat. They do proper afternoon tea. 7 days 12noon-10pm, Sun till 6pm. Bar till 3am.

675 2/B1 **The Griffin** 266 Bath Street On corner of Elmbank St across from the King's Theatre. The Griffin rooms have always been on that corner and until recently dispensed the basic pie, beans 'n' chips as standard. That seems to have gone now but the grub in the Griffin and Griffinette next door is decent and the rooms are classic. 7 days, lunch and LO 9pm. Bar 12midnight. 657/'UNSPOILT' PUBS.

676 2/XA1 **Brel** www.barbrelrestaurant.com · **Ashton Lane** Always-busy bar in West End lane where teams of students and the rest of us teem, especially at weekends. Pots of moules/frites help the many euro brews go down. Popular, stuff-your-face type of lunches and serried ranks of outside tables up the back. Lunch and food till 9.45pm (10.30pm weekends), bar 12midnight. 671/OUTSIDE DRINKING.

677 2/D3 **Bar Soba** www.barsoba.co.uk · **11 Mitchell Lane** Up the narrow lane off Buchanan St and next to the Lighthouse design centre, a bright, contemporary room and an ambitious fusion menu: Japanese and Malaysian staples reasonably accomplished. 7 days 12noon-10pm. Bar 12midnight.

Cool Bars

678 2/C3 ✓**Arches** www.thearches.co.uk · 0901 022 0300 (box office) · **253 Argyle Street** The boho bar/café of the essential Arches Theatre, the club and experimental theatre space refurbished with millennium money. Design by Timorous/Taller, this is an obvious pre-club pre-theatre space, but works at any time. Food and DJs and lots going on. Even if you're only in Glasgow for the weekend, you should come here for the vibe. Food 12noon-9pm.

679 2/XA1 ✓**The Goat** www.thegoat.co.uk · 0141 357 7373 · **1287 Argyle Street** Up west near Kelvingrove Gallery, a comfortable, friendly, sitting-room pub (with mezzanine and upstairs snug), not obviously 'cool' but known for its laid-back vibe and reasonable food. Big windows and pavement terrace look down Argyle St; a great corner for people gazing and a Glasgow-affirming experience. 7 days. Food 12noon-9pm, bar 12midnight.

680 2/E4 ✓**The Brunswick Hotel Bar** www.brunswickhotel.co.uk · 0141 552 0001 · **104 Brunswick Street** This small Merchant City hotel and its ground-level bar/restaurant has stood the style test of times and almost 20 years on is still a cool hangout for a mixed crowd, especially at Sunday brunch and all over the weekend. Very decent grub (537/PIZZA).

681 2/E3 ✓**Hummingbird** www.socialanimal.co.uk · **186 Bath Street** To be honest, I don't know if this is cool or not, it's certainly over the top in its attempt to be so. Transformed from another venture that had loadsa dosh lavished on it (the private members' Hallion Club), the bird hummed into vibrant view with no expense spared by the G1 group and quickly became 'it'. The 'Balearic' basement level has a beach vibe and a very questionable 'tub', and there are 3 floors of theme and thin people with great haircuts. You can book a booth or have a penthouse party. By the time you read this, though, the party may be over. Oh, and they do food (but don't go there). 5pm-3am.

682 2/XA1 **The Belle** 617 Great Western Road Laid-back West End pub between Byres Rd and Kelvin Bridge. Good selection of wines and beers including Krusovice light and dark on draft. Great coffee, daytime light snacks, mixed crowd. Open fire. Occasional light music. 7 days. LO 11.45pm.

683 2/D3 **Bar 10** 10 Mitchell Lane Halfway up Buchanan St pedestrian precinct on the left in the narrow lane that also houses the Lighthouse design centre. There's an NYC look about this joint that is so loved by its habitués, they still pack it at weekends over 12 years after it arrived. Ben Kelly design has worn well. Food till 7pm, DJs and pre-club preparations. 7 days till midnight. **Bar Soba**, great for cocktails and especially its pan-Asian menu, is opposite in the lane.

684 2/E3 **Bar 91** 91 Candleriggs A better bar among many of this ilk hereabouts, food also is well-considered and put together, though it stops at 6pm to make way for pre-club ministrations (and till 12midnight).

685 2/XA1
ATMOS
FREE

✓✓ **Kelvingrove Art Gallery & Museum** 0141 287 2699 · www.glasgowmuseums.com · Argyle Street (west end by Kelvingrove Park) Huge Victorian sandstone edifice with awesome atrium. On the ground floor is a natural history/Scottish history museum. The upper salons contain the city's superb British and European art collection. A prodigious success, with literally millions of visitors since it reopened '06 after major refurbishment. Endless interest and people-friendly presentations. See the world from a Glasgow point of view! (You go through 'Glasgow Stones' to get to 'Ancient Egypt'.) And it's all free, folks! 7 days. 10am-5pm (Fri/Sun from 11am).

686 2/XA5
FREE/
ADMISSION
NTS

✓✓ **The Burrell Collection, Pollok Park & Pollok House** 0141 287 2550 · www.nts.org.uk South of the river via A77 Kilmarnock Rd (over Jamaica St Bridge) about 5km, following signs from Pollokshaws Rd. Set in rural parkland, this award-winning modern gallery was built to house the eclectic acquisitions of Sir William Burrell. Showing a preference for medieval works, among the 8500 items the magpie magnate donated to the city in 1944 are artefacts from the Roman empire to Rodin. The building itself integrates old doorways and whole rooms reconstructed from Hutton Castle. Self-serve café and restaurant on the ground floor (Mon-Thu, Sat 10am-5pm, Fri and Sun 11am-5pm). **Pollok House** (0141 616 6410) and gardens further into the park (with works by Goya, El Greco and William Blake) is worth a detour and has, below stairs, the better tearooms; gardens to the river. Both open 7 days. 10am-5pm. 704/WALKS IN THE CITY.

687 2/XF3
FREE

✓ **Glasgow Cathedral & Provand's Lordship** 0141 552 6891/553 2557 · www.glasgowcathedral.org.uk · Castle Street Across the road from one another, they represent what remains of the oldest part of the city, which (as can be seen in the People's Palace, see below) was, in the early 18th century, merely a ribbon of streets from here to the river. The present cathedral, though established by St Mungo in AD 543, dates from the 12th century and is a fine example of the very real, if gloomy, Gothic. The house, built in 1471, is a museum which strives to convey a sense of medieval life. Watch you don't get run over when you re-emerge into the 21st century and try to cross the street. In the background, the Necropolis piled on the hill invites inspection and offers a viewpoint and the full Gothic perspective (though best not to go alone). Easy to do all of the above and St Mungo's Museum (below) together – allow half a day. Open 7 days. Times vary slightly.

688 2/XF5
ATMOS
FREE

✓ **The People's Palace** www.glasgowmuseums.com · 0141 271 2951 Approach via the Tron and London Road, then turn right into Glasgow Green. This has long been a folk museum *par excellence* wherein, since 1898, the history, folklore and artefacts of a proud city have been gathered, cherished and displayed. But this is much more than a mere museum; it is the heart and soul of the city and together with the Winter Gardens adjacent, shouldn't be missed, to know what Glasgow's about. Tearoom in the Tropics, among the palms and ferns of the Winter Gardens. Opening times as most other museums: Mon-Thu, Sat 10am-5pm, Fri & Sun 11am-5pm.

689 2/XA5
ADMISSION

✓ **Glasgow Science Centre** www.glasgowsciencecentre.org · 0871 540 1000 On south side of the Clyde opposite the SECC, Glasgow's newest attraction built with millennium dosh. Approach via the Clyde Arc ('squinty') Bridge or walk from SECC complex by Bell's Bridge. Impressive titanium-clad mall, Imax cinema and 127m-high tower. 4 floors of interactive exhibitions, planetarium and theatre. Separate tickets or combos. Book slot for tower (closed on windy days). Hours vary; generally 7 days 10am-5pm.

690 2/XF3 **St Mungo Museum of Religious Life & Art** www.glasgowmuseums.com ·
FREE 0141 553 2557 · **Castle Street** Part of the lovely and not-cherished-enough
cathedral precinct (see above), this houses art and artefacts representing the
world's 6 major religions arranged tactfully in an attractive stone building with a
Zen garden in the courtyard. 3 floors, 4 exhibition areas. The assemblage seems
like a good and worthwhile vision not quite realised, but in a city where sectarian-
ism is still an issue and a problem, this is a telling and informative display. 7 days
10am-5pm (Fri/Sun from 11am).

691 2/XA1 **Hunterian Museum & Art Gallery** www.hunterian.gla.ac.uk · 0141 330
FREE 4221/5431 · **University Avenue** On one side of the street, Scotland's oldest
museum with geological, archaeological and social history displayed in a venerable
building. The **University Chapel** and the cloisters should not be missed. Across
the street, a modern block holds part of Glasgow's exceptional civic collection –
Rembrandt to the Colourists and the Glasgow Boys, as well as one of the most
complete collections of any artist's work and personal effects to be found anywhere, viz that of Whistler. Fascinating stuff, even if you're not a fan. There's also a
print gallery and the superb **Mackintosh House** (729/MACKINTOSH). Mon-Sat
9.30am-5pm. Closed Sun.

▬▬▬ The Other Attractions

692 2/XA1 ✔✔**Museum Of Transport** www.glasgowmuseums.com · 0141 287
FREE 2720 · off **Argyle Street** behind the **Kelvin Hall** May not seem your
ticket to ride, but this is one of Scotland's most fascinating museums. Has something for everybody, especially kids. The reconstruction of a cobbled Glasgow street
c.1938 is an inspired evocation. There are trains, trams and unique collections of
cars, motorbikes and bicycles. And model ships in the Clyde room, in remembrance of a mighty river. Make a donation and the Mini splits in two. Mon-Thu, Sat
10am-5pm, Fri & Sun 11am-5pm. The Museum of Transport will be absorbed into
the new Zaha Hadid-designed **Riverside Museum** which will open on the banks
of the Clyde at Glasgow Harbour in summer 2011.

693 2/XA1 ✔✔**Botanic Gardens & Kibble Palace** www.glasgow.gov.uk · 0141
FREE 334 2422 · **Great Western Road** Smallish park close to River Kelvin
with riverside walks (702/WALKS IN THE CITY), and pretty much the 'dear green
place'. Kibble Palace (built 1873; major renovation 2006) is the distinctive domed
glasshouse with statues set among lush ferns and shrubbery from around the
(mostly temperate) world. 'Killer Plant House' especially popular. Main range
arranged through smell and colour and seasonality. A wonderful place to muse and
wander. Gardens open till dusk; palace 10am-4.45pm (4.15pm in winter).

694 2/D3 ✔✔**Gallery Of Modern Art** www.glasgowmuseums.com · 0141 229
FREE 1996 · **Queen Street** Central, controversial and housed in former
Stirling's Library, Glasgow's big visual arts attraction opened in a hail of art-world
bickering in 1996. Main point is: does it reflect Glasgow's eminence as a provenance of cutting edge or conceptual work (all those Turner and Becks Prize nomi-
nees and winners?). Murmurs stilled of late by more representative exhibitions and
new acquisition fund. Leaving aside the quibbling, it should definitely be on your
Glasgow hit list. Mon-Wed, Sat 10am-5pm, Thu 10am-8pm, Fri & Sun 11am-5pm.

695 2/F4   ✓ **The Barrows** East End (Pronounced 'Barras') The sprawling street and indoor market area around the Gallowgate. Almost 20 years ago when I first wrote this book, the Barras was pure dead brilliant, a real slab of Glasgow life. Its glory days are over but, as with all great markets, it's full of character and characters and it's still just about possible to find bargains if not collectibles. Everything from clairvoyants to the latest scam. Sat & Sun only 10am-5pm.

696 2/B1   **The Tenement House** www.nts.org.uk · 0141 333 0183 · 145 Buccleuch
NTS   **Street** Near Charing Cross but can approach from near the end of Sauchiehall St
ADMISSION   and over the hill. Typical 'respectable' Glasgow tenement, kept under a bell-jar since Our Agnes moved out in 1965. She lived there with her mother since 1911 and wasn't one for new-fangled things. It's a touch claustrophobic when busy and is distinctly voyeuristic, but, well... your house would be interesting, too, in 50 years if the clock were stopped. Daily, Mar-Oct 1-5pm. Reception on ground floor.

697 2/E4   **Sharmanka Kinetic Gallery & Theatre** www.sharmanka.com · 0141 552
ADMISSION   **7080 · 64 Osborne Street** Off King St in the Merchant City. A small and intimate experience cf most others on this page, but an extraordinary one. The gallery/theatre of Russian emigré Eduard Bersindsky shows his meticulous and amazing mechanical sculptures. Performances Thu 7pm, Sun 3pm & 7pm. Other times by arrangement.

698 2/XA5   **Greenbank Gardens** www.nts.org.uk · 0141 616 5126 · **Clarkston** 10km
NTS   southwest of centre via Kilmarnock Road, Eastwood Toll, Clarkston Toll and Mearns Road, then signposted (3km). A spacious oasis in the suburbs; formal gardens and 'working' walled garden, parterre and woodland walks around elegant Georgian house. Very Scottish. Gardens open all year 9.30am-dusk, shop/tearoom Apr-Oct 11am-5pm, Nov-Mar Sat & Sun 2-4pm.

699 2/E3   **City Chambers** www.glasgow.gov.uk · 0141 287 4018 · **George Square** The
FREE   hugely impressive building along the whole east side of Glasgow's municipal central square. This is a wonderfully evocative monument of the days when Glasgow was the Second City of the Empire. Guided tours Mon-Fri 10.30am and 2.30pm (subject to availability).

700 9/L25   **Finlaystone Country Estate** www.finlaystone.co.uk · 01475 540505 ·
ADMISSION   **30km west of city centre via M8/A8** Signed off dual carriageway just before Port Glasgow. Delightful gardens and woods around mansion house with many pottering places and longer trails (and ranger service). Estate open all year round 10am-5pm. Visitor centre and the Celtic Tree tearoom. Spectacular bluebells in May, colour therapy in autumn.

701 2/A4   **The Waverley** www.waverleyexcursions.co.uk · 0845 130 4647 'The
ADMISSION   World's Last Sea-going Paddle Steamer' which plied the Clyde in the glorious 'Doon the Water' days had a £7M lottery-funded refit. Definitely the way to see the West Coast. Sailings from Glasgow's Anderson Quay (by Kingston Bridge) to Rothesay, Kyles of Bute, Arran. Other days leaves from Ayr or Greenock, many destinations. Call for complex timetable. Bar, restaurants, live bands: it's a party!

Paisley Abbey Report: 1889/ABBEYS.

Bothwell Castle, Uddingston Report: 1788/RUINS.

The Best Walks In The City

See p. 12 for walk codes.

702 2/XA1
2/XB1
2/XC1
2-13+KM
XCIRC
BIKES
1-A-1

Kelvin Walkway A path along the banks of Glasgow's other river, the Kelvin, which enters the Clyde unobtrusively at Yorkhill but first meanders through some of the most interesting parts and parks of the northwest city. Walk starts at Kelvingrove Park through the University and Hillhead district under Kelvin Bridge and on to the celebrated Botanic Gardens (693/OTHER ATTRACTIONS). The trail then goes north, under the Forth and Clyde Canal (*see below*) to the Arcadian fields of Dawsholm Park (5km), Killermont (posh golf course) and Kirkintilloch (13km from start). Since the river and the canal shadow each other for much of their routes, it's possible, with a map, to go out by one waterway and return by the other (e.g. start at Great Western Road, return Maryhill Road).
START Usual start at the Eildon St (off Woodlands Road) gate of Kelvingrove Park or Kelvin Bridge. Street parking only.

703 2/XC1
ANY KM
XCIRC
BIKES
1-A-1

Forth & Clyde Canal Towpath The canal, opened in 1790, reopened 2002 as the Millennium Link. Once a major short cut for fishing boats and trade between Europe and America, it provides a fascinating look round the back of the city from a pathway that stretches on a spur from Port Dundas just north of the M8 to the main canal at the end of Lochburn Road off Maryhill Road, and then east all the way to Kirkintilloch and Falkirk (Falkirk Wheel: 08700 500208; 4/BIG ATTRACTIONS), and west through Maryhill and Drumchapel to Bowling and the Clyde (60km). Good option is go as far as Croy and take very regular train service back. Much of the route is through the forsaken or redeveloped industrial heart of the city, past waste ground, warehouses and high flats, but there are open stretches and curious corners and, by Bishopbriggs, it's a rural waterway. More info from British Waterways (0141 332 6936).
START (1) Top of Firhill Road (great view of city from Ruchill Park, 100m further on – 714/BEST VIEWS). (2) Lochburn Road (see above) at the confluence from which to go east or west to the Clyde. (3) Top of Crow Road, Anniesland where there is a canalside pub, **Lock 27** (669/DRINK OUTDOORS), with tables outside, real ale and food (12noon-evening). (4) Bishopbriggs Sports Centre, Balmuildy Road. From here it is 6km to Maryhill and 1km in other direction to the 'country churchyard' of Cadder or 3km to Kirkintilloch. All starts have some parking.

704 2/XA5

Pollok Country Park www.glasgow.gov.uk The park that (apart from the area around the gallery and the house – 686/MAIN ATTRACTIONS) most feels like a real country park. Numerous trails through woods and meadows. The leisurely guided walks with the park rangers can be educative and more fun than you would think (0141 632 7054 for details). Burrell Collection and Pollok House and Gardens are obvious highlights. There's a good restaurant and an old-fashioned tearoom in the basement of the latter serving an excellent range of hot, home-made dishes, soups, salads, sandwiches as well as the usual cakes and tasties. 7 days 10am-4.30pm (0141 616 6410). Enter by Haggs Rd or by Haggs Castle Golf Course. By car you are directed to the entry road off Pollokshaws Rd and then to the car park in front of the Burrell. Train to Pollokshaws West from Glasgow Central Station.

705 10/L25
5-20KM
CAN BE CIRC
BIKES
1-A-2

Mugdock Country Park www.mugdock-country-park.org.uk · 0141 956 6100 Not perhaps within the city, but one of the nearest and easiest escapes. Park which includes Mugdock Woods (SSSI) and 2 castles is northwest of Milngavie. Regular train from Queen St Station takes 20 minutes, then follow route of the West Highland Way for 4km across Drumclog Moor to south edge of the park. By car to Milngavie by A81 park is 5km north. Well signed. 5 car parks; the main one includes Craigend Visitor Centre (9am-9pm), Stables Tearoom (10am-5pm daily), craft gallery and theatre. There's also a garden centre and farm shop. Many trails marked out and further afield rambles. This is a godsend between Glasgow and the Highland hills.

Cathkin Braes South edge of city with views. Report: 712/BEST VIEWS.

Easy Walks Outside The City

See p. 12 for walk codes.

706 **10/M25**
10+KM
CAN BE CIRC
MTBIKES
2-B-2

Campsie Fells www.eastdunbarton.gov.uk Range of hills 25km north of city best reached via Kirkintilloch or Cumbernauld/Kilsyth. Encompasses area that includes the Kilsyth Hills, Fintry Hills and Carron Valley between. (1) Good approach from A803, Kilsyth main street up the Tak-me-Doon (*sic*) road. Park by the golf club and follow path by the burn. It's possible to take in the two hills to left as well as Tomtain (453m), the most easterly of the tops, in a good afternoon; views to the east. (2) Small car park on the south side of the B818 road to Fintry at the west end of the Carron Valley reservoir opposite the access road to Todholes Farm and new wind farm. Follow tracks along reservoir to ascend Meikle Bin (570m) to the right, the second-highest peak in the Campsies. (3) The bonny village of Fintry is a good start/base for the Fintry Hills and Earl's Seat (578m). (4) Campsie Glen – a sliver of glen in the hills. Approach via Clachan of Campsie on A81 (decent tearoom) or from viewpoint high on the hill on B822 from Lennoxtown-Fintry. This is the easy Campsie introduction.

707 **10/L26**
2-10KM
CAN BE CIRC
MTBIKES
1-A-2

Gleniffer Braes www.renfrewshire.gov.uk · **Paisley** Ridge to the south of Paisley (15km from Glasgow) has been a favourite walking-place for centuries. M8 or Paisley Road West to town centre then south via B774/B775 (Causeyside St then Neilston Rd) and sharp right after 3km to Glenfield Rd. Park/start at Robertson Park (signed). Here there are superb views and walks marked to east and west. 500m along Glenfield Rd is a car park/ranger centre (0141 884 3794). Walk up through gardens and formal parkland and then west along marked paths and trails.

708 **9/K25**
15/16KM
CIRC
MTBIKES
1-B-2

Greenock Cut 45km west of Glasgow. Can approach via Port Glasgow but simplest route is from A78 road to Largs. Travelling south from Greenock take first left after IBM, brown-signed Loch Thom/Cornalees. Lochside 5km up winding road. Park at Cornalees Bridge Centre (01475 521458). Walk left along lochside road to Overton (5km) then path is signed. The Cut, an aqueduct built in 1827 to supply water to Greenock and its 31 mills, is now a historic monument. Great views from the mast along the Cut though it is a detour. Another route to the right from Cornalees leads through a glen of birch, rowan and oak to the Kelly Cut. Both trails described on board at the car park.

709 **9/K25**
Clyde Muirshiel www.clydemuirshiel.co.uk General name for vast area of 'Inverclyde' west of city, including Greenock Cut (see above), Lochwinnoch, Castle Semple Country Park and Lunderston Bay, a stretch of coastline near the Cloch Lighthouse on the A770 south of Gourock for littoral amblings. Best wildish bit is around Muirshiel Centre itself, Muirshiel Country Park (01505 842803), with trails, a waterfall and Windy Hill (350m). Nothing arduous, but a breath of air. The hen harrier hunts here. From M8 junction 29, take A737 Lochwinnoch, then B786 to top of Calder Glen Road. Follow brown signs.

710 10/L25
5KM
CIRC
XBIKES
NO DOGS
1-A-1

The Whangie On A809 north from Bearsden about 8km after last roundabout and 2km after the Carbeth Inn, is the car park for the Queen's View (713/BEST VIEWS). Once you get to the summit of Auchineden Hill, take the path that drops down to the W (a half-right-angle) and look for crags on your right. This is the 'back door' of The Whangie. Carry on and you'll suddenly find yourself in a deep cleft in the rock face with sheer walls rising over 10m on either side. The Whangie is more than 100m long and at one point the walls narrow to less than 1m. Local mythology has it that The Whangie was made by the Devil, who lashed his tail in anticipation of a witchy rendezvous somewhere in the north, and carved a slice through the rock, where the path now goes.

711 10/M26
2-7KM
CIRC
BIKES
1-A-2

Chatelhérault www.southlanarkshire.gov.uk · **Near Hamilton** Junction 6 off M74, well signposted into Hamilton, follow road into centre, then bear left away from main road where it's signed for A723. The gates to the 'château' are about 3km outside town. A drive leads to the William Adam-designed hunting lodge of the Dukes of Hamilton, set amid ornamental gardens with a notable parterre and extensive grounds. Tracks along the deep, wooded glen of the Avon (ruins of Cadzow Castle) lead to distant glades. Good walks and ranger service (01698 426213). House open Mon-Thu & Sat 10am-4.30pm (Sun 12-4.30pm); walks at all times. The circular walk from the Visitor Centre is about 8km.

The Best Views Of The City & Beyond

712 2/XF5

Cathkin Braes, Queen Mary's Seat The southern ridge of the city on the B759 from Carmunnock to Cambuslang, about 12km from centre. Go south of river by Albert Bridge to Aikenhead Road which continues south as Carmunnock Road. Follow to Carmunnock, a delightfully rural village, and pick up the Cathkin Road. 2km along on the right is the Cathkin Braes Golf Club and 100m further on the left is the park. Marvellous views to north of the Campsies, Kilpatrick Hills, Ben Lomond and as far as Ben Ledi. Walks on the Braes on both sides of the road.

713 10/L25
1-A-1

Queen's View Auchineden Not so much a view of the city, more a perspective on Glasgow's Highland hinterland, this short walk and sweeping vista to the north has been a Glaswegian pilgrimage for generations. On A809 north from Bearsden about 8km after last roundabout and 2km after the Carbeth Inn, a very decent pub to repair to. Busy car park attests to popularity. The walk, along path cut into ridgeside, takes 40-50 minutes to the cairn, from which you can see The Cobbler (1937/HILLS), that other Glasgow favourite, Ben Ledi and sometimes as far as Ben Chonzie 50km away. The fine views of Loch Lomond are what Queen Victoria came for. Further on is The Whangie (710/EASY WALKS).

714 2/XC1

Ruchill Park Glasgow An unlikely but splendid panorama from this overlooked but well-kept park to the north of the city near the infamous Possilpark housing estate. Go to top of Firhill Road (past Partick Thistle football ground) over Forth and Clyde Canal (703/WALKS IN THE CITY) off Garscube Road where it becomes Maryhill Road. Best view is from around the flagpole; the whole city among its surrounding hills, from the Campsies to Gleniffer and Cathkin Braes (see above), becomes clear.

715 10/M25 **Bar Hill** Twechar, near Kirkintilloch 22km north of city, taking A803
  1-A-2 Kirkintilloch turnoff from M8, then the 'low' road to Kilsyth, the B8023, bearing left
at the 'black-and-white bridge'. Next to Twechar Quarry Inn, a path is signed for
Bar Hill and the Antonine Wall. Steepish climb for 2km; ignore the strange dome of
grass. Over to left in copse of trees are the remains of one of the forts on the wall
which was built across Scotland in the 2nd century AD. Ground plan explained on a
board. This is a special place with strong history vibes and airy views over the plain
to the city which came a long time after.

716 10/M26 **Blackhill** near Lesmahagow 28km south of city. Another marvellous outlook,
  1-A-2 but in the opposite direction from above. Take junction 10/11 on M74, then off the
B7078 signed Lanark, take the B7018. 4km along past Clarkston Farm, head uphill
for 1km and park by Water Board mound. Walk uphill through fields to right for
about 1km. Unprepossessing hill that unexpectedly reveals a vast vista of most of
east-central Scotland.

717 10/L26 **Paisley Abbey** www.paisleyabbey.org.uk · 0141 889 7654 · Paisley M8 to
Paisley; frequent trains from Central Station. Abbey Mon-Sat 10am-3.30pm. Every
so often on Abbey 'open days', the tower of this amazing edifice can be climbed.
The tower (restored 1926) is 50m high and from the top there's a grand view of the
Clyde. This is a rare experience, but phone the tourist information centre (0141 889
0711) or abbey itself (mornings) for details; could be your lucky day. Guided tours
by arrangement. 1889/GREAT ABBEYS.

718 9/K25 **Lyle Hill** Gourock Via M8 west to Greenock, then round the coast to relatively
genteel old resort of Gourock where the Free French worked in the yards during
the war. A monument has been erected to their memory on the top of Lyle Hill
above the town, from where you get one of the most dramatic views of the great
crossroads of the Clyde (Holy Loch, Gare Loch and Loch Long). Best vantage-point
is further along the road on other side by trig point. Follow British Rail station
signs, then Lyle Hill. There's another great view of the Clyde further down the
water at **Haylie, Largs**, the hill 3km from town reached via the A760 road to
Kilbirnie and Paisley. The island of Cumbrae lies in the sound and the sunset.

Campsie Fells & Gleniffer Braes Reports: 706/707/WALKS OUTSIDE THE CITY.

The Best Small Galleries

Apart from those listed previously (Main Attractions, Other Attractions), the following galleries are always worth looking into. The Glasgow Gallery Guide, *free from any of them, lists all the current exhibitions.*

719 2/E4 ✓✓ **Glasgow Print Studio** www.gpsart.co.uk · 0141 552 0704 · 25 & 48 King Street Influential and accessible upstairs gallery with print work on view and for sale from many of Scotland's leading and rising artists. Closed Sun and Mon. Print Shop over the road at 48.

720 2/E4 ✓✓ **Transmission Gallery** www.transmissiongallery.org · 0141 552 7141 · 45 King Street Cutting edge and often off-the-wall work from contemporary Scottish and international artists. Reflects Glasgow's increasing importance as a hot spot of conceptual art. Stuff you might disagree with. Closed Sun and Mon. Both Transmission and the Print Studio are in temporary locations on King St while a new art centre is being refurbished.

721 2/C4 ✓✓ **The Modern Institute** www.themoderninstitute.com · 0141 248 3711 · 73 Robertson Street Not really a gallery – more a concept. International reputation for cutting-edge art ideas and occasional events. By appointment. MI shows at London's pre-eminent, highly selective Frieze Art Fair.

722 2/D3 ✓✓ **The Glasgow Art Fair** www.glasgowartfair.com · George Square Held every year in tented pavilions in April. Some of the galleries on this page and many more are represented; selective but essential and good fun.

723 2/C2 ✓ **Compass Gallery** www.compassgallery.co.uk · 0141 221 6370 · 178 West Regent Street Glasgow's oldest established commercial contemporary art gallery. Their 'New Generation' exhibition in Jul-Aug shows work from new graduates of the art colleges and has heralded many a career. Combine with the other Gerber gallery (see below). Closed Sun.

724 2/C2 ✓ **Cyril Gerber Fine Art** www.gerberfineart.co.uk · 0141 221 3095 · 148 West Regent Street British paintings and especially the Scottish Colourists and 'name' contemporaries. Gerber and the Compass (see above) have Christmas exhibitions where small, accessible paintings can be bought for reasonable prices. Closed Sun.

725 2/C2 **Roger Billcliffe Gallery** www.billcliffegallery.com · 0141 332 4027 · 134 Blythswood Street Big, long-established gallery on 5 floors specialising in painting and decorative arts of the last 100 years. Roger, obviously this page had been incomplete without you!

726 2/XF3 **Sorcha Dallas** www.sorchadallas.com · 07812 605745 · 5 St Margaret's Place Deep in the East End, the secret salon of La Dallas where interesting new artists first come into the light. Phone first. Sorcha also usually does Frieze (see MI above).

Sharmanka Kinetic Gallery Report: 697/OTHER ATTRACTIONS.

The Mackintosh Trail

The great Scottish architect and designer Charles Rennie Mackintosh (1868–1928) had an extraordinary influence on contemporary design. Visit www.crmsociety.com

727 2/B1
ATMOS

✓ ✓ ✓ **Glasgow School of Art** www.gsa.ac.uk · 0141 353 4580 · **167 Renfrew Street** Mackintosh's supreme architectural triumph and 'Britain's Most Admired Building' 2009. It's enough almost to admire it from the street (and maybe best, since this is very much a working college) but there are guided tours at 11am and 2pm (Sat 10.30am, 11.30am, and many more in summer) of the sombre yet light interior, the halls and library. You might wonder if the building itself could be partly responsible for its remarkable output of acclaimed artists. Temporary exhibitions in the Mackintosh Gallery. The Tenement House (696/OTHER ATTRACTIONS) is nearby.

728 2/XC1
ADMISSION

✓ ✓ **Queen's Cross Church** www.queenscrosschurch.org.uk · 0141 946 6600 · **870 Garscube Road at Maryhill Road** Built 1896-99. Calm and simple, the antithesis of Victorian Gothic. If all churches had been built like this, we'd go more often. The HQ of the Charles Rennie Mackintosh Society which was founded in 1973. Mar-Oct Mon-Fri 10am-5pm, Sun 2-5pm (summer only). Nov-Feb Mon-Fri 10am-5pm.

729 2/C2
ADMISSION

✓ ✓ **The Mackintosh House** www.hunterian.gla.ac.uk · 0141 330 5431 · **University Avenue** Opposite and part of the Hunterian Art Gallery (691/MAIN ATTRACTIONS) within the University campus. The master's house has been transplanted and methodically reconstructed from the next street (they say even the light is the same). If you've ever wondered what the fuss is about, go and see how innovative and complete an artist, designer and architect he was, in this inspiring yet habitable set of rooms. Mon-Sat 9.30am-5pm. Closed Sun.

730 2/XA5
ATMOS
FREE

✓ ✓ **Scotland Street School Museum** www.glasgowmuseums.com · 0141 287 0500 · **225 Scotland Street** Opposite Shields Road underground station; best approach by car from Eglinton St (A77 Kilmarnock Road over Jamaica St Bridge). Entire school (from 1906) preserved as museum of education through Victorian/Edwardian and wartimes. Original, exquisite Mackintosh features, especially tiling, and powerfully redolent of happy school days. This is a uniquely evocative time capsule. Café and temporary exhibitions. Mon-Thu, Sat 10am-5pm, Fri & Sun 11am-5pm.

731 2/D3
ADMISSION

✓ **The Lighthouse** www.thelighthouse.co.uk · 0141 221 6362 · **Mitchell Lane, off Buchanan Street** Glasgow's legacy from its year as UK City of Architecture and Design. Changing exhibitions in Mackintosh's 1893-95 building for the *Glasgow Herald* newspaper. Though its future is uncertain at TGP, it has housed, over 6 floors, a shop and books, a café-bar, an interpretation centre and exhibition space. Fantastic rooftop views. Check hours.

732 9/K25
NTS
ATMOS
ADMISSION

✓ **The Hill House** www.nts.org.uk · 01436 673900 · **Upper Colquhoun Street, Helensburgh** Take Sinclair St off Princes St (at Romanesque tower and Tourist Information Centre) and go 2km uphill, taking left into Kennedy Dr and follow signs. A complete house incorporating Mackintosh's typical total unity of design, built for publisher Walter Blackie in 1902-4. Much to marvel over and wish that everybody else would go away and you could stay there for the night. There's even a library full of books to keep you occupied. Tearoom; gardens. Apr-Oct 1.30-5.30pm. Helensburgh is 45km northwest of city centre via Dumbarton (A82) and A814 up the north Clyde coast.

733 2/C2 **The Willow Tea Rooms** www.willowtearooms.co.uk · 0141 332 0521 · **Sauchiehall Street & Buchanan Street** The first is the café he designed (or what's left of it); a tea break on the trail. More than a little overrated.

734 2/XA5 **House For An Art Lover** www.houseforanartlover.co.uk · 0141 353 4770 ·
ADMISSION **10 Dumbreck Road, Bellahouston Park** Take the M8 west then the M77; turn right onto Dumbreck Road and it's on your left. These rooms were designed, nearly a century ago, specifically, it would seem, for willowy women to come and go, talking of Michelangelo. Detail is the essence of Mackintosh, and there's plenty here, but the overall effect is of space and light and a complete absence of clutter. Design shop and café (603/BEST TEAROOMS) on the ground floor. Phone for opening times.

Essential Culture

UNIQUE VENUES

735 2/XF4 ✓✓✓ **Barrowland Ballroom** www.glasgow-barrowland.com · 0141
ATMOS 552 4601 · **Gallowgate** When its neon lights are on, you can't miss it. The Barrowland is world-famous and for many bands one of their favourite gigs. It's tacky and a bit run-down, but distinctly venerable; and with its high stage and sprung dance floor, perfect for rock 'n' roll. The Glasgow audience is probably 'the best in the world'.

736 2/XD5 ✓✓ **The Citizens' Theatre** www.citz.co.uk · 0141 429 0022 · **Gorbals**
ATMOS **Street** Fabulous main auditorium and 2 small studios. Drama at its very best. Though not all that it once was, it's still one of Britain's most influential theatres, especially for design. Refurbished with lottery funds. Love the theatre? Love this theatre!

737 2/XA5 ✓✓ **The Tramway** www.tramway.org · 0141 422 2023 · **25 Albert Drive**
ATMOS South Side studio, theatre and vast performance and exhibition space. Dynamic and influential with a varied, innovative programme from all over the world. New home of Scottish Ballet. **Secret Garden** behind (1531/HIDDEN GARDENS). Worth a visit.

738 2/B1 ✓ **CCA** www.cca-glasgow.com · 0141 332 7521 · **Centre for Contemporary Arts, 350 Sauchiehall Street** Major refurbishment of central arts-lab complex for all kinds of performance and visual arts presentation, though curiously little wall space. Impressive atrium/courtyard houses cool café/restaurant called Tempus. Watch press for CCA programme.

739 2/B1 ✓ **ABC** www.abcglasgow.com · 0141 332 2232 · **Sauchiehall Street** Purposeful conversion of old ABC film centre in middle of Sauchiehall St into large-capacity live-music venue with intimate ambience, clubrooms downstairs and light bar overlooking street. See *The List* for programme.

740 2/C4 ✓ **The Arches** www.thearches.co.uk · 0870 240 7528 · **253 Argyle Street** Experimental and vital theatre on a budget in the railway arches under Central Station. Director Andy Arnold's gong must surely be in the post! Opening times vary. Weekend clubs among the best. Bar/café cool place to hang and even talk.

741 2/E4 **Tron Theatre** www.tron.co.uk · 0141 552 4267 · 63 Trongate Contemporary Scottish theatre and other interesting performance, especially music. Great café-bar with food before and *après*.

742 2/C1 **Glasgow Film Theatre** www.gft.org.uk · 0141 332 6535 · Rose Street Known affectionately as the GFT, has café/bar and 2 screens for essential art-house flicks. Home to the Glasgow Film Festival (see below).

743 2/B2 **King Tut's Wah Wah Hut** www.kingtuts.co.uk · 0141 221 5279 · 272 St Vincent Street Every bit as good as its namesake in Alphabet City used to be; the room for interesting new bands, make-or-break atmosphere and cramped. Bands on the club circuit play to a damp and appreciative crowd. See flyers and *The List* for details.

UNIQUE FESTIVALS

Celtic Connections www.celticconnections.com · 0141 353 8000 3 weeks in Jan. Festival with attitude and atmosphere.

Glasgow Film Festival www.glasgowfilmfestival.org · 0141 332 6535 Mid Feb. Growing in stature. Screenings at GFT, CCA and Cineworld.

Aye Write www.ayewrite.com · 0844 847 1683 (Ticketweb) Newish book and writers' fest in mid March. Centred on Mitchell Library (nice caff).

Glasgow International www.glasgowinternational.org · 0141 552 6027 Biennial contemporary visual arts in selected venues celebrating Glasgow's pre-eminence in producing significant new artists. Biennial: in 2010, 2012, etc.

Glasgow Art Fair www.glasgowartfair.com · 0141 552 6027 4 days in Apr.

West End Festival www.westendfestival.co.uk · 0141 341 0844 2 weeks in Jun. Neighbourhood and arts festival that includes parade in Byres Rd and a lot of drinking.

Glasgow International Jazz Festival www.jazzfest.co.uk · 0141 552 3552 1 week in Jul. Scotland's most credible jazz (in its widest sense) programme over different venues.

Merchant City Festival www.merchantcityfestival.com · 0141 552 6027 A weekend in mid Sep in quarter to east of George Sq. A great new festival waiting to spill out of its quarter. Future uncertain at TGP.

Glasgay www.glasgay.co.uk Mid Nov. Modest but eclectic programme for gays and straight people alike over several days and venues.

Hogmanay www.hogmanay.net · 0141 552 6027 31 Dec. Not on the same scale as Edinburgh but friendly. Usually a stage in George Sq (ticketed).

Section 4

Regional Hotels & Restaurants

744 9/J22
12 ROOMS
TEL · TV
NO PETS
£85+/
£45-60

✓✓ **Airds Hotel** www.airds-hotel.com · 01631 730236 · Port Appin 32km north of Oban, 4km off A828. Airds has long been one of the foremost northern hostelries and a legendary gourmet experience. Shaun and Jenny McKivragan continue this tradition and with care and attention, extensive refurbishing and a great team under Robert Templeton McKay, brought Airds firmly to the forefront of the 'civilised escape in a hectic world' market. Contemporary-cosy might describe bedrooms and lounges (and conservatory dining room). Dinner is the culmination of a hard day on the croquet lawn or gazing over the bay. Attentive, unobtrusive service and confident cuisine naturel from chef Paul Burns who's connected with all things growing and harvested locally: eg he will take guests mushrooming in autumn. 2 elegant suites, one with patio, one with balcony. Port Appin is one of Scotland's most charming places. The Lismore passenger ferry is 2km away (2219/MAGIC ISLANDS). Bring a bike (or hire locally) and come home to Airds!

£32+ **EAT** One of the best meals you will find in the North, a destination in itself.

745 9/H24
22 ROOMS
TEL · TV
DA
£45-60

✓✓ **Crinan Hotel** www.crinanhotel.com · 01546 830261 · Crinan 8km off A816. On coast, 60km south of Oban (Lochgilphead 12km) at head of the Crinan Canal which joins Loch Fyne with the sea. Nick Ryan's landmark hotel in a stunning setting and some of the best seaviews in the UK. Outside on the quay is the boat which has landed those massive prawns, sweet clams and other creatures with legs or valves, which are cooked very simply and brought to your table. Nick's own beautiful boat outside your window completes the view. This hotel has long housed one of the great seafood restaurants in the UK; the chef has that sure, light touch. Nick's wife's (the notable artist, Frances Macdonald) pictures of these shorelines and those of son, Ross, are hung around you and for sale. Both lounges on the third floor offer the perfect sunset setting for your aperitif. Last but not least, there are beautiful flowers.

£32+/ £15 **EAT** Choice of 'Westward' dining room or perfect pub grub in bar.

746 9/J22
7 ROOMS
FEB-NOV
TV
NO PETS
£45-60

✓✓ **Dun Na Mara** www.dunnamara.com · 01631 720233 · Benderloch Off A828 Oban-Fort William road, 12km north of Oban. Contemporary conversion of seaside mansion in a stunning setting with beach below and a perfect vista from all front (3) bedrooms, breakfast room and lounge. A dream guest house in immaculate (mainly white) taste retaining beautiful original features. Former architects are now your unobtrusive hosts. In summer book well ahead.

747 9/J24
17 ROOMS
TEL · TV
DA
ATMOS
£38-45

✓✓ **George Hotel** www.thegeorgehotel.co.uk · 01499 302111 · Inveraray On the main street of an interesting town on Loch Fyne with credible attractions both here (the castle, the *Arctic Penguin*, etc) and nearby. I've decided to award 2 ticks mainly because this ancient inn (1770), still in the capable and friendly hands of the Clark family, has fantastic atmosphere and not just in the bar. Rooms refurbished tastefully in a Highland-chic kind of way. Downstairs open fire, great grub. The Clarks have recently taken over the First House (actually the first house in the town), adding another 6 B&B rooms with some great loch views. It's round the back of the main hotel. All of this is exceptionally good value.
EAT Gastropub grub in multichambered stone and wood setting. Good ales, wines and staple/classic-led menu.

748 9/G25
5 ROOMS
APR-OCT
£60-85

✓✓ **Kilberry Inn** 01880 770223 · near Tarbert Small Knapdale roadside inn with famously good food. Simple, stylish cottage-courtyard rooms. Beautiful drive out on B8024, the Tarbert-Lochgilphead coast road. 2-tick gastropub food as good as it gets (1288/GASTROPUBS). David out front, amiable and attentive but not too much. Clare in the kitchen. Your deal will include dinner.

749 9/J26
3 ROOMS
+ 3 SELF-
CATERING
TV
NO KIDS
NO PETS
£60-85

✓ **Balmory Hall** www.balmoryhall.com · 01700 500669 · **Ascog, Isle of Bute** 6km Rothesay towards Mount Stuart (1823/COUNTRY HOUSES). Grand but liveable and lived-in big hoose up road 150m from 30mph sign. A country-house hotel with guest house intimacy. Deer on the lawn. 3 excellent self-catering apartments all in the house and a sweet little lodge at the foot of the drive. Impeccable appointments, fabulous bathrooms! Famously good breakfast, supper at the Smiddy (1305/GASTROPUBS) 7km or Brechin's Brasserie in Rothesay which does great home cooking. Balmory is *the* top stay on Bute.

750 9/J25
11 ROOMS
TEL · TV
NO KIDS
£60-85+

✓ **An Lochan** 01700 811239 · **Tighnabruaich** Roger and Bea McKie turned this seaside mansion into one of the best hotels in the west of Scotland and launched their An Lochan brand, now also in Glasgow (512/BEST BISTROS) and Perthshire near Gleneagles (880/PERTHSHIRE HOTELS). AA and others agree. Lovely rooms, many looking over to Bute, comfy furnishings and a plethora of pictures. Bea leads great out-front service and chef Paul Scott creates a Modern Scottish menu with lots of seafood in the bistro/brasserie and conservatory dining room with 'the view'. The Shinty Bar is cool. Doon the Water was never as good as this.

751 9/H23
11 ROOMS
TEL · TV
£60-85

✓ **The Manor House** www.manorhouseoban.com · 01631 562087 · **Oban** On south coast road out of town towards Kerrera ferry, overlooking bay. Understated elegance in contemporary style and a restaurant that serves (in an intimate dining room) probably the most fine-dining dinner in town. Daily changing menu. Bedrooms small but probably the cosiest (the competition ain't great). More delightful than deluxe. Nice bar. A very civilised lodging.

752 9/H23
12 ROOMS
MAR-NOV
TV
£38-45

✓ **Glenburnie Hotel** www.glenburnie.co.uk · 01631 562089 · **Oban** Corran Esplanade. In the middle of a broad sweep of hotels overlooking the bay, this is the best! Amiable Graeme Strachan's a natural innkeeper so everything in his seaside mansion is welcoming and easy on the eye. Great detail: home-made muesli and fruit for breakfast; nice furnishings. No dinner but he'll tell you where to go. Book.

753 9/H23
5 ROOMS
FEB-NOV
TV · NO KIDS
NO PETS
£45-60

✓ **Lerags House** www.leragshouse.com · 01631 563381 · **near Oban** 7km south of Oban. 4km from A816, a very particular guest house unobtrusively brilliant (even the sign off the road is low-key). Mansion in deep country with con-temporary feel and style. Lovely gardens in almost estuarine setting. Charlie and Bella Miller from Australia do good rooms and excellent food. Dinner inclusive. Fixed menu; neat wine list including selected Oz wines. A cool and calming place.

754 9/J23
3 ROOMS
TV
£38-45

✓ **Roineabhal** www.roineabhal.com · 01866 833207 · **Kilchrenan** Another great place to stay near Kilchrenan (see Taychreggan below and Ardanaiseig, 1121/COUNTRY HOUSE HOTELS) deep in the Loch Awe interior (10km from the A85 road to Oban, near Taynuilt). This is a good deal less expensive. Roger and Maria Soep call this a Highland country house (pronounced 'Ron-ay-val') – it is really a gorgeous guest house in a family home; good pictures (they are quite arty). Intimate (you eat round the same table) but all in excellent taste, especially the set-menu dinner. You don't have to have dinner but you should (and one day I will). Wine provided but you can BYOB.

755 9/J24
74 ROOMS
TEL · TV
£38-45

✓ **Loch Fyne Hotel** www.crerarhotels.com · 01499 302148 · **Inveraray** A surprisingly large and decidedly decent hotel in this charming town. On main A83 towards Lochgilphead overlooking loch. Part of the Crerar Group, the remains of British Trust Hotels; this one of their best. Pleasing, simple design makeover with a touch of tartan. Good bistro. Pool and spa facilities. But they do take coach parties.

756 9/J23   **Taychreggan** www.taychregganhotel.co.uk · 01866 833211 · **Kilchrenan**
18 ROOMS   Signed off A85 just before Taynuilt, 30km from Oban and nestling on a bluff by
TEL · TV   Loch Awe in imposing countryside. Quay of the old Portsonachan ferry is nearby.
£85+   The hotel has boats. With a spruce refurbishment, stylish internal courtyard, new
rooms and water lapping at garden's edge, this remains an attractive prospect.
American owners also have Culloden House (995/BEST HIGHLAND HOTELS).

757 9/J25   **Kilfinan Hotel** www.kilfinanhotel.com · 01700 821201 · **Kilfinan** 13km from
11 ROOMS   Tighnabruaich on B8000. A much-loved inn on the beautiful single-track road that
TEL · TV   skirts Loch Fyne. The Wyatts have taken over this classic, quiet getaway inn (quiet
£45-60   as the graveyard adjacent) with long-standing manager and people person,
Madalon. Relaxing rooms, great cooking from Helen Wyatt in dining room or bar;
sensible wine list. For a not-too-expensive retreat on a quiet peninsula, this is a
good bet and a very nice place to bring kids. 1136/HOTELS THAT WELCOME KIDS.

758 9/H24   **Loch Melfort Hotel** www.lochmelfort.co.uk · 01852 200233 · **Arduaine**
25 ROOMS   30km south of Oban on A816. This landmark hotel on the beautiful road between
FEB-DEC   Oban and Campbeltown has had its ups and downs. Now new owners seem
TEL · TV   determined to restore it to its rightful place. You start with the view of Loch Shuna
£60+   which you get from most rooms (including all the extension rooms which come
with either balcony or patio). Those in the main mansion are more traditional but
are pleasantly large. Same view dominates the dining room and the Chartroom bar
with pub-food menu (seafood specials). Hotel has the same access road as
Arduaine, an extraordinary back garden in which to wander. 1518/GARDENS.

759 9/H25   **Stonefield Castle Hotel** www.stonefieldhotels.com · 01880 820836 ·
33 ROOMS   **Tarbert** Just outside town on the A83, a castle evoking the 20th more than pre-
TEL · TV   ceding centuries. Splendid luxuriant gardens leading down to Loch Fyne. Rhodies
DA   in spring, hydrangeas in summer. Dining room with baronial splendour and stag-
£45-60   gering views. Friendly, flexible staff; overall, it seems quintessentially Scottish and
ok, especially for families. Recent refurbishments by owners Oxford Hotels have
tidied things up. 4 'principal' rooms, but 'standards' with loch views are fine.

Kames Hotel 01700 811489by · **Tighnabruaich** Report: 1176/SEASIDE INNS.

✓✓ **Isle Of Eriska** 01631 720371 20km north of Oban. 1118/COUNTRY-
HOUSE HOTELS.

✓✓ **Ardanaiseig** 01866 833333 · **Loch Awe** 1121/COUNTRY-HOUSE
HOTELS.

RESTAURANTS

760 9/J24   ✓ **Inver Cottage** www.invercottage.co.uk · 01369 860537 ·
£15-22   **Strathlachlan, Loch Fyne** South of Strachur on B8000, the scenic south
road by Loch Fyne, a cottage bar/bistro overlooking loch and ruins of Castle
Lachlan. Home baking and cooking at its best. Comfort food and surroundings.
Lovely walk to the ruins (40 minutes return) before or after. A real find! Apr-Nov.
All-day menus till 5pm. Dinner Wed-Sun (7 days Jul/Aug). LO 8.30pm.

761 9/K25   ✓ **Chatters** www.chattersdunoon.co.uk · 01369 706402 · **58 John Street,**
£22-32   **Dunoon** Rosie Macinnes' long-established and excellent restaurant is a good
reason for getting the ferry to Dunoon; the Cowal peninsula also awaits your explorations (and Younger Gardens: 1503/GARDENS). Bar menu and à la carte, a small
garden for drinks or lunch on a good day and a garden room when not. All delightful. I haven't been for ages: reports, please! Wed-Sat only, lunch and dinner.

762 9/H23
ATMOS
£15-22

✓ **The Seafood Temple** 01631 560000 · Gallanach Road, Oban On the south coast road out of town, adjacent Oban Sailing Club in a converted glass-fronted building. Stylish, simple conversion with conversation-numbing views over the lawn and out to sea. John Ogden's quirky approach but non-compromised, fresh-as-fresh seafood at great prices (the Grand Platter Magnifique @ £55 for 2). Quaffable wines. Thu-Sun (closed Sun in winter) from 5pm. Book.

763 9/G25
DA
£22-32

Pascal 01880 820263 · Castle Street, Tarbert Round the corner from The Corner House on quayside. The bistro venture of one Pascal Thezé, your inimitable host and chef. Extensive menu with many fish dishes. Apr-Oct, 6-10pm.

764 9/J25
£15-22

Portavadie Marina www.portavadiemarina.com · 01700 811075 Off the B8000. A new, sheltered marina that's popped up at the mouth of Loch Fyne opposite Tarbert, has a brand new steel-and-glass restaurant and yachty complex that serves ok food from breakfast to late. For people messing about off boats and the legions who go just to look at them. 7 days 9am-11pm (12midnight weekends).

If you're in Oban...

765 9/H23
WHERE TO STAY

✓✓**Dun Na Mara** 01631 720233 · Benderloch A guest house off the main A828 Oban-Fort William road at Benderloch 12km north of Oban. Gorgeous setting with beach adjacent and a fab contemporary conversion of seaside mansion. No ordinary B&B by the sea. Report: 746/BEST ARGYLL.

✓**The Manor House** www.manorhouseoban.com · 01631 562087 · Gallanach Road South of centre and ferry terminal. Best in town. Report: 751/BEST ARGYLL.

✓**Glenburnie Hotel** www.glenburnie.co.uk · 01631 562089 · Corran Esplanade From tea and shortbread on arrival and lovely rooms, it's clear this is a superior bed for the night. See 752/ARGYLL HOTELS.

59 ROOMS
TEL · TV
£60-05

Caledonian Hotel www.obancaledonian.com · 01855 821582 Lashings of dosh spent on this refurbished seafront hotel. Can't beat the captain's rooms – comfort and contemporary facilities. Dining room and café and bar. In the centre of things, the port and the people, so it can be noisy but is the best of the main hotels (until the Argyll opens in '11).

13 ROOMS
DEC-OCT
TEL · TV
£45-60

The Kimberley 01631 571115 · Dalriach Road Above the centre (2 minutes from main street). Solid Victorian mansion converted tastefully and with friendly Scottish owners. Nice public rooms including conservatory restaurant. With contemporary bedrooms and bathrooms it's a cut above the rest and good value.

11 ROOMS
MAR-NOV
TV
£30-38

Barriemore Hotel www.barriemore-hotel.co.uk · 01631 566356 · Corran Esplanade Last in the long sweep of hotels on the Esplanade road to Ganavan and better than most, a reputation established years ago – some changes of owners later, it's still a nice guest house with great views (and a very big dog).

13 ROOMS
TV
£38-45

Alltavona www.alltavona.co.uk · 01631 565067 · Corran Esplanade Another (and surprisingly large) good guest house/hotel on the Esplanade overlooking the bay. Contemporary rooms. Good breakfast (fresh OJ).

S.Y. Hostel 01631 562025 · Esplanade Good location on the front

WHERE TO EAT

✓ **The Seafood Temple** 01631 566000 · Gallanach Road Top but tiny
seafood spot. Report: 762/BEST ARGYLL.

£22-32 ✓ **Coast** 01631 569900 · 104 George Street Middle of the main street on
corner of John St. Richard (in the kitchen) and Nicola (out front) Fowler have
created the best (non-seafood) restaurant in Oban. Modern British menu by a
pedigree chef in contemporary, laid-back room. Excellent value for this quality and
no fuss. Menu changes seasonally. Awards attest to enduring appeal. Open all
year. 7 days lunch & LO 9.30pm.(Closed Sun in winter.) Best book.

£22-32 ✓ **Ee-Usk** www.eeusk.com · 01631 565666 & **Piazza** 01631 563628 ·
North Pier These 2 adjacent identical contemporary steel-and-glass houses
on the corner of the bay are both the ambitious creation and abiding passion of
the Macleod family. Macleod père runs a tight ship at Ee-Usk, a bright, modern
seafood café with great views. Wild halibut, haddock and cod locally sourced (they
know its origins and the fishermen personally),hand-cut chips; home-made starters and puds. **Piazza** run by Callum Macleod purveys standard though good standard Italian fare. Both are routinely packed. 7 days lunch & LO 9.30pm. All year.

£22-32 ✓ **The Waterfront At The Pier** www.waterfrontoban.co.uk · 01631
563110 In the port, by the station, in the midst of all, a place that's serious
about seafood. 'From pier to pan' is about right. Blackboard (well, TV-screen)
menu and the usuals à la carte. Big on oysters. Airy upstairs diner and large
ground-floor café/bar (a seafood, ie fish 'n' chips, bar-meal menu, though not at
all bad). Many locals, many tourists. Open lunch and LO 9pm-ish. All year.

£32+ ✓ **The Manor House** The best hotel dining room in town on an elevated
spot. Creative cuisines, fresh seafood and other good things from long-established chef team, Patrick and Sean. Book. 751/ARGYLL HOTELS

✓ **Fish & Chips In Oban** Oban has called itself the 'seafood capital of
Scotland' and for good reason. Not only is there a choice of seafood restau-
rants (above), there are 3 good fish 'n' chip shops, 2 with cafés: **Nories**, the **Oban
Fish & Chip Shop** and the **George St Fish 'n' Chip Shop**. See 1349/FISH & CHIPS.

£15-22 ✓ **Julie's Coffee House** 01631 565952 · 33 Stafford Street Opposite Oban
Whisky Visitor Centre. Only 10 tables, so fills up. Nice approach to food (excellent home baking) and customers. Best coffee shop in town. 7 days 10am-5pm.

Oban Chocolate Coffeeshop 01631 566099 · Corran Esplanade The place
to go for coffee, cake and of course chocolate. Chocs are made on the premises.
You can have the hot variety. Croissants for breakfast. 10am-5pm, Sun 12.30-4pm.

The Kitchen Garden www.kitchengardenoban.co.uk · 01631 566332 ·
14 George Street Deli-café that's often busy; you may have to queue for the
upstairs gallery caff. Not a bad cup of coffee, a sandwich and hot dishes. Great
whisky selection and a plethora of cheese. 7 days 9.30am-5pm, Sun 10am-4pm.
Deli has some great selected munchies, kitchen stuff and a good cheese counter.

£15 OR LESS **Coast Café** 01631 569900 · Off George Street at 104 Its parent restaurant is
Coast (above), this the new kid in the lane for soup 'n' sandwiches out of the same
kitchen; same friendly staff. 9am-4pm, Sun 10.30am-3.30pm (not Sun in winter).

Tourist Office 01631 563122 · Argyll Square Open all year.

766 9/K28
221 ROOMS
TEL · TV
£85+

✓✓ **Turnberry** www.turnberry.co.uk · 01655 331000 · Turnberry Not just a hotel on the Ayrshire coast, more a way of life centred on golf. Looks over the 2 celebrated courses (home to the Open '09) and Ailsa Craig, the enigmatic lump of rock in the sea (2046/GREAT GOLF COURSES). All that should be expected of a world-class hotel except, perhaps, the urban buzz; but plenty of golf reminiscing and time moving slowly. The spa complex adjacent has state-of-the-art treatments with deals for day visitors and a nice pool. Colin Montgomerie Golf Academy takes all sorts. The Club House has the Tappie Tourie Grill open from breakfast till late, looking over the greens. In the hotel, serene and after major refurbishment, stylish lounges include The Grand Tea Room and the main restaurant – a fabulous room with a view. Rooms in rolling refurbishment in many categories reflected in the price, though none of course are cheap.

£22-32+ **EAT** Main restaurant '1906', when the hotel began. Fine dining in grand style.

767 9/K28
6 SUITES
+ COTTAGES
APR-OCT
TEL · NO PETS
£85+

✓ **Culzean Castle** www.culzeanexperience.org · 01655 760615 · near Maybole 18km south of Ayr, this is accommodation in the suites of Culzean (1762/CASTLES) and includes the famous Eisenhower apartment, so a bed for the night rarely comes as posh. The second floor (you enter by the original 1920s lift) has some fabulous views. Rates are expensive but include afternoon tea. Dinner is available. The cliff-top setting, the gardens and the vast grounds are superb.

768 9/K26
42 ROOMS
TEL · TV
£60-85

✓ **Lochgreen House** www.costley.biz · 01292 313343 · Troon Top hotel of the Bill Costley group which is so preeminent in this neck of the woods, Lochgreen (adjacent to Royal Troon Golf Course) the most full-on upmarket – a newer extension gives 42 rooms. The **Brig o' Doon** at Alloway is the romance-and-Rabbie Burns hotel (01292 442466), with a self-catering house, **Doonbrae**, opposite (1258/HOUSE PARTIES) in gorgeous gardens, while **Highgrove** (01292 312511), a bit more intimate, is just outside Troon. All operate at a high standard. The Costleys also have the **Ellisland Hotel** in Ayr (779/AYR) and a good roadside inn, the **Cochrane** at Gatehead (1310/GASTROPUBS) and the new Soutar Johnnie's.

£32+ **EAT** **Lochgreen:** The top restaurant – probably – here (also the Brasserie) but consistently high quality throughout the group.

769 9/K27
5 ROOMS
TEL · TV
NO PETS
£45-60
£15-22

✓ **The Alloway Inn** www.costley.biz · 01292 442336 · Ayr North Park on Alloway Rd, almost feels like the country. Cosy, well-appointed rooms with bathrooms relatively lavish. Also part of the Costley empire (see above), this more a classy country pub with rooms. Good bathrooms. Rammed with happy Ayrshire eaters at weekends. Can walk to douce wee Alloway, heart of the Burns industry. **EAT** The Costleys' well thought-out comfort-food menu. Book weekends.

770 10/L27
4 ROOMS
TEL · TV
£38-45

✓ **The Sorn Inn** www.sorninn.com · 01290 551305 · 35 Main Street, Sorn 8km east of Mauchline on the B743 off the A76. Traditional inn in rural setting and pleasant village in deepest Ayrshire. The Grant family have established a big reputation for food with a continuing clutch of awards including consecutive Michelin Bib Gourmands. There are 4 delightful, great-value rooms with WiFi, etc. **EAT** People travel from miles around to eat here. Restaurant and pub meals. Craig Grant in the kitchen. See 1287/GASTROPUBS.

771 9/L28
6+1 ROOMS
TEL · TV
NO KIDS/PETS
£85+

Enterkine House www.enterkine.com · 01292 521608 · **near Annbank**
10km from Ayr in beautiful grounds. Self-consciously upmarket, 'informally formal' country-house hotel with pleasantly traditional public rooms. Paul Moffat presides over conservatory restaurant with good local reputation. Occasionally a piano is played. Woodland Lodge under the trees is a quirky, romantic hideaway and a new, permanent marquee indicates a concerted effort in the wedding market.

772 9/K27
30 ROOMS
TEL · TV
NO PETS
£60-85

Piersland Hotel www.piersland.co.uk · 01292 314747 · **Craig End Road, Troon** Opposite Portland Golf Course which is next to Royal Troon (2047/GREAT GOLF). Mansion house of character and ambience much favoured for weddings. Wood-panelling, open fires, lovely gardens only a 'drive' away from the courses (no preferential booking on Royal, but Portland usually possible) and lots of great golf nearby. Refurbished rooms best. Eat in the Redbowl Bar or Restaurant.

773 9/L27
50 ROOMS
TEL · TV
£38-45

The Park Hotel www.theparkhotel.uk.com · 01563 545999 · **Kilmarnock** Rugby Park ie adjacent Kilmarnock's football stadium. Contemporary business and family hotel better than chains of Travelodge ilk. Good café/restaurant. Sports facilities at the ground opposite. Weddings and dinner-dances do occur.

774 9/K28
11 RMS · TV
TEL · NO PETS
£38-45
£22-32

Wilding's Hotel & Restaurant 01655 331401 · **Maidens** Run by Brian Sage, restauranteur, this is perhaps more a restaurant with rooms. Contemporary and comfortable rooms overlook the serene harbour in this coastal village. **EAT** A beautiful spot and excellent gastropub-style menu in 2 large, buzzing rooms. Food LO 9pm. They come from all over the county, so book at weekends.

✓✓ **Glenapp Castle** www.glenappcastle.com · 01465 831212 Discreet and distinguished. A jewel in the Scottish crown here in deepest South Ayrshire. Report: 1117/SUPERLATIVE COUNTRY-HOUSE HOTELS.

4 ROOMS
TV
£38-45

Dunure Inn www.dunureinn.co.uk · 01292 500549 · **Dunure** On the A719, the minor but beautiful coast road south of Ayr. Harbourside pub with contemporary rooms (and 2 cottages). Report: 1307/GASTROPUBS.

RESTAURANTS

775 9/K26
£22-32

✓✓ **Braidwoods** www.braidwoods.co.uk · 01294 833544 · **near Dalry** Simplest approach is from the section of A78 north of Irvine; take B714 for Dalry. Cottage restaurant discreetly signed 5km on left. Michelin-star dining doesn't get more casually accomplished: impeccable, light food, always the best meal in the shire. Wed/Sun lunch (not Sun lunch in summer) and Tue-Sat dinner.

776 10/N27
£22-32

✓ **Ristorante La Vigna** www.lavigna.co.uk · 01555 664320 · **40 Wellgate, Lanark** Here for more than 25 years, this famously good Italian restaurant in a Lanark back street is an unexpected find in the Lanarkshire badlands. Superb wine list. This is no ordinary tratt! Lunch Mon-Sat, dinner 7 days.

777 9/K26
£22-32

✓ **Nardini** www.nardinis.co.uk · 01475 675000 · **Largs** On the Esplanade. Legendary seaside salon is back, trading somewhat on the past. Still, in a town hoaching with new eateries (Ad Lib, Room and the estimable **Lounge** above RBS), I prefer this new Nardini (nowt to do with the original family). Still buzzing in big rooms; Italian fare and snowdrifts of ice cream. Go back! 12noon-10pm.

✓ **MacCallums** 01292 319339 · **Troon** Report: 1330/SEAFOOD RESTAURANTS.

Fins 01475 568989 · **Fairlie near Largs** Report: 1339/SEAFOOD RESTAURANTS.

GASTROPUB GRUB IN AYRSHIRE

Ayrshire has many good gastropubs (partly down to the Costleys). All are routinely packed with happy Ayrshire eaters who travel and treat themselves. Book at weekends.

✓ **The Sorn Inn** 01290 551305 · Mauchline 770/AYRSHIRE HOTELS.

✓ **The Alloway Inn** 01292 313343 · Alloway Report: 769/AYRSHIRE HOTELS.

✓ **Souter Johnnie's** 01655 760653 · Kirkoswald Report: 1297/GASTROPUBS.

778 9/L27 **The Wheatsheaf** www.wheatsheafsymington.co.uk · 01563 830307 · Symington Village inn off main A77 with big local reputation for wholesome pub grub: the steak pie is famous. No fuss, great service. 11am-10pm. 7 days. 1295/GASTROPUBS.

The Cochrane 01563 570122 · Gatehead Report: 1370/GASTROPUBS.
Carrick Lodge Hotel 01292 262846 · Ayr Report: 779/AYR.
Dunure Inn 01292 500547 · Dunure Report: 1307/GASTROPUBS.

▰ If you're in Ayr...

779 9/K27 **WHERE TO STAY**

44 ROOMS
TEL · TV
£45-60
Fairfield House www.fairfieldhotel.co.uk · 01292 267461 · Fairfield Road 1km centre on the front. Solid, decent, suburban. 'Deluxe' facilities include pool/sauna/steam, and conservatory brasserie. 3 rooms have sea view.

49 ROOMS
TEL · TV
£60-85
Western House Hotel 08700 555510 · Craigie Road Very much part of Ayr Racecourse. Close to the big roundabout into Ayr on A77 from north. Former jockey dorm, now a contemporary bed for the night. 10 rooms in old mansion, the rest in 2 adjacent blocks. Lacking a little in charm but a good business bet.

9 ROOMS
TEL · TV
£60-85
The Ellisland www.costley.biz · 01292 260111 · 19 Racecourse Road On road to Alloway. Another makeover by the Costley group who have the Alloway Inn (above), Doonbrae (1258/HOUSE PARTIES) and others. Rooms vary but mostly large and well appointed. Decent restaurant with the Costleys' irresistible comfort food.

6 ROOMS
NO PETS
£30 OR LESS
The Richmond www.richmond-guest-house.co.uk · 01292 265153 · 38 Park Circus Best of bunch in a sedate terrace near the centre. Haven't stayed in a while but readers do tell.

Piersland 01292 314747 · Troon 12km north of Ayr. 772/AYRSHIRE HOTELS.

Enterkine House 01292 521608 · Annbank 12km Ayr town centre across ring road. Country house comforts. 771/AYRSHIRE HOTELS.

The Sorn Inn 01290 551305 · near Mauchline 25km east. Top gourmet pub with rooms. 770/AYRSHIRE HOTELS.

✓ **Lochgreen House** 01292 313343 · Monktonhall Road, Troon White seaside mansion near famous golf courses. Flagship hotel of Costley family (see below and all over Ayrshire). Report: 768/AYRSHIRE HOTELS.

✓ **The Alloway Inn** 01292 442336 3km from centre on road to Alloway. Small, well-appointed and superior gastropub. Report: 769/AYRSHIRE HOTELS.

✓ **Savoy Park** 01292 266112 · 16 Racecourse Road Interesting period mansion run by the Hendersons. Very Scots, very Ayrshire. 1227/SCOTTISH HOTELS.

WHERE TO EAT

£15-22 ✓ **Carrick Lodge Hotel** www.carricklodgehotel.co.uk · 01292 262846 · 46 Carrick Road On main road out of town in Alloway direction. Jim and Tracey Murdoch have created probably the most popular dining rooms in town. Huge kitchen team producing à la carte menu of wholesome pub food. 7 very pleasant rooms above. Book Fri/Sat. Lunch & 5.30-9pm.

Beresford Wine Bar www.costley.biz · 2 Academy Street Bistro, deli and art gallery, the new must-go place in Ayr at TGP and latest venture of the Costley clan (see Alloway Inn above). Med-style informal food. 7 days lunch & LO 10pm.

The Lido www.lido-troon.com · 01292 310088 · 11 West Portland Street, Troon Contemporary café-bar in Troon up the road. Italo-American buzzing diner from breakfast to supper. A stylish spot. 7 days 9am-10/10.30pm.

Fouters 01292 261391 · 2 Academy Street Long-established favourite Ayr dining spot, the bistro in a basement, but reports, please.

Cecchini's www.cecchinis.com · 01292 317171 · 72 Fort Street, Ayr & 39 Portland Street, Troon & Clyde Marina, Ardrossan Excellent Italian and Mediterranean restaurants run by the estimable Cecchini family. Also in Ardrossan where the Arran ferry comes in. Mon-Sat, lunch & LO 10pm.

£15-22 **Scott's** www.scotts-troon.com · 01292 315315 · Troon Harbour road within the marina about 2km downtown Troon. A self-consciously stylish, contemporary bar/restaurant upstairs overlooking the surprisingly packed marina. Same people have **Elliots** in **Prestwick**. Food ok, bling in evidence. 7 days. All day LO 10/11pm.

£15-22 **The Rupee Room** 01292 283002 · Wellington Square Ordinary-looking restaurant on the square serving the denizens of Ayr; they do fish 'n' chips but also rather good Indian food that's exactly what you want. 7 days. Lunch & LO 11pm.

Ayr India 01292 261026 · 1A Alloway Place & 01292 263731 · 10 Seafield Road Cleverly named, serviceable Indian restaurants in the town centre.

✓✓ **MacCallum's Of Troon Oyster Bar** This faraway dock on the bay has both the best restaurant hereabouts and also the best fish 'n' chip takeaway in the Wee Hurrie (see below). Report: 1330/SEAFOOD RESTAURANTS.

✓✓ **The Wee Hurrie** Ayr The best fish 'n' chips on the coast. See MacCallum (above) and report: 1348/FISH & CHIPS.

✓✓ **Mancini's** Ayr Ice cream and a' that. Report: 1435/ICE CREAM.

✓ **The Alloway Inn** 01292 442336 Restaurant of hotel above. The best just outside town with great pub-grub. Hugely popular. LO 9/9.30pm.

✓ **The Tudor Restaurant** 8 Beresford Terrace Superb all-round caff. They don't make 'em like this any more! Report: 1396/TEAROOMS.

Tourist Office 01292 290300 Open all year.

780 11/J30
10 ROOMS
TEL · TV
DA
£85+

£32+

✓✓ **Knockinaam Lodge** www.knockinaamlodge.com · 01776 810471 · **Portpatrick** Tucked away on dream cove, historic country house full of fresh flowers, great food, sea air and sympatico but smart service. Staff do stay. Sian and David Ibbotson balance a family home and a top-class get-away-from-it-all hotel. Rooms traditional but top-drawer. 1119/COUNTRY-HOUSE HOTELS.
EAT Best meal in the South from the outstanding and long- established Michelin chef in Scotland, Tony Pierce. Fixed menu – lots of unexpected treats.

781 11/N30
8 ROOMS
NO KIDS
TEL · TV
£45-60

✓ **Cavens** www.cavens.com · 01387 880234 · **Kirkbean** 20km south Dumfries via A710, Cavens is signed from Kirkbean. This elegant mansion in 6 landscaped acres has been converted by Angus and Jane Fordyce into a homely, informal Caven-haven of peace and quiet – great base for touring the South West. Lots of public space so you can even get away from each other. Angus's simple, good cooking using locally sourced ingredients: lots from Loch Arthur (1460/FARM SHOPS) including the excellent granola for breakfast. Gardens to wander: new cottage garden supplies dinner. Inexpensive to take over the lot. 1259/HOUSE PARTIES.
EAT Best food the quarter. Simple 2-choice menu like going to a dinner party but without having to get on with the guests.

782 11/M30
10 ROOMS
FEB-DEC
TEL · TV
£45-60

✓ **The Ship Inn** 01557 814217 · **Gatehouse of Fleet** Main street of delightful village with good forest walking all round. Refurbished to a good contemporary standard: light oak everywhere, plasma screens, nice bathrooms in simple and elegant rooms above. Great pub/bistro food make this the most attractive stay in the ville.

783 11/K30
17 ROOMS
FEB-DEC
TEL · TV
£85+

Kirroughtree Hotel www.kirroughtreehouse.co.uk · 01671 402141 · **Newton Stewart** On A712. Built 1719, Rabbie Burns was once here. Extensive country house draped and plushed up by the people who have a small chain of carefully run hotels and gorgeous Glenapp (1117/COUNTRY-HOUSE HOTELS). Original panelled hall and stairs, some spacious rooms the epitome of country-house living; nice grounds. Food here gets 3 AA rosettes: long-standing chef Ralph Mueller's menu may be your main reason for coming. Closed mid Jan to mid Feb.

784 11/J30
9 ROOMS
TEL · TV
ATMOS
£60-85

Corsewall Lighthouse Hotel www.lighthousehotel.co.uk · 01776 853220 · **Stranraer** A718 to Kirkcolm 3km, B738 to Corsewall 6km (follow signs). Wild location on cliff top. Cosily furnished clever but snug conversion: go with someone you like. The adjacent fully functioning lighthouse (since 1817) makes for surreal evenings. 3 suites are outside the lighthouse and 2 are further away. All have the sea and sky views. Small dining room. Food fine (it's a long way to the chipper).

785 11/N31
20 ROOMS
FEB-NOV
TEL · TV · DA
£60-85

Balcary Bay www.balcary-bay-hotel.co.uk · 01556 640311 · **Auchencairn** 20km south of Castle Douglas and Dalbeattie. Off A711 at end of shore road and as close to the water as you can get without getting wet. Ideal for walking, bird watching and outdoor pursuits (dogs welcome). Kitchen continues a strong commitment to local produce. A well-run hideaway and good for a romantic break!

786 11/N30
15 ROOMS
TEL · TV
DA
£38-45

Clonyard House www.clonyardhotel.co.uk · 01556 630372 · **Colvend** On Solway Coast road near Rockcliffe and Kippford (1562/COASTAL VILLAGES; 2037/COASTAL WALKS) but not on sea. Later extension to house provides 11 bedrooms adjacent to patio garden with own private access and... aviary! Friendly family and good for kids; decent pub grub. A refurbishment wouldn't go amiss but hey...

787 11/M31

Good Spots in Kirkcudbright Pronounced 'cur-*coo*-bree'; a gem of a town. On a High Street filled with posh B&Bs, the Cowans' **Gladstone House** (01557 331734) stands out. Only 3 (lovely attic) rooms so book well ahead.

16 ROOMS
TEL · TV
£38-45

Selkirk Arms www.selkirkarmshotel.co.uk · 01557 330402 · **High Street** Much more your 'proper hotel' (a Best Western). Owner/manager Douglas McDavid runs a tight but friendly ship. 16 of the best medium-expensive rooms in this most interesting of southwest towns. Bar food and garden.

788 11/N30
5 ROOMS
TV · KIDS
£30-38

Anchor Hotel 01556 620205 · **Kippford** Seaside hotel in cute village 3km off main A710. Basic accommodation but great pub atmosphere and extensive food operation; seafood menu (local lobster, pints of prawns). See 1318/GASTROPUBS.

Cally Palace 01557 814341 Report: 1135/KID-FRIENDLY HOTELS.
Aston Hotel 01387 272410 Report: 798/DUMFRIES.

RESTAURANTS

789 11/N29
£22-32

✓ **Auld Alliance** www.auldalliancedumfries.com · 01387 255689 · **53 St Michael Street, Dumfries** Direction Caerlaverock. Brave French guys Thierry Deliege and Julien Sarret took over Dumfries's only decent restaurant (the late Linen Room) and give it a very good go of Franco-Ecosse food somewhere between bistro and fine dining. Good luck! Dinner only Tue-Sun.

790
11/M28
£22-32

✓ **Blackaddie Hotel** www.blackaddiehotel.cok · 01659 50270 · **Sanquhar** I haven't visited this hotel in the less-travelled quarter of the south west but something is happening here: Ian McAndrew, a former Michelin chef and perhaps to be so again, is creating a foodie destination in these hills. There's even a cookery school. Can't wait to get there myself. Phone or log on for details.

791
11/M29
£22-32

✓ **Three Glens** 01848 200057 · **Moniaive** Suddenly ('09) there are 2 great places to eat in Moniaive which is a pleasant wee town between Thornhill and New Galloway north west of Dumfries. This is a contemporary cottage conversion with a pasta/wood-ovened-pizza place and interesting daily specials. And it's good! Dinner only, Tue-Sun.

792
11/M29
ATMOS
£15 OR LESS

✓ **Green Tea House** 07752 099193 · **Moniaive** And this is the other place (see above) except it's been here for ages and it's quite unique. A tea house right enough with an old-schoolroom ambience but Catherine Braid has created a caff/bistro in the back of beyond that's kinda brilliant. 5 daily soups, toasties (her signature haggis, cheese and peach chutney) and in summer a full menu 6-9pm.

793 11/M30
£15-22

✓ **Carlo's** 01556 503977 · **211 King Street, Castle Douglas** Here over 20 years, the Bignami family restaurant with Carlo in the kitchen is your absolute best option. Bustling tratt atmosphere (and including Dumfries) – this is the best Italian food in the South. Open Tue-Sat 6-9pm.

794 11/M30 **The Masonic Arms** www.themasonic-arms.co.uk · **01557 814335** ·
£15-22 **Gatehouse Of Fleet** New owners are rebuilding the big reputation this place always had for food. 3 separate rooms and atmosphere but same menu featuring local produce. Good vegetarian choices and kids' menu. Lunch and LO 8.45pm.

795 11/J30 **Campbell's** www.campbellsrestaurant.co.uk · **01776 810314** · **Portpatrick**
£15-22 Robert and Diane Campbell's café since 1998. Unpretentious fishy fare but offering something for everyone, including vegetarians. They have a boat, so crab and lobster a good, fresh bet. Lunch and LO 9.30pm. Closed Mon.

796 11/J30 **The Crown** www.crownportpatrick.com · **01776 810261** · **Portpatrick**
£15-22 Harbourside hotel and pub with better-than-average grub. Goes like a fair in summer in lounge, conservatory and outside.7 days. LO 10pm. Competition from the **Waterfront** (01776 810800) next door. The Crown has better atmosphere.

797 11/M31 **Kirkpatrick's** 01557 330888 · **Kirkcudbright** Scottish restaurant much welcomed
£15-22 in this much-visited town; upstairs and round corner from Main St. Dinner is where Tom Kirkpatrick shows his stuff. 7 days 6-9pm. Tapas twist on Thursdays.

▇ If you're in Dumfries...

798 11/N29 **WHERE TO STAY**
71 ROOMS **Aston Hotel** 01387 272410 · **Bankend Road** Newish hotel in the Crichton
TEL · TV Estate (signposted from centre), a curious 100-acre suburb of listed sandstone
£45-60 buildings including a conference centre. Contemporary-furnished hotel with brasserie. A bit far to walk to town but best bet for modern facilities and decent food.

7/4 ROOMS **Criffel Inn** www.criffel-inn.co.uk · **01387 850305** · **New Abbey &**
TV **Abbey Arms** 01387 850489 · **New Abbey** 12 km south of Dumfries A710. 2
£30-38 old-style pubs on either side of the green in this lovely wee village where Sweetheart Abbey is the main attraction (1892/ABBEYS). Criffel best for food and rooms. Locals seem to patronise the bar in both. This is basic accommodation.

✓ **Cavens** www.cavens.com · **01387 880234** · **Kirkbean** 20km from Dumfries by A710. Report: 781/SOUTHWEST HOTELS. And very civilised dining!

WHERE TO EAT
✓ **Auld Alliance** www.auldalliancedumfries.com · **01387 255689** · **53 St Michael Street** The area's fine dining. Report: 789/SOUTHWEST RESTAURANTS.

£15-22 **Hullabaloo** www.hullabaloorestaurant.co.uk · **01387 259679** At the Robert Burns Centre, also home to an art-house cinema. Hard to reach by car, so walk across the bridge over the river. Lighter food by day. Some say it's not as good as you'd wish. Closing time varies but usually 11am-8.30pm. Closed Sun/Mon dinner.

£15-22 **The Brasserie @ The Aston** 01387 272410 On edge of town near the university and infirmary; follow signs for the Crichton (see Aston Hotel above). Pleasant room with bar. Contemporary menu. 7 days. Lunch & LO 9.30pm.

£15-22 **Bruno's** 01387 255757 · **3 Balmoral Road** Off Annan Rd. Very long-established old-style Italian eaterie beside **Balmoral** chippy (1358/FISH & CHIPS). Interior (they close the blinds) but home cooking and real. 6-10pm, closed Tue.

£15-22 **Pizzeria Il Fiume** www.pizzeriailfiume.co.uk · 01387 265154 · **Dock Park**
Near St Michael's Bridge, underneath Riverside pub. Usual Italian menu but ok
pizzas and the best in town for cosy tratt atmosphere. 5.30-10pm daily.

£15-22 **Globe Inn** www.globeinndumfries.co.uk · 01387 252335 · **56 High Street**
Historic (17th century) pub made internationally famous as Robert Burns' howff
(1915/BURNS). Decent lunches and suppers by arrangement. Best found on foot.

✓ **Cavens** www.cavens.com · 01387 880234 · **Kirkbean** In a town not tops
for eating out, Cavens is only 20 minutes away (781/BEST SOUTHWEST).

The Best Hotels & Restaurants In Central Scotland

799 10/L23
14 ROOMS
TEL · TV
ATMOS
£45-85

✓✓ **Monachyle Mhor** www.monachylemhor.com · 01877 384622 · **near Balquhidder** Along the ribbon of road that skirts Loch Voil 7 km beyond the village (which is 4km) from the A84 Callander-Crianlarich road. Relatively remote (1171/GET-AWAY HOTELS) and splendid location for this informal and pink farmhouse hotel with great food, fabulous sexy, contemporary rooms and altogether good vibes. Boutique in the back of beyond.

£22-32
EAT It's a long way to go for dinner, but currently some of the best dining in Scotland to be had here. A great team on the stoves and sometimes Tom Lewis, when he's not away being Tom Lewis.

800 10/M24
14 ROOMS
TEL · TV
ATMOS
£85+

✓✓ **The Roman Camp** www.romancamphotel.co.uk · 01877 330003 · **Callander** Nothing much changes nor needs to in Ian and Marion Brown's top-of-the-Trossachs hotel, though they're always freshening it up: new bathrooms have underfloor heating, flat-screen TVs on their way at TGP. Behind the main street (at east or Stirling end), away from the tourist throng and with extensive gardens on the River Teith; another, more elegant world. Roman ruins are nearby. The house, built for the Dukes of Perth, has been a hotel since the war. Rooms low-ceilinged and snug; some small, many magnificent; period furnishings. In the old building corridors do creak. Delightful drawing room and conservatory. Oval dining room very sympatico. Private chapel should a prayer come on and, of course, some weddings. Rods for fishing – the river swishes past the lawn.

£32+
EAT Dining room effortlessly the best food in town with a great and long-standing chef – Ian McNaught.

801 10/M24
14 ROOMS
(8 SUITES)
TEL · TV
ATMOS
£85+

✓✓ **Cromlix House** www.cromlixhouse.com · 01786 822125 · **Dunblane** 3km from A9 and 4km from town on B8033; follow signs for Perth, then Kinbuck. A leisurely drive through old estate with splendid mature woodlands to this spacious country mansion both sumptuous and homely. Not much changes here in its old-style atmosphere but best to leave well alone. No leisure facilities but unnecessary with woods to walk and 3000 acres of meadows and fishing lochs. House Loch is serenity itself. Private chapel.

£32+
EAT Chef Steven MacCallum, great conservatory and cosy dining rooms.

802 10/M23
5 ROOMS
TEL · TV
£45-60

✓ **Creagan House** www.creaganhouse.co.uk · 01877 384638 · **Strathyre** End of the village on main A84 for Crianlarich (as above). Gordon & Cherry Gunn's very personally run Creagan House is the place to eat in Rob Roy and Callander country. They have 5 inexpensive rooms, small but a home from home. You eat in an impressive baronial dining room. There are many hills to walk and forest trails that start in the lovely garden (1939/HILLS). Closed Feb.
EAT Gordon's been in that kitchen creatively cooking for nigh on 25 years. They do take Wed and Thu off, which I think we can allow.

803 10/M24
16 ROOMS
TEL · TV
£45-60

✓ **Lake Hotel** www.lake-hotel.com · 01877 385258 · **Port Of Menteith** A very lake-side hotel on the Lake of Menteith in the purple heart of the Trossachs. Good centre for touring and walking and the lake always swarms with fishermen and wee boats. The Inchmahome ferry leaves from nearby (1902/MARY, CHARLIE & BOB). 5 rooms overlooking the lake, to be refurbished at TGP, are premium, but probably worth the extra. Conservatory restaurant for sunset supper or lazy lunch; also bar menu. All rooms are light and quiet; this is a romantic spot.
EAT Different menus to choose from in bar and conservatory but all stylish and well done. Lovely fishcakes. LO 9.30pm.

804 10/N24
10 ROOMS
TEL · TV
NO PETS
£45-60

✓ **Adamo Hotel** www.adamohotels.com · 01786 833268 · **Bridge of Allan** Main street of pleasant town (good shops and restaurants). Surprisingly and self-consciously 'stylish' and modern with cool interiors and art (though the 'Green Lady' is a curious choice). Fineish dining good value in an urbane setting. Nice bar.

805 10/M25
3 ROOMS
TEL
£30-45

✓ **Cross Keys** www.kippencrosskeys.com · 01786 870293 · **Kippen** Main street of dreamy little village above the Forth flood plain not far from Stirling. 3 pleasant, airy rooms above a pub that's getting an increasing reputation for a warm welcome and excellent food (1292/GASTROPUBS).

806 10/M25
12 ROOMS
TV
£45-60

Black Bull www.blackbullhotel.com · 01360 550215 · **Killearn** In this good-looking village, 30 minutes north of Glasgow between Loch Lomond and the Campsies, a good conversion of an old inn and now a restaurant-with rooms kinda thing. Bar and bistro with same menu and conservatory restaurant at weekends. Rooms simple and decent value (487/HOTELS OUTSIDE GLASGOW). In Killearn check also **The Old Mill** (1306/GASTROPUBS).

807 10/M24
210 ROOMS
TEL · TV
£60-85

Dunblane Hydro www.dunblanehydrohotel.com · 01786 822551 · **Dunblane** One of the huge hydro hotels left over from the last health boom, being refurbished by recent new owners Hilton at TGP. Nice views for some and a long walk down corridors for most. Leisure facilities include pool. Likely to remain a dinner-dance and wedded world when complete.

808 9/K23
14+16
ROOMS
ATMOS
£30-45

Inverarnan Hotel/The Drover's Inn & Lodge www.thedroversinn.co.uk · 01301 704234 · **Inverarnan** North of Ardlui on Loch Lomond and 12km south of Crianlarich on the A82. Much the same as it was when it was 'pub of the year 1705'; bare floors, open fires and heavy drinking (1264/BLOODY GOOD PUBS). The lodge on the other side of the road is modern. Highland hoolies here much recommended. Bar staff wearing kilts look like they're meant to. Rooms not Gleneagles but highly individual and some surprises (1 in hotel, 4 in lodge house have jacuzzis and 4-poster beds). A wild place in the wilderness. Expect atmosphere not service. Neither places have phones, only a couple have TV and mobiles probably don't work. Hey, you're away!

809 10/M24
4 ROOMS · TV
NO PETS
£38-45

The Inn at Kippen www.theinnatkippen.co.uk · 01786 871010 · **Kippen** Middle of village on road in from Loch Lomond direction. A village-inn experience though recent changes of hands have diminished its former stylish appeal. Rooms, though, are good value.

810 10/M24
6 ROOMS
MAR-NOV
NO PETS/KIDS
£30-38

Arden House www.ardenhouse.org.uk · 01877 330235 · **Callander** Bracklinn Rd off Main St at Stirling end and uphill. Superior B&B in elegant mansion. This one used to be featured in that seminal Sunday night series, *Dr Finlay's Casebook* and for oldies is still redolent of Tannochbrae.

 DeVere Cameron House 01389 755565 · Loch Lomond Report: 482/OUTSIDE TOWN HOTELS.

 Mar Hall 0141 312 9999 · Bishopton Opulent country house on big scale near Glasgow and airport. Report: 484/HOTELS OUTSIDE GLASGOW.

✓ **Lodge on Loch Lomond** 01436 860201 · Loch Lomond Report: 485/OUTSIDE TOWN HOTELS.

RESTAURANTS

811 10/N25
£15 OR LESS/
£32+

✓**Glenskirlie House & Castle** www.glenskirliehouse.com · 01324 840201 · **Banknock** On A803 Kilsyth-Bonnybridge road, junction 4 off M80 Glasgow-Stirling. The Macaloney family have one of Central Scotland's foodie destinations in this many-roomed mansion in an unlikely spot (though near M80 – 2km – and Falkirk/Stirling). Victorian house and new 'castle' offer fine dining and more informal bar and menu respectively. House for lunch and dinner (not Mon), castle evenings only (not Wed). Modern British menus with Scottish sourcing.

812 10/N24
£15 OR LESS

The Allan Water Café www.bridgeofallan.com · **Bridge of Allan** ·Caff that's been here for ever at end of the main street in Bridge of Allan now has big brassy, glassy extension and it occupies the whole block. Original features and clientele still remain in the old bit. It's all down to fish 'n' chips and the family ice cream (Bechelli's). 1441/ICE CREAM. 7 days, 8am-8.30pm.

813 10/M24
£15 OR LESS

Atrium 01877 331611 · **Main Street, Callander** Above CCW (Caledonian) outdoor shop. Unprepossessing approach through shop and upstairs to light, spacious mezzanine self-service restaurant probably best easy-eat choice in a stopover town. Home-made comfort food and especially good puds. Daytime only (till 5pm).

✓ ✓**Roman Camp** **Callander** Report: 800/CENTRAL HOTELS.

✓ ✓**Monachyle Mhor** **Balquhidder** Report: 799/CENTRAL HOTELS.

✓ ✓**Cromlix** **Dunblane** Report: 801/CENTRAL HOTELS.

✓**Creagan House** Strathyre Report: 802/CENTRAL HOTELS.

✓**Lake Hotel** **Port Of Menteith** Report: 803/CENTRAL HOTELS.

✓**Cross Keys** **Kippen** Report: 805/CENTRAL HOTELS.

If you're in Stirling...

814 10/N24
96 ROOMS
TEL · TV
£45-85

WHERE TO STAY

Barceló Stirling Highland www.barcelo-hotels.co.uk · 01786 475444 · **Spittal Street** Reasonably sympathetic conversion of former school (with modern accommodation block) in the historic section of town on road up to castle. Serviceable businessy hotel in prime location; light 17m pool. Scholars restaurant.

32/11 ROOMS
TEL · TV
£38-85

Halo Royal Hotel www.royal-stirling.co.uk · 01786 832284 · **Bridge of Allan** Middle of main street of the civilised suburb/adjacent town where the money is. Stately mansion with good service and ok restaurant. Also 100m along same street, the **Royal Lodge** (01786 834166). Both a better-than-average billet.

7 ROOMS
TEL · TV
£38-45

Osta www.osta.uk.com · 01786 430890 · **78 Upper Craigs** In the centre of the unintelligible town road system. A former bank building now transformed by the emerging Adamo group (see 804/CENTRAL HOTELS) and the most contemporary hotel in town. The main thing here is the busy, brasserie-like restaurant.

9 ROOMS
TEL · TV
£45-60

Park Lodge www.parklodge.net · 01786 474862 · **32 Park Terrace** Off main King's Park Rd, 500m from centre. Posh-ish hotel in Victorian/Georgian town (they say 'country') house near the park and golf course. Objets and lawns. French chef/proprietor. Michelin-mentioned. Some weddings.

4 ROOMS
TEL · TV
£38-45

Portcullis Hotel www.theportcullishotel.com · 01786 472290 · **Castle Wynd** Jim and Lynne Walker's pub with rooms, no more than a cannonball's throw from the castle and one of the best locations in town. Pub and pub food (home-made and popular, though basic); upstairs only 4 rooms, but 3 have brilliant views of Castle, graveyard, town and plain. Food till 8pm.

76 ROOMS
TEL · TV
NO PETS
£38-45

Stirling Management Centre www.smc.stir.ac.uk · 01786 451666 Not a hotel, but as good as. Fully serviced rooms on university campus (7km from centre in Bridge of Allan which has a good choice of restaurants). Excellent leisure facilities nearby. No atmosphere but a business-like option.

✓ **Adamo** www.adamohotels.com · 01786 833268 · **Bridge of Allan** Near Stirling; Bridge of Allan is the best place to be. Report: 804/CENTRAL HOTELS.

S.Y. Hostel 01786 473442 On road up to castle in recently renovated jail is this new-style hostel, though still very SYH (1229/HOSTELS). **Willy Wallace Hostel**, 77 Murray Pl at Friars St (01786 446773) is more funky. Upstairs in busy centre with caffs and pubs nearby. Unimposing entrance but bunkrooms for 54.

WHERE TO EAT

£22-32

✓ **Hermann's** www.hermanns.co.uk · 01786 450632 · **Mar Place** Many would say Stirling's best. A house on road up (and very close) to the castle. Hermann Aschaber's (with Scottish wife, Kay) corner of Austria where schnitzels and strudels figure along with Scottish fare. 2-floor, ambient, well-run rooms. Conservatory best. LO 9.30pm.

Zingerman's Bar & Grill www.zingermans.co.uk · 01786 463222 · **52 Port Street** Creation of Clive Ramsay who used to have a great deli and café in Bridge of Allan (they still trade under his name): a bar/restaurant which knows what it's doing and is all things to all people. Guzzle or graze. LO 9.30/10.30pm.

£15 OR LESS

Corrieri's 01786 472089 On road to Bridge of Allan at Causewayhead. For 70 years this excellent café/restaurant near busy corner below the Wallace Monument serving pasta/pizza and ice-cream as it should be. A genuine family .caff. LO 9.30pm. Closed Tue.

£15-22

Birds & Bees www.thebirdsandthebees-stirling.com · 01786 473663 Between Stirling and Bridge of Allan at Causewayhead. Towards Stirling, first on right (Easter Cornton Rd): popular pub grub. A roadhouse which is the Scottish *pétanque* (*boules*) centre. Good for kids. Terrace. 7 days. LO 9.15/10pm.

£15 OR LESS

Allan Water Café www.bridgeofallan.com · **Bridge of Allan** 8km up the road in Bridge of Allan main street near bridge itself. Great café, the best fish 'n' chips 'n' ice cream. Nostalgia no longer, now it's just massive. See 1441/ICE CREAM.

Osta www.osta.uk.com · 01786 430890 City-centre modern grazing and dining. See *Where To Stay* (above).

Tourist Office 01786 479901 Open all year.

The Best Hotels & Restaurants In The Borders

815 10/R27
11 ROOMS
TEL · TV
£60-85

✓ **The Townhouse** www.thetownhousemelrose.co.uk · 01896 822645 · **Melrose** Longstanding Burt's (below) has spawned a stylish little sister across the street. Charming and boutiqueish with a coherent, elegant look by Michael Vee Decor (from down the street) but nothing too over the top. In the whole of the Borders, this is probably the only hotel you could call 'contemporary'. Dining room and busy brasserie confidently positioned between Burt's' fine dining and its gastrogrub bar. The Hendersons (père et fils) here and over the road for a wee while now. They have this town down to an 'M' (for Melrose).

816 10/R27
20 ROOMS
TEL · TV
DA
£45-60

✓ **Burt's** www.burtshotel.co.uk · 01896 822285 · **Melrose** In Market Sq/main street; some (double-glazed) rooms overlook. Busy bars, especially for food, and it's not hard to see why. The dining room is *where to fine dine* in this part of the Borders. Traditional but comfortably modernised small town hotel, though some rooms feel small. Convenient location for Borders reveries and roving (1893/ABBEYS; 1956/HILL WALKS; 1523/GARDENS). Where to stay for the Sevens, but try getting in!

£32+

EAT Bar serves top gastropub food; an AA Pub of the Year (1289/GASTROPUBS). Main restaurant in beautiful garden room. Both in a class of their own hereabouts.

817 10/S27
4 ROOMS
TV
NO PETS
£38-45

✓ **Edenwater House** www.edenwaterhouse.co.uk · 01573 224070 · **Ednam, near Kelso** Find Ednam on Kelso–Swinton road B6461, 4 km. Discreet manse-type house beside old kirk and graveyard overlooking the said Eden Water, the lovely garden and tranquil green countryside – 'bucolic' is the word that comes to mind. You have the run of the home of Jeff and Jacqui Kelly. Jacqui's flair in the kitchen and down-to-earth approach and Jeff's carefully wrought wine list (he has a 'wine club' in the outhouse) make this the secret Borders dinner destination.

EAT Possibly the best meal in the counties. Jacqui Kelly is a longstanding, unassuming and underestimated cook. Non-residents must book.

818 10/Q26
8 ROOMS
TEL · TV
NO PETS
£45-60

✓ **Horseshoe Inn** www.horseshoeinn.co.uk · 01721 730225 · **Eddleston, near Peebles** On the A703 (8km Peebles, 30km Edinburgh), a recreated, reconstructed coaching inn and a convivial and contemporary stopover with famously good food that continues to win awards for chef/proprietor Patrick Bardoulet. Rooms in the old village school behind are peaceful and better than anything down the road in Peebles. Stumble there replete after dinner.

£22-32

EAT Sumptuous dining rooms and a destination for dinner. At weekends it's so busy you have to be seated in the bistro by 7.15pm. The restaurant books 7.30-9.30pm. From Cherubs (ie the kids' menu) to the full 7-course tasting menu, it's here to be adored.

819 10/Q27
13 ROOMS
TEL · TV
£85+

✓ **Cringletie House** www.cringletie.com · 01721 725750 · **Peebles** Country house 5km from town just off A703 Edinburgh road (35km). Late 19th-century Scottish baronial house in 28 acres. Quintessential Peeblesshire: comfortable and civilised with an imperturbable air of calm. Restful garden view from every room. Top disabled facilities including a lift! Conservatory, lounges up and downstairs; gracious dining room. Walled kitchen garden.

£32+

EAT Craig Gibson tasting menu and à la carte in fine and proper situation. And lovely afternoon tea for Borders tootlers.

820 10/S27
22 ROOMS
TEL · TV
£60-85

✓**Roxburghe Hotel** www.roxburghe.net · 01573 450331 · near Kelso
The consummate country-house hotel in the Borders. Owned by the Duke and Duchess of Roxburghe, who have a personal input. Rooms distinctive, all light with garden views. Owls hoot at night and once – no, twice, a crow fell down my chimney. This was good luck! The 18-hole golf course has major appeal – it's challenging and championship standard and in a beautiful riverside setting. Non-residents can play (2065/GREAT GOLF). 'Health and Beauty Suite' for golf widows. While dining is not a strong point, the bar and dining room and the personable, not overbearing service make it a treat to eat. Compared with other country-house hotels, the Roxburghe is good value. Serene garden, perfect policies!

821 10/P27
5 ROOMS
MAR-DEC
TEL · TV
£38-45

✓**Skirling House** www.skirlinghouse.com · 01899 860274 · Skirling On A72. 3km from Biggar as you come into Skirling village. In an Arts and Crafts house (by Ramsay Traquair, son of Phoebe), Bob and Isobel Hunter have created a rural guest house which is the epitome of taste. From the toiletries to the white doves in the doocot, the hens from which your breakfast eggs come and the garden produce, it's just perfect. Bob cooks (set menu), Isobel out front. Skirling continues to win awards.

822 10/R26
8+2 ROOMS
MAR-JAN
TEL · TV · DA
£38-45

✓**Black Bull** 01578 722208 · Lauder Main street near the clock of strip of town on A68 that leads to the real Border Country. Eminent especially for its food (1290/GASTROPUBS), it also has 8 (and 2 family) very pleasant rooms above the many-chambered pub; a popular local. New management '09 but values remain.
EAT The best gastropub south of the capital.

823 10/R26
10 ROOMS
TEL · TV
£38-60

Lodge At Carfraemill www.carfraemill.co.uk · 01578 750750 · near Lauder On A68 roundabout 8km north of Lauder. Old coaching-type lodging. Rooms are old-style and all different – it sure beats a motel! Old-style cooking, a good stop on the road for grub ('Jo's Kitchen' LO 9pm, all-day menu Sat/Sun) and a gateway to the Borders. Nice for kids.

824 10/R27
38 ROOMS
TEL · TV · ECO
£60-85

Dryburgh Abbey Hotel www.dryburgh.co.uk · 01835 822261 · near St Boswells Secluded, elegant 19th-century house in abbey (1891/ABBEYS) grounds banking River Tweed. Peaceful and beautiful location; small swimming pool a bit tatty now. Not big on atmosphere despite surroundings, and rather average dining in very pink room. But lovely riverside walks. And the abbey: pure romance by moonlight.

825 10/Q27
12 ROOMS
+ 5 LODGES
TEL · TV
£60-85

Philipburn www.philipburnhousehotel.co.uk · 01750 720747 · Selkirk 1km from town centre on A707 Peebles Rd. Excellent, privately owned hotel for families, walkers, weekend away from it all. Selkirk is a good Borders base. Restaurant and bar-bistro and comfy rooms, some more luxurious than others. Spa and pool underway at TGP. 1138/HOTELS THAT WELCOME KIDS.

826 10/S27
32 ROOMS
TEL · TV
£38-45

Ednam House www.ednamhouse.com · 01573 224168 · Kelso Just off town square overlooking River Tweed; majestic Georgian mansion with very old original features including some of the guests! In the same family (the Brooks) since 1928, it has dated in a comforting way: guests quietly getting on with the main business of fishing and dozing off in an old armchair. The restaurant's river view is, however, the main attraction in a great garden room with an unfortunate carpet. Only half the bedrooms have view.

827 10/R27
5 ROOMS
TV
£38-45

Clint Lodge www.clintlodge.co.uk · 01835 822027 · **St Boswells** On B6356 (1638/SCENIC ROUTES) between Dryburgh Abbey (1891/ABBEYS) and Smailholm Tower (1852/MONUMENTS). Small country guest house in great border country with tranquil views from rooms. Nice conservatory pre dinner. Very good home cooking and service from Bill and Heather Walker then a splendid Border breakfast.

828 10/R27
3 ROOMS
TV
£30-38

Fauhope www.melrose.bordernet.co.uk · 01896 823184 · **Melrose** Borders house in sylvan setting overlooking Tweed. Lovely front rooms, terrace and terraced lawns. Only 3 rooms but in more guides than mine (*Best B&Bs, Michelin*), so must book. Family dogs much in evidence.

829 10/R28
4 RMS · TV
MAR-OCT
NO C/ CARDS
£30 OR LESS

Hundalee House www.accommodation-scotland.org · 01835 863011 · **Jedburgh** 1km south of Jedburgh off A68. Lovely 1700 manor house in 10-acre garden. Brilliant value, great base, views of Cheviot hills. Near the famously old Capon Tree.

S.Y. Hostels Very good in the Borders. Report: 1151/HOSTELS.

Glentress Hotel near Peebles Report: 1134/HOTELS THAT WELCOME KIDS

Wheatsheaf Swinton Report: 1295/GASTROPUBS.

Traquair Arms Innerleithen Report: 1167/ROADSIDE INNS.

RESTAURANTS

830 10/Q27
£15-32

✓✓**Osso** 01721 724477 · **Innerleithen Road, Peebles** Aka the main street at the Innerleithen end. Ally McGrath's perfectly judged and effective bistro-cum-tearoom-cum-restaurant that changes through the day from lightsome lunch to scones and cakes to superb dining-out experience at night. And no city prices or pretensions in sight. For tourists and locals he's pressed the Peebles button big-time. Lunch 7 days through to dinner (Tue-Sat). LO 8.45pm.

831 10/R27
£15-22

✓**Marmion's** www.marmionsbrasserie.co.uk · 01896 822245 · **Buccleuch Street, Melrose** Near the abbey. Local fave bistro for a long time, its original formula and atmosphere unchanged by new owners a couple of years back. Open for breakfast, lunch and dinner with a bistro rather than brasserie menu. The reliably good repast in the Borders foodie capital. LO 8.45pm. Closed Sun.

832 10/R27
£22-32

✓**Chapters** www.melrose.bordernet.co.uk · 01896 823217 · **Gattonside, near Melrose** Over the River Tweed (you could walk by footbridge as quick as going round by car). Kevin and Nicki Winsland's surprising bistro is a real find. Huge choice from à la carte and specials in a periodically changing menu. Good atmosphere. Tue-Sat dinner only.

✓**Burts & Townhouse** Melrose · **Cringletie** Peebles (see above) Burt's for best dining hereabouts (including the two-tick gastropub and the brasserie at the Townhouse), Cringletie for country treat (Cringletie is just outside Peebles). Reports: 816/815/BORDERS HOTELS, 1289/GASTROPUBS (Burt's).

£15 OR LESS

✓**Turnbulls** 01450 372020 · **Hawick** By 'the Horse', ie Oliver Place, this recent arrival is thought by some to be the best thing to happen to Hawick for years. Not hard to see why. 9.30am-5pm (café till 4pm). Report: 1450/DELIS.

833 10/R27 **The Hoebridge Inn** www.thehoebridgeinn.com · 01896 823082 ·
£15-22 **Gattonside, near Melrose** At Earlston end of village, signed towards the river. Long reputation for superior and imaginative pub food with some flair, though not a lot of atmosphere. Lunch Tue-Sun, dinner Tue-Sat. LO 9.30pm.

834 10/R27 **Monte Cassino** www.melrose.bordernet.co.uk · 01896 820082 · **Melrose**
£15-22 Great setting, occupying old station building just up from main square. Cheerful, non-pretentious and locally popular Italian with pasta/pizza staples and the odd ok special. LO 9.45pm. Closed Mon.

835 10/Q27 **Courthouse** 01721 723537 · **Peebles** Facing the end of the High St near the bridge. Upstairs in the former courthouse, a vaulted main room with terrace and garden. Popular, with an eclectic menu. Changes afoot at TGP can only make it even better. Reports, please! 7 days 12noon-9pm.

836 10/Q27 **Sunflower Restaurant** www.thesunflower.net · 01721 722420 ·
£15-22 **Bridgegate, Peebles** Off the main street at Veitches corner. Long-standing spot for restaurant, a local fave. 3 small rooms, so book for dinner at weekends. Integrity and design in café menu during day and nice for kids. They take vegetarian food seriously (and have their own cookbook). Thu/Fri/Sat for dinner 7–9 pm. Lunch 7 days.

£15-22 **Giacopazzi's & Oblo's** 01890 752527 · **Eyemouth** Great fish 'n' chips and ice-cream plus upstairs bistro near harbour of this fishy and friendly town. Report: 1355/FISH 'N' CHIPS.

837 10/R28 **Brydons** 01450 372672 · **16 High Street, Hawick** Once Brydons were bakers,
£15-22 now they have this oddly funky family caff-cum-restaurant. Home cooking, good folk – this is a totally Hawick experience. 8am-4.30pm. Closed Sun (1377/CAFÉS).

838 10/R28 **Damascus Drum Café & Books** 0786 7530709 · **2 Silver Street, Hawick**
£15 OR LESS Near tourist information centre. Surprisingly contemporary, laid-back second-hand bookshop and caff in a backstreet of this cultural backwater. Comfy seats. Home-made soups, quiche and bagels (1322/VEGETARIAN RESTAURANTS)... and rugs. Mon-Sat 10am-5pm.

839 10/S27 **The Cobbles Inn** 01573 223548 · **Kelso** Off a corner of the main square
£15-22 behind the Cross Keys Hotel. Popular local pub-grub (more grub than pub) restaurant in a town with not a lot of good options. The Meiklejohns run a tight and friendly ship and care about their suppliers (mostly local). Bar and restaurant menu (evenings). Good ales. Live music Fri. Lunch and LO 9pm. Closed Sun/Mon.

Auld Crosskeys Inn Denholm Report: 1292/GASTROPUBS.
The Craw Inn Auchencrow Report: 1168/ROADSIDE INNS.
Woodside near Ancrum Report: 1395/TEAROOMS.
Under The Sun Kelso Report: 1376/CAFÉS.

See Section 2 for Edinburgh Hotels & Restaurants just outside the city.

840 10/P25
16 ROOMS
TEL · TV
NO KIDS
NO PETS
£85+

£15-32+

✓✓ **Champany Inn** www.champany.com · 01506 834532 · **near Linlithgow** Excellent restaurant with rooms near M9 junction 3 (Edinburgh-Stirling), 30 minutes from Edinburgh city centre, 15 minutes from the airport. Convenient high standard hotel adjacent to nationally famous restaurant (118/HOTELS OUTSIDE EDINBURGH) especially if you love your meat well-hung and properly presented. Superlative wine list, especially South African vintages from the restaurant, available to buy from The Cellar (12noon-10pm, 7 days). **EAT** Accolades confirm the best meal in West Lothian. Casual dining in the Chop 'n' Ale House. Angus beef (hung 3 weeks, butchered on premises), home-made sausages, Gruinart oysters.

841 10/R25
83 ROOMS
TEL · TV
£60-85

✓ **Marine Hotel** www.macdonaldhotels.co.uk · 01620 892406 · **North Berwick** The old seaside hotel of North Berwick underwent a long and extensive re-fit and re-emerged as a spa and conference centre. Done in the sombre/elegant, corporate style à la mode with lots of public space and everywhere (except the leisure area) the great views of the Links and the sea. Dining fine though not 'Fine'; small pool and other 'vital' facilities. Top suites have telescopes as well as the fluffy towels.

842 10/Q25
26 ROOMS
TEL · TV
£45-60

Kilspindie House www.kilspindie.co.uk · 01875 870682 · **Aberlady** Old-style village inn taken over by Edinburgh restauranteur of repute, Malcolm Duck. Rooms adequate and upgraded but hotel excels not surprisingly in the food department. Bar menu and proper dining. Excellent wine list. **EAT** Ducks Restaurant and Bar with à la carte and plats du jour. Gastropub dining on the coast – well sourced, all home-made, from the bread to the ice cream.

843 10/R25
12 ROOMS
TEL · TV
£30-38

The Rocks www.experiencetherocks.co.uk · 01368 862287 · **Dunbar** Not signed but at the east (ie Edinburgh) and John Muir Park end of Dunbar with great views across to the rocky harbour area, a hotel with big local reputation for food. Rooms vary – you would want 'the view'. Big beds, all the mod cons. **EAT** They do come from far and wide (but no signage so you'll need satnav). Big food operation downstairs. Seafood and the rest in bar and 'Piano Room'. They have the inexplicable touch. Must book weekends.

844 10/R25
13 ROOMS
TEL · TV
NO PETS
£45-60

Nether Abbey www.netherabbey.co.uk · 01620 892802 · **20 Dirleton Avenue, North Berwick** On way in on 'Coastal Trail' from Gullane. Long-established family 'seaside' hotel with major drop-in bar/restaurant operation – the Fly-Half Bar and Grill (well- and locally sourced dishes). Busy downstairs, comfy up. The same people have 12 Quality Street (below).

845 10/R25
12 ROOMS
TEL · TV
£45-85

Open Arms www.openarmshotel.com · 01620 850241 · **Dirleton** Dirleton is 4km from Gullane towards North Berwick. Comfortable, cosy and countrified hotel in tiny village opposite ancient ruins. If this were in France it might be a 'Hotel du Charme', but in need of TLC at TGP. Location means it's a golfers' haven; special packages available. Nice public rooms with much lounging space. 'Deveaus' Restaurant LO 9pm.

846 10/R26
18 ROOMS
TEL · TV
£38-45

Tweeddale Arms 01620 810240 · Gifford One of two inns in this heart of East Lothian village 9km from the A1 at Haddington, within easy reach of Edinburgh. Set among rich farming country, Gifford is conservative and couthy. Some bedrooms small, but public rooms pleasant and comfy in a country way. Recent new owners stepping up the food side, with a daily-changing menu using local produce.

✓✓ **The Dakota** 0870 423 4293 · South Queensferry Report: 119/HOTELS OUTSIDE EDINBURGH. Designed for travellers.

✓ **Orocco Pier** 0131 331 1298 · South Queensferry Report: 122/HOTELS OUTSIDE EDINBURGH. Boutique on the water. And the bridge.

RESTAURANTS: EAST LOTHIAN

847 10/R25
£32+

✓✓ **La Potinière** www.la-potiniere.co.uk · 01620 843214 · Gullane On the main street of this golfing mecca. This small, discreet restaurant has been an East Lothian destination for decades. Keith Marley and Mary Runciman, who share the cooking, have carried on and consolidated its reputation since 2003. The room is not of the bustling bistro variety but just right for gentle, perhaps genteel, appreciation of their simply excellent 2-choice, locally sourced menu. Far and away the best dining in East Lothian. Lunch Wed-Sun, Dinner Wed-Sat (Sun in summer). LO 8.30pm.

848
10/Q25
£15-32

✓ **The Glasshouse** www.theglasshouseateskmills.com · 0131 273 5240 · Station Road, Musselburgh An unlikely find perhaps off the high street in Musselburgh, but a good one. Coming from Edinburgh, turn hard right after the bridge, pass Tesco on the left, next turning on left then pass Links Coachworks on your left. Beyond the car park in the pleasingly restored Eskmills (they used to make fishing lines) complex, an airy urban dining room with accessible and very good Modern British menu with good vegetarian choice. Chef Steven Thompson in the unnecessarily visible kitchen. Courtyard outside; weddings spill out from adjacent function room. Tue-Sat. Lunch and LO 9.30pm.

849 10/R25
£15 OR LESS

✓ **Fenton Barns** www.fentonbarnsfarmshop.com · 01620 850294 · near Drem Farmshop/deli but also a great café with delicious food home-made from the mainly local produce they sell; hot dishes till 3.30pm then scrumptious cake. Not licensed. Daily till 4.30pm. See 1464/FARMSHOPS.

850 10/R25
£15-32

✓ **Creel** www.creelrestaurant.co.uk · 01368 863279 · Lamer Street, Dunbar Scotsman Logan Thorburn went out in the world and learned to be a top-end chef. He returned to this discreet corner of old Dunbar near the harbour and from a tiny kitchen produces sound and simple, almost rustic menus. Local, of course, and not just seafood. Very bistro. Thu-Sun lunch and Thu-Sat dinner.

851 10/R25
£15-22

✓ **Osteria** 01620 890589 · High Street, North Berwick The restaurant in downtown small town set up by the legendary Italian chef from Edinburgh, called just simply Cosmo, at the age of 75. Well, he's 80 now so 'family' run it but its old-fashioned values in menu and service make this the smart and reliably good place to eat. Good Italian wine list. Closed Sun and Mon lunch. LO 10pm.

852 10/R25
£15-22

The Old Clubhouse www.oldclubhouse.com · 01620 842008 · East Links Road, Gullane Behind main street, on corner of Green. Large woody clubhouse; a bar/bistro serving a long menu (of the burgers/pasta/nachos variety) all day till 9.30pm. Great busy atmosphere. Surprising wine selection.

853 10/R25
£15 OR LESS

The Linton www.lintonhotel.com · 01620 860202 · **East Linton** Classic small country village hotel; friendly and welcoming. Simple, quiet rooms and notable locally for bar meals and dining. Has an unusual upstairs walled garden.

854 10/Q25
£15-22

Restaurant 102 0131 665 3535 · **102 New Street, Musselburgh** 2 gals run this contemporary room behind the main street in Musselburgh. Hits the local spot perfectly. Changing menu and 'favourites'. Good value. Breakfast on Sun. 12noon-8.45pm (later Fri/Sat). 7 days.

855 10/R25
£15 OR LESS

Tyneside Tavern www.tynesidetavern.co.uk · 01620 822221 · **Haddington** On the edge of the town centre on the road to Gifford by Poldrate Mill where there is a bistro. I prefer this welcoming pub-grub pub: the room, the menu, the whole approach – simple. Expect good home-made mince 'n' tatties and apple crumble. 7 days. Sat 12noon-9pm, Sun 1-7.30pm.

Goblin Ha' Hotel 01620 810244 · **Gifford** Report: 1314/GASTROPUBS, 273/EDINBURGH KID-FRIENDLY.

RESTAURANTS: WEST LOTHIAN

856 10/N25
£15-22

✓ **Livingston's** www.livingstons-restaurant.co.uk · 01506 846565 · **Linlithgow** Through arch at east end of High St opposite PO. Cottage conversion with conservatory and garden – a quiet bistro with imaginative modern Franco-Scottish cuisine. A bit formal but easily the best in town and shire. Straightforward menu; good vegetarian. Tue-Sat, lunch and dinner. Closed Jan.

857 10/P25
£15-22

✓ **The Boathouse** 0131 331 5429 · **South Queensferry** Enter from main street or down steps to terrace overlooking shingly beach and excellent views of the bridge (398/MAIN ATTRACTIONS). South Q picking up these days and this wine bar/bistro/restaurant fills a big gap. Nothing too fancy but mainly seafood in a lucky location. Times vary but you can eat 7 days till 9.30pm.

858 10/N25
£15-32

Epulum www.epulum.net · 01506 844411 · **121 High Street, Linlithgow** At the Falkirk end of the street. Funky, conscientious café/restaurant embracing all the current foody concerns, ie they have 'an ethos'. All home-made, properly sourced, free-range and where appropriate, 'slow'. Great light food. 7 days all day. Dinner Thu-Sat LO 9pm.

✓✓ **Champany Inn** 01506 834532 · **South Queensferry** See *Hotels In The Lothians*, above.

✓✓ **The Dakota** 0870 423 4293 · **South Queensferry** Report: 119/HOTELS OUTSIDE EDINBURGH.

✓ **Orocco Pier** 0131 331 1298 · **South Queensferry** Report: 122/HOTELS OUTSIDE EDINBURGH.

859 10/R23
144 ROOMS
TEL · TV
NO PETS
£85+

✓✓ **Old Course** www.oldcoursehotel.co.uk · 01334 474371 · **St Andrews** Arriving in St Andrews on the A91, you come to the Old Course and this world-renowned hotel first. It has an elegant presence, is surrounded by greens and is full of golfers coming and going. It was designed by NY architects with Americans in mind. Rooms, most overlooking the famous course and sea, are immaculate and tastefully done with no facility or expense spared, as with the Sands Brasserie and fine-dining Road Hole Grill up top. Bar here also for lingering views and a big choice of drams. Truly great for golf, but anyone could unwind here, towelled in luxury. Excellent Kohler (the hotel's US owners) 'water spa' with 20m pool, thermal suite and some top treatments (1241/BEST SPAS). No preferential treatment on the Old Course adjacent but the hotel has its own course, Dukes, 5km away.

£32+/
£22-32

EAT Road Hole Grill for spectacular dinner, especially in late light summer. Sands for lighter and later food. Nice afternoon tea.

860 10/Q24
30 ROOMS
TEL · TV
£85+

✓ **Balbirnie House** www.balbirnie.co.uk · 01592 610066 · **Markinch** Signed from the road system around Glenrothes (3km) in surprisingly sylvan setting of Balbirnie Country Park. One of the most sociable and comfortable country-house hotels in the land, with high, if traditional, standards in service and decor personally overseen by the Russell family. Library Bar leads on to tranquil garden. Choice of dining and a good wine list. No leisure facilities. Nice wedding/honeymoon destination. Good golf in the park.

£32+

EAT An elegant hotel for lunch and dinner in Orangery or downstairs bistro.

861 10/R23
24 ROOMS
+ 2 LODGES
TEL · TV · ECO
£60-85

✓ **Rufflets** www.rufflets.co.uk · 01334 472594 · **St Andrews** 4km from centre via Argyle St opposite West Port along Strathkinness Low Rd past university buildings and playing fields. Calm, elegant feel to this country-house hotel on edge of town. The celebrated gardens are a joy. Garden-restaurant fine dining; lovely lounges, especially for afternoon tea. Cosy rooms with half on garden. New conference/wedding suite but it's in a separate building so the serenity remains mainly intact (except for photo calls on the lawns).

862 10/R23
209 ROOMS
+ 2 LODGES
TEL · TV
£60-85

✓ **Fairmont St Andrews (aka St Andrews Bay)** 01334 837000 · **near St Andrews** 8km east on A917 to Crail overlooking eponymous bay. Smart modern edifice in rolling greens. Soulless perhaps, but every facility a golfing family could need. It does have a championship course and service at the Fairmont is top. There's a Taste of Scotland approach in the Squire, a brasserie-type restaurant in an immense atrium. Fine dining in Esperante up top – Mediterranean menu (closed Mon/Tue), or the Clubhouse on the green with its signature fish 'n' chips.

863 10/R23
8 ROOMS
TV · NO KIDS
£45-60

✓ **Old Station** www.theoldstation.co.uk · 01334 880505 · **near St Andrews** On B9131 (Anstruther road) off A917 from St Andrews. Individualist makeover of old station with themed rooms and a contemporary look. Great detail and consideration for guests: library, putting green, snooker and ping-pong. Conservatory dining room, comfy lounge with log fire. 2 suites in a railway carriage in the garden! B&B only.

864 10/R24
17 ROOMS
+2 COTTAGES
£38-45

Cambo Estate www.camboestate.com · 01333 450054 · **near Crail** 2km east of Crail on A917. Huge country pile in glorious gardens on the coastal road between St Andrews and Crail. Rooms arranged in apartments (and 2 cottages), but this is self catering in the grand if quirky manner (breakfast and dinner can be arranged). A real period piece and not expensive. Grounds are always superb, especially in spring (the snowdrops!); great walks and Kingsbarns golf and beach adjacent (2059/GREAT GOLF). Rattle around, pretend you're house guests and be grateful you don't have to pay the bills.

865 10/P25
17 ROOMS
TEL · TV
NO PETS
UNDER £38

29 Bruce Street 01383 840041 · **Dunfermline** Very central (and adjacent main car park) conversion of townhouse into Italian restaurant (Ristorante Alberto) and contemporary boutique-style rooms. Bar/club adjacent. Well targeted to urban traveller, though you may well feel the noise. Not so far from the motorway. Good value.

866 10/R24
5 ROOMS
TV
£38-45

The Ship Inn www.ship-elie.com · 01333 330246 · **Elie** 5 basic rooms by the sea in Rock View adjacent to the pub that is notable for food, cricket and the good life in an excellent neuk of Fife. Summer only.
EAT The pub (next door) is an institution in Elie and reason enough for going there (1293/GASTROPUBS).

867 10/P25
20 ROOMS
TEL · TV
£38-45

Woodside Hotel www.thewoodsidehotel.co.uk · 01383 860328 · **Aberdour** Historic inn in main street of pleasant village with prize-winning rail station, castle and church (1862/CHURCHES), coastal walk and beach. This is where to come from Edinburgh (by train) with your bit on the side. Old-style accommodation.

868 10/P25
5 ROOMS
TV
£38-45

Forth View www.forthviewhotel.co.uk · 01383 860402 · **Aberdour** Over the sea from Edinburgh, an old-fashioned hideaway on the point and the undercliff just outside Aberdour (you can walk round the bay: 300m). A jagged pier and view of the water and the sunset. A Room With A View is the seafood dining room; public area small. Family-run historic house. Steep approach by car from Silver Sands car park. They do pick you up from the famously floral station.

 The Peat Inn near Cupar & St Andrews The Peat Inn has great accommodation behind the restaurant (see below). 20 minutes from St Andrews.

For accommodation in St Andrews, see p. 165.

RESTAURANTS

869 10/Q24
£32+
ATMOS

 The Peat Inn www.thepeatinn.co.uk · 01334 840206 · near Cupar & St Andrews Legendary restaurant (with 8 luxury suites) at an eponymous crossroads of Fife. Geoffrey and Katherine Smeddle have maintained its reputation, and indeed developed it as one of the great contemporary dining-out experiences in the land. A tasting menu, plats du jour and a seasonal à la carte offer loads of hard choice, and how Geoffrey and just 3 other chefs turn over the number of tables spread comfortably through the cottagey rooms, is quite extraordinary. Unlike many top chefs, he's always there (*and* he writes a foody column in the *Sunday Herald*). The Peat Inn is way in the country (though close to St Andrews) so the rooms come in handy. And then there's breakfast! Superb wine list, especially French. Lunch & LO 9pm Tue-Sat.

870 10/R24
£22-32
ATMOS

The Cellar 01333 310378 · **Anstruther** For nigh-on 30 years, this classic bistro has pioneered and served some of the best fish you'll eat in Scotland. Off a courtyard behind the Fisheries Museum in this busy East Neuk town (1563/COASTAL VILLAGES) – you'd never think this was a restaurant from the approach but inside is a comforting oasis of epicurean delight. Peter Jukes sources only the best produce and he does mean *the* best. Even the Anstruther crabs want to crawl in here. One meat dish, excellent complementary wine list. Pure, simple food and timeless atmosphere. Lunch Thu-Sun (not Thu in winter). Dinner Mon-Sat (not Mon in winter). 1326/SEAFOOD RESTAURANTS.

871 10/R24 ✓ **Sangster's** www.sangsters.co.uk · 01333 331001 · Main Street, Elie
£22-32   Michelin-starred chef and the missus' unobtrusive and unpretentious restaurant is perfect for charmed and charming little Elie, the secret neuk of many a moneyed Edinburger and other lovers of the good life. Usually 3 choices, simply described and presented; the chef's signature elegant pairings of fine ingredients. And stand-out value for money. Only a few tables so must book, especially for dinner. Lunch Wed-Fri & Sun. Dinner Wed-Sat.

872 10/Q23 ✓ **Ostler's Close** www.ostlersclose.co.uk · 01334 655574 · Temperance
£22-32   Close, Cupar Down a close off the main street, Amanda and Jimmy Graham run a bistro/restaurant that has been on the gastronomic map and a reason for coming to Cupar for well over 20 years. Intimate, cottagey rooms. Amanda out front also does puds, Jimmy a star in the kitchen. Often organic and from their garden, big on mushrooms and other wild things, lots of fish choice – the handwritten menu sums up their approach. Everything is carefully considered, sourced and combined. Cupar is only 20 minutes from St Andrews. Go to it! Sat lunch & Tue-Sat dinner LO 9.30pm. Must book.

873 10/P25 ✓ **The Wee Restaurant** www.theweerestaurant.co.uk · 01383 616263 ·
£22-32   Main Street, North Queensferry Just over the Road Bridge from Edinburgh and in the shadow of the Rail Bridge (398/MAIN ATTRACTIONS). Wee, it is: a few tables up a few stairs from the street. Owner/chef Craig Wood and missus, Vicki, live through the back, bake the bread in the morning and prepare their no-fuss menu with commitment (to good food) and aplomb. There's nowhere as good as this anywhere nearby except Edinburgh. Neat wine list. Michelin Bib. Lunch Tue-Sun, dinner Tue-Sat.

874 10/Q25 **Harvey McGuire's** www.harveymcguires.co.uk · 01334 828888 · Pitscottie
£15-22   Between Cupar and St Andrews. At rural crossroads, a diner-inn with a bit of a' things to a' folk (including art). Big servings of the grub we like served with thought and panache by the Harvey boy (well, actually chef Grant MacNicol, it is confusing). They have a deli in Church St, St Andrews. 7 days lunch and LO 9.30pm.

£15 OR LESS **Fish & Chips In Fife: Valente's Kirkcaldy, The Anstruther Fish Bar, The Wee Chippie, The Pittenweem Fish & Chip Bar** 4 great fish 'n' chip shops with queues every day. All good, that's why! 1361/1365/FISH & CHIPS.

875 10/R24 **Wok & Spice** 01333 730888 · St Monans On A917 turning past St Monans.
£15 OR LESS Not a caff but a takeaway. Sizzling woks, proper rice, a taste of real Malaysian food (please don't have the chips). This would work anywhere but when in Fife, order here (they deliver between Largo and Crail). 7 days 4.30pm till whenever.

✓ **The Seafood Restaurants** www.theseafoodrestaurant.com · 01334 479475 · St Andrews & 01333 730327 · St Monans Both excellent, unpretentious restaurants by the Butler family in perfect, if very different, settings. Reports: 1328/1329/SEAFOOD RESTAURANTS.

✓ **The Grange Inn** St Andrews Report: 1294/GASTROPUBS.

✓ **The Ship Inn** Elie Report: 1293/GASTROPUBS.

✓ **The Vine Leaf** St Andrews See *Where to Eat in St Andrews*, p. 166.

Many of the places below are mentioned in Scotland- or Fife-wide categories.

876 10/R23   WHERE TO STAY

4 ROOMS
NO KIDS/PETS
£38-45

✓**18 Queen's Terrace** www.18queensterrace.com · 01334 478849
Family home run by the enthusiastic Jill Hardie. Her lounge, gardens, very
individual and spacious bedrooms and lovely breakfast are yours. Very central; hard
to beat, really!

68 ROOMS
TEL · TV
£45-60

Rusacks www.rusacks-hotel.co.uk · 01334 474321 · Pilmour Links Long-
standing golfy hotel near all courses and overlooking the 1st and 18th of the Old.
Nice sun-lounge and breakfast overlooking the greens. Jack Nicklaus looms large.
Reliable and quite classy for a Macdonald Hotel. Good 'packages'.

22 ROOMS
TEL · TV
NO PETS
£60-85

Albany Hotel 01334 477737 · 56 North Street Townhouse hotel with
surprising number of rooms and beautiful back garden. 50% of rooms overlook
and are individually (though not in a boutique sense) done; 3 have outside decks
and there's a suite with a patio. Bar and basement restaurant, 'The Garden'. A very
St Andrews kind of a hostelry.

13 ROOMS
TEL · TV
£38-45

Ogstons On North Street www.ogstonsonnorthst.com · 01334 473387 ·
127 North Street Corner of Murray Park where there are numerous guest-house
options. Boutique-ish rooms above restaurant and often-busy bar. Lizard bar in
basement, the Oakrooms on street level is quite civilised café-bar. Comfy, contemporary rooms, perhaps best for students and their mates, rather than their
parents.

20 RMS · TEL
TV · NO KIDS
NO PETS
£45-60

Greyfriars 01334 474906 · 129 North Street And immediately adjacent to
Ogstons (above), another bar/restaurant with rooms above with a very similar
offering. Perhaps even more self-consciously contemporary: a more recent
makeover. Restaurant not bad; a busy, sports-on-TV kind of billet for the night.

6 ROOMS
TV · NO PETS
£45-60

5 Pilmour Place www.5pilmourplace.com · 01334 478665 Adjacent 18th
green of Old Course. Contemporary-style guest house with lounge. The Wrights
have got it, well... right, and are notably obliging. Great breakfast choice.

✓✓**Old Course Hotel** 01334 474371 Report: 859/FIFE HOTELS.

✓**Rufflets** 01334 472594 Report: 861/FIFE HOTELS.

✓**Fairmont (St Andrews Bay)** 01334 837000 Report: 862/FIFE HOTELS.

✓**Old Station** 01334 880505 Report: 863/FIFE HOTELS.

WHERE TO EAT

£22-32 ✓ **The Vine Leaf** 01334 477497 · 131 South Street Inauspicious entrance passage belies what has been for 25 years the best all-round restaurant in town. Eclectic menu that covers all bases, including good vegetarian options and good wines. Morag and Ian Hamilton know how to look after you and what you like (especially for pud). David Joy's calming pictures adorn (perhaps over-adorn) the walls; they do sell. Tue-Sat from 7pm.

£15-22 **The Doll's House** www.houserestaurants.com · 01334 477422 · Church Square Very central café/restaurant that caters well for kids (and their parents). Eclectic range, smiley people and tables outside in summer. Same people have **The Grill House** in St Mary's Place, a real townhouse with 3 different rooms and young staff. And they also have:

£15-22 **The Glasshouse** www.houserestaurants.com · 01334 473673 · 80 North Street Contemporary building with few tables downstairs and a few up. Bright, buzzy surroundings of metal, brick and glass. Mainly Italian (pasta and thin stone-oven pizza and specials). 7 days 11am-10pm.

£15-22 **Nahm-Jim** 01334 474000 · Crails Lane & **L'Orient** 01334 470000 · 62 Market Street 2 fused fusion restaurants with the same owner and with Japanese and Thai food. Generally good press, and good news for St Andrews. 7 days 12noon-12midnight (but often close earlier).

£22-32 **Balaka Bangladeshi Restaurant** www.balaka.com · 01334 474825 · 3 Alexandra Place One of those Best Curry in Scotland winners. But certainly as good as many in 'the city' (they have Dil Se in Dundee; 929/DUNDEE RESTAU-RANTS). Celebrated herb and spice garden out back which supplies others in St Andrews. Handily open later than most.

£15 OR LESS **North Point** North Street Top of the street. Great little caff (daytime only). Coffee, salads, home-made stuff – soup, scones and crumble of the day. 8.30am-5pm (opens 10am on Sun).

✓ ✓ **The Peat Inn** 01334 840 206 15km southwest. Only 20 minutes to the best meal around. Report: 869/FIFE RESTAURANTS.

✓ **The Seafood Restaurant** 01334 479475 Top seafood, top view (Old Course and the sea). Report: 1328/SEAFOOD RESTAURANTS.

✓ **Grange Inn** 01334 472670 4km east off Anstruther road A917. Very popular country pub in several rooms with local reputation. Report: 1294/GAS-TROPUBS.

Janetta's 31 South Street Known for ice-cream, but popular caff. Open 7 days till 5pm. Report: 1437/ICE CREAM.

The Best Hotels & Restaurants In Perthshire & Tayside

877 10/M22
26 ROOMS
TEL · NO KIDS
NO PETS
£85+

✓✓ **Ardeonaig** www.ardeonaighotel.co.uk · 01567 820400 · **South Shore, Loch Tay** This lochside inn ain't easy to get to (midway Killin and Kenmore on bumpy single-track) but that's what it's about (1182/GET-AWAY HOTELS). In this airy, uplifting setting looking over the lawn and the loch to Ben Lawyers, South African Pete Grottgens has created a love letter to his homeland and one of Scotland's most stylish hotels. Everything – public rooms, bedrooms, (especially the round, thatched rondavels along the banks of the Finglen Burn), the dining and most certainly the service (from largely SA staff) – is exemplary. No TVs but a lovely library up top and a menu of activities on loch or hill. The hotel leases 3000 acres for stalking or photo stalking with Dounnen bothy for lunch, providing transport up and offering mountain bikes back. Hill or chill?

£32+ **EAT** Chef/proprietor Pete in the kitchen where from 2 tables a night you can watch him at work. Dining room, wine cellar and bistro (breakfast and lunch) with outside tables and the view. All run with flair and precision.

878 10/P22
25+16
ROOMS
TEL · TV
DA
£85+

✓ **Ballathie House** www.ballathiehousehotel.com · 01250 883268 · **near Perth** A true country-house hotel on the Tay that you fall in love with, especially if you hunt, shoot, fish or just want to lounge around. Comfortingly old-style, the river and the astonishing trees are the thing. Good dining, great fishing; good for a weekend away. Riverside rooms are over the lawn (150m walk for breakfast; or room service) and uniform but you taste the Tay. Also cheaper, motel-like Sportsman's Lodge adjacent main house. Love the approach: red squirrels, copper beeches, golden corn. Estate café and farmshop 1km (1467/FARMSHOPS).

£32+ **EAT** Chef Andrew Wilkie. Local and estate produce, especially beef/lamb.

879 10/Q22
6 ROOMS
TEL · TV
£60-85

✓ **Castleton House** www.castletonglamis.co.uk · 01307 840340 · **Eassie, near Glamis** 13km west of Forfar, 25km north of Dundee. Approach from Glamis, 5km southwest on A94. Unlikely, perhaps unprepossessing location for a delightful, very civilised country-house hotel meticulously run by the Websters and their excellent, mainly local staff. Chef is Matt Dobson from the Websters' other excellent country-house hotel, Raemoir (936/BEST NORTHEAST). Best Angus option by far. Our First Minister and his missus often dine here.

£22-32 **EAT** Pleasing conservatory restaurant. All foodie formalities observed.

880 10/N24
12 ROOMS
+2 ADJACENT
TEL · TV
£38-45

✓ **An Lochan** 01259 781252 · **Tormaukin, near Auchterarder** 12km south of Auchterarder and Gleneagles via A823 or via A91 east of Stirling and the charmingly called Yetts o' Muckhart. The old Tormaukin inn taken over and considerably polished up by the intrepid Mackay family venturing far from their base in Tignabruaich (750/ARGYLL HOTELS) and their largely seafood restaurant in Glasgow (512/BISTROS) – both rebranded with the 'An Lochan' name. So here now an almost boutique hotel in the heart of the glen (Glen Devon) and a restaurant that demonstrates their uncompromising and simple approach to gastronomy (under chef Gary Noble). Rooms pleasant and unpretentious. Menu majors on local meat and game.

881 10/M23
11 ROOMS
TEL · TV
NO PETS
£60-85

✓ **Royal Hotel** www.royalhotel.co.uk · 01764 679200 · **Comrie** Central square of cosy town, a surprisingly stylish small-town hotel. Excellent restaurant with good light (and a light touch from chef David Milsom); pub out back with ale and atmosphere. Nice rugs and pictures. A pleasing touch of understated class in the county bit of the country. Bar meals. Both restaurant and bar LO 9pm.

882 10/N21
13 ROOMS
TEL · TV
NO KIDS
£38-45

✓**Craigatin House** www.craigatinhouse.co.uk · 01796 472478 · **Pitlochry** The house, built 1820s, is now a stylish guest house on road north out of Pitlochry. Aspiring perhaps to be part of the cool/hip hotels network, this is definitely the coolest in this town built for tourism. Martin and Andrea Anderson are your obliging hosts. More guest house than hotel, with rooms in the main mansion and courtyard. Rooms have simple good taste with great bathrooms. Breakfast in conservatory which opens to serene garden.

883 10/P21
17 ROOMS
TEL · TV
£38-45

✓**Dalmunzie Castle** www.dalmunzie.com · 01250 885224 · **Spittal o' Glenshee** 3 km from Perth-Braemar road close to Glenshee ski slopes and good base for Royal Deeside without Deeside prices. 9 hole golf-course for fun. Highland-lodge feel. Hills all around and burn besides; a truly peaceful outlook. Food mention in Michelin, fire in the hall!

884 10/Q22
17 ROOMS
TEL · TV
£38-45

✓**Lands of Loyal** 01828 633151 · **Alyth** Been here forever and under new ownership '08 (the Websters, who have Castleton, above). This Victorian mansion on the Loyal Hill with fantastic views from the south-facing rooms and the rambling terraced garden, has a real presence and extraordinary interior, especially the woody atrium. Awaiting the Webster treatment at TGP. Meanwhile, an aperitif on that terrace! Nice dining rooms (3) with open fires (2) and bar. An all-round great hotel experience.

885 10/P22
98 ROOMS
TEL · TV
£85+

✓**(Hilton) Dunkeld House** www.hilton.co.uk/dunkeld · 01350 727771 · **Dunkeld** Former home of Duke of Atholl, a very large impressive country house on the banks of the Tay in beautiful grounds (some time-share) outside Dunkeld. Leisure complex with good pool, etc and many other activities laid on eg quad bikes, clay pigeons. Very decent menu. Fine for kids. Pleasant walks. Not cheap but often deals available. Rooms in old house best. Many weddings.

886 10/N22
11 ROOMS
TEL · TV
£45-60

✓**Fortingall House** 01887 830367 · **near Aberfeldy** Historic roadhouse hotel 8km Aberfeldy on the road to gorgeous Glen Lyon. Refurbished to a high, boutique-style standard. Adjacent the kirkyard and the Fortingall Yew, the famous 'oldest tree in Europe'. Part of the local estate, with their own decor and produce. Decent dining and Ewe public bar. Garden.

887 10/R22
3 ROOMS
ATMOS
£38-45

✓**Evie Castle** 01241 830434 · **Inverkeilor, near Arbroath** 10km north of Arbroath off the A92 on the backroad to Lunan at a bend on the road marked 'Ethiebarns'. An ancient sandstone castle dating from the 14th century and in very good nick. Home of the Morgan family and also of the ghost of Cardinal Beaton. Fabulous public and bedrooms at your disposal; breakfast in the 'Tudor kitchen'. Dinner by arrangement but Gordons and the But 'n' Ben are nearby (see below). This is a very superior guest house!

888 10/P23
34 ROOMS
TEL · TV
£45-60

Huntingtower Hotel www.huntingtowerhotel.co.uk · 01738 583771 · **near Perth** Crieff road (1km off A85, 3km west of ring route A9 signed). Elegant, modernised mansionhouse outside town. Good gardens with spectacular copper beech and other trees. Subdued, panelled restaurant with decent menu (especially lunch) and wine list. Businesslike service.

889 10/N21
20 ROOMS
TEL · TV
NO PETS
£45-60

Pine Trees Hotel www.pinetreeshotel.co.uk · 01796 472121 · **Pitlochry** A safe and sophisticated haven in visitor-ville – it's above the town and above all that (there are many mansions here). Take Larchwood Rd off west end of main street. Woody gardens, woody interior. Scots owners. Traditional but with taste (nice rugs).

890 10/N21
13 ROOMS
TEL · TV
DA
£45-60

East Haugh House www.easthaugh.co.uk · **01796 473121** · near **Pitlochry** On south approach to Pitlochry from A9, a mansion house built 18th century; part of the Atholl estate. Notable for hunting/shooting and especially fishing with a beat on the Tay and a full-time ghillie, and for very decent food in dining room or bar. Family-run with popular proprietor Neil McGown cheffing for the Two Sisters restaurant and one of those daughters out front. Nice rooms especially up top, romantic with it (8 rooms have 4-posters). A top retreat near the Tay.
EAT Award-winning chef. Fish/game: good sourcing.

891 10/N21
10 ROOMS
MAR-NOV
TEL · TV
DA
£60-85

Killiecrankie Hotel www.killiecrankiehotel.co.uk · **01796 473220** · **Killie- crankie** 5km north of Pitlochry off A9 on B8079 signed Killiecrankie. Lovely road- side inn well known for food with cosy rooms upstairs and down. Delightful garden supplying kitchen. Conservatory and bar. Very family (and conscientiously) run.
EAT Bar and conservatory seasonal menus and dining room with daily menu. Casual and even more casual.

892 10/M22
42 ROOMS
TEL · TV
£38-45

Kenmore Hotel www.kenmorehotel.com · **01887 830205** · **Kenmore** Ancient coaching inn (16th century) in quaint conservation village. Good prospect for golfing with preferential rates at the adjacent Taymouth Castle and fishing. On the river (Tay) itself with terrace and restaurant overlooking it. Layout bitty, food so-so but real fires (and Robert Burns was definitely here). Room expansion immi- nent at TGP.

893 10/Q21
10 ROOMS
TEL · TV
NO PETS
£38-45

Glen Clova Hotel www.clova.com · **01575 550350** Near end of Glen Clova, one of the great Angus Glens (1594/GLENS), on B955 25km north of Kirriemuir. A walk/climb/country retreat hotel; very comfy. Superb walking nearby. Often full. Also bunkhouse accommodation behind. Luxury lodges out back (2 with another 6 coming at TGP) have hot tubs and fluffy downies. This place a very civilised Scottish inn in the hills and great value. The lovely Claire is everywhere.

894 10/M22
7 ROOMS
TEL · DA
£32-45

Dalshian Guest House www.dalshian.co.uk · **01796 472173** · near **Pitlochry** Historic house in lovely gardens just off the A9 6km south towards Ballinluig (road signed 'Croftinloan and Dalshian'). Martin and Heather Walls' old hoose and their hospitalities make for a very civilised retreat. Good fishing prospect. Logierait Inn nearby for dinner (see below). Good value.

895 10/M21
28 ROOMS
TEL · TV
£38-45

Dunalastair Hotel www.dunalastair.co.uk · **01882 632323** · **Kinloch Rannoch** Dominates one side of cute Victorian village square on this road (B8019) that stabs into the wild heart of Scotland. 30km Pitlochry on A9 (station for Edinburgh train) and 30km Rannoch station further up (station for Glasgow train). Schiehallion overlooks and must be climbed (1961/MUNROS); many other easy hikes. Welcoming Highland lodge that can point you in the direction of many outdoor activities. Newer rooms on tartan edge and pics need a radical rethink, but on the whole pleasant hotel with good bar for locals.

896 10/N23
10 RMS · TEL
TV · NO PETS
£60-85

Coll Earn House **01764 663553** · **Auchterarder** Signposted from main street. Extravagant Victorian mansion with exceptional stained glass. Comfy rooms, huge beds. Pleasant garden.

✓✓✓ **Gleneagles** **01764 662231** Report: 1116/COUNTRY-HOUSE HOTELS.

✓✓ **Kinloch House** **01250 884237** · **Blairgowrie** 5km west of Blairgowrie on A923 to Dunkeld. Quintessential Perthshire comfort and joy. Report: 1120/COUNTRY-HOUSE HOTELS.

✓ ✓ **Crieff Hydro** 01764 655555 Superb for many reasons, especially kids. Quintessentially Scottish. Report: 1122/HOTELS THAT WELCOME KIDS.

✓ ✓ **The Bield at Blackruthven** 01738 583238 Report: 1231/RETREATS.

✓ ✓ **The Barley Bree** Muthill · 01764 681451 Report: 1162/ROADSIDE INNS.

✓ **The Inn on the Tay** Grandtully · 01887 840760 Report: 1166/ROADSIDE INNS.

RESTAURANTS

897 10/N24
£32+

✓ ✓+ **Andrew Fairlie at Gleneagles** www.gleneagles.com · 01764 694267 The 'other' fine-dining restaurant apart from main dining room in this deluxe resort hotel (1116/COUNTRY-HOUSE HOTELS) and comfortably the best meal to be had in this and many other counties. Mr Fairlie comes with a big reputation, 2 Michelin stars and good PR. Understated opulence in interior room and confident French food of a very superior nature. Andrew, who stares from the wall while generally keeping to the kitchen, reminds us that Scotland is becoming as good a country to eat out in as any. Mon-Sat dinner only. LO 10pm.

898 10/P23
£22-32

✓ ✓ **Deans @ Let's Eat** www.letseatperth.co.uk · 01738 643377 · Kinnoull Street, Perth Perth's long-established premier and probably most popular eaterie. Fine contemporary dining and great value. Must book weekends. Chef/proprietor Willie Deans very much in charge. Tue-Sat lunch and LO 9.30pm.

899 10/P23
£22-32

✓ **63 Tay Street** www.63taystreet.co.uk · 01738 441451 · Perth On the new riverside road and walk. Set up in the early noughties by chef Jeremy Wares, 63 quickly became the other place to eat in Perth. Now the province of another chef, Graeme Pallister from Parklands. It continues to win awards. Sat night 3-course dinner with fancy bits is a must-book. Tue-Sat lunch, LO 9pm.

900 10/R22
£22-32

✓ **Gordon's** www.gordonsrestaurant.co.uk · 01241 830364 · Inverkeilor Halfway between Arbroath and Montrose on the main street. A restaurant with rooms (4) which has won loadsa accolades for Gordon and son Gary in the kitchen. It's been here for almost 25 years! Splendid people doing good Franco-Scot cooking. Seasonal menu. May lack atmosphere but it's the best meal for miles. Lunch and dinner. Closed Sun/Mon (Sun in summer). LO 8.45pm. Best book.

901 10/P23
£15-22

✓ **Apron Stage** 01738 8288885 · King Street, Stanley 3km from A9 just north of Perth. Shona and Jane's tiny local but magic bistro in the main street of sleepy village. It was chef Shona Drysdale who along with Tony Heath established Let's Eat (above) – this is where Shona came for a quieter life. Only 5 tables, so tight space and limited choices, but simply good. Fri lunch and dinner Wed-Sat.

902 10/R22
£15-22

✓ **The But 'n' Ben** 01241 877223 · Auchmithie 2km off A92 north from Arbroath, 8km to town or 4km by cliff-top walk. Village on cliff top where a ravine leads to a small cove and quay. Adjacent cottages converted into a cosy restaurant. Menus vary but all very Scottish and informal, emphasising fresh fish and seafood. The brilliant couthy creation of Margaret Horn after 30 years and still in the family, it's now run by son Angus (in the kitchen) and Margo out front assuring a warm welcome and consistency for a huge loyal following. Lunch and dinner with famous Sunday high tea.

903 10/N23 · £22-32   ✓ **Yann's** 01764 650111 · **Crieff**   Bistro of the small mansion-house hotel on the Perth road out of town, ticked because this really is where to eat around here. Very French. Book weekends, well in advance. Lunch and LO 9pm. Closed Mon/Tue.

904 10/P22   ✓ **The Antiquary** 01250 873232 · **Blairgowrie**   Back of road through town by the river and back of Roy Sim's spacious antique emporium but worth finding for excellent home cooking using best locally sourced (all within 25 miles) ingredients. Daily specials and afternoon tea. Proprietor/chefs Daz out front and Ben in the kitchen making a very good go of it here. Occasional dinners in the showroom using the plethora of antique dining tables. 10am-5pm (till 9pm Wed-Sat), Sun 10am-6pm. Closed Mon.
Cargills next door is a decent, long-established family bistro option.

905 10/N23 · £15-22   ✓ **Delivino** 01764 655665 · **6 King Street, Crieff**   Just off the main street. As it says on the tin, a deli counter and wine bar, but mainly an Italian bistro where ladies may lunch. Pizza, daily pastas. Perfectly Crieff! 10am-6pm (8pm Fri/Sat). Closed Sun.

906 10/N22 · £15 OR LESS   ✓ **Logierait Inn** 01796 482423 · **near Ballinluig**   8km south of Pitlochry. An inn (and self-catering lodges) by the River Tay 2km from the main A9 on A827 to Aberfeldy. Reputation for food is such that it has fairly limited opening hours but is always busy and you may have to book. Excellent gastropub grub. Wed-Sun. Evenings only LO 8.30pm.

907 10/N21 · £15-32   **Old Armoury** www.theoldarmouryrestaurant.com · 01796 474281 · **Pitlochry**   On road from main street that winds down to Salmon Ladder. Old Black Watch armoury gives spacious, light ambience and nice terrace/tea garden. Changing hands at TGP.

908 10/P22 · £15-22   **Darjeeling** 01350 727427 · **Main Street, Dunkeld**   Perfectly good local Indian restaurant along clean, contemporary lines. A welcome variant to beef and banoffee pie in these parts – the best place to eat full stop. 7 days, lunch & LO 10.30pm.

909 10/N21 · £22-32   **Port-na-Craig** www.portnacraig.com · 01796 472777 · **Pitlochry**   Just by the Pitlochry Theatre, cottage style bistro with courtyard in a 17th-century inn. Informal and friendly with a Modern European menu. Especially handy pre- and post-theatre.

910 10/M23 · £15-22   **Deil's Cauldron** www.deilscauldron.co.uk · 01764 670352 · **Comrie**   On bend of the A85 main road through town and corner of the road to Glen Lednock. Cottage restaurant with quietly effective menu includes staples and very good steaks, and eclectic tapas menu in bar area. Seriously good wine list; cosy ambience. Loyal clientele keep this Perthshire secret. Lunch Tue-Sun, dinner Tue-Sat.

The Best Places To Stay In & Around Dundee

911 10/Q23
151 ROOMS
TEL · TV
NO PETS
£45-60

✓ **The Apex** www.apexhotels.co.uk · 01382 202404 · West Victoria Dock Road There are now 4 Apex hotels in Edinburgh (74/INDIVIDUAL HOTELS) (and one in London) where there are many 4/5 stars to choose from. Here in Dundee this 21st-century edifice is in a league of its own. After some years now it's still the only place to stay! Overlooking both bridge and new dock and with good detail in the modern facilities (including the Yu spa and pool; 1247/SPAS). Not cheap (for Dundee) but very good value compared to elsewhere. Metro restaurant also one of the city's reliably good eats. Rooms facing the firth and out to sea are best. Big waterfront developments are promised nearer the bridge; the beauty of the Apex location is its urban serenity with dreamy views of a non-bustling waterfront.

EAT Acceptable brasserie and grazing menu overlooking quiet waters.

912 10/Q23
128 ROOMS
TEL · TV
£45-60

Hilton www.hilton.co.uk/dundee · 01382 229271 On riverside by Olympic Centre near Discovery Point. Big changes expected in this area of Dundee's Waterfront, including smartening up of this old block. Serviceable, mainly business hotel with little charm but reasonable facilities. Tired compared to Apex (above). Living Well leisure centre with ok pool. Rooms facing south have some great Tay views.

913 10/Q23
98 ROOMS
TEL · TV
£45-60

The Landmark www.thelandmarkdundee.com · 01382 641122 On western edge of the city (Perth direction) on the Kingsway ring road, the Landmark arose from the swallowing-up and complete makeover of the long-established Swallow Hotel. Functional, business-like and big on weddings, this is a reasonable choice in a city where there ain't much. The gardens are nice. Tiny pool and gym.

914 10/Q23
52 RMS · TEL
TV · £45-60

The Queen's Hotel www.queenshotel-dundee.com · 01382 322515 · 160 Nethergate Little charm but convenient location, having found itself in the middle of the cultural quarter adjacent DCA (2148/PUBLIC GALLERIES) and Dundee Rep. Back rooms (about 50%) overlooking distant River Tay are best.

915 10/Q23
4 ROOMS
TV · NO KIDS
NO PETS
£30-38

Number Twenty-Five 01382 200399 · 25 South Tay Street In the aforesaid cultural quarter near Dundee Rep Theatre and DCA (2148/PUBLIC GALLERIES). Dundee's boutique hotel. Rooms above café/bar and restaurant with niteclub in basement (busy Wed and weekends) so an up-for-it rather than escape-from-it bed for the night. Continental breakfast in room. Rooms, though clean and modern, seem a bit of an afterthought but they're good value.

916 10/Q23
11 ROOMS
(9 EN SUITE)
£30-38

Fisherman's Tavern www.fishermanstavern.co.uk · 01382 775941 · Fort Street, Broughty Ferry Near the river/sea. 17th-century fisherman's cottage converted to a pub in 1827. Rooms above and adjacent cottages much more recent! Excellent real ales and pub menu, but also nearby Ship Inn (922/DUNDEE RESTAURANTS) which is preferred for eats (Tavern does lunch only).

917 10/Q23
38 RMS · TEL
TV · £38-45

Woodlands www.bw-woodlandshotel.co.uk · 01382 480033 · Broughty Ferry In the 'burbs, signed up Abercromby St. High-falutin' house in substantial acreage. Good disabled access. Popular wedding venue; small pool and gym.

The nearest really good hotel to Dundee is:
✓ **Castleton House** near Glamis 28km north. Report: 879/TAYSIDE HOTELS.

The Best Places To Eat In & Around Dundee

918
10/Q23
£15 OR LESS

✓ **Jute at Dundee Contemporary Arts** www.dca.org.uk · 01382 909246 · Perth Road Jute, the downstairs bar/restaurant of Dundee's acclaimed art centre, DCA, is the most convivial place in town to eat – no contest. Chef Chris Wilson offers a menu far superior to any old arts venue, especially one which is all things to all people. Bar and restaurant: your rendezvous in Dundee. A good kids' menu. Book weekends. All day 10.30am-9.30pm.

919
10/Q23
£15-22

✓ **The Playwright** www.theplaywright.co.uk · 01382 223113 · Tay Square On the square adjacent and taking its point of reference from the estimable Dundee Repertory Theatre, this upstairs bistro has plugged the informal but informed contemporary-dining gap in Dundee and gets good notices from public and critics alike. Good Modern British cookery. Lunch and LO 9/10pm. Closed Sun.

920
10/Q23
£15-22

✓ **Bon Appétit** www.bonappetit-dundee.com · 01382 809000 · Exchange Street Near Commercial St. Owners Audrey and John Batchelor spent 16 years in France then returned to Dundee to 'make a difference'. Well, they have: in a culinary desert and with no French chefs they created an authentic French café with food as good as any bistro de la gare you'll find in any obscure town on your hols. All Francophile faves from moules frites to mousse au chocolat done just so. Menu changes every 6 weeks. All excellent value. Lunch and LO 10pm. Closed Sun.

921
10/Q23
£15-22

✓ **The Agacan** 01382 644227 · 113 Perth Road Fabled bistro for Turkish eats and wine. OTT frontage, much art on the walls; and the furniture. Bohemian ambience. You smell the meat (veggies go meze). 5-9/10pm. Closed Mon.

922
10/Q23
£15-22
ATMOS

✓ **The Ship Inn** 01382 779176 · Broughty Ferry On the front. Weathered by the River Tay since the 1800s, this cosy pub has sustained smugglers, fishermen and foody folk alike. Bar and upstairs restaurant; no-nonsense Scottish menu and a fabulous picture window overlooking the Tay. Lunch and bar food till 7.30pm, restaurant 8.30pm (9.30pm weekends).

923
10/R23
£22-32

✓ **Fraser's** 01382 730890 · Broughty Ferry Though it's been here for years, this sometime restaurant is a bit of a local secret. Dick Fraser chef/owner keeps this place almost as a hobby and only opens on Fri/Sat for set 5-course dinner: Modern Scottish dining real good and excellent wine selection. Must book.

924
10/Q23
£15 OR LESS

✓ **The Parrot Café** 01382 206277 · 91 Perth Road Many caffs around here but Val Ireland holds her own coz she makes her own (bread, cakes, scones, soups, blackboard specials) with a regular following of students and ladies who lunch and tea. No cellophaned muffins in sight. 2 delicious hot-lunch options. The craft of home baking is alive here. Tue-Sat 10am-5pm (4pm Sat).

925 10/Q23
£15 OR LESS

✓ **Fisher & Donaldson** www.fisheranddonaldson.com · Whitehall Street, off Nethergate Traditional but forwards-facing bakers – the very best in Scotland (1425/BAKERS) with busy little tearoom. Snacks and all their fine fare. Mon-Sat 8am-4.45pm (shop till 5.15pm).

926
10/Q23
£15-22

The Italian www.theitalian.co.uk · 01382 206444 · 36 Commercial Street 2-floored restaurant in city centre aptly named – it is *the* Italian. Somewhere between a tratt and a restaurant with well-chosen wine list, white linen and excellent service. Look no further than this. 7 days lunch & LO 9.30pm.

927
10/Q23
£15 OR LESS

Visocchi's 01382 779297 · 40 Gray Street, Broughty Ferry Following from the original Kirriemuir caff (now no relation): a busy tratt and ice-cream parlour. Over 3 generations they've been making mouth-watering Italian ice creams (*amaretto, cassata*, etc.) alongside home-made pasta and snacks. Hard work and integrity evident here. Till 8pm (4pm Tue, 10pm Fri/Sat). Closed Mon.

928
10/Q23

The Parlour 01382 203588 · West Port Opposite the more prominent Globe Bar, this wee caff at the end of the row of shops is easily missed but loyal locals and students pack it for home-made light food, soups, salads and big slabs of cakes. Lunch and LO 5pm, 7pm Sat. Closed Sun. Good vegetarian.

929
10/Q23
£22-32

Dil Se www.dilse-restaurant.co.uk · 01382 221501 · 99-101 Perth Road Bangladeshi restaurant; on two floors and food from all over the subcontinent but it's for curries, ain't it? Related to Balaka in St Andrews, this is just a bit smarter than the competition. Lunch and dinner Sun-Thu, open all day Fri & Sat. Till late!

930
10/R23
£15-22

The Glass Pavilion 01382 732738 · Broughty Ferry On 'The Esplanade' over-looking the Tay so you'd think it would be easy to find! Actually it's tricky and maybe easier to walk from Broughty Ferry Castle and harbour east to Monifieth, about 1.5km. Food so-so, but glass pavilion right enough, a contemporary reconstruction of an Art Deco gem. The pictures of Broughty Ferry beach and Esplanade in days gone by are a revelation (corridor by the toilets) and worth the journey alone. Nice coffee and chat, and walk further to Barnhill Rock Garden. A bracing and educative outing.

931
10/Q23
£15-22

Taychreggan Hotel 01382 778626 · 4 Ellieslea Road, West Ferry On main road between Dundee and Broughty Ferry signed just before the latter. Mansionhouse hotel (may be ok stopover) with big local reputation for food, espe-cially high teas and suppers. Fairly standard fare but reliably good. Surprising malt whisky selection. Lunch, high tea (5-6pm; from 4pm on Sun) & LO 9pm.

932
10/Q23
£15-22

Dundee Rep Café Bar Restaurant 01382 206699 · Tay Square Part of Dundee's celebrated Rep, a café meeting place in the foyer worth a visit in its own right for food and civilised surroundings. Loads better than many cultural caffs with serious options in à la carte and blackboard specials. Lunch and LO 9pm. Closed Sun.

If you're in Perth...

933 10/P23   **WHERE TO STAY**

34 ROOMS
TEL · TV
£45-60

Huntingtower Hotel www.huntingtowerhotel.co.uk · 01738 583771 Crieff road (1km off A85, 3km west of ring route A9 signed). Decent modernised mansion-house hotel outside town. Good gardens. Subdued, panelled restaurant; decent menu (especially lunch) and wine list. Business-like service. A Best West.

15 ROOMS
TEL · TV
£60-85

Parklands www.theparklandshotel.com · 01738 622451 · 2 St Leonard's Bank Near station overlooking expansive green parkland of North Inch. Reasonable town mansion hotel with a reputation for food under chef/proprietor Graeme Pallister who cooks at 63 Tay Street (see above).

23 ROOMS
£45-60

New County Hotel www.newcountyhotel.com · 01738 623355 · 22 County Place And 'new' it is, all spruced up and probably as close as Perth hotels come to 'boutique'. Comfy bedrooms and public areas include Gavin's, the pub and the estimable Opus One restaurant. Busy street and tricky parking but fine in a county-town-chic kind of way.
EAT Chef Ryan Young and David Cochrane produce a surprising, great-value menu which Joanna Blythman awarded $9/_{10}$. Lunch Thu-Sat, dinner Tue-Sat. LO 8.45pm.

39 ROOMS
TEL · TV
£45-60

Royal George www.theroyalgeorgehotel.co.uk · 01738 624455 · Tay Street By the Perth Bridge over the Tay to the A93 to Blairgowrie, near Dundee road and motorway system. Bridge is illuminated at night. Georgian proportions and nostalgic niceties, eg dainty bright flowers in the garden, twinkly chandeliers; feels comfortably replete, like an old-style town hotel after a wedding. Big on high tea, especially Sun. Mums, farmers and visiting clergy get comfy here.

WHERE TO EAT

£22-32

Café Tabou 01738 446698 · 4 St John's Place Central corner of a pedestrianised square; from outside and in, it feels like an unassuming café de la place but locals love it. French staff, French wine and a reasonable pass at French country food from chef Marek Michalate. Mon-Sat lunch and LO 9.30pm.

£15-22

Keracher's www.kerachers-restaurant.co.uk · 01738 449777 · Corner of South & Scott Streets Upstairs diner run by notable local seafood supplier. Great fish and seafood of course; some meat and vegetarian choice. Good ingredients and service. Dinner only Tue-Sat. LO 'depends'.

£15-22

Duncan's in Perth 01738 626016 · 33 George Street James Duncan's bistro-style restaurant: a local favourite in a long-established site and good value. Lunch & dinner. Closed Sun/Mon.

£15-22

The Bothy 01738 449792 · 33 Kinnoull Street A creation of Glasgow's expansive G1 group, this version of their Bothy in Glasgow's West End. Capitalising on the rediscovery of Scottish roots in cuisine, this appeals to Perth residents and passing tourists alike. Food and 'the look' are all designed in, including staff in kilts. Food till 10pm bar 11.30pm.

£15-22

Breizh 01738 444427 · 28 High Street Breizh, the Breton name for Brittany, is a buzzy and inexpensive eating-out choice. Galettes galore, salads, grillades, good pizza and some home-made puds. Good fun place. 7 days lunch & LO 9/9.30pm.

✓✓ **Deans @ Let's Eat** 01738 643377 898/PERTHSHIRE RESTAURANTS.

✓ **63 Tay Street** 01738 441451 899/PERTHSHIRE RESTAURANTS.

£15-22

Holdgate's Fish Teas South Street A classic for over 100 years!

Tourist Office 01738 636103 · Lower City Mills Open all year.

The Best Hotels & Restaurants In The North East

Excludes the city of Aberdeen (except Marcliffe); for Aberdeen see p. 179–80. Speyside listings on p. 183.

934 8/S19
42 ROOMS
TEL · TV
£85+

✓✓ **Marcliffe of Pitfodels** www.marcliffe.com · 01224 861000 · **North Deeside Road** En route to Royal Deeside 5km from Union St. On the edge of town, a successful mix of intimate and spacious, the old (mansion house) and the newer wing. Personally run by the Spence family: Stewart Spence the consummate hotelier. His many pics on the piano with the famous and political (both Margarets – the princess and the T) attest to this hotel's enduring primacy. 2 excellent restaurants, breakfast in light conservatory. Nice courtyard and terrace overlooking gardens. Hugely popular spa facilities but no pool. Honeymoon suites are fab and there are many weddings but this understated hotel (yah-boo to boutique) caters for all sorts, not only the great and good of Aberdeen. Unquestionably one of the best all-round hotels in Scotland; staying here always a pleasure.

935 8/Q20
12 ROOMS
FEB-DEC
TEL · TV
£85+

✓✓ **Darroch Learg** www.darrochlearg.co.uk · 01339 755443 · **Ballater** On main A93 at edge of town. The Franks maintain high standards at this Deeside mansion especially for food. With a relaxed ambience, old and understated style and an excellent conservatory dining room, it's a Deeside destination. Oft-awarded chef David Mutter has been there since '95 – a long time in chef world. Some great views of grounds (8 rooms at the front) and Grampian hills. No bar, but civilised drinks before and *après*. They also run the Station Restaurant in Ballater itself, part of the station which Queen Victoria made famous (she's still there on the platform!). Fairly basic grub there.

£32+

EAT Conservatory dining room still one of best restaurants in the North East. Great wine list. Nice garden view.

936 8/R20
20 ROOMS
+ SELF-
CATERING
TEL · TV
ATMOS
£85+

✓✓ **Raemoir House** www.raemoir.com · 01330 824884 · **Banchory** 5km north from town via A980 off main street. Mansion in the country just off the Deeside conveyor belt; quirky, romantic – it has something which sets it apart. Old-fashioned, very individual comfy rooms given contemporary details. Flowers everywhere, candles at night. Stable annex and self-catering apartments. Extensive grounds (helicopter pad). Owners David and Verity Webster who also have Castleton (879/PERTHSHIRE HOTELS) and no-nonsense chef Dougie Scobie ensure that dinner's a treat. There's lots of public space to slouch about in. Staff largely local. This place has the all-important serenity.

937 8/R19
27 ROOMS
TEL · TV
£85+

✓ **Pittodrie House** www.macdonaldhotels.co.uk · 01467 681444 · **Pitcaple** Large 'family' mansion house on estate in one of the best bits of Aberdeenshire with Bennachie above (1952/HILLS). 40km Aberdeen but 'only 30 minutes from airport' via A96. Follow signs off B9002. Lots of activities available on the estate, croquet lawn, billiards, many comfortable rooms. Exquisite walled garden 500m from house (937/GARDENS) and great walk around. A Macdonald hotel (and possibly their best) with very individual rooms in old house and a new extension out back. Nice pictures, great whisky bar. Many weddings!

938 8/Q20
6 ROOMS
TEL · TV
GF · DA
£45-60

✓ **The Auld Kirk** 01339 755762 · **Ballater** On Braemar road heading out of town. It is indeed an auld kirk and Peter Graydon and Tony Fuell make the most of the ecclesiastical shapes and ambience. Bedrooms (2 standards) are tasteful, contemporary boutique-style with a new suite up-top on the way at TGP. Growing reputation for dinner in purply-chandeliered vestry (closed Sun) and daytime coffee shop (a good one is welcome in Ballater).

939 8/T19
27 RMS · TV
TEL · NO PETS
£38-45
£22-32

Udny Arms 01358 789444 · Newburgh A975 off A92. Village pub famous for food and with some character needed serious TLC on last visit. So reports, please. Golf course Cruden Bay (2055/GREAT GOLF) 16km north and walks beside Ythan estuary (1750/WILDLIFE).
EAT Good grub in bar or dining room with plans to restore its former reputation at TGP. Lunch; LO 9.30pm. Once, it is said, Sticky Toffee Pudding was invented here.

940 8/Q20
45 ROOMS
TEL · TV
NO PETS
£85+

Hilton Craigendarroch www.hilton.co.uk/craigendarroch · 01339 755858 · **Ballater** On the Braemar road (A93). Part of a country-club/time-share operation with elegant dining, good leisure facilities and discreet resort-in-the-woods feel. 2 restaurants: an informal one by the pool (like a leisure-centre caff) and the self-conscious Oaks (Thu-Sun) – no Topshop tops, please. Lodges can be available on short lets, a good idea for a group holiday or weekend.

941 8/S18
22 ROOMS
(5 IN LODGE)
TEL · TV
£85+

Meldrum House www.meldrumhousegolf.co.uk · 01651 872294 · **Oldmeldrum** 1km from village, 30km north of Aberdeen via A947 Banff road. Immediately impressive and solid establishment – Scottish baronial style. Set amid new 18-hole golf course (private membership, but guests can use), landscaped and managed to high standard (great practice range). Rooms large with atmosphere and nice furnishing – many original antiques and pictures. New lodge adding 13 contemporary rooms for 2010 in stable block opposite. A lot of cash being spent here at TGP, so former cachet may be restored. Reports, please. Expect weddings.

942 8/S18
3 ROOMS
TEL · TV
£30-38

The Red Garth www.redgarth.com · 01651 872353 · **Oldmeldrum** There is a hotel in Oldmeldrum that has kept its act together over the years. This family-run inn (signed from main road system) only has 3 rooms but it's great value; bar meals are very popular locally. Nice flowers.

943 8/R18
18 ROOMS
TEL · TV
NO PETS
£45-60

Castle Hotel www.castlehotel.uk.com · 01466 792696 · **Huntly** Behind the spooky, eyeless ruin of Huntly Castle; approach from town through castle entrance and then over River Deveron up hugely impressive drive. Former dowager house of the Dukes of Gordon, family-run and not bad value for the grandeur/setting – tourists and business travellers keep it busy.

944 8/R19
12 ROOMS
TEL · TV
£38-45

Grant Arms www.grantarmshotel.com · 01467 651226 · **Monymusk** The village inn on a remarkable small square, a good centre for walking, close to the 'Castle Trail' (1776/CASTLES; 1833/COUNTRY HOUSES) and with fishing rights on the Don. Rooms in hotel and 6 chalets around a courtyard (old stables). Good ambience and decent grub in the pub.

RESTAURANTS

945
8/T18
£22-32

✓ ✓ **Eat On The Green** www.eatonthegreen.co.uk · 01651 842337 · **Udny Green, near Ellon** Former pub now restaurant on the green of a cute village in deepest Aberdeenshire. In fact, if one restaurant epitomised the region, this would be it – loved in its locale, folk come from miles around for this celebratory though unpretentious food that's great value. Chef/proprietor Craig Wilson and a great team are going places but they don't need to – we'll come to them! Book especially for a Sat night (prix fixe) out. Wed-Sun lunch, LO 9pm.

946 8/S20
£22-32

✓ **The (Art Deco) Carron Restaurant** www.carron-restaurant.co.uk · 01569 760460 · **20 Carron Street, Stonehaven** Discreet location off main street near the square. They use 'art deco' in the title, but you couldn't miss the reference in this fantastic period piece faithfully restored and embellished.

Lighting could be softer, but they don't make 'em like that any more. Chef/proprietor Robert Cleever, a Modern Scottish menu, and friendly and efficient service. Closed Sun/Mon.

947
8/S20
£15-22

✓ **Milton Restaurant** www.themilton.co.uk · 01330 844566 On main A93 Royal Deeside road 4km east of Banchory opposite the entrance to Crathes (1505/GARDENS; 1834/COUNTRY HOUSES). Roadside and surprisingly contemporary restaurant in old steading adjacent craft village of varying quality (not related). Light and exceedingly pleasant space. All-day menu from brunch to dinner so they cater for everything (and rather well). Mon-Sat 9.30am-9.30pm. Sun 10.30am-6pm. Can be awash with weddings.

948
8/Q20
£22-32

✓ **The Green Inn** www.green-inn.com · 01339 755701 · Victoria Road, Ballater Small frontage, surprisingly opens out at back. The O'Halloran family maintain the enduring reputation of this Deeside destination for dining. Understated and dependable. Book weekends. 3 inexpensive rooms upstairs. Dinner only Mon-Sat 7-9pm.

949
8/R20
£15-22

White Cottage www.whitecottage.eu · 01398 885757 · near Aboyne On the main A93 outside Aboyne from Aberdeen. John Inches' now long-standing roadside white cottage (conservatory attached) serving Modern British menu to loyal locals and travellers. Now calling itself a diner, reflected by the comfort-food staples on the all-home-made menu. All home made. Thu-Mon 11am-7pm and Sat dinner (may extend hours in season).

950
8/R17
£15 OR LESS/
£32+

The County Hotel www.thecountyhotel.com · 01261 815353 · Banff Francophile dining options in dear sleepy Banff. Bistro, restaurant and bar (lunches and bar suppers Mon-Sat). Dining menu has tartiflette, proper terrine and salade champêtre. There are burgers et al in the bar. Food here is quite a find (there's a letter from Alex Salmond saying how much he liked it).

✓ **Tolbooth** 01569 762287 · Stonehaven Excellent location on Stonehaven Harbour; gives great lobster. 1334/SEAFOOD RESTAURANTS.

✓ **Lairhillock Inn** www.lairhillock.co.uk · 01569 730001 · near Stonehaven 15km south of Aberdeen off A92. Excellent country pub and restaurant, good for kids. Report: 964/ABERDEEN RESTAURANTS; 1302/GASTROPUBS.

✓✓ **The Black-Faced Sheep** Aboyne Report: 1388/TEAROOMS.

✓ **The Creel Inn** Catterline Report: 1299/GASTROPUBS.

✓ **The Raemoir Garden Centre** Report: 2201/GARDEN CENTRES.

✓ **The Falls of Feugh** Banchory Report: 1394/TEAROOMS.

The Best Places To Stay In & Around Aberdeen

951 8/T19
80 ROOMS
TEL · TV
NO PETS
£85+

✓ **Malmaison** www.malmaison.com · 01224 327370 · 49 Queen's Road
On the main road west from Union St, the first major new hotel in Aberdeen for years. Usual design values of the brand here put to notably good use. Excellent, ambient and large brasserie with the Mal 'homegrown and local' menu. Espa spa, no pool. Rooms cosy and cool.

952 8/T19
7 ROOMS
TEL · TV
NO KIDS
NO PETS
£30-60

✓ **The Globe Inn** www.travelodge.co.uk · 01224 624258 · 15 Silver
Street Rooms above the Globe, the civilised pub in a street off Union St (1320/GASTROPUBS). Pub has good reputation for ales, food (and does live music Tue and weekends, so no early to bed). Accommodation is reasonably priced and very serviceable. Breakfast is continental and comes on a pre-packed tray with flasks – not a strong point. Since decent value and individuality are hard to find in Aberdeen, book ahead. Parking is cheap inside nearby square.

953 8/S20
40 ROOMS
TEL · TV
NO PETS
£60-85

Maryculter House Hotel www.maryculterhousehotel.com · 01224
732124 · Maryculter Out of town, 7km further on than Ardoe (below). Excellent setting on banks of Dee: riverside walks and an old graveyard and ruined chapel in the Priory. The hotel is on the site of a 13th-century preceptory. Newer annex; rooms overlook river. Poacher's Bar is special, dining room not though food has improved of late. At weekends this hotel is a wedding factory!

954 8/S20
110 ROOMS
TEL · TV
£85+

Ardoe House www.mercure-uk.com · 0870 194 2104 · Blairs 12km south-west of centre on South Deeside (possible to turn off the A92 from Stonehaven and the south at the first bridge and get to the hotel avoiding the city). The Dee is nearby on other side of road from hotel. A granite chunk of Scottish Baronial with few, but more individual (they call them 'feature') rooms and an annex where most rooms are feature-less but have pleasant country views. Restaurant so-so. Leisure facilities adjacent corporate but all-round, reliable business hotel.

955 8/T19
49 RMS · TEL
TV · NO PETS
£38-60

Carmelite www.carmelitehotels.com · 01224 589101 · Stirling Street
A boutique hotel. Very central in the quarter below Union St near the port. 3 types of room, all very 'modern'. Most have good light, including bathrooms. Suites themed: Japanese, antique, etc. Bar and restaurant. Not as smart as you might expect and they think they are.

956 8/T19
17 RMS · TEL
TV · NO PETS
£38-85

City Centre Hotel www.aberdeencitycentrehotel.co.uk · 01224 658406 ·
Belmont Street Beneath and part of the Vodka Bar in a busy street off Union St. Opened '09, an upmarket hotel (though not cheap) for urban sophisticates and whoever you meet in the night. Voddy-fuelled sessions await.

957 8/T19
77 ROOMS
TEL · TV
£60-85

Thistle Caledonian Hotel www.thistlehotels.com · 01224 640233 · Union
Terrace Victorian edifice, one of 3 Thistles in the city. Of several city centre hotels just off Union St, this always somehow seems the easiest to deal with; the most likely to be calm and efficient. Dining room and on-street bar/brasserie. Some nice suites overlooking the gardens.

958 8/T19
34 ROOMS
TEL · TV
NO PETS
£38-85

Atholl Hotel www.atholl-aberdeen.com · 01224 323505 · 54 King's Gate
On a busy road in west towards Hazelhead. An Aberdeen stalwart. I've never stayed, but many an Aberdonian would attest that this is the best among many mansions. The Atholl people say it's 'in a class of its own'. So they're proud of their reputation and this is a very good thing.

959 8/T19
65 ROOMS
TEL · TV
£30-60

The Brentwood Hotel www.brentwood-hotel.co.uk · 01224 595440 · **101 Crown Street** In an area of many hotels and guest houses to the south of Union St, this one's somewhat garish though flower-covered appearance belies a surprisingly commodious hostelry that is a better prospect than most. An adequate business hotel on a budget. Close to Union St and bars/restaurants. Bar meals in subterranean 'Carriages' recommended; the ale is real (8 on tap).

960 8/T19
155 ROOMS
TEL · TV
NO PETS
£38-45

Express by Holiday Inn www.hieaberdeen.co.uk · 01224 623500 · **Chapel Street** In the middle of West End nightlife zone. Chain, of course, but a better than average bedbox in a central location for, say, urban weekend breakers. Contemporary and convenient. You'd eat out (there's plenty to choose from) and there's the legendary all-night bakery opposite. Room price varies.

961 8/T19

Hostels SYHA www.syha.org.uk · **8 Queen's Road** On an arterial road to west. Grade 1 hostel 2km from centre (plenty buses). No café. Rooms mainly for 4-6 people. You can stay out late. Other hostels and self-catering flats c/o University, of which the best is the **Robert Gordon** (01224 262134). Campus in Old Aberdeen is good place to be though 2km city centre has university-halls accommodation (01224 272664). Both these vacation-times only.

✓ ✓ **Marcliffe of Pitfodels** www.marcliffe.com · 01224 861000 · **North Deeside Road** (en route to Royal Deeside 5km from Union St). Aberdeen's premiere hotel: nothing else is remotely close for comfort and service. Report: 934/NORTHEAST HOTELS.

The Best Places To Eat In Aberdeen

BISTROS & CAFÉ BARS

962 8/T19
ATMOS
£15-22

✓ **Café 52** www.cafe52.net · 01224 590094 · **52 The Green** Not easy for a non-Aberdonian to find but close to – below – east end of Union St. Go down steps or approach via Market St. You'd agree this place was 'a little bit different' and it has a boho, verging-on-chaotic buzz. A sliver of a cosy bistro with outside tables and a big presence in this slowly emerging quarter. Chef/owner Steve Bothwell keeps customers happy with unusual dishes but comforting combinations prevail. Busy at (good-value) lunch. Lunch and LO 9.30pm (bar 12midnight). 4.30pm Sun.

963 8/T19
£15-22

✓ **The Foyer** www.aberdeenfoyer.com · 01224 582277 · **82a Crown Street** Remarkable in that this busy, contemporary restaurant with good Modern British seasonal menu and great service is part of a local charity helping homeless and disadvantaged people. No hint of charity evident, but you can satisfy your conscience as well as your appetite in smart surroundings. Lunch onwards LO 10pm. Closed Sun/Mon. Foyer also have café-bar at His Majesty's Theatre (lunch and 5-7pm pre-theatre menu; later on theatre nights).

964 8/T19
ATMOS
£15-22/
£22-32

✓ **The Lairhillock Inn** www.lairhillock.co.uk · 01569 730001 Not in the city at all, but a roadside inn at a country crossroads to the south, reached from either the road to Stonehaven or the South Deeside Rd west. Easiest is: head south on main A92, turn off at Durris then 5km. Famous for pub food (1302/GAS-TROPUBS) and informal atmosphere in conservatory and bar. Newish owners have restored most of former reputation. Restaurant adjacent, **Crynoch**, has more ambitious menu, excellent cheeseboard and malt selection. Restaurant: dinner & Sun lunch. Closed Mon. LO 9pm. Inn: 7 days lunch & LO 9pm (10pm Fri/Sat).

965 8/T19
ATMOS
£15-22

✓ **Le Café Bohème** 01224 210677 · Windmill Brae Authentic French bistro, atmosphere and food behind a discreet frontage in an area that gets drunk at weekends. Here all is calm with style and good service. Food proper French, à la carte and plats du jour. Best place to eat by far in this part of the city centre. Lunch and LO 9pm. Closed Sun/Mon.

966 8/T19
£15-22

✓ **Olive Tree** 01224 208877 · 32 Queens Road Off-centre but a significant part of smart dining in the Granite City. From the start Mike Reilly certainly made sure it had the look and the good management, and nothing much has changed. Fine dining bistro and **Black Olive** brasserie in conservatory annex. Tangible difference in offering – brazz very pleasant and affordable, restaurant, a good restaurant. Service and presentation tip-top in both. The Olive Branch adjacent is curiously more Spar than special. Mon-Sat Lunch & LO 10pm, Black Olive till 11pm.

967 8/S19
ATMOS
£15-22

✓ **The Broadstraik Inn** www.broadstraikinn.co.uk · 01224 743217 · Elrick Not in the city but on the main A944 to Alford at Elrick near Westhill, about 12km city centre. Roadside pub since 1905 now gastrofied and civilised by Jackie Spence and Chris Wills. Growing reputation for good food and smart service; well worth the drive (1296/GASTROPUBS). 7 days lunch, LO 8.45pm.

968 8/T19
£15-22

The Square www.1thesquare.com · 01224 646362 · 1 Golden Square Enter by South Silver St off Union St near Music Hall. Long-established restaurant in a spacious, modern room, contemporary menu, friendly service and relaxing ambience. Lunch and dinner LO 10/11pm. Closed Sun.

969 8/T19
£15-22

Howie's www.howies.uk.com · 01224 639500 · 50 Chapel Street Follows successful formula made in Edinburgh in classic/contemporary bistro style, this discreetly fronted restaurant presses all the right Aberdonian buttons (yes, including the price!). Along with The Square (above), it is reliable. 7 days, lunch and LO 10pm.

970 8/T19
£15-22

Bistro Verde 01224 586180 · The Green Down steps from east end of Union St and opposite Café 52 (above). Hard to find in a car but 'off Market St'. Unpretentious, mainly fish restaurant with blackboard daily catch. Nice, friendly place. Lunch and LO 10pm. Closed Sun/Mon.

971 8/T19
£15 OR LESS

Food Story 01224 622293 · 22 Rose Street Central café/takeaway with artisan, ethical approach and well-sourced produce. Daytime only; they also do outside catering. Hours vary but early-6pm (5pm Sat, 4.30pm Sun).

972 8/T19
£15 OR LESS

Beautiful Mountain www.thebeautifulmountain.com · 01224 645353 · 11 Belmont Street In an area of many eateries, this unpretentious caff stands out. Takeaway and tables jammed together in 2 rooms upstairs. Great combos and ingredients – just better and probably healthier! LO 4.30pm. Closed Sun.

973 8/T19
ATMOS
£15-22

✓ **The Victoria** 01224 621381 · Upstairs at 140 Union Street Not a bistro or café-bar as such, more a luncheon- and tearoom, but too good not to include here. Excellent as always on a recent visit. Same staircase and foyer as adjacent jewellery-and-gift emporium so an odd alliance. Great light menu, everything home- and terribly well-made including the bread and the biscuits and in July (actually all year), a lemonade. Soup and Eve's Pudding for a song – perfect! Gillian and Gordon Harold keeping Aberdeen happy and well fed. 9am-5pm (6.30pm Thu). Closed Sun.

SEAFOOD

974 8/T19
£32+
ATMOS

✓ **Silver Darling** www.silverdarling.co.uk · 01224 576229 · **Pocra Quay**
Didier Dejean still on the stoves in this exemplary seafood bistro in a perfect spot. Not so easy to find – head for Beach Esplanade, the lighthouse and harbour mouth (Pocra Quay). The light winks and ghostly boats glide past. Upstairs dining room not large (best to book) and you so want to be by the window. Different menu for lunch and dinner, depends on the catch and season. Apposite wines, wicked desserts. Some may say the Silver Darling has lost its sheen but this is still the best and most dynamic location of any seafood restaurant in the land. Mon-Fri lunch, Mon-Sat dinner 7-9.30pm (but always phone first to check times).

975 8/T19
£22-32

✓ **Atlantis at the Mariner Hotel** www.themarinerhotel.co.uk · 01224 591403 · **349 Great Western Road** Those that know where to go in Aberdeen for excellent fish and seafood may not necessarily go to Silver Darling, but come here off centre and in a hotel but always busy. Hotel dining room atmosphere is not too evident (tables in conservatory) and the fish very good. Bar menu also available. Moderately priced wines. Lunch (not Sat) and dinner LO 9pm.

ITALIAN

976 8/T19
£15-22

Rustico 01224 658444 · **Corner of Union Row & Summer Street** 50m from Union St. If this were French I'd say it had the *je ne sais quoi*, but it is most definitely Italian (Sicilian actually). Tony and Niko's love for Sicily evident (their brill photos on the walls) though Niko is Greek. And the food is well above the tratt average: everything home made, including the puds. As good a tratt as you'll find. Lunch and LO 10pm. Closed Sun lunch.

977 8/T19
£15 OR LESS

Carmine's Pizza 01224 624145 · **32 Union Terrace** This tiny slice of a room for *the* best pizza in town and behind, slaving over a hot stove, the eponymous, much-loved but often quite grumpy chef. Take away (to the Gardens opposite). Real authentic pasta in basic spag/tag and penne variants. Lunch and 4.30-6.45pm. Closed Sun.

EASTERN

978 8/T19
£22-32

✓ **Yatai** www.yatai.co.uk · 01224 591403 · **75 Skene Street** Round the corner from the end of Union Terrace. Surprisingly authentic and sympatico Japanese diner by friendly, quite big Aberdonian boys who fill up their tiny kitchen. Most tables upstairs. Varied menu means you don't have to eat raw fish; dishes come when they're ready. Daily specials best. Go carefully on those slippy floors. Yatai was Oriental Restaurant of the Year at the Scottish Restaurant Awards '09. Lunch Tue/Wed/Fri/Sat. LO 10pm. Closed Mon.

979 8/T19
£15-22

Jewel In The Crown www.thejewelinthecrown.com · 01224 210288 · **145 Crown Street** Way down the street on corner with Affleck. Great North Indian food all home made and authentic. Possibly the best curry in town – always arguments about that, natch, though not from the 4 sons of Farooq Ahmed who work like a football team to make this place a top spot. Lunch and LO 11pm. 7 days.

980 8/T19
£22-32

Nargile www.nargile.co.uk · 01224 636093 · **77 Skene Street** Turkish survivor that has made its regulars happy for over 20 years. Turkish owner, who also spawned the **Meze Café** at 3 Rose St (great takeaway and open very late ie 3/4am). Reliable meze, kebabs, swordfish, etc and good puds. Lunch Fri/Sat. Dinner only LO 11pm. Closed Sun.

Hammerton Stores 1444/GOOD DELIS.
The Globe 1320/GASTROPUBS.

The Best Hotels & Restaurants In Speyside

981
8/Q18
25 ROOMS
TEL · TV
NO PETS
£60-85

✓ **Craigellachie Hotel** www.craigellachie.com · 01340 881204 · **Craigellachie** The quintessential Speyside hotel, off A941 Elgin to Perth may be trading a little on former glory. Especially good for fishing, but well placed for walking (Speyside Way runs along bottom of garden; see 1975/LONG WALKS) and distillery visits (1484/WHISKY). Rooms ok – you want one of the Master Rooms that overlook the river. The food is well regarded and the Quaich bar could keep a whisky lover amused for years: probably one of Scotland's best places for a dram.

982
8/Q18
5 ROOMS
TEL · TV
£45-60

✓ **The Mash Tun** 01340 881771 · **8 Broomfield Square, Aberlour** Off main street behind the church by lovely river meadow park. A restaurant/pub with rooms above (all named after whiskies). They call themselves a whisky bar and this is a very Malt Trail destination that's boutique standard and informal and better value than most. Pub has nice ambience and good grub. LO 9pm.

983
8/N19
12 ROOMS
TEL · TV
£60-85

Muckrach Lodge 01479 851257 · **Dulnain Bridge** Off Carrbridge road out of Dulnain Bridge which is off A95 Aviemore-Grantown road. Country manor presiding over bucolic demesne to the river. Andy Picheta and Rebecca Ferrand's labour of country-house love on Speyside. Refurbishment (as always) ongoing, so 'done' rooms are best. Nice bar leading on to deck terrace, and conservatory restaurant.

984 8/N19
23 ROOMS
TEL · TV
NO PETS
£60-85

Eight Acres Hotel www.crerarhotels.com · 01343 548811 · **Elgin** Formerly the Mansion House, now with a small, mainly Scottish chain. Sits discreetly under the monument to the last Duke of Gordon and near the big Tesco store. Comfortable and elegant mansion house in a comfortable and gentle town with leisure facilities, including small pool/gym and drop-in (very small) bistro. Nice dining room (the Papillon Restaurant – not tried).

985 8/Q18
16 ROOMS
TEL · TV
£38-45

Dowan's Hotel www.dowanshotel.com · 01340 871488 · **Aberlour** Above river and charming town signed off the A85 from Grantown. Solid mansion and solid Speyside hospitality though oddly you approach from the back. Inside all is pleasant and comfortable and there are 150 malts in the bar. Fishermen-friendly and inexpensive.

986
8/P18
11 ROOMS
TEL · TV
£45-60

Archiestown Hotel www.archiestownhotel.co.uk · 0870 950 6282 · **Archiestown** Main street of small village in heart of Speyside near Cardhu Distillery (1490/WHISKY). A village inn/hotel with comfortable rooms and decent food in a pleasant bistro setting (LO 8.30pm). Fishers and people who don't mind a bit of attitude from the hosts. Locals stay away but others do recommend.

RESTAURANTS

987
8/Q18
£15-22

La Faisanderie 01340 821273 · **Dufftown** The Whisky Trail with Eric Obry's French twist. A small Franco-Scots affair, corner of The Square and Balvenie St, near the steeple. A welcome departure for these parts – and well known as *the place* to eat. Lunch and dinner daily LO 8.30pm (winter hours may vary).

988
8/Q18
£15 OR LESS

Glenfiddich Restaurant 01340 820363 · **Church Street, Dufftown** Near the town clock. Enough to send a modern Scot gibbering into his Irn Bru cocktail, others may be in unreconstructed heaven. This is the complete opposite of La Faisanderie above. Although they say 'award-winning', the food is fairly ghastly but this is as camp as the Black Watch on manoeuvres. Packed with paraphernalia and yes, happy punters. 7 days (LO 9pm, winter hours vary).

The Best Hotels & Restaurants In The Highlands

See also Inverness, p. 195–97; Skye, p. 382 and 387; Outer Hebrides, p. 395.

989
9/K21
17 ROOMS
TV
ATMOS
£85+

✓✓ **Inverlochy Castle** www.inverlochycastlehotel.com · 01397 702177 · **Fort William** 5km from town on A82 Inverness road, Scotland's flagship Highland hotel filled with sumptuous furnishings, elegant decor and occasional film stars, luminaries and royalty. Owner Mr Chai insists on old-style hospitality. As you sit in the atrium after dinner – perhaps with someone tinkling the piano – marvelling at the ceiling and stylish people swish up and down the staircase, you know this is no ordinary country-house hotel. And it has all you expect of a 'castle'; the epitome of grandeur and service. Huge comfortable bedrooms, the antlered billiard room, acres of rhododendrons, trout in the lake, tennis and a lovely terrace. The big Ben is over there.
EAT This dining destination is open to non residents. Philip Carnegie 6 years on these sacred stoves. Jacket and tie for dinner.

990
7/H16
5 ROOMS
TEL · TV
NO KIDS
ATMOS
£85+

✓✓ **Pool House Hotel** www.poolhousehotel.com · 01445 781272 · **Poolewe** Formerly owned by Osgood MacKenzie who founded the gardens up the road (1504/GARDENS). The Harrisons have transformed with immaculate style and sheer determination this Highland home into one of the must-do stopovers in the land. Their dream of creating something truly special has been materialising over years and still it doesn't stop. For 2010/11 they've introduced a new BBQ pavilion in the ornamental and kitchen garden on the lochside. Guests can take boat trips and then cook their catch. The restaurant will do dinners weekends only (but check). The bar/snooker room has excellent malt selection. There are only 5 but all fabulously themed suites, including new 'Indian' single suite with amazing bed, and the Boathouse overlooking the river mouth and out to the bay. Late '10 there will be a dog-friendly cottage in the garden. Rooms are meticulously assembled and hand-painted by daughter Liz. Bathrooms are simply fabulous. This has been a labour of love for the whole family and for this standard, is great value. They close Mon. See also 70/PLACES WE SHOULD LOVE MORE.

991
8/N17
9 ROOMS
(2 SUITES)
TEL · TV
£85+

✓✓ **The Boath House** www.boath-house.com · 01667 454896 · **Auldearn** Signed from the main A96 3km east of Nairn. A small country-house hotel in a classic and immaculately restored mansion – Don and Wendy Matheson's family home with serene grassy grounds, got a much-deserved Michelin star '09. Comfy public rooms with local artists' pics. Bedrooms (3 woodland, 2 lake, 2 downstairs with their own conservatory and a cottage over-by) are home from home with great bathrooms. 6-course (no choice, so declare diet first) dinner simply delicious, much of it foraged and farmed nearby. Chef Charlie Lockley is at the top of his game. Service impeccable; friendly and local. Delightful grounds with walled garden from whence your salad, a lake where deer come to drink and a big heron waits motionless for its dinner; you watch while having yours. Beautiful Brodie nearby (1701/CASTLES).
EAT Mr Lockley: intuitive, great judgement, Michelin-starred and 4 AA rosettes. Cooking: organic, slow and from the kitchen garden. Set menu.

992
6/J14
7 ROOMS
MAR–DEC
TEL · TV
NO KIDS

✓✓ **The Albannach** www.thealbannach.co.uk · 01571 844407 · **Lochinver** 2km up road to Baddidarach as you come into Lochinver on the A837 at the bridge. Lesley and Colin's uniquely beautiful boutique hotel in the north: ancient splendid landscape around you, contemporary splendid comfort to return to. The steading suite overlooks 'the Croft' from its own conservatory and hot tub. 'The Penthouse' has its own terrace. Though Lesley (with Colin on puds) has been turning out a wonderful 5-course fixed (so declare diets and fads up front) for years, it wasn't till '09 that the Albannach got its Michelin star. The very good news is that there's 9 tables so non-residents can dine. Lochinver got lucky! Suilven over there from a relatively midge-free terrace.

EAT When in far-flung Assynt, you really *must* eat at the Albannach.

✓✓ **Rocpool Reserve** www.rocpool.com · 01463 240089 · Culduthel Road, Inverness Above the town and above all that (ordinary stuff), a determinably urbane hotel now owned by the people who have Inverlochy (above). Though look and feel are poles apart, service is similarly top. Room categories somewhat offputting (1057/INVERNESS HOTELS) but exceed expectations.

EAT Albert Roux's only restaurant north of the border – simple French food brilliantly done for a fraction of what you'd pay in London.

✓✓ **Glenmoriston Townhouse** www.glenmoristontownhouse.com · 01463 223777 · 20 Nessbank, Inverness Along riverside opposite Eden Court Theatre. No expense spared in the conversion of this long-reputed hotel (and the one next door) into a chic boutique and very urban hotel in the ascendant city of Inverness. Rooms split 50/50 between main hotel and adjacent Windsor House, the latter refurbished to urban-chic standard; with rooms overlooking the river, the old building is more traditional. Piano bar, top restaurant – Abstract – and bistro/brasserie, Contrast where breakfast is served, so more convenient when staying above. All in all a smart, well-oiled operation.

EAT Abstract could be NY or London or Edinburgh (where it is actually: 127/BEST EDINBURGH RESTAURANTS). Great staff (mainly French), excellent wine lists and malts. Contrast buzzier and more casual. Summer BBQs.

✓✓ **Culloden House** www.cullodenhouse.co.uk · 01463 790461 · Inverness 5km east of town near A9, follow signs for Culloden village, not the battlefield. Easiest approach from A96 Nairn road, turn right at first roundabout after the mall. Hugely impressive Georgian mansion and lawn a big green duvet on edge of suburbia and, of course, history. Near town and airport. Demonstrates that sometimes old-style is the best style. Lovely big bedrooms overlooking the policies. Some fab suites in separate garden house. Elegant dining in beautifully conserved room under chef Michael Simpson. The mansion is adjacent to an emerging and restored 4-acre walled garden, a major project to be completed 2010. Fabulous trees including redwoods, tennis courts. A very civilised experience courtesy of Culloden's caring American owners.

✓ **The Cross** www.thecross.co.uk · 01540 661166 · Kingussie Off main street at traffic lights 200m uphill then left into glen. Tasteful hotel and superb restaurant in converted tweed mill by the river which gurgles outside most windows. Comfy rooms refurbishing and de-pining at TGP. David and Katie Young, considerate hosts, will help you get the most from the wonderful area around.

✓✓ EAT Deal probably includes dinner which is so what you want. But also open to non-residents for what is after all these years still the best restaurant in the region. 2 choices each course. David and long-standing Beca still on stoves. Fabulous wine list! Closed most Sun/Mon.

✓ **Dower House** www.thedowerhouse.co.uk · 01463 870090 · near Muir Of Ord On A862 between Beauly and Dingwall, 18km northwest of Inverness and 2km north of village after the railway bridge. Charming, personal place; you are the house guest of Robyn (in the kitchen) and Mena Aitchison, your consummate hosts. Cottagey-style, lived-in, small country house, with comfy public rooms and lovely garden with pond for G&T moments.

£22-32   **EAT** Robyn Aitchison's cooking: simple and sophisticated. Fixed menu. They do a packed lunch if you're going fishing.

998
7/L18
7 ROOMS
+5 COTTAGES
TEL · TV
£85+

✓ **Loch Ness Lodge** www.loch-ness-lodge.com · 01456 459469 · near **Abriachan** On the A82, 18km south of Inverness by the Clansman Hotel which you can't miss on the road. The Lodge is set back above the road and loch, a surprising new build and labour of love of the Sutherland family – siblings Scott and Iona. A top stopover and especially for exclusive use, well out of the tourist tide that washes down to Drumnadrochit. Comfortable and all things considered. Spa and hot tubs. Fine dining with fixed menu from chef Ross Fraser (haven't tried at TGP). Your lodging on the loch (also self-catering cottages).

999
7/M18
11 ROOMS
+2 COTTAGES
TEL · TV · DA
£60-85

✓ **Dunain Par Hotel** www.dunainparkhotel.co.uk · 01463 230512 · **Inverness** 6km southwest of town on A82 Fort William road. Mansion-house just off the road, a lived-in, civilised and old-style alternative to hotels in town for those on business or pleasure. Some good deals out of season. Gorgeous gardens; real countryside beyond. Notable restaurant in various cosy dining rooms with sound Scottish menu. Excellent wine and malt list. Enviro-friendly garden where the cottages are and your contemplations come.

1000
7/N16
6 ROOMS
+3 COTTAGES
TEL · NO PETS
£85+

✓ **Glenmorangie House at Cadboll** www.theglenmorangiehouse.com · 01862 871671 · near **Fearn** South of Tain 10km east of A9. Old mansion in open grounds overlooking a distant sea. Owned, like the distillery, by Louis Vuitton Moët Hennessy so expect some luxury (understated in public areas but all-embracing in bedrooms after a £300k refurbishment). No leisure facilities but no shortage of distraction around (the 'seaboard villages', the dolphins, Anta/Tain Pottery; 2159/2160/SHOPPING). Open fires and communal, house-party atmosphere. Fixed dinner round one table, honesty bar, great service.

1001
6/J15
15 ROOMS
APR-OCT
TEL
NO KIDS · DA
£60-85

✓ **The Summer Isles Hotel** www.summerisleshotel.co.uk · 01854 622282 · **Achiltibuie** 40km from Ullapool with views over the isles; Stac Polly and Suilven are close by to climb. A long-established romantic retreat on the strand at Achiltibuie, it recently changed hands but enchantment remains as do the Michelin-star dinners with chef Chris Firth-Bernard. Adjacent pub offers similar quality food at half the price (1291/GASTROPUBS). 2 great suites, 11 rooms in the house and William's, a fab crofter's cottage on the hill. Lots to do outdoors including nearby boat trips and don't miss one (or two) of the great views of Scotland nearby (1651/VIEWS).
EAT Formal dining: don't be late! Fixed (truly individual) menu, trolleys of puds and cheese: the big moment. Sunsets. Bar menu is great value.

1002
6/N15
22 ROOMS
TEL · TV
£60-85

✓ **Royal Marine Hotel** www.royalmarinehotel.co.uk · 01408 621252 · **Golf Road, Brora** Turn-of-the-century mansion house by Robert Lorimer overlooking the harbour below and self-catering apartment block newly built overlooking the golf course. Ambition to be on par with great golf hotels elsewhere. Contemporary public rooms; bedrooms vary. Spa has good pool. Restaurant in dining room, Lorimer's, and bar have similar menus and complementary atmosphere.

1003
6/P12
14 ROOMS
TEL · TV
£45-60

✓ **Forss House Hotel** www.forsshousehotel.co.uk · 01847 861201 · near **Thurso** 8km west on A836. The Richards' welcoming Georgian mansion house set in 20 (rare in these parts) woodland acres by the meandering River Forss is the best hotel in Scotland's north-east corner. Popular restaurant (you should book), nearly 300 malts in the bar, comfortable spacious rooms and 6 additional rooms in cottages in the grounds. Breakfast in the conservatory then walks: there's an old mill and a waterfall. Fishing is big here.

1004
9/J22
20 ROOMS
TEL · TV
£60-85

✓ **Holly Tree** www.hollytreehotel.co.uk · 01631 740292 · **Kentallen** On A828 Fort William (Ballachulish)–Oban road, 8km south of Ballachulish Bridge. On road and sea and once the railway; it was formerly a station. Convenient location and superb setting on Loch Linnhe with fab views from bedrooms and dining room. Appropriate location for surf 'n' turf menu. Nice for kids. New pool and the jetty on the sea outside. 1132/HOTELS THAT WELCOME KIDS.

1005
7/L17
21 ROOMS
TEL · TV
DA
£45-60

✓ **Coul House Contin** www.coulhousehotel.com · 01997 421487 · **near Strathpeffer** Comfortable country-house hotel on the edge of the wilds with some lovely public rooms recently refurbished with all elegance intact (especially the octagonal dining room). Well-kept lawns with new bog garden and duck pond. An accessible, not-too-posh country-house retreat. Varied menu: à la carte and specials under chef Garry More. Good vegetarian choice. Well-priced wines. All great value.

1006
7/M18
16 ROOMS
TEL · TV
£85+

Bunchrew House www.bunchrew-inverness.co.uk · 01463 234917 · **near Inverness** On A862 Beauly road only 5km from Inverness yet completely removed from town; on the wooded shore of the Beauly Firth. Almost completely positioned as a wedding hotel, but midweek stays possible. An atmospheric place.

1007
7/N17
44 ROOMS
TEL · TV
£45-60

Golf View www.golfviewhotelnairn.co.uk · 01667 452301 · **Nairn** Seafront on Inverness side of town. Not so much golf, more beach view but near the famous course (2056/GREAT GOLF). Well appointed, refurbished rooms with conservatory restaurant and leisure facilities including good pool for kids and tennis courts. Some dreamy views of the sea.

1008
9/J21
27 ROOMS
TEL · TV
£45-60

Onich Hotel www.onich-fortwilliam.co.uk · 01855 821214 · **Onich by Fort William** 16km south on main A82, one of many roadside and in this case, lochside hotels which are an alternative to taking your chances in Fort William. Onich is good value with good public space; some bedrooms overlook Loch Linnhe. Busy bars, grassy terrace and nice garden to beach.

✓ ✓ **The Torridon** www.lochtorridonhotel.com · 01445 791242 · **Loch Torridon, near Kinlochewe** At the end of Glen Torridon in immense scenery. Highland Lodge atmosphere, big hills to climb. Now with adjacent **Torridon Inn** (inexpensive, with bar and bistro). Report: 1183/GET-AWAY HOTELS.

✓ ✓ **Ackergill Tower** 01955 603556 · **near Wick** Report: 1250/HOUSE PARTIES.

✓ ✓ **House Over-By** 01470 571258 · **Skye** Report: 2221/SKYE HOTELS.

✓ **Eilean Iarmain** 01470 833332 · **Skye** Report: 2223/SKYE HOTELS.

✓ **Kinloch Lodge** 01470 833333 · **Skye** Report: 2222/SKYE HOTELS.

✓ **Scarista House** 01859 550238 · **South Harris** Report: 2237/ISLAND HOTELS.

Best Less Expensive Highland Hotels

1009
6/K15
13 ROOMS
+ BUNKS
TEL
ATMOS
£60-85

The Ceilidh Place www.ceilidhplace.com · 01854 612103 · Ullapool 'Books, Music, Art' and Life: Jean Urquhart's oasis of hospitality, craic and culture in the Highlands. What started out in the 1970s as a coffee/exhibition shop in a boat shed, spread along the row of cottages and now comprises a restaurant, bookshop, café/bar (and performance) area with bedrooms upstairs. Bar and restaurant go all day from famously good breakfast to dinner menu from 6.30pm (LO 9pm). Always convivial and great, friendly service. Bunkhouse across the road offers cheaper accommodation: stay 'luxuriously rough'. Live music and events through the year (check the website), or you can simply sit in the lounge upstairs with honesty bar or on the terrace overlooking Ullapool where the boats come in.

£22-32

EAT Bar and restaurant areas in one big, happy room. All-day menu till 6.30pm then supper. Puts the craic into casual dining.

1010 6/L12
7 ROOMS
APR-OCT
TV
NO PETS
£38-45

Mackay's www.visitmackays.com · 01971 511202 · Durness Gloriously remote but actually in the centre of a straggled-out township. Small (7 rooms, 8 tables) but perfectly conceived and formed hotel at the corner of north-west Scotland (literally where the road turns south again). In the Mackay family for generations. Fiona and Robbie have transformed this solid old house into the coolest spot in this northern hemisphere where in summer the light lingers forever. Wood and slate. Discreet but efficient service. Comfy beds. No bar but all-day food; LO 9pm. Many interesting distractions nearby (2080/ GOLF, 1843/MONUMENTS, Smoo Cave, etc). They got it just right.

1011 5/M20
5 ROOMS
TV
£30-45

Coig na Shee www.coignashee.co.uk · 01540 670109 · Newtonmore Road out of Newtonmore (which is just off the A9) for Fort William. Mansion house with light, contemporary feel and furnishings. B&B only – nice breakfast, though dinner also by request (and Blasta in the village is very good – 1049/BEST HIGHLAND RESTAURANTS). Friendly proprietors. Exceptional value.

1012 6/N16
3 RMS · TEL
TV · NO PETS
£38-45

2 Quail www.2quail.com · 01862 811811 · Castle Street, Dornoch As you arrive from south. For a long time a pre-eminent destination in the region, especially for the restaurant which is no more. The rooms above and the breakfast, however, remain, and Kerensa Carr will make you very comfortable and welcome.

1013
9/J20
13 ROOMS
MAR-NOV
ATMOS
£38-85

Glenfinnan House Hotel www.glenfinnanhouse.com · 01397 722235 · Glenfinnan Victorian mansion with lawns down to Loch Shiel and the Glenfinnan Monument over the water. No shortbread-tin twee or tartan carpet here; instead a warm welcome from the MacFarlanes and managers the Gibsons. And everything just gets better here. Refurbished bar has not lost its great atmosphere. A cruise on this stunning loch (01687 470322) or row boat at the foot of the lawn! Great for kids. 1226/SCOTTISH HOTELS.

1014
7/L19
30 ROOMS
TEL · TV
£45-60

Lovat Arms 0845 450 1100 · Fort Augustus On edge of town, the road south to Fort William. Refurbished by the family of the people who brought us Torridon (1183/GET-AWAY HOTELS), into a contemporary, comfortable roadside hotel, unquestionably the best hotel hereabouts. Brasserie menu and lovely, light dining rooms for table d'hôte and breakfast. Good looks and smart service in the heart of the Great Glen.

1015
9/K20
4 ROOMS
MAR-OCT
TV · NO PETS
£30-38

✓**Corriechoille Lodge** www.corriechoille.com · 01397 712002 · by Spean Bridge 4 (riverside) km out of Spean Bridge on the small road by the station. Justin and Lucy Swabey's hideaway house facing the mountains. Beautiful corner of the country with spectacular views towards the Grey Corries and Aonach Mor. Lovely set dinner, cosy rooms. (No kids under 7 years.) 2 turf-roofed self-catering chalets over by. Great walks begin here. Also 1192/GET-AWAY HOTELS.

1016 7/L18
12 ROOMS
NO PETS
£38-45

✓**The Loch Ness Inn** 01456 450991 · Lewiston by Drumnadrochit Just off the A82 1km from the monster mash of Drumnadrochit. A functional roadhouse hotel, quite the best in the area and with a notable restaurant that's invariably full. The estimable Judy Fish from the Applecross Inn, 1190/GETAWAY HOTELS, has a hand in this.
EAT Lewiston Restaurant, the best meal on the long road between Inverness and Fort Augustus, but may have to book.

1017 9/K21
9 ROOMS
£45-60

✓**Lime Tree Studios** 01397 701806 · Achintore Road, Fort William At the roundabout as you come from the south. Regional and local art gallery with rooms above and a good restaurant that fills all the gaps in Fort William. Simple, contemporary, convivial atmosphere in tasteful public rooms of the Old Manse.

1018 7/H17
11 ROOMS
APR-OCT
DA
£60-85

✓**Tigh-an-Eilean** 01520 755251 · Shieldaig Lovely, cosily furnished hotel on waterfront overlooks Scots Pine island on loch. The Fields run a pleasant house and now the adjacent Coastal Kitchen, the pub transformed with upstairs bistro and deck overlooking the loch. Some live music. An all-round cool spot at the heart of a Highland village.

1019 6/P15
19 ROOMS
TEL · TV
£38-45

✓**Bridge Hotel** 01431 821100 · Dunrobin Street, Helmsdale End of the main street and along from the Mirage (1045/BEST HIGHLAND RESTAURANTS) in this historic and atmospheric village which coyly reveals its considerable charm when you look (67/PLACES WE SHOULD LOVE MORE). Overlooking the bridge, glen and sentinel church, this hotel is surprisingly commodious. Animals, art and science everywhere – antlertastic (there are more deer here than in your average glen). Conscientious management and good service. Spacious public rooms, a cosy bar. Lots of game on an ambitious menu (venison their speciality). Nice jams for breakfast.

1020 9/K20
8 ROOMS
TEL · TV
£45-60

✓**Old Pines** www.oldpines.co.uk · 01397 712324 · near Spean Bridge 3km Spean Bridge via B8004 for Garlochy at Commando Monument. Open-plan pine cabin with log fires, neat bedrooms and a huge polytunnel (where bits of your dinner come from). A very comfy, unpretentious hotel with great food; à la carte menu open to non-residents. And see 1130/HOTELS THAT WELCOME KIDS.

1021 7/K20
26 ROOMS
MAR-NOV
TEL · TV
£45-60

Glengarry Castle www.glengarry.net · 01809 501254 · Invergarry A family-run hotel in the Highlands for almost 50 years, in the charge of the younger MacCallums. Rhodies, honeysuckle as you walk to the loch. Magnificent trees and a ruined castle in the grounds the stronghold of the Macdonells: you may remember the famous portrait by Raeburn – the epitome of the fashionable Highland chief. Romantic destination in every way. Big rooms.

1022 7/H18
14/15
ROOMS
TEL · TV
£38-60

The Plockton Inn www.plocktoninn.co.uk · 01599 544222 · Plockton
The Plockton Hotel www.plocktonhotel.co.uk · 01599 544274 · Plockton
Two possible stays in perfect Plockton (1555/COASTAL VILLAGES). The village is why we come. The inn is away from the front. Some good cask ale in bar. Very basic rooms. 7 rooms in hotel and 7 in more contemporary annex over the street. Bistro: mainly seafood. Tables on terrace in summer, back garden for kids. The Plockton Hotel is by the water's edge and is busier and buzzier. Pub and pub meals seem always packed. May be noisy weekends.

1023
8/N19
32 ROOMS
TEL · TV
£38-45

Boat Hotel www.boathotel.co.uk · 01479 831258 · Boat of Garten Centre of village overlooking the steam train line and near golf course (2070/GOOD GOLF). Great old-style (Victorian/1920s) hotel in rolling refurbishment so rooms vary (you want the deluxe). There are also 6 chalet-type garden rooms: ok and quiet. Decent restaurant, the Capercaillie, a bar locals use and a hotel bar with bar food.

1024 6/N16
24 ROOMS
TEL · TV
£45-85+

Dornoch Castle Hotel 01862 810216 · Dornoch Main street of delightful northern town with nice beaches, great golf and a cathedral made famous by the new Madonna (rather than the original). Very castle-like (from 15th century), up-and-down building where rooms vary hugely, as do prices. Garden Restaurant (yes, on the garden) is thought well of for food though I'm not so sure: reports, please!

1025 6/M13
19 ROOMS
TEL · TV
£45-60

Tongue Hotel www.tonguehotel.co.uk · 01847 611206 · Tongue One of 2 hotels in Tongue at the centre of the north coast where Ben Loyal rises. This the most presentable though a little more expensive. Nicely turned-out rooms. Lounge bar and dining room. Very Highland. The Brass Tap pub downstairs has a good Highland atmosphere.

1026 7/M17
9 ROOMS
TV
£38-45

The Anderson www.theanderson.co.uk · 01381 620236 · Fortrose Main street of town in the middle of the Black Isle. Restaurant, bar and reasonable rooms in very individual hotel notable for an extraordinary bottled ales and whisky collection and then the grub. Rooms have a certain boho and well-chosen charm. US owners diligent in their pursuit of approvals. They have mine.
EAT Joanna Blythman gave them $9/_{10}$ and you really can't do better than that. Anne Anderson manages a long, interesting and daily-changing menu.

1027 7/K18
8 ROOMS
TEL · TV
£45-60

Tomich Hotel www.tomichhotel.co.uk · 01456 415399 · Tomich, near **Drumnadrochit** The inn of a quiet conservation village, part of an old estate on the edge of Guisachan Forest. Near fantastic Plodda Falls (1610/WATERFALLS) and Glen Affric (1589/GLENS). Rooms pleasant and cosy. Use of pool nearby in farm steading (9am-9pm); especially good for fishing holidays. 25km drive from Drumnadrochit by A831. Nice bar, though fewer locals these days.

1028 7/J19
4 ROOMS
FEB-DEC
£45-80

Grants At Craigellachie 01599 511331 · Ratagan, near Kyle Of Lochalsh On the west side of Loch Duich on the road to Glenelg off the A87 28km south of Kyle. A little (and they do mean 'little') restaurant with rooms in a family house and created garden in a splendid landscape. Bedrooms/suites also not large but a very personally run, superior guest house with good food.

✓ **The Smiddy House** 01397 712335 · Spean Bridge A notable restaurant with rooms. Report: 1046/BEST HIGHLAND RESTAURANTS.

6 GREAT HIGHLAND B&Bs

1029 9/K21
3 ROOMS
MAR-NOV
£45-60

✓✓ **The Grange** www.thegrange-scotland.co.uk · 01397 705516 · **Fort William** Probably the best rooms for the night in Fort William. All in the best possible taste and with views of Loch Linnhe. Reports: 1080/FORT WILLIAM.

1030 7/G19
3 ROOMS
£30-38

✓ **Tigh An Dochais** 01471 820022 · **Broadford, Skye** Signed and on the road coming into Broadford from the south (the bridge and ferries). Stunning contemporary building by award-winning architects Dualchas, this long, light house makes the most of its location. Bedrooms open out to and practically merge with the littoral. Breakfast in upstairs lounge; bread home made, etc. A superb introduction to Skye.

1031 7/M20
3 ROOMS
FEB-NOV
£30-38

✓ **The Rumblie** www.rumblie.com · 01528 544766 · **Laggan near Newtonmore** Off the A9 on the A86 midway between Dalwhinnie and Newtonmore to this eco-friendly and people-friendly B&B which takes its green agenda seriously. Organic breakfast; evening meal by arrangement (or go to Blasta in Newtonmore, below). Nice garden; bike hire nearby at Wolftrax.

1032 6/J16
3 ROOMS
MAR-OCT
TV · NO KIDS
£45-60

The Old Smiddy www.oldsmiddyguesthouse.co.uk · 01445 731696 · **Laide** Readers' letters sent us here, as elsewhere on this page. Landlady Julie Clements keeps the place on the map (Gruinard Bay, Wester Ross on the A832). She's a fine cook and does serious dinners (book then BYOB) including non-residents'.

1033 6/K15
3 ROOMS
TV
NO C/ CARDS
£38-45

Tanglewood House www.tanglewoodhouse.co.uk · 01854 612059 · **Ullapool** Just outside town on A835 south overlook Loch Broom. Family guest house very personally run by Anne Holloway who reckons she serves the best dinner to be had in Ullapool. Having eaten here recently I can attest to this. And it's available to non-residents. All rooms have great view of lovely Loch Broom; there's a boat if you feel like a row on it.
EAT Fixed-menu (so phone fads ahead), delicious 4-course dinner overlooking the loch. You join other guests like a dinner party. Sunset and supper to savour.

1034 6/K13
3 ROOMS
£30-38

Scourie Guest House www.scourieguesthouse.btinternet.co.uk · 01971 502001 · **Scourie** This cosy wee guest house off the A894 at Scourie (turn right going north into the village opposite the hotel and Spar shop. It's signposted B&B No. 55 and is not to be confused with either the Scourie Hotel or Scourie Lodge). Now this place really is small, with breakfast and dinner in a tiny conservatory. The Stephens are welcoming hosts all year round (there's nowhere else open in the winter to stay or eat). They make more effort than most to look after you.

Best Restaurants In The Highlands

1035 7/H18 · £15-22 · ✓ **The Potting Shed** 01520 744440 · **Applecross** In north Applecross along the strand at the back of a gorgeous walled garden. 6 years in restoration after 50 years of neglect – you enter via a pergola of roses (in summer). A destination coffee shop/restaurant like the Inn (1190/GET-AWAY HOTELS) putting Applecross on the map. Everything home made and often from the garden. Full menu lunch and dinner and excellent cakes. 7 days Mar-Oct.

1036 6/L15 · £15-22 · ✓ **Carron Restaurant** www.carron-restaurant.co.uk · 01520 722488 · **Strathcarron** On A890 round Loch Carron (joins A87 Kyle of Lochalsh road) just south of Strathcarron. Peter and Michelle Teago's roadside diner and grill started by Peter's dad over 30 years ago is a destination and not just locally. With absolutely everything home made, including the bread, the puds, the chips, and sourced locally as a matter of course (salad leaves from Attadale Gardens down the road; 1528/GARDENS), this place looks like just another caff but is far from it. 'Honest to goodness' it is. Apr-Nov, 10.30am-9pm. Closed Sun.

1037 8/P17 · £15-22 · ✓ **The Bakehouse** 01309 691826 · **Findhorn** Follow the one-way system round end-of-the-road village and you can't miss it. Owners had the great deli at the Findhorn Community (1447/DELIS, 1230/RETREATS). This is a brilliant coffee shop/restaurant where you eat ethically and really well. Home made/home grown/organic naturally and part of the slow-food movement so all individually prepared. A new destination in the North and a treat to eat. 7 days. 10am-5pm. Open later in summer. Bakery behind.

1038 7/N19 · £15-22 · ✓ **Ord Bán Restaurant Café** www.ordban.com · 01479 810005 · **Coylumbridge** Ross and Polly Cameron and Gordon have turned this funky old room at the Rothiemurchus Visitor Centre on the A951 Cairngorm Road, 5km from Aviemore from a drop-in caff to the destination bistro in the area. Well thought out, conscientious and determinedly locally sourced. A la carte specials. 7 days 9.30am-5.30pm, Thu-Sat 6.30-9pm. Live music nights. Winter hours vary.

1039 8/P18 · £22-32 · ✓ **The Glass House** www.theglasshouse-grantown.co.uk · 01479 872980 · **Grant Road, Grantown On Spey** Parallel to Main St. Steve and Karen Robertson's conservatory restaurant is the dining destination in these Speyside parts – loyal local lientele and lucky visitors who find it. No-nonsense Modern British menu that's excellent value. Closed Sun evening, Tue lunch and Mon.

1040 9/H22 · £22-32 · ✓ **Whitehouse** www.thewhitehouserestaurant.co.uk · 01967 421777 · **Lochaline, Ardnamurchan** Sits above the ferry port as the Mull boats come in, a restaurant adjacent the village shop with all the right/best principles: local produce, organic, simple and slow cooking means you may wait but (apart from the ferry) where are you going, anyway? Ingredients from Mull and Lochaber – the bay, the woods and the hedgerow. Quiet days in Ardnamurchan begin here. Perfect! Apr-Oct. 11am-afternoon tea-dinner LO 9.30pm. Closed Sun evening and Mon.

1041 7/H18 · £15-22 · ✓ **Plockton Shores** 01599 544263 · **Plockton** On the foreshore of lovely little Plockton, an all-purpose eaterie with fine home cooking making the most of location and hinterland (for ingredients). Breakfast, lunch and dinner (LO 9pm). Decent vegetarian choice.

1042 5/M17
£15-22

✓ **Sutor Creek** www.sutorcreek.co.uk · 01381 600855 · 21 Bank Street, Cromarty Near the seafront. An end-of-the-road diner that's there when you need it most (in Cromarty: 1558/COASTAL VILLAGES). Folk do travel to Sarah and Colin Munro's family-friendly and neighbourhood-friendly spot. Wood-fired oven turning out great crispy pizza and more; many specials. Seafood from the harbour. 7 days in season. Closed Mon/Tue May/Jun and Sep. Fri-Sun in winter. LO 9pm.

1043 7/H18
ATMOS
£22-32

✓ **The Waterside Seafood Restaurant** 01599 534813 · Kyle of Lochalsh · www.theseafoodrestaurant.com Not so much waterside as station-side, though by the busy port, off the road to Skye and with that bridge in the distance. *Brief Encounter* location actually on the platform lends atmosphere. Seafood from Kyle/Mallaig/Skye ie very local, and vegetarian selection. Lunch and LO 9pm. Closed Sun/Mon.

1044 7/H18
£15-22

✓ **The Seafood Restaurant** www.theseafoodrestaurant.com · 01599 544423 · Plockton Same folk as above and once again on the platform of a working railway station. No droopy sandwiches here, just good home cooking. Snacks in the day then blackboard specials and evening menu later. 10am-9.30pm in summer. Weekends only in winter. Brilliant faraway-bistro atmosphere. Take the trail or the train! (Also 1555/COASTAL VILLAGES).

1045 6/P15
£15-22

✓ **La Mirage** www.lamirage.org · 01431 821615 · Dunrobin Street, Helmsdale Near the Bridge Hotel. A bright little gem in the Sutherland straths and once a homage to Barbara Cartland, the romantic novelist, who lived nearby in this gorgeous wee village by the sea (67/PLACES WE SHOULD LOVE MORE). Snacks of every kind all day and great home cooking and baking from Don, son-in-law of Nancy Sinclair who famously put this caff on the map (her pic's on the wall). Great fish and chips. All year 11am-9pm.

1046 9/K20
£15-22

✓ **Russell's @ Smiddy House** www.smiddyhouse.co.uk · 01397 712335 · Spean Bridge Near junction of A82 for Skye on A86 for Laggan, Messrs Bryson and Russell's carefully run guest house or restaurant with (4) rooms. Good, unpretentious fare all home made. Fish selection and great chargrill steaks. Especially good for vegetarian food and diets. Hugely popular so best to book. Afternoon tea in light lounge with great choice of teas and tier of tea things. 7 days in summer, lunch & LO 9.30pm. Wed-Sun winter.

1047 6/K14
MAR-OCT
£15-22

✓ **Kylesku Hotel** www.kyleskuhotel.co.uk · 01971 502231 · near Kylestrome On A894; tucked down beside Loch Glencoul where the boat leaves to see Britain's 'highest waterfall' (1606/WATERFALLS). Small quayside pub/hotel (8 pretty basic rooms) serving great seafood in seafood setting with mighty Quinag behind (1935/HILLS). Food in bar or residents-only dining room. 12noon-9pm. See also 1303/GASTROPUBS.

1048 7/N19
£15 OR LESS

The Boathouse www.kincraig.com · 01540 651394 · Kincraig 2km from village towards Feshiebridge along Loch Insh. Part of Loch Insh Water Sports (2105/WATER SPORTS), a balcony restaurant overlooking beach and loch. Serene setting and ambience, friendly young staff (but they come and go). Some vegetarian; home-made puds. Bar menu and home baking till 6pm; supper till 9pm, bar 11pm. Check winter hours.

1049 7/M20
£15-22

Blasta www.blasta-restaurant.co.uk · 01540 673231 · Newtonmore Main street opposite the beautiful town hall. A well-priced, conscientiously run restaurant in the heart of Cairngorms National Park, with a reputation for delicious dinner and friendly service. Evenings only. Check days out of season.

1050 7/N17
£15 OR LESS

The Classroom 01667 455999 · Cawdor Street, Nairn At top end of main shopping street; Cawdor St is a continuation. Contemporary makeover in this conservative, golfy town. Under new owners '09. Bar/restaurant and afternoon tea with nice cakes. 7 days. LO 9.30pm.
Nearby at 10 High St, **The Kist** bistro (01667 459412) has a good reputation, and next door the **Victoria Tearoom** offers Nairn ladies somewhere to take a toastie.

1051 6/J14
£22-32

Riverside Bistro www.piesbypost.co.uk · 01571 844356 · Lochinver On way into town on A837. This Lochinver larder is notable mainly for vast array of Ian Stewart's home-made pies, calorific cakes and fab focaccia. The banoffi pie here is truly wicked. You can eat in or take away. Conservatories out front and back. Bistro on riverside serves very popular meals at night; using local seafood, venison, vegetarian – something for everyone including, apparently, Michael Winner (though don't let that put you off). Evening menu from 6.30pm.
The **Caberfeidh** pub (01571 844391) next door, with great Scottish (haddock 'n' chips, mince 'n' tatties) pub grub, all home made and locally sourced, adds to the excellent Lochinver options.

1052 7/M16
£22-32

The Oystercatcher www.the-oystercatcher.co.uk · 01862 871560 · Portmahomack On promontory of the Dornoch Firth (Tain 15km) this hidden seaside village (the only east-coast village that faces west) could bring back beach-plootering memories. Restaurant (a bistro by day – they switch rooms) is a destination in itself. Not a seaside caff: the wine list and malt choice are truly extraordinary. Food is inventive, multi-ingredient, somewhat rich, but always interesting. Café dining, lunch and dinner. Closed Nov-Feb and Mon/Tue. Best book for dinner.

1053 6/K15
£15-22

The Arch Inn 01854 612836 · West Shore Street, Ullapool West from ferry terminal. Pub across the road from the lochside: the locals' pub-grub choice. Dinner only Tue-Sat. LO 9pm.

1054 6/H16
£15-22

Blueprint Café 01445 712397 · Gairloch Main part of strung-out village opposite Mountain Restaurant. Contemporary café/restaurant with mixed menu including ok pizza, pasta and specials. Café lunch then evening menu LO 8.45pm. Closed Sun/Mon.

1055 6/M15
£15

Falls of Shin Visitor Centre www.fallsofshin.co.uk · 01549 402231 · near Lairg Self-serve café/ restaurant in visitor centre and shop across road from Falls of Shin on the Achany Glen road 8km south of Lairg (1615/WATERFALLS). Excellent home-made food better than it probably has to be in an unlikely outpost of Harrods: Mohammed al Fayed's Highland estate is here. (He's erected a statue of himself – a not-unexpected vanity and a bit of a hoot.) But somebody in that kitchen cooks like your mum. 9.30am-6pm; winter 10am-5pm. Food LO 4.30pm.

1056 7/M16
£15-22

Carnegie Lodge 01862 894039 · Tain At top of the town signed from A9 (ring road). It's a Tain thing, but the Wynes have turned this curiously suburban road-house/motel into the place to eat around here. Straight-up scrumptious food, big helpings, great value. They also have 8 rooms. Lunch & LO 9pm.

The Best Places To Stay In & Around Inverness

1057 7/M18
11 ROOMS
TEL · TV
NO PETS
£85+

✓✓ **Rocpool Reserve** www.rocpool.com · 01463 240089 · 14 Culduthel Road Just out of centre, looks down from above (some view from terrace). The very self-consciously presented boutique hotel followed Rocpool Restaurant (see below) but is now owned by the people who have Inverlochy Castle (993/HIGHLAND HOTELS). Each room a design statement. Divided into 'Hip', 'Chic' or 'Decadent'. You may feel you have to live up to the titles. 2 rooms have hot tubs on outdoor decks. Probably best to have someone to shag in these circumstances. Bar and restaurant the Scottish outpost of Albert Roux who has assembled a great team and a great menu most definitely worth sampling even as a non-resident (see below).

✓✓ **Glenmoriston** 01463 223777 · Ness Bank The smart stay and fabulous food experience lives up to expectations. 994/HIGHLAND HOTELS.

✓✓ **Boath House** 01667 454896 · Auldearn Half an hour east on A96. Excellence, elegance and very fine dining! 991/HIGHLAND HOTELS.

✓✓ **Culloden House** 01463 790461 5km east near (but not adjacent) the battlefield. Gracious living, splendid grounds. 995/HIGHLANDS HOTELS.

✓ **Dunain Park Hotel** 01463 230512 6km southwest on A82 Fort William road. Comfy country house just outside town. 999/HIGHLANDS HOTELS.

1058 7/M18
7 ROOMS
TEL · TV
£45-60

✓ **The Heathmount** www.heathmounthotel.com · 01463 235877 Kingsmills, then centre (from Eastgate Mall). Fiona Newton's quite groovy boutique-style hotel with popular, and at weekends very busy, bar/restaurant. High standard of mod-con; rich boudoir decor with personal attention to detail. Famously, some rooms have TVs in the shower. Very good value at the price.

1059 7/M18
76 ROOMS
TEL · TV
£38-45

Columba Hotel 01463 231391 · 7 Ness Walk An excellent central location overlooking the main bridge over the Ness and across the river to the castle. Pleasant and friendly, contemporary feel. Rooms vary, some small; river views best. Nice bar with grub; upstairs restaurant has castle views.

1060 7/M18
70 ROOMS
TEL · TV
£60-85

Royal Highland Hotel www.royalhighlandhotel.co.uk · 01463 231926 · Academy Street Literally on top of the station; continuing refurbishment under new owners. Nice staircase. Some rather average rooms. A surreal start to the day in the very interior breakfast room (The Wallace). Very much in the centre of things but definitely more functional than flash.

1061 7/M18
83 ROOMS
TEL · TV
£60-85

Marriott Hotel www.marriott.com · 01463 237166 · Culcabock Road In suburban area south of centre near A9. Modern, very well-appointed with pleasant garden. Best of the chain hotels. Leisure facilities include small pool.

1062 7/M18
10, 7 ROOMS
TV
£38-45

The Alexander/Felstead www.thealexander.net · 01463 231151/712266/ 231634 2 hotels on Ness Bank, along the river opposite Eden Court and very central. The Alexander is contemporary with nice uniformity in block out back. Other rooms are bigger. Felstead offers old-style comfort. Both B&B only. Many other hotels in this street. These ones are good value.

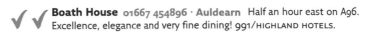

1063 7/M18 **Moyness House** www.moyness.co.uk · 01463 233836 · 6 Bruce Gardens
7 ROOMS Accolade-gathering and TripAdvisor-rated suburban guest house over bridge south
TV of river but 10 minutes' walk to centre and on-street parking. Friendly family
£38-45 house. B&B only. The writer Neil Gunn used to live here!

Bunchrew House Hotel 01463 234917 4km north on the road to Beauly on
firth shore. Wedding hotel but weekdays possible. Report: 1030/HIGHLAND HOTELS.

1064 7/M18 **3 Good Hostels: SY Hostel** www.syha.org.uk · 01463 231771 · Victoria
Drive Large official hostel (SYHA). More funky are the **Student Hostel**,
8 Culduthel Rd (01463 236556), and 3 doors down **Bazpackers** (01463 717663).

1065 7/M18 **Camping & Caravan Parks** Most central (2km) at **Bught Park**
www.invernesscaravanpark.com · 01463 236920 Well-equipped and large-
scale site on flat river meadow. Many facilities. Approach via A82 Fort William road.

▉ The Best Places To Eat In Inverness

£22-32 ✓✓ **Boath House** www.boath-house.com · 01667 454896 · Auldearn
Well out of town, but worth drive. Just off A96 3km east of Nairn. 30mins
from Inverness. Chef Charlie Lockely got his Michelin star and was Scottish Chef of
the Year '09. A very fine-dining night out. 991/HIGHLAND HOTELS.

1066 7/M18 ✓✓ **Abstract @ The Glenmoriston** 01463 223777 · 20 Nessbank ·
£32+ www.abstractrestaurant.com Along the river. The top-end restaurant
in town, part of Barry Larsen's Glenmoriston Hotel (see above). A sophisticated
dining experience – the 8-course 'temptation' menu or à la carte under chef Will
Hay. The 'market menu' (under £30) a good-value option. No Michelin recognition
yet but often comes close. Abstract opened in Edinburgh '07 with similar formula.
Dinner Tue-Sat. LO 9.30pm.

1067 7/M18 ✓✓ **Rocpool Reserve** www.rocpool.com · 01463 240089 · Culduthel
£32+ Road 3 rooms, private dining and terrace overlooking town. The Albert
Roux experience (he is here occasionally) – a classic French à la carte at great
prices. Elegant, non-poncey food. A real treat! 7 days. Lunch & LO 10pm.

1068 7/M18 ✓ **Rocpool** www.rocpool.com · 01463 717274 · Ness Walk Corner of main
£15-22 bridge over river. Stephen Devlin's excellent modern diner with accent on
inexpensive daytime and eclectic evening menu. Still the consistently good place
to eat in the centre of Inverness. Look no further! Forerunner of the Reserve
(above). 7 days. LO 9.45pm. Closed Sun lunch.

1069 7/M18 ✓ **Café One** 01463 226200 · 10 Castle Street Near the castle. Contemporary
£22-32 decor and cuisine well run, well presented. Menu changes monthly, carefully
sourced ingredients – good pricing for this standard of food and service. Express
menu a good deal. Yet another restaurant for Inverness to be pleased about.
Breakfast, lunch, dinner LO 9.30pm. Closed Sun.

1070 7/M18 ✓ **Contrast** 01463 227889 · Ness Bank Part of the Glenmoriston Hotel, the
£15-22 bistro/brasserie contrasts with fine-dining Abstract adjacent (see above).
Genuinely quite French, informal and light à la carte. Outside tables overlook the
river. Summer BBQ. Lunch and LO 9.30pm.

1071 7/M18
£15-22
The Mustard Seed 01463 220220 · 16 Fraser Street Catriona Bissett's cool restaurant in architectural riverside room with good attitude and ambience. Contemporary menu, ok wine. A restaurant that would not be out of place in any city on the up. 7 days 12noon-4pm, 6-10pm.

1072 7/M18
£15-22
The Kitchen on the River 01463 259119 · 15 Huntly Street As it says, 'on the river'. Still an emerging location in emerging Inverness, this a new building almost opposite its parent, The Mustard Seed (see above). On 3 floors (when busy) so waiters work hard as does the kitchen which you can watch on screen – it all comes right in the end. 7 days lunch & LO 10pm.

1073 7/M18
£15 OR LESS
Delices de Bretagne 01463 712422 · 6 Stephens Brae Just up from Girvans (see below), another café/restaurant. This one brings 'a taste of France to Inverness'. So croissants, croques and crèpes... and baked potatoes. The patisserie is fine but not a patch on the real *chose*, the crêpes on the other hand are light and welcome in the land of the heavy carb. Nice coffee. 9am-5.30pm. Closed Sun.

1074 7/M18
£22-32/
£15-22
Riva & Pazzo's 01463 237377 · 4 Ness Walk Prominent (adjacent main bridge) Italian restaurant and (upstairs) tratt. Probably best in town. By the Girvans (see below). Contemporary room overlooking riverside. Decent Italian menu. Riva lunch & LO 9.30pm, Pazzo's evenings only (pasta and pizza only), LO 10pm.

1075 7/M18
£22-32
Riverhouse Restaurant 01463 222033 · Greig Street Over the pedestrian bridge. Intimate restaurant with contemporary food from Alan Little's open kitchen. Gets busy so can feel cramped but excellent reputation. Lunch Tue-Sat, dinner Tue-Sun, LO 9pm. Closed Sun in winter.

1076 7/M18
£15-22
River Café www.rivercafeandrestaurant.co.uk · 01463 714884 · Bank Street On town side of the river near pedestrian bridge. Small, friendly café/restaurant. Solid and unpretentious evening menu and ladies who lunch. 7 days LO 9pm. May close Sun in winter.

1077 7/M18
£15 22
Raja 01463 237190 · Post Office Lane Downstairs in the lane (between Church St and Academy St, behind Queensgate) is the best of several curry houses. It's been here since 1982 and it's usually packed. Says it all!

1078 7/M18
£15-22
Red Pepper 01463 237111 · 74 Church Street The cooler coffee-shop by the people that brought us the Mustard Seed (above). Daytime caffeine-hit with bespoke sandwiches, etc. 7.30am-4.30pm. Closed Sun.

1079 7/M18
£15-22
La Tortilla Asesina www.latortillaasesina.co.uk · 01463 709809 · Top of Castle Street Near castle and hostels (see above). Reasonably authentic Spanish restaurant serving the UK version of tapas ie 2/3 portions as a meal. All the faves and some variants are here with lots *de dia*. The rioja and the beers are here, of course. 7 days. LO 10pm (bar later).

✓**Girvans** Stephens Brae Behind M&S. Fast-turnover food for all folks. Report: 1370/CAFÉS.

✓**Castle Restaurant** Castle Street Legendary caff of the Highlands. Hardest-working kitchen in the North. Report: 1369/CAFÉS.

If you're in Fort William...

WHERE TO STAY

9 ROOMS
TEL
£30-38

✓ **Lime Tree Studios** www.limetreefortwilliam.co.uk · 01397 701806 Achintore road as you come from south, the last hotel of many near the end of main street. Combines regional art-gallery space in the old manse with rooms above and a newer extension. Bar/restaurant with open kitchen and terrace. David Wilson (his art on the walls) and Charlotte Wright run a convivial, cosmopolitan inn.

3 ROOMS
MAR-NOV
TV · NO KIDS
NO PETS
£45-60

✓ **The Grange** www.thegrange-scotland.co.uk · 01397 705516 · Grange Road Overlooks the loch and the main road south. Look for Ashburn House on main A82 turning into Ashburn Lane. Joan and John Campbell have been running this superlative, contemporary B&B in bereft Fort William for years. Discreet, almost suburban house but great views from garden terrace and fresh, modern rooms with great bathrooms. B&B only. Joan was 'Landlady of the Year' '09. New, gorgeous garden room on the way '10/11.

27 ROOMS
TEL · TV
£38-45

The Moorings www.moorings-fortwilliam.co.uk · 01397 772797 · Banavie 5km out on A830 Corpach/Mallaig by the Caledonian Canal by Neptune's Staircase (some rooms overlook). Good location, pub dining best. Serviceable enough.

Onich Hotel 01855 821214 · Onich 16km south on A82. Lochside; good value. 1008/HIGHLANDS HOTELS.

S.Y. Hostel 0870 004 1120 · Glen Nevis 5km from Fort William by picturesque but busy Glen Nevis road. The Ben is above. Grade 1. Many other hostels in area (ask for list at tourist information centre) but especially **FW Backpackers** 01397 700711 · Alma Road.

Achintee Farm 01397 702240 On approach to Ben Nevis main route and adjacent Ben Nevis Inn (see below). Guest house/self catering and bunkhouse. A walkers' haven.

Camping/Caravan Site 01397 702191 · Glen Nevis Near hostel. Well-run site, mainly caravans (also for rent). Many facilities including restaurants.

✓ ✓ **Inverlochy Castle** 01397 702177 5km out on A82 Inverness road. In the forefront of hotels in Scotland. Victorian elegance, classically stylish and impeccable service. The restaurant is open to non-residents but this is not casual dining. 989/HIGHLANDS HOTELS.

WHERE TO EAT

£15-22

Crannog At The Waterfront aka The Seafood Restaurant www.oceanandoak.co.uk · 01397 705589 Finlay Finlayson's long-established landmark restaurant on the waterfront. Freshly caught seafood mainly (one meat/one vegetarian) in informal bistro setting. Good wine list. All year. 7 days. Lunch & LO 9pm.

£15-22

Lime Tree Restaurant 01397 701806 · Cameron Square Achintore Rd at roundabout as you arrive from south, or at the south end of the main street. Restaurant of boutiquey hotel (see above) with good atmosphere, open kitchen and terrace. 4 starters/mains/desserts. Local sourcing and Scottish cheeses, neat wine list. Lunch and LO 9pm.

Ben Nevis Inn www.ben-nevis-inn.co.uk · 01397 701227 · **Achintee** On main approach to the Ben itself. Reach across river by footbridge from visitor centre or by road on right after Inverlochy/Glen Nevis roundabout on A82 (marked 'Claggan and Achintee'; 3km). Excellent atmosphere inn in converted farm building. Good grub/ale and walking chat. LO 9pm. Weekends only in winter.

Loch Leven Seafood Café Worth the 15km drive. 1335/SEAFOOD RESTAURANTS.

◼ If you're around Wick & Thurso...

WHERE TO STAY

✓ **Forss House** www.forsshousehotel.co.uk · 01847 861201 · **near Thurso** 8km west to Tongue off A836. Best in the North West. A haven of hospitality in woody policies in a region where you may long for a tree. Restaurant open to non-residents. Report: 1003/HIGHLAND HOTELS.

✓ **Ulbster Arms Hotel** www.ulbsterarmshotel.co.uk · 01847 831641 · **Halkirk** In middle of village off A9 10km south of Thurso. By the river which is there to be fished (the hotel has 13 beats). Refurbished to comfy standard, unusually contemporary up Caithness way. Dining more traditional. You would want one of the 6 deluxe rooms.

Portland Arms 01593 721721 · **Lybster** On main A9 20km south of Wick and 45km south of Thurso by A895. A coaching inn since 1851; still hospitable, though no longer in private hands. Small rooms are a bit, well, small but this is a homely hotel with decent food in a choice of settings (a good drop-in for pub grub). Log fires. Feels part of the community. While in Lybster, pop down and see Waterlines (nice restoration, poignant story).

S.Y. Hostel 0870 004119 · **Canisbay** John o' Groats (7km). Wick 25km. Regular bus service. Furthest-flung youth hostel on the mainland. Thurso has **Sandra's** at 24-26 Princes Street (01847 894575). Cheap 'n' cheerful with snack bar adjacent.

WHERE TO EAT

✓✓ **Captain's Galley** www.captainsgalley.co.uk · 01847 894999 · **Scrabster** The best dinner to be had on this coast. Seafood with simplicity and integrity. Report: 1327/SEAFOOD RESTAURANTS.

Le Bistro 01847 893737 · **Trail Street, Thurso** On the main road through at the end of the pedestrianised main street. If you have to eat in Thurso, this is the local choice. Long-established, decent grub. Lunch Tue-Sat, dinner Wed-Sat.

Bord de L'Eau 01955 604400 · **Market Street, Wick** By the bridge, on the waterside. Passably French bistro (menu in French as well as English) where locals might go for the night out. Atmosphere bypass. Lunch Tue-Sat, dinner Tue-Sun.

The Tempest Café 01847 892500 · **Thurso** On harbour adjacent Tempest Surf shop. Laid-back, surfey, kind of waiting-on-the-wave place. Travel books remind us of the world out there. Nice home-made soup, all-day breakfast, butties, cakes etc. LO 4.30pm.

Tourist Offices 01847 893155 · **Whitechapel Road, Wick** Open all year. Riverside, Thurso Apr-Oct.

EDINBURGH
BARS & CLUBS

1082 1/D2 ✓✓ **New Town Bar** www.newtownbar.co.uk · 26 Dublin Street · 0131 538 7775 Grown-up and cosmo watering hole for mixed, mainly older crowd. Bear-friendly (especially the 2nd Sat of the month). Basement has skilfully hung drapes to compartmentalise action. 7 days till 12midnight/1am, weekends 2am. Food 12-5; Sunday roast (we mean food!).

1083 1/D2 ✓ **GHQ** 0131 550 1780 · 4 Picardy Place Chandeliered bar and basement club by Glasgow's G1 Group in the heart of the Pink Triangle. Club is flexi-space with dance depending on crowd. Banquettes can be booked (for watching and gossip). 7 days 5pm-3am. Young crowd.

1084 1/E2 ✓ **CC Bloom's** www.ccbloomshotel.com · 0131 556 9331 · Greenside Place The long-established last stand, now a bit worse for wear, like much of the clientele. Bar and small dancefloors up and downstairs. Cruisy, of course (your last chance before 'The Gardens'). 7 days 7pm-3am.

1085 1/E1 **Planet** 0131 524 0061 · Greenside Place Scouting for girls in this bar in the strip below the Playhouse. An unthreatening vibe (except for the door dykes). 7 days till 1am.

1086 1/E2 **Café Habana** www.cafehabanaeh1.com · 0131 558 1270 · 22 Greenside Place Adjacent CCs above. Banging music. Young crowd. Quite tiny really, so usu-ally rammed. Line-up on the mezzanine so coming in is like arriving on the beach at Mykonos: you are immediately checked out, ie probably dismissed, then you can relax. Outside tables. 7 days noon-1am.

1087 1/XE1 **Priscilla's** 0131 554 8962 · Albert Place On the right of Leith Walk going down. 'Cabaret Bar' and well... rough as fuck. But friendly and mixed. Karaoke stage, some drag shows; many smokers. 7 days 12noon-1am. Lisa looks on.

1088 1/B3 **Frenchie's** 0131 225 7651 · Rose Street Lane North Near Castle St. Oldest gay bar, quite removed from the East End Pink Triangle. Hence more intimate but no less trashy. Age before beauty so suits all. 7 days till 11pm. (1am Fri/sat.)

1089 1/F2 **The Regent** 0131 661 8198 · Corner of Abbeyhill Adjacent well-known cruis-ing gardens. Friendly locals, relaxed, straight friendly. Even have ales (Deuchars, Cally 80/- and guests). 7 days till 1am.

OTHER PLACES

1090 1/D1
£15 OR LESS ✓ **Blue Moon Café** www.bluemooncafe.co.uk · 0131 556 2788 · Barony Street Long-running neighbourhood caff with juice bar (Sejuiced) attached; enter round the corner on Broughton St. Always busy with lively mixed crowd for food and drink and goss. **Out of the Blue** gay accessories and book shop next door. If you arrive in Edinburgh and don't know anybody, come here first. Food 7 days till 10-ish; bar 11/11.30pm. (294/CAFÉS)

1091 1/D1
£15 OR LESS ✓ **Café Nom de Plume** 0131 478 1372 · 60 Broughton Street Part of the LGBT Centre. Proper café-bistro with changing à la carte home-made food and nice people sitting around. So 2 civilised caffs within 100 metres at the heart of the gay zone. 7 days 12noon-9.30pm/10pm food, bar later.

1092 1/D1 **No. 18** 0131 553 3222 · 18 Albert Place Sauna for gentlemen (mainly older). Discreet doorway halfway down Leith Walk. Dark room. Mon–Sat 12noon-10pm. Sun 2-10pm (only a fiver after 8pm).

1093 1/D1 **Steamworks** 0131 477 3567 · Broughton Market At the end of Barony St off Broughton St at the Blue Moon. Modern, Euro-style wet and dry areas. Cubies. Café. Dark room. Mixed crowd. Part of the Village Apartments (see below). 7 days 11am-10pm.

GUEST HOUSES

1094 1/E1
5 ROOMS · TV
£45-60

✓**Ardmor House** www.ardmorhouse.com · 0131 554 4944 · 74 Pilrig Street Quiet mix of contemporary and original design meet in this stylish guest house run by Robin and Lola the doggie. Family room so straight-friendly. They have very nice flats to rent, too.

1095 1/D1
4 ROOMS · TV
£30 OR LESS

✓**Village Apartments** www.villageapartments.co.uk · 0131 556 5094 · Broughton Market Attached to Steamworks (above), 4 tastefully turned-out flatlets, central especially for the gay village (between the New Town and the Blue Moon). Is ticked though I have never stayed (nor been invited). Men only.

1096 1/E1
6 ROOMS · TV
£30 OR LESS

Garlands www.garlands.demon.co.uk · 0131 554 4205 · 48 Pilrig Street Another guest house on Pilrig St, Garlands is more old-style and probably more gay than Ardmor (above).

GLASGOW
BARS & CLUBS

1097 2/E3 ✓**Delmonica's** 0141 552 4802 · 68 Virginia Street Glasgow-stylish pub with long bar and open plan in quiet lane in Merchant City gay quarter. Pleasant and airy during day but busy and sceney at night, especially weekends. 'It's nice if your face fits'. 7 days till 12midnight (then the PL, below).

1098 2/E3 ✓**Moda** 0141 553 2553 · 58 Virginia Street Another fashionable bar by the G1 group between Delmonica's and the Polo Lounge so you're on the same beat. 5pm-1am, 3am weekends.

1099 2/E3 ✓**Polo Lounge** 0141 553 1221 · 84 Wilson Street Long-established venue with stylish decor, period furnishings. Gents' club meets Euro-lounge ambience. 3am licence; otherwise till 1am. Downstairs disco at weekends (with admission).

1100 2/C3 **Waterloo Bar** 0141 229 5891 · 306 Argyle Street Scotland's oldest gay bar and it tells. But an unpretentious down-to-earth vibe so refreshing in its way. Old-established bar and clientele. You might not fancy anybody but they're a friendly old bunch. 7 days till 12midnight.

1101 2/E4 **Court Bar** 0141 552 2463 · 69 Hutcheson Street Centre of Merchant City area. Long-going small bar that's straight till mid evening then turns into a fairy. 7 days till 12midnight.

1102 2/E4 **Bennet's** www.bennetsnightclub.co.uk · 0141 552 5761 · 80 Glassford Street In the beginning and in the end... Bennet's. Relentless, unashamed disco fun without attitude on 2 floors. Wed-Sun 11pm-3am, Tue is 'traditionally' straight night, first Fri of the month is ladies' night.

1103 **Revolver** www.revolverglasgow.com · 0141 553 2456 · **6a John Street** In
2/E3 basement opposite Italian Centre. Civilised subterranea. Free juke box, pool, ale.
Some uniform nights. Most of the men will be men. 7 days all day to 12midnight.

OTHER PLACES

1104 ✓ **The Pipeworks** 0141 552 5502 · **5 Metropole Lane** East of St Enoch
2/D4 Centre, near Slater Menswear, down an unlikely lane. Glasgow's most full-on
(and modern) sauna. 7 days 12noon-11pm, all night Sat/Sun.

1105 **The Lane** 0141 221 1802 · **60 Robertson Street** Near Waterloo (above), other
2/C4 side of Argyle St, lane on right. You 'look for the green light'. Sauna and private
club. You wouldn't call it upmarket, that cabin fever! 7 days, afternoons till 7/8pm.

1106 **Relax Central** 0141 221 0415 · **3rd Floor, 27 Union Street** Between Central
2/D3 Station and Argyle St. Small, friendly sauna. Limited facilities but regular clientele.

ABERDEEN

1107 **Cheerz** 01224 594511 · **2 Exchange Street** Evening gay bar and club later on.
8/T19 Haven't been! 7 days 6pm-12 midnight. Club till 2/3am.

1108 **Hyploc** 01224 580744 · **72 Commerce Street** Bar in emerging gay quarter.
8/T19 12noon-12 midnight.

1109 **Club Foundation** **Carnegie's Brae** Opposite the Tunnels, a straight club
8/T19 below Union St. This is a gay but straight-friendly club. Wed-Sun 11pm-3am.

1110 **Wellman's Health Studio** www.wellmans-health-studio.co.uk · 01224
8/T19 211441 · **218 Holburn Street** To complete Aberdeen's transformation in 3 years
from gay dead zone to well-endowed, a sauna with all you could want. 12noon-
10pm (earlier Sat/Sun).

DUNDEE

1111 **Out** 01382 200660 · **124 Seagate** Bar and dancefloor. Everybody knows every-
10/Q23 body else, but not you. This may have its advantages. Wed-Sun till 2.30am. Also ...

1112 **Brooklyns** 01382 200660 · **St Andrews Lane** Behind and above Out (above).
10/Q23 Small bar, a pre-club bar on disco nights (reduced tickets available at bar). Wed-
Sun 7pm-12midnight (11pm Sun).

1113 **Gauger** 01382 226840 · **75 Seagate** Near the above. Pub with disco Fri/Sat.
10/Q23 Till 12midnight 7 days. Non-threatening haven in sometimes scary zone.

1114 **Jock's Health Club** 01382 451986 · **11 Princes Street** Recent arrival on
10/Q23 Dundee gay scene: sauna with all the usual heat.

HOTELS ELSEWHERE

1115 **Colquhonnie House Hotel** www.thecolquhonniehotel.co.uk · 01975
8/Q19 651210 · **Strathdon** In the Don valley, deepest Aberdeenshire. An unlikely find in
10 ROOMS the Highlands, this roadside (A944) lodge adjacent the Lonach (village) Hall takes
TV · GF · DA all sorts but is very positively gay-friendly (they fly the flag as well as the saltire).
£30-38 Good base for the Castle Trail, active stuff (fishing rights on the Don) or just chilling out. Local bar is, you will understand, not a gay bar.

Section 5
Particular Places to Eat & Stay in Scotland

Scotland the best

Superlative Country-House Hotels

1116
10/N24
232 ROOMS
TEL · TV
£85+

✓✓✓ **Gleneagles** Auchterarder · www.gleneagles.com · 01764 662231 Off A9 Perth-Stirling road and signed. Scotland's truly luxurious resort hotel. For facilities on the grand scale others pale into insignificance; an international destination. Comfort and style and they've thought of everything. Sport and leisure activities include shooting, riding, fishing, off-roading (even kids' jeeps), 2 pools with outdoor tub and for inactivity the Espa spa is gorgeous (1243/SPAS). Gleneagles golf (3 courses) is world-renowned; the 40th Ryder Cup is coming 2014. Both traditional luxurious and contemporary luxurious (by Amanda Rosa) in the main house; the new wing Braid House contemporary and remote (in the 'handset to control temperature, lights, curtains and fireplace' sense). Strathearn Restaurant is a foodie heaven but expensive. Casual dining in Deseo: lighter, brighter Mediterranean; there are 2 other restaurants. Andrew Fairlie's intimate dining room is considered by many to offer Scotland's best fine dining (879/PERTHSHIRE RESTAURANTS). Gleneagles could be anywhere but it is quintessentially Scottish. It has airs and graces but it's a friendly old place. Sometimes they'll cut you a deal!

1117
11/J29
17 ROOMS
EASTER-OCT
TEL · TV
DA
£85+

✓✓ **Glenapp Castle** near Ballantrae · www.glenappcastle.com · 01465 831212 Relais and Chateaux luxury in South Ayrshire south of Ballantrae. Very discreet entrance (first right turn after village: no sign, and entryphone system – don't bother without a reservation or appointment). Home of Inchcape family for most of 20th century, opened as a hotel in first year of 21st. Run by Graham and Fay Cowan (Fay's family has several hotels but this is their flagship). Fabulous restoration on a house that fell into disuse in the 1990s. Excellent and considerate service, top-notch food, impeccable interiors. The rooms are all individually beautiful, the suites are enormous. Quality costs but the price includes just about everything, so relax and join this effortless house party. Kids can have separate high tea. Tennis, lovely walks in superb grounds (especially May and Sep) kept by almost as many gardeners as there are chefs. A southern secret though with many accolades. **EAT** Recent arrival Adam Stokes: I'd be amazed if he didn't get Michelin star back.

1118
9/J22
16 ROOMS
7 SUITES
2 COTTAGES
FEB-DEC
TEL · TV
£85+

✓✓ **Isle of Eriska** Ledaig · www.eriska-hotel.co.uk · 01631 720371 20km north of Oban (signed from A85 near Benderloch Castle). Hotel, spa and they do say, island! As you drive over the Victorian iron bridge, you enter a more tranquil and gracious world. Its 300 acres are a sanctuary for wildlife; you are not the only guests. The famous badgers come almost every night to the door of the bar for their milk and peanuts. Comfortable baronial house with fastidious service and facilities. Rooms (named after islands) are very individual. Two 2-bedroom and five 1-bedroom suites in spa outbuilding are more contemporary, with private terraces and hot tubs. Picturesque 9-hole golf, great 17m pool and gym excellent in summer when it opens on to the garden. Also putting, tennis and clay shooting; it's all there if you feel like action, but it's very pleasant just to stay still. Espa treatment rooms (3) and Verandah Café with deck adjacent for lunch. Dining, with a Scottish flavour and impeccable local ingredients from a rich backyard and bay, in elegantly remodelled dining room under chef Robert MacPherson.

1119
11/J30
9 ROOMS
MAR-DEC
TEL · TV
DA
£85+

✓✓ **Knockinaam Lodge** Portpatrick · www.knockinaamlodge.com · 01776 810471 An ideal place to lie low; an historic Victorian house nestled on a cove. The Irish coastline is the only thing on the horizon, apart from discreet service and excellent food. Winston Churchill was once very comfortable here, too! Superb wine (especially French) and whisky list. 15km south of Stranraer, off A77 near Lochans but get directions. Further report 780/SOUTH-WEST HOTELS. **EAT** Tony Pierce – Scotland's longest-standing Michelin chef. Tasting set menu (advise requirements). An understated foodie treat.

1120	✓ ✓ **Kinloch House** near Blairgowrie · www.kinlochhouse.com ·
10/P22	01250 884237 5km west on A923 to Dunkeld. Quintessential rural
18 ROOMS	Scottish comfort and joy. Beautiful mansion among the green fields and woods of
TEL · TV	Perthshire, home to exemplary hosts the Allen family. Always welcoming: open
£85+	fires, oak-panelled hall and portrait gallery with comfy rooms and informal but sure

✓ ✓ **Kinloch House** near Blairgowrie · www.kinlochhouse.com · 01250 884237 5km west on A923 to Dunkeld. Quintessential rural Scottish comfort and joy. Beautiful mansion among the green fields and woods of Perthshire, home to exemplary hosts the Allen family. Always welcoming: open fires, oak-panelled hall and portrait gallery with comfy rooms and informal but sure service. Fine south-facing views. Surprising 35-foot pool (and other facilities) you may have to yourself. 3 suites. Enjoy!

EAT Excellent food: Graeme Allen and the guys – Andrew, Steven and dessert maestro David Orrock – in the kitchen. Top wine list (especially French).

1121
9/J23
16 ROOMS
FEB-DEC
TEL · TV
DA
£85+
ATMOS

✓ **Ardanaiseig** Loch Awe · www.ardanaiseig.com · 01866 833333 16km from Taynuilt signed from main A85 to Oban down beautiful winding road and 7km from Kilchrenan. In sheltered landscaped gardens dotted with ongoing sculpture project to complement this rambling gothic mansion's collection of selected antiques (proprietor owns antique business in London) overlooking an enchanting loch. Peaty water on tap and all amongst great trees. Genuine 'faux' grand that works. Outside by the loch, deer wander and bats flap at dusk. Pure romance. Chef Gary Goldie gets it just right. The Boatshed suite, with its boat and its loch, is simply idyllic. Not surprisingly, there are many weddings.

✓ **Ballathie House** Kinclaven, near Blairgowrie & Perth · 01250 883268 · www.ballathiehousehotel.com Superb situation on River Tay. Handy for Perth and probably the best place to stay near the town. Full report and codes: 878/PERTHSHIRE HOTELS.

✓ ✓ **Cromlix House** Dunblane · www.cromlixhouse.com · 01786 822125 Near A9 north of Perth, 4km Dunblane. Quintessential country-house hotel in the most beautiful grounds. Report: 801/CENTRAL HOTELS.

✓ ✓ **Raemoir House** Banchory · 01330 824884 5km north from town via A980. A gem in the North East. Historical with contemporary comforts and excellent dining. Report: 936/NORTHEAST HOTELS.

Hotels That Welcome Kids

1122
10/N23
214 ROOMS
+SELF-
CATERING
TEL · TV
£38-45

✓ ✓ **Crieff Hydro** Crieff · www.crieffhydro.com · 01764 655555 A national institution and still a family business; your family is part of theirs. Approach via High St, then follow signs. Vast Victorian pile with activities for all from bowlers to babies. Still run by the Leckies from hydropathic beginnings but with continuous refurbishments, including the fabulous winter gardens moving graciously with the times (fine coffee shop: freshly squeezed OJ and must-have donuts). New sports hall (the Hub), café and kids' centre '07 as good as any local authority facility. Formal chandeliered dining room (Meikle's) and the Brasserie (best for food Med-style; open all day). Great tennis courts, riding school, 2 pools. Tiny cinema shows family movies; nature talks, donkey rides. Kids endlessly entertained (even while you eat). Chalets (52) in grounds are among the best in Scotland. Great for family get-togethers. Populism with probity and no preciousness: when in doubt, resort to this resort!

1123
9/J27
36 ROOMS
TEL · TV
£45-60

✓ **Auchrannie** Brodick, Arran · www.auchrannie.co.uk · 01770 302234 Much expanded from the original house, the new block is perfect for a family holiday. Loadsa activities on tap including 2 pools, racquet court, spa and outdoor stuff (from out back) on rivers, trails and hills of Arran. All rooms can take 2 adults and 2 kids. Main restaurant is a bit motorway services but 2 other options include fine-ish dining in Eighteen69 (phone-monitoring service and hotel can arrange babysitting). This is where kids will begin their lifelong love of Arran.

1124
9/J22
59 ROOMS
TEL · TV
£38-85

✓ **Isles of Glencoe Hotel** Ballachulish · www.islesofglencoe.com · 01855 811602 Beside the A82 Crianlarich to Fort William: a modern hotel and leisure centre jutting out onto Loch Leven. Adventure playground outside and nature trails. Conservatory restaurant overlooking the water. Lochaber Watersports next door have all kind of boats from pedalos to kayaks and bikes. Hotel has pool. 2 different standards of family rooms (Deck Dens work well). Snacks in the restaurant all day. Glencoe and 2 ski areas nearby.

1125
7/E15
5 ROOMS
MAR-DEC
£60-85

✓ **Scarista House** Harris · www.scaristahouse.com · 01859 550238 20km south of Tarbert on west coast of South Harris, just over an hour to Stornoway. Big, comfortable former manse overlooking amazing beach (1573/BEACHES); and golf course (2074/GOOD GOLF). Lots of other great countryside around. The Martins have 3 school-age kids and yours may muck in with them (including 6pm supper). Laid-back but civilised ambience.

1126
7/E14
7 ROOMS
MAY-SEP
£38-45

✓ **Baile-Na-Cille** Timsgarry, Lewis · www.baillenacille.com · 01851 672242 Far far into the sunset on the west of Lewis 60km Stornoway so a plane/ferry and drive to somewhere you and the kids can leave it all behind. Exquisite, vast beach, garden, tennis, games room. No TV, phone or mobile reception (but WiFi in the lounge). Plenty books. There are a couple of places nearby for lunch (2281/OUTER HEBRIDES). The kids will never forget it.

1127
9/F23
16 & 27
ROOMS
APR-OCT
£45-60

✓ **Argyll Hotel** & **St Columba Hotels** Iona · www.argyllhoteliona.co.uk & www.stcolumba-hotel.co.uk · 01681 700334 & 01681 700304 The 2 Iona hotels owned by a consortium of local people on this charmed and blessed little island. Holidays here are remembered forever. Both hotels fairly basic but child- and people-in-general-friendly. Unhurried, hassle-free; kids run free. Beautiful gardens. Both open Apr-Oct.

1128
9/J20
13 ROOMS
MAR-NOV
£38-85
ATMOS

✓ **Glenfinnan House** Glenfinnan · www.glenfinnanhouse.com · 01397 722235 Just off the Road to the Isles (the A830 from Fort William to Mallaig). Very large Highland hoose with so many rooms and such large gardens you can be as noisy as you like. Great introduction to the Highland heartland; music, scenery and local characters. Comfy rooms: no phone or TV but fresh flowers and you won't need a key. Row on the loch from the foot of the lawn. Midge-eater in the garden is necessary. 1013/INEXPENSIVE HIGHLAND HOTELS.

1129
9/G22
10 ROOMS
MAR-NOV
£38-45

✓ **Calgary Hotel** near Dervaig, Mull · www.calgary.co.uk · 01688 400256 20km south of Tobermory (and a long way from Balamory), a roadside hotel/ bistro/gallery and a very laid-back place. Main features are beautiful wood out back (with art in it, but an adventure land for kids) and Mull's famously fab beach adjacent. 2 great family rooms. 2241/ISLAND HOTELS.

1130
9/K20
8 ROOMS
£45-60

✓ **Old Pines** near Spean Bridge · www.oldpines.co.uk · 01397 712324 3km Spean Bridge via B8004 for Gairlochy at Commando Monument. A ranch-like hotel in a good spot north of Fort William. This hotel has long had a big reputation not only for food but also for welcoming kids. The Dalleys have kids too and welcome yours. Separate mealtimes with real food then a great dinner for the adults. Very safe, easy environment with chickens and woods to run.

1131
10/N22
6 ROOMS
TV
£38-45

Inn on the Tay Grandtully · www.theinnonthetay.co.uk · 01887 840760 Road and riverside inn in small village of Aberfeldy. This stretch of river famous for its rapids so usually plenty of raft and canoe action. Stylish refurbishment by Josie and Geoff determined to make it family-friendly. Some rooms have 3 beds but only adults pay. 4 overlook and you are soothed to sleep by the river. Nice lounge and café/bar with river deck.

1132
9/J22
20 ROOMS
TEL · TV
£60-85

Holly Tree Hotel Kentallen · www.hollytreehotel.co.uk · 01631 740292 On A828 Fort William-Oban road south of Ballachulish. Long-established roadside and seaside hotel in great setting. Many rooms have the view. Garden on the shore with pier. Former railway station with Mackintosh references (sic). Surf 'n' turf restaurant, bar and surprising swimming pool.

1133
10/Q27
128 ROOMS
TEL · TV
£60-85

Peebles Hydro Peebles · www.peebleshydro.co.uk · 01721 720602 One of the first Victorian hydros and a complete resort for families; it has that well-worn look but it doesn't matter too much if they run amok. Huge grounds, corridors (you get lost) and floors of rooms. Pool and leisure facilities. Entertainment and baby-sitting services. Traditional and refreshingly untrendy. Rooms vary. Dining room is vast and hotel-like. Lazels downstairs is light, contemporary for lunch and tea. Many family rooms. Now owned by reputable small chain from the South West (who have the Cally Pally below) so expect improvements 2010.

1134
10/Q27
14 ROOMS
TEL · TV
£30-38

Glentress Hotel near Peebles · www.glentress.org.uk · 01721 720100 3km east of Peebles on the main A72 road to Innerleithen. Roadside lodge ideally situated for families who do the outdoors together, especially cycling. Adjacent Glentress Mountain Bike Centre (2091/CYCLING); hotel itself hires bikes (though not for kids). Restaurant ain't bad. Family rooms. Perfect little Peebles nearby.

1135
11/M30
56 ROOMS
TEL · TV
£45-60

The Cally Palace Gatehouse of Fleet · www.callypalace.co.uk · 01557 814341 The big all-round family and golf hotel in the South West in charming village with safe, woody walks in the grounds and beaches nearby. Leisure facilities include pool and tennis. 500 acres of forest good for cycling (bike hire can be arranged). There are allegedly red squirrels. 9 family rooms. Kids' tea at 5pm. See 1519/GARDENS.

1136
9/J25
11 ROOMS
TEL · TV
£45-60

Kilfinan Hotel Kilfinan · www.kilfinanhotel.com · 01700 821201 North of Tignabruaich on B8000 close to but not on Loch Fyne in the country heart of Cowal and Argyll. A long-established coaching inn with a good reputation for food, now in the hands of the Wyatts who have 3 kids and will welcome yours. Proper kids' menu. Chickens and ducks and a fairy bridge; wild walks nearby. A relaxing and easy place for all.

1137
7/N19
175 ROOMS
TEL · TV
£85+

Hilton Coylumbridge near Aviemore · www.hilton.co.uk/coylumbridge · 01479 810661 8km from Aviemore Centre on B970 road to ski slopes and nearest hotel to them. 2 pools of decent size, sauna, flume, etc. Plenty to do in summer and winter (1710/KIDS) and certainly where to go when it rains. Best of the often-criticised Aviemore concrete blocks, the most facilities, huge shed with kids' play area (the Funhouse). Whole hotel kidtastic in school hols.

1138
10/Q27
12 ROOMS
+ 5 LODGES
TEL · TV
£60-85

Philipburn Selkirk · www.philipburnhousehotel.co.uk · 01750 720747 1km town centre on Peebles Rd. Privately owned and well-run hotel in middle of Borders. Comfy rooms and easy-eat bistro restaurant with separate kids' meal-time. Giant chess in the garden, indoor pool (and spa) on the way at TGP. Other physical (kids' adventure playground in woods at Bowhill, salmon-leaping and -watching centre 2km up the road) and more energetic pursuits at St Mary's Loch/ Grey Mare's Tail (1609/WATERFALLS) nearby.

√ **Comrie Croft** near Comrie · 01764 670140 Hostel accommodation on a working farm with basic or quite posh camping in the woods in beautiful heart of Perthshire setting. Report 1140/HOSTELS.

Stonefield Castle Hotel Tarbert · www.stonefieldhotels.com · 01880 820836 Outside Tarbert on A83 on slopes of Loch Fyne with wonderful views. A real castle with 60 acres of woody grounds to explore. Report: 822/ARGYLL HOTELS.

Pierhouse Port Appin · 01631 730302 Report: 759/SEASIDE INNS.

The Best Hostels

For hostels in Edinburgh, see p. 39; for Glasgow, see p. 94. SYHA Info: 01786 891400. Central reservations (SYHA) 0870 155 3255. www.syha.org.uk

1139
6/L15

√√√ **Carbisdale Castle SYH** Culrain, near Bonar Bridge · www.carbisdale.org · 0870 004 1109 The flagship hostel of the SYHA, an Edwardian castle in terraced gardens overlooking the Kyle of Sutherland on the edge of the Highlands. Once the home of the exiled King of Norway, it still contains original works of art (nothing of great value though the sculptures lend elegance). The library, ballroom, lounges are all in use and it's only a few quid a night. Some private rooms. Kitchens and café. Bike hire in summer; lots of scenic walks. Station (from Inverness) 1km up steep hill. Buses: Inverness/Thurso/Lairg. 75km Inverness, 330km Edinburgh. You can hire the whole place for parties and it has its own ghost (1257/HOUSE PARTIES).

1140
10/M23

√ **Comrie Croft** near Comrie · www.comriecroft.com · 01764 670140 On A85 Comrie-Crieff/Perth road 3km before Comrie. 2 self-contained buildings: the Farmhouse and the Lodge and courtyard of a working farm in beautiful coun-tryside including a loch and a mountain. Excellent facilities including shop, games

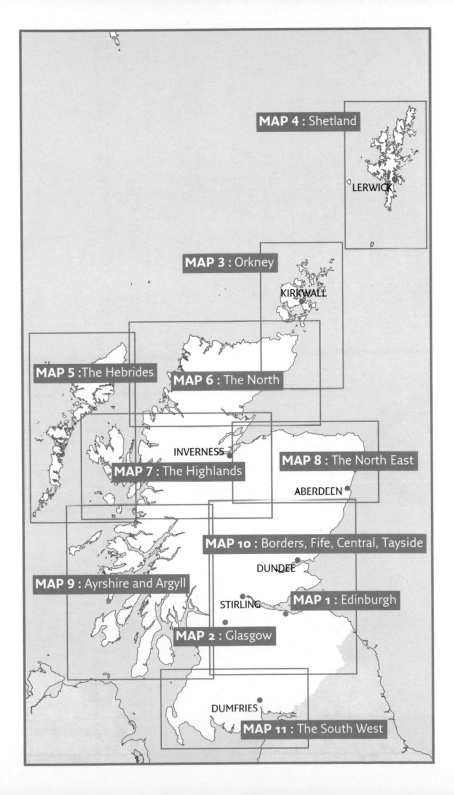

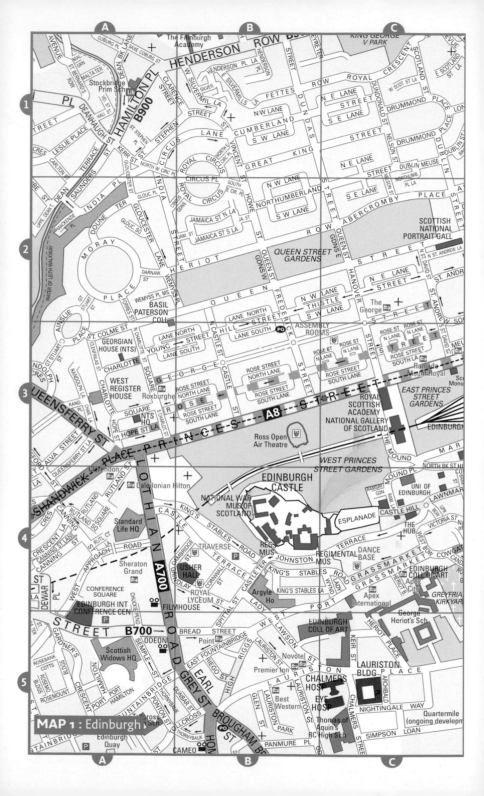

MAP 1 : Edinburgh

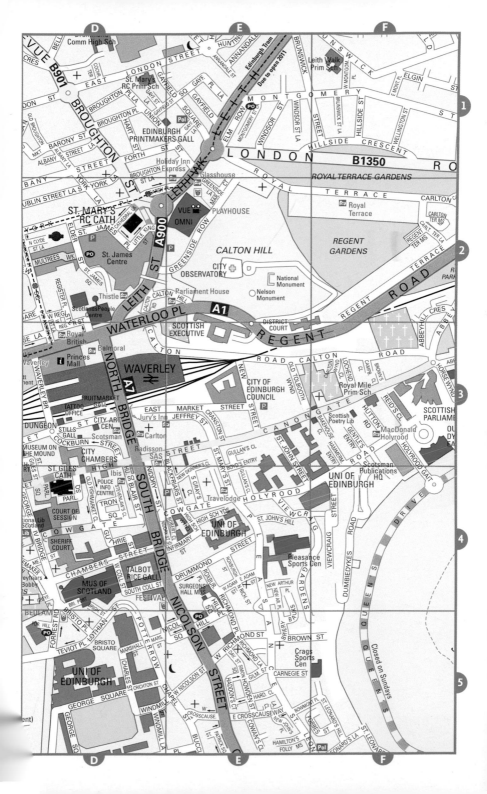

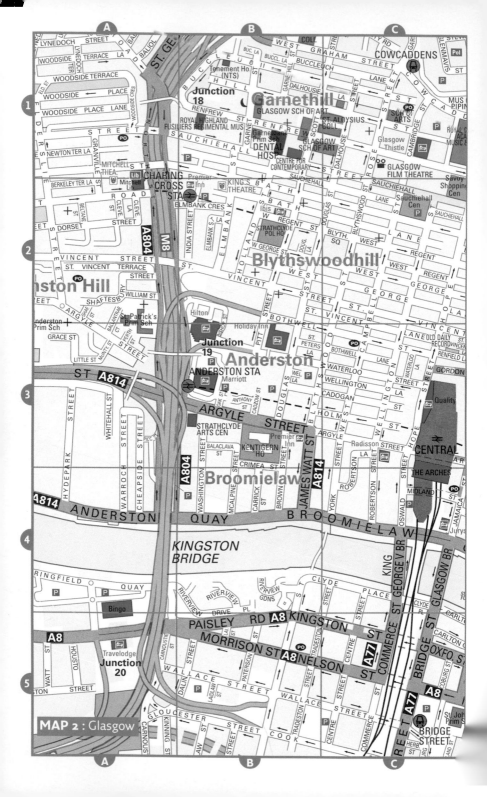

MAP 2 : Glasgow

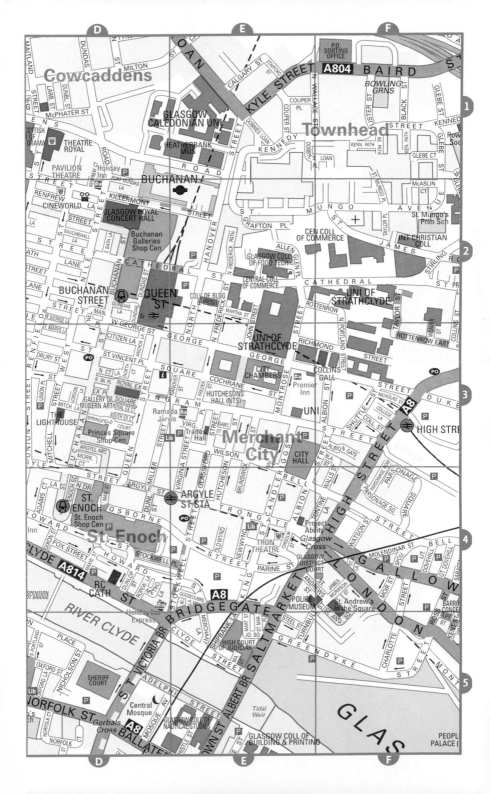

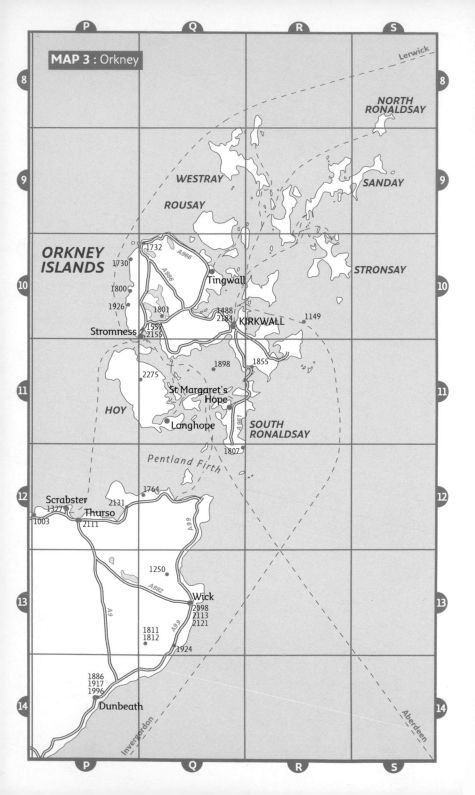

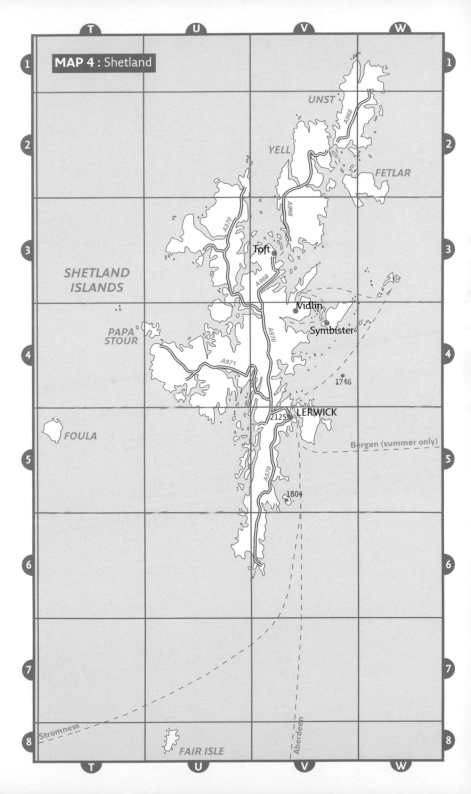

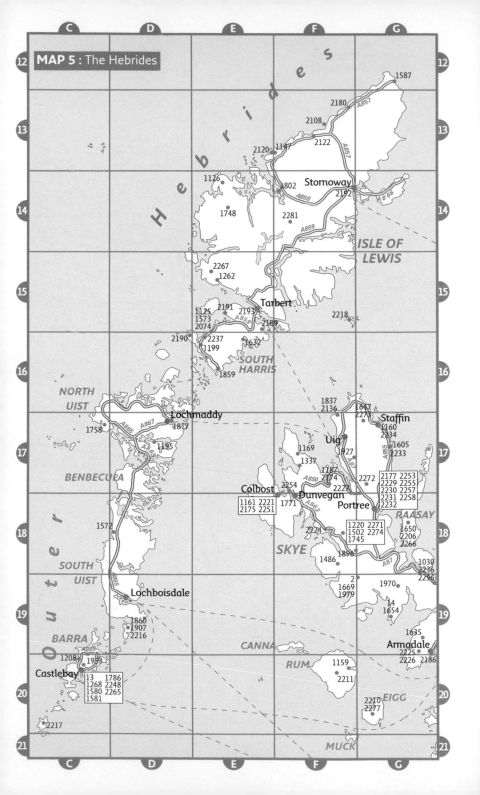

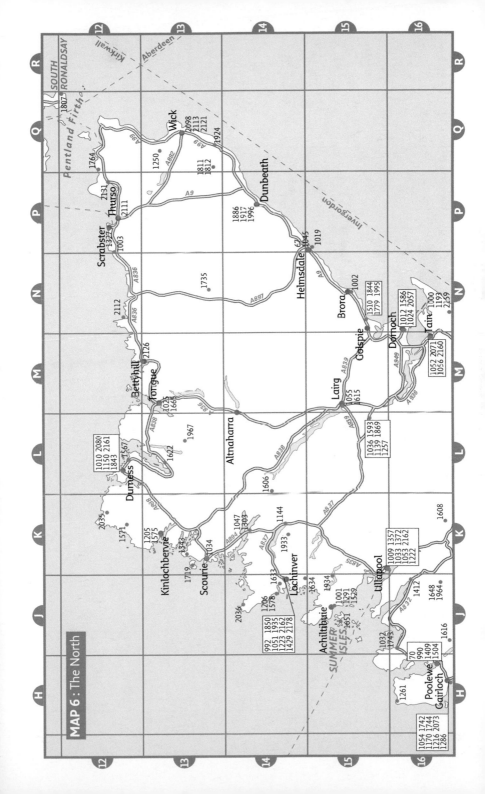

MAP 6 : The North

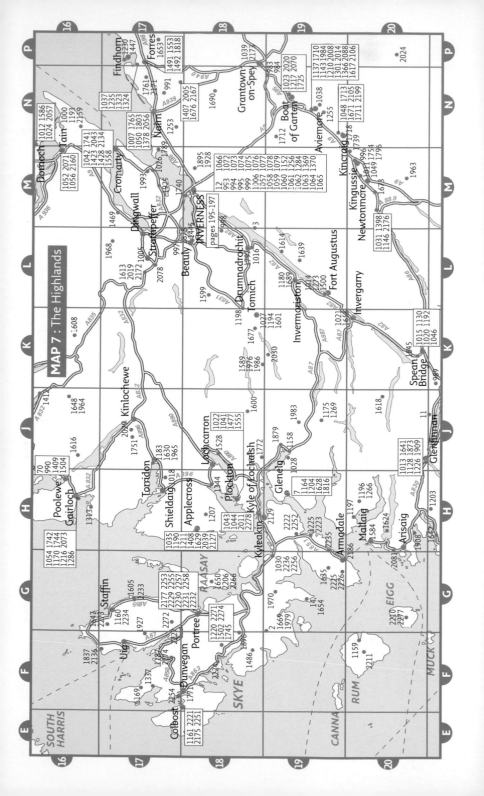

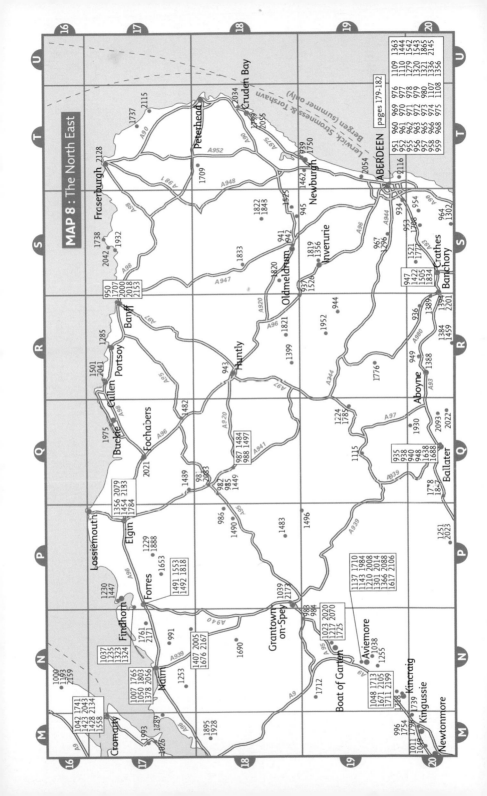

MAP 8 : The North East

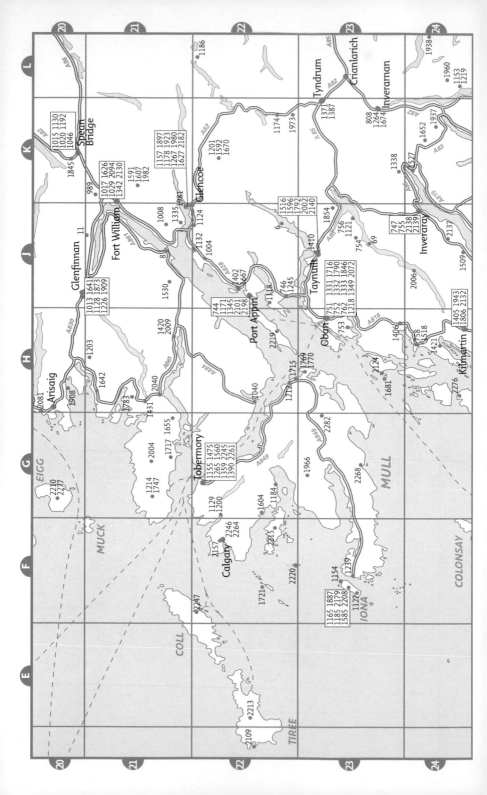

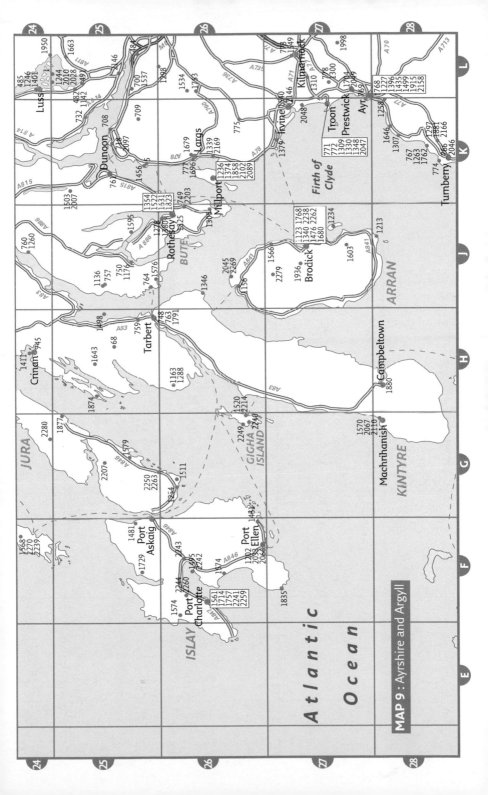

MAP 9 : Ayrshire and Argyll

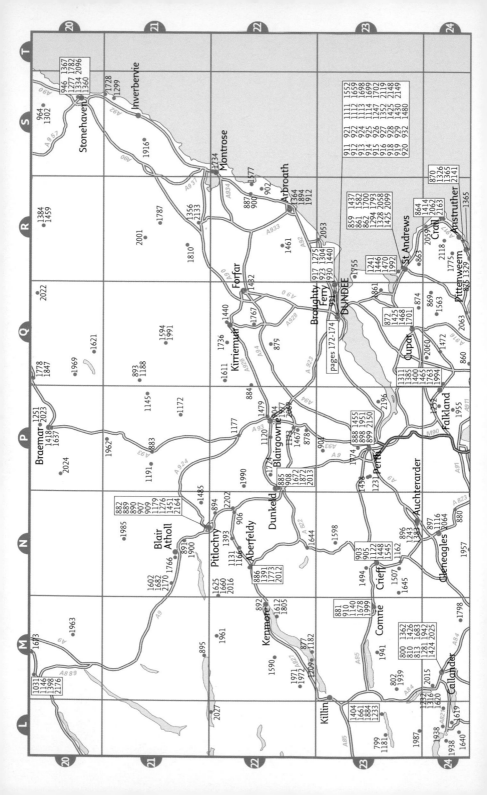

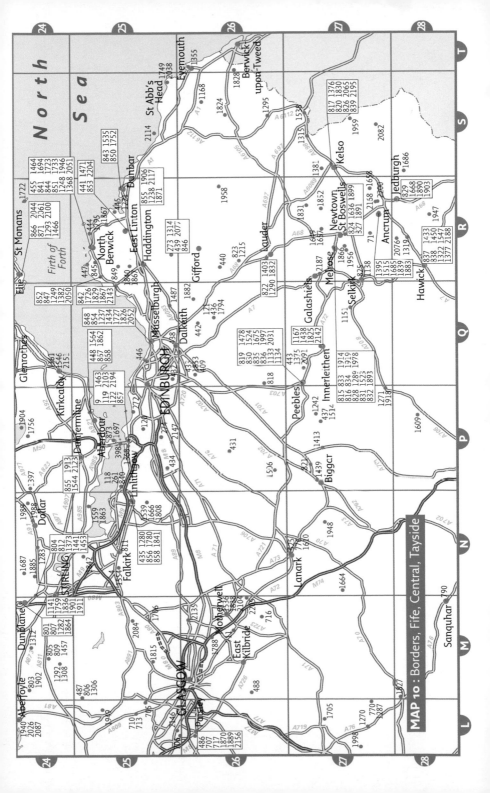

MAP 10 : Borders, Fife, Central, Tayside

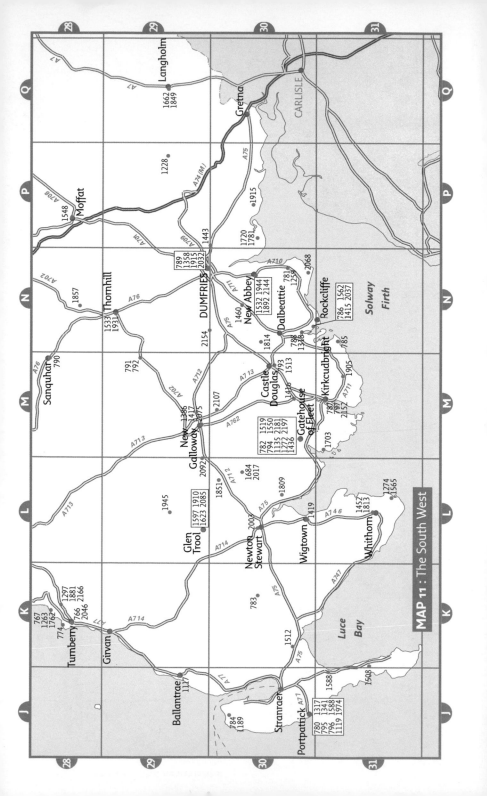

MAP 11 : The South West

room, kitchen and lounges. Mountain bikes for hire; trails. Eco-friendly camping in the woods, including Swedish katas for hire with own wood-burning stoves. Good place to take kids.

1141
10/N24

✓ **Stirling SYH** Stirling · www.stirlinghostel.co.uk · 0870 004 1149
Modern conversion in great part of town, close to castle, adjacent ancient graveyard and with fine views from some rooms. One of the new hotel-like hostels with student-hall standard and facilities. Many oldies and international tourists. Breakfast included or self-catering. Access till 2am.

1142
9/L25

✓ **Loch Lomond SYH** Alexandria · www.syha.org.uk · 0870 004 1149
Built in 1866 by George Martin, the tobacco baron (as opposed to the other one who produced the Beatles), this is hostelling on the grand scale. Towers and turrets, galleried upper-hall, space for banqueting and a splendid view across the loch, of where you're going tomorrow. 30km Glasgow. Station (Balloch) 4km. Buses 200m. Access till midnight. Some private accommodation.

1143
7/N19

✓ **Aviemore Bunkhouse** Aviemore · www.aviemore-bunkhouse.com · 01479 811181 Near station. Main road into Aviemore from south (A95) off Coylumbridge road to Cairngorm. By the river. Part of Old Bridge Inn (1301/GAS-TROPUBS) so great food adjacent. Ensuite rooms for 6/8 and family rooms available. All year.

1144
6/K14

✓ **Inchnadamph Lodge** Assynt · www.inch-lodge.co.uk · 01571 822218
25km north of Ullapool on A837 road to Lochinver and Sutherland. Well appointed mansion house for individuals or groups in geology-gazing, hill-walking, mountain-rearing Assynt. Kitchen, canteen (dinner not provided but self-service breakfast), DVDs. Some twin rooms.

1145
10/P21

✓ **Prosen Hostel** Glen Prosen · www.prosenhostel.co.uk · 01575 540238
Glen Prosen, the gentlest, most beautiful and wooded of the Angus glens (1594/GLENS). 10km from start of glen at Dykehead and part of tiny Prosen village (well, church) at the end of the road. An SYH 'green' hostel; wood-burning stove, internet. Tidy rooms for 4 and 6. Grassy sward, lovely terrace and red squirrels.

1146
7/M20

✓ **Pottery Bunkhouse** Laggan Bridge · www.potterybunkhouse.co.uk · 01528 544231 On A889 east-west near Loch Laggan, 12km from A9 at Dalwhinnie. Homely bunkhouse and great home-bakes caff (1398/TEAROOMS). Lounge overlooking hills (and has TV); wood stove, hot tub on deck. All year (tea-room Easter-Oct).

1147
5/F13

✓ **Na Gearrannan** near Carloway, North Lewis The remarkable hostel in a village of blackhouses is an idyllic spot. See 2120/MUSEUMS. Also:
Am Bothan Harris · www.ambothan.com · 01859 520251 At Leverburgh in the south of South Harris, a bunkhouse handbuilt and personally run – a bright, cool building with well-lived-in feel. Good disabled facilities. Caff, shop nearby. One of 8 hostels in Scotland given 5 Stars by VisitScotland.

1148
7
ATMOS

✓ **Hostelling in the Hebrides** www.syha.org.uk Simple hostelling in the crofting communities of Lewis, Harris and the Uists. Run by a trust to maintain standards in the spirit of Highland hospitality with local crofters acting as wardens. Lewis, Harris and one each in North and South Uist. The Black House cottages on the west of Lewis at Gearrannan (see above) are exceptional. Check local tourist information centres for details (2281/OUTER HEBRIDES).

1149
3/R10

✓ **Bis Geos** Isle of Westray, Orkney · bis-geos.co.uk · 01857 677420
Remote and fabulous: this is how this traditionally rebuilt croft is described, because I still haven't been. Sounds like perhaps 2 ticks may be due. Exceptional standard with nautical theme. Conservatory overlooks the wild ocean. Minibus from the ferry. Sleeps 12. 2 cottages.

1150
6/L12

✓ **Lazy Crofter Bunkhouse** Durness · www.durnesshostel.com · 07803 927642 Adjacent (and with the same owners as) Mackay's Hotel (1010/LESS EXPENSIVE HIGHLANDS). A small, woody chalet (sleeps 12 in 4 rooms) in good location for exploring Durness, Cape Wrath, etc (2035/COASTAL WALKS, 1567/BEACHES). No pub in the hotel but great eats all day. Kitchen and outdoor terrace.

1151
10/Q27

The Borders SYH www.syha.org.uk *There are some ideal wee hostels in this hill-walking tract of Scotland (where it all began). These 2 are especially good, one grand, one very small.*

Melrose 01896 822521 Grade 1, 81 beds, very popular. Well-appointed mansion on meadow 250m by riverside from the abbey. Nice pub nearby (the Ship).
Broadmeadows 8km from Selkirk off A708, the first hostel in Scotland (1931) is a cosy howff with a stove and a view.

1152
7/M18

Inverness Student Hostel 8 Culduthel Road · www.scotlands-top-hostels.com · 01463 236556 Best independent hostel in town uphill from town centre (some dorms have views). Run by same folk who have the great Edinburgh one (114/HOSTELS), with similar laid-back atmosphere and camaraderie. **Bazpackers** 100m downhill, similar vibe.

1153
9/L24

Rowardennan SYH Loch Lomond · www.syha.co.uk · 01360 870259 The hostel at the end of the road up the east (less touristy) side of Loch Lomond from Balmaha and Drymen. Large, well managed and modernised and on a water-side site. On West Highland Way and obvious base for climbing Ben Lomond (1960/MUNROS). Good all-round activity centre and lawns to the loch of your dreams. Rowardennan Hotel boozer nearby. Can do private rooms.

1154
9/F23

Iona Hostel Iona · www.ionahostel.co.uk · 01681 700781Bunkhouse at north tip of island 2km from ferry on John Maclean's farm. This feels like the edge of the world looking over to Staffa and beyond; beach besides. Open all year. 5 rooms, sleeps 21. Iona is, of course, very special (2208/ISLANDS).

1155
9/G22

Tobermory SYH Mull · www.syha.org.uk · 0870 004 1151 Looks out to Tobermory Bay. Central, relatively high-standard hostel very busy in summer. 39 places in 7 rooms (4 on front). Kitchen. Internet. Sweet garden terrace. Near ferry to Ardnamurchan; main Oban ferry 35km away (1560/COASTAL VILLAGES). Mar-Oct.

1156
9/J26

Lochranza Youth Hostel SYH Lochranza · www.syha.org.uk · 0870 004 1140 On left approaching village from south – Victorian house overlooking fab bay and castle ruins. Swans dip at dawn. Full self-catering facilities. Comfortable sitting room. Major refurbishment '09. Mar-Nov.

1157
9/J21

Glencoe SYH Glencoe · www.glencoehostel.co.uk · 0870 004 1122 Deep in the glen itself, 3km off A82/4km by back road from Glencoe village and 33km from Fort William. Modern timber house near river; especially handy for climbers and walkers. Laundry, drying room. Clachaig pub, 2km for good food and craic. (Also 1627/SCENIC ROUTES; 1923/ENCHANTING PLACES; 1897/BATTLEGROUNDS; 1267/PUBS; 1981/SERIOUS WALKS.)

1158 **Ratagan SYH** 0870 004 1147 29km from Kyle of Lochalsh, 3km Shiel Bridge
7/J19 (on A87). A much-loved Highland hostel on the shore of Loch Duich and well situated for walking and exploring some of Scotland's most celebrated scenery, eg 5
Sisters of Kintail/Cluanie Ridge (1983/SERIOUS WALKS), Glenelg (1628/SCENIC
ROUTES; 1816/PREHISTORIC SITES), Falls of Glomach (1600/WATERFALLS). From
Glenelg there's the short and dramatic crossing to Skye through the Kylerhea narrows (continuous, summer only), quite the best way to go.

1159 **Kinloch Castle** Rum · 01687 462037 The hostel on first and second floor (53
7/F20 beds) in one of the most opulent castle-fantasies in the Highlands, though you
ATMOS don't get to use those bathrooms. Hostel operates to allow visitors to experience
the rich natural wildlife, grandeur and peace of Rum. Self-catering. See Rum:
2211/ISLANDS.

1160 **Dun Flodigarry** near Staffin, Skye · www.hostelflodigarry.co.uk · 01470
7/G17 552212 In far north 32km from Portree beside Flodigarry Country House Hotel,
which has a decent bistro, pub and is amidst big scenery. Overlooks sea.
Bunkrooms for 2-6 and 3 singles (holds up to 40) and great refectory. Open all
year.

The Best Roadside, Seaside & Countryside Inns

1161 ✓✓**The Three Chimneys** Colbost, Skye · www.threechimneys.co.uk ·
7/F18 01470 511258 7km west of Dunvegan on B884 to Glendale. Rooms in a
6 ROOMS new build across the yard from the much-loved and much-awarded Three
TEL · TV Chimneys restaurant (2251/SKYE RESTAURANTS) called **The House Over-by**.
£85+ Roadside, yes but few cars come by and there's the smell of the sea. Calm and
contemporary split-level rooms with own doors to the sward. Breakfast lounge
which doubles as a predinner lounge in the evening. A model of its kind in the
Highlands, hence often full. Be sure to book for dinner!

1162 ✓✓**The Barley Bree** Muthill, near Crieff www.barleybree.com ·
10/N23 01764 681451 Stylish, excellent value restaurant with rooms above on
5 ROOMS main road through the village. Great food, tasteful and comfortable rooms. Must
TV be the French connection (chef Fabrice Bouteloup). Bar/restaurant open for lunch
£38-45 (Wed-Sat) and dinner (closed Mon). Not much to do in Muthill itself but the amaz-
ATMOS ing Drummond Gardens are nearby (1507/GARDENS) and there's Crieff and Comrie.

1163 9/H26 ✓✓**Kilberry Inn** near Tarbert, Argyll · www.kilberryinn.com · 01880
5 ROOMS 770223 Half-way round the Knapdale peninsula on the single-track
APR-OCT B8024 (1163/SCENIC ROUTES), the long and breathtaking way to Lochgilphead.
TV · DA Homely roadside inn with simple, classy rooms and excellent cooking (1288/GAS-
£60-85 TROPUBS). Michelin Bib Gourmand and Restaurant of the Year '09 at 'the Awards'.

1164 ✓**Glenelg Inn** Glenelg · www.glenelg-inn.com · 01599 522273 At the
7/H19 end of that great road over the hill from Shiel Bridge on the A87 (1628/SCENIC
6 ROOMS +1 ROUTES)...well, not quite the end because you can drive further round to ethereal
£38-45 Loch Hourn, but this halt is a civilised hostelry to repair to. Decent food, good
ATMOS drinking, snug lounge. Garden with tables and views. Rooms basic but it all has
the atmosphere that came from the Mains. From Glenelg, take the best route to
Skye (7/FAVOURITE JOURNEYS).

1165
9/F23
16 ROOMS
APR-OCT
£45-60

✓ **Argyll Hotel** Iona · www.argyllhoteliona.co.uk · 01681 700334 On beautiful, turquoise bay between Iona and Mull on road between ferry and abbey. Day trippers come and go; you should stay! A charming hotel on a remarkable island. Cosy rooms (1 suite), good food (especially vegetarian) fresh from the organic garden. The real peace and quiet and that's just sitting on the bench outside – it's Colourist country and this is where they would have stayed too. Nice for kids (1127/HOTELS THAT WELCOME KIDS).

1166
10/N22
5 ROOMS
TV
£38-45

✓ **Inn on the Tay** Grandtully · www.theinnonthetay.co.uk · 01887 840760 Recent conversion of roadside inn that also has a commanding position on the riverbank where rapids tax all the helmeted rafters and canoeists of Perthshire – so constant entertainment. Contemporary café/bar with good food, residents' lounge, outside deck and comfortable modern bedrooms – some with 3 beds, so a good family or ménage à trois option.

1167
10/Q27
14 ROOMS
TEL · TV
£38-45

✓ **Traquair Arms** Innerleithen · www.traquairarmshotel.co.uk · 01896 830229 100m from the A72 Gala-Peebles road towards Traquair, a popular village and country inn that caters for all kinds of folk (and, at weekends, large numbers of them). Notable for bar meals, real ale and family facilities. Rooms refurbished to a decent standard. David and Jane Roger making a fair go of it here. Beer garden out back. Much cycling nearby and the Tweed.

1168
10/S26
3 ROOMS
£30-38

Craw Inn Auchencrow, near Reston · www.thecrawinn.co.uk · 01890 761253 5 km A1 and well worth short detour into Berwickshire countryside. Quintessential inn with cosy pub and dining room. Funky furniture, simple rooms. Food decent, wines extraordinary. Lunch and dinner.

1169
7/F17
5 ROOMS
£30 OR LESS

The Stein Inn Waternish, Skye · www.stein-inn.co.uk · 01470 592362 Off B886 the Dunvegan-Portree road, about 10km Dunvegan. In row of cottages on water side. The 'oldest inn on Skye' with great pub (open fire, ok grub). Small rooms above are not great but Waternish is a special spot and there's an excellent seafood restaurant adjacent (2254/SEAFOOD RESTAURANTS).

1170
7/H16
17 ROOMS
TEL · TV · DA
£38-45

Old Inn Gairloch · www.theoldinn.net · 01445 712006 Southern approach on A832, tucked away by river and 'old bridge'. Excellent pub for food in bar, lounge and restaurant and tables by the river. Music (Fri and as advertised). Also own the hotel up the road but you'd want to stay here. Nice, simple rooms (and the pub goes like a fair). Routinely recommended in pub guides; their ale is good.

1171
10/M24
12 ROOMS
TEL · TV
NO PETS
£38-60

Pierhouse Port Appin · www.pierhousehotel.co.uk · 01631 730302 An inn at the end of the road (the minor road that leads off the A828 Oban to Fort William) and at the end of the 'pier', where the tiny passenger ferry leaves for Lismore (2219/MAGIC ISLANDS). A bistro restaurant with decent seafood (1345/SEAFOOD RESTAURANTS) in great setting. Comfy motel-type rooms (more expensive overlook the sea and island) and conservatory restaurant and lounge. Good place to take kids and a great yachty stop.

1172
10/P21
6 ROOMS
DA
£38-45

Glenisla Hotel Kirkton Of Glenisla · www.glenisla-hotel.com · 01575 582223 20km northwest of Kirriemuir via B951 at head of this secluded storybook glen. A home from home: hearty food, real ale and local colour. Fishers, stalkers, trekkers and walkers (notable stopover on the Cateran Trail; 1977/LONG WALKS) all come by for grub, grog and a chat along the way (pub closed Mon). Neat rooms look into countryside but still await their wee makeover.

1173
10/P22
5 ROOMS
TV
£45-60

Meikleour Hotel Meikleour · www.meikleour-inn.co.uk · 01250 883206
Just off the A93 Perth-Blairgowrie road (on the B984) by and behind the famously
high beech hedge (a Perthshire landmark). Roadside inn with quiet accommodation and food in dining room or (more convivially) the bar. Refurbishing of rooms
in progress.

1174
9/K22
10 ROOMS
TEL · TV
£38-45

Bridge of Orchy Hotel Bridge of Orchy · www.bridgeoforchy.co.uk ·
01838 400208 Unmissable on the A82 (the road to Glencoe, Fort William and
Skye) 11km north of Tyndrum. Old inn extensively refurbished and a great stopover
for motorists and walkers. Simple, quite stylish rooms. A la carte menu and specials in pub/conservatory. Good spot for the malt or a munch on the West
Highland Way (1976/LONG WALKS). Food LO 9pm. The 50-bed bunkhouse is very
cheap.

1175 7/J19
12 ROOMS
+BUNKHOUSE
TEL
£30-38/
£45-60

Cluanie Inn Glenmoriston · www.cluanieinn.com · 01320 340238 On main
road to Skye 15km before Shiel Bridge, a traditional inn surrounded by the mountain summits that attract walkers and travellers – the 5 Sisters, the Ridge and the
Saddle (1983/SERIOUS WALKS). Club house adjacent has some group accommodation while inn rooms can be high-spec – one with sauna, one with jacuzzi! Bar
food LO 9pm. Rooms do vary. Friendly staff.

1176
9/J25
10 RMS · TV
£38-45
ATMOS

The Kames Hotel by Tighnabruaich · www.kames-hotel.com · 01700
811489 Frequented by passing yachtsmen who moor down below and pop up for
lunch. Great seaside setting on the Doon-the-Water shore, and atmospheric bar.
Owners (3) have taste and TLC with a calming colour scheme, friendly staff and
Philippa Elliott's pretty good photography. All simply stylish and a good vibe.

1177
10/P22
17 ROOMS
TV · DA
£38-45

Bridge of Cally Hotel Bridge of Cally · www.bridgeofcallyhotel.com ·
01250 886231 Wayside pub on a bend of the road between Blairgowrie and
Glenshee/Braemar (the ski zone and Royal Deeside). Cosy and inexpensive
between gentle Perthshire and the wilder Grampians. Staging post on the Cateran
Trail (1977/LONG WALKS). Rooms quiet and pleasant and good value. Restaurant
and bar meals till 9pm.

1178
9/J21
23 ROOMS
TV · NO PETS
£30-38

Clachaig Inn Glencoe · www.clachaig.com · 01855 811252 Basic but decent
accommodation; you will sleep well, especially after walking/climbing/drinking,
which is what most people are doing here. Great atmosphere both inside and out.
Food available bar/lounge and dining room till 9pm. Ales aplenty; 1267/PUBS. 4
lodges out back. Harry Potter and film crew were once here.

1179 10/N21
16 ROOMS
TEL · TV · DA
£38-45

Moulin Hotel Pitlochry · www.moulinhotel.co.uk · 01796 472196
Kirkmichael Rd; at the landmark crossroads on the A924. Basic rooms above and
beside notable pub for excellent pub food and especially ales – they brew their
own out the back. (1276/REAL ALES). There is an annexe across the street.

1180
7/L19
8 ROOMS
TEL · TV
£38-45

Glenmoriston Arms Hotel Invermoriston, Loch Ness · 01320 351206 ·
www.glenmoriston-arms-hotel.co.uk On main A82 between Inverness (45km)
and Fort Augustus (10km) at the Glen Moriston corner, and a worthwhile corner of
this famous loch side to explore. Busy local bar, fishermen's tales. Bistro over-by
(7 days summer, Thu-Sat in winter). Bar meals look ok and extensive malt list –
certainly a good place to drink them. Inn-like bedrooms.

✓ ✓ **Ardeonaig** Loch Tay · 01567 820400 On tiny ribbon of road,
lochside luxury with superb dining. 1182/GET-AWAY HOTELS.

✓ **The Applecross Inn** Applecross · www.applecross.uk.com/inn · 01520 744262 The legendary end of the road, seaside inn on the shore opposite Applecross. Report: 1190/GET AWAY HOTELS.

✓ **The Ship Inn** Gatehouse of Fleet · www.theshipinngatehouse.co.uk · 01557 814217 Old inn on corner of main street of this most charming Galloway town. Recent refurbishment, great grub. Report: 782/SOUTHWEST HOTELS.

✓ **The Harbour Inn** Islay · 01496 810330 **& The Port Charlotte Hotel** 01496 850360 2 waterfront inns on faraway Islay: one in town, the other in charming Port Charlotte. 2242/2241/ISLAND HOTELS.

✓ **The Sorn Inn** Sorn, Ayrshire · www.sorninn.com · 01290 551305 1287/GASTROPUBS.

Anchor Hotel Kippford · 01556 620205 Pub grub with rooms in superb Solway setting. 788/SOUTHWEST HOTELS/RESTAURANTS.

The Best Restaurants With Rooms

✓✓ **The Sorn Inn** Sorn · 01290 551305 8km east of Mauchline on the B743, half an hour from Ayr. 770/AYRSHIRE HOTELS.

✓✓ **The Peat Inn** near Cupar · 01334 840206 At eponymous Fife crossroads. Long-established brilliant restaurant under masterchef Geoffrey Smeddle. And swish suites. 869/FIFE RESTAURANTS.

✓✓ **The Three Chimneys** Colbost, Skye · 01470 511258 State-of-the-art dining and contemporary rooms far away in the west. Near Dunvegan. But you'll be lucky to get in. 2221/SKYE HOTELS.

✓✓ **The Barley Bree** Muthill, near Crieff · 01764 681451 French guy in the kitchen, Scots partner on decor and design have transformed this old pub in a sleepy village to a destination. 1162/ROADSIDE INNS.

✓✓ **The Horseshoe Inn** Eddleston, near Peebles · 01721 730225 New-ish Borders destination. Bistro and restaurant and rooms in old school behind. Designed to impress. 818/BORDERS HOTELS.

✓✓ **The Cross** Kingussie · 01540 661166 Rooms upstairs in converted tweed mill. Downstairs the best restaurant and wine list in the region. 996/HIGHLAND HOTELS.

✓✓ **Mackay's** Durness · 01971 511202 Contemporary makeover of long-established hotel in the far North West. 1010/LESS EXPENSIVE HIGHLAND HOTELS.

✓✓ **The Cross Keys** Kippen · 01786 870293 Long established but recently revitalised gastropub with rooms above in foodie village main street. 1292/GASTROPUBS.

✓ ✓ **Kilberry Inn** Kilberry near Tarbert · 01880 770223 1163/ROADSIDE INNS.

✓ **The Alloway Inn** Ayr · 01292 442336 Just outside Alloway in deepest Burns country. Cosy rooms. Gastropub food. 796/AYRSHIRE HOTELS.

✓ **The Ship Inn** Elie · 01333 330246 Destination pub for food and pubness with rooms adjacent on shore road.

✓ **Yann's At Glenearn House** Crieff · 01764 650111 Victorian mansion with 5 rooms above the very French and the best bistro in the county. 903/PERTHSHIRE RESTAURANTS.

✓ **The Mash Tun** Aberlour · 01340 881771 Boutique-style rooms above pub in whisky country. 982/SPEYSIDE.

✓ **The Green Inn** Ballater · 01339 755701 Long-established best restaurant in Deeside tourist town. 948/NORTHEAST RESTAURANTS.

✓ **The Inn on the Tay** Grandtully, near Aberfeldy · 01887 840760 Another made-over inn, this on the banks of the rushing River Tay. Great for kids. 1166/ROADSIDE INNS.

✓ **Creagan House** Strathyre · 01877 384638 Rob Roy and Trossachs country. On the road west and to the islands. 802/CENTRAL HOTELS.

✓ **Smiddy House** Spean Bridge · 01397 712335 Comfy roadside inn and best casual food in Fort William area. 1046/BEST HIGHLAND RESTAURANTS.

✓ **Wildings Hotel** Maidens · 01655 331401 Huge local reputation for food; refurbished rooms overlook the sea. 774/AYRSHIRE HOTELS.

✓ **The Wheatsheaf** Swinton, Berwickshire · 01890 860257 10 all-different bedrooms above gastropub of long standing. 1295/GASTROPUBS.

The Inn At Kippen Kippen · 01786 871010 Excellent bar and restaurant in centre of village just off the road from Stirling to Loch Lomond. 809/CENTRAL HOTELS.

Dunure Inn Dunure · 01292 500549 South of Ayr. 1307/GASTROPUBS.

Kilspindie House Aberlady · 01875 870682 Main street of East Lothian village. 842/LOTHIAN HOTELS.

Grants At Craigellachie Ratagan, near Kyle of Lochalsh · 01599 511331 1028/INEXPENSIVE HIGHLAND HOTELS.

The Rocks Dunbar · 01368 862287 At east end of town. Overlooking harbour area. Big local reputation for food. 843/LOTHIAN HOTELS.

The Great Get-Away-From-It-All Hotels

1181
10/L23
14 ROOMS
TEL · TV
ATMOS
£45-85+

Monachyle Mhor near Balquhidder · www.monachylemhor.com · 01877 384622 Not so remote, but seems so once you've negotiated the thread of road along Loch Voil from Balquhidder (only 11km from the A84 Callander-Crianlarich road). Incongruously pink farmhouse overlooking Loch Voil from the magnificent Balquhidder Braes where the children Tom and Madeleine and Dick Lewis grew up; then turned it into the first really cool boutique hotel in the Highlands. Contemporary, calm and sexy. 7 rooms in courtyard annexe, 6 in main building, 1 out back. Now all completely gorgeous, especially the baths and bathrooms. Bar locals and visitors use. Tom on stoves (when he's not food festing) cooking up some of the best food in the North. Friendly, cosy, inexpensive for this standard; a place to relax summer or winter. Safaris, walking and farmyard or photography courses and a shop that stocks the 'brand': a Mhor-ish experience.

1182
10/M22
20 ROOMS
TEL
£45-85+

Ardeonaig Loch Tay · www.ardeonaighotel.co.uk · 01567 820400 On narrow, scenic south Loch Tay road midway between Kenmore and Killin. An airy inn by the water opposite Ben Lawers. South African chef/proprietor Pete Grottgens making the most of this perfect lochside location. Stylish rooms, including self-contained rondawels arranged round edge of lawns to the shore. Great bar and excellent dining with top urban service standards. See also 877/BEST TAYSIDE. Library with cool books and dreamy view of the ben. You could flop around here for days unwinding but activities include guided walks, stalking, photography (on hotel's 3000 acres of moor and hill) and there's a bothy for lunch and a boathouse. Room rate includes dinner but you wouldn't go anywhere else.

1183
7/J17
12 ROOMS
TEL · TV
NO KIDS
£85+

The Torridon Glen Torridon, near Kinlochewe · 01445 791242 · www.lochtorridonhotel.com Impressive former hunting lodge on lochside, surrounded by majestic mountains. A comfortable but cosy family-run baronial house with very relaxed atmosphere: an all-round Highland experience. Focuses on outdoor activities like clay-pigeon shoots, kayaking, gorge-scrambling, mountain biking or fishing with 2 full-time guides/instructors. Lots of walking possibilities nearby including the Torridon big 3: Beinn Alligin (1965/MUNROS), Liathach right in front of the hotel and Beinn Eighe. This great hotel has spawned a cheaper travel lodge option: **The Torridon Inn** in adjacent block with own bar and bistro. An excellent budget choice (12 rooms). Main hotel has fine dining room under chef Kevin Broome, does a nice afternoon tea and has a fantastic malts bar for a dram in the dwindling day (1495/WHISKY).

1184 9/G22
7 ROOMS
+3 COTTAGES
MAR-NOV
TV
£60-85

Tiroran House Isle of Mull · tiroran.com · 01681 705232 Southwest corner on road to Iona from Craignure then B8035 round Loch na Keal. 1 hour Tobermory. Family-friendly small country house in fabulous gardens by the sea, under conscientious owners Laurence and Katie Mackay (Katie a Cordon Bleu cook). Near Iona and Ulva ferry; you won't miss Tobermory. Excellent food from sea and organic kitchen garden. Lovely rooms. Sea eagles fly over, otters flop in the bay.

1185
9/F23
15 ROOMS
(1 SUITE)
APR-OCT
£45-60

Argyll Hotel Iona · www.argyllhoteliona.co.uk · 01681 700334 Quintessential island hotel on the best of small islands just large enough to get away for walks and explore (2208/ISLANDS). You can hire bikes (or bring). Abbey is nearby (1887/ABBEYS). 3 lounges (1 with TV, 1 with sun) and 1 lovely suite (with wood-burning stove). Good home-grown/made food from their famous organic garden.

1186 9/L22
5 ROOMS
MID FEB-
MID NOV
£38-45

✓ **Moor of Rannoch Hotel** Rannoch Station · www.moorofrannoch.co.uk
01882 633238 Beyond Pitlochry and the Trossachs and far west via Loch
Tummel and Loch Rannoch (B8019 and B8846) so a wonderful journey to the edge
of Rannoch Moor and adjacent station (so you could get the sleeper from London
and be here for breakfast. 4 trains either way each day via Glasgow). Literally the
end of the road but an exceptional find in the middle of nowhere. Cosy, wood-
panelled rooms, ok restaurant, though gourmets may grumble. Nevertheless a
quintessential Highland inn. Great walking.

1187 7/F17
8 ROOMS
MAR-DEC
£85+

✓ **Greshornish Country House** www.greshornishhouse.com · 01470
582345 · Skye Off the A850 Portree-Dunvegan road about half-way then
6km along Loch Greshornish to delightful isolation. It's a long way to another
good dinner so you're expected to eat in (but lovely menu from Greshornish Loch
starters to impressive Scottish cheese). Comfy but airy rooms presented with great
taste (nice pics) by the Colquhouns. Log fires, billiard room, candlelit dinners. A
superb retreat which you can have for exclusive use.

1188
10/Q21
10 ROOMS
TEL · TV
NO PETS
£38-45

✓ **Glen Clova Hotel** www.clova.com · 01575 550350 · near Kirriemuir
Well, not that near Kirriemuir; 25km north up the glen on B955 from
Dykehead. Rooms all en-suite and surprisingly well appointed. Climbers' bar (till all
hours). Superb walking hereabouts (eg Loch Brandy and the classic path to Loch
Muick). A laid-back get-away though lots of families drive up on a Sunday for
lunch. Also has a bunkhouse (cheap) and 2 new 'luxury' lodges. 6 more in the off-
ing at TGP, with hot tubs. Great value, great craic! Calmer, greener and more basic
is **Prosen Hostel** at the head of Glen Prosen, probably the most beautiful and
unspoiled of the glens. No pub, no interference (1145/HOSTELS).

1189 11/J30
6 ROOMS
+ SUITES
TEL · TV
£60-85

✓ **Corsewall Lighthouse Hotel** www.lighthousehotel.co.uk · 01776
853220 · near Stranraer Only 20 minutes from Stranraer (via A718 to
Kirkcolm) and follow signs, but way up on the peninsula and as it suggests a hotel
made out of a working lighthouse. Romantic and offbeat, but only ok food.
Attractions nearby include Portpatrick 30 minutes away through the maze of quiet
backroads.

1190 7/H18
8 ROOMS
£30-38

✓ **Applecross Inn** www.applecross.uk.com/inn · 01520 744262 ·
Applecross At the end of the road (the Pass of the Cattle which is often
snowed up in winter, so you can really disappear) north of Kyle of Lochalsh and
west of Strathcarron. After a spectacular journey, this water-side inn is a haven of
hospitality. Buzzes all seasons. Rooms small (1+7 best). Judy Fish, a great team
and a real chef look after you. Poignant visitor centre (2127/HERITAGE), walled garden, lovely walks (2039/COASTAL WALKS) and even a real pizza hut in summer
(1408/COFFEE SHOPS) easily enough to keep you happy in Applecross for days.

1191
10/P21
17 ROOMS
TEL · TV
£38-45

✓ **Dalmunzie Castle** www.dalmunzie.com · 01250 885224 · Spittal of
Glenshee 3km off Blairgowrie-Braemar road and near Glenshee skiing. By
riverside and surrounded by bare hills, this laird's house is warm and welcoming
but splendidly remote. Some great rooms, Michelin-mentioned dining, bar and 9-
hole golf course. See also 883/PERTHSHIRE.

1192 9/K20
5 ROOMS
MAR-OCT
TV · NO PETS
£30-38

✓ **Corriechoille Lodge** www.corriechoille.com · 01397 712002 · by
Spean Bridge 3km from south Bridge via road by station. Lovely road and
spectacularly situated; it's great to arrive. Justin and Lucy share their perfect
retreat with you in house and 2 turf-covered chalets out back. Set-menu dinner.
All round serenity! Report 1115/HIGHLAND HOTELS.

1193 7/N16
9 ROOMS
TEL · NO PETS
£60-85

✓ **Glenmorangie House** Cadboll by Fearn, near Tain · 01862 871671 · www.theglenmorangiehouse.com On the little peninsula east of Tain off A9 (10km). Comfortable mansion with house-party atmosphere. Owned by LVMH; recently refurbished bedrooms are luxurious. Report: 1000/HIGHLAND HOTELS.

1194 7/K20
10 ROOMS
£38-45

Tomdoun Hotel www.tomdoun.com · 01809 511218 · near Invergarry 20km from Invergarry, 9km off the A87 to Kyle of Lochalsh. An ivy-covered Victorian coaching inn that replaced a much older one; off the beaten track but perfect (we do mean perfect) for fishing and walking (Loch Quoich and Knoydart, in the last wilderness). Superb views over Glengarry and Bonnie Prince Charlie's country. House-party atmosphere, mix-match furniture, loadsa malts and nice dogs. Reports, please, on food!

1195 5/D17
10 ROOMS
MAR-JAN
DA
£45-60

Langass Lodge North Uist · www.langasslodge.co.uk · 01876 580285 On the A867 which runs through the middle of the Uists, 7km south of Lochmaddy, 500m from the road. Small, hideaway hotel with garden and island outlook, though the entrance ain't so lovely. Half of rooms in extension to stylish standard but others in hotel ok. Nice bar and dining overlooking the garden. Kid-friendly and you can bring the dog. Uists are wonderful to explore and there's prehistoric stuff nearby and a great (2.5km) walk. 1817/PREHISTORIC, 1572/BEACHES.

1196 7/H20
4 ROOMS
MAR-OCT
NO PETS
£30 OR LESS

The Pier House www.pierhouseknoydart.co.uk · 01687 462347 · Inverie, Knoydart Currently the only restaurant on far-away Knoydart, though good grub at the pub nearby (1266/BLOODY GOOD PUBS). Accessible on foot (sic) from Kinlochourn (25km) or Bruce Watt's boat from Mallaig (Mon-Fri summer; Mon, Wed, Fri winter. 01687 462320). Friendly couple offer warm hospitality in their home and notably good seafood; rovers return.

1197 7/H20
4 ROOMS
+ LODGE
APR-SEP
NO PETS
£38-45

Doune Stone Lodge www.doune-knoydart.co.uk/stlodge.html · 01687 462667 · Knoydart As above, on this remote peninsula and this great spot on the west tip overlooking a bay on the Sound of Sleat. They have own boats so pick you up from Mallaig and drop you round the inlets for walking. Otherwise 8km from Inverie. Rooms and lodge for up to 14. Only lodge in winter. Excellent home-cooked dinner, breakfast and packed lunch.

1198 7/K18
8 ROOMS
TEL · TV
£45-60

Tomich Hotel www.tomichhotel.co.uk · 01456 415399 · near Cannich 8km from Cannich which is 25km from Drumnadrochit. Fabulous Plodda Falls are nearby (1601/WATERFALLS). Cosy country inn in conservation village with added bonus of use of swimming pool in nearby steading. Faraway feel, surprising bar round the back where what's left of the locals do linger. Good base for outdoorsy weekend. Glen Affric across the way.

✓✓ **Knockinaam Lodge** near Portpatrick · 01776 810471 Report: 780/SOUTH WEST HOTELS.

✓✓ **Glenapp Castle** Ballantrae · 01465 831212 Report: 1117/COUNTRY-HOUSE HOTELS.

✓✓ **Three Chimneys** Skye · 01470 511258 Report: 1161/ROADSIDE INNS, 2251/SKYE RESTAURANTS.

✓✓ **Mackay's** Durness · 01971 511202 Report: 1010/LESS EXPENSIVE HIGHLAND HOTELS.

✓ **Glenelg Inn** Glenelg · 01599 522273 Report: 1164/ROADSIDE INNS.

✓ **Broad Bay House** Lewis · 01851 820990 Report: 2281/HEBRIDES.

Great Wild Camping Up North

In Scotland the Best *we don't do caravans. In fact, because I spend a lot of time behind them on Highland roads, WE HATE CARAVANS and ain't mad about campervans, either. Wild camping is a different matter, provided you are sensitive to the environment and respect the rights of farmers and other landowners.*

1199
5/E16

✓ **South Harris** West coast south of Tarbert where the boat comes in. 35km to Stornoway. Follow road and you reach some truly splendid beaches (eg Scarista 1573/BEACHES). You could treat yourself to dinner at Scarista House (2237/ISLAND HOTELS). Graze on your own private sunset and swim in a turquoise sea.

1200 9/G22

✓ **Calgary Beach** Mull 10km from Dervaig, where there are toilets, picnic tables and BBQs but no other facilities – this is classic wild camping but you won't be alone. The laid-back Calgary Hotel and Dovecot Restaurant are on hand for shelter and sustenance. Also on Mull south of Killiechronan on the gentle shore of **Loch na Keal**, there is nothing but the sky and the sea and you have it all to yourself. Ben More is in the background (1966/MUNROS). Both sublime!

1201 9/K22

✓ **Glen Etive** near Ballachulish & Glencoe One of Scotland's great unofficial camping grounds. Along the road/river side in a classic glen (1592/GLENS) guarded where it joins the pass into Glencoe by the awesome Buachaille Etive Mor. Innumerable grassy terraces and small meadows on which climbers and walkers have camped for generations, and pools to bathe in (1670/SWIMMING HOLES). The famous Kingshouse Pub is 2km from the foot of the glen for sustenance, malt whisky and comparing midge bites.

1202 9/F26

Kintra Islay Bowmore-Port Ellen road, take Oa turn-off then follow signs 7km. Long beach one way, wild coastal walk the other. Camping (and room for a few campervans) on grassy strand looking out to sea; basic facilities in farmyard – shower, toilet, washing machine.

1203 9/H21

Lochailort A 12km stretch south from Lochailort on the A861, along the southern shore of the sea loch itself. A flat, rocky and grassy foreshore with a splendid seascape and backed by brooding mountains. Nearby is Loch nan Uamh where Bonnie Prince Charlie landed (1908/MARY, CHARLIE & BOB). Once past the salmon farm laboratories, you're in calendar scenery; the Glenuig Inn at the southern end is the pub to repair to. No facilities except the sea.

1204 7/H19

Glenelg Near the village of Glenelg itself which is over the amazing hill from Shiel Bridge (1628/SCENIC ROUTES). Village has great pub, the Glenelg Inn (1164/INNS) and a shop. Best spots 1km from village on road to Skye ferry on the strand.

1205 6/K13

Oldshoremore near Kinlochbervie 3km from village and supplies. Gorgeous beach (1575/BEACHES) and **Polin**, next cove. On the way to **Sandwood Bay** where the camping is legendary (but you have to carry everything 7km).

1206 6/J14

Achmelvich near Lochinver Signed off the fabulous Lochinver to Drumbeg road (1633/SCENIC ROUTES) or walk from village 3km via Ardroe (and a great spot to watch otters that have been there for generations). There is an official campsite adjacent horrible caravan park, but walk further north towards Stoer. The beach at **Alltan na Bradhan** with the ruins of the old mill is fabulous. Best sea-swimming on this coast. Directions: 1578/BEACHES.

1207 **7/H18** **On the Road to Applecross** The road that winds up the mountain from the A896 that takes you to Applecross (1629/SCENIC ROUTES) is one of the most dramatic in Scotland or anywhere. At the plateau before you descend to the coast, the landscape is lunar and the views to die for. Camp here (wind permitting) with the gods. Once over and 8km downhill there's the foreshore for more leisurely camping and proper campsite with caff (see next page).

1208 **5/C20** **Barra** www.isleofbarra.com Lots of quiet places but you may as well be next to an amazing beach – one by 'the airport' where the little Otters come and go has added interest (and mobile phone reception – unlike rest of the island) but the twin crescent beaches on **Vatersay** are too beautiful to miss (1580/BEACHES).

1209 **10/M22** **Loch Tay** South bank between Kenmore and Killin. A single-track road. Stunning views of the loch and Ben Lawers. Very woody in places. Great variety of potential pitches. Great restaurant half-way, the Ardeonaig Hotel (an expensive treat, but excellent; see 1182/GET-AWAY HOTELS).

Camping With The Kids

Caravan sites and camp grounds that are especially kid-friendly, with good facilities and a range of things to do (including a good pub).
Key: HIRE Caravans for rent NO HIRE No rental caravans available
X C'VAN Number of caravan pitches X TENT Number of tent pitches
FLEXIBLE They take caravans and tents according to demand.

1210 **7/N19** **240 TENTS** **DEC-OCT** **NO HIRE** ✓**Glen More Camp Site** near Aviemore · 01479 861271 9km Aviemore on the road to the ski slopes, B970. Across the road from Glen More Visitor Centre and adjacent to Loch Morlich Watersports Centre (2106/WATER SPORTS). Extensive grassy site on lochside with trees and mountain views. Loads of activities include watery ones, reindeer (1710/KIDS) and at the Coylumbridge Hotel (1137/HOTELS THAT WELCOME KIDS) there's a pool and the Fun House, a separate building full of stuff to amuse kids of all ages. Shop at site entrance; café (does breakfast).

1211 **7/H18** **FLEXIBLE** **APR-OCT** **NO HIRE** ✓**Applecross Campsite** www.applecross.uk.com/campsite · 01520 744268 First thing you come to as you approach the coast after your hair-raising drive over the *bealach*, the mountain pass. Grassy meadow in farm setting 1km sea. Usual facilities and Flower Tunnel café (1408/COFFEE SHOPS) Apr-Oct till 9pm, till 5pm Mon and Tue. A green, grassy safe haven.

1212 **9/H22** **80 TENTS** **30 C'VAN** **APR-MID OCT** **NO HIRE** ✓**Shieling Holidays** Craignure, Mull · www.shielingholidays.co.uk · 01680 812496 35km from Tobermory right where the ferry docks. Great views and a no-nonsense, thought-of-everything camp park. Self-catering shielings (carpeted cottage tents with heaters and ensuite facilities) or hostel beds. Loads to do and see, including nearby Torosay and Duart Castles (1770/1769/CASTLES); the fun Mull Light Railway next door; and a pool at the Isle of Mull Hostel open to the plebs (1km).

1213 **9/J28** **TENTS** **APR-OCT** ✓**Sealshore** Kildonan, Arran · 01770 820320 In the south of the island, the emerging fun place to be, Kildonan (2279/ARRAN HOTELS) with a long littoral to wander and open views to Pladda Island. Smallish, intimate greenfield site (40+) for campers and caravans. BBQ, dayroom and hotel adjacent for grub and pub. 'We're always in the UK top 20,' says Mr Deigton who will brook no nonsense from naughty kids or naughty parents. Sleep with the seals!

1214 9/G21
FLEXIBLE
APR-OCT

✓ **Resipole Farm** Loch Sunart, Ardnamurchan · **www.resipole.co.uk** · **01967 431235** Arrive via Corran Ferry (8/JOURNEYS) or from Mallaig or Fort William route via Lochailort (1642/SCENIC ROUTES). Extensive grassy landing on lochside with all mod cons including shop, dishwashers, washing machines. Quiet days in Ardnamurchan are all around you.

1215 10/R26
60 TENTS
MAR-OCT
NO HIRE

Carfraemill Camping & Caravanning Site aka Lauder Camping & Caravanning Club www.campingandcaravanningclub.co.uk · 01578 750697 Just off A697 where it joins the A68 near Oxton. Small, sheltered and friendly campsite in the green countryside with a buttercup meadow and a trickling burn. 4 chalets for hire on site. Good gateway to the Borders (Melrose 20km). The Lodge (or Jo's Kitchen as it is also known) adjacent has great family restaurant where kids made very welcome (play area and the food they like, etc).

1216 7/H16
MANY TENTS
100 C'VAN
HIRE

Sands Holiday Centre Gairloch · www.highlandcaravancamping.co.uk · 01445 712152 4km Gairloch (road to Melvaig) with views to the islands, a large park with dunes and its own sandy beach. Kids' play area but plenty to do and see in Gairloch itself – a great pub, the Old Inn, for adults (1170/ROADSIDE INNS). Well equipped shop, mountain bikes for hire; great camping in dunes plus walking, fishing, etc.

1217 8/N19
37 TENTS
HIRE

Boat of Garten Caravan Park www.boatofgartenholidaypark.com · 01479 831652 In village itself, a medium-sized, slightly regimented site tailored to families with play area for the kids and cots for rent. Cabins if the Scottish weather gets too much. Not the most rural or attractive site in the Highlands, but lots on doorstep, including kid-brilliant Landmark Centre (1712/KIDS) and Loch Garten ospreys (1725/BIRDS). Good bistro 100m.

1218 9/H23
MANY TENTS
SOME C'VAN
MAR-OCT
NO HIRE

Oban Divers Caravan Park Oban · www.obandivers.co.uk · 01631 562755 3km out of Oban. Quiet, clean and friendly ground with stream running through. All sorts of 'extras' such as undercover cooking area, BBQ, adventure playground. No dogs. The **Oban Caravan & Camping Park** www.obancaravanpark.com · 01631 562425 is adjacent at Gallanachmore overlooking sea and easier to find. Well-run family site with shop and ducks!

1219 9/L24
20 TENTS
100 C'VAN
MAR-JAN
HIRE

Cashel Caravan & Campsite Rowardennan · 01360 870234 Forestry Commission site on the quieter shores of Loch Lomond in Queen Elizabeth Forest Park. Fewer pitches than previously but more organised. Excellent facilities and tons to do in the surrounding area which includes Ben Lomond and plootering by the loch.

1220 7/F18
FLEXIBLE
JAN-DEC

Sligachan Skye · 01478 650204 The camp site you see at the major bend in the road on the A87 going north to Portree from the bridge and the ferries. Sligachan is major hotel landmark and all its facilities include all-day bistro/Seumas' bar. Lovely site by river with many walks from here. Warden lives on site. Pitch up and check in. Laundry facilities.

1221 10/R25
APR-SEP

Lochhouses Farm near North Berwick · www.featherdown.co.uk · 01420 80804 Old arable farm 2km A198 between Tyninghame (445/EDINBURGH BEACHES) and North Berwick. Wild camping but 'cottage tents' have flushing loos, wood stove, etc. Farm animals abound and the beaches here are fantastic (in the John Muir Country Park). Part of the Featherdown 'civilised camping on farms' business. Safe and real nice rural experience for kids.

The Best Very Scottish Hotels

1222 6/K15
23 ROOMS
TEL
ATMOS
£60-85/
£30 OR LESS

✓✓ The Ceilidh Place Ullapool · www.ceilidhplace.com · 01854 612103 Off main street near port for the Hebrides. Inimitable Jean Urquhart's place which, more than any other in the Highlands, encapsulates Scottish traditional culture and hospitality and interprets it in a contemporary manner. Caters for all sorts: hotel rooms are above (with a truly comfortable lounge – you help yourself to drinks) and a bistro/bar below with occasional live music and performance (ceilidh-style). A bunkhouse across the way with cheap and cheerful accommodation and a bookshop where you can browse through the best of all Scottish literature. Though it was long ago that the Ceilidh Place put Ullapool on the must-visit map of Scotland, it has moved effortlessly with the times. More detail: 1009/LESS EXPENSIVE HIGHLAND HOTELS.

1223 6/J14
5 ROOMS
MAR-DEC
TEL
£38-45

✓✓ The Albannach Lochinver · www.thealbannach.co.uk · 01571 844407 2km up road to Baddidarach as you come from south into Lochinver on A837, at the bridge. Lovely 18th-century house in one of Scotland's most scenic areas, Assynt, where the mountains can take your breath away even without going up them (1933/1935/FAVOURITE HILLS). The outbuilding overlooking the croft is the latest of their gorgeous 3 suites. There's also the Loft and the Penthouse, with outside cliff-enclosed terrace. Great walk behind house to Archemelvich beach – otters on the way – and Colin's 'secret' beach nearby (1578/BEACHES). Non-residents can, and should, eat. Lesley's fixed-menu dinner now with Michelin star is nature on a plate. All in all, an urban-boutique-hotel experience in a glorious landscape.

1224 8/Q18
16 ROOMS
FEB-DEC
TEL · TV
£85+

✓ Kildrummy Castle Hotel www.kildrummycastlehotel.co.uk · 01975 571288 · near Alford 60km west of Aberdeen via A944, through some fine bucolic scenery and the green Don valley to this spectacular location with real Highlands aura. Well placed if you're on the Castle Trail, this comfortable chunk of Scottish Baronial has the redolent ruins of Kildrummy Castle on the opposite bluff and a gorgeful of gardens between. Some rooms small, but all very Scottish. Romantic in autumn when the gardens are good. Faber family preside.

1225 7/H19
12 ROOMS
+4 SUITES
TEL · TV
£60-85/
£85+
ATMOS

✓ Eilean Iarmain Skye · www.eilean-iarmain.co.uk · 01471 833332 Sleat area on south of island, this snug Gaelic inn nestles in the bay and is the classic island hostelry: the word 'location' could easily be repeated more than 3 times. Bedrooms in hotel best but cottage over by is quieter. New suites in adjacent steading more expensive but more contemporary. Food decent in dining room and with more atmosphere in the bar. Mystic shore walks. Gallery with selected exhibitions and shop by the quay. This hostelry is very Highland as well as very Scottish, it's all said in Gaelic and its charm is subtle but sure. Not all mod cons are considered necessary.

1226 9/J20
13+ ROOMS
MAR-NOV
£38-85
ATMOS

✓ Glenfinnan House Hotel Glenfinnan · www.glenfinnanhouse.com · 01397 722235 Off the Road to the Isles (A830 Fort William to Mallaig). The MacFarlanes have owned this legendary hotel in this historic house for 30 years (1909/MARY, CHARLIE & BOB); managers, the Gibsons keep it soundly sympatico. Refurbishment has retained its charm; the huge rooms remain yet intimate and cosy with open fires. Impromptu sessions and ceilidhs wherever there's a gathering in the bar. Solitude still achievable in the grounds, or fishing or dreaming on Loch Shiel at foot of the lawn (row boat and a cruise boat nearby). Day trips to Skye and the small islands. Quintessential!

1227 9/L28
15 ROOMS
TEL · TV
£38-45

Savoy Park 16 Racecourse Road, Ayr · www.savoypark.com · 01292 266112 In a street and area of indifferent hotels this one, owned and run by the Henderson family for over 40 years, is a real Scottish gem. Many weddings here. Period features, lovely garden, recently reddened-up lounge and not too much tartan: a warm, cosy, homespun atmosphere. And round one of the fireplaces: 'blessed be God for his giftis'.

Crieff Hydro Crieff · 01764 655555 *The* Scottish family hotel. Report: 1122/ HOTELS FOR KIDS.

Stonefield Castle Tarbert · 01880 820836 Report: 759/ARGYLL HOTELS.

▬▬▬ Real Retreats

1228
11/P29

✓✓✓**Samye Ling** Eskdalemuir, near Lockerbie & Dumfries · www.samyeling.org · 01387 373232 Bus or train to Lockerbie/ Carlisle then bus (Mon-Sat 0871 200 2233) or taxi (01576 470480). Community consists of an extraordinary and inspiring temple incongruous in these Border parts. The complex comprises main house (with some accommodation), dorm and guest-house blocks many single rooms, a café (open 7 days 9am-5pm) and shop. Further up the hill, real retreats – months and years – in annexes. Much of Samye Ling, a world centre for Tibetan Buddhism, is still under construction under the supervision of Tibetan masters, but they offer daily and longer stays (£23 dorm to £36 single room, '09) and courses in all aspects of Buddhism, meditation, tai chi, yoga, etc. Daily timetable from prayers at 6am and work period. Breakfast/lunch and soup, etc for supper at 6pm; all vegetarian. Busy, thriving community atmosphere; some space cases and holier-than-thous, but rewarding and unique and thriving. This is Buddhism, pure and simple. See also World Peace Centre (below).

1229
8/P17
ATMOS

✓✓**Pluscarden** between Forres & Elgin · www.pluscardenabbey.org · fax: 01343 890258 Signed from the main A96 (11km from Elgin) in a sheltered glen south-facing with a background of wooded hillside, this is the only medieval monastery in the UK still inhabited by monks. It's a deeply calming place. The (Benedictine) community keep walled gardens and bees. 8 services a day in the glorious chapel (1888/ABBEYS) which visitors can attend. Retreat for men (14 places) and women (separate, self-catering) with 2 week maximum and no obligatory charge. Write to the Guest Master, Pluscarden Abbey, by Elgin IV30 8VA; no telephone bookings. Men eat with the monks (mainly vegetarian). Restoration/building work always in progress (of the abbey and of the spirit).

1230
8/P17

✓✓**Findhorn Community** Findhorn, near Forres · www.findhorn.org · 01309 690311 The world-famous spiritual community (and foundation) begun by Peter and Eileen Caddy and Dorothy Maclean in 1962, a village of mainly caravans and cabins on the way into Findhorn on the B9011. Open as an ordinary caravan park and visitors can join the community as 'short-term guests' eating and working on-site but probably staying at recommended B&Bs. Full programme of courses and residential workshops in spiritual growth/dance/ healing, etc. Course accommodation mainly at Cluny Hill College in Forres. Many other aspects and facilities available in this cosmopolitan and well-organised eco village. Casual visitors can take a tour. Excellent shop (1447/DELIS) and café – the Blue Angel (1323/VEGETARIAN), and the Universal Hall has a great music and performance programme.

1231 ✓ ✓ **The Bield at Blackruthven** Tibbermore · 01738 583238 ·
10/P23   www.bieldatblackruthven.org.uk Take Crieff road (A85) from Perth
and A9/ring road past Huntingtower then left for Tibbermore. 2km. 'Bield' an old
Scottish word for a place of refuge and shelter also means to nurture, succour,
encourage. All are possible here. A Georgian home with outbuildings containing
accommodation, lounges, meeting rooms in 30 gorgeous garden acres with a
swimming pool and a chapel (in an old carpenter's workshop) which are always
open. More like a country-house hotel but there are prayers, courses and support
if you want it. No guests on Mon, so 6 days max. Very cheap for this level of comfort. It is beautiful, peaceful and all very tasteful. Meals and self catering. Serenity!

1232 ✓ **Lendrick Lodge** Brig o' Turk · www.lendricklodge.com · 01877
10/L24   376263 On A821 scenic road through the Trossachs, 15km from Callander.
Near road but in beautiful grounds with gurgling river. An organised retreat and
get away from it all 'yoga and healing' centre. Yoga/reiki and shamanic teaching
throughout year. Can take up to 50 people and run 2 courses at the same time.
Individual rooms and full board if required. New 'River Retreat' in separate building overlooking the river has a pool and 2 ensuite rooms.

1233 ✓ **Dhanakosa** Balquhidder · www.dhanakosa.com · 01877 384213 3km
10/L23   village on Loch Voilside 9km from A84 Callander-Crianlarich road. Gentle
Buddhist place with ongoing retreat programmes (1 week or weekends in winter).
Guidance and group sessions. Meditation room. Rooms hold 2–6 and are ensuite.
Vegetarian food. Beautiful serene setting on Balquhidder Braes.

1234 ✓ **The World Peace Centre** Holy Island · www.holyisle.org · 01770
9/J27   601100 Take a ferry from Lamlash on Arran (ferry 01770 700463/600998) to
find yourself part of a Tibetan (albeit contemporary) mystery. Escape from the
madding crowd on the mainland and compose your spirit or just refresh. Built by
Samye Ling Abbots on this tiny Celtic refuge, the centre offers a range of activities
to help purge the soul or restore the faith. Day trippers, holiday-breakers and mul-
tifaiths welcome. Can accommodate 60. Conference/ gathering centre. Do phone
ahead. Ferries very limited in winter.

1235 ✓ **Shambala** Findhorn · www.shambala-retreat.org · 01309 690690
8/P17   Adjacent to the Findhorn community and across the road facing the bay, this
comfortable, airy mansion house caters for individual or group retreats with daily
meditations and some courses. Buddhist library, sauna and massage and shop
with directly supplied Nepalese and Tibetan stuff. Organic vegetarian cuisine. Can
accommodate up to 24 in single/twin/group rooms. Not connected to Findhorn
except spiritually. A very nice spot to centre on. A surprising roof terrace overlooks
a serene sea.

1236 **College of the Holy Spirit** Millport, Island of Cumbrae · 01475 530353 ·
9/K26   www.argyllandtheisles.org.uk/cumbrae.html Continuous ferry service from
Largs (hourly in winter), then 6km bus journey to Millport. Off main street through
gate in the wall, into grounds of the Cathedral of the Isles (1858/CHURCHES) and
another more peaceful world. A retreat for the Episcopal Church since 1884, there
are 16 comfortable rooms, all renovated 2003, some ensuite, in the college next to
the church with B&B. Also half/full board. Morning and night prayer each day,
Eucharist on Sun and delightful concerts in summer. Warden available for direction and spiritual counselling. Fine library. Bike hire available on island. And the
island's great café (1374/CAFÉS).

1237
10/Q25

Carberry Towers Musselburgh · www.carberrytower.com · 0131 665 3135
Sitting in extensive, well-kept grounds 3km south of Musselburgh, parts of this
fine old house date back to the 15th century. Now a Christian residential and
conference centre with beautiful refurbished rooms in the house and accommodation in new block 50m away (student-hall standard). 60 rooms in total on the
estate. Courses for church workers/group weekends which visitors may sometimes join. Not a quiet retreat but inexpensive for a break with great facilities; high
on 'renewal', low on rock 'n' roll. But they receive everyone.

1238
10/R25

Nunraw Abbey Garvald, near Haddington · www.nunraw.org.uk · 01620
830228 Cistercian community earning its daily bread with a working farm in the
land surrounding the abbey but visitors can come and stay for a while and get
their heads together in the Sancta Maria Guest House (a house for visitors is part
of their doctrine). Payment by donation. Very Catholic monastic ambience
throughout. Guest house is 1km from the monastery, a modern complex built to a
traditional Cistercian pattern. Services in the abbey are open to visitors.

1239
9/F25

Camas Adventure Centre Mull · www.iona.org.uk/camas_home.php ·
01681 700404 Part of Iona Community near Fionnphort in south of island. Good
bus service then a 20-minute yomp over the moor. On a rocky coast with limited
electricity, no cars, TV or noise except the waves and the gulls. Outdoor activities
(eg canoeing, hillwalking). 2 dorms; share chores. Week-long stays. Individuals or
groups. You'll probably have to relate, but this spiritual place invokes the simple
outdoor life and also enjoins the life where you're not alone. May-Sep.

■ The Best Spas

All these spas offer day visits and specific treatments.

1240
10/P25

✓✓ **One Spa** The Sheraton Grand Hotel, Edinburgh · 0131 221 7777 ·
www.one-spa.net Considered the best spa in the city; and on loads of
national/international lists. And probably the best thing about the hotel which is
very centrally situated on Festival Sq opposite the Usher Hall (78/MAJOR EDIN-
BURGH HOTELS). As well as the usual (but reasonably spacious) pool there's
another one which extends outdoors dangling infinity-style over Conference Sq at
the back of the hotel. Decent gym. Exotic hydrotherapy and a host of treatments.
Day and half-day tickets and of course gift vouchers available.

1241
10/R23

✓✓ **The Kohler Waters Spa** The Old Course Hotel, St Andrews ·
www.oldcoursehotel.co.uk · 01334 474371 In the lovely Old Course
golfing resort (859/FIFE HOTELS), this beautifully designed leisure and treatment
suite, though small, is one of many reasons for staying. The spa was designed by
the team who created the original Cow Shed at Babington House. Owners of the
hotel, the Kohler Company produces iconic kitchens and bathrooms in the US and
have other luxury resorts. Here the gym looks out over the Old Course (and there's
a roof-top hot tub). In the main suite there's a 20-metre pool, monsoon showers,
saunas, crystal steam rooms and several treatment rooms. Non-residents must
purchase 100 minutes minimum.

1242
10/P27

✓✓ **Stobo Castle** Stobo, near Peebles · www.stobocastle.co.uk ·
01721 725300 Border baronial mansion 10km south of Peebles in
beautiful countryside of towering trees and trickling burns. Dawyk Botanic
Gardens nearby (1514/GARDENS) and there are Japanese Water Gardens in the

grounds. Mainly a hotel but day visits possible; the spa is the heart of the whole pampering experience. Over 70 treatments. Not too much emphasis on exercise. Classic, standard rooms and suites; also lodge. Bespoke treatment for men and women. You do feel they know what they are doing; all medical peculiarities accounted for. Deals often available for days and half days.

1243
10/N23
✓ ✓ **The Spa** Gleneagles Hotel, Auchterarder · www.gleneagles.com · 01764 662231 The leisure suites at Gleneagles have always offered (obviously) one of the best spa experiences. A recent relocation and redesign by the brilliant Amanda Rosa has made it practically irresistible with or without golf fatigue. It offers Espa body treatments and uses all their oils and unguents. Treatments vary from the usual aromatherapy and facials to hot-stone therapy and Balinese and ayurvedic applications. Luxuriate!

1244
9/L25
✓ ✓ **The Spa** Cameron House Hotel, Loch Lomond · 01389 713659 · www.devere.co.uk The spa of the recently made-over De Vere Cameron House Hotel is 5km along the road and lochside at the Carrick, the new 18-hole golf course. Spa inculcates the Kirsten Florien philosophy, which revolves around hydrotherapy, aromatherapy and thalassotherapy, balnotherapy and pelotherapy (whatever they are) with a host of products including the 'highly acclaimed, ageless Caviar Collection'. There's a pool, an outside (sheltered) deck, bar and restaurant. When you've made enough dosh to afford this (or somebody treats you), you really can relax.

1245
9/J22
✓ **The Spa** Isle of Eriska Hotel, Ledaig · www.eriska-hotel.co.uk · 01631 720371 The Isle of Eriska ('hotel/spa/island'), one of Scotland's most comfy country-house hotels (1118/COUNTRY-HOUSE HOTELS), is 20km north of Oban. Apart from the usual indulgences they have created a lovely spa separate from the main building in the gardens overlooking the new 9-hole golf course. There's a pool and gym, the Verandah Café with terrace and several treatment rooms using Espa products. Perfect tranquillity.

1246
9/L24
✓ **The Spa In The Walled Garden** Luss · www.lochlomond.com · 01436 655315 The more leisurely side of Loch Lomond Golf Club, this stunning contemporary spa suite (designed by Donna Vallone) is what it says on the tin. Thermal suites, treatment and relaxation rooms open on to small, private gardens and then the walled garden itself with its fabulous glass houses, a visit to which is another form of relaxation. Espa products.

1247
10/Q23
Yu Spa Apex City Quay Hotel, Dundee · www.apexhotels.co.uk · 01382 309309 The inexpensive and accessible spa is part of the overall offering at this central business hotel, most definitely the best in the city (911/DUNDEE HOTELS). The spa and swimming pool occupy a corner of the ground floor. Therapies combine the ethos and products from Elemis in over 50 treatments for men and women. Japanese-inspired wooden hot tubs, herb-infused steam room and sauna. Everything you need before you go out and face Dundee.

1248
10/R25
The Spa The Macdonald Marine Hotel, North Berwick · 01620 897333 · www.macdonaldhotels.co.uk The spa in the renovated Marine Hotel which has been here forever overlooking the golf course. Salt-water hydro pool, aroma steam room, bio sauna, a cold therapy room and a serenity relaxation room all contribute to a well-thought-out suite of facilities removed from the main hustle and bustle of the hotel. Decleor products are offered in a wide range of treatments which includes a men's menu.

For The Best House Parties

Places you can rent for families or friends and have to yourselves: exclusive use.

1249
10/R25
ATMOS

✓ ✓ **Greywalls** Gullane · www.greywalls.co.uk · 01620 842144 36km east of Edinburgh off A198 beyond Gullane towards North Berwick. The fabulous former hotel is now available only for exclusive use. Overlooks Muirfield, the championship course, and is close to several of Scotland's top courses. The Lutyens-designed manor house and the gardens attributed to Gertrude Jekyll are simply superb, especially in summer, and the public rooms are the epitome of taste and comfiness at all times. Dining arranged to suit. 20 rooms and the Colonel's House. This is house-party living as it's supposed to be.

1250
6/Q13

✓ ✓ **Ackergill Tower** near Wick · www.ackergilltower.co.uk · 01955 603556 Deluxe retreat totally geared for parties and groups (mostly corporates). 5 times a year, eg Valentine's/Hogmanay, you can join their house parties. Fixed price (3-night minimum stay), all-inclusive: this means fab-atmosphere dinners (huge fires, candlelight) but you may not eat in the same place twice. Host of activities (there's even an 'opera house') and outside, the wild coast. A perfect treat/retreat. Individual prices on request. You'll probably have to mingle.

1251
8/P20

✓ ✓ **Mar Lodge Estate** near Braemar · www.ntsholidays.com · 0844 493 2173 For exclusive use, there are several remarkable properties including apartments in the big hoose in the NTS-run, 72,000-acre estate 15km from Braemar. Classic Highland scenery superb in any season with the upper waters of the River Dee running through it. 5 apartments in main mansion and 2 other houses sleeping 8 and 10. Public rooms including library, billiard room and ballroom can be hired separately. Expensive of course but not, divided between all your mates. Live like the royals down the road but without the servants.

1252
10/P24

✓ **Myres Castle** near Auchtermuchty · www.myrescastle.com · 01337 828350 2 km Auchtermuchty on Falkland road. Well-preserved castle/family home in stunningly beautiful gardens. High country life though at a price. 9 rooms individually refurbished to exceptional standard. Formal dining room, evocative Victorian kitchen and impressive billiard room. The perfect setting for a murder mystery shindig. Central to all Fife attractions especially Falkland and St Andrews. £350 per person per night at TGP, can take 18. Dinners up to 20.

1253
8/N17

✓ **Drynachan Lodge** near Nairn · www.cawdor.com · 01667 402402 This fab 19th-century hunting lodge is on the Cawdor Estate south of Nairn. The castle is signed from all over (1765/CASTLES). While there are many cottages here for let this is the big house (sleeps 22) and was personally decked out by Lady Isabella Cawdor. Like all things on the estate it's done with great taste. Fully staffed and catered, it's like a hip shooting lodge. But it'll cost ya.

1254
9/G26

✓ **Jura House** Jura · 01496 820315 In the south of this long, long, fabulous island (2207/MAGICAL ISLANDS) near the ferry at Feolin (8km), the grand old and family house of the Ardfin estate. Not too posh inside; outside enchanting gardens (1511/GARDENS) and a short skip to your own beach. 3 floors, billiard room. Self-catering or arrange for cook. Nice Aga. There's always the Antlers (2263/ ISLAND RESTAURANTS) 5km away at Craighouse. Sleeps 15. £1900 a week.

1255
8/N19

✓ **Inshriach House** near Aviemore · www.inshriachhouse.com · 01540 651341 On the B970 back road between Inverdrurie and Feshiebridge, 8km south of Aviemore. Atmospheric, comfy, lived-in Edwardian country house with gorgeous public rooms, highly individual bedrooms, gardens and small estate. Close to spectacular Loch an Eilean (1617/LOCHS) and Inshriach (2119/GARDEN CENTRES) with its famous cakes and bird-watching, but loads to do round here. Self-catering or ask Ord Ban to do it (1308/BEST HIGHLAND RESTAURANTS). Up to 17 can stay. From £2k-3.5k per week. One of the most laid-back options on this page. They even have a festival – The Insider – in the grounds in June. And we know where that came from!

1256
7/M17
✓ **Castle Stuart** Inverness · www.castlestuart.com · 01463 790745 15 minutes city centre on airport road via A96 Aberdeen road. Authentic pile of 17th-century history; a real castle experience complete with ghost. Antique in every sense. Guided tour on arrival. 8 bedrooms (can take 16). £2k per night. Quite snobby people live here and naughty houseguests won't be welcome.

1257
6/L15
Carbisdale Castle Culrain, near Bonar Bridge · www.carbisdale.org · 01549 421232 Another castle and hugely impressive but on a per head basis, very inexpensive. Carbisdale is the flagship hostel of the SYHA (1139/BEST HOSTELS for directions). From Nov-Feb you can hire the whole place so big Highland hoolies over Xmas/Hogmanay are an option. More than 150 people can be accommodated in the 32 rooms (varying from singles to 12-bed dorms). Per-night price around £1500 plus. Bring your own chef or muck in. Other SYHA hostels can be hired Oct-May. 0845 293 7373.

1258
9/K28
Doonbrae Alloway · www.costley.biz · 01292 442466 In heart of unspoilt village still evocative of Burns whose birthplace, gardens and Tam o' Shanter graveyard are nearby. Opposite and part of **Brig o' Doon Hotel** (768/AYRSHIRE HOTELS), much favoured for weddings. This refurbished mansion is separate and you can have it to yourself. On Doon banks in delightful gardens. Self-catering or eat at hotel. 5 suites.

1259
11/N30
Cavens Kirkbean · www.cavens.com · 01387 880234 Off A710, the Solway Coast road 20km south of Dumfries. Well appointed mansion in gorgeous grounds near a beach. Up to 12 accommodated and very reasonable compared to many grand houses of this type. Angus's dinner-party cooking. 781/SOUTHWEST HOTELS.

1260
9/J24
Castle Lachlan Loch Fyne · www.castlelachlan.com · 01369 860669 For directions see Inver Cottage, the tearoom on the estate (760/ARGYLL RESTAURANTS). Stunning setting in heart of Scotland scenery, the 18th-century ancestral home of the Clan Maclachlan. Snooker room; all-weather tennis. Self-catering but dining can be arranged. Sleeps up to 15 (22 for dinner). £2-3K per week. Sumptuous surroundings for rock stars and weddings and the like.

1261
6/H16
Rua Reidh Lighthouse Melvaig near Gairloch · www.ruareidh.co.uk · 01445 771263 End of the road 20km from Gairloch but yes, you can have this lighthouse to yourself. Sleeps up to 24 in 9 bedrooms (from £500 for 2 nights low season to £1900 7 nights New Year at TGP). Gairloch has good food/pub options but you do or arrange your own catering. Plus the sea and the scenery!

1262
5/E15
ATMOS
Amhuinnsuidhe Castle Harris · www.amhuinnsuidhe.com · 01859 560200 North from Tarbert then west into the faraway strand (for directions see Lost Glen 2267/FANTASTIC ISLAND WALKS). Staffed, fab food and gothic Victorian castle/shooting and fishing lodge (the salmon arrive in a foaming mass at the river mouth). 9 bedrooms take 16 guests: mainly sporting groups but individuals can join at certain times for a mixed house party. Grand interiors and top fishing on 9 lochs and rivers.

Cambo near Crail · www.camboestate.com · 01333 450313 Old, interesting mansion in beautiful grounds near St Andrews. Up to 17 separate rooms available and B&B. Very reasonable rates. Report: 864/FIFE HOTELS.

1263
9/K28
NTS

Culzean Castle: Eisenhower Apartment South Ayrshire · 01655 760615 · www.culzeanexperience.org The second-floor apartment once stayed in by the wartime Supreme Allied Commander in Europe and later president of the United States. It has 6 suites and public rooms available singly or for exclusive use. Spectacular both in and out. Dinner can be provided; the grounds are superb.

National Trust for Scotland *has many other interesting properties they rent out for weekends or longer. 0131 243 9331 or www.nts.org.uk for details.*

The Landmark Trust *also have 18 mostly fabulous properties in Scotland including* **The Pineapple** *(1842/MONUMENTS),* **Auchenleck House** *in Ayrshire which sleeps 13 and the wonderful* **Ascog House** *or* **Meikle House** *on the Isle of Bute which sleep 9 and 10 respectively. Phone 01628 825925 to get their beautiful handbook (properties throughout the UK) or see www.landmarktrust.org.uk*

✓ **Loch Ness Lodge** Loch Ness · www.loch-ness-lodge.com · 01456 459469 Overlooking the loch on A82 south of Inverness. 7 rooms and 5 cottages. £2k exclusive use. Report: 998/HIGHLAND HOTELS.

✓ **Greshornish Country House** Skye · www.greshornishhouse.com · 01470 582345 Comfy country house to yourself; lovely rooms. Lochside in the middle of Skye. Report: 1187/GET-AWAY-FROM-IT-ALL.

Scotland's Great Guest Houses

✓✓ **Balmory Hall** Isle of Bute · 01700 500669 In Ascog, 6km from Rothesay towards Mount Stuart. Report: 749/ARGYLL HOTELS.

✓✓ **Dun Na Mara** Benderloch · 01631 720233 Off the A828 Fort William road. 12 km north of Oban. Report: 746/ARGYLL HOTELS.

✓✓ **Skirling House** near Biggar · 01899 860274 On the A72 3km from Biggar. Excellent food. Report: 821/BORDERS HOTELS.

✓ **Lerags House** near Oban · 01631 563381 7km south of Oban and 4 km from the main A816. Excellent food. Report: 753/ARGYLL HOTELS.

✓ **Edenwater House** Ednam, near Kelso · 01733 224370 On the Kelso-Swinton Rd B6461. 4km from Kelso. Excellent food. Report: 817/BORDERS HOTELS.

✓ **Coig Na Shee** Newtonmore · 01540 670109 Just outside the village towards Fort William, just off the A9. Report: 1011/INEXPENSIVE HIGHLAND HOTELS.

✓ **Roineabhal** near Kilchrenan, Loch Awe · 01866 833207 10km from the A85 road to Oban near Taynuilt. Report: 754/ARGYLL HOTELS.

Old Station   near St Andrews · 01334 880505 On B9131, the Anstruther road off the A917 St Andrews-Crail (3km). Report: 863/FIFE HOTELS.

Doune Stone Lodge   Knoydart · 01687 462667 Remote but comfy house on this faraway peninsula. Will collect from Mallaig. Boat excursions and wonderful walks. Great food. Report: 1197/GET-AWAY HOTELS.

The Bield   Tibbermore, near Perth · 01738 583238 Crieff road, from Perth off the ring road. Report: 1231/RETREATS.

Craigatin House   Pitlochry · 01796 472478 Surprisingly stylish guest house in this traditional tourist town. Report: 882/PERTHSHIRE HOTELS.

Tanglewood House   near Ullapool · 01854 612059 Beautiful house overlooking Loch Broom. Bedrooms and dining have the view. Report: 1033/GREAT HIGHLAND B&BS.

Clint Lodge   near St Boswells · 01899 860274 Near Dryburgh Abbey in Scott country. Report: 827/BORDERS HOTELS.

Section 6

Good Food & Drink

scotland the best

Bloody Good Pubs

Pubs in Edinburgh and Glasgow are listed in their own sections.

1264
9/K23
ATMOS

✓✓ **Drover's Inn** Inverarnan · www.thedroversinn.co.uk A famously Scottish drinking den/hotel on the edge of the Highlands just north of Ardlui at the head of Loch Lomond and 12km south of Crianlarich on the A82. Smoky, low-ceilinged rooms, open ranges, whisky in the jar, stuffed animals in the hall and kilted barmen; this is nevertheless the antithesis of the contrived Scottish tourist pub. Food till 9pm. Also see 808/HOTELS CENTRAL.

1265
9/G22
ATMOS

✓✓ **The Mishnish** Tobermory · www.mishnish.co.uk The Mish has always been the real Tobermory and it's been in the Macleod family since, well, since 1869 so they are somewhat connected. And so will you be in this classic island hostelry with rooms (10), a restaurant upstairs (One Up) but most importantly – the pub. 7 days till late. Often live music from Scottish traditional to DJs and indie especially Sat. Different rooms, nooks and crannies. Great pub grub, open fire. Something, as they say, for everybody.

1266
7/H20
ATMOS

✓ **Old Forge** Inverie, Knoydart · www.theoldforge.co.uk 01687 462267 A warm haven for visitors who have found their way to this peninsula. Suddenly you're part of the community, real ales and real characters, excellent pub grub. Lunch and LO 9pm. Stay along the road at brilliant guest house (1196/GET-AWAY HOTELS) or bunk along the road (info@knoydart.org).

1267
9/J21
ATMOS

✓ **Clachaig Inn** Glencoe · www.clachaig.com · 01855 811252 Deep in the glen itself down the road signed off the A82, 5km from Glencoe village. Both the pub with its wood-burning stove and the lounge are woody and welcoming. Backdoor best for muddy boots or those averse to leather-studded furniture. Real ale and real climbers and walkers. Handy if you're in the hostel 2km down road or camping. Decent food in bar/lounge and good, inexpensive accommodation including 4 lodges. Many ales and a beer fest in Oct.

1268
5/C20
ATMOS

Castlebay Bar Barra · www.castlebay-hotel.co.uk Adjacent to Castlebay Hotel. A deceptively average-seeming but brilliant bar. All human life is here. More Irish than all the Irish makeovers on the mainland. Occasional live music including the Vatersay Boys; conversations with strangers. Report: 2248/ISLAND HOTELS.

1269
7/J19

Cluanie Inn Loch Cluanie · www.cluanieinn.com · 01320 340238 On A87 at head of Loch Cluanie 15km before Shiel Bridge on the long road to Kyle of Lochalsh. A wayside inn with good pub food, a restaurant and the accommodation walkers want. Good base for climbing/walking (especially the 5 Sisters of Kintail, 1983/SERIOUS WALKS). A cosy refuge. LO 9pm for food.

1270
10/L27
ATMOS

Poosie Nansie's Mauchline Main street of this Ayrshire village where Burns lived in 1788. This pub there then, those characters still there at the bar. 4 of his children buried (yes, 4) in the churchyard opposite. A room in the pub left as was. Living heritage at its most real! Lunch and 6-8pm Fri/Sat. Otherwise just the ale.

1271
10/P27

Tibbie Shiels Inn Borders · www.tibbieshielsinn.com Off A708 Moffat-Selkirk road. Has its own particular place in Scottish culture, especially literature (1918/LITERARY PLACES) and in the Border hills southwest of Selkirk where it nestles between 2 romantic lochs. On Southern Upland Way (1609/WATERFALLS) a good place to stop and refuel though food is not a strong point. Very busy on Sun.

1272
11/M30

The Murray Arms & The Masonic Arms Gatehouse of Fleet 2 adjacent unrelated pubs that just fit perfectly into the life of this great wee town. The Masonic is the best for food with great atmosphere. Masonic symbols still on the walls of the upstairs rooms. The Murray Arms has a Burns *Scots Wha' Ha'e* connection. **The Ship** (782/SOUTHWEST HOTELS) on the main street is the newer, more stylish kid on the block.

1273
7/L19

Lock Inn Fort Augustus Busy canalside (Caledonian Canal which joins Loch Ness in the distance) pub for locals and visitors. Good grub downstairs or up if you want (overlooking lock). Pub staples well done; reasonable malts. Food LO 9.30pm. Some live music. Seats on the canal in summer where boats go by very slowly.

1274
11/L31
ATMOS

The Steampacket Inn www.steampacketinn.com · 01988 500334 · Isle of Whithorn · The hub of atmosphere wee village at the end of the road (1565/COASTAL VILLAGES) south. On harbour that fills and empties with the tide. Great for ales and food (brunch and LO 9pm all year). 7 rooms upstairs.

▋ Great Pubs For Real Ale

For real-ale pubs in Edinburgh, see p. 74, Glasgow p. 123.

1275
10/Q23
ATMOS

✓**Fisherman's Tavern** Broughty Ferry · www.fishermanstavern.co.uk In Dundee, but not too far to go for great atmosphere and the best collection of ales in the area. In Fort St near the seafront. Regular ales and many guests. Low-ceilinged and friendly. Inexpensive accommodation adjacent and pub grub better of late (916/DUNDEE HOTELS).

1276
10/N21
ATMOS

✓**Moulin Inn/Hotel** Pitlochry · www.moulinhotel.co.uk 4km uphill from main street on road to Bridge of Cally, an inn at a picturesque crossroads since 1695. Some rooms and reputation for pub grub, but also for cosy bar and brewery out back from which comes 'Moulin Light', 'Ale of Atholl' and others. Live music some Sun. Food (LO 9.30pm) is... ok.

1277
10/S20

✓**Marine Hotel** Stonehaven · www.marinehotelstonehaven.co.uk Popular local on great harbour front with seats outside and always a crowd. 4/5 guest ales, big Belgian and wheat-beer selection and food till 9pm. New upstairs dining room. Open all day.

1278
9/J26

✓**The Port Royal** Port Bannatyne, near Rothesay Seafront on Kames Bay in Bute. A 'Russian' tavern with latkas and sauerkraut with your stroganoff. Some live music. 5 rooms upstairs and a great selection of ales. Brill atmosphere.

1279
8/T19

✓**The Prince of Wales** Aberdeen St Nicholas Lane, just off Union St at George St. An all-round great pub always mentioned in guides and one of the best places in the city for real ale: Old Peculier, Caledonian 80/- and guest beers. Very cheap self-service food at lunchtime. Lots of wood, flagstones, booths. Macaroni cheese. Large area but gets very crowded. 7 days, 11am-midnight (11pm Sun).

1280
10/N25

The Four Marys Linlithgow · www.thefourmarys.co.uk Main street near road up to palace so handy for a pint after schlepping around the historical attractions. Mentioned in most beer guides. 7 ales on tap including various guests. Beer festivals May and Oct. Notable malt whisky collection and popular locally for lunches (daily) and evening meals (LO 8.45pm); weekends 12noon-food LO.

1281 **The Lade Inn** Callander At Kilmahog, the western approach to the town at the
10/M24 beginning of road into the Trossachs – so a good place to stop. Inn known for
food, also brews its own ale (Waylade, Ladeback, etc) but runs an ale shop
adjacent with well over 100 of Scotland's finest. Shop 12noon-6pm. Pub food till
8.45pm.

1282 **The Tappit Hen** Dunblane By the cathedral. Good ales (usually Deuchars and
10/J26 4 guests and many malts), atmosphere and occasional live music. A good find in
these parts.

1283 **The Woolpack** Tillicoultry Via Upper Mill St (signed 'Mill Glen') from main
10/N24 street on your way to the Ochils. They come far and wide to this ancient pub. Bar
food and a changing selection of ales which they know how to keep. Sup after a
stroll.

1284 **Clachnaharry Inn** Inverness On A862 Inverness-Beauly road just outside
7/M18 Inverness overlooking firth and railway, with beer garden. Long list of regulars
posted, 5/6 on tap. Local fave for pub food (12noon-9pm). A Belhaven pub.

1285 **The Shore Inn** Portsoy Down at the harbour, good atmosphere (and ales).
8/R17 Food during day in summer, weekends only in winter. Plays centre stage at the
Traditional Boats fest (38/EVENTS). May be quiet other times, but a great pub on
the quayside corner.

1286 **The Old Inn** Gairloch Southern approach on A832 near golf course, an 'old inn'
7/H16 across an old bridge; a goodly selection of malts. Some real ales in the cellar.
Tourists and locals mix in season, live music some nights. Rooms above make this
an all-round good reason to stop in Gairloch (1170/ROADSIDE INNS).

The Masonic Arms Gatehouse of Fleet 794/SOUTHWEST RESTAURANTS.
The Steam Packet Isle of Whithorn 1274/BLOODY GOOD PUBS.
The 2 pubs in the South West that look after their ale (and their drinkers).

The Best Gastropubs

Gastropubs in Edinburgh and Glasgow are listed in their own sections.

1287
10/L27
ATMOS
✓✓ **The Sorn Inn** Sorn · www.sorninn.com · 01290 551305 Main street of village, 8km east of Mauchline, 25 km Ayr. Pub with rooms and big reputation for food. Restaurants and tables in bar. Family-run (the Grants with chef Craig Grant). 'Inspector's Favourite '09'; Michelin Bib Gourmand. Everything just so and made to order. An exemplary rural gastropub experience. Lunch and LO 9pm. All day Sat/Sun. LO Sun 6.30pm.

1288
9/H26
✓✓ **Kilberry Inn** 01880 770223 · near Tarbert, Argyll On the single-track B8024 that follows the coast of the Knapdale peninsula between Lochgilphead and Tarbert, this is out on its own. Bib Gourmand and both Rural Restaurant of the Year and Overall Winner '09 (Scottish Restaurant Awards). Clare Johnson is a great cook and everything is well sourced; the lounges have a smart, pubby ambience with relaxed, unobtrusive service led by Clare's bloke David. So make that journey (1643/SCENIC ROUTES). Lunch and dinner. LO 9pm. Closed Mon. Apr-Oct. Weekends Nov/Dec.

1289
10/R27
✓✓ **Burt's** Melrose · www.burtshotel.co.uk · 01896 822285 The bar of the estimable hotel on Melrose's main street (816/BORDER HOTELS) and some might say even better than their fine-dining restaurant. A la carte specials with pub faves like fish 'n' chips and beef olives and more adventurous choices. Big rugby-player helpings. 7 days lunch and LO 10pm.

1290
10/R26
✓✓ **Black Bull** Lauder · www.blackbull-lauder.com · 01578 722208 Main street of A68 ribbon town between Edinburgh and the Borders, near enough the city to be a destination meal. 8 individual rooms above, different dining areas below. Some great Modern British cooking; good wine list. 7 days. LO 9pm.

1291
6/J15
✓✓ **The Summer Isles Hotel Bar** Achiltibuie · 01854 622282 · www.summerisleshotel.co.uk The adjacent bar of this long-established romantic hotel on the foreshore facing the isles and the sunset (1001/HIGHLAND HOTELS). All the superior qualities of their famous (Michelin) food operation available at less than half the price in the cosy bistro-like bar with tiny terrace. Great seafood and vegetarian. Apr-Oct, lunch and LO 8.30pm.

1292
10/M24
DA
✓✓ **The Cross Keys** Kippen · www.kippencrosskeys.co.uk · 01786 870293 Here forever in this quiet backwater town off the A811 15km west of Stirling. Debby Macgregor and Brian Horsburgh transformed this dependable pub for grub into a stopover not just for Sunday lunch but for a weekend stay. 3 rooms upstairs, open fires and great food in bar or lounge areas below. Seriously thought-over and irresistible gastropub food. Beer garden. Lunch and LO 9pm.

1293
10/R24
ATMOS
✓✓ **Ship Inn** Elie · www.ship-elie.com Pub on the bay at Elie, the perfect toon in the picturesque East Neuk of Fife (1563/COASTAL VILLAGES). In summer a huge food operation: bar, back room, next door and upstairs (latter has good view; book weekends). Same menu throughout; blackboard specials. On warm days the terrace overlooking the beach goes like Bondi. LO 9/9.30pm. Also has 5 rooms adjacent in summer (01333 330246). They love cricket.

1294
10/R23
ATMOS
✓✓ **The Grange Inn** St Andrews · 01334 472670 4km out of town off Anstruther/Crail road A917. Perennially popular; rightly so. Mike and Lena Singer have built on long reputation of this almost Englishy pub with cosy

rooms and comfort food with flair. Lunch (not Sat) and dinner (not Sun evening or Mon) LO 8.30pm. Must book weekends.

1295
10/S26
✓ **The Wheatsheaf** Swinton · www.wheatsheaf-swinton.co.uk · 01890 860257 A hotel pub in an undistinguished village about halfway between Kelso and Berwick (18km) on the B6461. In deepest, flattest Berwickshire, owners Chris and Jan Winson serve up the best pub grub you've had since England (they're also involved in the Fisherman's Arms at Birgham; see below). 10 rooms adjacent and in cottages. An all-round good hostelry. Lunch and 6-9pm.

1296
8/S19
✓ **The Broadstraik Inn** Westhill · www.broadstraikinn.co.uk · 01224 743217 On main A944 Aberdeen-Alford road, 12km from city centre and well worth the drive. Jackie Spence and Chris Wills have transformed this long-running roadside pub into an all-round pub and pub-food destination. Bar and restaurant area. Great for families, with real-food kids' menu. Blackboard specials. Very busy weekends. 7 days lunch and LO 8.45pm.

1297
9/K28
✓ **Souter Johnnie's Inn** Kirkoswald · www.costley.biz · 01655 760653 On A77 between Girvan and Ayr. Contemporary and ambitious transformation of old hotel and adjacent buildings to form the new Costley (see Cochrane Inn below) complex that includes a tearoom, deli/shop, ice-cream factory and bakers (2166/SCOTTISH SHOPPING). This, the pub, offers the usual sound gastropub menu with a Scottish emphasis. All good stuff. 7 days, lunch and LO 9pm.

1298
9/L26
✓ **Fox and Hounds** Houston · www.foxandhoundshouston.co.uk On B790 village main street in Renfrewshire, 30km west of Glasgow by M8 junction 29 (A726), then cross back under motorway on B790. Village pub home to Houston brewery with great ales, excellent pub food and dining room upstairs for family meals and suppers. Folk come from miles. Sunday roasts. Fine for kids. Lunch and LO 8.45pm (later Fri/Sat). Restaurant: 01505 612448. Bar till 12midnight.

1299
10/S21
✓ **The Creel Inn** Catterline, near Stonehaven · 01569 750254 2km from main A92 Arbroath-Stonehaven road 8km south Stonehaven (signed) perching above the bay from where the lobsters come. And lots of other seafood. Good wine; huge speciality beer selection. Cove itself has a haunting beauty. Catterline is Joan Eardley (the notable artist) territory. It's also famous for this pub and though food is not quite what it was, it's always buzzing. 7 days lunch and LO 9pm.

1300
9/L27
✓ **Wheatsheaf Inn** Symington · www.wheatsheafsymington.co.uk · 01563 830307 2km A77. Pleasant village off the unpleasant A77 with this busy coaching inn opposite church. Folk come from miles around to eat (book at weekends) honest-to-goodness pub fare in various rooms (roast beef every Sunday). Menu on boards. Beer garden. LO 9.30pm.

1301
7/N19
✓ **Old Bridge Inn** Aviemore · www.oldbridgeinn.co.uk/aviemore Off Coylumbridge road at south end of Aviemore as you come in from A9 or Kincraig. 100m main street but sits in hollow. An old inn like it says with basic à la carte and more interesting blackboard specials. Three cask ales on tap. Kids' menu that is not just pizza and chips; ski-bums welcome. Lunch and 6-9pm. In summer, tables over road by the river. Hostel adjacent (1143/HOSTELS). LO 9.30pm.

1302
8/S20
ATMOS
✓ **Lairhillock Inn** near Netherley, Stonehaven · www.lairhillock.co.uk · 01569 730001 Long a landmark pub for good grub at a country crossroads. 7 days lunch and dinner. Fine for kids. Superb cheese selection, notable malts and ales. Can approach from South Deeside road, but simplest direction for strangers

is: 15km south of Aberdeen by main A92 towards Stonehaven, then signed Durris, go 5km to country crossroads. **The Crynoch Restaurant** is adjacent (964/ABERDEEN RESTAURANTS).

1303
6/K14

✓ **Kylesku Hotel** Kylesku · www.kyleskuhotel.co.uk · 01971 502231 Off A894 between Scourie and Lochinver in Sutherland. A hotel and pub with a great quayside location on Loch Glencoul where boats leave for trips to see the 'highest waterfall in Europe' (1606/WATERFALLS, 1047/BEST HIGHLAND RESTAU-RANTS). Friendly bar/bistro atmosphere with local fish, seafood (especially with legs and claws) including interesting specials, eg spineys – the tails of squat lobsters; yummy desserts. Lunch and 6-9pm Mar-Oct.

1304
10/Q23

✓ **The Ship Inn** Broughty Ferry · Excellent seafront (Tay estuary – there are dolphins and the pub can supply binoculars) snug pub with food upstairs and down (best tables at window upstairs). Famous for clootie dumpling and other classic gastropub fare. 7 days, lunch and 5-9pm (922/DUNDEE RESTAURANTS).

1305
9/J26

✓ **Smiddy Bar at the Kingarth Hotel** Isle of Bute · 01700 831662 · www.kingarthhotel.com 13 km Rothesay 4km after Mount Stuart (1823/COUNTRY HOUSES). Good, friendly old inn probably serving the best food on the island. Blackboard menu and à la carte. The atmosphere is just right. Outside deck. Open all year. Food LO 8pm (9pm Fri/Sat).

1306
10/M25

✓ **Old Mill** Main Street, Killearn · www.old-mill-killearn.co.uk · 01360 550068 More than one notable inn in this village (806/CENTRAL HOTELS) but this is cosy, friendly and all an old pub should be (old here is from 1774). Pub and restaurant. Log fires, nice for kids. Garden. 7 days 12noon-9pm (Sun 8pm).

1307
9/K28

Dunure Inn Dunure · www.dunureinn.co.uk · 01292 500549 Just off A719 coast road 10km south of Ayr. The inn of the charming wee village not much more than a ruined castle and an old harbour on the picturesque coast south of Ayr (1646/SCENIC ROUTES). This restaurant with rooms overlooks the harbour and has been building a good reputation for food since recent new ownership (the Munro family) and major transformation. Good, seafood-led gastropub and good atmos-phere inside and out. Some live music. 7 days, lunch and LO 8.30pm.

1308
10/M24

The Inn at Kippen Kippen · www.theinnatkippen.co.uk · 01786 871010 The place that originally put Kippen on the foodie map. Somewhat diminished by recent changes in ownership but with the deli (1457/DELIS), the butcher's and the Cross Keys (see above) on the up, Kippen is something of a foodie destination in central Scotland. 3 rooms above. Food might be improved, but a pleasant ambi-ence. 7 days, lunch and LO 9pm. Bar 11pm/1am.

1309
9/K27

Apple Inn Troon · 01292 318819 Small, unpretentious and somewhat unatmospheric pub on Irvine road out of Troon. Great eclectic, Med-influenced menu with staples and some flair. Lunch and LO 9.30pm (10pm weekends).

1310
9/L27

Cochrane Inn Gatehead · www.costley.biz · 01563 570122 Part of the Costley hotel empire (768/HOTELS IN AYRSHIRE). A trim and cosy ivy-covered, very inn-like inn – most agreeable. On A759 Troon to Kilmarnock and 2km A71 Kilmarnock-Irvine road. A bugger to get to (locals know how), but excellent gour-met pub with huge local reputation; must book weekends. Lunch and LO 9pm.

1311
10/P24

The Stag Inn Falkland · 01337 858327 Off square on Mill Wynd on the wee green in kind of idyllic wee Falkland. Good atmosphere with stone and wood and log fire. Grub not gastro but decent. Lunch and LO 9.30pm. Winter hours may vary. Also in the square, the Italian place: **Luigino** (01337 857224) does passable wood-oven pizza, pasta, etc. Both open 7 days. LO 8-9.30pm depending on the day.

1312
10/M24
Lion & Unicorn Thornhill · www.lion-unicorn.co.uk · 01786 850204 On A873 off A84 road between the M9 and Callander and near Lake of Menteith in the Trossachs. On main road through nondescript village. They come from miles around for pub grub and sizzling steaks. Cosy dining areas, open fires and garden. Changing menu, not too fancy. 7 days. LO 9pm.

1313
7/H16
Badachro Inn Badachro, near Gairloch · 01445 741255 South of Gairloch off A832, then B8056 to Redpoint. A spectacular road and fantastic setting for this waterside pub. Great beer and wine list with lots by the glass and great home-made pub grub. Probably tick-worthy but le patron comes with a bit of attitude that some visitors could do without. A great deck overlooks the rocky bay. 7 days 12noon-3pm, 6-9pm.

1314
10/R26
Goblin Ha' Hotel Gifford · www.goblinha.com · 01620 810244 Twee village in East Lothian heartland; one of 2 hotels. This one, with the great name, serves a decent pub lunch and supper (6-9pm; 9.30pm on Fri and Sat) in recently exten-sively refurbished lounge and pub. Conservatory, terrace and beer garden are great for kids and for grown-ups. A well-run Punch Tavern.

1315
10/S27
Fisherman's Arms Birgham, near Kelso · 01890 830230 In small Tweedside village 6km from Kelso on Coldstream road. A very village pub, friendly and local. Decent food, no pretence. Garden terrace. Sunday carvery. Closed Mon.

1316
10/L24
The Byre Brig o' Turk · 01877 376292 Off A821 at Callander end of the village adjacent Dundarroch Hotel and Loch Achray. Country inn in deepest Trossachs, with more owner changes than I've had sleepless nights. New guys '09 seem good. Less gastro, more basic pub grub in cosy, firelit rooms with outside decks in summer. Byre probably the best of nearby options in Brig o' Turk village and Loch Venacher café. LO 9pm. Can walk from here to Duke's Pass (1640/SCENIC ROUTES).

1317
11/J30
The Crown Portpatrick · 01776 810261 Hugely popular pub on harbour with tables outside in summer. Light, airy conservatory at back serving freshly caught fish. 12 rooms above. Locals and Irish who sail over for lunch (sic). LO 10pm.

1318
11/N30
The Anchor Kippford · 01556 620205 A defining pub of this popular coastal village on the 'Scottish Riviera'. Nothing too gastro, more whole and hearty but a huge throughput in bar and lounges and especially outside tables. Overlooking the tranquil cove. Lunch and LO 9pm.

1319
10/R28
The Auld Cross Keys Inn Denholm, near Hawick · 01450 870305 Not a lot to recommend in Hawick, so this village pub with rooms is worth the 8km journey on the A698 Jedburgh road. On the Green, with pub and dining lounges through the back. Blackboard menu, heaps of choice. Real fire and candles. Sun carvery. Food LO 8pm. 3 rooms if you want to stay.

1320
8/T19
The Globe Inn Aberdeen Urban and urbane bar in North Silver Street – a place to drink coffee as well as lager, but without self-conscious, pretentious 'café-bar' atmosphere. Known for its food at lunch and 5-7.45pm (not weekends) and for live music Tue and weekends – jazz and blues in the corner. The Globe Inn has rooms upstairs (952/ABERDEEN HOTELS) so not a bad place to base a weekend in Aberdeen.

1321 8/T19   **Ma Cameron's Inn** Aberdeen In Little Belmont Street, the 'oldest pub in the city' (though the old bit is actually a small portion of the sprawling whole – but there's a good snug). No nonsense oasis in buzzy street. Food from a huge menu including all (we mean all) the pub staples: lunch and early evening. Terrace up top for smokers and their mates.

Moulin Inn Pitlochry Report: 1179/ROADSIDE INNS.
Old Clubhouse Gullane Report: 852/LOTHIANS HOTELS.
Old Inn Gairloch Report: 1170/ROADSIDE INNS.
The Masonic Arms Gatehouse of Fleet Report: 794/SOUTHWEST RESTAURANTS.
The Ship Inn Gatehouse of Fleet Report: 782/SOUTHWEST HOTELS.

The Best Vegetarian Restaurants

Not surprisingly, perhaps, there are few completely vegetarian restaurants in Scotland. But there are lots in Edinburgh (see p. 57) and some in Glasgow (see p. 113).

1322 10/R28 ATMOS £15 OR LESS   ✓**Damascus Drum** Hawick · 07707 856123 One of the notable cafés of the Borders (838/BORDER RESTAURANTS), Chris Ryan's bookshop and haven of civil- • isation is not strictly vegetarian but is mostly, and it gets a tick a) coz it's quirky and good and b) for sticking it out in this least favourite of towns where men and rugby and meat still rule. Coffee/cake, hot dish of the day, quiches and borek (sic). Great atmosphere. Mon-Sat 9am-5pm.

1323 8/P17 £15 OR LESS   ✓**Blue Angel at Findhorn Community** Findhorn You will go a long way in the North to find real vegetarian food, so it may be worth the detour from the main A96 Inverness–Elgin road, to Findhorn and the famous community (1230/RETREATS) where there is a great deli (1447/DELIS) and this pleasant caff by the hall at the end of the (old) runway. 7 days till 5pm and evenings if event in the hall. (Hot food till 3pm.)

1324 8/P17 £15-22   ✓**The Bakehouse** Findhorn · 01309 691826 Same neck of the woods as Blue Angel (above) and its owners loosely connected. Not strictly vegetarian but lots of vegetarian choice; all ethical and 'slow'. Bread and cakes from the bakery behind. Lovely, conscientious cookery. 7 days 10am-5pm (evenings in summer).

1325 9/J26 £15 OR LESS   ✓**Musicker** High Street, Rothesay · 01700 502287 Beside the castle, up from the ferry. Great pastries, paninis and soups, range of coffee (soya milk if wished). Nice books, old juke box, newspapers, bluesy: jazz CDs for sale. Friendly, relaxed. Leslie says the new coffee machine is just right. Tue-Sat 10am-5pm.

✓**Woodside** near Ancram On B6400 near Monteviot House, a tearoom in a walled garden (1515/GARDENS). Organic, simple food. Report: 1395/TEAROOMS.

The Best Vegetarian-Friendly Places

HIGHLANDS
The Ceilidh Place Ullapool · 01854 612103 1009/INEXPENSIVE HIGHLAND HOTELS.
Café One Inverness · 01463 226200 1069/INVERNESS.
Three Chimneys Skye · 01470 511258 2251/SKYE RESTAURANTS.
Café Arriba Skye · 01478 611830 2257/SKYE RESTAURANTS.

The Waterside Seafood Restaurant Kyle of Lochalsh 1043/BEST HIGHLAND RESTAURANTS.

Riverside Bistro Lochinver · 01571 844356 1051/BEST HIGHLAND RESTAURANTS.

Old Pines near Spean Bridge · 01397 712324 1020/LESS EXPENSIVE HIGHLAND HOTELS.

Russell's @ Smiddy House Spean Bridge · 01397 712335 1046/BEST HIGHLAND RESTAURANTS.

Carron Restaurant Loch Carron · 01520 722488 1036/BEST HIGHLAND RESTAURANTS.

Plockton Shores Plockton · 01599 544263 1041/BEST HIGHLAND RESTAURANTS.

Summer Isles Hotel Bar Achiltibuie · 01854 622282 1291/GASTROPUBS.

Coul House Contin · 01997 421487 1005/HIGHLAND HOTELS.

NORTH EAST
The Foyer Aberdeen · 01224 582277 963/ABERDEEN RESTAURANTS.

Beautiful Mountain Aberdeen · 01224 645353 972/ABERDEEN RESTAURANTS.

Milton Restaurant Crathes · 01330 844566 947/NORTHEAST HOTELS.

ARGYLL & ISLES
Argyll Hotel Iona · 01681 700334 1163/SEASIDE INNS.

St Columba Hotel Iona · 01681 700304 2282/MULL.

Inver Cottage Loch Fyne · 01369 860537 760/ARGYLL RESTAURANTS.

The Green Welly Stop Tyndrum · 01838 400271 1387/TEAROOMS.

An Lochan Tighnabruaich · 01700 811239 750/ARGYLL HOTELS.

Julie's Coffee House Oban · 01631 565952 765/OBAN.

Kilmartin House Café Kilmartin · 01546 510278 1405/TEAROOMS.

FIFE & LOTHIANS
Pillars of Hercules near Falkland · 01337 857749 1400/BEST TEAROOMS.

Ostler's Close Cupar · 01334 655574 872/FIFE RESTAURANTS.

The Vine Leaf St Andrews · 01334 477497 876/ST ANDREWS.

Old Clubhouse Gullane · 01620 842008 852/EAST LOTHIAN RESTAURANTS.

Livingston's Linlithgow · 01506 846565 856/WEST LOTHIAN RESTAURANTS.

CENTRAL
Deans @ Let's Eat Perth · 01738 643377 898/PERTHSHIRE RESTAURANTS.

Monachyle Mhor near Balquhidder · 01877 384622 1181/GET-AWAY HOTELS.

Indulge Auchterarder · 01764 660033 1383/TEAROOMS.

Parrot Café Dundee · 01382 206277 924/DUNDEE RESTAURANTS.

Jute Dundee · 01382 909246 918/DUNDEE RESTAURANTS.

The Parlour Dundee · 01382 203588 928/DUNDEE RESTAURANTS.

SOUTH & SOUTH WEST
Marmions Melrose · 01896 822245 831/BORDERS RESTAURANTS.

Philipburn Selkirk · 01750 20747 825/BORDERS HOTELS.

The Masonic Arms Gatehouse of Fleet · 01557 81433 794/SOUTHWEST RESTAURANTS.

The Sunflower Peebles · 01721 722420 836/BORDERS RESTAURANTS.

Osso Peebles · 01721 724477 830/BORDERS RESTAURANTS.

ORKNEY
Woodwick House Evie · 01856 751330 2283/ORKNEY.

The Best Seafood Restaurants

For seafood restaurants in Edinburgh, see p. 55; for Glasgow, see p. 112.

1326
10/R24
£22-32
ATMOS

✓✓ **The Cellar** Anstruther · 01333 310378 From a time when seafood restaurants were few as were good restaurants full stop, the Cellar has set a shining example from its cosy neuk of Fife of how assiduously sourced ingredients (and especially seafood) served simply is what makes a restaurant meal great. And of all those shiny diners that have since lit up the coasts, the Cellar's darker but timeless atmosphere still sets exactly the right tone for the fish supper you won't forget. 870/FIFE RESTAURANTS.

1327
6/P12
£22-32

✓✓ **The Captain's Galley** Scrabster · www.captainsgalley.co.uk · 01847 894999 In the Galley there is a very firm and sure hand on the tiller. This is the place to eat on the north coast and a reputation built on total integrity with a conservation, sustainability and slow-food ethos throughout. Chef/proprietor Jim Cowie and his missus know exactly where everything comes from – salad from their poly tunnel and daily-landed fish from the boats and the bay is all personally selected. Those crabs actually choose Jim's creels. Menu short (usually 4 choices) and to the point, as are opening hours. Dinner only Tue-Sat 7-9pm. Best book: this was UK Seafood Restaurant of the Year 2009.

1328
10/R23
£22-32

✓✓ **The Seafood Restaurant** St Andrews · 01334 479475 · www.the-seafoodrestaurant.com In a landmark position overlooking the Old Course and the bay, this glass-walled pavilion is the top spot in the town and for a sunset supper is hard to beat. Great wines, nice puds but mainly fish pure and simple (usually 1 meat option). 7 days lunch and dinner LO 10pm.

1329
10/R24
£22-32

✓✓ **The Seafood Restaurant** St Monans, Fife · 01333 730327 · www.theseafoodrestaurant.com West end of East Neuk village. As St Andrews (above), Butler family offer simple title and no fuss in the menu either. Conservatory and terrace overlooks sea, waves lap, gulls mew, etc. Superb, out-of-the-way setting. Chef/proprietor Craig Millar rattles the pans. Bar menu Wed-Sun lunch and dinner LO 10pm.

1330
9/K27
£22-32

✓✓ **MacCallum's of Troon Oyster Bar** Troon · 01292 319339 Right down at the quayside. Follow signs for Troon ferry, past the woodpiles. 3km from centre. Red-brick building with discreet sign, so eyes peeled. Lovely fish (big on oysters and 'catch of the day'), great atmosphere and unpretentious. Tue-Sat lunch and LO 9.30pm. Sun lunch only. Adjacent fish 'n' chip shop is one of the best in the land (1348/FISH & CHIPS).

1331
9/H23
£22-32

✓✓ **The Seafood Temple** Oban · 01631 566000 Top spot perhaps of the 3 great seafood restaurants in Oban (see below), the 'Seafood Capital of Scotland'. Wonderful setting overlooking the bay and across to the town. Simple, local and great value – one surf 'n' turf, otherwise only seafood. But this place *is* tiny! Report: 762/ARGYLL RESTAURANTS.

1332
9/H23
£22-32

✓ **The Waterfront** Oban · www.waterfrontoban.co.uk · 01631 563110 On the waterfront at the station and upstairs from unimposing entrance a light, airy room (formerly the Seaman's Mission) above the busy bar which is serving some of the best seafood around in an authentic setting. Specials change daily. The fish leap upstairs and onto your plate. Somewhere in Oban to linger on the way to the ferry. Open all year. Lunch and LO 9pm.

1333
9/H23
£22-32

✓ **Ee-Usk** Oban · www.eeusk.com · 01631 565666 Landmark new-build on the north pier by the hospitable Macleods (adjacent an Italian restaurant in a similar building which they also run – the Piazza). A full-on seafront caff with urban-bistro feel, great views and fish from that sea. Goes like a ferry. Good wee wine list. 7 days lunch and LO 9.30pm.

1334
10/S20
£22-32

✓ **The Tolbooth** Stonehaven · 01569 762287 On corner of harbour, long one of the best restaurants in the area in a great setting (reputedly the oldest building in town). Upstairs bistro, a light room with picture windows on to beach and harbour no longer landing much fish but local fishermen do supply crab, langoustine, great lobster and the odd halibut. Fresh, simple and decent value.

1335
9/J21
£22-32

✓ **Loch Leven Seafood Café** near Kinlochleven · 01855 821048 · www.lochlevenseafoodcafe.co.uk Leave the A82 at north Ballachulish, 15km south of Fort William, then 7km on B863 down the side of Loch Leven to this shellfish tankery, shop and bright, airy restaurant. A la carte of scallops, mussels, clams, lobster, crab and specials. Excellent wine list. Reciprocal fine products from places they export to, like Spain. Best food in the area. Lunch and 6-9pm. 7 days in summer. Wed-Fri in winter.

1336
8/T19
£22-32
ATMOS

✓ **Silver Darling** Aberdeen · www.silverdarling.co.uk · 01224 576229 Down by harbour. For many years one of the best restaurants in the city and the North East; a stunning location. 974/ABERDEEN RESTAURANTS.

1337
7/F17
£22-32
ATMOS

✓ **Lochbay Seafood** Skye · www.lochbay-seafood-restaurant.co.uk · 01470 592235 12km north Dunvegan; A850 to Portree, B886 Waternish peninsula coastal route. A scenic Skye drive leads you to the door of this small cottage at end of the village row where David and Alison Wilkinson have been at their 'simply sublime seafood' for many seasons now. Overlooks water where your scallops, prawns and oysters are surfaced. Main dishes served unfussily with puds like clootie dumpling. Small, with nice bistro atmosphere. Best book. Apr-Oct; lunch and LO 8.30-ish. Tue-Sat (open Mon dinner Jun-Aug).

1338
9/K23
£15-22

✓ **Loch Fyne Oysters** Loch Fyne · 01499 600264 On A83 the Loch Lomond to Inveraray road, 20km Inveraray/11km Rest and Be Thankful. Landmark roadside restaurant and all-round seafood experience on the way out west. Though Loch Fyne Seafood is a huge UK chain, this is the original (and not actually in the chain after management buy-out). People come from afar for the oysters and the smokery fare, especially the kippers. Spacious and with many banquettes though somewhat refectory-ish! House white (other whites and whisky) well chosen. Same menu all day; LO 8pm (later in summer). Shop sells every conceivable packaging of salmon and other Scots produce; shop 7.30pm.

1339
9/K26
£15-22

✓ **Fins** Fairlie, near Largs · 01475 568989 On main A78 south of Fairlie a seafood bistro, smokery (Fencebay), shop and craft/cookshop (2169/SHOPPING). Roadside fish farm, bistro, farmshop and cookshop: an all-round day-out experience. Best place to eat for miles in either direction. Simple, straightforward good cookin' and the wine list is similarly to the point. Nice conservatory; like the geraniums. Lunch and dinner LO 8.30/9pm. Closed Mon.

1340
9/L26
£22-32

✓ **Creelers** Brodick, Arran · www.creelers.co.uk · 01770 302810 Just outside Brodick on road north to castle beside Aromatics-led gift plaza; the cheese shop is nice (1476/CHEESES). Excellent seafood bistro – great food, fun staff though as always on islands they come and go (good reputation '09). They smoke their own. Easter-Oct. Closed Mon.

1341
11/J30
£22-32

Campbell's Portpatrick · www.campbellsrestaurant.co.uk · 01776 810314 Friendly, harbourside restaurant in much-visited Portpatrick. Some meat dishes, but mainly seafood. Their own boat brings back crab and lobster (and sea bass and pollack). 7 days lunch and LO 10pm. Closed Jan-Mar and Mon.

1342
9/K21
£22-32

Crannog at the Waterfront Fort William · www.oceanandoak.co.uk · 01397 705589 Long-established landmark and destination restaurant. Nice bright contemporary setting, not only great seafood but a real sense of place in this rainy town. 7 days, lunch and LO 9pm (later weekends).

1343
6/K13
£15-22

Shorehouse Café Tarbet, near Scourie · 01971 502251 Charming recently rebuilt conservatory restaurant on cove where boats leave for Handa Island bird reserve (1719/BIRDS). Julian catches your seafood from his boat and Jackie cooks it; they have the Rick Stein seal of approval. Home-made puds. Located at end of unclassified road off the A894 between Laxford Bridge and Scourie; best phone to check openings (esp Sun). Apr-Sep: Mon-Sat 12-8pm; some Suns. Licensed.

1344
7/H18
£22-32

Kishorn Seafood Bar Kishorn · www.kishornseafoodbar.co.uk · 01520 733240 On A896 at Kishorn on the road between Lochcarron (Inverness) and Sheildaig near the road over the hill to Applecross (1629/SCENIC ROUTES). Fresh local seafood in a roadside diner: Kishorn oysters, Applecross crab; lobsters in a tank out back. Light, bright and a real find in the middle of beautiful nowhere courtesy of the enthusiastic Viv Rollo. Apr-Oct daily 10am-5pm (9pm Jul/Aug). Sun 12noon-5pm.

1345
9/J22
£15-22

The Pierhouse Port Appin · www.pierhousehotel.co.uk · 01631 730302 At the end of the minor road and 3km from the A828 Oban-Fort William road in Port Appin village right by the tiny 'pier' where the passenger ferry leaves for Lismore. This is a place that people will always want to come to and they have through several changes of ownership. Currently well run with great locally caught seafood (Lismore oysters, Mallaig flatfish, hand-dived shellfish) which comes fresh to the door by boat. Lively atmosphere, wine and that wonderful view. Report: 1171/INNS.

1346
9/J26
£15 OR LESS

The Seafood Cabin Skipness · 01880 760207 Adjacent Skipness Castle, signed from Claonaig where the CalMac ferry from Lochranza arrives. Cabin, outdoor seating and indoor options in perfect spot for their fresh and local seafood, snacks and cakes. Mussels come further (Loch Etive). Smoked stuff from Creelers in Arran. Jun-Sep 11-6pm. Closed Sat.

✓✓**Applecross Inn** 01520 744262 · Applecross The inn at the end of the road. Great seafood care of Judy Fish; classic fish 'n' chips. 1190/GET-AWAY HOTELS.

✓**Café Fish** Tobermory · 01688 301253 1190/MULL RESTAURANTS.

The Best Fish & Chip Shops

1347
1/B1
✓ ✓ **L'Alba D'Oro** Henderson Row, Edinburgh Near corner with Dundas St. Large selection of deep-fried goodies, including vegetarian savouries. Inexpensive proper pasta, real pizzas and superb, surprising Italian wine to go in adjacent takeaway **Anima**, a stools-at-the-window diner (315/TAKEAWAYS). This is still the chip shop of the future. Open till 12midnight. 194/EDINBURGH PIZZA.

1348
9/K27
✓ ✓ **The Wee Hurrie** Troon · 01292 319340 Famed and fabulous, the Wee Hurrie is part of MacCallum's oyster and fish restaurant (see 1330/SEAFOOD RESTAURANTS for directions because it's a fair walk from the town centre). Big range of fresh daily fish displayed and to select. Light tempuras, even salads to go. Tue-Sun 12noon-8pm (9pm Fri/Sat).

1349
9/H23
✓ ✓ **Fish & Chips in Oban** Oban has declared itself the 'Seafood Capital of Scotland', with 3 good seafood restaurants but also these 3 great chip shops. All are in George St by the bay. **Nories** at 88 has been here over 50 years. They are uncompromising about the lard but they do great F&C (12noon-10.30pm; closed Sun). **Oban Fish & Chip Shop** is the fancy newcomer at 116 with coley, hake and home-made fishcakes along with 'sustainable' haddock and cod. They do use vegetable oil (11.30am-10pm 7 days). Both Nories and the Oban have sit-in caffs. Many locals advise that the best fish 'n' chips in town is from the **George St Fish & Chip Shop** behind the Caledonian Hotel near the square. All here is bright and fresh. They do use beef dripping and keep the menu small. 7 days 10am-11pm. Wherever you get 'em, Oban's waterfront is the perfect place to scoff 'em.

1350
1/D1
✓ **The Rapido** 77 Broughton Street, Edinburgh Legendary chippie. Popular with late-nighters stumbling back down the hill to the New Town, including the flotsam of the 'Pink Triangle'. 1.30am (3.30am Fri/Sat).

1351
1/E1
✓ **The Deep Sea** Leith Walk, Edinburgh Opposite Playhouse. Open late and often has queues (which are quickly dispatched). Haddock has to be 'of a certain size'. Traditional menu. One of the best fish suppers with which to feed your hangover. 2am-ish (3am Fri/Sat).

1352
10/Q23
✓ **Deep Sea** 81 Nethergate, Dundee At bottom end of Perth Rd; very central. The Sterpaio family have been serving the Dundonians excellent fish 'n' chips for almost 75 years (you read that correctly); great range of fish in groundnut (the most expensive) oil. Café with aproned waitress service is a classic. So very traditional, so very tasty. Mon-Sat, 9.30am-6.40pm (7pm carry-out).

1353
2/XA1
✓ **Philadelphia** 445 Great Western Road, Glasgow Adjacent Big Blue (537/PIZZA) and La Parmigiana (523/BEST ITALIAN RESTAURANTS), owned by same family. Since 1930, a Glasgow fixture and fresher fryer than most. 7 days 12noon-12midnight (Fri/Sat 3am).

1354
9/J26
✓ **West End** 1 Gallowgate, Rothesay Change of owners over the years but the West End is a Rothesay must-do, hence always a queue. Only haddock, but wide range of other fries and fresh pizza. We can't make head nor tail of their hours, but they're mostly open! Closed 2-4pm.

1355
10/T26
✓ **Giacopazzi's** Eyemouth Harbour by the fish market (or what's left of it). A caff and takeaway with the catch on its doorstep. Dispensing excellent fish and chips and their award-winning ice cream quietly here in the far-flung south-

east corner of Scotland since 1900. 7 days 11am-9pm. Upstairs to **Oblo's Bistro** (01890 752527). Sun-Thu 10am-midnight, Fri & Sat 10am-1am.

1356
8/P17

✓ **The Ashvale** Aberdeen, Elgin, Inverurie, Ellon, Banchory, Brechin Original restaurant (1985) at 46 Great Western Rd; 3 other city branches. Restaurant/takeaway à la Harry Ramsden (stuck to dripping for long enough but changed to vegetable oil in '09). Various sizes of haddock, sole, plaice. Home-made stovies, etc, all served fresh so you may wait. Hours vary.

1357
6/K15

Seaforth Chippy Ullapool Adjacent ferry terminal. Part of Seaforth Hotel with upstairs bistro but best to stick to fish and chips and walk the harbour. Some question in Ullapool whether it's the Seaforth or the one round the corner but I'll stick with this. Chips often pale but fish don't get any fresher. 7 days till 9.30pm.

1358
11/N29

Balmoral Balmoral Road, Dumfries Seems as old and essential as the Bard himself. Using rapeseed oil, it's the best chip in the south. Out the Annan road heading east, 1km from centre. LO 10pm (9pm Sun/Mon).

1359
9/G22

The Fish & Chip Van aka The Fisherman's Pier Tobermory Parked by the clock on Fisherman's Pier, this van has almost achieved the status of a destination restaurant. Always a queue. Fresh and al fresco. All year. 12.30-9pm. Closed Sun.

1360
10/S20

Sandy's Market Square, Stonehaven The established Stoney chipper, and always busy despite interlopers (see the Bay, below). Daily, LO 10pm, 9pm Sun. Big haddock like the old days.

AND THESE THAT STICK TO LARD

1361
10/Q24

✓ ✓ **Valente's** 73 Overton Road, Kirkcaldy · 01592 651991 Ask directions or satnav to this superb chippy in east of town (not the high street one); worth the detour and the queue when you get there. They also make ice cream. LO 10.25pm. Branch at 73 Henry Rd (01592 203600). Closed Wed.

1362
10/M24

✓ ✓ **Mhor Fish** Callander · www.mhor.net Main street near square. Legendary café taken over by the ambitious and industrious Lewis family of Monachyle Mhor (1181/GET-AWAY HOTELS). Unprepossessing frontage but here, Dick Lewis adds a fresh-fish counter and general panache but doesn't tamper with the basic product: the fish tea with fresh Scrabster-landed fish and great chips. Fish here is to love; they have demonstrations of filleting and oyster-opening and other fishy stories regularly in the upstairs room. They use dripping but they explain why. 7 days till 9pm. The takeaway next door is open later.

1363
8/T19

✓ **The New Dolphin** Chapel Street, Aberdeen Despite the pre-eminence of the Ashvale in Aberdeen, many would rather swear by this small, always-busy place just off Union St. They both swear by lard. Till 1am; 3/4am weekends.

1364
10/R22

✓ **Peppo's** 53 Ladybridge Street, Arbroath By the harbour where those fish come in. Fresh as that and chips in dripping. Peppo here since 1951; John and Frank Orsi carry on a great family tradition feeding the hordes. 7 days 4pm-8pm (it's a teatime thing).

1365
10/R24

✓ **The Anstruther Fish Bar** Anstruther · www.anstrutherfishbar.co.uk On the front (1563/COASTAL VILLAGES). Often listed as the best fish 'n' chips in Scotland/UK/Universe and the continuous queue suggests they may be right. Sit in or walk round the harbour. There's also the ice cream. 7 days 11.30am-10pm. Or go west 100m to the **Wee Chippie**. 7 days till 10pm. Many locals prefer **The**

Pittenweem Fish & Chip Bar. Tiny door in the wall in Main St next to clock tower in next town along. NB: both Pittenweem and the Wee use vegetable oil.

1366
7/N19
✓**Harkai's** Aviemore On main road through town at south end as you come in from A9. Here since 1965 with a big local reputation and though a long way from the sea, this is a chipper that takes itself seriously. (Perhaps less so 'the environment': no obvious sustainable fish policy.) 7 days LO 8.30pm (9pm Jul/Aug).

1367
10/S20
The Bay Stonehaven On the prom towards the open-air pool (2096/SWIMMING POOLS), a newer chip shop to add to Sandy's (above) in this well-fried town. Bay is the local choice. 7 days till 10pm.

1368
10/R25
The North Berwick Fry 11 Quality Street, North Berwick Adjacent tourist information centre. Here forever in this seaside town. A long, thin diner and next door, the chippie. Best to take your poke (or box) to the front (or to the gardens opposite). Big reputation, always busy. 7 days 11.30am-12midnight.

Great Cafés

For cafés in Edinburgh, see p. 67, Glasgow, p. 115.

1369
7/M18
✓✓**The Castle Restaurant** Inverness On road that winds up to the castle from the main street, near the tourist information centre and the hostels. No pandering to tourists here, but this great caff has been serving chips with everything for 40 years though these (crinkle cuts) are not their strong point. Pork chops, perfect fried eggs, prawn cocktail to crumbles. They work damned hard. In Inverness or anywhere nearby, you'll be pushed to find better-value grub than this. (But see below.) 9am-8.25pm (sic). Closed Sun.

1370
7/M17
✓✓**Girvans** 2 Stephens Brae, Inverness Behind Marks & Spencer at the end of pedestrian street. A different proposition to the Castle (above), more up-market – more perhaps a restaurant – but the atmosphere is of a good old-fashioned caff serving everything from omelettes to full-blown comforting meals. Great all-day breakfast on Sun. Tempting cream-laden cakes. Always busy but no need to book. The Girvan family here 18 years! 7 days 9am-9pm (Sun from 10am).

1371
9/K23
✓✓**The Real Food Café** Tyndrum · www.therealfoodcafe.com Created from a Little Chef on the main A82 just before the junction Oban/Fort William and what a difference. Excellent food for the road, conscientiously prepared, seriously sourced, eg using coley (more sustainable) rather than cod, the antithesis of frozen, fast and couldn't-care-less. Fish 'n' chips, burgers, breakfasts, pies – all home-made. Lounge with wood-burning stove. Birds to watch. This is no ordinary pitstop! 7 days 10am-10pm.

1372
6/K15
✓**The Tea Store** Argyll Street, Ullapool · www.theteastore.co.uk In the street parallel to and one up from the waterfront. Excellent, unpretentious café serving all-day fry-ups and other snacks. Great home baking including those strawberry tarts in season. Best in Ullapool (or Lewis where you might be heading). All year. 8.30am-4.30pm. Sun 9am-3pm. (Winter hours vary.)

1373
10/N24

✓ **Allan Water Café** Henderson Street, Bridge of Allan The main street, beside the eponymous bridge. Worth coming over from Stirling (8km) for a takeaway or a seat in the caff (a steel-and-glass extension somewhat lacking in charm) for great fish 'n' chips and the ice cream (1441/ICE CREAM). Nice people here. 7 days, 8am-8.30pm.

1374
9/K26
ATMOS

✓ **The Ritz Café** Millport See Millport, see the Ritz. Since 1906 and now in its fourth generation, the classic café on the Clyde. Once overshadowed by Nardini's and a short ferry journey away (from Largs, continuous; then 6km), it should be an essential part of any visit to this part of the coast, and Millport is not entirely without charm. Toasties, rolls, the famous 'hot peas'. Exellent ice cream (especially with melted marshmallow). Something of 'things past'. 7 days, 10am-9pm in season. Other hours vary.

1375
10/Q27
ATMOS

✓ **The Hub** near Innerleithen · www.thehubintheforest.co.uk · 01721 721736 At entranceway 'the trail head' to Glentress Forest Park on A72 5km from Peebles. Glentress is mountain bike mecca so this US-style caff in a shack serves shorts-and-lycra-clad allsorts with big appetites. All-day breakfasts from Forsyth's the butchers (plus vegetarian) and other fuel food including multifarious flapjacks. Outdoor terrace strewn with bikes and bikeists. Cool spot. 7 days till 6pm (7pm Sat/Sun) & till 10pm Wed (night biking!).

1376
10/S27

Under The Sun Roxburgh Street, Kelso · 01573 225179 Just off the square. Fraser and Kirstin Murray's café and 'fairtrade centre' Under the Sun has also been under my radar. Opened a while but we didn't get on to it till recently. Curious mix of kids' stuff for sale and busy caff. Home baking, hot dishes, big-choice menu with integrity. 9.30am-6pm (5pm Sat). Closed Sun.

1377
10/R18

Brydons 16 High Street, Hawick · 01877 376267 Cool, family-run and friendly caff in Hawick main street serving breakfast through to tea. Has the real caff atmosphere. Hot food like mince 'n' tatties, macaroni cheese. This was the food I was brought up on and I went to that damned high school. Surprising collection of teapots. 8am-4.30pm. Closed Sun.

1378
7/N17

Basil Harbour Café Nairn Down by Nairn's unexpected harbour (signed from A96) and overlooking the unexpected boats. No-nonsense caff and takeaway that becomes a wee bistro at night (Wed-Sat, 6-9pm). Shut when we came by on a Monday holiday but great local reputation. Caff 10am-5pm.

1379
9/K27

The Melbourne 72 Hamilton Street, Saltcoats A tatty but authentic 1950s leftover with good coffee, good panini, breakfasts, filled rolls, etc. Juke box nearly as cool as the lassies behind the counter! Used as a film location (*Late Night Shopping*). Damned fine! Daily 9am-4pm.

1380
9/J26

Ettrick Bay Café Bute End of the road from Port Bannatyne near Rothesay in the middle of the bay and the beach looking over to Arran-Kintyre so this is the café 'with the view'. Here forever, a family caff from seaside days gone by. Honest, home-made menu including their famous garlic mussels and Alec's lavish cakes. 7 days 10am-5pm.

The Best Tearooms & Coffee Shops

For Edinburgh, see p. 65, for Glasgow, p. 114.

1381
10/S27
✓ ✓ **The Terrace** Floors Castle, Kelso Top garden tearoom inside and out an old outbuilding that forms one side of the estate walled garden (2295/GARDEN CENTRES) some distance from the castle (1830/COUNTRY HOUSES). Superb, home-made, unpretentious: hot dishes and baking: home-cured ham, salads and irresistible cakes and puds and pies. Shop with deli stuff. And the terrace: bliss. 7 days 12noon-5pm, hot food till 2.30pm then toasties. Open all year.

1382
10/R25
✓ ✓ **Falko** Gullane Main street of genteel village (though too much house building seems likely to lower the dulcet tone) on corner. A bakery/coffee shop (though the bakery is actually in Edinburgh) that calls itself a konditerai because those gorgeous cakes and breads are German, Austrian and Swiss and they change with the seasons (stollen comes in October). Master baker and proprietor Falko has fingers many sweet pies. 8am-5.30pm, Sun from 11am. Closed Mon.

1383
10/N23
✓ ✓ **Indulge** Auchterarder · 01764 660033 Aptly named and as befits the town where Gleneagles presides, a top tearoom/restaurant at the bottom end of long main street. Eclectic, comforting hot-meal menu, irresistible desserts and some good old-fashioned cakes to wash down with Darjeeling. 9am-5pm (4pm Sat). Closed Sun.

1384
8/R20
✓ ✓ **Finzean Tearoom** Finzean · www.finzean.com · 01330 850710 The tearoom and farmshop of the Finzean (pronounced 'fing-in') estate on backroad between Aboyne and Banchory, a very worthwhile detour. Great food, great views. See 1459/FARMSHOPS. 7 days 9am-5pm. Sun from 12noon.

1385
10/Q24
✓ ✓ **Kind Kyttock's Kitchen** Falkland Folk come to Falkland (1763/CASTLES; 1955/HILL WALKS) for many reasons, not least for afternoon tea at KKK: Quentin Dalrymple keeping it in the family with great attention to detail and to you. Omelettes, pizza, toasties, baked potatoes, top cake list. A visit to Falkland wouldn't be the same without it! 10.30am-5.30pm (4.30pm in winter). Sat supper in summer.

1386
11/M29
✓ ✓ **Kitty's Tearoom** New Galloway Main street of town in the forest. Absolutely splendid. Sylvia Brown's steady hand in the kitchen, great cakes, good tea in proper china and conversations between local ladies. Great salads. High tea 4-6pm very popular, including 'a roast'. All this but you must take cake. It's an Alan Bennett world. 11am-5pm (6pm Sat/Sun), Easter-Oct. Tue-Sun.

1387
9/K23
✓ ✓ **The Green Welly Stop** Tyndrum · www.thegreenwellystop.co.uk On A82, a strategically placed all-round super services on the drive to Oban or Fort William (just before the road divides), with a Scottish produce shop, a gas station, a snack stop which does pizzas (open later) and a self-service restaurant: great comfort food at a much higher standard than any motorway in the land. Food prepared to order, excellent cakes and puds, fresh OJ and fast, friendly service. Shop stuffed with everything Scottish you don't and do need (including this book). 7 days, 8.30am-5.30pm (5pm in winter). Snack stop till 9/10pm.

1388
8/R20
✓ ✓ **The Black-Faced Sheep** Aboyne · 01339 887311 Near main Royal Deeside road through Aboyne (A93) and Mark Ronson's excellent coffee shop/gift shop is well-loved by locals (and regulars from all over) but is thankfully missed by the bus parties hurtling towards Balmoral. Home-made breads and

cakes, light specials; good coffee (real capp and espresso from Elektra machine). His love affair with Italy means own-label wines and olive oil. 10am-5pm, Sun from 11am. Also, some fascinating furniture and knick-knacks.

1389
8/R20

✓ ✓ **Raemoir Garden Centre** Banchory On A980 off main A93, the Deeside road through town, about 3km. You have to beat a path through the garden (centre) to the tearoom though it's a good 'un (2201/GARDEN CENTRES). The caff is superb with excellent home baking and a full hot-meal menu. Big scones, lashings of cream. Expansion 2010 with roadside faster foodstop. There's no stopping these guys! 7 days till 5pm (Sun 4.30pm). Centre till 5.30pm.

1390
9/G22

✓ ✓ **Glengorm Farm Coffee Shop** near Tobermory · 01688 302321 First right on Tobermory-Dervaig road (7km). Organic food served in well refurbished stable block. Soups, cakes, venison burgers among other hot meals and delicious salads from their famous garden (they supply other Mull restaurants). All you need after a walk in the grounds of this great estate (2282/MULL HOTELS) ...and the *best* cappuccino on Mull. Open all year LO 4.30pm. Closed Wed.

1391
10/S22

✓ ✓ **The Watermill** Aberfeldy · www.aberfeldywatermill.com · 01887 822896 Off Main St direction Kenmore near the Birks (2012/WOODLAND WALKS). Downstairs caff on riverside in a conserved mill. Much more than its extensive bookshop with well-laid-out travel, kids' and beautiful tome sections. Upstairs a notable and remakable gallery. Waiter service in busy caff with inside and terrace seating. Soups, quiches, home baking. 10am-5.30pm (Sun 11am-5pm). Signed from all over, this is your destination in Aberfeldy!

1392
2/F4
ATMOS

✓ ✓ **Café Gandolfi** Glasgow · www.cafegandolfi.com Glasgow's definitive tearoom, long-standing and a formula that has not been bettered – hence mentioned again on this page. Also in Glasgow the more recent and decidedly boho **Tchai-Ovna**. No chintz nor cream teas here, just good tchai and chat. Reports: 594/602/GLASGOW TEAROOMS.

1393
10/N22

✓ **Legends & The Highland Chocolatier** Grantully, near Aberfeldy Main street of village on the Tay where the rivers are as busy with rafters as the road with traffic. Gift and famously good home made chocolate shop and through the back a good tearoom for light snacks, home-made stuff, great tea list and of course hot chocolate. 10am-5pm. Closed Mon.

1394
8/S20

✓ **The Falls of Feugh** Banchory · www.fallsoffeugh.com · 01330 822123 Over bridge south from town, the B974 for Fettercairn (signed), a restaurant-cum-tearoom by a local beauty spot, the tumbling Falls. Ann Taylor's labour of love with à la carte menu, specials and great bakes. A model of how it should be done, here on the Deeside teaside where there are more than a few places to choose from (see above and below). All year. 7 days till 5pm (4pm in winter). Closed Mon/Tue.

1395
10/R27

✓ **Woodside** near Ancrum On B6400 off A68 at Ancrum turnoff. The caff in the shack at the back of the Woodside Garden Centre in the walled garden of Monteviot House (1515/GARDENS). Simple, delicious, mostly organic and locally sourced home baking: soup, sandwiches, quiche and cakes. Outside tables on sheltered lawn. 10am-5pm.

1396
9/L28

✓ **Tudor Restaurant** 8 Beresford Terrace, Ayr Near Odeon and Burns Monument Sq. High tea from 3.15pm, breakfast all day. Roomy, well-used, full of life. Bakery counter at front (fab cream donuts and bacon butties as they're supposed to be) and locals from bairns to OAPs in the body of the kirk. 10am-9pm Mon-Sat, 12noon-8pm Sun.

1397
10/P24
✓ **The Powmill Milkbar** near Kinross On the A977 Kinross (on the M90, junction 6) to Kincardine Bridge road, a real milk bar and a real slice of Scottish craic and cake. Apple pie, moist fly cemeteries, big meringues – an essential stop on any Sunday run (but open every day). The paper plates do little justice to the confections they bear, but they are part of the deal, so don't complain! Hot meals, great salads. Good place to take kids. 7 days, 9am-5pm (6pm summer, 4pm winter). And then: 1989/GLEN & RIVER WALKS.

1398
7/M20
✓ **Laggan Coffeeshop** near Laggan · www.potterybunkhouse.co.uk On A889 from Dalwhinnie on A9 that leads to A86, the road west to Spean Bridge and Kyle. Lovely Linda's road sign points you to this former pottery, craft shop and bunkhouse (1146/HOSTELS). Great home baking, scones, soup, sarnies and the most yummy cakes. Near great spot for forest walks and river swimming (1673/PICNICS). May-Oct 7 days till 5pm.

1399
8/R18
✓ **The Tearoom at Clatt** near Alford & Inverurie In the village hall in the hamlet of Clatt where local ladies display great home-made Scottish baking – like a weekly sale of work. Take A96 north of Inverurie, then B9002 follow sign for Auchleven, then Clatt. Great countryside. Weekends Apr-Oct 12noon-4pm. One of the great tea and scone experiences in the world (you'll see what I mean).

1400
10/Q24
✓ **Pillars Of Hercules** near Falkland · www.pillars.co.uk · 01337 857749 Rustic tearoom on organic farm on A912 2km from village towards Strathmiglo and the motorway. Excellent, homely place and fare and all PC. Home-made cakes, soup, etc. See also 1465/FARM SHOPS. 7 days 10am-5pm (shop till 6pm).

1401
9/L24
✓ **The Coach House** Luss, Loch Lomond · www.lochlomondtrading.com Long after the soap *Take The High Road* which was set here ended, this village still throngs with visitors. Rowena Grove's lovely caff goes like the proverbial fair. Not all home-made but good soups, quiches and stokies. Big tea selection, lashings of cream. Some outside seating. Nice loos. 7 days 10am-5pm.

1402
9/J22
✓ **Castle Stalker View** Portnacroish · www.castlestalkerview.co.uk On A828 Oban-Fort William about halfway. Modern-build café/gift shop with soup 'n' salad menu and home baking. Nice people so a popular local rendezvous as well as you and me just passing through. The main thing is the extraordinary view (1667/VIEWS). Mar-Oct 9.30am-5.30pm, winter Wed-Sun 10am-4pm.

1403
10/R26
✓ **Flat Cat Gallery Coffee Shop** Lauder · www.flatgallery.co.uk Opposite Eagle Hotel on Market St. Speeding through Lauder (note speed camera at Edinburgh end) you might miss this cool coffee spot and serious gallery. Always interesting work including furniture from Harestanes down the road; and ethnic things. Home baking. 7 days till 5pm.

1404
10/L23
✓ **Library Tearoom** Balquhidder Centre of village opposite church (1884/GRAVEYARDS) where many walks start. Includes great view (1661/VIEWS) and near long walk to Brig o' Turk (1987/GLEN WALKS). Excellent bakes, soup, salad and famous chocolate cake. Only a few tables. Apr-Oct, 10.30am-5.30pm. Closed Tue.

1405
9/H24
£15 OR LESS
✓ **Kilmartin House Café** Kilmartin · 01546 510278 Attached to early-peoples' museum (2132/MUSEUMS) in Kilmartin Glen and on main road north of Lochgilphead. Organic garden produce including tisanes for the revitalising that

the great range of home-made lunches (and dinners) don't fix. Good vegetarian choices. 7 days, hot food till 3pm, cakes till 5pm and dinner Thu-Sat in summer.

1406
9/H23

✓ **The Quaich Café** Kilmelford · 01852 200271 On road south from Oban to Campbeltown, Anne Saunders' village store and through the back, upstairs an unlikely great wee café; in the evenings, a restaurant. Home baking and snack meals by day 10.30am-4.30pm, then lovely home-made comfort food/local-produce-driven menu like your really-good-cook mum makes. Tue-Sat. LO 9pm.

1407
8/N17

✓ **Logie Steading** near Forres South of town towards Grantown (A940) – 10km. Or from Carrbridge via B9007. See 2005/WOODLAND WALKS (**Randolph's Leap**). In a lovely spot near the River Findhorn, a courtyard of fine things (2167/ SHOPPING) and Emma Swan's superior tearoom – home bakes and snacks; sound local sourcing. Hot food till 3pm. 7 days 10.30am-5pm. Apr-Dec.

1408
7/H18

The Flower Tunnel Applecross · www.applecross.uk.com/flower_tunnel In campsite (1211/CAMPING WITH KIDS) as you arrive in Applecross after amazing journey (1629/SCENIC ROUTES). Coffee-shop in greenhouse full of plants and outdoor seating. Famous (well, locally) pizzas. Apr-Oct. 7 days till 9pm.

1409
7/H16

Bridge Cottage Poolewe In village and near Inverewe Gardens (1504/GARDENS), cottage right enough with crafts/pictures up stairs and parlour teashop down. Salads, soups, baked potatoes, big cakes; local produce. 10.30am-4.30pm (winter hours vary). Closed Wed. Closed Nov.

1410
9/J23

Robin's Nest Main Street, Taynuilt Off the A85 (leading to Bonawe 2140/MUSEUMS and Glen Etive Cruises). Tiny home-baking caff with unusual soups and snacks as well as the good WRI kind of cakes. Easter-Oct 7 days 10am-5pm, Thu-Sun in winter.

1411
9/H25

Crinan Coffee Shop Crinan · www.crinanhotel.com Run by the hotel people (745/BEST HOTELS ARGYLL) – I guess they opened this because Crinan had to have a good coffee shop too. Fascinating village for yachties and anyone with time to while away, this place overlooks the busy canal basin where boats are always going through. The Canadian girl makes the most excellent cakes, bread and scones. Easter-Oct 9am-5.30pm.

1412
6/J16

Maggie's Tearoom Dundonnell On A832 in Wester Ross, the road to Inverewe Gardens and Gairloch. Roadside cottage with great view. Home-made hot dishes, salads and bakes. Season only. Closed Sun.

1413
10/P27

Laurel Bank Broughton · 01899 830462 On A701 near Biggar southwest of Edinburgh. Cottage tearoom, bistro and bar; local, friendly and a tad traditional. Nice coffee, home baking and Broughton Ales. 9am-11pm in summer, winter hours may vary.

1414
10/R24

Crail Harbour Tearoom Crail At last in cute little Crail, a tearoom where you need it on the road going down to the harbour. Gallery with pics from the owner. Lovely, sheltered terrace overlooking the shore. Dressed crab from the harbour, herring and dill, flaky salmon and cakes. Perfect! 7 days 10.30am-5pm. Apr-Nov.

1415
11/N30

Garden Room Teashop Rockcliffe On main road in/out of this seaside cul de sac. Best on sunny days when you can sit in the sheltered garden. Snacks and cakes (though not all home-made). 10.30am-5.30pm. Closed Mon/Tue.

1416 **The Schoolhouse** Ringford On the A75 10km west of Castle Douglas. I've long
11/M30 hurtled past this roadside tearoom in an old school that's always got loads of cars
parked outside. Not surprisingly, this is because folk love the Lawries' fresh cooking with integrity and commitment. It's all made here. Can take away. 8.30am-
5.30pm. Closed Wed except Jul/Aug.

1417 **The Smithy** New Galloway This little village has for a long time been a tea-
11/M29 room terminus because of Kitty's (see above), but new owners at the Smithy by
the burn are doing good stuff and the location is Sunday best. Home baking,
soups, omelettes. Let's hope there's tea enough for two. Mar-Oct 10am-5pm.

1418 **Gordons Tearoom** Braemar We haven't been but hear good reports about
10/P20 Gordons. There's got to be a demand for a decent place in this touristy town. All
home-made and friendly (they say). Reports, please. 7 days 10am-5pm. Sat/Sun
till 8pm for dinner.

1419 **Reading Glasses** Wigtown Few good eating places in Wigtown Booktown but
11/L30 this tiny caff at the back of yet another bookshop is a rest and respite from all that
browsing. 3-wifie operation with named, locally sourced ingredients, soup with
Creetown's Wigwam bread and home-made cakes. Can be as packed as a book-
shelf. 7 days Easter-Oct. 10am-5pm.

1420 **The Ariundle Centre** Strontian · www.ariundle.co.uk At beginning of walk
9/H21 in Ariundle Woods (2009/WOODLAND WALKS) in wonderful Ardnamurchan.
Bungalow tearoom with knits and knick-knacks. Hot dishes, home bakes. Lovely
home-made candlelit dinners 6.30-8.30pm (whenever) and a bunkhouse.

1421 **Crafty Kitchen** Ardfern Down the Ardfern B8002 road (4km) from A816 Oban-
9/H24 Lochgilphead road, the classier yachty haven of the Craignish peninsula. More
kitchen craft than crafty craft: great home-made cakes and special hot dishes
emerge along with superior burgers and fries. Tue-Sun 10am-5pm. Weekends only
Nov/Dec. Closed Jan-Mar.

1422 **Horsemill Restaurant** Crathes Castle, near Banchory · 01330 844525
8/S20 Adjacent magnificent Crathes (1834/COUNTRY HOUSES; 1505/GARDENS) so lots of
reasons to go off the Deeside road (A93) and up the drive. More tearoom than
restaurant in contemporary conversion of steadings around a pleasant courtyard.
Soup 'n' sandwich kinda menu. Gets mobbed. Open all year till 4.30pm.

1423 **The Pantry** Cromarty In great wee town in Black Isle 45km northeast of
7/M17 Inverness (1558/COASTAL VILLAGES) on corner of Church St. Excellent home baking,
soups and a decent cup of coffee. Easter-end Oct. 10.30am-4.30pm.

1424 **Dun Whinny's** Callander Off main street at Glasgow road, a welcoming wee
10/M24 (not twee) tearoom; not run by wifies. Banoffee pie kind of thing and clootie
dumpling. There's a few naff caffs in Callander. This one still ok in my book. It's all
home made. 7 days till 5pm.

✓ ✓ **Gloagburn Farm & Coffee Shop** Tibbermore near Perth
1458/FARM SHOPS.
✓ **The Corn Kist** Milton Haugh, near Arbroath 1461/FARM SHOPS.

✓ **Inshriach** Aviemore 2199/GARDEN CENTRES.

The Best Scotch Bakers

1425
10/Q23

✓✓ **Fisher & Donaldson** Dundee, St Andrews & Cupar ·
www.fisheranddonaldson.com Main or original branch in Cupar and a new kind of factory outlet up by Tesco and 3 in Dundee and St Andrews. Superior contemporary bakers along traditional lines (born 1919) – surprising (and a pity) that they haven't gone further, although they do supply selected outlets (eg Jenners in Edinburgh with pastries and the most excellent Dr Floyd's bread which is as good as anything you could make yourself). Sample also their yum yums, Danish pastries, other breads and signature mini apple and rhubarb pies. Main square, Cupar; Church St, St Andrews; Whitehall St, 300 Perth Rd and Lochee, Dundee. Dundee Whitehall and Cupar have good tearooms (925/BEST DUNDEE) and the factory one is fab.

1426
10/M24

✓✓ **Mhor Bread** Callander West end of main street in busy touristy town. Here forever but taken on by the irrepressible Lewis family of Monachyle Mhor (1181/GETAWAY HOTELS) so those pies, cakes, the biggest, possibly the best, tattie scones and sublime doughnuts in Scotland have all been thrust into the 21st century; your picnic on the Braes is sorted. Adjacent café does the bake stuff plus sandwiches, omelettes and always, the scone. Callander transformed (but still some way to go)! 7 days 7am-5pm (Sun from 9am, tearoom till 4.30pm).

1427
2/B1

✓ **Bradford's** 245 Sauchiehall Street, Glasgow Also suburban branches – they have not over-expanded; for a bakery chain, some lines seem almost home-made. Certainly better than all the industrial 'home' bakers around. Individual fruit pies, for example, are uniquely yummy, and the all-important Scotch pie pastry is exemplary. Report: 610/GLASGOW CAFFS.

1428
7/M17

✓ **Cromarty Bakery** Bank Street, Cromarty One of the many reasons to visit this picturesque seaside town. Abundance of speciality cakes, organic bread, rolls and pies, baked daily on premises. Top oatcakes! Also tea, coffee, hot savouries and takeaway. Produce available elsewhere in the area, eg the Storehouse at Evanton (1469/FARMSHOPS). 8.30am-5.30pm; Sat till 4 pm. Closed Sun.

1429
6/J14

✓ **Riverside Bistro** Lochinver · www.piesbypost.co.uk On way into town from Ullapool, etc. A bistro/restaurant rightly famous for their brilliant pies from takeaway counter. Huge variety of savoury and fruit from traditional to exotic. And irresistible puds. Ready sustenance, indulgence; or get 'em by post. 7 days.

1430
10/Q23

Goodfellow & Steven Dundee, Perth & Fife The other bakers in the Fife/Dundee belt (not a patch on Fisher & Donaldson; but hey). G&S have several branches in Dundee, Perth and Fife. Good commercial Scotch baking with the kind of cakes that used to be a treat.

1431
9/H21

The Bakehouse Acharacle, Ardnamurchan Helen Macgillvray's roadside bakery unprepossessing, tiny inside but great bakes including bread, pastries and especially savouries. Top pork pie in Scotland. Stock up for picnics at Singing Sands (2040/COASTAL WALKS) or Castle Tioram shore (1793/RUINS). All year. Closed Sun.

1432
10/Q22

McLaren's Forfar Town centre next to Queens Hotel and in Kirriemuir. Best in town to sample the famous Forfar bridie, a meaty shortcrust pastie hugely underestimated as a national delicacy. They're so much better than the gross and grossly overhyped Cornish pasty but have never progressed beyond this part of Perthshire; though one of the best examples is the home-made bridie that can be found in the café at Glamis (1767/CASTLES). **Saddler's** in North St, Forfar do them too.

The Really Good Delis

For Edinburgh and Glasgow delis, see p. 71 and p. 120.

1444
8/T19

✓ ✓ **Hammerton Stores** 336 Great Western Road, Aberdeen · www.hammertonstore.co.uk · 01224 324449 On the road west to Deeside. Susan Watson's love affair with life, not strictly speaking a deli, more a superior provisioner where essentials include art and cool pottery and travelling rugs. Wines, beers, cheeses and brands are all carefully selected. Tables outside where you can snack and reflect how nice it would be to have a place like this in your neighbourhood. 7 days 8am-7pm (Sun 6pm).

1445
7/L18

✓ ✓ **The Corner on the Square** 1 High Street, Beauly · 01463 783000 · www.corneronthesquare.co.uk On said corner of the square on right heading west. Good find hereabouts mainly because of its sit-in coffee-shop fare including great baking, quiches, scones, soups, etc. Well-cared-for cheeses and Cromarty bakes (1428/BAKERIES). Lunch 12noon-3pm, shop and snacks 9am-5.30pm (Sat 5pm). Closed Sun.

1446
10/R23

✓ ✓ **I.J. Mellis** St Andrews · www.mellischeese.co.uk Started out as the cheese guy, now more of a very select deli for food that's good and 'slow'. Coffees, hams, sausages, olives and seasonal stuff like apples and mushrooms (branches vary), so smells mingle. Irresistible! Branches also in Edinburgh (325/EDINBURGH DELIS) and Glasgow (642/GLASGOW DELIS). 7 days though times vary. See also 1473/CHEESES.

1447
8/P17

✓ **Phoenix Findhorn Community** Findhorn · www.phoenixshop.co.uk Serving the wider community and the eco village itself (1230/RETREATS) and therefore pursuing a conscientious approach, this has become an exemplary and very high-quality deli, worth the detour from the A96 Inverness-Elgin road. Packed and carefully selected shelves; as much for pleasurable eating as for healthy. Best organic fruit and veg in the North East. The excellent **Bakehouse** café in Findhorn itself owned by the folk who used to have the deli for superb ethical eats (1037/LESS EXPENSIVE HIGHLAND RESTAURANTS). Till 6pm (weekends 5pm).

1448
10/N23

✓ **2 Damned Fine Delis in Crieff: McNee's** Main Street Near the town clock. Deli/bakers/chocolatiers. More like an old-fashioned grocer. Great home-baking and ready-made meals, home-roasted meats and some sweety and touristy things creeping in... well, after 20 years! 9am-6pm (Sun 9.30am-4pm). **J.L. Gill** West end, near right turn to Crianlarich And the real McCoy, here 70 years. Unpredictable choice of provisions: honey, tinned tuna, 10 kinds of oatcakes, lotsa whisky. A real old-style, still the best-style gem. 8.45am-5.30pm. Closed Sun.

1449
8/Q18

✓ **Spey Larder** Main Street, Aberlour · www.speylarder.com In deepest Speyside. Beautiful old shop (1864) spacious and full of great, often local produce (honeys, bread, game in winter, Speyside chanterelles and of course whisky). Nice cheese counter. All year. Closed Sun. 9am-5.30pm.

1450
10/R28

✓ **Turnbull's** Hawick · 01450 372020 By 'the Horse' in main street, a much-needed shot in the foodie arm in old Hawick which has waited a long time for olive oil to drip into the diet. Now this attractive, eclectic deli/café supplies the lot and makes life better. Tables a bit cramped for soup/salad/sandwich menu but where else would you go (perhaps Damascus Drum; 832/BORDERS RESTAURANTS)? 9.30am-5pm (food till 4pm). Closed Sun.

1451
10/N21

The Scottish Delis www.scottish-deli.co.uk · 01796 473322 · **Pitlochry** & 01350 7280828 · **Dunkeld** & **The Farm Shop at Highland Safaris** 01887 822821 · **Dull, Aberfeldy** Pitlochry shop is just off the main street (West Moulin Rd); Dunkeld Main St. All have great takeaway food and ready meals: traiteur-style and cafés with home baking. They have the '3 corners of Perthshire' covered. Charcuterie, cheese, etc. 7 days.

1542
11/L13

Ravenstone Deli Whithorn · 01988 500329 Main street up from Whithorn Story Visitor Centre. James Barton and Sara Guild's essential deli, bakery, butcher, pizzeria and coffee shop. Good cheese and olive selection, local produce, some organics, excellent daily bread (baked on premises). Home-cured bacon, home-made sausages and meat locally sourced. Pizzas prêt-a-porter from deli counter. An all-round good thing! 8.30am-5pm. Closed Sun/Mon.

1453
10/N24

Clive Ramsay Main Street, Bridge of Allan · www.cliveramsay.com Here for years but both this and the café/bistro adjacent have fallen into other (both different) hands and Mr Ramsay has moved on. Still a decent deli in pleasant B of A for fruit/veg, cheese, olives, seeds and well-chosen usuals. 7 days 7am-7pm.

1454
8/P17

Gordon & MacPhail South Street, Elgin Purveyors of fine wines, cheeses, meats, Mediterranean goodies, unusual breads and other epicurean delights to the good burghers of Elgin for nigh on a century. Traditional shopkeeping, in the style of the 'family grocer'. G & M are widely known as bottlers of lesser-known high-quality malts ('Connoisseurs' range) – on sale here as well as every other whisky you've ever heard of and many you ain't. Some rare real ales by the bottle too. Mon-Sat 9am-5.15pm.

1455
10/P23

Provender Brown 23 George Street, Perth · 01738 587300 As we might expect, a decent deli in the town/city where several good restaurants reside, there's a big farmers' market (first in Scotland) and many folk aren't short of a bob or two. P&B are good for olives, vacuum-packed products and especially cheese. 9am-5pm (till 5.30pm Thu-Sat). Closed Sun.

1456
9/K25

Mearns T. McCaskie Wemyss Bay Now in its third generation, a butcher of integrity and repute: home-cured bacon, sausages, pies, cheeses, fine wines and other delights. Picnic anyone? 8am-5.30pm (5pm Sat). Closed Sun.

1457
10/M24

Berits & Brown Kippen · 01786 870077 The original of possible emerging deli franchise (there's another in Glasgow). Not hugely original but nice enough. Café with bespoke sandwiches from counter, soup, etc. Adds to Kippen's 'foodie village' credentials (great butcher's, Skinner's, opposite). 10am-5pm.

Gloagburn Farm & Coffee Shop Tibbermore, near Perth Excellent sit-in coffee shop/restaurant but also deli with selected local/organic produce. Report: 1458/FARM SHOPS.

The Pillars of Hercules near Falkland · 01337 857749 Organic grocers with tearoom (1400/TEAROOMS) and outstanding farm shop. Report: 1465/FARM SHOPS.

The Really Good Farm Shops

1458
10/P23

✓✓ **Gloagburn Farm & Coffee Shop** Tibbermore Off A85 Perth-
Methven and Crieff road from A9 and ring road at Huntingtower, signed
Tibbermore (Tibbermore also signed off A9 from Stirling just before Perth). Through
village, second farm on right: a family (the Nivens') farm shop with ducks on the
pond and Tamworth pigs out back – excellent fresh produce and inside a deli and
café where food (hot dishes, cakes, etc) is exemplary. Hot and other food till 5pm.
Vacuum-packed meats, frozen meals, fruit 'n' veg. A destination place only 15
minutes from Perth. Open all year 9am-5.30pm (4pm winter). 7 days.

1459
8/R20

✓✓ **Finzean Farm Shop & Tearoom** Deeside · 01330 850710 On the
south side of the river on B976 between Banchory and Aboyne. Kate and
Catriona's foodie haven in glorious open countryside with views to the hills from
the terrace. Local and carefully sourced produce beautifully presented fresh and
frozen. Meat from the estate. Cool cookbooks. Hot dishes till 3pm. Cakes that
don't rely on cream. 7 days 9am-5pm.

1460
11/N30

✓✓ **Loch Arthur Creamery & Farm Shop** Beeswing, near Dumfries
Run by Camphill Trust, this is the genuine article tucked away in a working dairy farm with a strong organic agenda. Great baking, famous organic veg,
those cheeses (see p. 260, Scottish Cheeses) and the UK's best granola. Tiny shop
but stock expanded of late. From Beeswing take New Abbey road 1km. Mon-Fri
9am-5.30pm, Sat 10am-3pm. Closed Sun.

1461
10/R22

✓✓ **Milton Haugh Farm Shop** Carmyllie · 01241 860579 Off A92
Dundee-Arbroath road at Carnoustie, follow Forfar road, then signs. Faraway farm on B961 that's enormously popular. Great range of fruit and veg, meats
and selected deli fare with own-label meals, jams, etc. 5 kinds of excellent oatcakes. Excellent Corn Kist Coffee Shop with home-made cakes, soups and specials,
so from far and wide you come. 9am-5pm (Sun from 10am). Café 10am-4pm.

1462
8/T19

✓ **The Store** Westfield, Foveran, near Udny Station · 01358 788083 Off
A90 this beautiful farm shop is a foodlovers' haven and a base for their Aberdeen Angus (well-hung and tender) operation which also supplies their shop in
Edinburgh (330/EDINBURGH). Range of vacuum-packed other meats, cooked meals
and all the stuff including fruit and veg to have with them. 7 days 10am-5pm.

1463
10/P25

✓ **West Craigie Farm** near South Queensferry · 0131 319 1048 Take the
South Queensferry exit from dual carriageway north from Edinburgh, A90 to
Forth Road Bridge. Farm is signed 2km. Nowhere on this page demonstrates the
growth, potential and appeal of farm shops more than this. A short time ago it was
a farm on the edge of town where you could PYO or buy fruit (and fudge) from a
back door of the byre. Now you enter a lofty emporium packed with farm/deli
goodies and sit on a terrace taking tea and cake overlooking rows and fields of
fruit like vineyards in France while the city shimmers in the distance. PYO berries
(not just strawbs and rasps) from mid Jun-late Aug. All year 9-5pm.

1464
10/R25

✓ **Fenton Barns Farm Shop** near North Berwick · 01620 850294 Off A1
for Dirleton, Mhairi and Roy's country emporium/caff is between Drem and
Dirleton on Fenton Barns retail and craft parklet, an old airfield complex. They also
look after the Fruitmarket Gallery Café in Edinburgh (279/TEAROOMS) and St Giles'
Cathedral coffee shop – how do they do it? Organic meats, free-range eggs, home-
made pies, soups, terrines, selected fruit and veg, Roy's great coffee and their signature cool as coffee shop in the back. 849/EAST LOTHIAN EATS. 7 days 10am-5pm.

1465
10/Q24
☕

✔ **The Pillars of Hercules** near Falkland · www.pillars.co.uk · 01337 857749 On A912 2km from town towards Strathmiglo and motorway. A pillar of the organic community. Grocers with tearoom (1400/TEAROOMS) on farm/nursery where you can PYO herbs and flowers. Always fruit/veg and great selection of dry goods that's a long way from Sainsbury's and here long before the organic boom. 7 days 10-6pm.

1466
10/R24

✔ **Ardross Farm** near Elie · 01333 330415 Between St Monance and Elie on the A917 Fife coastal route. East Neuk farm shop known mainly for its own meat but with long list (42) of seasonal dug vegetables, Fiona's pies, readymade meals. The Pollock family have been here over a century and they're big supporters of UK farm produce as well as their own. 7 days 9am-5.30pm, Sun 9am-4pm. Closed Mon/Tue in winter.

1467
10/P22

Ballathie Kinclaven, near Blairgowrie · 01250 876219 On the Ballathie estate adjacent the famous hotel (878/BEST PERTHSHIRE), a tearoom and shop around a courtyard with estate produce, especially meat and game and other choice foods. Tearoom has great burgers and home-made cakes. Some readymade meals. 9.30am-5.30pm (Sun from 10am). Closed Mon.

1468
10/Q23
☕

Cairnie Fruit Farm (and Maze) near Cupar · 01334 655610 A truly a(maze)ing conversion of a fruit farm into a major family attraction (1701/KIDS), demonstrating if nothing else the inexorable rise of the strawberry. Here this and other berries can be picked, purchased and eaten in all manner of cakes with other farm produce and snack food. Main thing though is the kids' area outside. 10am-5pm. Closed Mon Sep-Dec. Farm is 4km north of Cupar on minor road past the hospital or 3km from main A92, signed near Kilmany.

1469
7/M17
☕

The Storehouse near Evanton · 01349 830038 Roadside farm shop and destination diner on A9 north of Inverness south of Alness overlooking the Firth. Locally sourced meats, veg and greens and a big selection of preserves, etc; some trinketry. (Now some readers take exception to this word but I'm sticking with it: the produce just ain't as fresh farm shop as others on this page.) However, there's no doubting that they've got the food right – the self-service restaurant goes like a fair with all things irresistible but not very good for you. Often queues. Lashings of cream. 7 days 9am-6pm, Sun 10am-5pm.

1470
10/R23
☕

Allanhill near St Andrews · 01334 477998 6km out of town off Anstruther/Crail road A917 past the Grange (1294/GASTROPUBS). Simple farm shop and café with tables out in the field and kids' stuff including animals and hay bales. Great views to St Andrews Bay. Known mainly for excellent soft fruits including the elusive blueberry. Tearoom has excellent strawberry cakes and a top scone. Only open 100 days: May-Sep.

1471
10/R25

Knowes Farm Shop Farm near East Linton · 01620 860010 Close to A1 on A198 to North Berwick just before Tyninghame. Farm cottage converted into spacious, integrity food store. Organic veg and herbs, home-made pâtés and pavlova. Lots of eggs and the chickens in the field. All year 9.30am-5pm. They supply other farm shops, restaurants, etc with their excellent home-grown veg.

1472
10/Q24
☕

Muddy Boots Balmalcolm · 07843 630762 On A914 from A92 south of Cupar, a farm shop with kitchen and crafts and some integrity over their produce; and now a full-on kids' playground. Their home-grown fruit and veg is high quality (the *best* raspberries) and they're keen to educate and inspire kids into good country practice. All year 7 days 9am-6pm (10am-5pm Sun).

Scottish Cheeses

Mull or Tobermory Cheddar www.isleofmullcheese.co.uk From Sgriob-Ruadh Farm (pronounced 'Skibrua'). Comes in big 50lb cheeses and 1lb truckles. Good, strong cheddar, one of the very best in UK. (See Arran Cheeseshop, below).

Dunsyre Blue/Lanark Blue Made by Humphrey Errington at Carnwath. Next to Stilton, **Dunsyre** (made from the unpasteurised milk of Ayrshire cows) is the best blue in the UK. It is soft, rather like Dolcelatte. **Lanark,** the original, is Scotland's Roquefort and made from ewes' milk. Both can vary seasonally but are always excellent. Go on, live dangerously – unpasteurise your life.

Locharthur Cheese www.locharthur.org.uk Anything from this (Camphill Trust) South West creamery is worth a nibble: the cheddar, **Criffel** (mild), **Kebbuck** (shaped like a dinosaur's tooth, semi-soft). Widely available but have their own shop (see below).
Bonnet Hard goats' milk cheese from Anne Dorwood's farm at Stewarton in Ayrshire. Also a very good cheddar (and sheep's-milk cheddar).

Wester Lawrenceton Farm Cheeses Forres Pam Rodway's excellent organic cheeses: **Carola, Califer** (goats' milk) and the hard-to-get **Sweetmilk Cheddar**. On sale Findhorn shop and Gordon & MacPhail (1537/DELIS).

Craigmyle Cheeses Torphins, Royal Deeside Lovely **Wummle** (wee or muckle) and the delicate, crumbly, organic **Clachnaben**. New, enterprising, already award-winning.

Highland Fine Cheeses From the Stone family in Tain. 6 cheeses including **Crowdie** (traditional curd cheese), **Caboc** and **Strathdon Blue** (award winner) and their excellent cheddar **Blairliath**.

Bishop Kennedy A semi-soft, runny, cows'-milk cheese that hums. Note also **Anster** – crumbly, white and tasty from the St Andrews Cheese Company.

Arran Cheeses Award-winning variety. See their cheese shop outside Brodick, below.

... AND WHERE TO FIND THEM
The delis on pp. 71, 120 and 256-57 will have good selections (especially Valvona's in Edinburgh and Delizique in Glasgow).

1473
10/M26
10/P25
10/R23
8/T19

✓✓ **I.J. Mellis** Edinburgh, Glasgow, St Andrews & Aberdeen · www.mellischeese.co.uk 30a Victoria St, far end of Morningside Rd and Baker's Pl, Stockbridge (Edinburgh), 492 Great Western Rd (Glasgow), 149 South St (St Andrews), 201 Rosemount Pl (Aberdeen). A real cheesemonger. Smell and taste before you buy. Cheeses from all over the UK in prime condition. Daily and seasonal specials. (324/EDINBURGH DELIS, 642/GLASGOW DELIS, 1446/DELIS.)

1474
1/XA1

✓ **Herbie** 66 Raeburn Place, William Street & North West Circus Place, Edinburgh · www.herbieofedinburgh.co.uk Excellent selection – everything here is the right stuff. Great bread, bagels, etc from independent baker, home-made houmous and with Scottish cheeses, it's practically impossible here to find a Brie or a blue in less than perfect condition. William St (West End) is the takeaway of choice hereabouts.

1475
9/G22

✓ **Sgriob-Ruadh Farm** Tobermory Head out on road to Dervaig, take turning for Glengorm (great coffee shop; 1390/TEAROOMS) and watch for sign and track to farm. Past big glass barn where they live and follow path to distant doorway into the cheese factory and farm shop (though all there is are lovely shit-covered fresh eggs and their cheddar). Honesty box when nobody working.

1476
9/J27

Arran Cheeseshop Arran 5km Brodick, road to castle and Corrie. Excellent selection of their own (the well-known cheddars) but many others especially crowdie, Camembert, Brie, Arran white (like Cheshire) and award-winning blue. Selected others. See them being made. 7 days. 9.30am-5.30pm (5pm in winter).

1477
7/H18

West Highland Dairy www.westhighlanddairy.co.uk · 01599 577203 · Achmore, near Plockton Mr and Mrs Biss still running their great farm dairy shop selling their own cheeses (goats' and cows' milk), yoghurt, ice cream and cheesecake. Mar-Dec. Signed from village. Highland sylvan setting but no cows in sight. If you're making the trip specially, phone first to check they're open (usually 10am-4.30pm).

1478
10/Q27

Riley's High Street, Peebles · 01721 729202 Bridge end. Small, ok deli especially for ham, salamis and cheeses. 10am-5pm. Closed Sun.

1479
10/P22

McDonald's Cheese Shop Rattray, near Blairgowrie · 01250 872493 Long-established emporium of cheese (80 varieties selected by owner Caroline Robertson). You can buy a whole wheel of Gruyère. 9am-5pm. Closed Sun/Mon.

1480
10/Q23

The Cheesery Dundee · www.thecheesery.co.uk · 01382 202160 In Exchange St where there are a couple of food stops, eg Sa'vor next door for take-away food with integrity, but this cheese place is a foody oasis in downtown Dundee. Tue-Sat 9.30am-5.30pm.

Loch Arthur Creamery Beeswing Off A75, A711 road to New Abbey. Excellent for their cheeses and other very good things. 1460/FARM SHOPS.

House Of Bruar near Blair Atholl Roadside emporium. 2170/SHOPPING.

Falls of Shin Visitor Centre near Lairg Harrods of the North. 2172/SHOPPING.

Peter MacLennan 28 High Street, Fort William.

Scottish Speciality Food North Ballachulish By Leven Hotel.

The Kitchen Garden Oban 765/OBAN.

Jenners Department Store Princes Street, Edinburgh Top floor.

Corner on the Square Main Street, Beauly 1445/DELIS.

Whisky: The Best Distillery Tours

The process is basically the same in every distillery, but some are more atmospheric and some have more interesting tours, like these below. www.scotchwhisky.net is a great site on all things whisky.

1481
9/F25
ATMOS

✓✓ **The Islay Malts** www.islaywhiskysociety.com Plenty to choose from including, in the north:
Caol Ila (Mon-Fri, times vary Feb-Nov; 01496 302769);
the wholly independent **Bruichladdich** (3 tours daily Mon-Fri, twice daily on Sat, 01496 850221); and
Kilchoman, the brand new Wills kid, daily tours not Sun (not Sat in winter) with great café; 2280/ISLAY (01496 850011).
In the south near Port Ellen, 3 of the world's great malts are in a row on a mystic coast. The distilleries here look like distilleries ought to.
Lagavulin (01496 302749) and **Laphroaig** (01496 302418) offer fascinating tours where your guide will lay on the anecdotes as well as the process and you get a feel for the life and history as well as the product of these world-famous places. At Laphroaig you can join their 'Friend' scheme (free) and own a piece of their hallowed ground. Tours 7 days a week Mar-Oct, Mon-Fri in winter. Tour times vary.
Ardbeg (01496 302244) is perhaps the most visitor-oriented and has a really good café – 2280/ISLAY RESTAURANTS – and makes the most of its (dark olive) brand. All these distilleries are in settings that entirely justify the romantic hyperbole of their advertising. Worth seeing from the outside as well as the factory floor.
Bowmore (01496 810441) has professional, more commercial, 1-hour tours twice a day (with video show and the usual dram) and is perhaps the most convenient.

1482
8/Q17
ATMOS

✓ **Strathisla** Keith · 01542 783044 The oldest working distillery in the Highlands, literally on the strath of the Isla River and methinks the most evocative atmosphere of all the Speyside distilleries. Tastefully reconstructed, this is a very classy halt for the malt. Used as the 'heart' of Chivas Regal, the malt not commonly available is still a fine dram. You wait for a tour group to gather; there's a dram at the beginning and the end. Mar-Oct 10am-4pm (Sun from 12.30pm).

1483
8/P18

✓ **The Glenlivet** Minmore · www.theglenlivet.com · 01340 821720 Starting as an illicit dram celebrated as far south as Edinburgh, George Smith licensed the brand in 1824 and founded this distillery in 1858, registering the already mighty name so anyone else had to use a prefix. After successions and mergers, independence was lost in 1978 when Seagrams took over. Now owned by Pernod Ricard. The famous Josie's Well, from which the water springs, is underground but small parties and a walk-through which is not on a gantry make the tour satisfying and as popular, especially with Americans, as the product. Excellent reception centre with bar/restaurant and shop. Apr-Oct 9.30am-4pm. Sun 12-4pm.

1484
8/Q18

✓ **Glenfiddich** Dufftown · www.glenfiddich.com · 01340 820373 Outside town on the A941 to Craigellachie by the ruins of Balvenie Castle. Well-oiled tourist operation and the only distillery where you can see the whole process from barley to bar. The only major distillery that's free (including dram). Also now runs an artists in residence scheme with changing exhibitions over the summer in gallery adjacent car park (01340 821565 for details). All year 9.30am-4.30pm, not weekends in winter. Good café.
On the same road you can see a whisky-related craft that hasn't changed.
Speyside Cooperage is 1km from Craigellachie. See those poor guys from the gantry (no chance to slack). All year Mon-Fri 9.30am-4.30pm. Good coffee shop.

1485
10/N21

✓ **Edradour** near Pitlochry · www.edradour.co.uk · 01796 472095
Picturesque and as romantic as you can imagine the smallest distillery in
Scotland to be, producing single malts for blends since 1825 and limited quanti-
ties of the Edradour (since 1986) as well as the House of Lords' own brand. Guided
tour of charming cottage complex every 20 minutes. 4km from Pitlochry off
Kirkmichael road, A924; signed after Moulin village. Complex opening hours
though open all year, 7 days.

1486
7/F18

Talisker Carbost, Isle of Skye From Sligachan-Dunvegan road (A863) take
B8009 for Carbost and Glen Brittle along the south side of Loch Harport for 5km.
Skye's only distillery; since 1830 they've been making this classic after-dinner malt
from barley and the burn that runs off the Hawkhill behind. A dram before the informative 40-minute tour. Good visitor centre. Apr-Oct 9.30am-5pm (set times in
winter; 01478 614308). Great gifts nearby (2175/CRAFT SHOPS). Nice pub for grub
and music nearby: the Old Inn at Carbost.

1487
10/Q25

Glenkinchie Pencaitland, near Edinburgh · 01875 342004 Only 25km from
city centre (via A68 and A6093 before Pathhead), signposted and so very popular.
Founded in 1837 in a pastoral place 3km from village, with its own bowling green;
a country trip and a whisky tour. State-of-the-art visitor centre. Summer daily till
5pm. Closed 4pm and weekends in winter.

1488
3/Q10

Highland Park Kirkwall, Orkney · www.highlandpark.co.uk · 01856 874619
2km from town on main A961 road south to South Ronaldsay. The whisky is great
(the 18 Years Old won The Best Spirit in the World '05) and the award-winning
tour one of the best. The most northerly whisky in a class and a bottle of its own.
You walk through the floor maltings and you can touch the warm barley and fair
smell the peat. Good combination of the industrial and the traditional. Tours every
half hour. Open all year Mon-Fri 10am-5pm. Afternoons only in winter.

THE BEST OF THE SPEYSIDE WHISKY TRAIL
Well signposted but a bewildering number of tours, though not at every distillery.
Many are in featureless industrial complexes but these (with Strathisla, The Glenlivet
and Glenfiddich above) are the best:

1489
8/Q17

Glen Grant Rothes · 01340 832118 In Rothes on the A941 Elgin to Perth road.
Not the most picturesque but a distillery tour with an added attraction, viz. the
gardens and orchard reconstructed around the shallow bowl of the glen of the
burn that runs through the distillery: there's a delightful Dram Pavilion. The
French own this one too: reflect as you sit in the library and listen to the founder
before you leave. Feb-Dec 9.30am-5pm, from 12pm on Sun. Last tour 4pm.

1490
8/P18

Cardhu (or Cardow) Carron · 01340 872555 Off B9102 from Craigellachie to
Grantown through deepest Speyside, a small if charming distillery with its own
community, a millpond, picnic tables, etc. Owned by United Distillers, Cardhu is
the 'heart of Johnnie Walker' (which, amazingly, has another 30 malts in it). Open
all year round, Mon-Fri (7 days Jul/Aug). Hours vary.

1491
8/P17

Benromach Forres · www.benromach.com · 01309 675968 Signed from
the A96 through road. The smallest working distillery so no bus tours or big
tourist operation. Human beings with time for a chat. Rescued by Gordon &
MacPhail (1454/DELIS) and reopened 1999. The Malt Whisky Centre is a good
introduction; you may need no other tour even if you've never heard of the brand.
Apr-Sep 9.30am-5pm (Sun in Jun-Aug only 12noon-4pm). Winter 10am-4pm.

1492   **Dallas Dhu** near Forres · 01309 676548 Not really near the Spey (3km south
8/P17   of Forres on B9010) and no longer a working distillery (ceased 1983), but instant
HS   history provided by Historic Scotland and you don't have to go round on a tour.
The wax workers are a bit spooky; the product itself is more life-like. Historic
Scotland opening hours. Closed Thu/Fri.

1493   **Scotch Whisky Heritage Centre** Edinburgh · 0131 220 0441 ·
1/C4   www.whisky-heritage.co.uk On Castlehill on last stretch to castle (you cannot
miss it). Not a distillery of course, but a visitor attraction to celebrate all things a
tourist can take in about Scotland's main export. Shop has huge range. 7 days
10am-5pm (extended hours in summer).

1494   **Promotional Tours: Glenturret** near Crieff **& Aberfeldy** A recent trend
10/N23 has been to make over distilleries into interactive ads for certain brands of blends.
The quaint old Glenturret distillery by Crieff is now the Famous Grouse Experience
(daily all year 08450 451800) while Aberfeldy distillery is now Dewar's World of
Whisky (all year, call for times 01887 822010) though it also includes Aberfeldy
(the whisky, not the town or the band). The branding density is tiresome but the
production tours are super-professional.

Whisky: The Best Malts Selections

EDINBURGH

✓ ✓ **Scotch Malt Whisky Society** The Vaults, 87 Giles Street, Leith &
28 Queen Street · www.smws.com Your search will end here. More a
club (with membership); visitors must be signed in.

✓ **Royal Mile Whiskies** 379 High Street · www.royalmilewhiskies.com
Whisky Magazine Retailer of the Year. Also in London.

Bennet's 8 Leven Street · www.bennets.co.uk 333/UNIQUE EDINBURGH PUBS.

Kay's Bar 39 Jamaica Street 339/UNIQUE EDINBURGH PUBS.

The Bow Bar 80 West Bow · www.bowbar.com 354/EDINBURGH REAL-ALE
PUBS.

Cadenhead's 172 Canongate · www.wmcadenhead.com The shop with the
lot.

Canny Man 237 Morningside Road 163/EDINBURGH PUBS.

The Malt Shovel 11 Cockburn Street 100 whiskies and all.

Blue Blazer Corner Spittal & Bread Streets 357/EDINBURGH REAL-ALE PUBS.

GLASGOW

✓ ✓ **The Pot Still** 154 Hope Street · www.thepotstill.co.uk
450 different bottles of single malt. And proud of it.

The Bon Accord 153 North Street · www.thebonaccord.com 662/GLASGOW
REAL-ALE PUBS.

The Lismore 206 Dumbarton Road 655/UNIQUE GLASGOW PUBS.

Ubiquitous Chip Ashton Lane · www.ubiquitouschip.co.uk Restaurant, bistro and great bar on the corner.

Ben Nevis Argyle Street · www.geocities.com/bennevisbar Far west end of the street. 656/UNIQUE GLASGOW PUBS.

REST OF SCOTLAND

1495
9/F26
✓ ✓ **Lochside Hotel** Bowmore, Islay · www.lochsidehotel.co.uk More Islay malts than you ever imagined in friendly local near the Bowmore Distillery. And on the lochside.

✓ ✓ **Torridon Inn** near Kinlochewe Classic Highland hotel and 300 malts shelf by shelf. And the mountains! 1183/GET-AWAY HOTELS.

✓ ✓ **Clachaig Inn** Glencoe Over 100 malts to go with the range of ales and the range of thirsty hillwalkers. 1267/BLOODY GOOD PUBS.

✓ ✓ **The Drover's Inn** Inverarnan Same as above, with around 75 to choose from and the right atmosphere to drink them in. 1264/BLOODY GOOD PUBS.

✓ ✓ **The Oystercatcher** Portmahomack Gordon Robertson's exceptional malt (and wine) collection in quality restaurant in far-flung village. 1052/HIGHLAND RESTAURANTS.

✓ ✓ **Forss House** near Thurso Hotel bar on north coast. Often a wee wind outside. Warm up with one of the 300 well-presented malts. 1003/BEST HIGHLAND.

1496
8/P19
✓ ✓ **Minmore House** Glenlivet Beautiful, comfy country-house hotel right next to the distillery.

✓ **The Quaich Bar** at The Craigellachie Hotel Whiskies arranged around cosy bar of this essential Speyside hotel and the river below. 981/SPEYSIDE.

✓ **Knockinaam Lodge** Portpatrick Comfortable country-house hotel; especially good Lowland selection including the local Bladnoch. 780/SOUTH WEST HOTELS.

✓ **The Piano Bar at the Glenmoriston Townhouse** Inverness Easy-to-decipher malt list in superior, stylish surroundings. 994/HIGHLAND HOTELS.

✓ **The Anderson** Fortrose Amazing collection of malts (and beers) in town hotel bar. 1026/LESS EXPENSIVE HIGHLANDS.

✓ **Ardanaiseig Hotel** Loch Awe · www.ardanaiseig.com A dram's a must after dinner in the bar looking over the lawn to the loch. 1121/COUNTRY-HOUSE HOTELS.

✓ **Glenmoriston Arms Hotel** Invermoriston On A82 between Inverness and Fort Augustus. Growing collection of malts in lovely roadside inn with new owners. 1180/ROADSIDE INNS.

✓ Dunain Park Hotel   Inverness   After dinner in one of the best places to eat hereabouts, there's a serious malts list to mull over. 999/HIGHLAND HOTELS.

✓ Hotel Eilean Iarmain   Skye   Also known as the Isleornsay Hotel (2223/ISLAND HOTELS); not the biggest range but one of the best places to drink (it).

Kinloch House Hotel   near Blairgowrie   1120/COUNTRY-HOUSE HOTELS.

Gordon & MacPhail   Elgin   The whisky provisioner and bottlers of the Connoisseurs brand you see in other shops and bars all over. From these humble beginnings over 100 years ago, they now supply their exclusive and rarity range to the world. Mon-Sat till 5.15pm (5pm Wed). Closed Sun. 1454/DELIS.

1497
8/Q18
The Whisky Shop   Dufftown · www.whiskyshopdufftown.co.uk   The whisky shop in the main street (by the clock tower) at the heart of whisky country. Within a few miles of numerous distilleries and their sales operations, this place stocks all the product (including many halfs). 10am-6pm Mon-Sat, 2-4pm Sun.

1498
9/H25
Loch Fyne Whiskies   Inveraray · www.lfw.co.uk   Beyond the church on the A83, a shop with 400 malts to choose from; and whisky ware.

1499
9/L27
Robbie's Drams   Ayr · www.robbiesdrams.com   In Sandgate near the bridge. By bottle or case a huge selection; also beers and wines.

Fox & Hounds   Houston   1298/GASTROPUBS.

Taychreggan Hotel Bar   West Ferry, Dundee   931/DUNDEE EAT & DRINK.

Fisherman's Tavern   Broughty Ferry   916/DUNDEE HOTELS.

1500
7/L19
Lock Inn   Fort Augustus   Canalside setting by the Caledonian Canal, good food and plenty whisky.

1501
8/R17
Seafield Hotel Bar   Cullen   Main street of Moray coast town. 150+ malts on offer.

1502
7/F18
Sligachan Hotel   Skye · www.sligachan.co.uk · 01478 650204   On A87 (A850) 11km south of Portree. Over 250 malts in Seamus' huge cabin bar. Good ale selection, including their own (the Cuillin Brewery is here).

Pittodrie House Hotel   Pitcaple   In the snug. 937/NORTHEAST HOTELS.

The Lairhillock Inn   near Stonehaven   Public bar. 1302/GASTROPUBS.

Section 7

Outdoor Places

The Best Gardens

☕ signifies **notable** tearoom. FREE/ ADMISSION *indicates entry fee due - or not.*
NTS *indicates a garden under the care of the National Trust for Scotland.*

1503
9/K25
ADMISSION
☕

✓✓ **The Younger Botanic Garden** www.rbge.org.uk · Benmore
12km Dunoon on the A815 to Strachur. An 'outstation' of the Royal Botanic in Edinburgh, gifted to the nation by Harry Younger in 1928, but the first plantations dating from 1820. Walks clearly marked through formal gardens, woody grounds and the 'pinetum' where the air is often so sweet and spicy it can seem like the elixir of life. Redwood avenue, terraced hill sides, views; a garden of different moods and fine proportions. Good walk, 'Puck's Glen', nearby (2007/WOODLAND WALKS). Café. Mar-Oct 10am-6pm (5pm Oct-Mar).

1504
7/H16
NTS
ADMISSION
☕

✓✓ **Inverewe** www.nts.org.uk · Poolewe On A832, 80km south of Ullapool. The world-famous gardens on a promontory of Loch Ewe. Begun in 1862, Osgood Mackenzie made it his life's work and people have come from all over the world ever since to admire his efforts. Helped by the ameliorating effect of the Gulf Stream, the 'wild' garden became the model for many others. The guided tours (1.30pm Mon-Fri Apr-Sep) are probably the best way to get the most out of this extensive garden or go in the evening when it's quiet! Shop, visitor centre till 5pm. Gardens all year till dusk.

1505
8/S20
NTS
ADMISSION
☕

✓✓ **Crathes** www.nts.org.uk · near Banchory 25km west of Aberdeen and just off A93 on Royal Deeside. One of the most interesting tower houses (1834/COUNTRY HOUSES) surrounded by mind-blowing topiary and walled gardens of inspired design and tranquil atmosphere. Keen gardeners will be in their scented heaven. The Golden Garden (after Gertrude Jekyll) works particularly well and there's a wild garden beyond the old wall that many people miss. All in all, a very *House and Garden* experience though in summer it's stuffed with people as well as plants. Grounds open all year 9.30am-sunset.

1506
10/P26
ATMOS

✓✓ **Little Sparta** www.littlesparta.co.uk · 07826 495677 · near Dunsyre Near Biggar southwest of Edinburgh off A702 (5km), go through village then signed. House in bare hill country the home of conceptual artist and national treasure, Ian Hamilton Finlay who died 2006. Gardens lovingly created over years, full of thought-provoking art/sculpture/perspectives. Unlike anywhere else. A privilege to visit but it is fragile; no dogs or little kids. Jun-Sep, Wed/Fri/Sun 2.30-5pm, but check the website as the Trust may change times.

1507
10/N23
ADMISSION

✓✓ **Drummond Castle Gardens** www.drummondcastlegardens.co.uk · Muthill Near Crieff; signed from A822, 2km from Muthill then up a long avenue, the most exquisite formal gardens viewed first from the terrace by the house. A boxwood parterre of a vast St Andrew's Cross in yellow and red (especially antirrhinums and roses), the Drummond colours, with extraordinary sundial centrepiece; 5 gardeners keep every leaf in place. 7 days Easter and May-Oct 1-5pm (last admission). House not open to public.

1508
11/K31
ADMISSION
☕

✓✓ **Logan Botanical Gardens** www.rbge.org.uk · near Sandhead 16km south of Stranraer by A77/A716 and 2km on from Sandhead. Remarkable outstation of the Edinburgh Botanics amongst sheltering woodland in the mild South West. Compact and full of pleasant southern surprises. Less crowded than other 'exotic' gardens. Walled and woodland gardens and the 'Tasmanian Creek'. The Gunnera Bog is quite extraterrestrial. Coffee shop decent. Mar-Oct; 7 days, 10am-5pm (6pm Apr-Sep).

1509
9/J24
NTS
ADMISSION

✓ ✓ **Crarae** www.nts.org.uk · Inverary 16km southeast on A83 to Lochgilphead. The most gorgeous of the famed gardens of Argyll. And in any season. The wooded banks of Loch Fyne with gushing burn are as lush as the jungles of Borneo. All year 9.30am till dusk. Visitor centre Apr-Sep.

1510
6/N15
ADMISSION

✓ ✓ **Dunrobin Castle Gardens** Golspie On A9 1km north of town. The Versailles-inspired gardens that sit below the opulent Highland chateau of the Dukes of Sutherland (1779/CASTLES). Terraced, parterred and immaculate, they stretch to the sea. 30 gardeners once tended them, now there are 4 but little has changed since they impressed a more exclusive clientele. Apr-Oct 10.30am-last admission 4pm (5pm Jun-Aug).

1511
9/G26
ATMOS
ADMISSION

✓ ✓ **Jura House Walled Garden** www.jurahouseandgardens.co.uk · Ardfin, Jura Around 8km from the ferry on the only road. Park opposite and follow track into woods. The most beautiful not-overtended walled garden can be part of a walk that takes you ultimately (though steep) to the beach and the 'Misty Pools'. Beautiful in rain (frequent) or shine and a place of utmost serenity. Open all year 9am-5pm. Tea tent on the lawn with lovely cakes (Jun-Sep).

1512
11/K30

✓ **Glenwhan** near Glen Luce, near Solway Coast Signed from A75 and close to more famous **Castle Kennedy** (also very much worth a visit), this the more edifying labour of love. Up through beechy (and in May) bluebell woods and through backyards to horticultural haven teased from bracken and gorse moorland from 1979. Open moorland still beckons at the top of the network of trails through a carefully planted but wild botanical wonder. Many seats for contemplations, some sculpture. Easter-Sep 10am-5pm.

1513
11/M30
☕

✓ **Threave** near Castle Douglas 64 acres of magnificent Victorian landscaping in incomparable setting overlooking Galloway coastline. Gardeners shouldn't miss the walled kitchen garden. Horticulturally inspiring; and daunting. The garden is part of a vast estate which includes the castle and a wildfowl reserve. Explore on an easy 4km walk. Open Feb-Dec 10am-dusk.

1514
10/P27
ADMISSION

✓ **Dawyck** www.rgbe.org.uk · Stobo On B712 Moffat road off A72 Biggar/Peebles road, 2km from Stobo. An outstation of the Edinburgh Botanics, though tree planting here goes back 300 years. Sloping grounds around the gurgling Scrape burn which trickles into the Tweed. Landscaped woody pathways for meditative walks. Famous for shrubs, blue Himalayan poppies and Douglas Firs. Rare Plant Trail and great walk on drovers' road nearby, 2km off Stobo Rd before Dawyck entrance. Visitor centre with café and shop. Mar-Oct 10am-5pm.

1515
10/R27
ADMISSION

✓ **Monteviot House Garden & Woodside Nursery** near Ancrum & Jedburgh Off A68 at Ancrum, the B6400 to Nisbet (3km), first there's Woodside on left (the Victorian walled garden for the house – separate but don't miss) then the mainly formal gardens of the house (the home of the Tory MP Michael Ancram, the Marquess of Lothian); terraced to the river (Teviot). All extraordinarily pleasant. Woodside has an organic demonstrations section, other events and a great tearoom (1395/TEAROOMS, 2200/GARDEN CENTRES). House: 2 weeks in Jul 1-5pm. Gardens: Apr-Oct 12noon-5pm.

1516
9/J23
HONESTY BOX

✓ **Angus's Garden** www.barguillean.co.uk · Taynuilt 7km from village (which is 12km from Oban on the A85) along the Glen Lonan road. Take first right after Barguillean Garden Centre. A garden laid out by the family who own the centre in memory of their son Angus, a reporter who was killed reporting on the war in Cyprus. On the slopes around Angus's Loch, brimful of lilies and ducks and (rescued) swans. Informal mix of tended and uncultivated (though wild prevails), a more poignant remembrance is hard to imagine as you while an hour away in this peaceful place. Open all year.

1517
1/XF4
ADMISSION

✓ **Dr Neil's (Secret) Garden** Edinburgh Not many people know about this superb, almost private garden on the shores of Duddingston Loch. At the end of the road through Holyrood Park, just past Duddingston church, enter through the manse gates. Turn right. At end of the manse lawn, in the corner a gate leads to an extraordinary terraced garden bordering the loch. With wild Arthur's Seat above, you'd swear you were in Argyll. The labour of love of one Claudia Poitier and many volunteers, this is an enchanting corner of the city. 7 days dawn-dusk. The 'skating minister' of the Raeburn painting took off from here.

1518
9/H24
NTS
ADMISSION

✓ **Arduaine Garden** www.arduaine-garden.org.uk · near Kilmelford 28km south of Oban on A816, one of Argyll's undiscovered arcadias gifted to the NTS who in '09 announced that due to cuts, it may have to close. There's a stay of execution for 2010 but a local action group is working to keep it open (your support needed!). The creation of this microclimate in which the rich, diverse vegetation flourished, was influenced by Osgood Mackenzie of Inverewe and its restoration is a testimony to the 20 years' hard labour of the famous Wright brothers. Enter/park by Loch Melfort hotel, gate 100m. Until dusk.

1519
11/M30
ADMISSION

✓ **Cally Gardens** www.callygardens.co.uk · **Gatehouse of Fleet** Off the A75 at Gatehouse and through the gateway to Cally Palace Hotel (1135/HOTELS THAT WELCOME KIDS), this walled garden discreetly signed off to the left before you reach the hotel. Built in the 1770s as the kitchen garden of the big house, the seat of the Murray-Ushers, it was rescued in 1987 by Michael Wickenden who has transformed it into a haven for gardeners and has meticulously gathered, introduced, nurtured and recorded herbaceous plants (over 3000), many of which you can't find anywhere else. Serious stuff but a joy to visit. Easter-Sep. Tue-Fri 2-5.30pm. Sat/Sun 10am-5.30pm.

1520
9/G26
ADMISSION

✓ **Achamore Gardens** www.gigha.org.uk · **Isle of Gigha** 1km from ferry. Walk or cycle (bike hire by ferry); an easy 2km trip. The big house (which does top B&B; 2240/ISLAND HOTELS) on the island set in 65 acres. Lush tropical plants mingle with early-flourishing rhodies (Feb-March): all due to the mild climate and the devotion of the gardeners. 2 marked walks (40 minutes/2 hours) start from the walled garden (green route takes in the sea view of Islay and Jura). Density and variety of shrubs, pond plants and trees revealed as you meander in this enchanting spot. Leaflet guides at entrance. New interpretation centre 2010. Open all year dawn to dusk. Honesty box. 2214/MAGICAL ISLANDS.

1521
8/S20

✓ **Drum Castle Rose Garden** www.nts.org.uk · **near Banchory** 1km from A93, the Deeside road. In the grounds of Drum Castle (the Irvine ancestral home – though nothing to do with my family) a superb walled garden that is a homage to the rose and encapsulating 4 centuries of its horticulture. 4 areas (17th-20th centuries). Fabulous, Jul/Aug especially. Open Easter-Oct 10am-6pm.

1522
9/J26
ADMISSION

Ascog Hall Fernery www.ascoghallfernery.co.uk · **Rothesay** Outside town on road to Mount Stuart (1823/COUNTRY HOUSES), worth stopping at this small garden and very small Victorian Fern House. Green and lush and dripping! Easter-Oct, 10am-5pm. Closed Mon/Tue. And don't miss Rothesay's Victorian men's loos (which women can visit, too); they are not small.

1523 **Priorwood** www.nts.org.uk · **Melrose** Next to Melrose Abbey, a tranquil
10/R27 secret garden behind high walls which specialises in growing flowers and plants
ADMISSION for drying. Picking, drying and arranging is continuously in progress. Samples for
NTS sale. Run by enthusiasts on behalf of the NTS, they're always willing to talk
stamens with you. Also includes an historical apple orchard with trees through the
ages. Mon-Sat 10am-5pm; Sun 1-5pm. Closed 4pm winter. Dried flower demos
and a superior shop.

1524 **Kailzie Gardens** www.kailziegardens.com · **Peebles** On B7062 Traquair
10/Q27 road. Informal woodland gardens just out of town; not extensive but eminently
ADMISSION strollable. Old-fashioned roses and wilder bits. Courtyard teashop. Kids' corner and
much ado about ospreys (Apr-Jul). Fishing ponds popular. Apr-Oct 11am-5.30pm
(restricted access in winter).

1525 **Pitmedden Garden** www.nts.org.uk · **near Ellon** 35km north of Aberdeen
8/S18 and 10km west of main A92. Formal French gardens recreated in 1950s on site of
ADMISSION Sir Alex Seaton's 17th-century ones. The 4 great parterres, 3 based on designs for
NTS gardens at Holyrood Palace, are best viewed from the terrace. Charming farm-
☕ house 'museum' seems transplanted. For lovers of symmetry and an orderly
universe only (but there is a woodland walk with wildlife garden area). May-Oct
1-5.30pm.

1526 **Pittodrie House** www.macdonaldhotels.co.uk · **near Inverurie** An
8/R19 exceptional walled garden in the grounds of Pittodrie House Hotel at Chapel of
Garioch in Aberdeenshire (937/NORTHEAST HOTELS). Different gardens compart-
mentalised by hedges. 500m from house and curiously unvisited by many of the
guests, this secret and sheltered haven is both a kitchen garden and a place for
meditations and reflections (and possibly wedding photos).

1527 **Ardkinglas Woodland** www.ardkinglass.com · **Cairndow** Off the A83 Loch
9/K24 Lomond to Inveraray road. Through village to signed car park and these mature
ADMISSION woodlands in the grounds of Ardkinglas House on the southern bank near the
head of Loch Fyne. Fine pines include the 'tallest tree in Britain'. Magical at dawn
or dusk. 2km Loch Fyne Oysters (1338/SEAFOOD RESTAURANTS) where there is also a
tree-shop garden centre especially for trees and shrubs.

1528 **Attadale Gardens** www.attadale.com · **Strathcarron** On A890 from Kyle of
7/J18 Lochalsh and A87 just south of Strathcarron. Lovely West Highland home (to the
ADMISSION Macphersons) and (painters') gardens near Loch Carron. Exotic specials, water gar-
dens, sculpture, great rhodies May/Jun. Nursery and kitchen garden. Fern and
Japanese gardens. Good café/restaurant nearby (1036/HIGHLAND RESTAURANTS).
Apr-Oct 10am-5pm. Closed Sun.

1529 **Achiltibuie Garden** www.thehydroponicum.com · 01854 622202 ·
6/J15 **Achiltibuie** The 'Garden of the Future': the long-established indoor water world
ADMISSION known as the Hydroponicum moved '09: same people, new venture still being
constructed and developed at TGP. Intention is to build an even greener, more
sustainable garden with plants thriving without soil in their various microclimates.
An inspiring project for all budding gardeners. Check by phone or online for details.

1530 **Ard-Daraich Hill Garden** www.arddaraich.co.uk · 01855 841348 · **Ardgour**
9/J21 3 km south Ardgour at Corran Ferry (8/JOURNEYS) on A861 to Strontian. Private,
labour of love hill and wild garden where you are at liberty to wander. Once the
home of Constance Spry. Specialising in rhodies, shrubs, trees. Nursery/small garden centre. Open all year, 7 days. Lovely rooms to stay over; home-garden produce.

1531 **The Hidden Gardens** www.thehiddengardens.org.uk · Glasgow This
2/XA5 garden oasis in the asphalt jungle of Glasgow's South Side opened in the disused
wasteland behind The Tramway performance and studio space in 2003. A project
of environmental theatre group nva working with landscape architects City Design
Co-operative, this is a very modern approach to an age-old challenge – how to
make and keep a sanctuary in the city! It's ageing gracefully. Nice caff (616/GLAS-
GOW KIDS). Open 10am-8pm (winter hours vary). Closed Mon.

1532 **Shambellie Walled Garden** New Abbey, near Dumfries Near but not part
11/N30 of Shambellie House, the National Museum of Costume. Leaving village towards
ADMISSION Dumfries, turn left on the road for Beeswing; the garden is on the right 150m. Few
gardens on these pages are quite such a labour of love as this, the walled garden
rescued by Sheila Cameron for no other reason than that 'she had to' and transformed with cash and graft into this lovingly attended oasis. See the pics of what
she and her brother started with. Some plant sales. Sat/Sun/Mon 10am-4pm in
season.

All the following host exceptional gardens.

Royal Botanic Garden Edinburgh 410/OTHER ATTRACTIONS.
Botanic Garden & Kibble Palace Glasgow 693/OTHER ATTRACTIONS.
Kildrummy Castle Hotel 1224/SCOTTISH HOTELS.
Stonefield Castle 759/ARGYLL HOTELS.
Castle of Mey 1764/CASTLES.
Cawdor Castle 1765/CASTLES.
Brodick Castle 1768/CASTLES.
Torosay Castle 1770/CASTLES.
Dunvegan Castle 1771/CASTLES.
Mount Stuart 1823/COUNTRY HOUSES.
Manderston 1824/COUNTRY HOUSES.
Floors Castle 1830/COUNTRY HOUSES.

*If you are interested in learning more about all the above gardens and many others, I
would recommend to you* **Scotland for Gardeners** *by Kenneth Cox, published by
Birlinn.*

The Best Country Parks

1533
11/N29

✓ ✓ **Drumlanrig Castle** www.drumlanrig.com · 01848 330248 ·
Thornhill On A76, 7km north of Thornhill in the west Borders in whose
romance and history it's steeped, much more than merely a country park; spend a
good day, both inside the castle and in the grounds. Apart from *that* art collection
(Rembrandt, Holbein and you may remember the Leonardo got stolen, then recov-
ered; it should be back 2010) and the courtyard of shops, the delights include: a
great wee tearoom; woodland and riverside walks; an adventure playground; regular events programme, including a farmers' market last Sun of the month (Feb-
Oct); and bike hire for explorations along the Nith. Open Mar-Oct 10am-5pm.
(House: Apr-Aug 11am-4pm.)

1534
9/L26

✓ **Muirshiel** www.clydemuirsheil.co.uk · near Lochwinnoch Via Largs
(A760) or Glasgow (M8, junction 29 A737 then A760 5km south of Johnstone). North from village on Kilmacolm road for 3km then signed. Muirshiel is
name given to wider area but park proper begins 6km on road along the Calder
valley. Despite proximity of conurbation, this is a wild and enchanting place for
walks, picnics, etc. Trails marked to waterfall and summit views. Extensive events
programme. Go look for hen harriers. See also 709/GLASGOW WALKS. Escape!

1535
10/R25
ECO

John Muir Country Park www.eastlothian.gov.uk · near Dunbar Named
after the 19th-century conservationist who founded America's national parks (and
the Sierra Club) and who was born in Dunbar (his birthplace is now an interactive
museum at 126 High St). This swathe of coastline to the west of the town (known
locally as Tyninghame) is an important estuarine nature reserve but is good for
family walks and beachcombing (445/EDINBURGH BEACHES). Can enter via B6370
off A198 to North Berwick or by 'cliff-top' trail from Dunbar or from car park on
road into Dunbar from west at West Barns (1752/WILDLIFE).

1536
10/M26

Strathclyde Park near Hamilton & Motherwell 15km southeast of Glasgow.
Take M8/A725 interchange or M74 junction 5 or 6. Scotland's most popular country park, especially for water sports. From canoeing to parascending; you can hire
gear. Also excavated Roman bath house, playgrounds, sports pitches and pleasant
walks. Nearby Baron's Haugh and Dalzell Country Park notable for their nature
trails and gardens. The 'Scotland's Theme Park' fairground and the horrid Alona
Hotel remind us what country parks should not be about.

1537
9/L25

Finlaystone Estate www.finlaystone.co.uk · Langbank, near Greenock
A8 to Greenock, Houston direction at Langbank, then signed. Grand mansion
home to Chief of Clan Macmillan set in formal gardens in wooded estate. Lots of
facilities ('Celtic' tearoom, craft shop, etc), leafy walks, walled garden. Rare magic.
Oct-Mar weekends only, Apr-Sep daily until 5pm.

1538
10/S27

Hirsel Country Park www.hirselcountrypark.co.uk · Coldstream On A697,
north edge town (direction Kelso). 3000 acres the grounds of Hirsel House (not
open public). 2-4km walks through farmland and woods including lovely languid
lake. Museum, tearoom and craft units at the Homestead.

1539
10/N25

Muiravonside Country Park near Linlithgow 4km southwest of Linlithgow
on B825. Also signed from junction 4 of M9 Edinburgh/Stirling. Former farm
estate now run by the local authority with 170 acres of woodland walks, parkland,
picnic sites and a visitor centre for school parties or anyone else with an interest in
birds, bees and badgers. Ranger service does guided walks Apr-Sep. Great place to
walk off that lunch at the not-too-distant Champany Inn (261/BURGERS).

1540
9/K27
Eglinton near Irvine By main A78 Largs/Ayr road signed from Irvine/Kilwinning intersection. Spacious lungful of Ayrshire. Visitor centre with interpretation of absolutely everything. Park always open, visitor centre Easter–Oct. Network of walks.

✓✓**Culzean Castle Park** Superb and hugely popular. 1762/CASTLES.

✓**Haddo House** Aberdeenshire Beautiful grounds. 1822/COUNTRY HOUSES.

Mugdock Country Park near Milngavie Marvellous park close to Glasgow. 5 car parks around the vast site. 705/CITY WALKS.

Tentsmuir near Tayport Estuarine; John Muir, on Tay. 1755/WILDLIFE.
Kelburne Country Centre Largs 1696/KIDS.

The Best Town Parks

1541
1/C3
✓✓**Princes Street Gardens** Edinburgh South side of Princes St. The greenery that launched a thousand postcards, now under threat from a thousand events. This former loch, drained when the New Town was built, is divided by the Mound. The eastern half has pitch and putt, Winter Wonderland and the Scott Monument (453/BEST VIEWS), the western has its much-photographed fountain, open-air café, space for locals and tourists to sprawl on the grass when sunny, and the Ross Bandstand – heart of Edinburgh's Hogmanay (66/BEST EVENTS) and the International Festival's fireworks concert (51/EVENTS). Louts with lager, senior citizens on benches, dazed tourists: all our lives are here. Till dusk.

1542
8/T19
✓✓**Hazelhead Park** Aberdeen Via Queens Rd, 3km centre. Extraordinary park where the Aberdonians' mysterious gardening skills are magnificently in evidence. Many facilities including a maze, pets' corner, wonderful tacky tearoom and there are lawns, memorials and botanical splendours aplenty especially azalea garden in spring and roses in summer. Great sculpture.

1543
8/T19
✓**Duthie Park** Aberdeen Riverside Dr along River Dee from the bridge carrying main A92 Stonehaven road. The other large well-kept park with duck pond, bandstand, hugely impressive summer rose gardens, carved sculptures and the famous David Welch Winter Garden of subtropical palms/ferns, etc; under restoration (9.30am-7.30pm summer, winter at dusk).

1544
10/P25
✓**Pittencrieff Park** Dunfermline The extensive park alongside the Abbey and Palace ruins gifted to the town in 1903 by Carnegie. Open areas, glasshouses, pavilion (more a function room) but most notably a deep verdant glen criss-crossed with pathways. Great kids' play area. Lush, full of birds, good after rain.

1545
10/N23
✓**Macrosty Park** www.perthshire.co.uk · Crieff On your left as you leave Crieff for Comrie and Crianlarich; for parking ask locally. A perfect green place on sloping ground to the River Earn (good level walk – Lady Mary's Walk) with tearooms, kids' area, mature trees and superb bandstand. A fine old park.

1546
10/Q24
Beveridge Park Kirkcaldy Also in Fife, another big municipal park with a duck and boat pond, wide-open spaces and many amusements (eg bowling, tennis, putting, plootering). **Ravenscraig** a coastal park on the main road east to Dysart is an excellent place to walk. Great prospect of the firth and its coves and cruise.

1547
10/R28
Wilton Lodge Park Hawick Hawick not overfull of visitor attractions, but it does have a nice park with facilities and diversions enough for everyone, eg the civic gallery, rugby pitches (they quite like rugby in Hawick), a large kids' playground, a seasonal café and lots of riverside walks by the Teviot. Lots of my school friends lost their virginity in the shed here. All-round open-air recreation centre. South end of town by A7. PS: the shed, like our virginities, is long gone.

1548
11/P28
Station Park www.visitmoffat.co.uk · Moffat On your right as you enter the town from the M74. Well-proportioned people's park; boating pond (with giant swans) main feature. Annan water alongside offers nice walking. Notable also for the monument to Air Chief Marshall Hugh Dowding, Commander in Chief during the Battle of Britain. 'Never... was so much owed by so many to so few'.

1549
9/L27
Dean Castle Park www.deancastle.com · Kilmarnock A77 south first turnoff for Kilmarnock then signed; from Ayr A77 north, 3rd turnoff. Surprising green and woody oasis in suburban Kilmarnock; lawns and woods around restored castle and courtyard. Riding centre. Burns Rose Garden.

1550
11/M30
Garries Park Gatehouse of Fleet Notable for its tiny perfect garden which you enter under an arch from the main street of this South West village. A wee gem especially for its large flowers. Leads to bigger public space, but pause in the garden and smell those roses. Then go to the Ship (782/SOUTHWEST HOTELS).

1551
2/XC5
Rouken Glen & Linn Park Glasgow Both on south side of river. Rouken Glen via Pollokshaws/Kilmarnock road to Eastwood Toll then right. Good place to park is second left, Davieland Rd beside pond. Across park from here (or beside main Rouken Glen road) is main visitor area with info centre, garden centre, a café, kids' play area and woodland walks. Linn Park via Aikenhead and Carmunnock road. After King's Park on left, take right to Simshill Rd and park at golf course beyond houses. A long route there, but worth it; this is one of the undiscovered Elysiums of a city which boasts 60 parks. Activities, wildlife walks, kids' nature trails, horse-riding and Alexander Greek Thomson's **Holmwood House**; open Easter-Oct 12noon-5pm (NTS).

1552
10/Q23
Camperdown Park www.camperdownpark.com · Dundee Calling itself a country park, Camperdown is the main recreational breathing space for the city and hosts a plethora of distractions (a golf course, a wildlife complex, mansion house, etc). Situated beyond Kingsway, the ring-route; go via Coupar Angus turnoff. Best walks across the A923 in Templeton Woods. **Balgray Park** also excellent.

1553
8/P17
Grant Park Forres Frequent winner of the Bonny Bloom competitions (a board proclaims their awards) and with its balance of ornamental gardens, open parkland and woody hill side, this is obviously a carefully tended rose. Good municipal facilities like pitch and putt, playground. Cricket in summer and topping topiary. Through woods on Cluny Hill to the Nelson Tower for a little more exercise.

1554
10/N25
Callander Park Falkirk Park on edge of town centre, signed from all over. Overlooked by high-rise blocks and near busy road system, this is nevertheless a beautiful green space with a big hoose (heritage museum), woods and lawns. Comes alive in May as venue for Big in Falkirk (30/EVENTS).

The Most Interesting Coastal Villages

1555
7/H18
✓ **Plockton** www.plockton.com · near Kyle of Lochalsh A Highland gem of a place 8km over the hill from Kyle, clustered around inlets of a wooded bay on Loch Carron. Cottage gardens down to the bay and palm trees! Some great walks over headlands. Plockton Inn and on the front the Plockton Hotel offer reasonable rooms and pub grub (1022/LESS EXPENSIVE HIGHLAND HOTELS) and there's also the estimable Plockton Shores (1041/BEST HIGHLAND RESTAURANTS). Calum's Seal Trips are a treat (seals and dolphins almost guaranteed): 01599 544306. It's not hard to feel connected with this village (so many people do).

1556
8/R17
✓ **Moray Coast Fishing Villages** From Speybay (where the Spey slips into the sea) along to Fraserburgh, some of Scotland's best coastal scenery and many interesting villages in cliff/cove and beach settings. For the best beaches, see 1569/BEACHES. Especially notable are **Portsoy** with 17th-century harbour – and see 38/EVENTS and 1285/PUBS; **Sandend** with its own popular beach and a fabulous one nearby; **Pennan** made famous by the film *Local Hero*; **Gardenstown** with a walk along the water's edge to **Crovie** (pronounced 'Crivee') the epitome of a coast-clinging community (near Troup Head; 1738/BIRDS); and **Cullen**, a larger community with a couple of hotels and a great wide beach.

1557
3/Q10
✓ **Stromness** Orkney Mainland 24km from Kirkwall and a different kettle of fish. Hugging the shore and with narrow streets and wynds, it has a unique atmosphere, both maritime and European. Some of the most singular shops you'll see anywhere and the Orkney folk going about their business. Park near harbour and walk down the cobbled main street if you don't want to scrape your paintwork (2283/ORKNEY; 2155/GALLERIES).

1558
7/M17
✓ **Cromarty** near Inverness At end of road across Black Isle from Inverness (45km northeast), does take longer than you think (well, 30 minutes). Village with dreamy times-gone-by atmosphere, without being twee. Lots of kids running about and a pink strand of beach. Delights to discover include: the east kirk, plain and aesthetic with countryside through the windows behind the altar; Hugh (the geologist) Miller's cottage/Courthouse museum (2134/BEST HISTORY & HERITAGE); The Pantry (1423/TEAROOMS); Cromarty Bakery (1428/BEST SCOTCH BAKERS); the perfect, wee restaurant Sutor Creek (1042/BEST HIGHLAND RESTAURANTS); the shore and cliff walk (2043/COASTAL WALKS); the Pirates' Cemetery and of course the dolphins (1741/DOLPHINS).

1559
10/N25
Culross near Dunfermline By A994 from Dunfermline or junction 1 of M90 just over Forth Road Bridge (15km). Old centre conserved and restored by NTS. Mainly residential and not awash with craft and coffee shops. More historical than merely quaint; a community of careful custodians lives in the white and yellow red-pantiled houses. Footsteps echo in the cobbled wynds. Palace and Town House open Easter-Oct 12noon-5pm, weekends Sep/Oct. Interesting back gardens and lovely church at top of hill (1863/CHURCHES).

1560
9/G22
Tobermory Mull Not so much a village or setting for a kids' TV show (the late lamented *Balamory*), rather the main town of Mull, set around a hill on superb Tobermory Bay. Ferry port for Ardnamurchan, but main Oban ferry is 35km away at Craignure. Usually a bustling harbour front with quieter streets behind; a quintessential island atmosphere. Some good inexpensive hotels (and quayside hostel) well situated to explore the whole island. 2282/MULL; 2246/ISLAND HOTELS; 1155/BEST HOSTELS.

1561 **Port Charlotte** Islay A township on the Rhinns of Islay, the western peninsula.
9/F26 By A846 from the ports, Askaig and Ellen via Bridgend. Rows of whitewashed, well-kept cottages along and back from shoreline. On road in, there's an island museum and a coffee/bookshop. Also a 'town' beach and one between Port Charlotte and Bruichladdich (and especially the one with the war memorial nearby). Quiet and charming, not merely quaint. 2280/ISLAY; 2241/ISLAND HOTELS; 1757/WILDLIFE CENTRES.

1562 **Rockcliffe** near Dumfries 25km south on Solway Coast road, A710. On the
11/N30 'Scottish Riviera', the rocky part of the coast around to Kippford (2037/COASTAL WALKS). A good rock-scrambling foreshore though not so clean, and a village with few houses and Baron's Craig hotel; set back with views (27 moderately expensive rooms) but a somewhat gloomy presence. Garden Tearoom in village (1415/TEAROOMS) is nice or repair to the Anchor (1318/GASTROPUBS) in Kippford.

1563 **East Neuk Villages** www.eastneukwide.co.uk The quintessential quaint
10/R24 wee fishing villages along the bit of Fife that forms the mouth of the Firth of Forth, **Crail, Anstruther, Pittenweem, St Monans** and **Elie** all have different characters and attractions especially Crail (1414/TEAROOMS) and Pittenweem harbours, Anstruther as main centre and home of Fisheries Museum (see also 1365/FISH & CHIPS; 1722/ BIRDS) and perfect Elie (864/866/FIFE HOTELS; 1293/GASTROPUBS; 2061/GREAT GOLF). Or see St Andrews. Cycling good, traffic in summer not.

1564 **Aberdour** www.aberdour.org.uk Between Dunfermline and Kirkcaldy and
10/P25 near Forth Road Bridge (10km east from junction 1 of M90) or, better still, go by train from Edinburgh (frequent service: Dundee or Kirkcaldy); delightful station. Walks round harbour and to headland, Silver Sands beach 1km (448/EDINBURGH BEACHES), castle ruins. 1862/CHURCHES; 867/FIFE HOTELS.

1565 **Isle of Whithorn** www.isleofwhithorn.com Strange faraway village at end of
11/L31 the road, 35km south Newton Stewart, 6km Whithorn (1813/PREHISTORIC SITES). Mystical harbour where low tide does mean low, saintly shoreline, a sea angler's pub, the Steam Packet – very good pub grub (1274/BLOODY GOOD PUBS). Ninian's chapel round the headland underwhelming but you pass the poignant memorial to the *Solway Harvester*. Everybody visiting IoW seems to walk this way. Great deli/pizzeria – Ravenstones 1452/DELIS. In Whithorn en route.

1566 **Corrie** www.arran.uk.com · Arran Last but not least, the bonniest bit of Arran
9/J27 (apart from Kildonan and the glens and the rest), best reached by bike from Brodick (01770 302377 or 302868). Many walks from here including Goat Fell but nice just to sit or potter on the foreshore. Hotel not quite up to expectations. The village shop is an art gallery like most of the village itself: animal sculptures on the foreshore and even the boats in the slips of harbours are aesthetic.

Fantastic Beaches & Bays

1567
6/L12
✓ ✓ **Pete's Beach** near Durness The One of many great beaches on the North Coast (see below) that I've called my own. The hill above it is called Ceannabeinne; you find it 7km east of Durness. Coming from Tongue it's just after where Loch Eriboll comes out to the sea and the road hits the coast again (there's a layby opposite). It's a small perfect cove flanked by walls of coral-pink rock and shallow turquoise sea. Splendid from above (land rises to a bluff with a huge boulder) and from below. Of course I was gutted to find '09 that this wasn't just my beach but also Fiona and Robbie's who walk their dogs here every Sunday at some unearthly (actually earthly) hour of the AM. Ok, it is for all of us.

1568
9/F24
✓ ✓ **Kiloran Beach** Colonsay 9km from quay and hotel, past Colonsay House; parking and access on hill side. Often described as the finest beach in the Hebrides, it doesn't disappoint though it has changed character recently (a shallower sandbar traps tidal run-off). Craggy cliffs on one side, negotiable rocks on the other, tiers of grassy dunes between. Do go to the end! The island was once bought as a picnic spot. This beach was probably the reason why.

1569
8
✓ ✓ **Moray Coast** www.moray.gov.uk Many great beaches along coast from Spey Bay to Fraserburgh, notably **Cullen** and **Lossiemouth** (town beaches) and **New Aberdour** (1km from New Aberdour village on B9031, 15km west of Fraserburgh) and **Rosehearty** (8km west of Fraserburgh) both quieter places for walks and picnics. 2 of the great secret beaches on this coast are:
✓ ✓ **Sunnyside** Where you walk past the incredible ruins of Findlater Castle on the cliff top (how did they build it? A place, on its grassed-over roof, for a picnic) and down to a cove which on my sunny day was simply perfect. Take a left from Sandend 16km west of Banff, follow road for 2km, turn right, park in the farmyard. Walk from here past dovecote, 1km to cliff, then left. Also signed from A98. See also 2041/COASTAL WALKS.
Cullykhan Bay East of Gardenstown signed from the coast road (200m to small car park). A small beach but great littoral for beach scrambling and full of surprises (1932/ENCHANTING PLACES).

1570
9/G28
✓ ✓ **Macrihanish** At the bottom of the Kintyre peninsula 10km from Campbeltown. Walk north from Machrihanish village or golf course, or from the car park on the main A83 to Tayinloan and Tarbert at point where it hits/leaves the coast. A joyously long strand (8km) of unspoiled orange-pink sand backed by dunes and facing the 'steepe Atlantic Stream' all the way to Newfoundland (2067/GOLF IN GREAT PLACES).

1571
6/K12
✓ ✓ **Sandwood Bay** Kinlochbervie This mile-long sandy strand with its old Stack is legendary but there's the problem: too PLU come here and you may have to share its glorious isolation. Inaccessibility is its saving grace: it's a 7km walk from the sign off the road at Balchrick (near the cattle grid) which is 6km from Kinlochbervie; allow 3-4hrs return plus time there. More venturesome is the walk from the north and Cape Wrath (2035/COASTAL WALKS). Go easy and go in summer! Stock up at the Tardis-like Mackays near Badcall.

1572
5/D18
✓ ✓ **South Uist** www.southuist.com Deserted but for birds, an almost unbroken strand of beach running for miles down the west coast; the machair is best in early summer (follow the Machair Way). Take any road off the spinal A865; usually less than 2km. Good spot to try is turnoff at Tobha Mor 25km north of Lochboisdale; real blackhouses and a chapel on the way to the sea. Listen to those birds – this is as far away as you can get from Hoxton.

1573 ✓ ✓ **Scarista Beach & the Beaches of South Harris** On road south of
5/E15 Tarbert (20km) to Rodel. Scarista is so beautiful that people have been
married there. Hotel over the road is worth staying just for this, but is also a great
retreat; 2 excellent self-catering cottages. 2237/ISLAND HOTELS. Golf on the links
(2074/GOLF IN GREAT PLACES). The coast has many extraordinary beaches. You may
want to camp (1199/CAMPING). It's fab here in early evening. The sun also rises.

1574 ✓ ✓ **Saligo, Machir Bay & The Big Strand** Islay The first two are bays
9/F26 on NW of island via A847 road to Port Charlotte, then B8018 past Loch
Gorm. Wide beaches; remains of war fortifications in deep dunes, Machir perhaps
best for beach bums but Saligo is one of the most pleasingly aesthetic beaches...
anywhere. The Big Strand on Laggan Bay: along Bowmore-Port Ellen road take Oa
turnoff, follow Kintra signs. There's camping and great walks in either direction,
8km of glorious sand and dunes (contains the Machrie Golf Course). All these are
airy ambles under a wide sky. 2066/GOLF IN GREAT PLACES; 2033/COASTAL WALKS.

1575 ✓ **Oldshoremore** The beach you pass on the road to Balchrick, only 3km
6/K13 from Kinlochbervie. It's easy to reach and a beautiful spot: the water is clear
and perfect for swimming, and there are rocky walks and quiet places. **Polin**,
500m north, is a cove you might have to yourself. (1205/CAMPING)

1576 ✓ **Ostal Beach/Kilbride Bay** Millhouse, near Tighnabruaich 3km from
9/J25 Millhouse on B8000 signed Ardlamont (not Portvadie, the ferry), a track to
right before white house (often with a chain across to restrict access). Park and
walk 1.5km, turning right after lochan. You arrive on a perfect white sandy crescent known locally as Ostal and, in certain conditions, a mystical place to swim
and picnic. Arran's north coast is like a Greek island in the bay. **Ettrick Bay on
Bute** is another good beach with this view and a brilliant wee café (1374/CAFÉS).

1577 ✓ **Lunan Bay** near Montrose 5km from main A92 road to Aberdeen and
10/R22 5km of deep red crescent beach under a wide northern sky. But 'n' Ben,
Auchmithie, is an excellent place to start or finish (902/PERTHSHIRE EATS) and good
approach (from south), although Gordon's restaurant at Inverkeilor is closer
(900/PERTHSHIRE EATS). You can climb up to the Red Castle. An evocative North
Sea strand, Lunan is often deserted. **St Cyrus** north of Montrose (a nature reserve)
also a serene littoral to wander. Walk 2km south of village.

1578 ✓ **The Secret Beach** near Achmelvich Approach from Archmelvich car
6/J14 park going north (it's the next proper bay round) or Lochinver-Stoer/Drumbeg
road (less of a walk; 1633/SCENIC ROUTES); layby on right 3km after Archmelvich
turnoff, 250m beyond sign for Cathair Estate. Park on right (going north) and walk
towards sea on left following stream (a sign points to 'Mill'). Well-defined path.
Called **Alltan na Bradhan**, it's the site of an old mill (grinding wheels still there),
perfect for camping and the best sea for swimming in the area. And pretty special.

1579 **Lowlandman's Bay** Jura Not strictly a beach (there is a sandy strand before
9/G25 the headland) but a rocky foreshore with ethereal atmosphere; great light and
space. Only seals break the spell. Go right at 3-arch bridge to first group of houses
(Knockdrome), through yard on left and right around cottages to track to
Ardmenish. After deer fences, bay is visible on your right, 1km walk away.

1580 **Vatersay** Outer Hebrides The tiny island joined by a causeway to Barra. Twin
5/C20 crescent beaches on either side of the isthmus, one shallow and sheltered visible
from Castlebay, the other an ocean beach with more rollers. Dunes/machair; safe
swimming. Poignant memorial to a 19th-century shipwreck in the Ocean Bay and

another (on the way here) to a plane crash during the war; the wreckage is still there. There's a helluva hill between Barra and Vatersay if you're cycling.

1581 **Seal Bay** www.isleofbarra.com · Barra 5km Castlebay on west coast, 2km
5/C20 after Isle of Barra Hotel through gate across machair where road right is signed Allathasdal a Deas (after a sandy then a rockier cove). A flat, rocky Hebridean shore and skerries where seals flop into the water and eye you with intense curiosity. The better-beach type beach is next to the ghastly hotel that you pass.

1582 **West Sands** St Andrews As a town beach, this is hard to beat; it dominates
10/R23 the view to west. Wide swathe not too unclean and sea swimmable. Golf courses behind. Consistently gets 'the blue flag', but beach buffs may prefer **Kinshaldy** (1755/WILDLIFE) or **Kingsbarns** (10km south on Crail road) where there is a great beach walk taking in the Cammo Estate (with its gardens) and skirting the great Kingsbarns Golf Course or **Elie** (28km south).

1583 **North Coast** West of Thurso are some of Britain's most unspoiled and unsung
6 beaches. No beach bums, no Beach Boys. There are so many great little coves, you can have one to yourself even on a hot day, but those to mention are: **Strathy** and **Armadale** (35km west Thurso), **Farr** and **Torrisdale** (48km) and **Cold-backie** (65km). My favourite is elevated to the top of this category. 1567/BEACHES.

1584 **Sands of Morar** near Mallaig 70km west of Fort William and 6km from
7/H20 Mallaig by newly improved road, these easily accessible beaches may seem over-populated on summer days and the south stretch nearest to Arisaig may have one too many caravan parks, but they go on for miles and there's enough space for everybody. The sand's supposed to be silver but in fact it's a very pleasing pink. Lots of rocky bits for exploration. One of the best beachy bits (the bay before the estuary) is 'Camusdarrach', signed from the main road (where *Local Hero* was filmed); further from the road, it is quieter and a very good swathe of sand. Traigh, the golf course makes good use of the dunes (2081/GOOD GOLF).

1585 **The Bay at the Back of the Ocean** Iona Easy 2km walk from the ferry from
9/F23 Fionnphort, south of Mull (2208/MAGICAL ISLANDS) or bike hire from store on your left as you walk into the village (01681 700357). Mostly paved road. John Smith, who is buried by the abbey, once told me that this was one of his favourite places. 2 great inexpensive hotels on Iona, the Argyll and St Columba (2282/BEST OF MULL).

1586 **Dornoch (& Embo Beaches)** The wide and extensive sandy beach of this
6/N16 pleasant town at the mouth of the Dornoch Firth famous also for its golf links. 4km north, Embo Sands starts with ghastly caravan city, but walk north towards Golspie. Embo is twinned with Kaunakakai, Hawaii. We can dream!

1587 **Port of Ness** Isle of Lewis Also signed Port Nis, this is the beach at the north
5/G12 end of the Hebrides: keep driving. Some interesting stops on the way (2120/2122/ MUSEUMS) until you get to this tiny bay and harbour down the hill at the end of the road. Anthony Barber's Harbour View Gallery full of his own work (which you find in many other galleries and even postcards) is worth a visit (Mon-Sat 10am-5pm).

1588 **2 Beaches in the far South West** Killantringan Bay, near Portpatrick Off
11/J30 A77 before Portpatrick signed 'Dunskey Gardens' in summer, follow road signed Killantringan Lighthouse (dirt track). Park 1km before lighthouse or walk from Portpatrick following the Southern Upland Way. Beautiful bay for exploration. **Sandhead Beach** A716 south of Stranraer. Shallow, safe waters of Luce Bay (8km of sands). Perfect for families (in their damned caravans).

The Great Glens

1589
7/K18

✓ ✓ ✓ **Glen Affric** www.glenaffric.org Beyond Cannich at end of Glen Urquhart A831, 20km from Drumnadrochit on Loch Ness. A dramatic gorge that strikes westwards into the wild heart of Scotland. Superb for rambles (1986/GLEN & RIVER WALKS), expeditions, Munro-bagging (further in beyond Loch Affric) and even just tootling through in the car. Shaped by the Hydro Board, Loch Benevean also adds to the drama. One of the best places in Scotland to understand the beauty of Scots Pine. Cycling good (bike hire in Cannich and at the campsite; 01456 415364) as is the detour to Tomich and Plodda Falls (1601/WATERFALLS). Stop at Dog Falls (1677/PICNICS) but do go to the end of the glen.

1590
10/M22

✓ ✓ ✓ **Glen Lyon** www.glenlyon.org · near Aberfeldy One of Scotland's crucial places historically and geographically, much favoured by fishers/walkers/Munro-baggers. Wordsworth, Tennyson, Gladstone and Baden Powell all sang its praises. The Lyon is a classic Highland river tumbling through corries, gorges and riverine meadows. Several Munros are within its watershed and rise gloriously on either side. Road all the way to the loch side (30km). Eagles soar over the remoter tops at the head of the glen. The **Post Office Coffee Shop** does a roaring trade and the **Fortingal Hotel** on the way in is excellent (886/PERTHSHIRE).

1591
9/K21

✓ ✓ **Glen Nevis** www.glen-nevis.co.uk · Fort William Used by many a film director and easy to see why. Ben Nevis is only part of magnificent scenery. Many walks and convenient facilities (1607/WATERFALLS; 1982/SERIOUS WALKS). West Highland Way emerges here. Visitor centre; cross river to climb Ben Nevis. **Café Beag** nearby is a pleasant caff (summer only). This woody dramatic glen is a national treasure.

1592
9/K22

✓ ✓ **Glen Etive** Off from more exalted Glencoe and the A82 at Kingshouse, as anyone you meet there will tell you, this truly is a glen of glens. Treat with great respect while you make it your own. (1201/CAMPING, 1670/POOLS)

1593
6/L15

Strathcarron www.strathcarron.com · near Bonar Bridge You drive up the north bank of this Highland river from the bridge outside Ardgay (pronounced 'Ordguy') which is 3km over the bridge from Bonar Bridge. Road goes 15km to Croick and its remarkable church (1869/CHURCHES). The river gurgles and gushes along its rocky course to the Dornoch Firth and there are innumerable places to picnic, swim and stroll further up. Quite heavenly here on a warm day.

1594
10/Q21

The Angus Glens www.angusglens.co.uk **Glen Clova**, **Glen Prosen** and **Glen Isla** Isla for drama, Clova for walkers, Prosen for the soul. All via Kirriemuir. Isla to the west is a woody, approachable glen with a deep gorge, on B954 near Alyth (1611/WATERFALLS) and the cosy Glenisla Hotel (1172/INNS). Others via B955, to Dykehead then road bifurcates. Both glens stab into the heart of the Grampians. Minister's Walk goes between them from behind the kirk at Prosen village over the hill to B955 before Clova village (7km). Glen Clova is a walkers' paradise especially from Glendoll 24km from Dykehead; limit of road with new Ranger Centre. Viewpoint. Jock's Road to Braemar and the Capel Mounth to Ballater (both 24km). Clova Hotel (893/PERTHSHIRE HOTELS) with famous Loops of Brandy walk (2 hours, 2-B-2); stark and beautiful. Prosen Hostel at end of the road is a serene stopover (1145/HOSTELS).

1595
9/J25
2-B-2

Glendaruel www.glendaruel.com · Cowal Peninsula On the A886 between Colintraive and Strachur. Humble but perfectly formed glen of River Ruel, from Clachan in south (a kirk and an inn) through deciduous meadowland to more rugged grandeur 10km north. Easy walking and cycling. West road best. Kilmodan carved stones signed. Inver Cottage on Loch Fyne a great coffee/food stop (760/ARGYLL RESTAURANTS).

1596
9/J23
2-B-2

Glen Lonan near Taynuilt Between Taynuilt on A85 and A816 south of Oban. Another quiet wee glen, but all the right elements for walking, picnics, cycling and fishing or just a run in the car. Varying scenery, a bubbling burn (the River Lonan), some standing stones and not many folk. Angus's Garden at the Taynuilt end should not be missed (1516/GARDENS). No marked walks; now get lost!

1597
11/L29

Glen Trool near Newton Stewart 26km north by A714 via Bargrennan which is on the Southern Upland Way (1974/LONG WALKS). A gentle wooded glen within the vast Galloway Forest Park (one of the most charming, accessible parts) visitor centre 5km from Bargrennan. Pick up a walk brochure. Many options. (1910/MARY, CHARLIE & BOB) Start of the Merrick climb (1945/HILLS).

1598
10/N23

The Sma' Glen near Crieff Off the A85 to Perth, the A822 to Amulree and Aberfeldy. Sma' meaning small, this is the valley of the River Almond where the Mealls (lumpish, shapeless hills) fall steeply down to the road. Where the road turns away from the river, the long distance path to Loch Tay begins (28km). Sma' Glen, 8km, has good picnic spots, but they get busy and midgy in summer.

1599
7/L18

Strathfarrar www.glenaffric.org · near Beauly or Drumnadrochit Rare unspoiled glen accessed from A831 leaving Drumnadrochit on Loch Ness via Cannich (30km) or south from Beauly (15km). Signed at Struy. Arrive at gate-keeper's house. Access restricted to 25 cars per day (closed Tue and till 1.30pm on Wed). For access Mar-Oct, phone 01463 761260; there may be a curfew. 22km to head of glen past lochs. Good climbing, walking, fishing. The real peace and quiet!

The Most Spectacular Waterfalls

One aspect of Scotland that really is improved by rain. All the walks to these falls are graded 1-A-1 unless otherwise stated (see p. 12 for walk codes).

1600
7/J18
2-C-3

✓ ✓ **Falls of Glomach** 25km south of Kyle of Lochalsh off A87 near Shiel Bridge, past Kintail Centre at Morvich then 2km further up Glen Croe to bridge. Walk starts other side; there are other ways (eg from the SY Hostel in Glen Affric) but this is most straightforward. Allow 5/7 hours for the pilgrimage to one of Britain's highest falls. Path is steep but well trod. Glomach means gloomy and you might feel so, peering into the ravine; from precipice to pool, it's 200m. But to pay tribute, go down carefully to ledge. Vertigo factor and sense of achievement both fairly high. Consult *Where to Walk in Kintail, Glenelg & Lochalsh*, sold locally for the Kintail Mountain Rescue Team. Ranger service 01599 511231.

1601
7/K18

✓ ✓ **Plodda Falls** www.glenaffric.org · near Tomich, near Drumnadrochit A831 from Loch Ness to Cannich (20km), then 7km to Tomich, a further 5km up mainly woodland track to car park. 200m walk down through woods of Scots Pine and ancient Douglas Fir to one of the most enchanting woodland sites in Britain and the Victorian iron bridge over the brink of the 150m fall into the churning river below. The dawn chorus here must be amazing. Freezes into winter wonderland (ice climbers from Inverness take advantage). Good hotel in village (1027/INEXPENSIVE HIGHLANDS HOTELS).

1602
10/N21
☕

✓**Falls of Bruar** near Blair Atholl Close to the main A9 Perth-Inverness road, 12km north of Blair Atholl near House of Bruar shopping experience. (2170/SCOTTISH SHOPPING). Consequently, the short walk to lower falls is very consumer-led but less crowded than you might expect. The lichen-covered walls of the gorge below the upper falls (1km) are less ogled and more dramatic. Circular path is well marked but steep and rocky in places. Tempting to swim on hot days (1682/SWIMMING HOLES). 2.3km circular.

1603
9/J27
1-B-1

✓**Glenashdale Falls** Arran 5km walk from bridge on main road at Whiting Bay. Signed up the burn side, but uphill and further than you think, so allow 2 hours (return). Series of falls in a rocky gorge in the woods with paths so you get right down to the brim and the pools. Swim here, swim in heaven! There's another waterfall walk, **Eas Mor**, further south off the A841 at the second Kildonan turnoff.

1604
9/G22

Eas Fors Mull On the Dervaig to Fionnphort road 3km from Ulva Ferry; a series of cataracts tumbling down on either side of the road. Easily accessible from small car park on left going south (otherwise unmarked). There's a path down the side to the brink where the river plunges into the sea. On a warm day swimming in the sea below the fall is a rare exhilaration.

1605
7/G17
2-C-2

Lealt Falls Skye Impressive torrent of wild mountain water about 20km north of Portree on the A855. Look for sign: 'River Lealt'. There's a car park on a bend on right (going north). Walk to grassy ledges and look over or go down to the beach. **Kilt Rock**, a viewpoint much favoured by bus parties, is a few km further (you look over and along the cliffs). Also...
Eas Mor Glen Brittle near end of road. 24km from Sligachan. A mountain waterfall with the wild Cuillin behind and views to the sea. Approach as part of a serious scramble or merely a 30-minute Cuillin sampler. Start at the Memorial Hut, cross the road, bear right, cross burn and then follow path uphill.

1606
6/L14
2-C-3

Eas A' Chual Aluinn Kylesku Britain's highest waterfall near the head of Glencoul, is not easy to reach. Kylesku is between Scourie and Lochinver off the main A894, 20km south of Scourie. There are 2-hour cruises May-Sep (01971 502345) from outside the hotel (1047/BEST HIGHLAND RESTAURANTS). Falls are a rather distant prospect but you may be able to alight and get next boat. Baby seals an added attraction Jun-Aug. (Another boat trip from the same quay goes to **Kerracher Gardens** www.kerracher.co.uk, a lochside labour of love worth seeing.) There's also a track to the top of the falls from 5km north of the Skiag Bridge on the main road (4 hours return) but you will need to get directions locally. The water freefalls for 200m, which is 4 times further than Niagara (take pinch of salt here). There is a spectacular pulpit view down the cliff, 100m to right.

1607
9/K21
3-A-3

Steall Falls www.glen-nevis.co.uk · Glen Nevis, Fort William Take Glen Nevis road at the roundabout outside town centre and drive to the end (16km) through glen. Start from the second and final car park, following marked path uphill through the woody gorge with River Ness thrashing below. Glen eventually and dramatically opens out and there are great views of the long veils of the Falls. Precarious 3-wire bridge for which you will also need nerves of steel. You can cross further down or see the falls from a distance.

1608
7/K16

Corrieshalloch Gorge/Falls of Measach Junction of A832 and A835, 20km south of Ullapool; possible to walk down into the gorge from both roads. Most dramatic approach is from the car park on the A832 Gairloch road. Staircase to swing bridge from whence to consider how such a wee burn could make such a deep gash. Very impressive. A must-stop on the way to/from Ullapool.

1609 **The Grey Mare's Tail** between Moffat & Selkirk On the wildly scenic A708.
10/P28 About halfway, a car park and signs for waterfall. 8km from Tibby Shiels Inn (refreshments! 1271/BLOODY GOOD PUBS). The lower track takes 10/15 minutes to a viewing place still 500m from falls; the higher, on the other side of the Tail burn, threads between the austere hills and up to Loch Skene from which the falls overflow (45/60 minutes). Mountain goats.

1610 **The Falls of Clyde** www.swt.org.uk · New Lanark Dramatic falls in a long
10/N27 gorge of the Clyde. New Lanark, the conservation village of Robert Owen the social reformer, is signed from Lanark. It's hard to avoid the 'award-winning' tourist bazaar, but the riverbank has... a more natural appeal. The path to the Power Station is about 1km, but the route doesn't get interesting till after it, a 1km climb to the first fall (Cora Linn) and another 1km to the next (Bonnington Linn). There is a great Italian restaurant in Lanark (525/GLASGOW ITALIAN RESTAURANTS) and one of the mills is now a hotel. The strange uniformity of New Lanark is better when the other tourists have gone home.

1611 **Reekie Linn** Alyth 8km north of town on back roads to Kirriemuir on B951
10/Q22 between Bridge of Craigisla and Bridge of Lintrathen. A picnic site and car park on bend of road leads by 200m to the wooded gorge of Glen Isla with precipitous viewpoints of defile where Isla is squeezed and falls in tiers for 100ft. Walk further along the glen and look back. Peel Farm Shop/Tearoom, widely signposted, is disappointing.

1612 **Falls of Acharn** near Kenmore 5km along south side of Loch Tay on an
10/M22 unclassified road. Walk from just after the bridge going west in township of Acharn; falls are signed. Steepish start then 1km up side of gorge; waterfalls on other side. Can be circular route.

1613 **Falls of Rogie** www.ullapool.co.uk · near Strathpeffer Car park on A835
7/L17 Inverness-Ullapool road, 5km Contin/10km Strathpeffer. Accessibility makes short walk (250m) quite popular to these hurtling falls on the Blackwater River. Bridge (built by the Territorial Army) and salmon ladder (they leap in summer). Woodland trails 1-3km marked, include a circular route to Contin (2019/WOODLAND WALKS).

1614 **Foyers** Loch Ness On southern route from Fort Augustus to Inverness, the
7/L19 B862 (1639/SCENIC ROUTES) at the village of Foyers (35km from Inverness). Park next to shops and cross road, go through fence and down steep track to viewing places (slither-proof shoes advised). River Foyers falls 150m into foaming gorge below and then into Loch Ness throwing clouds of spray into the trees (you may get drenched).

1615 **Falls of Shin** www.fallsofshin.co.uk · near Lairg 6km east of town on signed
6/M15 road, car park and falls nearby are easily accessible. Not quite up to the splendours
⌨ of others on this page, but an excellent place to see salmon battling upstream (best Jun-Aug). Visitor centre with extensive shop; the café/restaurant is excellent (1055/BEST RESTAURANTS) and there's an adventure playground and other reasons to hang around in Sutherland.

The Lochs We Love

1616
7/J16 ✓✓ **Loch Maree** A832 between Kinlochewe and Gairloch. Dotted with islands covered in Scots Pine hiding some of the best examples of Viking graves and apparently a money tree in their midst. Easily viewed from the road which follows its length for 15km. Beinn Eighe rises behind you and the omniscient presence of Slioch is opposite. Aultroy Vistor Centre (5km Kinlochewe), fine walks from lochside car parks, among the largest original Scots Pine woodlands in the West Highlands.

1617
7/N19 ✓✓ **Loch An Eilean** 4km Inverdruie off the Coylumbridge road from Aviemore. Car park and info board. An enchanted loch in the heart of the Rothiemurchus Forest (2008/WOODLAND WALKS for directions). You can walk right round the loch (5km, allow 1.5 hours). This is classic Highland scenery, a calendar landscape of magnificent Scots Pine. But I get sad when I come here!

1618
7/J20 ✓ **Loch Arkaig** 25km Fort William. An enigmatic loch long renowned for its fishing. From the A82 beyond Spean Bridge (at the Commando Monument; 1845/MONUMENTS) cross the Caledonian Canal, then on by single-track road through the Clunes Forest and the Dark Mile past the Witches' Pool (a cauldron of dark water below cataracts) to the loch. Bonnie Prince Charlie came this way before and after Culloden; one of his refuge caves is marked on a trail.

1619
10/L24 **Loch Achray** near Brig o' Turk The small loch at the centre of the Trossachs between **Loch Katrine** (on which the SS *Sir Walter Scott* and the smaller *Lady of the Lake* makes 4 sailings a day – the morning one stops at the end of the loch; 01877 376316) and **Loch Venachar**. The A821 from Callander skirts both Venachar and Achray. Many picnic spots and a new fishing centre and Harbour Café on the main road by Loch Venachar. Ben Venue and Ben An rise above: great walks (1938/HILLS) and views. A one-way forest road goes round the other side of Loch Achray through Achray Forest (enter and leave from the Duke's Pass road between Aberfoyle and Brig o' Turk). Details of trails from forest visitor centre 3km north Aberfoyle. Bike hire at Loch Katrine/Callander/Aberfoyle – it's the best way to see these lochs.

1620
10/L24 **Glen Finglas Reservoir** Brig o' Turk And while we're on the subject of lochs in the Trossachs (see above) here's a great one to walk to. Although it's man-made it's a real beauty, surrounded by soft green hills and the odd burn bubbling in. Approach 'through' Brig o' Turk houses (past the caff) and park 2km up road, or from new car park 2km before Brig o' Turk from Callander. It's about 5km to the head of the loch and 18km on the Mell Trail round the hill or 12km to Balquhidder: a walk across the heart of Scotland (1987/GLEN WALKS). Ranger board gives details.

1621
10/Q20 **Loch Muick** near Ballater At head of road off B976, the South Dee road at Ballater. 14km up Glen Muick (pronounced 'Mick') to car park, visitor centre and 1km to loch side. Lochnagar rises above (1969/MUNROS) and walk also begins here for Capel Mounth and Glen Clova (1594/GLENS). 3-hour walk around loch and any number of ambles. The lodge where Vic met John is at the furthest point (well, it would be). Open aspect with grazing deer and not too much forestry. (Ranger's office 01339 755059.)

1622
6/L13 **Loch Eriboll** North Coast 90km west of Thurso. The long sea loch that indents into the North Coast for 15km and which you drive right round on the main A838 (40 minutes). Deepest natural anchorage in the UK, exhibiting every aspect of loch

side scenery including, alas, fish cages. Ben Hope stands near the head of the loch and there is a perfect beach (my own private Idaho) on the coast (1567/BEACHES). Walks from Hope.

1623 **Loch Trool** near Newton Stewart The small, celebrated loch in a bowl of the
11/L29 Galloway Hills reached via Bargrennan 14km north via A714 and 8km to end of road. Woodland visitor centre/café on the way. Get Galloway Forest Park brochure. Good walks but best viewed from Bruce's Stone (1910/MARY, CHARLIE & BOB) and the slopes of Merrick (1945/HILLS). An idyllic place.

1624 **Loch Morar** near Mallaig 70km west of Fort William by the A850 (a wildly
7/H20 scenic and much improved route). Morar village is 6km from Mallaig and a single track road leads away from the coast to the loch (only 500m but out of sight) then along it for 5km to Bracora. It's the prettiest part with wooded islets, small beaches, loch side meadows and bobbing boats. The road stops at a turning place but a track continues from Bracorina to Tarbet and it's possible to connect with a post boat and sail back to Mallaig on Loch Nevis though this will take some organising (check tourist information centre). Boat hire on the loch itself from Ewen Macdonald (01687 462520). Loch Morar, joined to the coast by the shortest river in Britain, also has the deepest water. There is a spookiness about it and just possibly a monster called Morag.

1625 **Loch Tummel** near Pitlochry West from Pitlochry on B8019 to Rannoch (and
10/N22 the end of the road), Loch Tummel comes into view, as it did for Queen Victoria, scintillating beneath you, and on a clear day with Schiehallion beyond (1660/VIEWS). This north side has good walks (2016/WOODLAND WALKS), but the south road from Faskally just outside Pitlochry is the one to take to get down to the lochside to picnic, etc.

1626 **Loch Lundavra** near Fort William Here's a secret loch in the hills, but not far
9/K21 from the well-trodden tracks through the glens and the sunny streets of Fort William. Go up Lundavra Rd from roundabout at west end of main street, out of town, over cattle grid and on (to end of road) 8km. You should have it to yourself; good picnic spots and great view of Ben Nevis. West Highland Way comes this way (1973/LONG WALKS).

Loch Lomond The biggest, maybe not the bonniest (1/BIG ATTRACTIONS) with major visitor centre and retail experience, **Lomond Shores**, at south end near Balloch.

Loch Ness The longest; you haven't heard the last of it (3/BIG ATTRACTIONS).

The Scenic Routes

1627
9/J21
NTS
ATMOS

√√√ **Glencoe** www.glencoe-nts.org.uk The A82 from Crianlarich to Ballachulish is a fine drive, but from the extraterrestrial Loch Ba onwards, there can be few roads anywhere that have direct contact with such imposing scenery. After Kingshouse and Buachaille Etive Mor on the left, the mountains and ridges rising on either side of Glencoe proper invoke the correct usage of the word 'awesome'. The new visitor centre, more discreet than the former near Glencoe village, sets the topographical and historical scene. (1267/BLOODY GOOD PUBS; 1981/SERIOUS WALKS; 1897/BATTLEGROUNDS; 1923/ENCHANTING PLACES; 1157/HOSTELS.)

1628
7/H19

√√ **Shiel Bridge-Glenelg** The switchback road that climbs from the A87 (Fort William 96km) at Shiel Bridge over the 'hill' and down to the coast opposite the Sleat Peninsula in Skye (short ferry to Kylerhea). As you climb you're almost as high as the surrounding summits and there's the classic view across Loch Duich to the 5 Sisters of Kintail. Coming back you think you're going straight into the loch! It's really worth driving to Glenelg (1816/PREHISTORIC SITES, 1204/CAMPING, 1164/INNS) and beyond to Arnisdale and ethereal Loch Hourn (16km).

1629
7/H18

√√ **Applecross** www.applecross.uk.com · 120km from Inverness. From Tornapress near Lochcarron for 18km. Leaving the A896 seems like leaving civilisation; the winding ribbon heads into monstrous mountains and the high plateau at the top is another planet. It's not for the faint hearted and Applecross is a relief to arrive in with its campsite/coffee shop and a faraway inn: the legendary Applecross Inn (1190/GET-AWAY HOTELS). Also see 1053/HIGHLAND RESTAURANTS, 1408/COFFEE SHOPS, 1207/1211/CAMPING. This hair-raising road rises 2000 feet in 6 miles. See how they built it at the Applecross Heritage Centre (2127/HERITAGE).

1630
7/J17

√√ **Glen Torridon** The A896 between Torridon and thence to Diabaig with staggering views along the route of the 3 mighty Torridon mountains: Beinn Eighe, Liathach and Beinn Alligin. If you want to climb them, there are various starts along this road – enquire and all other information at the NTS Countryside Centre at the Diabaig turnoff. Excellent two-tier accommodation at the Torridon (1183/GET-AWAY HOTELS). There is much to climb and clamber over here; or merely be amazed. See also 1648/VIEWS.

1631
9/J26

√ **Rothesay-Tighnabruaich** A886/A8003. The most celebrated part of this route is the latter, the A8003 down the side of Loch Riddon to Tighnabruaich along the hill sides with the breathtaking views of Bute and the Kyles (can be a lot of vegetation in summer – one good layby/viewpoint) but the whole way, with its diverse aspects of lochside, riverine and rocky scenery, is supernatural. Includes short crossing between Rhubodach and Colintraive. Great hotel/ restaurants at Tighnabruaich (750/ARGYLL HOTELS) and Kames (1176/SEASIDE INNS).

1632
5/E16
ATMOS

√ **The Golden Road** South Harris The main road in Harris follows the west coast, notable for bays and beaches (1573/BEACHES). This is the other one, winding round a series of coves and inlets with offshore skerries and a treeless rocky hinterland – classic Hebridean landscape, especially Finsbay. Good caff nearby (2281/HEBRIDES). Tweed is woven in this area; you can visit the crofts and there are 2 shops (2190/TWEED).

1633
6/J14

✓ **Lochinver–Drumbeg–Kylestrome** The coast road north from Lochinver (35km) is marvellous; essential Assynt. Actually best travelled north-south so that you leave the splendid vista of Eddrachilles Bay and pass through lochan, moor and even woodland, touching the coast again by sandy beaches (at Stoer a road leads 7km to the lighthouse and the walk to the Old Man of Stoer, 2036/ COASTAL WALKS) past the wonderful Secret Beach (1578/BEACHES) and approach Lochinver (possible detour to Auchmelvich and beaches) with one of the classic long views of Suilven. Get your pies in Lochinver (1051/LESS EXPENSIVE HIGHLAND).

1634
6/J14

Lochinver–Achiltibuie And south from Lochinver Achiltibuie is 40km from Ullapool; so this is the route from the north; 28km of winding road/unwinding Highland scenery; through glens, mountains and silver sea. Known locally as the 'wee mad road' (it is maddening if you're in a hurry). Passes Achin's Bookshop (2178/SHOPPING), the path to Kirkaig Falls and the mighty Suilven. Near Achiltibuie is one (or two) of the most uplifting views in Scotland (1649/VIEWS).

1635
7/G19

Sleat Peninsula Skye The unclassified road off the A851 (main Sleat road) especially coming from south, i.e. take road at Ostaig near Gaelic College (great place to stay nearby: 2235/SKYE); it meets coast after 9km. Affords rare views of the Cuillins from a craggy coast. Returning to 'main' road south of Isleornsay, pop into the great hotel pub there (2223/SKYE HOTELS).

1636
10/R27

Leaderfoot–Clintmains near St Boswells The B6356 between the A68 (look out for Leaderfoot viaduct and signs for Dryburgh) and the B6404 Kelso-St Boswells road. This small road, busy in summer, links Scott's View and Dryburgh Abbey (1891/ABBEYS; find by following Abbey signs) and Smailholm Tower, and passes through classic Border/Tweedside scenery. 500m walk to the Wallace Statue is signed. Don't miss Irvine's View if you want to see the best of the Borders (827/VIEWS). Nice guest house (821/BORDER HOTELS).

1637
10/P20

Braemar–Linn Of Dee 12km of renowned Highland river scenery along the upper valley of the (Royal) Dee. The Linn (rapids) is at the end of the road and the mighty Dee is squeezed until it is no more than 1m wide, but there are river walks and the start of the great Glen Tilt walk to Blair Atholl (1984/SERIOUS WALKS). Deer abound.

1638
8/Q20

Ballater–Tomintoul The ski road to the Lecht, the A939 which leaves the Royal Deeside road (A93) west of Ballater before it gets really royal. A ribbon of road in the bare Grampians (though starts woody), past the sentinel ruin Corgarff (open to view, 250m walk) and the valley of the trickling Don. Road proceeds seriously uphill and main viewpoints are south of the Lecht. There is just nobody for miles. Walks in Glenlivet estates south of Tomintoul.

1639
7/L19

Fort Augustus–Dores near Inverness The B862 often single-track road that follows and latterly skirts Loch Ness. Quieter and more interesting than the main west bank A82. Starts in rugged country and follows the straight road built by Wade to tame the Highlands. Reaches the lochside at Foyers (1614/WATERFALLS) and goes all the way to Dores (15km from Inverness) where the dance music gathering, RockNess, is held in June (33/EVENTS). Paths to the shore of the loch. Fabulous untrodden woodlands near Errogie (marked) and the spooky graveyard adjacent Boleskin House where Aleister Crowley did his dark magic and Jimmy Page of Led Zeppelin may have done his. 35km total; worth taking slowly. Great start/finish is the **Boathouse** café at the Highland Club at Fort Augustus right at the southern tip of the loch (lunch and dinner in season).

1640 **The Duke's Pass, Aberfoyle-Brig o' Turk** Of the many roads through the
10/L24 Trossachs, this one is spectacular though gets busy; numerous possibilities for
stopping, exploration and great views. Good viewpoint 4km from Loch Achray
Hotel, above road and lay-by. One-way forest road goes round Loch Achray and 2
other lochs (Drunkie and Vennacher). Good hill walking starts (1938/1939/1940/
FAVOURITE HILLS) and Loch Katrine Ferry (2km) 4 times a day Apr-Oct (01877
376316). Bike hire at Loch Katrine, Aberfoyle and Callander.

1641 **Glenfinnan-Mallaig** The A830, aka the Road to the Isles. Through some of the
9/J20 most impressive and romantic landscapes in the Highlands, splendid in any
weather (it does rain rather a lot) to the coast at the Sands of Morar (1584/
BEACHES). This is deepest Bonnie Prince Charlie country (1909/MARY, CHARLIE &
BOB) and demonstrates what a misty eye he had for magnificent settings. A full-
throttle bikers' dream. The road is shadowed for much of the way by the West
Highland Railway, which is an even better way to enjoy the scenery (11/FAVOURITE
JOURNEYS). Road recently improved.

1642 **Lochailort-Acharacle** Off from the A830 above at Lochailort and turning south
9/H21 on the A861, the coastal section of this great scenery is superb especially in the
setting sun, or in May when the rhodies are out. Glen Uig Inn is rough and ready!
This is the road to the Castle Tioram shoreline, which should not be missed
(1783/RUINS), and glorious Ardnamurchan.

1643 **Knapdale: Lochgilphead-Tarbert** B8024 off the main A83 follows the coast
9/H25 for most of its route. Views to Jura are immense (and on a clear day, Ireland). Not
much happens here but in the middle in exactly the right place is a superb inn
(1163/ROADSIDE INNS, 1288/GASTROPUBS). Take it easy on this very Scottish 35km
of single track. Short walk to the Coves 3km before Kilberry.

1644 **Amulree-Kenmore** Unclassified single-track and very narrow road from the
10/N22 hill-country hamlet of Amulree to cosy Kenmore signed Glen Quaich. Past Loch
Freuchie, a steep climb takes you to a plateau ringed by magnificent (far)
mountains to Loch Tay. Steep descent to Loch Tay and Kenmore. Don't forget to
close the gates.

1645 **Muthill-Comrie** Pure Perthshire. A route which takes you through some of the
10/N23 best scenery in central Scotland and ends up (best this way round) in Comrie with
teashops and other pleasures (881/PERTHSHIRE HOTELS, 1678/PICNICS). Leave
Muthill (1162/ROADSIDE INNS) by Crieff road turning left (2km) into Drummond
Castle grounds up a glorious avenue of beech trees (gate open 2-5pm). Visit gar-
den (1507/GARDENS); continue through estate. At gate, go right, following signs for
Strowan. First junction, go left following signs (4km). At T-junction, go left to
Comrie (7km). Best have a map, but if not, who cares? It's all bonny!

1646 **The Heads of Ayr** The coast road south from Ayr to Culzean (1762/CASTLES) and
9/K28 Turnberry (766/AYRSHIRE HOTELS) includes these headlands, great views of Ailsa
Craig and Arran and some horrible caravan parks. The Electric Brae south of
Dunure village is famously worth stopping on (your car runs the opposite way to
the slope) and the Dunure Inn itself is now officially a great food stop in a lovely
harbourside setting (1307/GASTROPUBS). Culzean grounds are gorgeous.

The Classic Views

For views of and around Edinburgh and Glasgow see p. 89 and p. 131. No views from hill or mountain tops are included here.

1647
7/G17

✓ ✓ ✓ **The Quirang** Skye Best approach is from Uig direction taking the right-hand unclassified road off the hairpin of the A855 above and 2km from town signed 'Staffin via Quirang' (more usual approach from Staffin side is less of a revelation). View (and walk) from car park, the massive rock formations of a towering, contorted ridge. Solidified lava heaved and eroded into fantastic pinnacles. Fine views also across Staffin Bay to Wester Ross. (2273/ISLAND WALKS.)

1648
7/J16

✓ ✓ ✓ The views of **An Teallach** and **Liathach** An Teallach, that great favourite of Scottish hill walkers (40km south of Ullapool by the A835/A832), is best viewed from the side of Little Loch Broom or the A832 just before you get to Dundonnell (1412/TEAROOMS).
The classic view of the other great Torridon mountains (**Beinn Eighe**, pronounced 'Ben A', and **Liathach** together, 100km south by road from Ullapool) in Glen Torridon (1630/SCENIC ROUTES) 4km from Kinlochewe. This viewpoint is not marked but it's on the track around Loch Clair which is reached from the entrance to the Coulin estate off the A896, Glen Torridon road (be aware of stalking). Park outside gate; no cars allowed, 1km walk to lochside. These mountains have to be seen to be believed.

1649
10/R27

✓ ✓ **Irvine's View** St Boswells The full panorama from the Cheviots to the Lammermuirs. This the finest view in southern Scotland. It's only a furlong further than Scott's View, below: cross the road from Scott's View layby through the kissing gate, veering left uphill across rough pasture till you reach the double track. Head up till the track divides and take the right, lesser path. You'll see the fallen standing stone where I would like my bench (Borders Council!). The telecoms masts are ghastly but then I'm never without my moby either. Turn your back on them and gaze across the beautiful Borders to another country... you know, England.

1650
7/G18
2-B-2

✓ ✓ From **Raasay** www.raasay.com There are several fabulous views looking over to Skye from Raasay, the small island reached by ferry from Sconser (2206/MAGICAL ISLANDS). The panorama from Dun Caan, the hill in the centre of the island (444m) is of Munro proportions, producing an elation incommensurate with the small effort required to get there. Start from the road to the North End or ask at the hotel in Inverarish.

1651
6/J15

✓ ✓ **The Summer Isles** www.summer-isles.com · Achiltibuie The Summer Isles are a scattering of islands seen from the coast of Achiltibuie (and the lounge of the Summer Isles Hotel; 1001/HIGHLANDS HOTELS) and visited by boat from Ullapool. But the best place to see them, and the stunning perspective of this western shore, is on the road to Altandhu (has other spellings). Best approach is: from Achiltibuie, veer left through Polbain, past Polbain Stores, on and through Allandhu, past turning for Reiff and Blairbuie, then 500m ascending inland. There's a bench and a new path (sign for 'Viewpoint') 50m to little plateau with many cairns and this one of the ethereal views of Scotland. On this same road 500m round the corner, the distant mountains of Assynt all in a row: 2 jawdropping perspectives of the Highlands in 5 minutes.

1652   ✓ ✓ **The Rest and Be Thankful** On A83 Loch Lomond-Inveraray road
9/K24   where it's met by the B828 from Lochgoilhead. In summer the rest may
be from driving stress and you may not be thankful for the camera-toting masses,
but this was always one of the most accessible, rewarding viewpoints in the land.
Surprisingly, none of the encompassing hills are Munros but they are nonetheless
dramatic. Only a few carpets of conifer to smother the grandeur of the crags as
you look down the valley.

1653   ✓ **Califer** near Forres 7km from Forres on A96 to Elgin, turn right signed for
8/P17   'Pluscarden', follow this road for 5km back towards Forres. You are unaware
how high above the coastal plain you are and the layby is discreetly located. When
you walk across a small park with young memorial trees you are rewarded with a
truly remarkable sight – down across Findhorn Bay and the wide vista of the Moray
Firth to the Black Isle and Ben Wyvis. There is often fantastic light on this coast.

1654   ✓ **Elgol** Skye End of the road, the B8083, 22km from Broadford. The classic
7/G19   view of the Cuillins from across Loch Scavaig and of Soay and Rum. Cruises
(Apr-Oct) in the *Bella Jane* (0800 731 3089) or *The Misty Isle* (Apr-Oct, not Sun
01471 866288) to the famous corrie of Loch Coruisk, painted by Turner,
romanticised by Walter Scott. A journey you'll remember.

1655   **Camas Nan Geall** Ardnamurchan 12km Salen on B8007. 4km from
9/G21   Ardnamurchan's Natural History Centre (1717/KIDS) 65km Fort William. Coming
especially from the Kilchoan direction, a magnificent bay appears below you,
where the road first meets the sea. Almost symmetrical with high cliffs and a
perfect field (still cultivated) in the bowl fringed by a shingle beach. Car park viewpoint and there is a path down. Amazing Ardnamurchan!

1656   **Glengarry** www.glengarry.net 3km after Tomdoun turnoff on A87, Invergarry-
7/K20   Kyle of Lochalsh road. Layby with viewfinder. An uncluttered vista up and down
loch and glen with not a house in sight (pity about the salmon cages). Distant
peaks of Knoydart are identified, but not Loch Quoich nestling spookily and full of
fish in the wilderness at the head of the glen. Gaelic mouthfuls of mountains on
the orientation board. Bonnie Prince Charlie passed this way.

1657   **Scott's View** St Boswells Off A68 at Leaderfoot Bridge near St Boswells,
7/R27   signed Gattonside. The View, old Walter's favourite (the horses still stopped there
long after he'd gone), is 4km along the road (Dryburgh Abbey 3km further;
1891/ABBEYS). Magnificent sweep of his beloved Border country, but only in one
direction. If you cross the road and go through the kissing gate you're on the
approach to Irvine's View (see above... and beyond).

1658   **Peniel Heugh** near Ancrum While we're on the subject of great views in the
10/R27   Borders, you may look no further than this – the sentinel Borders symbol. Report:
1839/BEST MONUMENTS.

1659   **The Law** Dundee Few cities have such a single good viewpoint. To north of the
10/Q23   centre, it reveals the panoramic perspective of the city on the estuary of the silvery
Tay. Best to walk from town; the one-way system is a nightmare.

1660   **Queen's View** Loch Tummel, near Pitlochry 8km on B8019 to Kinloch
10/N22   Rannoch. Car park and 100m walk to rocky knoll where pioneers of tourism Queen
Victoria and Prince Albert were 'transported into ecstasies' by view of Loch
Tummel and Schiehallion (1625/LOCHS; 2016/WOODLAND WALKS). Their view was

flooded by a hydro scheme after World War II; more recently it spawned a whole view-driven visitor experience (costing a quid to park). It all... makes you wonder.

1661
10/L23
The Rallying Place of the Maclarens Balquhidder Short climb from behind the church (1884/GRAVEYARDS) along the track 150m then signed Creag an Turc, steep at first. Superb view down Loch Voil, the Balquhidder Braes and the real Rob Roy Country and great caff with home baking on your descent (1404/COFFEE SHOPS).

1662
11/Q29
The Malcolm Memorial Langholm 3km from Langholm and signed from main A7, a single-track road leads to a path to this obelisk raised to celebrate the military and masonic achievements of one John Malcolm. The eulogy is fulsome especially compared with that for Hugh MacDiarmid on the cairn by the stunning sculpture at the start of the path (1849/MEMORIALS). Views from the obelisk, however, are among the finest in the south, encompassing a vista from the Lakeland Fells and the Solway Firth to the wild Border hills. Path 1km.

1663
9/L25
Duncryne Hill Gartocharn Gartocharn is between Balloch and Drymen on the A811, and this view, was recommended by writer and outdoorsman Tom Weir as 'the finest viewpoint of any small hill in Scotland'. Turn up Duncryne road at the east end of village and park 1km on left by a small wood (a sign reads 'Woods reserved for Teddy bears'). The hill is only 470ft high and 'easy', but the view of Loch Lomond and the Kilpatrick Hills is superb.

1664
10/N27
1-A-2
Blackhill Lesmahagow 28km south of Glasgow. Another marvellous outlook, but in the opposite direction from above. Take junction 10/11 on M74, then off the B7078 signed Lanark, take the B7018. 4km along past Clarkston Farm, head uphill for 1km and park by Water Board mound. Walk uphill through fields to right for about 1km. Unprepossessing hill which unexpectedly reveals a vast vista of most of East Central Scotland (and most of the uphill is in the car).

1665
6/M13
Tongue From the causeway across the kyle, or better, follow the minor road to Melness Talmine on the west side, look south to Ben Loyal or north to the small islands off the coast.

1666
10/N25
Cairnpapple Hill near Linlithgow Volcanic geology, neolithic henge, east Scottish agriculture, the Forth plain, the Bridges, Grangemouth industrial complex and telecoms masts: not all pretty, but the whole of Scotland at a glance. For directions see 1808/PREHISTORIC SITES.

1667
9/J22
Castle Stalker View Portnacroish Near Port Appin on main A828 Oban-Fort William road. On right going south, the view has been commandeered by a café (1402/TEASHOPS) which ain't bad (closed in evenings) but viewpoint can be accessed at all times 50m away from car park. Always impressive, in certain lights the vista of Port Appin, the castle in the fore and Loch Linnhe, is ethereal.

1668
10/R28
Carter Bar English Border near Jedburgh On the A68 Edinburgh-Newcastle road, the last and first view in Scotland just happens to be superb. The Border hill country spread out before you for many long miles. The tear in my eye is not because of the wind, but because this was the landscape of my youth and where I spent my lightsome days.

Summer Picnics & Great Swimming Holes

Care should be taken when swimming in rivers; don't take them for granted. Kids should be watched. Most of these places are traditional local swimming and picnic spots where people have swum for years, but rivers continuously change their course and their nature. Wearing sandals or old sports shoes is a good idea.

1669
7/G19

✓✓ **The Fairy Pools** Glen Brittle, Skye On that rare hot day, this is one of the best places on Skye to head for; swimming in deep pools with the massif of the Cuillins around you. One pool has a stone bridge you can swim under. Head off A863 Dunvegan road from Sligachan Hotel then B8009 and Glen-brittle road. 7km down just as road begins to parallel the glen itself, you'll see a river coming off the hills. Park in layby on right. 1-2km walk. Swim with the fairies!

1670
9/K22

✓✓ **The Pools in Glen Etive** Glen Etive is a wild, enchanted place where people have been camping for years to walk and climb in Glencoe area. There are many grassy landings at the river side as well as these perfect pools for bathing. The first is about 5km from the main road, the A82 at Kingshouse, but just follow the river and find your own. Take midge cream for evening wear. Lots.

1671
7/N19

✓✓ **Feshiebridge** At the bridge itself on the B970 between Kingussie and Inverdruie near Aviemore. 4km from Kincraig. Great walks here into Glen Feshie and in nearby woodland, but under bridge a perfect spot for Highland swimming. Go down to left from south. Rocky ledges, clear water. One of the best but cold even in high summer. Further pools nearby, up river.

1672
10/P22

✓✓ **Rumbling Bridge & The Braan Walk** near Dunkeld Excellent stretch of cascading river with pools, rocky banks and ledges. Just off A9 heading north opposite first turning for Dunkeld, the A822 for Aberfeldy, Amulree (signed Crieff/Crianlarich). Car park on right after 4km. Connects with forest paths (the Braan Walk) to the Hermitage (2013/WOODLAND WALKS) – 2km. Fab picnic and swimming spot though take great care. This is the nearest Highland-type river to Edinburgh (about 1 hour).

1673
7/M20
ATMOS

✓✓ **Strathmashie** www.strathmashie.co.uk · near Newtonmore On A86 Newtonmore-Dalwhinnie (on A9) to Fort William road 7km from Laggan, watch for Forest sign. Car parks on either side of the road; the Druim an Aird car park has finder boards. Great swimming spot, but often campers. Viewpoints, waterfall, pines. If people are here don't despair – there are great forest walks and follow the river; there are many other great pools. Great café with home baking 5km towards the A9 (1398/TEAROOMS).

1674
9/K23
ATMOS

✓✓ **Rob Roy's Bathtub** The Falloch Falls, near Inverarnan A82 north of Ardlui and 3 km past the Drover's Inn (1264/BLOODY GOOD PUBS). Sign on the right (Picnic Area) going north. Park, then follow the path. Some pools on the rocky river course but 500m from car park you reach the main falls and below a perfect round natural pool 30m across. There's an overhanging rock face on one side and smooth slabs at the edge of the falls. Natural suntrap in summer, but the water is Baltic at all times.

1675
10/Q27

✓ **Neidpath** Peebles 2km from town on A72, Biggar road; sign for castle. Park by Hay Lodge Park and walk upriver or down the track to the castle when the gate is open, or the layby 100m beyond. Idyllic setting of a broad meander of the Tweed, with medieval Neidpath Castle, a sentinel above. Two pools (3m deep in average summer) linked by shallow rapids which the adventurous chute down on their backs. Usually a rope-swing on the oak tree at the upper pool. Also see (1997/GLEN & RIVER WALKS). Castle open May-Sep, Wed-Sun. TAKE CARE.

1676
8/N17
✔ **Randolph's Leap** near Forres Spectacular gorge on the mythical Findhorn which carves out some craggy scenery on its way to a gentle coast. This no-longer secret glade and fabulous swimming hole are behind a wall on a bend of the B9007 (see 2005/WOODLAND WALKS for directions) south of Forres and Nairn and near Logie Steading, a courtyard of good things (a board there maps out walks) and refreshment (1407/TEAROOMS). One Randolph or Alistair as the new tale tells, may have leapt here; we just bathe and picnic under the trees.

1677
7/K18
Dog Falls Glen Affric Half-way along Glen Affric road from Cannich before you come to the loch, a well-marked picnic spot and great place to swim in the peaty waters surrounded by the Caledonian Forest (with trails). Birds well sussed to picnic potential – your car covered in tits and cheeky chaffinches – Hitchcock or what? (1986/GLEN & RIVER WALKS). Falls (rapids really) to the left.

1678
10/M23
Near Comrie www.comrie.org.uk 2 great pools of different character near the neat little town in deepest Perthshire. **The Linn**, the town pool: go over humpback bridge from main A85 west to Lochearnhead, signed 'The Ross'. Take left fork then after 2km there's a parking place on left. River's relatively wide, very pleasant spot. For more adventurous, **Glenartney**, known locally as 'the cliffs': go over bridge, the Braco road after 3km signed Glenartney, past Cultybraggan training camp (no longer in use) and then MoD range on left just before the end-of-the-road sign (200m after boarded-up cottage on right, 5km from Comrie). Park and walk down to river in glen. What with the twin perils of the Army and the Comrie Angling Club, you might feel you have no right to be here, but you do and this stretch of river is marvellous. Respect the farmland. Follow the road further for more great picnic spots. Comrie has a great pub/hotel bistro (881/PERTHSHIRE HOTELS) and the Deil's Cauldron (910/PERTHSHIRE RESTAURANTS).

1679
9/K26
Greeto Falls Gogo Glen, Largs Well known locally so ask to find Flatt Rd. At top there's a car park and you follow the beautiful Gogo Glen path, past Cockmalone Cottage. Superb views of the Clyde. 3 pools to choose from in the Gogo Burn near the bridge.

1680
9/J27
North Sannox Burn Arran Park at the North Sannox Bridge on the A841 (road from Lochranza to Sannox Bay) and follow the track west to the deer fence and tree line (1km). Just past there you will find a great pool with small waterfall, dragonflies and perhaps even an eagle or two wheeling above.

1681
9/H23
Swimmers' Quarry Easdale Cross to Easdale on the wee boat (5-minute continuous service); see 2312/HISTORY for details. Do visit the museum but go beyond scattered houses following paths to slate quarries full of seawater since 1881 with clear water like an enormous boutique hotel swimming pool. The L-shaped one with its little bench is easiest, the water blue like the Aegean.

1682
10/N21
Falls of Bruar near Blair Atholl Just off A9, 12km north of Blair Atholl. 250m walk from **House of Bruar** car park and shopping experience (2170/SHOPPING) to lower fall (1602/WATERFALLS) where there is an accessible large deep pool by the bridge. Cold, fresh mountain water in a woody gorge. The proximity of the retail experience can make it all the more... naturally exhilarating.

1683 **The Scout Pool & The Bracklinn Falls** Callander The latter are a Callander
10/M24 must-see, easy-to-find (signposted from south end of Main St, up hill to golf
course then next car park up on right – from there it's a 15-minute walk). The
Scout Pool is a traditional swimming hole on same river so a summer thing only.
Follow road further 5km from Bracklinn car park till road goes on through iron
gate. Park on right. Downhill 150m cross wooden bridge then follow river path to
right 250m. Access to huge pool dammed by giant boulders, made less easy by
storms 2005, but a beautiful secret spot in the woods.

1684 **The Otter's Pool** New Galloway Forest A clearing in the forest reached by a
11/L30 track, the Raider's Road, running from 8km north of Laurieston on the A762, for
16km to Clatteringshaws Loch. The track, which is only open Apr-Oct, has a toll of
£2 and gets busy. It follows the Water of Dee and halfway down the road – the
Otter's Pool. A bronze otter used to mark the spot (it got nicked) and it's a place
mainly for kids and paddling; but when the dam runs off it can be deep enough to
swim. Road closes dusk. 2017/WOODLAND WALKS.

1685 **Ancrum** www.ancrum.com A secret place on the quiet Ale Water (out of vil-
10/R27 lage towards Lilliesleaf, 3km out 250m from farm sign to Hopton – a recessed gate
on the right before a bend and a rough track that locals know). A buttercup
meadow, a Border burn, a surprisingly deep pool to swim. Go to left of rough vegetation in defile, going downhill follow fence on your right. Cross further gate at
bottom (only 100m from road). Arcadia awaits beyond the meadow.

1686 **Towford** near Hounam & Jedburgh Another Borders burn with a surprising
10/S28 pool. This one legendary but hard to find. Deep in the Cheviots, nobody for miles.
It's where I went as a kid. Only the very intrepid tourist ventures here. Ask a local.

1687 **Paradise** Sheriffmuir, near Dunblane A pool at the foot of an unexpected
10/N24 leafy gorge on the moor between the Ochils and Strathallan. Here the Wharry
Burn is known locally as 'Paradise'. Take road from 'behind' Dunblane or Bridge of
Allan to the Sheriffmuir Inn (ok-ish!); head downhill (back) towards B of A. Park
1km after hump-back bridge. Head for the pylon nearest the river and you'll find
the pool. It can be midgy but it can be paradise.

1688 **Potarch Bridge & Cambus o' May** On The Dee 2 places: the first by the
8/Q20 reconstructed Victorian bridge (and near the hotel) 3km east of Kincardine O'Neill.
Cambus another stretch of river east of Ballater (6km). Locals swim, picnic on
rocks, etc, and there are forest walks on the other side of road. The brave jump off
the bridge at Cambus (in wetsuits). Great tearooms nearby: the Black Faced Sheep
in Aboyne (1388/TEAROOMS) and locally famous break-making Cranach adjacent.

1689 **Invermoriston** www.invermoriston.org On main Loch Ness road A82
7/L19 between Inverness and Fort Augustus, this is the best bit. River Moriston tumbles
under an ancient bridge. Perfectly Highland. Ledges for picnics, invigorating pools,
ozone-friendly. Nice beech woods. Follow signs 'Columba's Well', go under the
bridge to the 'wee house'. Tavern/bistro nearby (1180/INNS).

1690 **Dulsie Bridge** near Nairn 16km south of Nairn on the A939 to Grantown, this
8/N18 locally revered beauty spot is fabulous for summer swimming. The ancient arched
bridge spans the rocky gorge of the Findhorn (again see Randolph's Leap, above)
and there are ledges and even sandy beaches for picnics and from which to launch
yourself or paddle into the peaty waters. Fab in summer '09.

Strathcarron near Bonar Bridge Pick your spot (1593/GLENS).

Good Places To Take Kids

CENTRAL

1691
1/XA4
ECO

✓✓✓ **Edinburgh Zoo** www.edinburghzoo.org.uk · 0131 334 9171 · **Corstorphine Road, Edinburgh** 4km west of Princes St. A large and long-established zoo which is always evolving and where the natural world from the poles to the plains of Africa is ranged around Corstorphine Hill. Enough huge/exotic/ghastly creatures and friendly, amusing ones to fill an overstimulated day. The Budongo Trail chimp enclosure is first class. The penguins do their famous parade at 2.15pm. The beavers are brill, the koalas are cool as... Shop stocked with PC toys and souvenirs. Café. Open all year 7 days, Apr-Sep 9am-6pm, Oct-Mar till 5pm, Nov-Feb till 4.30pm.

✓✓ **Our Dynamic Earth** 0131 550 7800 · Holyrood Road, Edinburgh Edinburgh's major kids' attraction. Report 405/MAIN ATTRACTIONS.

✓✓ **Museum of Childhood** 0131 529 414242 · High Street, Edinburgh An Aladdin's cave of toys for all ages. 415/OTHER ATTRACTIONS.

1692
10/Q25

✓ **Edinburgh Butterfly Farm & Insect World** 0131 663 4932 · near **Dalkeith** · www.edinburgh-butterfly-world.co.uk On A7, signed Eskbank/ Galashiels from ring road (1km). Part of a garden centre complex. Beauty and the beasties in a creepy-crawly world: delightful butterflies but kids are more impressed by the glowing scorpions, locusts, iguanas and other assorted uglies. Red-kneed tarantula not for the faint hearted. 7 days, 9.30am-5.30pm (10am-5pm in winter).

✓ **Glasgow Science Centre** www.glasgowsciencecentre.org · 0141 420 5000 One of Glasgow's most flash attractions. State-of-the-art interactive, landmark tower and Imax. Report: 689/MAIN ATTRACTIONS.

1693
1/XA4

✓ **Gorgie City Farm** www.gorgiecityfarm.org.uk · 0131 337 4202 · 57 **Gorgie Road, Edinburgh** A working farm on busy road in the heart of the city. Friendly domestic animals and people, garden, great playground and café. All year 9am-4.30pm (4pm in winter). Free. Green and fluffy in the concrete jungle.

1694
10/R25

Yellowcraigs near Dirleton Beautiful beach 35km east of Edinburgh via A1, the A198, though Dirleton village then right, for 2km. Lovely, scenic beach and dunes (447/EDINBURGH BEACHES). Recent Treasure Island play pond in the woods is great for kids. Activity and sea air!

1695
1/D2

The Edinburgh Dungeon www.thedungeons.com · 0131 240 1000 · 31 Market Street, Edinburgh Multimillion très contrived experience takes you through a ghoulish history of Scottish nasties. Hammy of course, but kids will love the monorail. Times vary.

1696
9/K26

Kelburn Country Centre www.kelburncountrycentre.com · 01475 568685 · **Largs** 2km south of Largs on A78. Riding school, gardens, woodland walks up the Kelburn Glen and a visitor section with shops/exhibits/cafés. Wooden stockade for clambering kids; indoor playbarn with quite scary slides. Falconry displays (those long-suffering owls). The Plaisance indeed a pleasant place and the Secret Forest beckons. Stock up on ice cream at Nardini's famous caff (777/AYRSHIRE RESTAURANTS). 7 days 10am-6pm. Apr-Oct. Grounds only in winter 11-dusk.

✓✓ **Falkirk Wheel** Falkirk 4/MAIN ATTRACTIONS.

FIFE & DUNDEE

1697
10/P25

✔ **Deep Sea World** www.deepseaworld.com · 01383 411880 · **North Queensferry** The aquarium in a quarry which may be reaching its swim-by date. Habitats are viewed from a conveyor belt where you can stare at the fish as diverse divers teem around and above you. Maximum hard sell to this all-weather attraction 'the shark capital', but kids like it even when they've been queueing for aeons. Cute seals and sharp sharks! Café is fairly awful, but nice views. Open all year 7 days 10am-5pm; weekends till 6pm (last entry 1 hour before).

1698
10/Q23

✔ **Sensation** www.sensation.org.uk · 01382 228800 · **Dundee** Greenmarket across roundabout from Discovery Point and adjacent DCA (2148/GALLERIES). Purpose-built indoor info-tainment, this is an innovative and interactive games room with a message. 7 days 10am-5pm. Average visit time 2-3 hours.

1699
10/Q23
☕

✔ **Verdant Works** 01382 225282 · **West Henderson's Wynd, Dundee** Near Westport. Heritage museum that recreates workings of a jute mill. Sounds dull, but brilliant for kids and grown-ups. Report: 2119/MUSEUMS.

1700
10/R23

✔ **Craigton Park** 01334 473666 · **St Andrews** 3km southwest of St Andrews on the Pitscottie road (enter via Dukes Golf Course). An oasis of fun: bouncy castles, trampolines, putting, crazy golf, boating lake, a train through the grounds, adventure playgrounds and glasshouses. A perfect day's amusement especially for nippers. Easter-Sep 9am-4pm. Entrance charge covers all attractions.

1701
10/Q23

✔ **Cairnie Fruit Farm & Maze** 01334 655610 · **near Cupar** Leave town by minor road from main street heading past the hospital; signed (4km), or from main A92; signed near Kilmany (3km). A fruit and farm shop/café (1468/FARM SHOPS); hugely poppular due to extensive play area using farm materials to amuse kids and get them countrified. The maze in the maize field is major. Then there's strawberries for tea! May-Dec 9.30am-6pm (10am-5pm Sep-Dec and closed Mon).

1702
10/Q23

Camperdown Park www.camperdownpark.com · **Dundee** Large park just off the ring-road (Kingsway and A923 to Coupar Angus) with a wildlife centre and nearby play complex. Animal-handling at weekends. Over 80 species: bats, bears and wolves! All year; centre 10am-4.30pm, earlier in winter (1552/TOWN PARKS).

SOUTH & SOUTH WEST

1703
11/M31
ECO

✔✔ **Cream o' Galloway** www.creamogalloway.co.uk · **Rainton** There is something inherently good about a visitor attraction tbased on the incontrovertible fact that human beings love ice cream; especially presented with a 'pure and simple' message, organic café, burger barn, herb garden and fab adventure playground in the woods, part of 5km of child-friendly nature trails. Let's hear it for cows! All year 10am-6pm. Allow a few hours. Report: 1436/ICE CREAM.

1704
9/L27

✔ **Kidz Play** www.kidz-play.co.uk · 01292 475215 · **Prestwick** Off main street at Station Road, past station to beach and to right. Big shed soft play area for kids. Everything the little blighters will like in the throwing-themselves-around department. Shriek city. 7 days 9.30am-7pm.

1705
10/L27

✔ **Loudoun Castle** www.loudouncastle.co.uk · **near Galston** Theme park with big ambitions south of Glasgow. Off A71 Kilmarnock-Edinburgh road or from Glasgow via M77, then A719. Behind the ruins of the said Loudoun Castle (burned out in 1941), a fairground which includes the 'largest carousel in Europe', the Rat rollercoaster and the terrifying Barnstormer, has been transplanted in the old walled garden. Farm area. Nice setting. Open Easter-Aug.

1706
10/M25
Palacerigg Country Park www.northlan.gov.uk · 01236 720047 · **Cumbernauld** 6km east of Cumbernauld off A801. 740 acres of parkland; ranger service, nature trails, picnic area and kids' farm with rare breeds. Golf course and putting green. Changing exhibits about forestry, conservation, etc. Open all year 7 days; daylight hours. Café.

✓ ✓ **Drumlanrig Castle** near Dumfries 1533/COUNTRY PARKS.

NORTH EAST

1707
8/R17
✓ **Macduff Marine Aquarium** www.macduff-aquarium.org.uk On the seafront east of the harbour, a family attraction for this Moray Firth port. Small but under-rated, perhaps because neighbouring Banff gets more attention from tourists, though Duff House (2153/GALLERIES) gets fewer visitors than this child-friendly sea-life centre. All fish seem curiously happy with their lot and content to educate and entertain. Open all year 10am-5pm (last admission 4.15pm).

1708
8/S20
✓ **Storybook Glen** www.storybookglenaberdeen.co.uk · near Aberdeen Fibreglass fantasy land in verdant glen 16km south of Aberdeen via B9077, the South Deeside road, a nice drive. Characters from every fairy tale and nursery story dotted around 20-acre park. Their fixed manic stares give them a spooky resemblance to people you know. Older kids may find it tame: no guns, no big technology but nice for little 'uns. Indoor play area and quite wonderful gardens. 7 days, 10am-6pm (5pm in winter), weather permitting.

1709
8/T18
Aden www.aberdeenshire.gov.uk · **Mintlaw** (Pronounced 'Ah-den'). Country park just beyond Mintlaw on A950 16km from Peterhead. Former grounds of mansion with walks and organised activities and events. Farm buildings converted into Farming Heritage Centre, café, etc. Adventure playground. All year.

HIGHLANDS & ISLANDS

1710
7/N19
ECO
✓ **The Cairngorm Reindeer Herd** 01479 861228 · **Glenmore, near Aviemore** · www.reindeer-company.demon.co.uk At Glenmore Forest Park 12km Aviemore along Coylumbridge Rd, 100m behind Glenmore visitor centre. Stop at centre (shop, exhibition) to buy tickets and follow the guide in your vehicle up the mountain. From here, 20-minute walk. Real reindeer aplenty in authentic free-ranging habitat (when they come down off the cloudy hillside in winter with snow all around). They've come a long way from Sweden (in 1952). 1 hour 30 minute trip. They are so... small. 11am all year plus 2.30pm in summer. Wear appropriate footwear and phone if weather looks threatening.

1711
7/N19
✓ **Leault Farm** www.leaultfarm.co.uk · 01540 651310 · **near Kincraig** On the A9 but easier to find from the sign 1km south of Kincraig on the B9152. Working farm with daily sheepdog trials showing an extraordinary facility with dogs and sheep (and ducks). A great spectacle and totally authentic in this setting. Usually 4pm (possibly other times). Closed Sat. Sometimes pups to love.

1712
7/N19
✓ **Landmark Centre** www.landmark-centre.co.uk · 01479 841614 · **Carrbridge** A purpose-built tourist centre with audiovisual displays and a great deal of shopping. Great for kids messing about in the woods on slides, in a 'maze', etc, in a large adventure playground, Microworld or (especially squealy) the Wildwater Coaster. The Tower may be too much for Granny but there are fine forest views. Open all year 7 days till 6pm (5pm in winter, 7pm mid Jul-mid Aug). Disappointing caff.

1713
7/N19
ECO

The Highland Wildlife Park www.highlandwildlifepark.org · Kincraig · 01540 651270 On B9152 Aviemore-Kingussie. Large drive-through 'reserve' run by Royal Zoological Society with wandering herds of deer, bison, etc and pens of other animals. 'Habitats', but mostly cages. Cute, vicious little wildcats! Mercedes, UK's only captive polar bear on her tod in new 4-acre enclosure but the new Amur tiger cubs do have each other. Must be time to bring back bears, let the wolves go free and liven up the caravan parks. Open 10am-5pm (Jul/Aug 6pm, winter 4pm).

1714
9/F26
ECO

Islay Wildlife Information & Field Centre www.islay.co.uk · 01496 850288 · Port Charlotte Fascinating wildlife centre, activities and day trips. (1757/WILDLIFE; 2280/ISLAY). Excellent for getting kids interested in wildlife. Then go find it! Apr-Oct 10am-4pm. Closed Sat (Jul/Aug 7 days).

1715
9/H22

Mull Railway & Torosay Castle 01680 812494 · Mull This long-established chugalong train from the ferry at Craignure to Torosay Gardens and Castle (a 20-minute journey) is a lovely way to get there and lovely when you do (1770/CASTLES). It's so dinky, a bit of a must, really! Apr-Oct.

1716
9/H23
ECO

The Scottish Sealife Sanctuary www.sealsanctuary.co.uk · 01631 720386 · Oban 16km north on the A828. On the shore of Loch Creran, one of the oldest UK waterworlds still the best. Environmentally conscientious, they 'rescue' seals and house numerous aquatic life. Various aquaria, all kinds of fish going round, multi-level viewing otter enclosure and the seal thing. Feeding times posted: a theatrical sight. Café/shop/adventure playground. Summer, 10am-6pm. Check winter hours.

1717
9/G21
ECO

Natural History Centre www.ardnamurchannaturalhistorycentre.co.uk · 01972 500209 · Ardnamurchan A861 Strontian, B8007 Glenmore 14km. Photographer Michael McGregor's award-winning interactive exhibition (under different owners). Kids enjoy, adults impressed. A walk-through of wildlife including live pine martens (if you're lucky) and CCTV of more cautious creatures. Antler Tearoom. Apr-Oct Mon-Sat 10.30am-5.30pm, Sun from 12noon.

1718
8/N19

Loch Insh www.lochinsh.com · 01540 561272 · Kincraig Watersports centre but much more on B970 2km from Kincraig (near Kingussie and the A9). Beautiful loch and mountain setting, 2 small beaches and gentle water Lots of instruction available, wildlife boat trips, biking possibilites and Kids' Kingdom small adventure playground. Good café and terrace overlooking loch; the Boath House (991/BEST HIGHLAND RESTAURANTS). All-round active day out; there are chalets to stay longer.

The Best Places To See Birds

See p. 305–06 for Wildlife Reserves, many of which are good for bird-watching.

1719
6/K13

✓✓ **Handa Island** www.swt.org.uk · near Scourie Take the boat from Tarbet Pier 6km off A894 5km north of Scourie and land on a beautiful island run as a nature reserve by the Scottish Wildlife Trust. Boats (Apr-early Sep though fewer birds after Aug) are continuous depending on demand. Crossing 30 minutes. Small reception hut and 2.5km walk over island to cliffs which rise 350m and are layered in colonies: fulmars, shags and the UK's largest colony of guillemots. Allow 3-4 hours. Though you must take care not to disturb the birds, you'll be eye to eye with seals and bill to bill with razorbills. Eat at the seafood café on the cove when you return (1343/SEAFOOD RESTAURANTS). Mon-Sat. Last return 5pm.

1720
11/P30
ADMISSION
ECO

✓✓ **Caerlaverock** www.wwt.org.uk · near Dumfries 17km south on B725 near Bankend, signed from road. The WWT Caerlaverock Wetlands Centre (01387 770200) is an excellent place to see whooper swans, barnacle geese and more (countless hides, observatories, viewing towers). Has Fair Trade café as well as farmhouse-style accommodation for up to 14. More than just birds too: natterjack toads, badgers so not just for twitchers. Eastpark Farm, Caerlaverock. Centre open daily all year 10am-5pm.

1721
9/F22

✓✓ **Lunga & The Treshnish Islands** www.hebrideantrust.org · off Mull Sail from Iona or Fionnphort or Ulva ferry on Mull to these uninhabited islands on a 5/6-hour excursion which probably takes in Staffa and Fingal's Cave. Best time is May-Jul when birds are breeding. Talk of pufflings not making it because parents can't find sand eels seems premature here. Some trips allow 3 hours on Lunga. Razorbills, guillemots and a carpet of puffins oblivious to your presence. This is a memorable day. Boat trips (Ulva Ferry 08000 858786; or 01681 700338 from Fionnphort) from Iona or Oban. Trips dependent on sea conditions.

1722
10/R24

✓✓ **Isle of May** www.nlb.org.uk · Firth of Forth Island at mouth of Forth off Crail/ Anstruther reached by daily boat trip from Anstruther Harbour (01333 310054), May-Oct 9am-2.30pm depending on tides. Boats hold 40-50; trip 45 minutes; allows 3 hours ashore. Or quicker, smaller *Osprey Rib*. Can reserve the day before. Often no-shows so possible there and then. Island (including isthmus to Rona) 1.5km x 0.5km. Info centre and resident wardens. See guillemots, razorbills and kittiwakes on cliffs and shags, terns and thousands of puffins. Most populations increasing. This place is strange as well as beautiful. The puffins in early summer are, as always, engaging.

1723
10/R25

✓✓ **The Bass Rock** www.nlb.org.uk · 01620 892838 · off North Berwick 'Temple of gannets'. A guano-encrusted massif sticking out of the Forth: their largest island colony in the world. Davie Balfour was imprisoned here in RLS's *Catriona* (aka *Kidnapped II*). A variety of weather-dependent boat trips available May-Sep, including landings and 'safaris'. Extraordinary birds, extraordinary experience. Phone for details: 01620 890202, the Seabird Centre (below).

1724
10/P22
ECO

✓✓ **Loch of the Lowes** Dunkeld 4km northeast Dunkeld on A923 to Blairgowrie. Superbly managed (Scottish Wildlife Trust) site with double-floored hide (always open) and new hide (same hours as visitor centre) and permanent binoculars. Main attractions are the captivating ospreys (from early Apr-Aug). Nest 100m over loch and clearly visible. Their revival (almost 300 pairs now in UK) is well documented, including diary of movements, breeding history, etc. Also the near-at-hand endless fascination of watching wild birds including woodpeckers, and red squirrels feeding outside the picture window is a real treat. Great walks nearby (1990/GLEN WALKS) including to the other loch (Ordie).

1725
8/N19
ECO

✓✓ **Loch Garten** www.lochgarten.co.uk · Boat of Garten 3km village off B970 into Abernethy Forest. Famous for the ospreys and signed from all round. Best Apr-Jun. 2 car parks: the first has nature trails through Scots Pine woods and around loch; other has visitor centre with the main hide 250m away: TV screens, binoculars, other wild-bird viewing and informed chat. Here since 1954, that first pair have done wonders for local tourism – in fact, they and the RSPB and the army of determined volunteers practically invented eco-tourism! Och, but they are magnificent.

1726
10/Q25
ECO

✔ **The Scottish Ornithologists' Club House** www.the-soc.org.uk ·
near Aberlady On the A198 on the left going into Aberlady from Edinburgh
side, opposite Gosford Estate. Not a birdwatching site per se (though between the
Lagoon and the Seabird Centre, below and near Aberlady Reserve 2km), but an
archive and library and resource centre for all things related to and for lovers of
Scottish birds. Beautiful, light modern building looks across bay to reserve. Art
exhibitions and much to browse. Friendly staff. The Society published the definitive book *Birds of Scotland*. Open 10am-4pm (12-6pm weekends in summer). Go in
October, late afternoon, when the geese come in.

1727
10/Q25

✔ **The Lagoon** Musselburgh On east edge of town behind the racecourse
(follow road round, take turn-off signed Race Course Parking) at the estuarine
mouth of the River Esk. Waders, sea birds, ducks aplenty and often interesting
migrants on the mudflats and wide littoral. The Lagoon itself is a man-made pond
behind with hide and attracts big populations (both birds and binocs). This is the
nearest diverse-species area to Edinburgh (15km) and is one of the most significant migrant stopovers in the UK.

1728
10/S21

✔ **Fowlsheugh** www.rspb.org.uk · near Stonehaven 8km south of
Stonehaven and signed from A92 with path from Crawton. Sea-bird city on
2km of red sandstone cliffs up to 200 feet high; take great care. 80,000 pairs of 6
species especially guillemots, kittiwakes, razorbills and also fulmar, shag, puffins.
Possible to view the birds without disturbing them and see the 'layers' they
occupy on the cliff face. Best seen May-Jul.

1729
9/F25
ECO

✔ **Loch Gruinart, Loch Indaal** Islay RSPB reserve. Take A847 at Bridgend
then B8017 turning north and right for Gruinart. The mudflats and fields at
the head of the loch provide winter grazing for huge flocks of Barnacle and Green-
land geese. They arrive, as do flocks of fellow bird-watchers, in late Oct. Hides and
good vantage points near road. Don't miss beautiful Saligo Bay (1574/BEACHES).
The Rhinns and the Oa in the south also sustain a huge variety of bird life.

1730
3/P10

✔ **Marwick Head** www.rspb.org.uk · Orkney Mainland 40km northwest
of Kirkwall, via Finstown and Dounby; take left at Birsay after Loch of Isbister
cross the B9056 and park at Cumlaquoy. A 4km circular walk. Spectacular sea bird
breeding colony on 100m cliffs and nearby at the Loons Reserve, wet meadowland,
8 species of duck and many waders. Orkney sites include the Noup cliffs on
Westray, North Hill on Papa Westray and Copinsay, 3km east of the mainland.

1731
9/H22

Isle of Mull www.isle.of.mull.com Sea eagles. Since the reintroduction of
these magnificent eagles, there is now a hide with CCTV viewing. By appointment
only. Site changes every year. Contact Forest Enterprise (01631 566155) or ask at
the tourist information centre.

1732
3/Q10

Orkney Puffins Wildabout tours (01856 851011). Or go solo at Marwick Head
(see above), Brough of Birsay and Westray (which gets them first); check Kirkwall
tourist information centre for latest.

1733
10/R25
ECO

Scottish Seabird Centre www.seabird.org · 01620 890202 · North
Berwick Award-winning, interactive visitor attraction near Harbour overlooking
Bass Rock and Fidra (above). If you don't want to go out there, video and other
state-of-the-art technology makes you feel as if the birds are next to you. Viewing
deck for dramatic perspective of gannets diving (140kmph!) Excellent teashop
(seafood especially). 10am-6pm (4pm winter/5.30pm weekends).

1734 **Montrose Basin Wildlife Centre** www.swt.org.uk · 01674 676336 1.5km
10/S22 south of Montrose on the A92 to Arbroath. Accessible Scottish Wildlife Trust centre overlooks estuarine basin hosting residents and migrants. Good for twitchers
and kids. And autumn geese. Apr-Oct daily 10.30am-5pm. Call for winter hours.

1735 **Forsinard Nature Reserve** www.caithness.org · 01641 571225 44km from
6/N13 Helmsdale on the A897, or train stops on route to Wick/Thurso. RSPB (proposed
World Heritage Site) reserve, acquired after public appeal. 19,000 hectares of the
Flow Country and its birds: divers, plovers, merlins and hen harriers (CCTV pics).
Guided walks available. Reserve open all year; visitor centre Apr-Oct 9am-5.30pm.

1736 **Loch of Kinnordy** www.rspb.org.uk · Kirriemuir 4km west of town on B951,
10/Q22 an easily accessible site with 3 hides overlooking loch and wetland area managed
by RSPB. Geese in late autumn, gulls aplenty; always tickworthy. You may see the
vanishing ruglet butterfly.

1737 **Strathbeg** www.rspb.org.uk · near Fraserburgh 12km south off the A952
8/T17 Fraserburgh-Peterhead road, signed 'Nature Reserve' at Crimond. Wide, shallow
loch close to coastline, a 'magnet for migrating wildfowl'. Marsh/fen, dune and
meadow habitats. In winter 30,000 geese/widgeon/mallard/swans and occasional
rarities like cranes and egrets. Binoculars in reception centre and hides.

1738 **Troup Head** between Macduff and Fraserburgh, Moray Firth Near the
8/S17 cliff-clinging villages of Crovie and *Local Hero* Pennan on the coastal B9031.
Fantastic airy walk from the former (2042/COASTAL WALKS) or (closer) directly from
the road signed for Northfield following RSPB signs for 2km, then a 1.5km stroll
from car park. Puffins, kittiwakes, the whole shebang; and dolphins.

1739 **Inshriach Garden Centre** near Aviemore A (very good) garden centre, yes
8/M20 and tearoom (2199/GARDEN CENTRES) but also one of the best places to watch wild
☕ birds who swarm round the feeders hanging in the woods over the gorge. Voted
the most popular site by RSPB members '08. Red squirrels and great cakes are
other good reasons for going. Mar-Oct 10am-5pm. Closed Wed.

Where To See Dolphins, Whales, Porpoises & Seals

✓✓ *The coast around the North of Scotland offers some of the best places in
Europe from which to see whales and dolphins and, more ubiquitously, seals.
You don't have to go on boat trips, though of course you get closer, the boatman will
know where to find them and the trip itself can be exhilarating. Good operators are
listed below. Dolphins are most active on a rising tide especially May-Sep.*

MORAY & CROMARTY FIRTHS (near Inverness)
The best area in Scotland. The population of bottlenose dolphins in this area well
exceeds 100 and they can be seen all year (though mostly Jun-Sep).

1740 **The Dolphins & Seals of the Moray Firth Centre** 01463 731866 or 01343
7/M18 820339 Just north of the Kessock Bridge on the A9. Underwater microphones
pick up the chatterings of dolphins and porpoises and there's always somebody
there to explain. They keep an up-to-date list of recent sightings and all cruises
available. Summer only Mon-Sat 9.30am-4.30pm (closes for lunch 12.30-1pm).

1741
7/M17
Cromarty Any vantage around town is good especially South Sutor for coastal walk and an old lighthouse cottage has been converted into a research station run by Aberdeen University. **Chanonry Point, Fortrose**, through the golf course, east end of point beyond lighthouse is the *best* place to see dolphins from land in Britain. Occasional sightings can also be seen at **Balintore**, opposite Seaboard Memorial Hall; **Tarbert Ness** beyond **Portmahomack**, end of path through reserve further out along the Moray Firth possible at **Burghead**, **Lossiemouth** and **Buckie**, **Spey Bay** and **Portknockie**. Also check the Dolphin Space Programme, an accreditation scheme for boat operators: www.dolphinspace.org

NORTH WEST
On the west coast, especially near Gairloch the following places may offer sightings of orcas, dolphins and minke whales mainly in summer.

1742
7/H16
Rubha Reidh near Gairloch 20km north of Melvaig (unclassified road). Near Carn Dearg Youth Hostel west of Lonemore. Where road turns inland is good spot.

1743
6/J16
Greenstone Point north of Laide Off A832 (unclassified road) through Mellon Udrigle round Gruinard Bay. Harbour porpoises Apr-Dec, minke whales May-Oct.

1744
7/H16
Red Point of Gairloch By B8056 via Badachro round Loch Gairloch. High ground looking over North Minch and south to Loch Torridon. Harbour porpoises often along this coast. Good pub on the way (1313/GASTROPUBS).

1745
7/F18
Rubha Hunish Skye The far northwest finger of Skye. Walk from Duntulm Castle or Flodigarry. Dolphins and minke whales in autumn.

OTHER PLACES
1746 4/V4
Mousa Sound Shetland 20km south of Lerwick (1804/PREHISTORIC SITES).

1747
9/G21
Ardnamurchan The Point The most westerly point (and lighthouse) on this wildly beautiful peninsula. Go to end of road or park near Sanna Beach and walk round. Sanna Beach worth going to just to walk the strand. Visitor centre; tearoom.

1748
5/E14
Stornoway Isle of Lewis Heading out of town for Eye Peninsula, at Holm near Sandwick south of A866 or from Bayble Bay (all within walking distance).

The Most Recommended Sealife Cruises

Eco Ventures www.ecoventures.co.uk · 01381 600323 · **Cromarty** Intimate and informative tours, but pricey. 2 trips per day all year. Booking essential.

Moray Firth Cruises www.inverness-dolphin-cruises.co.uk · 01463 717900 · **Inverness** 4 trips per day Mar-Oct.

Gemini Explorer www.geminiexplorer.co.uk · 07747 626280 · **Buckie** More Moray Firth cruising in former lifeboat. Good facilities.

Gairloch Marine Life Centre & Cruises 01445 712636 · **Gairloch** Long-established and eco-credible operator in interesting West Coast area.

Summer Isles Cruises www.summer-isles-cruises.co.uk · 01854 622200 · **Achiltibuie** Seals and seabirds abound. 2 trips per day on large MV.

Hebridean Wildlife Cruises www.southernhebrides.com · 01680 814260 · Oban Company with a choice of bigger boats operating out of Oban and other west-coast locations. Go all over including St Kilda (2212/MAGICAL ISLANDS).

Wildlife Cruises www.jogferry.co.uk · 01955 611353 · John o' Groats Seals, puffins, seabirds. 2.30pm daily Jun-Sep. Large panoramic boat. Trips to Orkney.

Sea.Fari Adventures www.seafari.co.uk · Edinburgh · 0131 331 5000 & Oban · 01852 300003 & Skye · 01471 833316 Sealife adventure: eco-tours and trips in fast, inflatable boats out of **Easdale, Isle of Seil** 25km south Oban.

ON THE ISLANDS
Sea-Life Surveys www.sealifesurveys.com · Mull · 01688 302916 Various packages from relaxed half-hour to a more intense 8-hour. Good percentage of porpoise, dolphin and whale sightings.

Turus Mara www.turusmara.com · 08000 858786 · Mull Daytrips from Ulva Ferry. Various itineraries taking in bird colonies of Treshnish Isles, Staffa and Iona. Dolphins, whales, puffins and seals.

Whale Watching 01688 400264 · Dervaig, Mull 12-passenger MV *Flamer* leaves daily from Croig 5km Dervaig. Full day at sea.

Shetland Wildlife & The Company of Whales 01950 422483 · Shetland · www.shetlandwildlife.co.uk From day trips to 7-day wildlife holidays. Sealife, birds, whales and otters. Very professional adventuring.

Seabirds-and-seals.com 01595 540224 · Shetland Award-winning wildlife adventure cruises.

Island Cruising www.island-cruising.com · 01851 672381 · Lewis Wildlife, birdwatching and diving around Western Isles and St Kilda (2212/MAGICAL ISLANDS).

Seatrek www.seatrek.co.uk · 01851 672469 · Uig, Lewis Various excursions from the far west and into the west, including St Kilda (2212/MAGICAL ISLANDS).

Seaprobe Atlantis 0800 9804846 · Skye Based at Kyle; stays around Kyle of Lochalsh (conservation) area. Sit underwater in the gallery for better viewing.

WILDLIFE TOURS
Island Encounter Wildlife Safaris www.mullwildlife.co.uk · 01680 300441 · Mull All-day tour with local expert. Possible sightings of otters, eagles, seals and falcons. Numerous pick-up points including ferry terminals.

Isle of Mull Wildlife Expeditions www.torrbuan.com · 01688 500121 · Mull Long-established day-long trips. Eagles, sea eagles et al. They know where to go.

Wildabout www.wildaboutorkney.com · 01856 851011 · Orkney Various trips with experienced guides. Wildlife plus history and folklore. Interactive.

Out & About Tours 01851 612288 · Lewis Former countryside ranger leads groups of all sizes on 4/7-night guided walks and day trips of Lewis and Harris. Experience the landscape, culture and wildlife of the islands.

Calum's Seal Trips www.calums-sealtrips.com · 01599 544306 · **Plockton** Wildlife watching doesn't get tamer than this (or the animals) but nice for the kids and the coast around Plockton is stunning. You may see an otter and Calum always knows where the dolphins are. Check locally for departures.

Otters can be seen all over the northwest Highlands in sheltered inlets, especially early morning and late evening and on an ebb tide. Skye is one of best places in Europe to see them. Go with:

International Otter Survival Fund www.otter.org · 01471 822487 · **Broadford** They organise courses and trips for small numbers and 1-to-1 for all wildlife and might point you in the right direction. Mon-Fri.

Otter Haven www.forestry.gov.uk · **Kylerhea** Basically a viewing hide with CCTV, binoculars and a knowledgeable warden (not always there). Seabirds and seals too and a forest walk. 500m walk along a track from car park signposted on road out of Kylerhea (and from the ferry from Glenelg; 7/JOURNEYS).

▬ Great Wildlife Reserves

These wildlife reserves are not merely bird-watching places. Most of them are easy to get to from major centres; none requires permits.

1749
10/S25
✓✓ **St Abb's Head** www.nlb.org.uk · near Berwick 9km north of Eyemouth and 10km east of main A1. Spectacular cliff scenery (2038/COASTAL WALKS), a huge sea bird colony, rich marine life and varied flora. Good view from top of stacks, geos and cliff face full of serried ranks of guillemot, kittiwake, razorbill, etc. Hanging gardens of grasses and campion. Behind cliffs, grassland rolls down to the Mire Loch and its varied habitat of bird, insect, butterfly life and vegetation. The coffee shop at the car park does a mean scone.

1750
8/T19
ECO
✓✓ **Sands Of Forvie & The Ythan Estuary** www.jncc.gov.uk · Newburgh 25km north Aberdeen. Cross bridge outside Newburgh on A975 to Cruden Bay and park. Path follows Ythan estuary, bears north and enters the largest undisturbed dune system in the UK. Dunes in every aspect of formation. Collieston, a 17/18th-century fishing village, is 5km away. These habitats support the largest population of eiders in UK (especially Jun) and huge numbers of terns. It's easy to get lost here, so get lost!

1751
7/J17
ECO
✓ **Beinn Eighe** Bounded by the A832 south from Gairloch and A896 west of Kinlochewe, this first National Nature Reserve in Britain includes a remaining fragments of old Caledonian pinewood on the south shore of Loch Maree (largest in West Highlands) and rises to the rugged tops with their spectacular views and varied geology. Excellent wood and mountain trails with starts on both roads – from A832 on Loch Maree side there are woodland strolls. Starts to the Beinn and to Liatach are from the A896 Glen Torridon road (1648/VIEWS, 1630/SCENIC ROUTES). There are visitor centres on both roads.

1752
10/R25
ECO
John Muir Country Park www.eastlothian.gov.uk · **Dunbar** Vast park between Dunbar and North Berwick named after the Dunbar-born father of the conservation movement. Includes estuary of the Tyne; the park is also known as Tyninghame, and see 445/EDINBURGH BEACHES. Diverse habitats: cliffs, sand spits and woodland. Many bird species. Crabs, lichens, sea and marsh plants. Enter at

east extremity of Dunbar at Belhaven, off the B6370 from A1; or off A198 to North Berwick 3km from A1. Or better, walk from Dunbar by cliff-top trail (2km+).

1753 **Lochwinnoch** www.lochwinnoch.info 30km southwest of Glasgow via M8
9/L26 junction 28A then A737 past Johnstone onto A760. Also from Largs 20km via
RSPB A760. Reserve just outside village on lochside and comprises wetland and wood-land habitats. A serious nature centre, incorporating an observation tower. Hides and marked trails; and a birds-spotted board. Shop and coffee shop. Events programme. Good for kids. Visitor centre open daily 10am-5pm.

1754 **Insh Marshes** www.rspb.org.uk · Kingussie 4km from town along B970 (past
7/M20 Ruthven Barracks, 1796/RUINS), 2500 acres of Spey floodplain run by RSPB. Trail (3km) marked out through meadow and wetland and a note of species to look out for (including 6 types of orchid, 7 'red list' birds and half the UK population of goldeneye). Also 2 hides (250m and 450m) high above marshes, vantage points to see waterfowl, birds of prey, otters and deer. Declared a National Nature Reserve in 2003.

1755 **Tentsmuir** www.forestry.gov.uk · **between Newport & Leuchars** North tip
10/R23 of Fife at the mouth of the Tay, reached from Tayport or Leuchars via the B945. Follow signs for Kinshaldy Beach taking road that winds for 4km over flat then forested land. Park (car park closes 8.30pm in summer, much earlier in winter) and cross dunes to broad strand. Walks in both direction: west back to Tayport, east to Leuchars. Also 4km circular walk of beach and forest. Hide 2km away at Ice House Pond. Seals often watch from waves and bask in summer. Lots of butterflies. Waders aplenty and, to the east, one of UK's most significant populations of eider. Most wildfowl offshore. (Ranger: 01334 473047.)

1756 **Vane Farm** www.rspb.org.uk · **Loch Leven** RSPB reserve on south shore of
10/P24 Loch Leven, beside and bisected by B9097 off junction 5 of M90. Easily reached
⛉ visitor centre with observation lounge and education/orientation facilities. Hide
ECO nearer loch side reached by tunnel under road. Nature trail on hill behind through heath and birchwood (2km circular). Good place to introduce kids to nature watching. Centre 10am-5pm. Hides always open. Events: 01577 862355.

1757 **Islay Wildlife Information & Field Centre** www.islay.co.uk · **Port**
9/F26 **Charlotte** Jam-packed info centre that's very 'hands-on' and interactive. Up-to-
ECO date displays of geology, natural history (rocks, skeletons, sealife tanks). Recent-sightings-of-wildlife board, flora and fauna lists, video room, reference library. Kids' area and activity days. Great for kids. Apr-Oct 10am-4pm. Closed Sat (Jun-Aug 10am-5pm 7 days).

1758 **Balranald** www.rspb.org.uk · **North Uist** West coast of North Uist reached by
5/C17 the road from Lochmaddy, then the Bayhead turnoff at Clachan Stores (10km north). This most western, most faraway reach is one of the last redoubts of the disappearing corncrake. Catch its calling while you can.

Section 8

Historical Places

scotland the best

The Best Castles

NTS: *Under the care of the National Trust for Scotland. Hours vary. Admission.*
HS: *Historic Scotland. Standard hours are: Apr-end Sep, 7 days 9.30am-6.30pm. Oct 9.30am-4.30pm. Winter hours vary. Admission.*

1759
10/N24
HS

✓ ✓ ✓ Stirling Castle www.historic-scotland.gov.uk · 01786 450000
Dominating the town and the plain, this like Edinburgh Castle is worth the hype and the history. And like Edinburgh, it's a timeless attraction that can withstand waves of tourism as it survived the centuries of warfare for which it was built. Despite this primary function, it does seem a very civilised billet, with peaceful gardens and rampart walks from which the views are excellent, including the aerial view of the ghost outline of the King's Knot Garden (the cup and saucer, as they're known locally). Includes the Renaissance Palace of James V and the Great Hall of James IV restored to full magnificence. Some rock legends have played here in summer and there are dinners.

1760
1/B4
HS

✓ ✓ ✓ Edinburgh Castle www.historic-scotland.gov.uk City centre. Impressive from any angle and all the more so from inside. Despite the tides of tourists and time, it still enthrals. Superb perspectives of the city and of Scottish history. Stone of Destiny & the Crown Jewels are the Big Attractions. Café and restaurant (superb views) with efficient, but uninspiring catering operation; open only castle hours and to castle visitors. Report: 397/MAIN ATTRACTIONS.

1761
8/N17
NTS

✓ ✓ Brodie Castle www.nts.org.uk · 0844 493 2100 · near Nairn
6-7km west of Forres off main A96. More a (Z-plan) tower house than a castle, dating from 1567. In this century and like Cawdor nearby, the subject of family feuding – now resolved and under the calming influence of the NTS, its guides discreetly passing over such unpleasantness. With a minimum of historical hocum, this 16/17th-century, but mainly Victorian, country house is furnished from rugs to moulded ceilings in the most excellent taste. Every picture (very few gloomies) bears examination. The nursery and nanny's room, the guest rooms, indeed all the rooms, are eminently habitable. I could live in the library. Tearoom and informal walks in grounds. An avenue leads to a lake; in spring the daffodils are famous. Hours reduced by cuts but Apr-Oct and last tour (register on arrival) at 3.30pm. Closed Thu-Sat Apr/May and Oct. Grounds open all year till sunset.

1762
9/K28
NTS

✓ ✓ Culzean Castle www.culzeanexperience.org · Maybole 24km
south of Ayr on A719. Impossible to convey here the scale and the scope of the house and the country park. Allow some hours especially for the grounds. Castle is more like a country house and you examine from the other side of a rope. From the 12th century, but rebuilt by Robert Adam in 1775, a time of soaring ambition, its grandeur is almost out of place in this exposed cliff-top position. It was designed for entertaining, and the oval staircase is magnificent. Wartime associations (especially with President Eisenhower) plus the enduring fascination of the aristocracy. 560 acres of grounds including cliff-top walk, formal gardens, walled garden, Swan Pond (a must) and Happy Valley. Harmonious home farm is visitor centre with exhibits and shop, etc. Caff could be better. Open Apr-Nov 10.30am-5pm. Park AYR. Many special events. Culzean is pronounced 'Cullane'. And you can stay (767/AYRSHIRE HOTELS).

1763
10/Q24
NTS

✓ ✓ Falkland Palace www.historic-scotland.gov.uk · Falkland Middle
of farming Fife, 15km from M90 junction 8. Not a castle at all, but the hunting palace of the Stewart dynasty. Despite its recreational rather than political role, it's one of the landmark buildings in Scottish history and in the 16th century

was the finest Renaissance building in Britain. They all came here for archery, falconry and hunting boar and deer on the Lomonds; and for Royal Tennis which is displayed and explained. Still occupied by the Crichton-Stewarts, the house is dark and rich and redolent of those days of 'dancin and deray at Falkland on the Grene'. Mar-Oct 10am-5pm. Sun 1-5pm. Plant shop and events programme. Great walks from village (1955/HILL WALKS, 1994/GLEN WALKS). See also 1385/TEAROOMS and 1311/GASTROPUBS. Home of the Big Tent Festival in July.

1764
6/Q12
✓ ✓ **Castle of Mey** www.castleofmey.org.uk · 01847 851473 · near Thurso Actually near John o' Groats (off A836), castles don't get further-
🖫 flung than this. Stunted trees, frequent wind and a wild coast but the Queen
ADMISSION Mother famously fell in love with this dilapidated house in 1952, filled it with
ATMOS things she found and was given and turned it into one of the most human and endearing of the Royal (if not all aristocratic) residences. Guides in every room tell the story and if you didn't love her already, you will when you leave. Lovely walled garden and animal centre in converted granary with farm animals including North Country sheep – great for kids. Excellent tearoom. Charles and Camilla still visit. May-Sep (closed 2 weeks early Aug).

1765
7/N17
✓ **Cawdor Castle** www.cawdorcastle.com · Cawdor, near Nairn & Inverness The mighty Cawdor of Macbeth fame. Most of the family clear off
ADMISSION for the summer and leave their romantic yet habitable and yes... stylish castle, sylvan grounds and gurgling Cawdor Burn to you. Pictures from Claude to Craigie Aitcheson, a modern kitchen as fascinating as the enormous one of yore. Even the 'tartan passage' is nicely done. The burn is the colour of tea. An easy drive (25km) to Brodie (above) means you can see 2 of Scotland's most appealing castles in one day. Gardens are gorgeous. May-early Oct, 7 days, 10am-5pm (last admission), 9-hole golf.

1766
10/N21
✓ **Blair Castle** www.blair-castle.co.uk · 01796 481207 · Blair Atholl Impressive from the A9, the castle and the landscape of the Dukes of Atholl
ADMISSION (present duke not present); 10km north of Pitlochry. Hugely popular; almost a holi-day camp atmosphere. Numbered rooms chock-full of 'collections': costumes, toys, plates, weapons, stag skulls, walking sticks – so many things! Upstairs, the more usual stuffed apartments including the Jacobite bits. Walk in the policies (includes Hercules Garden with tranquil ponds). Apr-Oct 9.30am-4.30pm (last admission) daily.

1767
10/Q22
✓ **Glamis** www.glamis-castle.co.uk · Forfar 8km from Forfar via A94 or off main A929, Dundee-Aberdeen road (turnoff 10km north of Dundee, a
ADMISSION picturesque approach). Fairy-tale castle in majestic setting. Seat of the Strathmore family (Queen Mum spent her childhood here) for 600 years; every room an example of the interior of a certain period. Guided tours (continuous/50 minutes' duration). Restaurant/gallery shop haven for tourists (and for an excellent bridie; 1432/BAKERS). Mar-Oct 10am-6pm, Nov/Dec 10.30am-4.30pm. Italian Gardens and nature trail well worth 500m walk.

1768
9/J27
✓ **Brodick Castle** www.nts.org.uk · Arran 4km from town (bike hire 01770 302868). Impressive, well-maintained landmark castle, exotic formal gardens
NTS and extensive grounds. Goat Fell in the background and the sea through the trees. Dating from 13th century and until the 1950s the home of the Dukes of Hamilton. An over-antlered hall leads to liveable rooms with portraits and heirlooms, an atmosphere of long-ago afternoons. Tangible sense of relief in the kitchens now all the entertaining is over. Robert the Bruce's cell is less convincing. Easter-Oct; check hours. Marvellous grounds open all year.

1769
9/H23
☕
ADMISSION

Duart Castle www.duartcastle.com · Mull A fabulous setting for the 13th-century ancestral seat of the Clan Maclean and home to Sir Lachlan and Lady Maclean. Quite a few modifications over the centuries as methods of defence grew in sophistication but with walls as thick as a truck and the sheer isolation of the place it must have doomed any prospect of attack from the outset. Now a happier, homelier place, the only attacking that gets done these days is on scones in the superior tearoom. Apr Sun-Thu 11am-4pm. May-Oct 10.30am-5.30pm. Event programme in summer months includes evening tours with Sir himself.

1770
9/H23
ADMISSION

Torosay Castle www.torosay.com · Mull 3km from Craignure and the ferry. A Victorian *arriviste* in this strategic corner where Duart Castle had ruled for centuries. Not many apartments open but who could blame them – this is a family home, endearing and eccentric especially their more recent history (like Dad's Loch Ness Monster fixation). The heirlooms are valuable because they have been cherished and there's a human proportion to the house and its contents which is rare in such places. The gardens, attributed to Lorimer, are fabulous, especially the Italianate Statue Walk, and are open all year. The Mull Light Railway from Craignure is one way to go (1715/KIDS), the woodland walk another. Tearoom. Apr-Oct 10.30am-5pm. Gardens all year 9am-7pm.

1771
7/F18
ADMISSION

Dunvegan Castle www.dunvegancastle.com · Skye 3km Dunvegan village. Romantic history and setting, though more baronial than castellate, the result of mid-19th-century restoration that incorporated the disparate parts. The castle and the 30,000-acre estate now presided over by the 30th MacLeod of MacLeod with the task of repairing the roof, etc from the controversial disposal of the Cuillin. Your visit also helps. Necessary crowd management leads you through a series of rooms where the Fairy Flag, displayed above a table of exquisite marquetry, has pride of place. Gardens, perhaps lovelier than the house, down to the loch; boats leave the jetty 'to see the seals'. Busy café and gift shop at gate side car park. Open Mar-Oct 10am-5.30pm. Check the website for winter hours (closed winter 09/10).

1772
7/J18
ADMISSION

Eilean Donan www.eileandonancastle.com · Dornie On A87, 13km before Kyle of Lochalsh. A calendar favourite, often depicted illuminated; and once, with a balloon hovering over, an abiding image from a BBC promo. Inside is a very decent slice of history for the price. The Banqueting Hall with its Pipers' Gallery must make for splendid dinner parties for the Macraes. Much military regalia amongst the bric-a-brac, but also the impressive Raasay Punchbowl partaken of by Johnson and Boswell. Mystical views from ramparts as well as the human story below the stairs. Apr-Oct 10am-5pm; Mar & Nov 10am-3pm & open from 9am Jul/Aug.

1773
10/N22
ADMISSION

Castle Menzies Weem www.menzies.org · near Aberfeldy In Tay valley with spectacular ridge behind (**Walks In The Weem Forest**, part of the Tummel Valley Forest Park; separate car park). On B846, 7km west of Aberfeldy, through Weem. The 16th-century stronghold of the Menzies (pronounced 'Mingiss'), one of Scotland's oldest clans. Sparsely furnished with odd clan memorabilia, the house nevertheless conveys more of a sense of Jacobite times than many more brimful of bric-a-brac. Bonnie Prince Charlie stopped here on the way to Culloden. Open farmland situation, so manured rather than manicured grounds. No tearoom but tea and Tunnocks. Apr-Oct 10.30am-5pm, Sun 2-5pm.

1774
10/P23
ADMISSION

Scone Palace www.scone-palace.co.uk · near Perth On A93 road to Blairgowrie and Braemar. A 'great house', the home to the Earl of Mansfield and gorgeous grounds. Famous for the Stone of Scone (aka The Stone of Destiny) on which the kings of Scots were crowned, and the Queen Vic bedroom. Maze and pinetum. Many contented animals greet you and a plethora of peacocks. Animal

Game Fair and bloody Runrig! Apr–Oct 7 days 9.30am-5pm (last admission). Fri only in winter 10am-4pm.

1775 **Kellie Castle** www.nts.org.uk · near **Pittenweem** Major castle in Fife.
10/R24 Dating from 14th century and restored by Robert Lorimer, his influence evidenced
NTS by magnificent plaster ceilings and furniture. Notable mural by Phoebe Anna Traquair. The gardens, nursery and kitchen recall all the old Victorian virtues. The old-fashioned roses still bloom for us. Apr–Oct 1-5pm (Fri-Tue).

1776 **Craigievar** www.nts.org.uk · near **Banchory** 15km north of main A93
8/R19 Aberdeen-Braemar road between Banchory and Aboyne. A classic tower house,
NTS perfect like a porcelain miniature. Random windows, turrets, balustrades. Set amongst sloping lawns and tall trees. Limited access to halt deterioration means you are spared the shuffling hordes, but don't go unless you are respecter of NTS conventions. Conservation is a serious business here.

1777 **Drum Castle (the Irvine Ancestral Home)** www.drum-castle.org · near
8/S20 **Banchory** Please forgive this, one of the longest entries in the book! 1km off main
NTS A93 Aberdeen-Braemar road between Banchory and Peterculter and 20km from
ATMOS Aberdeen centre. For 24 generations this has been the seat of the Irvines. Our lot! Gifted to one William De Irwin by Robert the Bruce, it combines the original keep (the oldest intact tower house in Scotland), a Jacobean mansion and Victorian expansionism. I have 3 times signed the book in the Irvine Room and wandered through the accumulated history hopeful of identifying with something. Hugh Irvine, the family 'artist' whose extravagant self-portrait as the Angel Gabriel raised eyebrows in 1810, seems more interesting than most of my soldiering forebears. Give me a window seat in that library! Grounds have an exceptional walled rose garden (Easter-Oct 10am-6pm; 1521/GARDENS). House: Easter-Oct 12.30-5.30pm (from 11am Jul-Aug). Last admission 4.15pm. Tower can be climbed for great views. Some pleasant walks from the car park.

1778 **Balmoral** near **Ballater** On main A93 between Ballater and Braemar. Limited
8/Q20 house access (ie only the ballroom: public functions are held here when they're in
ADMISSION residence and some corporates). Grounds (open Apr-Jul) with Albert's wonderful trees are more rewarding. For royalty rooters only, and if you like Landseers… Crathie Church along the main road has a good rose window, an altar of Iona marble. John Brown is somewhere in the old graveyard down track from visitor centre, the memorial on the hill is worth a climb for a poignant moment and view of the policies. Crathie services have never been quite the same Sunday attraction since Di and Fergie on a prince's arm. Daily 10am-5pm, last admission 4.30pm. Apr-Jul.

1779 **Dunrobin Castle** **Golspie** The largest house in the Highlands, the home of the
6/N15 Dukes of Sutherland who once owned more land than anyone else in the British
ADMISSION Empire. It's the first Duke who occupies an accursed place in Scots history for his inhumane replacement, in these vast tracts, of people with sheep. His statue stands on Ben Bhraggie above the town (1844/MONUMENTS). Living the life of imperial grandees, the Sutherlands transformed the castle into a *château* and filled it with their obscene wealth. Once there were 100 servants for a house party of 20 and it had 30 gardeners. Now it's a leisure industry. The gardens are still fabulous (1510/GARDENS). The castle and separate museum are open Apr-mid Oct, usually 10.30am-4pm. Check for times (01408 633177).

Crathes near **Banchory** 1505/GARDENS; 1834/COUNTRY HOUSES.
Fyvie **Aberdeenshire** 1833/COUNTRY HOUSES.

The Most Interesting Ruins

HS: *Under the care of Historic Scotland. Standard hours are: Apr-end Sep 7 days 9.30am-5.30pm. Oct-Mar Mon-Sat 9.30am-4.30pm. Some variations with individual properties; call 0131 668 8831 to check. All HS properties carry admission. 'Friends of Historic Scotland' membership: 0131 668 8600 or any of the manned sites (annual charge but then free admission). www.historic-scotland.gov.uk*

1780
10/N25
HS
✓ ✓ ✓ **Linlithgow Palace** www.historic-scotland.gov.uk Impressive from the M9 and the south approach to this the most agreeable of West Lothian towns, but don't confuse the magnificent Renaissance edifice with St Michael's Church next door, topped with its controversial crown and spear spire. From the Great Hall, built for James I, King of Scots, with its huge adjacent kitchens, and the North Range with loch views, you get a real impression of the lavish lifestyle of the court. Not as busy as some HS attractions on this page but it is fabulous. King's Fountain restoration has added to the Palace appeal.

1781
10/P30
HS
✓ ✓ **Caerlaverock** www.wwt.org.uk · near Dumfries 17km south by B725. Follow signs for Wetlands Reserve (1720/BIRDS) but go past road end (can walk between). Fairy-tale fortress within double moat and manicured lawns, the daunting frontage being the apex of an unusual triangular shape. Since 1270, the bastion of the Maxwells, the Wardens of the West Marches. Destroyed by Bruce, besieged in 1640. The whole castle experience is here. Kids' adventure park.

1782
10/S20
✓ **Dunnottar Castle** www.dunnottarcastle.co.uk · near Stonehaven 3km south of Stonehaven on the coast road just off the A92. Like Slains further north, the ruins are impressively and precariously perched on a cliff top. Historical links with Wallace, Mary, Queen of Scots (the odd night) and even Oliver Cromwell, whose Roundheads besieged it in 1650. Mel Gibson's *Hamlet* was filmed here (bet you don't remember the film) and the Crown Jewels of Scotland were once held here. 400m walk from car park. Can walk along cliff top from Stonehaven (2km). Apr-Oct 9am-6pm, Sun 2-5pm. Winter hours vary.

1783
9/H21
ATMOS
✓ **Castle Tioram** www.tioram.org · near Acharacle Romantic ruin where you don't need the saga to sense the place, and maybe the mystery is better than the history. 5km from A861 just north of Acharacle signed 'Dorlin'. Beautiful drive, 5km then park by Dorlin Cottage. Serenely beautiful shoreline then walk across a short causeway. Pronounced 'Cheerum'. Musical beach at nearby Kentra Bay (2040/COASTAL WALKS).

1784
8/P17
HS
✓ **Elgin Cathedral** www.historic-scotland.gov.uk · Elgin Follow signs in town centre. Set in a meadow by the river, a tranquil corner of this busy market town, the scattered ruins and surrounding graveyard of what was once Scotland's finest cathedral. The nasty Wolf of Badenoch burned it down in 1390, but there are some 13th century and medieval renewals. The octagonal chapter-house is especially revered, but this is an impressive and evocative slice of history. HS have made great job of recent restorations. Now tower can be climbed. Around the corner, there's now a biblical garden planted with species mentioned in the Bible. Gardens open May-Sep, 10am-7.30pm daily.

1785
8/Q19
HS
ATMOS
✓ **Kildrummy Castle** www.historic-scotland.gov.uk · near Alford 15km southwest of Alford on A97 near the hotel (1224/SCOTTISH HOTELS) and across the gorge from its famous gardens. Most complete 13th-century castle in Scotland, an HQ for the Jacobite uprising of 1715 and an evocative and very Highland site.

Here the invitation in the old HS advertising to 'bring your imagination' is truly valid. Apr-Sep 9.30am-5.30pm. Now head for the gardens (400m).

1786
5/C20
HS

✓ **Kisimull Castle** Isle of Barra · 01871 810313 The medieval fortress, home of the MacNeils that sits on a rocky outcrop in the bay 200m offshore. Originally built in the 11th century, it was burnt in the 18th and restored by the 45th chief, an American architect, but was unfinished when he died in 1970. An essential pilgrimage for all MacNeils, it is fascinating and atmospheric for the rest of us, a grim exterior belying an unusual internal layout – a courtyard that seems unchanged and rooms betwixt renovation and decay. Open every day in season and has a gift shop. Easter-Sep, closes for 1 hour at lunch. Last boat 4.30pm.

1787
10/R21
HS

Edzell Castle www.historic-scotland.gov.uk · Edzell 3km village off main street, signed. Pleasing red sandstone ruin in bucolic setting – birds twitter, rabbits run. The notable walled parterre Renaissance garden created by Sir David Lindsay way back in 1604 is the oldest-preserved in Scotland. The wall niches are nice. Lotsa lobelias! Mary, Queen of Scots was here (she so got around). Gate on the road is closed at night.

1788
10/M26
HS

Bothwell Castle www.historic-scotland.gov.uk · Uddingston, Glasgow 15km east of city via M74, Uddingston turnoff into main street and follow signs. Hugely impressive 13th-century ruin, the home of the Black Douglas, overlooking Clyde (with fine walks). Remarkable considering proximity to city that there is hardly any 21st-century intrusion except yourself. Pay to go inside or just sit and watch the Clyde go by.

1789
7/M17
HS

Fort George www.historic-scotland.gov.uk · near Inverness On promontory of Moray Firth 18km northeast via A96 by village of Ardersier. A vast site and 'one of the most outstanding artillery fortifications in Europe'. Planned after Culloden as a base for George II's army and completed 1769, it has remained unaltered ever since and allows a very complete picture. May provoke palpitations in the Nationalist heart, but it's heaven for militarists and altogether impressive (don't miss the museum). It's hardly a ruin of course, and is still occupied by the Army.

1790
9/H23

Dunollie Castle Oban Just outside town via Corran Esplanade towards Ganavan. Best to walk to or park on Esplanade and then walk 1km. (Only small layby and broken gate on main road below castle.) Bit of a scramble up and a slither down (and the run itself is not 'safe'), but views are superb. More atmospheric than Dunstaffnage and not commercialised. You can climb one flight up, but the ruin is only a remnant of the great stronghold of the Lorn Kings that it was. The Macdougals, who took it over in the 12th century, still live in the house below.

1791
9/H25

Tarbert Castle www.tarbert-castle.co.uk · Tarbert, Argyll Strategically and dramatically overlooking the sheltered harbour of this epitome of a West Highland port. Unsafe to clamber over, it's for the timeless view rather than an evocation of tangible history that it's worth finding the way up. Local campaign to clean it up and make it more accessible 2010, Steps up from Harbour Rd.

1792
9/J23
HS

Kilchurn Castle www.kilchurncastle.com · Loch Awe The romantic ruin at the head of awesome Loch Awe (69/PLACES TO LOVE MORE), visited either by a short walk (1km) from car park off the main A85 5km east of Lochawe village (between the Stronmilchan turnoff and the Inveraray road). You go under the railway line. A very pleasant spot for loch reflections; and others.

1793
10/R23
HS

St Andrews Cathedral www.standrewscathedral.com · St Andrews
The ruins of the largest church in Scotland before the Reformation, a place of great influence and pilgrimage. St Rule's Tower and the jagged fragment of the huge West Front in their striking position at the convergence of the main streets and overlooking the sea, are remnants of its great glory.

1794
10/Q26
HS

Crichton Castle www.historic-scotland.gov.uk · near Pathhead 3km west of A68 at Pathhead (28km south of Edinburgh) or via A7 turning east, 3km south of Gorebridge. Massive Border keep dominating the Tyne valley in pristine country-side. Open Apr-Sep. Nearby is the 15th-century collegiate church. Summer Sun only, 2-5pm. They record Radio 3 religious music here. 500m walk from Crichton village. Good picnic spots below by the river though may be overgrown in summer.

1795
10/R25
HS

Tantallon Castle www.historic-scotland.gov.uk · North Berwick 5km east of town by coast road; 500m to dramatic cliff top setting with views to Bass Rock (1723/BIRDS). Dates from 1350 with massive 'curtain wall' to see it through stormy weather and stormy history. The Red Douglases and their friends kept the world at bay. Wonderful beach nearby (444/EDINBURGH BEACHES). Closed Thu/Fri in winter.

1796
7/M20
HS

Ruthven Barracks www.historic-scotland.gov.uk · Kingussie 2km along B970 and visible from A9 especially at night when it's illuminated, these former barracks built by the English Redcoats as part of the campaign to tame the Highlands after the first Jacobite rising in 1715, were actually destroyed by the Jacobites in 1746 after Culloden. It was here that Bonnie Prince Charlie sent his final order, 'Let every man seek his own safety', signalling the absolute end of the doomed cause. Life for the soldiers is well described and visualised. Open all year.

1797
7/L18
HS

Urquhart Castle www.historic-scotland.gov.uk · Drumnadrochit, Loch Ness 28km south of Inverness on A82. The classic Highland fortress on a promontory overlooking Loch Ness visited every year by bus loads and boat loads of tourists. Photo opportunities galore amongst the well-kept lawns and extensive ruins of the once formidable stronghold of the Picts and their scions, finally abandoned in the 18th century. Visitor facilities almost cope with demand.

1798
10/M24
HS

Doune Castle www.historic-scotland.gov.uk · Doune Follow signs from centre of village which is just off A84 Callander-Dunblane road. Overlooking the River Teith, the well-preserved ruin of a late 14th-century courtyard castle with a great hall and another draughty room where Mary, Queen of Scots once slept. Nice walk to the meadow begins on track to left of castle.

1799
8/T18
ATMOS

Slains Castle www.peterhead.org.uk · near Cruden Bay 32km north of Aberdeen and 2km west of Cruden Bay, from car park (Meikle Partens) on bend of the A795. You see its craggy outline then walk 1km. Obviously because of its loca-tion, but also because there's no reception centre/postcard shop or proper sign-posts, this is a ruin that talks. Your imagination, like Bram Stoker's (who was inspired after staying here, to write *Dracula*), can be cast to the winds. The seat of the Earls of Errol, it has been gradually disintegrating since the roof was removed in 1925. Once, it had the finest dining room in Scotland. The waves crash below, as always. Be careful!

The Best Prehistoric Sites

HS: *Historic Scotland. Standard hours: Apr-end Sep 7 days 9.30am-5.30pm; Oct 9.30am-4.30pm. Winter hours vary.*

1800
3/P10
HS
ADMISSION

✓ ✓ ✓ **Skara Brae** www.historic-scotland.gov.uk · Orkney Mainland 32km Kirkwall by A965/B9655 via Finstown and Dounby. Excellent visitor and orientation centre. Can be a windy (500m) walk to this remarkable shoreline site, the subterranean remains of a compact village 5,000 years old. It was engulfed by a sandstorm 600 years later and lay perfectly preserved until uncovered by the laird's dog after another storm in 1850. Now it permits one of the most evocative glimpses of truly ancient times in the UK.

1801
3/Q10
HS

✓ ✓ **The Standing Stones of Stenness** www.historic-scotland.gov.uk · Orkney Mainland Together with the **Ring of Brodgar** and the great chambered tomb of **Maes Howe**, all within easy distance of the A965, 18km from Kirkwall, these are as impressive ceremonial sites as you'll find anywhere. From same period as Skara Brae. The individual stones and the scale of the Ring are very imposing and deeply mysterious. The burial cairn is the finest megalithic tomb in the UK. 500m walk from the visitor centre. Guided tour only. Entry to tunnel only 1m high! Seen together, they will stimulate even the most jaded sense of wonder.

1802
5/F14
HS
ADMISSION
☕

✓ ✓ **The Callanish Stones** www.historic-scotland.gov.uk · Lewis 24km from Stornoway. Take Tarbert road and go right at Leurbost. The best preserved and most unusual combination of standing stones in a ring around a tomb, with radiating arms in cross shape. Predating Stonehenge, they were unearthed from the peat in the mid-19th century and are the Hebrides' major historical attraction. Other configurations nearby. At dawn nobody else is there (except camping New Agers). Visitor centre (out of sight) is good; nice caff. Closed Sun. Free.

1803
7/N17
HS
FREE
ATMOS

✓ **The Clava Cairns** www.historic-scotland.gov.uk · near Culloden, near Inverness Here long before the most infamous battle in Scottish and other histories; another special atmosphere. Not so well signed but continue along the B9006 towards Cawdor Castle, that other great historical landmark (1765/CASTLES), taking a right at the Culloden Moor Inn; follow signs for Clava Lodge holiday homes, picking up HS sign to right. Chambered cairns in a grove of trees. They're really just piles of stones but the death rattle echo from 5,000 years ago is perceptible to all especially when no one else is there. Remoteness probably inhibits New Age attentions and allows more private meditations in this extraterrestrial spot.

1804
4/V5
HS
ADMISSION

✓ **The Mousa Broch** www.historic-scotland.gov.uk · Shetland On small island of Mousa, off Shetland mainland 20km south of Lerwick, visible from main A970. To see it properly, take the *Solan IV* from Sandsayre Pier at Leebitton in Sandwick (01950 431367). Takes 15 minutes. Isolated in its island fastness, this is the best-preserved broch in Scotland. Walls are 13m high (originally 15m) and galleries run up the middle, in one case to the top. Solid as a rock, this example of a uniquely Scottish phenomenon would once have been a very des res. Also: **Jarlshof** in the far south next to Sumburgh airport has remnants and ruins from Neolithic to Viking times – 18th century, with especially impressive 'wheelhouses'.

1805
10/M22
ADMISSION

✓ **Crannog Centre** www.crannog.co.uk · Kenmore, near Aberfeldy On south Loch Tay road 1km Kenmore. Superb reconstruction of Iron Age dwelling (there are several under the loch). Credible and worthwhile archaeological project, great for kids: conveys history well. Displays in progress and human story told by pleasant costumed humans. Open Apr-Oct 10am-5.30pm, Nov 10-4pm.

1806
9/H24
HS

✓ **Kilmartin Glen** www.historic-scotland.gov.uk · near Lochgilphead, Templewood 2km south of Kilmartin and 1km (signed) from A816 and across road from car park, 2 distinct stone circles from a long period of history between 3000-1200 BC. Story and speculations described on boards. Pastoral countryside and wide skies. There are apparently 150 other sites in the vicinity, and an excellent museum/café (2132/MUSEUMS). See also Dunadd (1943/FAVOURITE HILLS) for an elevated perspective of the whole area.

1807
3/Q10
ADMISSION
ATMOS

✓ **Tomb of the Eagles** www.tomboftheeagles.co.uk · Orkney Mainland 33km south of Kirkwall at the foot of South Ronaldsay; signed from Burwick. A recent discovery, the excavation of this cliff cave is on private land. You call in at the visitor centre first and they'll tell you the whole story. There's a 2km walk then you go in on a skateboard – no, really! Allow time; ethereal stuff. Open all year, Apr-Oct 9.30am-5.30pm, Mar 10am-noon or by appointment; 01856 831339.

1808
10/N25
HS
ADMISSION

Cairnpapple Hill near Linlithgow, West Lothian Approach from the Bee-craigs road off west end of Linlithgow main street. Go past the Beecraigs turnoff and continue for 3km. Cairnpapple is signed. Astonishing Neolithic henge and later burial site on windy hill with views from Highlands to Pentlands. Atmosphere made even more strange by the very 21st-century communications mast next door. Cute visitor centre! Summer only 9.30am-5.30pm but can be accessed any time.

1809
11/L30
FREE

Cairnholy www.cairnholy.co.uk · between Newton Stewart & Gatehouse of Fleet 2km off main A75. Signed from road. A mini Callanish of standing stones around a burial cairn on very human scale and in a serene setting with another site (with chambered tomb) 150m up the farm track. Excellent view – sit and contemplate what went on 4,000-6,000 years ago. I have it on good authority that this is a great place to watch the sunrise over the Solway Firth.

1810
10/R21
FREE

The Brown and White Caterthuns Kirkton of Menmuir, near Brechin & Edzell 5km uphill from war memorial at Menmuir, then signed 1km: a steep pull. Layby with obvious path to both on either side of the road. White easiest (500m uphill). These iron-age hill top settlements give tremendous sense of scale and space and afford an impressive panorama of the Highland line. Colours refer to the heather-covered turf and stone of one and the massive collapsed ramparts of the White. Sit here for a while and picture the Pict.

1811
6/Q13
FREE

The Grey Cairns of Canster near Wick 20km south of Wick, a very straight road (signed for Cairns) heads west from the A9 for 8km. The cairns are instantly identifiable near the road and impressively complete. The 'horned cairn' is the best in the UK. In 2500 BC these stone-piled structures were used for the disposal of the dead. You can crawl inside them if you're agile (or at night, brave). There are many other sights signed off the A9/99 but also interesting and nearby is:

1812
6/Q13
FREE

Hill o' Many Stanes www.stonepages.com · near Wick Aptly named place with extraordinary number of small standing stones; 200 in 22 rows. If fan shape was complete, there would be 600. Their very purposeful layout is enigmatic and strange.

1813
11/L31
FREE

The Whithorn Story www.whithorn.com · Whithorn Excavation site (though not active), medieval priory, shrine of St Ninian, visitor centre and café. More than enough to keep the whole family occupied – enthusiastic staff. Christianity? Look where it got us: this is where it started in Scotland. (Also 1565/COASTAL VILLAGES.) Easter-Oct 10.30am-5pm daily.

1814
11/N30
FREE

The Motte of Ur near Dalbeattie Off B794 north of Dalbeattie and 6km from main A75 Castle Douglas to Dumfries road. Most extensive bailey earthwork castle in Scotland dating from 12th century. No walls or excavation visible but a great sense of scale and place. Go through village of Haugh and on for 2km south of. Looking down to right at farm buildings the minor road crosses a ford; park here, cross footbridge and head to right – the hillock is above the ford.

1815
10/M25
FREE

Bar Hill near Kirkintilloch A fine example of the low ruins of a Roman fort on the Antonine Wall which ran across Scotland for 200 years early AD. Great place for an out-of-town walk (715/GLASGOW VIEWS).

1816
7/H19
HS

The Brochs www.historic-scotland.gov.uk · Glenelg 110km from Fort William. Glenelg is 14km from the A87 at Shiel Bridge (1628/SCENIC ROUTES). 5km from Glenelg village in beautiful Glen Beag. The 2 brochs, Dun Trodden and Dun Telve, are the best preserved examples on the mainland of these mysterious 1st-century homesteads. Easy here to distinguish the twin stone walls that kept out the cold and the more disagreeable neighbours. The Wagon Café next door open in summer for tea and cake.

1817
5/D17
FREE

Barpa Lanyass North Uist 8km south of Lochmaddy, visible from main A867 road, like a stone hat on the hill (200m walk). A squashed beehive burial cairn dating from 1000 BC, the tomb of a chieftain. It's largely intact and the small and nimble can explore inside, crawling through the short entrance tunnel and down through the years. Nice hotel nearby (1195/GET-AWAY HOTELS) where a circular walk starts, taking in this site and the loch (direction board 2.5km).

1818
8/P17
FREE

Sueno's Stone Forres Signposted from main street at east end just off the A96 More late Dark Age than prehistoric, a 9th- or 10th-century carved stone, 6m high in its own glass case. Pictish, magnificent; arguments still over what it shows.

1819
8/S18
FREE

Aberdeenshire Prehistoric Trail: East Aquhorthies Stone Circle near Inverurie 4km from Inverurie. Signed from B993 from Inverurie to Monymusk. A circle of pinkish stones with 2 grey sentinels flanking a huge recumbent stone set in the rolling countryside of the Don Valley. Bennachie over there, then as now (1952/HILLS)!

1820
8/S18
FREE
ATMOS

Loanhead Of Daviot Stone Circle near Inverurie Head for the village of Daviot on B9001 from Inverurie; or Loanhead, signed off A920 road between Oldmeldrum and Insch. The site is 500m from top of village. Impressive and spooky circle of 11 stones and one recumbent from 4000/5000 BC. Unusual second circle adjacent encloses a cremation cemetery from 1500 BC. Remains of 32 people were found here. Obviously, an important place. God knows what they were up to.

1821
8/R18
ADMISSION

Archaeolink www.archaeolink.co.uk · 01464 851500 · near Insch, Aberdeenshire Geographically between the 2 sites above and within an area of many prehistoric remnants, a more recent interpretative centre. Impressively modern approach to history both from exterior and within, where interactive and audiovisual displays bring the food hunter-gatherer past into the culture hunter-gatherer present. Up the hill, 3 adaptable staff members alternate as Iron/Bronze/Stone Age natives or visiting Romans. Easter-Nov 10am-5pm. Winter 11am-4pm.

1848   **The Prop of Ythsie**   near Aberdeen   35km northwest of city near Ellon to west
8/S18   of A92, or pass on the Castle Trail since this monument commemorates one
George Gordon of Haddo House nearby, who was prime minister 1852-55 (the
good-looking guy in the first portrait you come to in the house; 1822/COUNTRY
HOUSES). Tower visible from all of rolling Aberdeenshire and there are reciprocal
views should you take the easy but unclear route up. On B999 Aberdeen-Tarves
road (Haddo-Pitmeddon on the Castle Trail) and 2km from entrance to house.
Take road for the Ythsie (pronounced 'icy') farms, car park 100m. Stone circle
nearby.

1849   **The Monument To Hugh MacDiarmid**   Langholm   Brilliant piece of modern
11/Q29   sculpture by Jake Harvey rapidly rusting on the hill above Langholm 3km from A7
at beginning of path to the Malcolm obelisk from where there are great views
(1662/VIEWS). MacDiarmid, our national poet, was born in Langholm in 1872 and,
though they never liked him much after he left, the monument was commissioned and a cairn beside it raised in 1992. The bare hills surround you.

1850   **Memorial to Norman MacCaig**   near Lochinver   Follow directions for the
6/J14   remarkable Achin's bookshop (2178/SHOPPING) which is at the start of the great
walk to Suilven (1933/HILLS). Simple memorial of Torridon sandstone to Scotland's
great poet who wrote so much about this landscape he loved: Assynt. Recent tree
removal leaves site a bit forlorn but some words writ here to guide us on the way.

1851   **Murray Monument**   near New Galloway   Above A712 road to Newton
11/L29   Stewart about halfway between. A fairly austere needle of granite to commemo-
rate a 'shepherd boy', one Alexander Murray, who rose to become a professor of
Oriental Languages at Edinburgh University in the early 19th century. A 10-minute
walk up for fine views of Galloway Hills; pleasant waterfall nearby. Just as he, bare-
foot ...

1852   **Smailholm Tower**   www.historic-scotland.gov.uk · near Kelso & St
10/R27   **Boswells** The classic Border tower which inspired Walter Scott; plenty of history
HS   and romance in a bucolic setting. Picnic or whatever. Good views from its crags.
ATMOS   Near main road B6404 or off smaller B6937 – well signposted. Open Apr-Sep
9.30am-6.30pm. But fine to visit at any time (1636/SCENIC ROUTES).

Scott Monument   Edinburgh   453/EDINBURGH VIEWS.

The Most Interesting Churches

*All 'generally open' unless otherwise stated; those marked * have public services.*

1853
10/Q26
ATMOS

✓✓✓ ***Rosslyn Chapel** www.rosslynchapel.org.uk · Roslin 12km south of Edinburgh city centre. Take A702, then A703 from ring-route road, marked Penicuik. Roslin village 2km from main road and chapel 500m from village crossroads above Roslin Glen. Medieval but firmly on the world map because of *The Da Vinci Code*. Grail seekers have been coming forever but now so many, it's guided tours only in summer. No doubting the atmosphere in this temple to the Templars and all holy meaningful stuff in a *Foucault's Pendulum* sense. But a special place. In restoration till 2010/11. Episcopalian. Mon-Sat 10am-5pm, 12noon-4.45pm Sun. Walk in the glen (433/WALKS OUTSIDE THE CITY). Coffee shop.

1854
9/J23
ATMOS

✓✓ ***St Conan's Kirk** Loch Awe A85 33km east of Oban. Perched amongst trees on the side of Loch Awe, this small but spacious church seems to incorporate every ecclesiastical architectural style. Its building was a labour of love for one Walter Campbell who was perhaps striving for beauty rather than consistency. Though modern (begun by him in 1881 and finished by his sister and a board of trustees in 1930), the result is a place of ethereal light and atmosphere, enhanced by and befitting the inherent spirituality of the setting. There's a spooky carved effigy of Robert the Bruce, a cosy cloister and the most amazing flying buttresses. Big atmosphere. 69/PLACES TO LOVE MORE.

1855
3/R12
ATMOS

✓✓ **The Italian Chapel** www.visitorkney.com · Lamb Holm, Orkney 8km south of Kirkwall at Lamb Holm, the first causeway on the way to St Margaret's Hope. In 1943, Italian PoWs transformed a Nissen hut, using the most meagre materials, into this remarkable ornate chapel. The meticulous *trompe l'œil* and wrought-iron work are a touching affirmation of faith. Open all year round, daylight hours. At the other end of the architectural scale, **St Magnus Cathedral** in Kirkwall is a great edifice, but also filled with spirituality.

1856
2/XC1
ADMISSION

✓✓ **Queen's Cross Church** www.crmsociety.com · 70 Garscube Road, Glasgow Set where Garscube Rd becomes Maryhill Rd at Springbank St. C.R. Mackintosh's only church. Fascinating and unpredictable in every part of its design. Some elements reminiscent of Glasgow School of Art (built in the same year 1897) and others, like the tower, evoke medieval architecture. Bold and innovative, now restored and functioning as the headquarters of The Mackintosh Society. Mon-Fri 10am-5pm, Sun 2pm-5pm. (Not Sun in winter.) Closed Sat. No services. (728/MACKINTOSH.)

1857
11/N28
ATMOS

✓ ***Durisdeer Parish Church** www.churchesinscotland.co.uk · near Abington & Thornhill Off A702 Abington-Thornhill road and near Drumlanrig (1533/COUNTRY PARKS). If I lived near this delightful village in the hills, I'd go to church more often. It's exquisite and the history of Scotland is in the stones. The Queensberry marbles (1709) are displayed in the north transept (enter behind church) and there's a cradle roll and a list of ministers from the 14th century. The plaque to the two brothers who died at Gallipoli is especially touching. Covenanter tales are writ on the gravestones.

1858
9/K26

✓ ***Cathedral Of The Isles** Millport, the Isle Of Cumbrae Frequent ferry service from Largs is met by bus for 6km journey to Millport. Lane from main street by Newton pub, 250m then through gate. The smallest cathedral in Europe, one of Butterfield's great works (other is Keble College in Oxford). Here, small is outstandingly beautiful and absolutely quiet except Sundays in summer when there are lovely concerts. 1236/RETREATS; 1374/CAFÉS.

1859 **St Clements** Rodel, South Harris Tarbert 40km. Classic island kirk in
5/E16 Hebridean landscape. Go by the Golden Road (1632/SCENIC ROUTES). Simple cruci-form structure with tower, which the adventurous can climb. Probably influenced by Iona. Now an empty but atmospheric shell, with blackened effigies and impor-tant monumental sculpture. Goats in the churchyard graze amongst the head-stones of all the young Harris lads lost at sea in the Great War. There are other fallen angels on the outside of the tower.

1860 ***St Michael's Chapel** Eriskay, near South Uist/Barra That rare example of
5/D19 an ordinary modern church without history or grand architecture, which has charm and serenity and imbues the sense of well-being that a religious centre should. The focal point of a relatively devout Catholic community who obviously care for it. Overlooking the Sound of Barra. A real delight whatever your religion.

1861 ***St Athernase** www.leuchars.org.uk · Leuchars The parish church in a
10/Q23 commanding position by the main A91 on a corner of what is essentially an Air Force base spans centuries of warfare and architecture. The Norman bell tower is remarkable – a wedding cake in stone.

1862 ***St Fillan's Church** Aberdour Behind ruined castle (HS) in this pleasant sea-
10/P25 side village (1564/COASTAL VILLAGES), a more agreeable old kirk would be hard to find. Restored from a 12th-century ruin in 1926, the warm stonework and stained glass create a very soothing atmosphere (church open at most times, but if closed the graveyard is very fine). Services 10.30am Sun & 6.30pm first Sun of the month.

1863 ***Culross Abbey Church** www.historic-scotland.gov.uk Top of Forth-side
10/N25 village of interesting buildings and windy streets (1559/COASTAL VILLAGES). Worth
HS hike up hill (signed 'Abbey'; ruins adjacent) for views and this well-loved and cared-for church. Great stained glass (see Sandy's window), and often full of flowers.

1864 ***Dunblane Cathedral** www.dunblanecathedral.org.uk A huge nave of a
10/M24 church built around a Norman tower (from David I) on the Allan Water and restored
HS 1892. The wondrously bright stained glass is mostly 20th century. The poisoned sisters buried under the altar helped change the course of Scottish history.

1865 ***St Machar's Cathedral** www.stmachar.com · Aberdeen The Chanonry in
8/T19 'Old Aberdeen' off St Machar's Drive about 2km from centre. Best seen as part of a walk round the old 'village within the city' occupied mainly by the university's old and modern buildings. Cathedral's fine granite nave and twin-spired West Front date from 15th century, on site of 6th-century Celtic church. Noted for heraldic ceiling and 19/20th-century stained glass. Seaton Park adjacent has pleasant Don-side walks and there's the old Brig o' Balgownie. Church open daily 9am-5pm.

1866 ***Bowden Kirk** near Melrose & Newtown St Boswells Signed from the A68
10/R27 (the A699), the kirk is 500m off the main street. Beneath the Eildons (1954/HILL WALKS) in classic rolling Border country, an atmospheric old kirk since the 17th century from 12th century beginnings. Beautiful setting and the village itself is one of the prettiest in southern Scotland. Sun service at 9.30am.

1867 ***The East Lothian Churches** At Aberlady, Whitekirk, Athelstaneford &
10/Q25 Garvald 4 charming churches in bucolic settings; quiet corners to explore and reflect. Easy to find. All have interesting local histories and in the case of

Athelstaneford, a national resonance: a 'vision' in the sky near here inspired the flag of Scotland, the saltire. The spooky Doocot Heritage Centre behind the church explains. Aberlady is my favourite, Garvald a days-gone-by village with pub.

1868
10/P25
Abercorn Church near South Queensferry Off A904. 4 km west of roundabout at Forth Bridge, just after village of Newton, Abercorn is signed. 11th-century kirk nestling among ancient yews in a sleepy hamlet, untouched since Covenanter days. St Ninian said to have preached to the Picts here and though hard to believe, Abercorn was once on a par with York and Lindisfarne in religious importance. Church always open. Walk in woods from corner stile or the Hopetoun Estate.

1869
6/L15
ATMOS
Croick Church www.croickchurch.com · Bonar Bridge 16km west of Ardgay, just over the river from Bonar Bridge and through the splendid glen of Strathcarron (1593/GLENS). This humble and charming church is remembered for its place in the story of the Highland Clearances. In May 1845, 90 folk took shelter in the graveyard around the church after they had been cleared from their homes in nearby Glencalvie. Not allowed even in the kirk, their plight did not go unnoticed and was reported in *The Times*. The harrowing account is there to read, and the messages they scratched on the windows. Sheep graze all around then and now.

1870
10/L26
*Thomas Coates Memorial Church www.fenet.net · Paisley Built by Coates (of thread fame), an imposing edifice, one of the grandest Baptist churches in Europe. A monument to God, prosperity and the Industrial Revolution. Opening hours Fri 2-4pm only or check 0141 889 9980. Service on Sun at 11am.

1871
10/R25
*The Lamp Of The Lothians St Mary's Collegiate www.stmaryskirk.com · Haddington Follow signs from east main street At the risk of sounding profane or at least trite, this church has its act together (both now and throughout ecclesiastical history). It's beautiful and in a fine setting on the Tyne, with good stained glass and interesting crypts and corners. But it's obviously very much at the centre of the community, a lamp as it were, in the Lothians. Guided tours, brass rubbings (Sat). Summer concert season. Coffee shop and gift shop. Don't miss Lady Kitty's garden, including the secret medicinal garden, a quiet spot to contemplate (if not sort out) your condition. Daily 11am-4pm (2pm-4.30pm Sun). Daily service 12noon.

1072
10/P22
*Dunkeld Cathedral www.dunkeldcathedral.org.uk In town centre by lane to the banks of the Tay at its most silvery. Medieval splendour amongst lofty trees. Notable for 13th-century choir and 15th-century nave and tower. Parish church open for edifying services and other spiritual purposes. Lovely summer recitals.

1873
9/J20
St Mary & St Finnan Church Glenfinnan On main A830 Fort William-Mallaig road (the Road to the Isles, 1641/SCENIC ROUTES), a beautiful (though inside a bit crumbly) Catholic church in a spectacular setting. Queen Vic said she never saw a lovelier or more romantic spot. Late 19th century. Open daily for quiet meditations.

1874
9/H25
HS
Keills Chapel www.historic-scotland.gov.uk · South of Crinan The chapel at the end of nowhere. From Lochgilphead, drive towards Crinan, but before you get there, turn south down the B8025 and follow it past lovely little Tayvallich for nearly 20km to the end. Park at the farm then walk the last 200m. You are 7km across the Sound from Jura, at the edge of Knapdale. Early-13th-century chapel houses some remarkable cross slabs, a 7th century cross and ghosts.

St Giles' Cathedral Edinburgh 416/OTHER ATTRACTIONS.
Glasgow Cathedral/University Chapel Glasgow 687/691/MAIN ATTRACTIONS.

The Most Interesting Graveyards

1875
2/XF2
ATMOS

✔✔ **Glasgow Necropolis** www.glasgowcathedral.org.uk The vast burial ground at the crest of the ridge, running down to the river, that was the focus of the original settlement of Glasgow. Everything began at the foot of this hill and, ultimately, ended at the top where many of the city's most famous (and infamous) sons and daughters are interred within the reach of the long shadow of John Knox's obelisk. Generally open (official times), but best if you can get the full spooky experience to yourself, though don't go alone. See 687/MAIN ATTRACTIONS.

1876
1
ATMOS

✔ **Edinburgh Canongate** On left of Royal Mile going down to Palace. Adam Smith and the tragic poet Robert Fergusson revered by Rabbie Burns (who raised the memorial stone in 1787 over his pauper's grave) are buried here in the heart of Auld Reekie. Tourists can easily miss this one. **Greyfriars** A place of ancient mystery, famous for the wee dog who guarded his master's grave for 14 years, for the plundering of graves in the early 18th century for the Anatomy School and for the graves of Allan Ramsay (prominent poet and burgher), James Hutton (the father of geology), William McGonagall (the 'world's worst poet') and sundry serious Highlanders. Annals of a great city are written on these stones. **Dean Cemetery** is an Edinburgh secret and my New Town circle won't let me speak of it here.

1877
9/G25

✔ **Isle of Jura** www.theisleofjura.co.uk Killchianaig graveyard in the north. Follow road as far as it goes to Inverlussa, graveyard is on right, just before hamlet. Mairi Ribeach apparently lived until she was 128. In the south at Keils (2km from road north out of Craighouse, bearing left past Keils houses and through the deer fence), her father is buried and he was 180! Both sites are beautiful, isolated and redolent of island history, with much to reflect on, not least the mysterious longevity of the inhabitants and that soon we may all live this long.

1878
7/L18

✔ **Chisholm Graveyard** near Beauly Last resting place of the Chisholms and 3 of the largest Celtic crosses you'll see anywhere, in a secret and atmospheric woodland setting. 15km west of Beauly on A831 to Struy after Aigas dam and 5km after golf course on right-hand side; 1km before Cnoc Hotel opposite Erchless Estate and through a white iron gate on right. Walk 150m on mossy path. Sublime!

1879
7/J19

✔ **Clachan Duich** near Inverinate A beautiful stonewalled graveyard at the head of Loch Duich just south of Inverinate and 20km south of Kyle of Lochalsh. A monument on a rise above, a ruined chapel and many, many Macraes, this a delightful place to wander with glorious views to the loch and the mountains.

1880
9/H28

Campbeltown Cemetery Odd, but one of the nicest things about this end-of-the-line town is the cemetery. It's at the end of a row of fascinating posh houses, the original merchant and mariner owners of which will be interred in the leafy plots next door. Still very much in use after centuries of commerce and seafaring disasters, it has crept up the terraces of a steep and lush overhanging bank. The white cross and row of WW2 headstones are particularly affecting.

1881
9/K28

Kirkoswald Kirkyard near Maybole & Girvan On main road through village between Ayr and Girvan. The graveyard around the ruined Kirk and famous as the burial place of the characters in Burns' most famous poem, *Tam o' Shanter*. A must for Burns fans and famous-grave seekers with Souter Johnnie and Kirkton Jean buried here. Pub across the road is a great grubstop and adjacent the House of Burns, turning the village into a major visitor destination (2166/SHOPPING).

1882 **Humbie Churchyard** Humbie, East Lothian 25km southeast of Edinburgh via
10/Q26 A68 (turnoff at Fala). This is as reassuring a place to be buried as you could wish for; if you're set on cremation, come here and think of earth. Deep in the woods with the burn besides; after hours the sprites and the spirits have a hell of a time.

1883 **Ancrum Churchyard** near Jedburgh The quintessential country churchyard;
10/R27 away from the village (2km along B6400), by a lazy river (the Ale Water) crossed to a farm by a humpback bridge and a chapel in ruins. Elegiac and deeply peaceful. Great river swimming spot nearby (1685/PICNICS).

1884 **Balquhidder Churchyard** Chiefly notable as the last resting place of one Rob
10/L23 Roy Macgregor who was buried in 1734 after causing a heap of trouble hereabouts and raised to immortality by Sir Walter Scott and then Michael Caton-Jones (the movie). Despite well-trodden path, setting is poignant. For best reflections head along Loch Voil to Inverlochlarig. Sunday evening concerts have been held in the kirk Jul/Aug (check with local tourist information centres). Nice walk from back corner to the waterfall and then to Rallying Place (1961/VIEWS). Great long walk to Brig o' Turk (1987/GLEN WALKS). Tearoom in **Old Library** in village is cosy and couthie, with very good cakes (1404/TEAROOMS).

1885 **Logie Old Kirk** near Stirling A crumbling chapel and an ancient graveyard at
10/N24 the foot of the Ochils. The wall is round to keep out the demons, a burn gurgles beside and there are some fine and very old stones going back to the 16th century. Take road for Wallace Monument off A91, 2km from Stirling, then first right. The old kirk is beyond the new. Continuing on this steep narrow road (then right at the T-junction) takes you onto the Ochils (1957/HILL WALKS).

1886 **Tout-Na-Guil** Dunbeath There are various spellings of this enchanting ceme-
6/P14 tery 5km from Dunbeath, Neil Gunn's birthplace. Found by walking up the 'Strath' he describes in his book *Highland River* (1917/LITERARY PLACES). With a white wall around it, this graveyard, which before the clearances once served a valley community of 400 souls, can be seen for miles. Ask at Heritage Centre for route.

The Great Abbeys

NTS: *Under the care of the National Trust for Scotland. Hours vary. Admission.*
HS: *Under the care of Historic Scotland. Standard hours are: Apr-end Sep Mon-Sat 9.30am-6.30pm; Sun 2-6.30pm. Oct-Mar Mon-Sat 9.30am-4.30pm; Sun 2-4.30pm.*

1887
9/F23
HS
ATMOS

✓ ✓ **Iona Abbey** www.historic-scotland.gov.uk This hugely significant place of pilgrimage for new age and old age pilgrims and tourists alike is reached from Fionnphort, southwest Mull, by frequent CalMac Ferry (a 5-minute crossing). Walk 1km. Here in 563 AD St Columba began his mission for a Celtic Church that changed the face of Europe. Cloisters, graveyard of Scottish kings and, marked by a modest stone, the inscription already faded by the weather, the grave of John Smith, the patron saint of New Labour. Ethereal, clear light through the unstained windows may illuminate your contemplations. Great sense of being part of a universal church and community. Regular services. Good shop (2179/SHOPPING). Residential courses (MacLeod Centre adjacent, 01681 700404) including a Christmas house party (2208/MAGICAL ISLANDS).

1888
8/P17
ATMOS

✓ ✓ **Pluscarden Abbey** www.pluscardenabbey.org · **between Forres & Elgin** The oldest abbey monastic community still working in the UK (1229/RETREATS) in one of the most spiritual of places. Founded by Alexander II in 1230 and being restored since 1948. Benedictine services (starting with Vigil and Lauds at 4.45am through Prime-Terce-Sext-None-Vespers at 5.30pm and Compline at 8pm) open to the public. The ancient honey-coloured walls, brilliant stained glass, monks' Gregorian chant: the whole effect is a truly uplifting experience. The bell rings down the valley. Services aside, open to visitors 4.30am-8.30pm.

1889
10/L26

✓ ✓ **Paisley Abbey** www.paisleyabbey.org.uk · 0141 889 7654 In the town centre. An abbey founded in 1163, razed (by the English) in 1307 and with successive deteriorations and renovations ever since. Major restoration in the 1920s brought it to present-day cathedral-like magnificence. Exceptional stained glass (the recent window complementing the formidable Strachan East Window), an impressive choir and an edifying sense of space. Sunday services are superb, especially full-dress communion and there are open days; phone for dates. Otherwise Abbey open all year Mon-Sat 10am-3.30pm. Café/shop.

1890
10/R28
HS

✓ ✓ **Jedburgh Abbey** www.historic-scotland.gov.uk The classic abbey ruin; conveys the most complete impression of the Border abbeys built under the patronage of David I in the 12th century. Its tower and remarkable Catherine window are still intact. Excavations have unearthed example of a 12th-century comb. It's now displayed in the excellent visitor centre which brilliantly illustrates the full story of the abbey's amazing history. Best view from across the Jed in the Glebe. May-Sep 9.30am-5.30pm, Oct-Mar until 4.30pm.

1891
10/R27
HS
ATMOS

✓ **Dryburgh Abbey** www.historic-scotland.gov.uk · **near St Boswells** One of the most evocative of ruins, an aesthetic attraction since the late 18th century. Sustained innumerable attacks from the English since its inauguration by Premonstratensian Canons in 1150. Celebrated by Sir Walter Scott, buried here in 1832 (with his biographer Lockhart at his feet), its setting, amongst huge cedar trees on the banks of the Tweed is one of pure historical romance. 4km A68. (1739/VIEWS.) Apr-Sep 9.30am-5.30pm, Oct-Mar till 4.30pm, Sun 2-4.30pm.

1892 **Sweetheart** New Abbey, near Dumfries 12km south by A710. The endearing
11/N30 and enduring warm red sandstone abbey in the shadow of Criffel, so named
HS because Devorguilla de Balliol, devoted to her husband (he of the Oxford college),
founded the abbey for Cistercian monks and kept his heart in a casket which is
buried with her here. No roof, but the tower is intact. OK tearoom (but 'orrible gift
shop): you can sit and gaze at the ruins while eating your Cream o' Galloway.

1893 **Melrose Abbey** www.historic-scotland.gov.uk Another romantic setting, the
10/R27 abbey seems to lend class to the whole town. Once again built by David I (what a
HS guy!) for Cistercian monks from Rievaulx from 1136. It once sustained a huge community, as evinced by the widespread excavations. There's a museum of abbey,
church and Roman relics; soon to include Robert the Bruce's heart, recently excavated in the gardens. Nice Tweed walks can start here. Same hours as Jed.

1894 **Arbroath Abbey** www.historic-scotland.gov.uk 25km north of Dundee.
10/R22 Founded in 1178 and endowed on an unparalleled scale, this is an important place
HS in Scots history. It's where the Declaration was signed in 1320 to appeal to the
Pope to release the Scots from the yoke of the English (you can buy facsimiles of
the yellow parchment; the original is in the Scottish Records Office in Edinburgh –
oh, and tea towels). It was to Arbroath that the Stone of Destiny (on which Scottish
kings were traditionally crowned) was returned after being 'stolen' from
Westminster Abbey in the 1950s and is now at Edinburgh Castle. Great
interpretation centre before you tour the ruins.

The Great Battlegrounds

NTS: *Under the care of the National Trust for Scotland. Hours vary.*

1895 ✓✓ **Culloden** www.nts.org.uk · Inverness Signed from A9 and A96 into
7/M18 Inverness and about 8km from town. The new, state-of-the-art visitor
NTS centre puts you in the picture, then there's a 10-minute 'rooftop walk' with per-
ATMOS spective or a 40-minute through-the-battlefield walk. Positions of the clans and
the troops marked out across the moor; flags enable you to get a real sense of
scale. If you go in spring you see how wet and miserable the moor can be (the battle took place on 16 April 1746). No matter how many other folk are there wandering down the lines, a visit to this most infamous of battlefields can still leave a
pain in the heart. Centre 9am-6pm (winter 11am-4pm). Ground open at all times
for more personal Cullodens.

1896 **Battle Of The Braes** Skye 10km Portree. Take main A850 road south for 3km
7/F18 then left, marked 'Braes' for 7km. Monument is on a rise on right. The last battle
fought on British soil and a significant place in Scots history. When the Clearances,
uninterrupted by any organised opposition, were virtually complete and vast tracts
of Scotland had been depopulated for sheep, the Skye crofters finally stood up in
1882 to the Government troops and said enough is enough. A cairn has been
erected near the spot where they fought on behalf of 'all the crofters of Gaeldom',
a battle which led eventually to the Crofters Act which has guaranteed their rights
ever since. At the end of this road at Peinchorran, there are fine views of Raasay
(which was devastated by clearances) and Glamaig, the conical Cuillin, across Loch
Sligachan.

1897 **Glencoe** Not much of a battle, of course, but one of the most infamous mas-
9/J21 sacres in British history. Much has been written (John Prebble's *Glencoe* and others)
and a discreetly located visitor centre provides audiovisual scenario. Macdonald
monument near Glencoe village and the walk to the more evocative Signal Rock
where the bonfire was lit, now a happy woodland trail in this doom-laden landscape. Many other great walks. See 1923/ENCHANTING PLACES, 1267/PUBS.

1898 **Scapa Flow** www.scapaflow.co.uk · **Orkney Mainland & Hoy** Scapa Flow,
3/Q11 surrounded by various of the southern Orkney islands, is one of the most sheltered
anchorages in Europe. Hence the huge presence in Orkney of ships and personnel
during both wars. The Germans scuttled 54 of their warships here in 1919 and
many still lie in the bay. The *Royal Oak* was torpedoed in 1939 with the loss of 833
men. Much still remains of the war years (especially if you're a diver, 2145/DIVING):
the rusting hulks, the shore fortifications, the Churchill Barriers and the ghosts of a
long-gone army at Scapa and Lyness on Hoy. Evocative visitor centre and naval
cemetery at Lyness. Open all year round. Excellent tour on MV *Guide* with remote
controlled camera exploring 3 wrecks (01856 811360). May-Sep.

1899 **Lilliard's Edge** near **St Boswells** On main A68, look for Lilliard's Edge Caravan
10/R27 Park 5km south of St Boswells; park and walk back towards St Boswells to the brim
of the hill (about 500m), then cross rough ground on right along ridge, following
tree-line hedge. Marvellous view attests to strategic location. 200m along, a cairn
marks the grave of Lilliard who, in 1545, joined the Battle of Ancrum Moor against
the English 'loons' under the Earl of Angus. 'And when her legs were cuttit off, she
fought upon her stumps'. An ancient poem etched on the stone records her
legendary... feet.

1900 **Killiecrankie** near **Pitlochry** The first battle of the Jacobite Risings where, in
10/N21 Jul 1689, the Highlanders lost their leader Viscount (aka Bonnie) Dundee, but won
NTS the battle, using the narrow Pass of Killiecrankie. One escaping soldier made a
famous leap. Well-depicted scenario in visitor centre; short walk to 'The Leap'.
Battle viewpoint and cairn is further along road to Blair Atholl, turning right and
doubling back near the Garry Guesthouse and on, almost to A9 underpass (3km
from visitor centre). You get the lie of the land from here. Many good walks.

1901 **Bannockburn** www.nts.org.uk · near **Stirling** 4km town centre via Glasgow
10/N24 road (it's well signposted) or junction 9 of M9 (3km), behind a sad hotel and car-
NTS rental centre. Some visitors might be perplexed as to why 24 Jun 1314 was such a
big deal for the Scots and, apart from the 50m walk to the flag-pole and the huge
statue, there's not a lot doing. But the battle against the English did finally secure
the place of Robert I (the Bruce) as King of Scots, paving the way for the final settlement with England 15 years later. The Heritage Centre does bring to life the
scale of the battle, the horror and the glory. The battlefield itself is thought to lie
around the orange building of the high school some distance away, and the best
place to see the famous wee burn is from below the magnificent Telford Bridge.
Ask at centre (5km by road). NTS arrange mega re-enactments in mid Sep.
Controversies still rage among scholars: eg did the English really scarper after only
an hour?

Mary, Charlie & Bob

HS: *Under the care of Historic Scotland. Standard hours are: Apr-end Sep 7 days 9.30am-5.30pm. Oct 9.30am-4.30pm; winter hours vary.*

MARY, QUEEN OF SCOTS (1542–87)
Linlithgow Palace Where she was born. 1780/RUINS.
Holyrood Palace Edinburgh And lived. 400/MAIN ATTRACTIONS.

1902
10/M24
HS
Inchmahome Priory www.historic-scotland.gov.uk · **Port of Menteith** The priory ruins on the island in Scotland's only lake, where the infant queen spent her early years cared for by Augustinian monks. Short boat journey from quay near lake hotel. Signal the ferryman by turning the board to the island, much as she did. Apr-Oct. 7 days. Last trip 4.30pm.

1903
10/R28
Mary, Queen of Scots' House Jedburgh In gardens via Smiths Wynd off main street. Historians quibble but this long-standing museum claims to be 'the' house where she fell ill in 1566 but still made it over to visit the injured Bothwell at Hermitage Castle 50km away. Tower house in good condition; displays and well-told saga. Mar-Nov 10am-4.30pm, Sun 11am-4.30pm. Winter hours vary.

1904
10/P24
HS
Loch Leven Castle www.historic-scotland.gov.uk · **near Kinross** Well-signed! The ultimate in romantic penitentiaries; on the island in the middle of the loch, clearly visible from the M90. Not much left of the ruin to fill out the fantasy, but this is where Mary spent 10 months in 1568 before her famous escape and her final attempt to get back the throne. Sailings Apr-Sep, 9.30am-5.30pm (last out 4.30pm) from pier at the National Game Angling Academy (Pier Bar/café serves as you wait) in small launch from Kirkgate Park. 7-minute trip, return as you like.

1905
11/M31
HS
Dundrennan Abbey www.historic-scotland.gov.uk · **near Auchencairn** Mary got around and there are innumerable places where she spent the night. This was where she spent her last one on Scottish soil, leaving next day from Port Mary (nothing to see there but a beach, 2km along the road skirting the sinister MoD range, the pier long gone). The Cistercian abbey (established 1142) which harboured her on her last night is now a tranquil ruin.

'In my end is my beginning,' she said, facing her execution 19 years later.

1906
10/R25
Her 'death mask' is displayed at **Lennoxlove House** **near Haddington** · www.lennoxlove.com; it does seem small for someone who was supposedly 6 feet tall! Lennoxlove on road to Gifford. Apr-Oct, Wed/Thu/Sun 1.30-4pm.

BONNIE PRINCE CHARLIE (1720–88)
1907
5/D19
Prince Charlie's Bay or Strand Eriskay The uncelebrated, unmarked and quietly beautiful beach where Charlie first landed in Scotland to begin the Jacobite Rebellion. Nothing much has changed (except the pier for Barra ferry is adjacent) and this crescent of sand with soft machair and a turquoise sea is still a special place. 1km from township heading south; approach from township not by the new ferry road. 2216/MAGICAL ISLANDS.

1908
7/H20
ATMOS
Loch Nan Uamh, The Prince's Cairn near Arisaig 7km from Lochailort on A830 (1642/SCENIC ROUTES), 48km Fort William. Signed from the road (100m layby), a path leads down to the left. This is the traditional spot (pronounced 'Loch

Na Nuan') where Charlie embarked for France in Sep 1746, having lost the battle and the cause. The rocky headland also overlooks the bay and skerries where he'd landed in July the year before to begin the campaign. This place was the beginning and the end and it has all the romance necessary to be utterly convincing. Is that a French ship out there in the mist?

1909
9/J20
NTS

Glenfinnan www.glenfinnan.org Here he raised his standard to rally the clans to the Jacobite cause. For a while on that day in Aug 1745 it looked as if few were coming. Then pipes were heard and 600 Camerons came marching from the valley (where the viaduct now spans). That must have been one helluva moment. It's thought that he actually stood on the higher ground but there is a powerful sense of place and history here. The visitor centre has an excellent map of Charlie's path through Scotland – somehow he touched all the most alluring places! Climb the tower or take the long view from Loch Shiel (1641/ROUTES). Nice church 1km (1895/CHURCHES) and a great hotel and bar (1226/VERY SCOTTISH HOTELS).

Culloden near Inverness 1982/BATTLEGROUNDS.

ROBERT I, THE BRUCE (1274–1329)

1910
11/L29

Bruce's Stone Glen Trool, near Newton Stewart 26km north by A714 via Bargrennan (8km to head of glen) on the Southern Upland Way (1974/LONG WALKS). The fair Glen Trool is a celebrated spot in Galloway Forest Park (1597/GLENS). The stone is signed (200m walk) and marks the area where Bruce's guerrilla band rained boulders onto the pursuing English in 1307 after routing the main army at Solway Moss. Good walks, including to Merrick which starts here (1945/HILLS).

1911
10/N24

Bannockburn near Stirling The climactic battle in 1314, when Bruce decisively whipped the English and secured the kingdom (though Scotland was not legally recognised as independent until 1329). The scale of the skirmish can be visualised at the heritage centre but not so readily in the field. 1901/BATTLEGROUNDS.

1912
10/R22
HS

Arbroath Abbey www.historic-scotland.gov.uk Not much of the Bruce trail here, but this is where the famous Declaration was signed that was the attempt of the Scots nobility united behind him to gain international recognition of the independence they had won on the battlefield. What it says is stirring stuff; the original is in Edinburgh. Great interpretation centre.

1913
10/P25
HS

Dunfermline Abbey Church www.historic-scotland.gov.uk Here, some tangible evidence: his tomb. Buried in 1329, his remains were discovered wrapped in gold cloth when the site was being cleared for the new church in 1818. Many of the other great kings, the Alexanders I and III, were not so readily identifiable (Bruce's ribcage had been cut to remove his heart). With great national emotion he was reinterred under the pulpit. The church (as opposed to the ruins and Norman nave adjacent) is open Easter-Oct, winter for services. Great café in Abbot House through graveyard (2123/MUSEUMS). Look up and see Robert carved on the skyline.

1914
10/R27
HS

Melrose Abbey www.historic-scotland.gov.uk On his deathbed Bruce asked that his heart be buried here after it was taken to the Crusades to aid the army in their battles. A likely lead casket thought to contain it was excavated from the chapter house and it did date from the period. It was reburied here and is marked with a stone. Let's believe in this!

The Important Literary Places

1915 **Robert Burns (1759-96)** www.robertburns.org · Alloway, Ayr & Dumfries
9/L28 A well-marked heritage trail through his life and haunts in Ayrshire and Dumfries-
shire. His 'howff' in Dumfries, the **Globe Inn**, is very atmospheric – established in
1610 and still going strong (798/DUMFRIES). Best is at **Alloway**. The Auld Brig o'
Doon and the Auld Kirk, where Tam o' Shanter saw the witches dance are evocative, and the Monument and surrounding gardens are lovely. 1km up the road, his
cottage birthplace, now run by the NTS, is to be the new centrepiece attraction.
(Tam o' Shanter Experience visitor centre gets mobbed but is not recommended.)
Ayr The Auld Kirk off main street by river; graveyard with diagram of where his
friends are buried; open at all times. **Dumfries** House where he spent his last
years and mausoleum 250m away at back of a kirkyard stuffed with extravagant
masonry. 10km north of Dumfries on A76 at **Ellisland Farm** (home 1788-91) is
the most interesting of all the sites. The farmhouse with genuine memorabilia, eg
his mirror, fishing-rod, a poem scratched on glass, original manuscripts. There's
his favourite walk by the river where he composed *Tam o' Shanter* and a strong
atmosphere about the place. Open 7 days summer, closed Sun/Mon in winter.
Poosie Nansie's, the pub he frequented in Mauchline, is a must (1270/PUBS).
Brow Well near Ruthwell on the B725 20km south of Dumfries and near
Caerlaverock (1808/BIRDS), is a much quieter place, a well with curative properties
where he went in the latter stages of his illness.

2009, the Year of Homecoming, raised Burns' profile considerably.

1916 **Lewis Grassic Gibbon (1901-35)** www.grassicgibbon.com · Arbuthnott,
10/S21 near Stonehaven Although James Leslie Mitchell left the area in 1917, this is
where he was born and spent his formative years. Visitor centre (01561 361668;
Apr-Oct 7 days 10am-4.30pm) at the end of the village (via B967, 16km south of
Stonehaven off main A92) has details of his life and can point you in the direction
of the places he writes about in his trilogy, *A Scots Quair*. The first part, *Sunset
Song*, is generally considered to be one of the great Scots novels and this area, the
Howe of the Mearns, is the place he so effectively evokes. Arbuthnott is
reminiscent of 'Kinraddie' and the churchyard 1km away on the other side of road
still has the atmosphere of that time of innocence before the war which pervades
the book. His ashes are here in a grave in a corner; the inscription: 'the kindness of
friends/the warmth of toil/the peace of rest'. From 1928 to when he died 7 years
later at the age of only 34, he wrote an incredible 17 books.

1917 **Neil Gunn (1891-1973)** www.neilgunn.org.uk · Dunbeath, near Wick
6/P14 Scotland's foremost writer on Highland life, only recently receiving the recognition
he deserves, was brought up in this North East fishing village and based 3 of his
greatest yarns here, particularly *Highland River*, which must stand in any literature
as a brilliant evocation of place. The **Strath** in which it is set is below the house (a
nondescript terraced house next to the shop) and makes for a great walk (1996/
GLEN & RIVER WALKS). There's a commemorative statue by the harbour, not quite
the harbour you imagine from the books. The excellent heritage centre depicts the
Strath on its floor and has a leaflet for you to follow. Gunn also lived for many
years near **Dingwall** and there is a memorial on the back road to Strathpeffer and
a wonderful view in a place he often walked (on A834, 4km from Dingwall).

1918 **James Hogg (1770-1835)** St Mary's Loch, Ettrick The Ettrick Shepherd who
10/P27 wrote one of the great works of Scottish literature, *Confessions of a Justified Sinner*,
was born, lived and died in the valleys of the **Yarrow** and the **Ettrick**, some of

the most starkly beautiful landscapes in Scotland. **St Mary's Loch** on the A708, 28km west of Selkirk: there's a commemorative statue looking over the loch and the adjacent and supernatural seeming Loch of the Lowes. On the strip of land between is **Tibbie Shiels** pub (and hotel), once a gathering place for the writer and his friends (e.g. Sir Walter Scott) and still a notable hostelry (1271/PUBS). Across the valley divide (11km on foot, part of the Southern Upland Way: 1974/ LONG WALKS), or 25km by road past the Gordon Inn, Yarrow is the remote village of **Ettrick**, another monument and his grave (and Tibbie Shiels') in the churchyard. The James Hogg exhibition is at Bowhill House Visitor Centre (01750 22204).

1919 **Sir Walter Scott (1771–1832)** Abbotsford, Melrose No other place in
10/R27 Scotland (and few anywhere) contains so much of a writer's life and work. This was the house he rebuilt from the farmhouse he moved to in 1812 in the countryside he did so much to popularise. The house, until recently lived in by his descendants, is run by trustees on a mission to raise millions for its upkeep. The library and study are pretty much as he left them with 9,000 rare books, antiquarian even in his day. Pleasant grounds and topiary and a walk by the Tweed which the house overlooks. His grave is at **Dryburgh Abbey** (1891/ABBEYS). There are monuments to Walt famously in Edinburgh (453/EDINBURGH IEWS) and in George Square, Glasgow. Plans afoot for a major festival in the Trossachs 2010 where **Loch Katrine** was the setting for Scott's *Lady of the Lake*, the most popular poem ever published (in 1810). House open Mar-Nov 9.30am-5pm; Sun 9.30am-5pm (in winter 11am-4pm).

1920 **Robert Louis Stevenson (1850–94)** Edinburgh Though Stevenson travelled
1 widely – lived in France, emigrated to America and died and was buried in Samoa – he spent his first 30 years in Edinburgh. He was born and brought up in the New Town, living at **17 Heriot Row** from 1857-80 which is still lived in (not open to the public). Most of his youth was spent in this newly built and expanding part of the city in an area bounded then by parkland and farms. Both the **Botanics** (410/OTHER ATTRACTIONS) and **Warriston Cemetery** are part of the landscape of his childhood. However, his fondest recollections were of the **Pentland Hills** and, virtually unchanged as they are, it's here that one is following most poignantly in his footsteps. The 'cottage' at **Swanston** (a delightful village with some remark- able thatched cottages reached via the city bypass/Colinton turnoff or from Oxgangs Rd and a bridge over the bypass; the village nestles in a grove of trees below the hills and is a good place to walk from), the ruins of **Glencorse Church** (ruins even then and where he later asked that a prayer be said for him) and **Colinton Manse** can all be seen, but not visited. Edinburgh has no dedicated Stevenson Museum, but **The Writers' Museum** at Makars' Court has exhibits (and of many other writers). The **Hawes Inn** in South Queensferry where he wrote *Kidnapped* has had its history obliterated by a brewery makeover.

1921 **J.K. Rowling (we don't give a lady's birthdate)** www.jkrowling.com ·
1 Edinburgh Scotland's most successful writer ever as the creator of Harry Potter, rich beyond dreams, was famously an impecunious single mother scribbling away in Edinburgh coffee shops. The most-mentioned is opposite the Festival Theatre and is now something else. The **Elephant House** (285/EDINBURGH COFFEE SHOPS) was another and gives you the idea. Harry Potter country as interpreted by Hollywood can be found at **Glenfinnan** (1909/MARY, CHARLIE & BOB) and **Glencoe** especially around the **Clachaig Inn** (1178/INNS). JK lives in 'writers' block' in Merchiston in Edinburgh (as do Ian Rankin and Alexander McCall Smith).

1922 **Irvine Welsh (b.1958)** www.irvinewelsh.net · Edinburgh Literary
1 immortality awaits confirmation. There are *Trainspotting* tours but **Robbie's Bar** might suffice (350/EDINBURGH UNSPOILT PUBS); you will hear the voices.

The Most Enchanting Places

1923
9/J21
2-B-2
ATMOS

The Lost Valley Glencoe The secret glen where the ill-fated Macdonalds hid the cattle they'd stolen from the Lowlands and which became (with politics and power struggles) their undoing. A narrow wooded cleft takes you between the imposing and gnarled '3 Sisters' Hills and over the threshold (God knows how the cattle got there) and into the huge bowl of Coire Gabhail. The place envelops you in its tragic history, more redolent perhaps than any of the massacre sites. Park on the A82 6.5km from the visitor centre 300m west of the white bungalow by the road (always cars parked here). Follow clear path down to and across the River Coe. Ascend keeping burn to left; 1.5km further up, it's best to ford it. Allow 3 hours. (1897/BATTLEGROUNDS.)

1924
3/Q13

The Whaligoe Steps Ulbster 10km south of Wick. 100m to car park off the A99 at the (modern) telephone box near sign for the Cairn of Get. Short walk from car park to remarkable structure hewn into sheer cliffs, 365 steps down to a grassy platform – the Bink – and an old fishing station. From 1792, creels of cod, haddock and ling were hauled up these steps for the merchants of Wick and Lybster. Consider these labours as you follow their footsteps in this wild and enchanting place. No rails and can be slippy. Take great care!

1925
1/D4

Under Edinburgh Old Town www.edinburgholdtown.org.uk Mary King's Close, a medieval street under the Royal Mile closed in 1753 (**The Real Mary King's Close** 0845 070 6244); and the Vaults under South Bridge – built in the 18th century and sealed up around the time of the Napoleonic Wars (**Mercat Tours** 0131 225 5445). History underfoot for unsuspecting tourists and locals alike. Glimpses of a rather smelly subterranean life way back then. It's dark during the day, and you wouldn't want to get locked in.

1926
3/P10

The Yesnaby Stacks www.visitorkney.com · Orkney Mainland A cliff top viewpoint that's so wild, so dramatic and, if you walk near the edge, so precarious that its supernaturalism verges on the uneasy. Shells of lookout posts from the war echo the melancholy spirit of the place. ('The bloody town's a bloody cuss/No bloody trains, no bloody bus/And no one cares for bloody us/In bloody Orkney' – first lines of a poem written then, a soldier's lament.) Near Skara Brae, it's about 30km from Kirkwall and way out west. Follow directions from Marwick Head (1730/1732/BIRDS).

1927
7/F17
ATMOS

The Fairy Glen Skye A place so strange, it's hard to believe that it's merely a geological phenomenon. Entering Uig on the A855 (becomes A87) from Portree, there's a turret on the left (Macrae's Folly). Take road on right marked Balnaknock for 2km and you enter an area of extraordinary conical hills which, in certain conditions of light and weather, seems to entirely justify its legendary provenance. Your mood may determine whether you believe they were good or bad fairies, but there's supposed to be an incredible 365 of these grassy hillocks, some 35m high – well, how else could they be here?

1928
7/M18

Clava Cairns near Culloden, Inverness Near Culloden (1895/BATTLEGROUNDS) these curious chambered cairns in a grove of trees near a river in the middle of 21st-century nowhere. This spot can make you feel a glow or goosepimples (1803/ PREHISTORIC SITES).

1929 **The Clootie Well** www.blackisle.org · between Tore on the A9 & Avoch
7/M17   Spooky place on the road towards Avoch and Cromarty 4km from the roundabout
ATMOS   at Tore north of Inverness. Easily missed, though there is a marked car park on the
right side of the road going east. What you see is hundreds of rags or clouts: pieces
of clothing hanging on the branches of trees around the spout of an ancient well
where the wearer might be healed. They go way back up the hill behind and
though some may have been here a long time, this place seems to have been
commodified like everywhere else so there's plenty of new socks and t-shirts with
messages. It is all fairly weird.

1930 **Burn o' Vat** www.visitdeeside.org.uk · near Ballater   This impressive and
8/Q20   rather spooky glacial curiosity on Royal Deeside is a popular spot and well worth
the short walk. 8km from Ballater towards Aberdeen on main A93, take B9119 for
Huntly for 2km to the car park at the Muir of Dinnet nature reserve – driving
through forests of strange spindly birch. Some scrambling to reach the huge 'pot'
from which the burn flows to Loch Kinord. SNH visitor centre. Forest walks, 1.1km
circular walk to vat, 7km to loch. Can be busy on fine weekends, odd when you
find it deserted.

1931 **Crichope Linn** near Thornhill   A supernatural sliver of glen inhabited by water
11/N29 spirits of various temperaments (and midges). Take road for Cample on A76
ATMOS   Dumfries to Kilmarnock road just south of Thornhill; at village (2km) there's a
wooden sign so take left for 2km. Discreet sign and gate in bank on right is easy to
miss, but park in quarry 100m further on. Take care – can be very wet and very
slippy. Gorge is a 10-minute schlep from the gate. We saw red squirrels! Durisdeer
Church nearby should not be missed (1857/CHURCHES).

1932 **Hell's Lum Cave** near Gardenstown, Moray Firth Coast   A reader, Pauline
8/S17   Hetherington, alerted us to this locally popular beach picnic and combing spot east
of Gardenstown off the B9031 signed for Cullykhan Bay. From car park (200m from
main road), you walk down to bay and can see on left a scar on the hill which
marks the 'lum', approached along the shoreline possibly via a defile known as the
Devil's Dining Room. Lots of local mythology surrounds this wild and beautiful
spot. In the cave itself you hear what sounds like children crying.

The Necropolis Glasgow   1875/GRAVEYARDS.
Loanhead of Daviot near Oldmeldrum   1820/PREHISTORIC SITES.

Section 9

Strolls, Walks & Hikes

Favourite Hills

Popular and notable hills in the various regions of Scotland but not including Munros or difficult climbs. Always best to remember that the weather can change very quickly. Take an OS map on higher tops. See p. 12 for walk codes.

1933
6/K14
2-C-3

✓ ✓ **Suilven** Lochinver From close or far away, this is one of Scotland's most awe-inspiring mountains. The 'sugar loaf' can seem almost insurmountable, but in good weather it's not so difficult. Route from Inverkirkaig 5km south of Lochinver on road to Achiltibuie, turns up track by Achin's Bookshop (2178/SCOTTISH SHOPPING) on the path for the Kirkaig Falls; once at the loch, you head for the Bealach, the central waistline through an unexpected dyke and follow track to the top. The slightly quicker route from the north (Glencanisp) following a stalkers' track that eventually leads to Elphin, also heads for the central breach in the mountain's defences. Either way it's a long walk in; 8km before the climb. Allow 8 hours return. At the top, the most enjoyable 100m in the land and below – amazing Assynt. 731m. Take OS map.

1934
6/J15
2-B-3

✓ ✓ **Stac Pollaidh/Polly** near Ullapool This hill described variously as 'perfect', 'preposterous' and 'great fun'; it certainly has character and, rising out of the Sutherland moors on the road to Achiltibuie off the A835 north from Ullapool, demands to be climbed. Route everyone takes is from the car park by Loch Lurgainn 8km from main road. New path takes you (either way) round the hill and up from the north side. The path to the pinnacles is exposed and can be off-putting. Best half day hill climb in the North. 613m. Allow 3-4 hours return.

1935
6/J14

✓ ✓ **Quinag** near Lochinver Like Stac Polly (above), this Corbett (pronounced 'Koonyag') has amazing presence and seems more formidable than it actually is. Park off the A894 to Kylesku. An up-and-down route can take in 6 or 7 tops in your 5-hour expedition (or curtail). Once again, awesome Assynt!

1936
9/J27
2-B-2
NTS

✓ **Goat Fell** Arran Starting from the car park at Cladach before Brodick Castle grounds 3km from town, or from Corrieburn Bridge south of Corrie further up the coast (12km). A worn path, a steady climb, rarely much of a scramble but a rewarding afternoon's exertion. Some scree and some view! 874m. Usually not a circular route. Allow 4 hours.

1937
9/K24
2-B-3

✓ **The Cobbler (aka Ben Arthur)** Arrochar Perennial favourite of the Glasgow hillwalker and, for sheer exhilaration, the most popular of 'the Arrochar Alps'. A motorway path ascends from the A83 on the other side of Loch Long from Arrochar (park in laybys near Succoth road end; there are always loads of cars) and takes 2.5-3 hours to traverse the up 'n' down route to the top. Just short of a Munro at 881m, it has 3 tops of which the north peak is the simplest scramble (central and south peaks for climbers). Where the way is not marked, consult.

• •

SIX MAGNIFICENT HILLS IN THE TROSSACHS

1938
10/L24
2-B-3

✓ **Ben Venue & Ben A'An** 2 celebrated tops in the Highland microcosm of the Trossachs around Loch Achray, 15km west of Callander; strenuous but not difficult and with superb views. Ben Venue (727m) is the more serious; allow 4-5 hours return. Start from Kinlochard side at Ledard or more usually from the Loch Katrine corner before Loch Achray Hotel. It's waymarked from new car park. Ben A'an (pronounced 'An') (415m) starts with a steep climb from the main A821 near the same corner along from the Tigh Mor mansions (just before the corner).

Scramble at top. Allow 2-3 hours. Very busy on fine days. The Byre at Brig o' Turk, under new owners (again), is decent.

1939
10/M23
2-B-3

Benn Shian Strathyre Another Trossachs favourite and not taxing. From village main road (the A74 to Lochearnhead), cross bridge opposite Monro Inn, turn left after 200m then path to right at 50m a steep start through woods. Overlooking village and views to Crianlarich and Ben Vorlich (see below). 600m. 3 hours return.

1940
10/L24
1-B-1

Doon Hill The Faerie Knowe, Aberfoyle Legendary hillock in Aberfoyle, only 1 hour up and back, so a gentle elevation into faerie land. The tree at the top is the home of the 'People of Quietness' and there was once a local minister who had the temerity to tell their secrets (in 1692). Go round it 7 times and your wish will be granted, go round backwards at your peril (you wouldn't, would you?). From main street take Manse Rd by garden centre. 1km past cemetery – then signed.

1941
10/M23
2-B-3

Ben Vorlich The big hill itself is also approached from the south Lochearn road; from Ardvorlich House 5km from A84. Enter 'East Gate' and follow signs for open hillside of Glen Vorlich. Track splits after 1.5km, take right then southeast side to come to north ridge of mountain. Allow 5 hours return.

1942
10/M24
2-B-3

Ben Ledi near Callander Another Corbett looking higher than it is with the Trossachs spread before you as you climb. West from town on A84 through Pass of Leny. First left over bridge to car park. Well trod path, ridge at top. Return via Stank Glen then follow river. Allow 4 hours.

• •

1943
10/H24
2-B-2
HS

✓ **Dunadd** Kilmartin, north of Lochgilphead Halfway from Kilmartin on A816. Less of a hill, more of a lump, but it's where they crowned the kings of Dalriada for half a millennium. Rocky staircases and soft, grassy top. Stand there when the Atlantic rain is sheeting in and... you get wet like even the kings did. Or when the light is good you can see the glen and distant coast. Kilmartin House Museum nearby for info and great food (2132/HISTORY, 1405/TEAROOMS).

1944
11/N30
2-A-2

Criffel New Abbey, near Dumfries 12km south by A710 to New Abbey, which Criffel dominates. It's only 569m, but seems higher. Exceptional views from top as far as English lakes and across to Borders. Granite lump with brilliant outcrops of quartzite. The annual race gets up and back to the Abbey Arms in under an hour; you can take it easier. Start 3km south of village, turnoff A710 100m from one of the curious painted bus shelters signed for Ardwell Mains Farm. Park before the farm buildings and get on up.

1945
11/L29
2-B-3

Merrick near Newton Stewart Go from bonnie Glen Trool via Bargrennan 14km north on the A714. Bruce's Stone is there at the start (1910/MARY, CHARLIE & BOB). The highest peak in Southern Scotland (843m), it's a strenuous though straightforward climb, a grassy ridge to the summit and glorious scenery. 4 hours.

1946
10/R25
BOTH 1-A-1

North Berwick Law The conical volcanic hill, a beacon in the East Lothian landscape. **Traprain Law** nearby, is higher, easy and celebrated by rock climbers, but has major prehistoric significance as a hill fort citadel of the Goddodin and a definite aura. NBL is also simple and rewarding – leave town by Law Rd, path marked beyond houses. Car park and picnic site. Views 'to the Cairngorms' (!) and along the Forth. Famous whalebone at the top.

1947
10/R28
2-A-2
Ruberslaw Denholm, near Hawick This smooth hummock above the Teviot valley affords views of 7 counties, including Northumberland. Millennium plaque on top. At 424m, it's a gentle climb taking about 1 hour from the usual start at Denholm Hill Farm (private land, be aware of livestock). Leave Denholm at corner of green by post office and go past war memorial. Take left after 2km to farm.

1948
10/N27
2-A-2
Tinto Hill near Biggar & Lanark A favourite climb in South/Central Scotland with easy access to start from Fallburn on the A73 near Symington, 10km south of Lanark. Park 100m behind Tinto Hills farm shop. Good, simple track there and back though it has its ups and downs before you get there. Braw views. 707m. Allow 2 hours though the annual racers do it in less than 30 minutes.

1949
10/L25
2-A-2
Dumgoyne near Blanefield Close to Glasgow and almost a mountain, so a popular non-strenuous hike. Huge presence, sits above A81 and Glengoyne Distillery (open to public). Approach from Strathblane War Memorial via Campsie Dene road. 7km track, allow 3–4 hours (or take the steep way up from the distillery). Refresh/replenish in Killearn (806/CENTRAL HOTELS, 1306/PUB FOOD). Take care on outcrops.

1950
9/L24
2-A-2
Conic Hill Balmaha, Loch Lomond An easier climb than the Ben up the road and a good place to view it from, Conic, on the Highland fault line, is one of the first Highland hills you reach from Glasgow. Stunning views also of Loch Lomond from its 358m peak. Ascend through woodland from the corner of Balmaha (the visitor centre) car park. Watch for buzzards and your footing on the final crumbly bits. Access all year with new Access Code. Easy walks also on the nearby island, Inchcailloch (2010/WOODLAND WALKS). 1.5 hours up.

1951
10/P23
1-A-1
Kinnoull Hill www.forestry.gov.uk · Perth Various starts from town (the path from beyond Branklyn Garden on the Dundee Rd is less frequented) to the wooded ridge above the Tay with its tower and incredible views to south from the precipitous cliffs. Surprisingly extensive area of hill side common and it's not difficult to get lost. The leaflet/map from Perth tourist information centre helps. Local lurv spot after dark.

1952
8/R19
2-B-2
Bennachie www.forestry.gov.uk · near Aberdeen The pilgrimage hill, an easy 528m often busy at weekends but never disappoints. Various trails take you to 'the Taps' from 3 main car parks. (1) From the new Bennachie Centre: 3km north of Inverurie on the A96, take left to chapel of Garioch (pronounced 'Geery'), then left (it's signed). Centre closed Mon. (2) 16km north of Inverurie on the A96, take the B9002 through Oyne, then signed on left – picnic here among the pines. (3) The Donview car park 5km north of Monymusk towards Blairdaff – the longer, gentler walk in. All car parks have trail-finders. From the fortified top you see what Aberdeenshire is about. 2 hours. Bennachie's soulmate, **Tap o' Noth**, is 20km west. Easy approach via Rhynie on A97 (then 3km).

1953
5/C20
Heaval Barra The mini-Matterhorn that rises above Castlebay is an easy and rewarding climb. At 1250ft, it's steep in places but never over-taxing. You see 'the road to Mingulay'. Start up hill through Castlebay, park behind the new-build house, find path via Our Lady of the Sea. 1.5 hours return.

Hill Walks

The following ranges of hills offer walks in various directions and more than one summit. They are all accessible and fairly easy. See p. 12 for walk codes.

1954
5

Walks on Skye www.skyewalk.co.uk Obviously many serious walks in and around the Cuillin (1970/MUNROS, 1979/SERIOUS WALKS), but almost infinite variety of others. Can do no better than read a great book, *50 Best Routes on Skye and Raasay* by Ralph Storer (available locally), which describes and grades many of the must-dos. And other pocket guides from the tourist information centre.

1955
10/P24
3-10KM
CIRC
XBIKES
2-A-2

Lomond Hills near Falkland The conservation village lies below a prominent ridge easily reached from the main street especially via Back Wynd (off which there's a car park). More usual approach to both East and West Lomond, the main tops, is from Craigmead car park 3km from village towards Leslie trail-finder board. The celebrated Lomonds (aka the Paps of Fife), aren't that high (West is 522m), but they can see and be seen for miles. Also: easy start from radio masts 3km up road from A912 east of Falkland. 1385/TEAROOM, 1311/GASTROPUBS (in village)
An easy rewarding single climb is **Bishop Hill**. Start 100m from the church in Scotlandwell. A steep path veers left and then there are several ways up. Allow 2 hours. Great view of Loch Leven, Fife and a good swathe of Central Scotland. Gliders glide over from the old airstrip below.

1956
10/R27
3KM
CIRC
XBIKES
1-A-2

The Eildons Melrose The 3 much-loved hills or paps visible from most of the Central Borders and easily climbed from the town of Melrose which nestles at their foot. Leave main sq by road to station (the Dingleton road), after 100m a path begins between 2 pebble-dash houses on the left. You climb the smaller first, then the highest central one (422m). You can make a circular route of it by returning to the golf course. Allow 2 hours. Good pub-grub options in Melrose; p. 157.

1957
10/N24
2-40KM
SOME CIRC
XBIKES
1/2-B-2

The Ochils www.friendsoftheochils.org.uk Usual approach from the 'hillfoot towns' at the foot of the glens that cut into their south-facing slopes, along the A91 Stirling-St Andrews road. Alva, Tillicoultry and Dollar all have impressive glen walks easily found from the main streets where tracks are marked (1988/GLEN & RIVER WALKS). Good start near Stirling from the Sheriffmuir road uphill from Bridge of Allan about 3km, look for pylons and a lay-by on the right (a reservoir just visible on the left). There are usually other cars here. A stile leads to the hills which stretch away to the east for 40km and afford great views for little effort from Dumyat (800 feet, 3 hour return) though the highest point is Ben Cleugh, 721m. Swimming place nearby is 'Paradise' (1687/PICNICS).

1958
10/R26
5-155KM
SOME CIRC
MTBIKES
1/2-B-2

The Lammermuirs www.lammermuirhills.com The hills southeast of Edinburgh that divide East Lothian's rich farmlands from the Borders' Tweed valley. Mostly high moorland but there's wooded gentle hill country in the watersheds of the southern rivers and spectacular coastal scenery between Cockburnspath and St Abbs Head (1749/WILDLIFE; 2038/COASTAL WALKS). Eastern part of the Southern Upland Way follows the Lammermuirs to the coast (1978/LONG WALKS). Many moorland walks begin at Whiteadder Reservoir car park (A1 to Haddington, the B6355 through Gifford), then 10km to a mysterious loch in the bowl of the hills. Excellent walks also around Abbey St Bathans; head off A1 at Cockburnspath. Through village to Toot Corner (signed 1km) and off to left, follow path above valley of Whiteadder to Edinshall Broch (2km). Further on, along river (1km), is a swing bridge and a fine place to swim. Circular walks possible; ask in village. The Yester estate near Gifford is nearer Edinburgh and a great foothill option (439/EDINBURGH WOODLAND WALKS).

1959 **The Cheviots** www.cheviot-hills.co.uk Not strictly in Scotland but they strad-
10/S27 dle the border and Border history. Many fine walks start from Kirk Yetholm (such
as the Pennine Way stretching 400km south to the Peak district and St Cuthbert's
Way; 1978/LONG WALKS) including an 8km circular route of typical Cheviot foothill
terrain. See *Walking in the Scottish Borders*, one of many excellent guides available
from Border tourist information centres. Most forays start at Wooler 20km from
Coldstream and the border. Cheviot itself (2676ft) a boggy plateau, Hedgehope via
the Harthope Burn more fun. Or look for Towford (1686/PICNICS).

The Campsie Fells near Glasgow 706/WALKS OUTSIDE GLASGOW.
The Pentland Hills near Edinburgh 431/WALKS OUTSIDE EDINBURGH.

Some Great Easy Munros

✓ ✓ *There are almost 300 hills in Scotland over 3000ft as tabled by Sir Hugh
Munro in 1891. Those selected here have been chosen for their relative ease
of access both to the bottom and thence to the top although you should only tackle
what is within your range of experience and ability. All these offer rewarding climbs.
None should be attempted without proper clothing (especially boots) and sustenance.
You may also need an OS map. Never underestimate how quickly weather conditions
can change in the Scottish mountains.*

1960 **Ben Lomond** Rowardennan, Loch Lomond Many folk's first Munro, given
9/L24 proximity to Glasgow (soul and city). It's not too taxing a climb and has rewarding
views (in good weather). 2 main ascents: the tourist route is easier, from toilet
block at Rowardennan car park (end of road from Drymen), well-trodden all the
way; or 500m up past Youth Hostel, a path follows burn – the Ptarmigan Route.
Steeper but quieter, more interesting. Circular walk possible. 974m. 3 hours up.

1961 **Schiehallion** near Kinloch Rannoch Fairy Hill of the Caledonians and a bit of
10/M22 a must (though very busy). New path c/o John Muir Trust over east flank. Start
Braes of Foss car park 10k from KR. 10km walk, ascent 750m. 5 hours. 1083m.

1962 **Carn Aosda** Glenshee One of the most accessible starting from Glenshee ski
10/M21 car park follow ski tow up. Ascent only 270m of 917m. So you can bag a Munro in
an hour. Easier still, take chairlift to Cairnwell, take in peak behind and then Carn
Aosda – hey, you're doing three Munros in a morning. The Grampian Highlands
unfold. Another easy (only 500m to climb) Munro nearby is **Cam an Tuirc** from a
start on the A93.

1963 **Meall Chuaich** Dalwhinnie Starting from verge of the A9 south of Cuaich at
7/M20 Cuaich cottages. Ascent only 623m, total walk 14km. Follow aqueduct to power
station then Loch Cuaich. An easily bagged 951m.

1964 **An Teallach** Torridon Sea-level start from Dundonnell on the A832 south of
7/J16 Ullapool. One of the most awesome Scots peaks but not the ordeal it looks. Path
well trod; great scrambling opportunities for the nimble. Peering over the pinnacle
of Lord Berkeley's Seat into the void is a jaw-drop. Take a day. Nice coffee shop
called Maggie's near start/finish (1412/TEAROOMS). 1,062m.

1965 **Beinn Alligin** Torridon The other great Torridon trek. Consult regarding start at
7/J17 NTS Countryside Centre on Torridon-Diabeg road. Car park by bridge on road to
Inveralligin and Diabeg, walk through woods over moor by river. Steepish pull up

onto the Horns of Alligin. You can cover 2 Munros in a circular route that takes you across the top of the world. 985m. Then you could tackle **Liathach**.

1966
9/G23

Ben More Mull The 'cool, high ben' sits in isolated splendour, the only Munro, bar the Cuillin, not on the mainland. Sea-level start from layby on the coast road B8073 that skirts the southern coast of Loch Na Keal at Dhiseig House, then a fairly clear path through the bleak landscape. Tricky near the top but there are fabulous views across the islands. 966m.

1967
6/L13

Ben Hope near Tongue The most northerly Munro and many a bagger's last; also a good one to start with. Steep and craggy with splendid views, the approach from the south is relatively easy and takes about 4 hours there and back. Go south from Hope (on the A38) on the unclassified road. 927m.

1968
7/L17

Ben Wyvis near Garve Standing apart from its northern neighbours, you can feel the presence of this mountain from a long way off. North of main A835 road Inverness-Ullapool and very accessible from it, park 6km north of Garve (48km from Inverness) and follow marked path by stream and through the shattered remnants of what was once a forest (replanting in progress). Leave the dereliction behind; the summit approach is by a soft, mossy ridge. Magnificent 1,046m.

1969
10/Q20

Lochnagar near Ballater Described as a fine, complex mountain, its nobility and mystique apparent from afar, not least Balmoral Castle. Approach via Glen Muick (pronounced 'Mick') road from Ballater to car park at Loch Muick (1612/LOCHS). Path to mountain well signed and well trodden. 18km return, allow 6-8 hours. Steep at top; the loch supernatural. Apparently on a clear day you can see the Forth Bridge. 1,155m.

1970
7/G19

Bla Bheinn Skye The magnificent massif, isolated from the other Cuillin, has a sea-level start and seems higher than it is. The *Munro Guide* describes it as 'exceptionally accessible'. It has an eerie jagged beauty and – though some scrambling is involved and it helps to have a head for exposed situations – there are no serious dangers. Take B8083 from Broadford to Elgol through Torrin, park 1km south of the head of Loch Slapin, walking west at Allt na Dunaiche along north bank of stream. Bla Bheinn (pronounced 'Blahven') is an enormously rewarding climb. Rapid descent for scree runners, but allow 8 hours. 928m.

1971
10/M22
NTS

Ben Lawers between Killin & Aberfeldy The massif of 7 summits including 6 Munros that dominate the north side of Loch Tay are linked by a twisting ridge 12km long that only once falls below 800m. If you're very fit, it's possible to do the lot in a day starting from the north or Glen Lyon side. Have an easier day of it knocking off Beinn Ghlas then Ben Lawers from the visitor centre (now closed) 5km off the A827. 4/5 hours.

1972
10/M22

Meall Nan Tarmachan The part of the ridge west of Lawers (above), which takes in a Munro and several tops, is one of the easiest Munro climbs and is immensely impressive. Start 1km further on from NTS visitor centre down 100m track and through gate. Slog to start. 12km walk, climb 800m, allow 6 hours.

Long Walks

✓ ✓ *These walks require preparation, route maps, very good boots etc. But don't carry too much. Sections are always possible. See p. 12 for walk codes.*

1973
9/K22
2-B-3
The West Highland Way www.west-highland-way.co.uk The 150km walk which starts at Milngavie 12km outside Glasgow and goes via some of Scotland's most celebrated scenery to emerge in Glen Nevis before the Ben. The route goes like this: Mugdock Moor-Drymen-Loch Lomond-Rowardennan-Inversnaid-Inverarnan-Crianlarich-Tyndrum-Bridge of Orchy-Rannoch Moor-Kingshouse Hotel-Glencoe-The Devil's Staircase-Kinlochleven. The latter part from Bridge of Orchy is the most dramatic. **The Bridge of Orchy Hotel** (01838 400208; 1174/ROADSIDE INNS – not cheap!) and **Kingshouse** (01855 851259) are both historic staging posts, as is the **Drover's Inn, Inverarnan** (808/CENTRAL HOTELS). It's a good idea to book accommodation (allowing time for muscle fatigue) and don't carry too much. Info leaflet/pack from shops or **Ranger Service** (01389 722600).
START Officially at Milngavie (pronounced 'Mull-guy') Railway Station (regular service from Glasgow Central, also buses from Buchanan St Bus Station), but actually from Milngavie shopping precinct 500m away. However, the countryside is close. Start from other end on Glen Nevis road from roundabout on A82 north from Fort William. The Way is well marked, but you must have a route map.

1974
11/J30
2-B-3
The Southern Upland Way www.southernuplandway.gov.uk 350km walk from Portpatrick south of Stranraer across the Rhinns of Galloway, much moorland, the Galloway Forest Park, the wild heartland of Southern Scotland, then through James Hogg country (1918/LITERARY PLACES) to the gentler east Borders and the sea at Pease Bay (official end, Cockburnspath). Route is Portpatrick-Stranraer-New Luce-Dalry-Sanquhar-Wanlockhead-Beattock-St Mary's Loch-Melrose-Lauder-Abbey St Bathans. The first and latter sections are the most obviously picturesque but highlights include Loch Trool, the Lowther Hills, St Mary's Loch, River Tweed. Usually walked west to east, the Southern Upland Way is a formidable undertaking... Info from **Ranger Service** (01835 825060).
START Portpatrick by the harbour and up along the cliffs past the lighthouse. Or Cockburnspath. Map is on side of shop at the Cross.

1975
8/Q17
1-A-3
The Speyside Way www.moray.gov.uk A long distance route which generally follows the valley of the River Spey from Buckie on the Moray Firth coast to Aviemore in the foothills of the Cairngorms and thence to Newtonmore, with side spurs to Dufftown up Glen Fiddich (7km) and to Tomintoul over the hill between the River Avon (pronounced 'A'rn') and the River Livet (24km). The main stem of the route largely follows the valley bottom, criss-crossing the Spey several times – a distance of around 100km, and is less strenuous than Southern Upland or West Highland Ways. The Tomintoul spur has more hill-walking character and rises to a great viewpoint at 600m. Throughout walk you are in whisky country with opportunities to visit Cardhu, Glenlivet and other distilleries nearby (1490/1483/WHISKY). Info from **Ranger Service** (01340 881266).
START Usual start is from coast end. Spey Bay is 8km north of Fochabers; the first marker is by the banks of shingle at the river mouth.

1976
7/K18
2-C-3
Glen Affric www.glenaffric.org In enchanting Glen Affric and Loch Affric beyond (1986/GLEN & RIVER WALKS; 1589/GLENS; 1677/PICNICS), some serious walking begins on the 32km Kintail trail. Done either west-east starting at the Morvich Outdoor Centre 2km from A87 near Shiel Bridge, or east-west starting at the Affric Lodge 15km west of Cannich. Route can include one of the approaches to the Falls of Glomach (1600/WATERFALLS).

1977 **The Cateran Trail** www.pkct.org Named after the Caterans who were
10/P22 marauding cattle thieves, this 100k hike crosses their old stamping ground, the
2-B-3 splendid hills and glens of Angus and Perthshire. Circular from a start at
Blairgowrie, it takes 4/5 days but also sections: Blairgowrie-Bridge of Cally-
Glenshee-Glen Isla-Alyth. Good inn options on the way (1172/1177/ROADSIDE INNS;
884/PERTHSHIRE HOTELS). All in splendid country; a well thought-out route.

1978 **St Cuthbert's Way** www.stcuthbertsway.fsnet.co.uk From Melrose in
10/R27 Scottish Borders (where St Cuthbert started his ministry) to Lindisfarne on Holy
2-A-3 Island off Northumberland (where he died) via St Boswells-Kirk Yetholm-Wooler.
100km but many sections easy. Bowden–Maxton and a stroll by the Tweed especially fine. Check local tourist information centres. Leaflets/maps available.

Serious Walks

✓ ✓ *None of these should be attempted without OS maps, proper equipment and
preparation. Hill or ridge walking experience may be essential.*

1979 **The Cuillin Mountains** www.isleofskye.com · Skye Much scrambling and, if
7/G19 you want it, serious climbing over these famously unforgiving peaks. The Red ones
3-C-3 are easier and many walks start at the Sligachan Hotel on the main Portree-
Broadford road. Every July there's a hill race up Glamaig; the conical one which
overlooks the hotel. Most of the Black Cuillin including the highest, Sgurr Alasdair
(993m), and Sgurr Dearg, 'the Inaccessible Pinnacle' (978m), can be attacked from
the campsite or the youth hostel in Glen Brittle. Good guides are *Introductory
Scrambles from Glen Brittle* by Charles Rhodes, or *50 Best Routes in Skye and Raasay*
by Ralph Storer, both available locally, but you will need a map. (2/BIG ATTRAC-
TIONS; 1160/HOSTELS; 1605/WATERFALLS; 1970/MUNROS; 1669/PICNICS.)

1980 **Aonach Eagach** Glencoe One of several possible major expeditions in the
9/J21 Glencoe area and one of the world's classic ridge walks. Not for the faint-hearted
3-C-3 or the ill-prepared. It's the ridge on your right for almost the whole length of the
glen from Altnafeadh to the road to the Clachaig Inn (rewarding refreshment). Start
from the main road. Car park opposite the one for the Lost Valley (1923/ENCHAN-
TING PLACES). Stiff pull up then the switchback path across. There is no turning
back. Scary pinnacles two-thirds over, then one more Munro and the knee-trem-
bling, scree-running descent. On your way, you'll have come close to heaven, seen
Lochaber in its immense glory and reconnoitred some fairly exposed edges and
pinnacles. Go with somebody good as I once did. (1627/SCENIC ROUTES; 1267/
BLOODY GOOD PUBS; 1157/HOSTELS; 1897/BATTLEGROUNDS.)

1981 **Buachaille Etive Mor** Glencoe In same area as above and another of the UK's
9/J21 best high-level hauls. Not as difficult or precarious as the Eagach and long loved by
3-C-3 climbers and walkers, with stunning views from its several false summits to the
actual top with its severe drops. Start on main Glencoe road. 5km past King's
House Hotel. Well-worn path. Allow 6/7 hours return.

1982 **Ben Nevis** Start on Glen Nevis road, 5km Fort William town centre (by bridge
9/K21 opposite youth hostel or from visitor centre) or signed from A82 after Glen Nevis
2-B-3 roundabout. Both lead to start at Achintee Farm and the Ben Nevis Inn (handy
afterwards; 1080/FORT WILLIAM). This is the most popular and safest route. Allow
the best part of a day (and I do mean the best – the weather can turn quickly
here). For the more interesting arete route, consult locally. Many people are killed

every year, even experienced climbers. It is the biggest, though not the best; you can see 100 Munros on a clear day (ie about once a year). You climb it because... well, because you have to. 1344m. 7 hours return.

1983
7/J19
3-C-3

The Five Sisters of Kintail & The Cluanie Ridge Both generally started from A87 along from Cluanie Inn (1269/BLOODY GOOD PUBS) and they will keep you right; usually walked east to west. Sisters is an uncomplicated but inspiring ridge walk, taking in 3 Munros and 2 tops. It's a hard pull up and you descend to a point 8km further up the road (so arrange transport). Many side spurs to vantage-points and wild views. The Cluanie or south ridge is a classic which covers 7 Munros. Starts at inn; 2 ways off back onto A876. Both can be walked in a single day (Cluanie allow 9 hours). (1158/HOSTELS.)

From the Kintail Centre at Morvich off A87 near Shiel Bridge another long distance walk starts to Glen Affric (1976/LONG WALKS).

1984
7/N19
3-C-3

Glen More Forest Park www.forestry.gov.uk from Coylumbridge and Loch Morlich; 32km. (2) joins (3) beyond Loch Morlich and both go through the Rothiemurchus Forest (2008/WOODLAND WALKS) and the famous **Lairig Ghru**, the ancient right of way through the Cairngorms which passes between Ben Macdui and Braeriach. Ascent is over 700m and going can be rough. This is one of the great Scottish trails. At end of Jun, the Lairig Ghru Race completes this course east-west in 3.5 hours, but generally this is a full-day trip. The famous shelter, Corrour Bothy between 'Devil's Point' and Carn A Mhaim, can be a halfway house. Near Linn of Dee, routes (1) and (2/3) converge and pass through the ancient Caledonian Forest of Mar. Going east-west is less gruelling and there's Aviemore to look forward to!

Glen Affric Or rather beyond Glen Affric and Loch Affric (1986/GLEN WALKS; 1589/GLENS), the serious walking begins (1976/LONG WALKS).

Glen & River Walks

See also Great Glens, p. 281. Walk codes are on p. 12.

1985
10/N21
UP TO 17KM
CIRC
XBIKES
1-B-2

✓ **Glen Tilt** Blair Atholl A walk of variable length in this classic Highland glen, easily accessible from the old Blair Rd off main Blair Atholl road near Bridge of Tilt Hotel, car park by the (very) old bridge. Trail leaflet from park office and local tourist information centres. Fine walking and unspoiled scenery begins only a short distance into the deeply wooded gorge of the River Tilt, but to cover the circular route you have to walk to 'Gilbert's Bridge' (9km return) or the longer trail to Gow's Bridge (17km return). Begin here also the great route into the Cairngorms leading to the Linn of Dee and Braemar, joining the track from Speyside which starts at Feshiebridge or Glenmore Forest (1984/SERIOUS WALKS).

1986
7/K18
5/8 KM
CIRC
BIKES
1-B-2

✓ **Glen Affric** www.glenaffric.org · Cannich, near Drumnadrochit Easy short walks are marked and hugely rewarding in this magnificent glen well known as the first stretch in the great east-west route to Kintail (1976/LONG WALKS) and the Falls of Glomach (1600/WATERFALLS). Starting point of this track into the wilds is at the end of the road at Loch Affric; there are many short and circular trails indicated here. Car park is beyond metal road 2km along forest track towards Affric Lodge (cars not allowed to lodge itself). Track closed in stalking season. Easier walks in famous Affric forest from car park at Dog Falls. 7km from Cannich (1677/PICNICS). Waterfalls and spooky tame birds. Good idea to hire bikes at Drumnadrochit or Cannich (01456 415364). Don't miss Glen Affric (1589/GLENS).

1987
10/L23
18KM · XCIRC
XBIKES
2-B-2

✓ **Balquhidder to Brig o' Turk** Easy amble through the heart of Scotland via Glenfinglas (1620/LOCHS) with a handy pub (1316/GASTROPUBS) and tearooms (1404/TEAROOMS) at either end. Not circular so best to arrange transport. Usually walked starting at Rob Roy graveyard (1884/GRAVEYARDS), then Ballimore and past Ben Vane to the reservoir and Brig o' Turk. B o' T start offers some great walk options.

1988
10/N24
3KM + TOPS
CIRC
XBIKES
1-A-2

✓ **Dollar Glen** Dollar The classic fairy glen in Central Scotland, positively hoaching with water spirits, reeking of ozone and euphoric after rain. Erosion has taken its toll and the path no longer goes deep into the gorge. 20km by A91 from Stirling or 18km from M90 at Kinross junction 6. You walk by the Burn of Care and the Burn of Sorrow. Start at side of the museum or golf club, or further up road (signed Castle Campbell) where there are 2 car parks, the top one 5 minutes from castle. The castle at head of glen is open 7 days till 6pm (Oct-Mar till 4pm) and has boggling views. There's a circular walk back or take off for the Ochil Tops, the hills surrounding the glen. There are also first-class walks (the hill trail is more rewarding than the Mill Trail) up the glens of the other hillfoot towns, Alva and Tillicoultry which also lead to the hills (1957/HILL WALKS).

1989
10/N24
3KM
CIRC
XBIKES
1-A-1

✓ **Rumbling Bridge** near Dollar Formed by another burn off the Ochils, an easier short walk in a glen with something of the chasmic experience and added delight of the unique double bridge (built 1713). At the end of one of the walkways under the bridge you are looking into a Scottish jungle landscape as the Romantics imagined. Near Powmill on A977 from Kinross (junction 6, M90) then 2km. Up the road is **The Powmill Milkbar** serving traditional and tasty home-made food for over 40 years. It's 5km west on the A977. Open 7 days till 5pm (6pm weekends) (1397/TEAROOMS). Go after your walk!

1990
10/P22
16KM
CIRC
BIKES
1-A-2

✔ **Loch Ordie** near Dunkeld Not a walk through a specific glen or riverside but one which follows many burns past lochs and ponds, skirts some impressive hills and is all in all a splendid and simple hike through glorious country almost Highland in nature but close to the Central Belt. Loch Ordie is halfway on a loop that starts at a bend on the A923 Blairgowrie road on left about 6km from Dunkeld after the turnoff for Loch of the Lowes. Deuchary Hill, the highest here at 509m, can be climbed on a non-circular path from the main circuit. This is one of the best, most scenic walks in Perthshire. 16km; allow 4/5 hours, mostly level.

1991
10/Q21

✔ **Glen Clova** www.clova.com Most walked of the Angus glens. Many start from end at Acharn especially west to Glen Doll (new ranger centre for orientation, etc). Also enquire at Glen Clova Hotel (1188/GET-AWAY HOTELS) – 2-hour Loops of (Loch) Brandy walk starts here – and repair there afterwards (great walkers' pub). Easy, rewarding walks!

1992
10/R23
1-A-1

✔ **The Lade Braes** St Andrews Unlike most walks here, this cuts through the town itself following the Kinness Burn. But you are removed from all that! Start at Westport at the traffic lights just after the garage on Bridge St or (marked) opposite 139 South St. Trailboard and signs. Through Coldshaugh Park (sidespur to Botanics on opposite bank) and the leafy glen and green sward at the edge of this beautiful town. Ends in a duck pond. You pass the back gardens of some very comfortable lives.

1993
7/M17
1-A-1

✔ **The Fairy Glen** Rosemarkie On the Black Isle. On Main A832, the road to Cromarty, 150 metres after the Plough Inn on the right, a car park and information board. Beautiful, easy 3km walk with gorge, 2 waterfalls and some great birdlife. Can finish on Rosemarkie beach to picnic and look for dolphins. Some superb trees.

1994
10/Q24
3KM
CIRC
XBIKES
1-A-2

Falkland Fife If you're in Falkland for the Palace (1763/CASTLES) or the tearoom (1385/TEAROOMS), add this amble up an enchanting glen to your day. Go through village then signed Cricket Club for Falkland Estate and School (an activity centre) – car park just inside gate (with map) – and gardens are behind it. Glen and refurbished path up the macadam road are obvious. Gushing burn, waterfalls – you can even walk behind one! Pub on return (1311/GASTROPUBS).

1995
6/N15
6KM
CIRC
XBIKES
1-B-1

The Big Burn Walk Golspie A non-taxing, perfect glen walk through lush diverse woodland. 3 different entrances including car park marked from A9 near Dunrobin Castle gates but most complete starts beyond Sutherland Arms and Sutherland Stonework at the end of the village. Go past derelict mill and under aqueduct following river. A supernature trail unfolds with ancient tangled trees, meadows, waterfalls, cliffs and much wildlife. 3km to falls, return via route to castle woods for best all-round intoxication.

1996
6/P14
XCIRC
XBIKES
1-B-1

The Strath at Dunbeath www.dunbeath-heritage.org.uk The glen or strath so eloquently evoked in Neil Gunn's *Highland River* (1917/LITERARY PLACES), a book which is as much about the geography as the history of his childhood. A path follows the river for many miles. A leaflet from the Dunbeath Heritage Centre points out places on the way as well as map on its entire floor. It's a spate river and in summer becomes a trickle; hard to imagine Gunn's salmon odyssey. It's only 500m to the broch, but it's worth going into the hinterland where it becomes quite mystical (1886/GRAVEYARDS).

1997 **Tweedside** Peebles The riverside trail that follows the Tweed from town (Hay
10/Q27 Lodge Park) past Neidpath Castle (1675/PICNICS) and on through classic Border
5/12KM wooded countryside crossing river either 2.5km out (5km round trip), or at Manor
CIRC Bridge 6km out (Lyne Footbridge, 12km). Pick up *Walking in the Scottish Borders*
XBIKES and other Tweedside trail guides at local tourist information centres.
1-A-1 Other good Tweedside walks between Dryburgh Abbey and Bemersyde House
grounds (1636/SCENIC ROUTES) and at Newton St Boswells by the golf course.

1998 **Failford Gorge** near Mauchline Woody gorge of the River Ayr. Start from
10/L27 bridge at Ayr end of village on B743 Ayr-Mauchline road (4km Mauchline). Easy,
3/5KM · CIRC marked trail. Pub in village great for ale (they brew their own 'Windie Goat'!) and
XBIKES local craic but better for food is the Sorn Inn east of Mauchline (1287/GASTROPUBS).
1-A-1 This is bucolic Ayrshire at its best.

1999 **Glen Lednock** near Comrie You can walk from Comrie or take car further up
10/M23 to monument or drive further into glen to reservoir (9km) for more open walks.
3/5KM From town take right off main A85 (to Lochearnhead) at Deil's Cauldron restaurant.
CIRC Walk and Deil's Cauldron (waterfall and gorge) are signed after 250m. Walk takes
XBIKES less than 1hr and emerges on road near Lord Melville's monument (climb for great
1-A-1 views back towards Crieff, about 25 minutes). Other walks up slopes to left after
you emerge from the tree-lined gorge road. There's also the start of a hike up Ben
Chonzie, 6km up glen at Coishavachan. This is one of the easiest Munros (931m),
with a good path and great views, especially to the northwest.

2000 **Bridge of Alvah** Banff Details: 2018/WOODLAND WALKS, mentioned here
8/R17 because the best bit is by the river and the bridge itself. The single span crossing
was built in 1772 and stands high above the river in a sheer-sided gorge. The river
below is deep and slow. In the right light it's almost Amazonian. Walk takes 1.5
hours from Duff House (2153/PUBLIC GALLERIES). There's a picture of Alvah upstairs
in the collection.

2001 **The Gannochy Bridge & The Rocks Of Solitude** near Edzell 2km north of
10/R21 village on B966 to Fettercairn. There's a lay-by after bridge and a wooden door on
2KM · XCIRC left (you're in the grounds of the Burn House). Through it is another world and a
XBIKES path above the rocky gorge of the River North Esk (1km). Huge stone ledges over
1-A-1 dark pools. You don't have to be alone (well maybe you do).

2002 9/J23 **Near Taynuilt** A walk (recommended by readers) combining education with
10KM recreation. Start behind Bonawe Ironworks (2140/HISTORY) and go along the river
CIRC side to a suspension bridge and thence to Inverawe Smokehouse (open to the
BIKES public; café). Walk back less interesting but all very nice. Best not to park in
1-A-1 Bonawe car park (for HS visitors, and it closes at 6pm).

2003 **Glen Trool** near Newton Stewart A simple non-climbing, well marked route
11/L30 round Loch Trool. A circular 8km but with many options. And a caff at the visitor
centre. 1597/GREAT GLENS.

2004 ✓✓ **Ardnamurchan** www.ardnamurchan.com For anyone who loves
9/G21 trees (or hills, great coastal scenery and raw nature), this far-flung -
peninsula is a revelation. Approach from south via Corran ferry on A82 south of
Fort William or north from Lochailort on A830 Mallaig–Fort William road
(1641/SCENIC ROUTES) or from Mull. Many marked and unmarked trails (see
Ariundle below) but consult internet or locally. To visit Ardnamurchan is to fall in
love with Scotland again and again. Woods especially around Loch Sunart. Good
family campsite at Resipole (1214/CAMPING) and lovely food at Lochaline (1040/
BEST HIGHLAND RESTAURANTS).

2005 ✓ **Randolph's Leap** near Forres Spectacular gorge of the plucky little
8/N17 Findhorn lined with beautiful beech woods and a great place to swim or picnic
1-4KM (1676/PICNICS), so listen up. Go either: 10km south of Forres on the A940 for
CIRC Grantown, then the B9007 for Ferness and Carrbridge. 1km from the sign for Logie
XBIKES Steading (2167/SHOPPING) and 300m from the narrow stone bridge, there's a pull-
1-A-2 over place on the bend. The woods are on the other side of the road. Or: take the
A939 south from Nairn or north from Grantown and at Ferness take the B9007 for
Forres. Approaching from this direction, it's about 6km along the road; the pull-
over is on your right. If you come to Logie Steading in this direction you've missed
it; don't – you will miss one of the sylvan secrets of the North. Trailboard at site
and at **Logie Steading** (from which it's a 3.5km walk return) and great café.

2006 ✓ **Lochaweside** Unclassified road on north side of loch between Kilchrenan
9/J24 and Ford, centred on Dalavich. Illustrated brochure available from local hotels
2-8KM around Kilchrenan and Dalavich post office, describes 6 walks in the mixed,
CIRC mature forest all starting from car parking places on the road. 3 starting from the
XBIKES Barnaline car park are trail-marked and could be followed without brochure. Avich
2-A-2 Falls route crosses River Avich after 2km with falls on return route. Inverinan Glen
is always nice. The timber trail from the Big Tree/Cruachan car park 2km south of
Dalavich takes in the loch, a waterfall and it's easy on the eye and foot (4km). The
track from the car park north of Kilchrenan on the B845 back to Taynuilt isn't on
the brochure, may be less travelled and also fine. Good pub at Kilchrenan. See
69/PLACES WE SHOULD LOVE MORE.

2007 9/K25 ✓ **Puck's Glen** www.forestry.gov.uk · near Dunoon Close to the gates of
3KM the Younger Botanic Garden at Benmore (1503/GARDENS) on the other side of
CIRC the A815 to Strachur 12km north of Dunoon. A short, exhilarating woodland walk
XBIKES from a convenient car park. Ascend through trees then down into a fairy glen,
1-A-1 follow the burn back to the road. Some swimming pools.

2008 ✓ **Rothiemurchus Forest** www.rothiemurchus.net · near Aviemore The
7/N19 place to experience the magic and the majesty of the great Caledonian Forest
1-A-2 and the beauty of Scots Pine. Approach from B970, the road that parallels the A9
from Coylumbridge to Kincraig/Kingussie. 2km from Inverdruie near Coylumbridge
follow sign for Loch an Eilean; one of the most perfect lochans in these or any
woods. Loch circuit 5km (1617/LOCHS). Info, sustenance and shopping at the
Rothiemurchus visitor centre at Inverdruie with wonderful Ord Ban café/restau-
rant.

2009
9/H21
5KM
CIRC
MTBIKES
1-A-2

✓ **Ariundle Oakwoods** Strontian 35km Fort William via Corran Ferry. Walk guide brochure at Strontian tourist information centre. Many walks around Loch Sunart and Ariundle: rare oak and other native species. You see how very different Scotland's landscape was before the Industrial Revolution used up the wood. Start over town bridge, turning right for Polloch. Go on past Ariundle Centre, with good home-baking café and park (1420/TEAROOMS). 2 walks; well marked.

2010 9/L25
3KM
CIRC
1-A-2

✓ **Inchcailloch Island** Loch Lomond The surprisingly large island near and easily accessed from Balmaha is criss-crossed with easy, interesting woodland walks with the loch always there through the trees. Pleasant afternoon option is to row there from Balmaha Boatyard (£10 a boat at TGP). They also run a regular ferry; 01360 870214.

2011 7/H18
CIRC
XBIKES
1-A-1

Balmacarra www.nts.org.uk · Lochalsh Woodland Garden 5km south Kyle of Lochalsh on A87. A woodland walk around the shore of Loch Alsh, centred on Lochalsh House. Mixed woodland in fairly formal garden setting where you are confined to paths. Views to Skye. A fragrant and verdant amble. Ranger service.

2012
10/N22
3-3KM
CIRC
XBIKES
1-A-2

The Birks o' Aberfeldy Circular walk through oak, beech and the birch (or birk) woods of the title, easily reached and signed from town main street (1km). Steep-sided wooded glen of the Moness Burn with attractive falls especially the higher one spanned by bridge where the 2 marked walks converge. This is where Burns 'spread the lightsome days' in his eponymous poem. Excellent tearoom, the Watermill, back in town (1391/TEAROOMS). Allow 2 hours.

2013
10/P22
3-2KM
CIRC
XBIKES
1-A-1

The Hermitage, Dunkeld www.visitdunkeld.com On A9 2km north of Dunkeld. Popular, easy, accessible walks along glen and gorge of River Braan with pavilion overlooking the Falls and, further on, Ossian's Cave. Also uphill Craig Vinean walks starts here to good viewpoint (2km). Several woody walks around Dunkeld/Birnam – there's a good leaflet from the tourist information centre. 2km along river is **Rumbling Bridge**, a deep gorge, and beyond it great spots for swimming (1672/SWIMMING HOLES).

2014
7/N19

Glenmore Forest Park www.forestry.gov.uk · near Aviemore Along from Coylumbridge (and adjacent Rothiemurchus) on road to ski resort, the forest trail area centred on Loch Morlich (sandy beaches, good swimming, water sports). Visitor centre has maps of walk and bike trails and an activity programme. Glenmore Lodge (01479 861256) is Scotland's Outdoor Training Centre and well worth a visit. They know a lot about walking!

2015
10/M24
2 OR 4KM
CIRC
XBIKES
1-A-1

Above the Pass of Leny Callander A walk through mixed forest (beech, oak, birch, pine) with great Trossachs views. Start from main car park on A84 4km north of Callander (Falls of Leny are on opposite side of road, 100m away). Various options marked and boarded where marshy, though area under construction at TGP '09. Another short but glorious walk is to the **Bracklinn falls** – signed off east end of Callander Main St; start by the golf course (1km. See also 1683/PICNICS.). Also loop to the Craggs (adding another 2km).

2016
10/N22
2 -15KM
CIRC
BIKES
1-B-2

Loch Tummel Walks near Pitlochry The mixed woodland north of Loch Tummel reached by the B8019 from Pitlochry to Rannoch. Visitor centre at Queen's View (1660/VIEWS), 01796 473123; and walks in the Allean Forest which take in some historical sites (a restored farmstead, standing stones) start nearby (2-4km). There are many other walks in area: the Forestry Commission brochure is worth following (available from visitor centre and local tourist information centres). (1625/LOCHS.)

2017 **The New Galloway Forest** www.forestry.gov.uk Huge area of forest and hill
11/L30 country with every type of trail including part of Southern Upland Way from Bargrennan to Dalry (1974/LONG WALKS). Visitor centres at Kirroughtree (5km Newton
Stewart) and Clatteringshaws Loch on the Queen's Way (9km New Galloway). Glen
and Loch Trool are very fine (1597/GLENS); the 'Retreat Oakwood' near Laurieston
has 5km trails. Kitty's in New Galloway has great cakes and tea (1386/TEAROOMS).
There's a river pool on the Raiders' Rd (1684/PICNICS). One could ramble on...

2018 8/R17 **Duff House** www.duffhouse.org.uk · **Banff** Duff House is the major
7KM attraction around here (2153/PUBLIC GALLERIES), but if you've time it would be a
CIRC pity to miss the wooded policies and the meadows and riverscape of the Deveron.
XBIKES To the Bridge of Alvah where you should be bound is about 7km return; 1.5 hours
1-A-2 return. See also 2000/GLEN & RIVER WALKS.

2019 7/L17 **Torrachilty Forest & Rogie Falls** www.forestry.gov.uk · **near Contin &**
1-4KM **Strathpeffer** Enter by old bridge just outside Contin on main A835 west to
CIRC Ullapool or further along (4km) at Rogie Falls car park. Shame to miss the falls
XBIKES (1613/WATERFALLS), but the woods and gorge are pleasant enough if it's merely a
1-A-2 stroll you need. Ben Wyvis further up the road is the big challenge (1968/MUNROS).

2020 **Abernethy Forest** **near Boat of Garten** 3km from village off B970, but hard
8/N19 to miss because the famous ospreys are signposted from all over (1725/BIRDS).
Nevertheless this woodland reserve is a tranquil place among native pinewoods
around Loch Mallachie with dells and trails. Many other birdies twittering around
your picnic. They don't dispose of the midges.

2021 **Fochabers** www.fochabers-heritage.org.uk On main A96 about 3km east of
8/Q17 town are some excellent woody and winding walks around the glen and Whiteash
Hill (2-5km). Further west on the **Moray Coast Culbin Forest**: head for Cloddy-
moss or Kentessack off A96 at Brodie Castle 12km east of Nairn (1761/CASTLES).
Acres of Sitka in a sandy coastal forest.

Where To Find Scots Pine

Scots Pine, with oak and birch etc, formed the great Caledonian Forest which once covered most of Scotland. Native Scots Pine is very different from the regimented rows of pine trees we associate with forestry plantations and which now drape much of the countryside. It is more like a deciduous tree with reddish bark and irregular foliage; no two ever look the same. The remnants of the great stands of pine are beautiful to see, mystical and majestic, a joy to walk among and no less worthy of conservation perhaps than a castle or a bird of prey. Here are some places you will find them:

Rothiemurchus Forest 2008/WOODLAND WALKS.

2022
8/Q20   **Glentanar** www.glentanar.co.uk · Royal Deeside Near Ballater, 10-15km southwest of Aboyne.

2023 8/P20   Around **Braemar** and **Grantown-On-Spey**.

2024
10/P20   Around **Linn of Dee** (1637/SCENIC ROUTES), especially the back road to Mar Lodge (1251/HOUSE PARTIES).

2025
10/M24   **Strathyre** near Callander South of village on right of main road after Loch Lubnaig.

2026
10/L24   **Achray Forest** www.forestry.gov.uk · near Aberfoyle Some pine near the Duke's Pass road, the A821 to Loch Katrine, and amongst the mixed woodland in the 'forest drive' to Loch Achray.

2027
10/L22   **Blackwood of Rannoch** www.rannoch.net South of Loch Rannoch, 30km west of Pitlochry via Kinloch Rannoch. Start from Carie, fair walk in. 250-year-old pines; an important site which may be trashed by a proposed resort for the rich.

2028
9/L25   **Rowardennan** Loch Lomond End of the road along east side of loch near Ben Lomond. Easily accessible pines near the loch side, picnic sites, etc.

2029
7/J17   Shores of **Loch Maree, Loch Torridon** and around **Loch Clair, Glen Torridon**. Both near the **Beinn Eighe National Nature Reserve** (1751/GREAT WILDLIFE RESERVES). Visitor centre on A832 north of Kinlochewe.

2030
7/L18   **Glen Affric** near Drumnadrochit 1589/GLENS. Biggest remnant of the Caledonian Forest in classic glen. Many strolls and hikes possible. Try Dog Falls (on main road) for Affric introduction.

Native pinewoods aren't found south of Perthshire, but there are fine plantation examples in southern Scotland at:

2031
10/Q27   **Glentress** near Peebles 7km on A72 to Innerleithen. Mature forest up the burn side, though surrounded by commercial forest.

2032
11/N29   **Shambellie Estate** near Dumfries 1km from New Abbey beside A710 at the Shambellie House, 100yds sign. Ancient stands of pine over the wall amongst other glorious trees; this is like virgin woodland. Planted 1775-80. Magnificent (and great new garden nearby: 1532/GARDENS in the trees).

Coastal Walks

2033
9/F26
XCIRC
XBIKES
2-B-2

✓✓ **Kintra** Islay On Bowmore-Port Ellen road take Oa turnoff: then Kintra signed 7km. Park in old farmyard by campsite (1202/WILD CAMPING). A fabulous beach (1574/BEACHES) runs in opposite direction and a notable golf course behind it (2066/GOLF IN GREAT PLACES). This walk leads along north coast of the Mull of Oa, an area of diverse beauty, sometimes pastoral, sometimes wild, with a wonderful shoreline. Many great picnic spots. Also on the Oa, the walk to the American Monument is spectacular (1.5km or 6km circular). See 1835/MONUMENTS.

2034
8/T18

✓✓ **The Bullers Of Buchan** near Peterhead 8km south of Peterhead on A975 road to/from Cruden Bay. Park and walk 100m to cottages. To the north is the walk to Boddam and Longhaven Nature Reserve along dramatic cliffs and south past Slains Castle (1799/RUINS). The Bullers is at start of walk, a sheer-sided 'hole' 75m deep with an outlet to the sea through a natural arch. Walk round the edge of it, looking down on layers of birds (who might try to dive-bomb you away from their nests); it's a wonder of nature on an awesome coast. Take great care (and a head for heights).

2035
6/K12

✓✓ **Cape Wrath & The Cliffs of Clo Mor** www.capewrath.org.uk Britain's most northwesterly point reached by ferry from 1km off the A838 4km south of Durness; a 10-minute crossing then 40-minute minibus ride to Cape. Ferry holds 12 and runs May-Sep (call for times: 01971 511343) or ferryman direct (07719 678729): John Morrison on his boat for 30 years. At 280m Clo Mor are high though not the highest cliffs in UK (which are all on islands St Kilda, Foula and Hoy); for cliffs, ask to be put off the bus (which is heading for the Stevenson lighthouse) and reduce the walk to 3km. There are around 8 trips a day, weather and MoD range permitting. Bikes are ok. Easter-Sep. In other direction, the 28km to Kinlochbervie is one of Britain's most wild and wonderful coastal walks. Beaches include Sandwood (1571/BEACHES). While in this North West area: **Smoo Cave** 2km east of Durness is worth a visit.

2036
6/J14
1-B-2

✓ **Old Man Of Stoer** near Lochinver The easy, exhilarating walk to the dramatic 70m sandstone sea stack. Start from lighthouse off unclassified road 14km north Lochinver. Park and follow sheep tracks; cliffs are high and steep. 7km round trip; 2/3 hours. Then find the Secret Beach (1578/BEACHES).

2037
11/N30
1-A-2

✓ **Rockcliffe to Kippford** An easy and can be circular stroll along the Scottish Riviera through woodland near the shore (2km) past the Mote of Mark, a Dark Age hill fort with views to Rough Island. The better cliff top walk is in the other direction to Castlehillpoint. Good teashop in Rockcliffe (1415/TEAROOMS) and famed waterside pub, the Anchor, in Kippford (1318/GASTROPUBS).

2038
10/S25
5-10KM
CIRC · XBIKES
1-B-2

✓ **St Abbs Head** Some of the most dramatic coastal scenery in southern Scotland, scary in a wind, rhapsodic on a blue summer's day. Extensive wildlife reserve and trails through coastal hills and vales to cliffs. Cars can go as far as lighthouse, but best to park at visitor centre near farm on St Abbs village road 3km from A1107 to Eyemouth and follow route (1749/WILDLIFE). Very nice caff here.

2039
7/H18

Applecross This far peninsula is marvellous for many reasons including staying alive and eating out (1629/SCENIC ROUTES), but there are fine walks in and around the foreshore of Applecross Bay including river and woodland strolls. All detailed in a 'scenic walks' leaflet available locally.

2040 9/H21
1OKM RET
XCIRC
BIKES
1-B-1

Singing Sands Ardnamurchan 2km north of Acharacle, signed for Arevegaig. 3km to Arevegaig and park before wooden bridge (gate may be locked). Cross wooden bridge, following track round side of Kentra Bay. Follow signs for Gorteneorn, and walk through forest track and woodland to beach. As you pound the sands they should sing to you whilst you bathe in the beautiful views of Rum, Eigg, Muck and Skye (and just possibly the sea). Check at tourist information centre for directions and other walks booklet. 'Beware unexploded mines', it says. Mmm!

2041 8/R17
8KM · XCIRC
XBIKES
1-A-1

East From Cullen Moray Coast This is the same walk mentioned with reference to Sunnyside (1569/BEACHES), a golden beach with a fabulous ruined castle (Findlater) that might be your destination. There's a track east along from harbour. 2 hours return. Superb coastline.

2042
8/S17

Crovie-Troup Head Moray Coast Another Moray Coast classic that takes in the extraordinary cliff-clinging village of Crovie and the bird-stacked cliffs of the headland. Start at car park and viewpoint above Crovie 15km east of Banff off B9031. Park and walk to end of village, then follow path to Troup Head. 5km return. Shorter walk (1.5km) from RSPB car park 2km off B9031 east of Crovie/Gardenstown, signed for Northfield. Big sky and sea and birdlife.

2043
7/M17
5KM
CIRC
XBIKES
1-A-1

The South Sutor Cromarty The walk, known locally as 'The 100 Steps' though there are a few more than that, from Cromarty village (1558/COASTAL VILLAGES, 1423/TEAROOMS, 1042/HIGHLAND RESTAURANTS) round the tip of the south promontory at the narrow entrance to the Cromarty Firth. East of village past bowling green then up through woods to headland. Good bench! Go further to top car park and viewpoint panel. Perhaps return by road. There may be dolphins in that sea!

2044
10/R24
2-B-2

The Chain Walk Elie Unique and adventurous headland scramble at the west end of Elie (and Earlsferry). Britain's only Via Ferrata? Go to end of the road then by path skirting golf course towards headland. Hand- and footholds carved into rock with chains to haul yourself up. Emerge by Shell Bay Caravan Park. Watch tide; don't go alone.

2045
9/J26
2-B-2

Cock of Arran Lochranza This round trip usually starts at Lochranza castle, a breathtaking coastal trail round the north end of the island (see 2269/FANTASTIC ISLAND WALKS). Great for twitchers, ramblers and fossil hunters. Strong boots advisable. Approximately 4 hours, around 12km.

2045A

Island Coasts See also Fantastic Walks in the Islands, p. 389, but 3 spectacular walks recommended by reader John Dera (of Bermuda) but not yet walked by me are:
Duirinish coast on **Skye**, a long (8-12 hours) route with some of the best 'coastal architecture' in the UK: sea arches, waterfalls, stacks. For starts, consult.
Minginish coast, also on **Skye**, with views to the small isles, Hebrides and the Cuillin with fantastic geology and sea eagles above. 6-8 hours.
The Westray Way on **Orkney** with splendid cliffs, huge numbers of birds, Old Man of Hoy and other breathtaking views. Takes about 4 hours.
I must get out more!

Section 10

Outdoor Activities

Scotland's Great Golf Courses

Those listed open to non-members and available to visitors (including women!) at most times, unless otherwise stated. Handicap certificates may be required.

AYRSHIRE

2046
9/K28

✓ ✓ ✓ **Turnberry** www.turnberry.co.uk · 01655 334032 Ailsa (championship), Kintyre and Arran courses. Possible by application, cheaper if you're at the hotel (766/AYRSHIRE HOTELS). Superb. Golf academy a great place to learn. Was home to the Open again '09.

2047
9/K27

✓ ✓ **Royal Old Course** www.royaltroon.co.uk · 01292 311555 · Troon Very difficult to get on. No wimmen. Staying at Marine Highland Hotel (01292 314444) helps. Easier is **The Portland Course** (also 01292 311555) across the road from Royal. And 772/AYRSHIRE HOTELS for the adjacent Piersland House Hotel.

2048
9/K27

✓ **Glasgow Gailes/Western Gailes** www.glasgowgailes-golf.com · 0141 942 2011/01294 311258 Superb links courses next to one another, 5km south of Irvine off A78.

2049
9/L27

Old Prestwick www.prestwickgc.co.uk · 01292 671020 Original home of the Open and 'every challenge you'd wish to meet'. Hotels opposite cost less than a round. Unlikely to get on weekends (Sat members only).

EAST LOTHIAN

2050
9/R25

✓ ✓ **Gullane No.1** www.gullanegolfclub.com · 01620 842255 One of 3 varied courses surrounding charming village on links and within driving distance (35km) of Edinburgh. Muirfield is nearby, but you need an introduction. Gullane is okay most days except Sat/Sun. (Handicap required for no.1 only – under 24 men, 30 ladies.) No.3 best for beginners. Visitor centre acts as clubhouse for non-members on nos. 2/3. Clubhouse for members/no.1 players only.

2051
9/R25

✓ ✓ **North Berwick East & West** www.northberwick.org.uk · 01620 892135 East (officially the Glen Golf Club) has stunning views. A superb cliff-top course and is not too long. West more taxing (especially the classic 'Redan') used for Open qualifying; a very fine links. Also has 9-hole kids' course (01620 892135).

2052
9/Q25

Musselburgh Links www.musselburgholdlinks.co.uk · 0131 665 5438 The original home of golf (really: golf recorded here in 1672), but this local authority-run 9-hole links is not exactly top turf and is enclosed by Musselburgh Racecourse. Nostalgia still appeals though. **Royal Musselburgh** (01875 810276) nearby compensates. It dates to 1774, fifth-oldest in Scotland. Busy mornings and Fri-Sun.

NORTH EAST

2053
10/R23

✓ ✓ **Carnoustie** www.carnoustiegolflinks.co.uk · 01241 802270 3 good links courses; even possible (with handicap cert) to get on the championship course (though weekends difficult). Every hole has character. **Buddon Links** is cheaper and relatively quiet. Combination tickets available. A well-managed and accessible course, increasingly a golfing must. Open held here '07.

2054
8/T19 ✓ **Murcar Links** www.murcar.co.uk · 01224 704354 · Aberdeen Getting on **Royal Aberdeen** Course is difficult for most people, but Murcar is a testing alternative, a seaside course 6km north of centre off Peterhead road signed at roundabout after Exhibition Centre. Handicap certificate needed. Other municipal courses include charming 9-hole at Hazelhead (in an excellent 3-course complex).

2055
8/T18 ✓ **Cruden Bay** www.crudenbaygolfclub.co.uk · 01779 812285 · near Peterhead On A975 40km north of Aberdeen. Designed by Tom Simpson and ranked in UK top 50, a spectacular links course with the intangible aura of bygone days. Quirky holes epitomise old-fashioned style. Weekends difficult to get on.

2056
7/N17 ✓ **Nairn** www.nairngolfclub.co.uk · 01667 453208 Traditional seaside links course and one of the easiest championship courses to get on. Good clubhouse, friendly folk. Nairn Dunbar on other side of town also has good links. Handicap certificate required.

2057
6/N16 ✓ **Royal Dornoch** www.royaldornoch.com · 01862 810219 Sutherland championship course laid out by Tom Morris in 1877. Recently declared 5th-best course in the world outside the US, but not busy or incessantly pounded. No poor holes. Stimulating sequences. Probably the most northerly great golf course in the world – and not impossible to get on. Sister course the **Struie** also a treat.

FIFE

2058
10/R23 ✓✓✓ **St Andrews** www.standrews.org.uk · 01334 466666 The home and Mecca of golf, very much part of the town and the largest golf complex in Europe. Old Course most central, celebrated. Application by ballot the day before (handicap cert needed). For Jubilee (1897, upgraded 1989) and Eden (1914, laid out by Harry S. Holt paying homage to the Old with large, sloping greens), apply the day before. New Course (1895, some rate the best) easiest access. Less demanding are the new Strathyrum and Balgove (upgraded 9-hole for beginners) courses. All 6 courses contiguous and 'in town'. The new Castle Course is a 320-acre clifftop course for all abilities and the Dukes Course (part of Old Course Hotel) 3km away is a great alternative to the links. Reservations (and ballot). There's a whole lot of golf to be had – get your money out!

2059
10/R24 ✓✓ **Kingsbarns** www.kingsbarns.com · 01334 460860 Between St Andrews and Crail. One of Fife's newest courses but one of its best. In the 'World Top 100'. Inviting, challenging and a beautiful location on a secret coast by Cammo House grounds. Not cheap.

2060
10/Q24 ✓ **Ladybank** www.ladybankgolf.co.uk · 01337 830814 Best inland course in Fife; Tom Morris-designed again. Very well kept and organised. Good facilities. Tree-lined and picturesque.

2061
10/R24 **Elie** www.golfhouseclub.co.uk · 01333 330301 Splendid open links maintained in top condition; can be windswept. The starter has his famous periscope and may be watching you. Adjacent 9-hole course, often busy with kids, is fun (01333 330955).

2062
10/R24 **Crail** www.crailgolfingsociety.co.uk · 01333 450686 Balcomie Links originally designed by the legendary Tom Morris, or Craighead Links new sweeping course. All holes in sight of sea. Not expensive; easy to get on.

2063
10/Q24

Lundin Links www.lundingolfclub.co.uk · 01333 320202 Challenging seaside course used as Open qualifier. Some devious contourings. In the village there is also a separate 9-hole course, Lundin Ladies, open to all (01333 320832).

ELSEWHERE

2064
10/N24

✓✓✓ **Gleneagles** www.gleneagles.com · 0800 389 3737 Legendary golf the mainstay of resort complex in perfect Perthshire (hotel 01764 662231; report: 1116/COUNTRY-HOUSE HOTELS). 4 courses including PGA centenary which will host Ryder Cup in 2014. No handicap certificates required.

2065
10/S27

✓✓ **Roxburghe Hotel Golf Course** www.roxburghe.net · 01573 450333 · near Kelso Only championship course in the Borders. Designed by Dave Thomas along banks of River Teviot. Part of the Floors Castle estate. Open to non-residents. Fairways bar/brasserie clubhouse. Report: 820/BORDER HOTELS.

Good Golf Courses In Great Places

2066
9/F26

✓ **Machrie** www.machrie.com · 01496 302310 · Isle of Islay 7km Port Ellen. Worth going to Islay (BA's airstrip adjacent course or CalMac ferry from Kennacraig, near Tarbert) just for the golf. The Machrie (Golf) Hotel is sparse but convenient. Old-fashioned course to be played by feel and instinct. Splendid, sometimes windy isolation with a warm bar and restaurant at the end of it. The notorious 17th, 'Iffrin' (it means Hell), vortex shaped from the dune system of marram and close-cropped grass, is one of many great holes. 18 holes.

2067
9/G28

✓ **Macrihanish** www.machgolf.com · 01586 810213 · by Campbeltown Amongst the dunes and links of the glorious 8km stretch of the Machrihanish Beach (1570/BEACHES). The Atlantic provides thunderous applause for your triumphs over a challenging course. 9/18 holes.

2068
11/N30

✓ **Southerness** www.southernessgolfclub.com · 01387 880677 · Solway Firth 25km south of Dumfries by A710. A championship course on links on the silt flats of the Firth. Despite its prestige, visitors do get on. Start times available 10-12pm and 2-4pm. There are few courses as good as this at these prices. Under the wide Solway sky, it's pure – southerness.

2069
10/P22

✓ **Rosemount** www.theblairgowriegolfclub.co.uk · 01250 872622 · Blairgowrie Off A93, south of Blairgowrie. An excellent, pampered and well-managed course in the middle of green Perthshire, an alternative perhaps to Gleneagles, being much easier to get on (most days) and rather cheaper (though not at weekends). 18 holes.

2070
8/N19

✓ **Boat of Garten** www.boatgolf.com · 01479 831282 Challenging, picturesque course in town where ospreys have been known to wheel overhead. Has been called the 'Gleneagles of the North'; certainly the best around, though not for novices. 18 holes.

2071
6/M16

✓ **Tain & Brora** www.tain-golfclub.co.uk · 01862 892314 & www.broragolf.co.uk · 01408 621911 2 northern courses that are a delight to play on. Tain designed by Tom Morris in 1890. Brora stunning with good clubhouse and coos on the course. With Royal Dornoch (above), they're a roving-golfer must.

2072 **Glencruitten** www.obangolf.com · 01631 562868 · Oban Picturesque course
9/H23 on the edge of town. Head south (A816) from Argyll Sq, bearing left at church.
Course is signed. Quite tricky with many blind holes. Can get busy, so phone first.
18 holes.

2073 **Gairloch** www.gairlochgolfclub.com · 01445 712407 Just as you come into
7/H16 town from the south on A832, it looks over the bay and down to a perfect, pink,
sandy beach. Small clubhouse with honesty box out of hours. Not the world's
most agonising course; in fact, on a clear day with views to Skye, you can forget
agonising over anything. 9 holes.

2074 **Harris Golf Club** www.harrisgolf.com · 01859 550226 · Scarista, Isle of
5/E16 Harris Phone number is for the secretary, but no need to phone – just turn up on
the road between Tarbert and Rodel and leave £10 in the box. First tee commands
one of the great views in golf and throughout this basic, but testing course, you
are looking out to sea over Scarista beach (1575/BEACHES) and bay. The sunset may
put you off your swing. 9 holes.

2075 **New Galloway** www.nggc.co.uk · 01644 420737 Local course on south edge
11/M29 of this fine wee toon. Almost all on a slope but affording great views of Loch Ken
and the Galloway Forest behind. No bunkers and only 9 short holes, but
exhilarating play. Easy on, except Sun. Just turn up.

2076 **Minto** www.mintogolf.co.uk · 01450 870220 · Denholm 9km east of Hawick.
10/R28 Spacious parkland in Teviot valley. Best holes 3rd, 12th and 16th.
Vertish Hill www.hawickgolfclub.com · 01450 372293 · Hawick A more
challenging hill course. Both among the best in Borders. 18. Best holes 2nd and
18th. An excellent guide to all the courses in the Borders is available from tourist
information centres: *Freedom of the Fairways.*

2077 **Gifford** www.giffordgolfclub.com · 01620 810591 Dinky inland course on the
10/R26 edge of a charming village, bypassed by the queue for the big East Lothian courses
and a guarded secret among the regulars. Generally ok, but phone starter (above)
for availability. I was touched when they wrote to thank me for this entry. 9 holes.

2078 **Strathpeffer** www.strathpeffergolf.co.uk · 01997 421219 Very hilly (and we
7/L17 do mean hilly) course full of character and with exhilarating Highland views. Small-
town friendliness. You are playing up there with the gods and some other old
codgers. 18 holes.

2079 **Elgin** www.elgingolfclub.com · 01343 542338 1km from town on A941 Perth
8/P17 road. Many memorable holes on moorland/parkland course in an area where links
may lure you to the coast (**Nairn, Lossiemouth**). 18 holes.

2080 **Durness** www.durnessgolfclub.org · 01971 511364 The most northerly golf
6/L12 course on mainland UK, on the wild headland by Balnakeil Bay, looking over to
Faraid Head. The last hole is 'over the sea'. Only open since 1988, it's already got
cult status. 2km west of Durness. 9 holes.

2081 **Traigh** www.traighgolf.co.uk · 01687 450337 · Arisaig A830 Fort William-
7/H20 Mallaig road, 2km north Arisaig. Pronounced 'try' – and you may want to. The
islands are set out like stones in the sea around you and there are 9 hilly holes of
fun. Has been called 'the most beautiful 9 holes in the world'.

The Best Cycling

EASY CYCLING

2082
10/S27

✓ **The Borders** The Borders with its gentle hills, river tracks and low urbanisation seems to be paving the cycleway both for mountain biking (see below) and for more leisurely and family pursuits. Good linkage and signage and many routes, eg the 4 Abbeys, the Tweed Cycleway, the Borderloop and individual trails. Guides available from tourist information centres for almost all the Border towns. There's ample choice for all abilities and ages. See also 7 Stanes (below).

2083
8/Q18
20KM
CAN BE CIRC

✓ **Speyside Way Craigellachie-Ballindalloch** The cycling part of the Way (1975/LONG WALKS), with great views; flat and no cars. Goes past distilleries. Circular by return on minor roads.
START Craigellachie by rangers' office.

2084
10/M25
55KM

Forth & Clyde Canal Glasgow-Falkirk Wheel East out of the city, urban at first then nice in the Kelvin Valley; Kilsyth Hills to the north. Falkirk Wheel should be seen (4/ATTRACTIONS).
START The Maryhill Locks, Maryhill Rd.

2085
11/L29
15KM
CAN BE CIRC

Glentrool near Newton Stewart Two routes from visitor centre (1623/LOCHS, 1910/MARY, CHARLIE & BOB). Deep in the forest and well signed. Briefly joins public road. The 7 Stanes sections can be difficult (see below).
START Glentrool visitor centre off A714. Bike hire at **Kirroughtree** and network of trails listed from here (see below).

2086 1
12KM/
VARIOUS
CIRC

Edinburgh Trails Edinburgh streets can be a nightmare for cyclists and there's lots of uphill graft. But there is a vast network of cycle and towpaths especially north of the New Town. Another good run is to Balerno from Union Canal towpath in Lower Gilmore Place. End at Balerno High School.

2087
10/L24
11KM
CAN BE CIRC

The Trossachs www.lochlomond-trossachs.org · near Aberfoyle & Callander Many low-level lochside trails. Consult tourist information centres. Nice run is Loch Ard Circle from Aberfoyle going west (signed Inversnaid Scenic Route).

2088
8/N19
20KM
CIRC

Loch an Eilean near Aviemore Lots of bike tracks here in the Rothiemurchus Forest. This one goes past one of Scotland's most beautiful lochs (1617/LOCHS) and you can go further to Loch Insh via Feshiebridge and around Glen Feshie. Probably best to get a route leaflet at Rothiemurchus Centre or Aviemore Visitor Centre.
START Signed from B970 at Coylumbridge.

2089
9/K26

Cumbrae Take ferry from Largs to beautiful Cumbrae Island (1374/CAFÉS). Four or five routes around the island. One stiff pull to a great viewpoint. Others stick to sea level. Consult leaflet from tourist information centre. All roads quiet.

MOUNTAIN BIKING

2090
10, 11

✓✓ **7 Stanes** www.7stanes.gov.uk · Borders & South West Ambitious and hugely popular network of bike trails in south of Scotland, different lengths and abilities in each place. Include **Glentress/The Tweed Valley** (see below), **Newcastleton**, **Forest of Ae**, **Dalbeattie**, **Mabie**, **Glentrool** (see above), and **Kirroughtree** (see above). Routes at all levels. Many challenges. Good signage throughout.

2091
10/Q27
✓ ✓ **Glentress Forest** www.thehubintheforest.co.uk · near Peebles
Specially constructed mountain-bike trails. Well signed and well used in this hugely popular national cycling centre. Great café (1375/CAFÉS).Trails for all levels, plenty of flowing descents and drops. **7 Stanes** cross-country route also starts nearby at Traquair.

2092
11/M29
25KM
CIRC
Clatteringshaws Near Glentrool (see above). Various routes around Clatteringshaws Loch in the Galloway Forest and Hills. Most are easy, but some serious climbs and descents. Visitor centre has tearoom.

2093 8/Q20
25KM
CIRC
Glen Tanner www.royal-deeside.org.uk · Deeside Good way to encounter this beautiful glen in the shadow of Mount Keen. Quite difficult in places. **START** Tombae on the B976 opposite junction of A97 and A93.

2094
7
XCIRC
Great Glen, Fort William-Loch Lochy Easy at first on the Caledonian Canal towpath. Later it gets hilly with long climbs. Great views. **START** Neptune's Staircase at Banavie, near Fort William.

2095
10
25KM
CIRC
Perthshire & Angus, Glenfernate-Blair Atholl Beautiful Highland trail that takes in forests, lochs and Glen Tilt (1985/GLEN WALKS). Mainly rough track. Follow directions from tourist information centre leaflets. **START** On the A924 14km east of Pitlochrie, 500m east of school.

The Only Open-Air Swimming Pools

2096
10/S20
✓ **Stonehaven Outdoor Pool** www.stonehavenopenairpool.co.uk · 01569 762134 · **Stonehaven** The Friends of Stonehaven Outdoor Pool won the day (eat your hearts out North Berwick) and saved a great pool that goes from length to strength. Fabulous 1930s Olympic-sized heated salt-water pool (85ft). Midnight swims in midsummer most Wednesdays (is that cool, or what?). Jun-Sep only: 10am-7.30pm (10am-6pm weekends). Heated salt-water heaven.

2097
9/K25
✓ **Gourock Bathing Pool** 01475 631561 · Gourock The only other open-air (proper) pool in Scotland that's still open! On coast road south of town 45km from Glasgow. 1950s-style leisure. Heated (to 88°), so it doesn't need to be a scorcher (brilliant, but choc-a-block when it is). Open May-early Sep weekdays until 8pm.

2098
6/Q13
✓ **The Trinkie** Wick On south or Pultney side of town, follow cliff walk up from harbour or by car through housing estate. 2km. Not an organised set-up but a pool sluiced and filled by the sea within a natural formation of rocks. A bracing stroll, never mind immersion. Needing a bit of whitewash '09. Wickers also go to the North Baths a short walk from the harbour (Wick side) and opposite the wee lighthouse. 2 rare open-air swim spots in the far north – midsummer swimming at midnight, anyone?

2099
10/R23
The Step Rock Pool St Andrews Shallow bathing pool between West Sands and East Sands beaches below the Aquarium and the Seafood Restaurant (1328/SEAFOOD). Since 1903 when the gentlemen used to swim here naked, a shallow alternative to the colder sea and more recently the East Sands Leisure Centre. Costumes advised these days.

Especially Good Watersports Centres

2100
10/R24

✓ **Elie Watersports** www.eliewatersports.com · 01333 330962 · Elie
Great beach location in totally charming wee town where there's enough
going on to occupy non-watersporters. Easy lagoon for first timers and open season
for inexperienced users. Wind-surfers, kayaks, water-ski. Also mountain bikes
and inflatable 'biscuits'. 866/FIFE HOTELS, 1293/GASTROPUBS, 2061/GREAT GOLF.

2101
9/J22

✓ **Linnhe Marina** www.linnhemarina.co.uk · 07721 503981 ·
Lettershuna, Port Appin 32km north of Oban on A828 near Portnacroish.
Established, personally run business in a fine sheltered spot for learning and
plootering. More manna than sports these days but they almost guarantee to get
you windsurfing over to the island in 2 hours. Individual or group instruction. Wayfarers, Luggers and fishing boats. Moorings. Row boats for hire. Castle Stalker and
Lismore are round the corner, seals and porpoises abound. May-Sep 9am-6pm.

2102
9/K26

✓ **Scottish National Watersports Centre** 01475 530757 · Cumbrae ·
www.nationalcentrecumbrae.org.uk Ferry from Largs (centre near ferry
terminal so 5km Millport) then learn all about how to pilot things that float. You
need to book – call them, then bob about 'doon the watter'. Great range of
courses. 2-bunkroom accommodation available.

2103
10/P25

✓ **Port Edgar** www.peyc.org.uk · 0131 331 3330 · South Queensferry At
end of village, under and beyond the Forth Road Bridge. Major marina and
water sports centre. Berth your boat, hire dinghies (big range). Big tuition programme for kids and adults including canoes. Home to Port Edgar yacht club.

2104
10/M26

✓ **Strathclyde Park** www.northlan.gov.uk · 01698 266155 Major water
sports centre 15km southeast of Glasgow and easily reached from Central
Scotland via M8 or M74 (junction 5 or 6). 200-acre loch and centre with instruction on sailing, canoeing, windsurfing, rowing, water-skiing. Hire canoes, Lasers
and Wayfarers, windsurfers and trimarans. Call booking office for sessions/times.

2105
7/N19

✓ **Loch Insh Watersports** www.lochinsh.com · 01540 651272 · Kincraig
On B970, 2km from Kincraig towards Kingussie and the A9. Marvellous loch
site launching from gently sloping dinky beach into shallow forgiving waters of
Loch Insh. Hire of canoes, dinghies and windsurfers as well as rowing boats; river
trips. Archery and mountain biking. An idyllic place to learn anything. Watch the
others and the sunset from the balcony restaurant (1048/BEST HIGHLAND RESTAURANTS). Sports Apr-Oct 9.30am-5.30pm.

2106
7/N19

✓ **Loch Morlich Watersports** www.lochmorlich.com · 01479 861221 ·
near Aviemore By Glenmore Forest Park, part of the plethora of outdoor
activities hereabouts (skiing, walking, etc). This is the loch you see from Cairngorm
and just as picturesque from the woody shore. Surprising coral-pink beach! Canoes,
kayaks, rowing boats and dinghies with instruction in everything. Evening hire possible. Coffee shop up top. Good campsite adjacent (1210/CAMPING WITH KIDS).

2107
11/M30

✓ **Galloway Sailing Centre** www.lochken.co.uk · 01644 420626 · Loch
Ken, near Castle Douglas 15km north on A713 to Ayr. Dinghies, windsurfers, canoes, kayaks, tuition, biking. Also the Climbing Tower so you can zipwire and take that leap of faith! All this by a serene and forgiving loch by the
Galloway Forest. Phone for times and courses. Open Mar-Nov.

The Best Surfing Beaches

A surprise for the sceptical: Scotland has some of the best surfing beaches in Europe.

WEST COAST

2108
5/F13
✓✓ **Isle of Lewis** Probably the best of the lot. Go north of Stornoway, north of Barvas, north of just about anywhere. Leave the A857 and your day job behind. Not the most scenic of sites, but the waves have come a long way, further than you have. Derek at Hebridean Surf Holidays (01851 705862) will tell you when and where to go.

2109
9/D22
✓ **Isle of Tiree** Exposed to all the Atlantic swells, gorgeous little Tiree ain't just great for windsurfing. Stay at Millhouse, self-catering hostel (01879 220435); good facilities.

2110
9/G28
✓ **Macrihanish** Near Campbeltown at the foot of the Mull of Kintyre. Long strand to choose from (1570/BEACHES). Clan Skates in Glasgow (0141 339 6523) usually has an up-to-date satellite map and an idea of both the west and (nearest to central belt) Pease Bay (see below).

NORTH COAST

2111
6/P12
✓ **Thurso** Surf City, well not quite, but it's a good base to find your own waves. Especially to the east of town at Dunnet Bay – a 5km long beach with excellent reefs at the north end. They say it has to be the best right-hand breaking wave on the planet! When it ain't breaking, go west to...

2112
6/N12
✓ **Melvich & Strathy Bay** Near Bettyhill on the North Coast halfway between Tongue and Thurso on the A836. From here to Cape Wrath the power and quality of the waves detonating on the shore have justified comparisons with Hawaii. And then there's **Brimsness**. All information from **Tempest Surf** in Thurso; 01847 892500 (1081/THURSO).

2113
6/Q13
Wick On the Thurso road at Ackergill to the south of Sinclair's Bay (1250/HOUSE PARTIES). Find the ruined castle and taking care, clamber down the gully to the beach. A monumental reef break, you are working against the backdrop of the decaying ruin drenched in history, spume and romance.

EAST COAST

2114
10/S25
✓ **Pease Bay** South of Dunbar near Cockburnspath on the A1. The nearest surfie heaven to the capital. The caravan site has parking and toilets. Very consistent surf here and popular. Info and surf school from **Momentum**; 07796 561615.

2115
8/T17
Rattray Head between Peterhead & Fraserburgh 5km off A90. Hostel/B&B 300m from secret 15km beach with cool surf. (B&B 01346 532236.)

2116
8/T19
Nigg Bay Just south of Aberdeen (not to be confused with Nigg across from Cromarty) and off the vast beach at Lunan Bay (1577/BEACHES) between Arbroath and Montrose. There's 4 spots around **Fraserburgh** ('the broch').

Section 11

Consuming Passions

Best History & Heritage

For Edinburgh museums, see p. 80–83; Glasgow museums, see p. 126–28.
☕ *signifies* **notable** *café.*

2117
10/R25
☕

✓ ✓ **National Museum of Flight** www.nms.ac.uk · 0131 247 4238 ·
near Haddington 3km from A1 south of town. In the old complex of hangars and Nissen huts at the side of East Fortune, an airfield dating to World War I (there's a tacky open-air market on Sun) with a large collection of planes from gliders to jets and especially wartime memorabilia respectfully restored and preserved. Inspired and inspiring displays; not just boys' stuff. Marvel at the bravery back then and sense the unremitting passage of time. From East Fortune the airship R34 made its historic Atlantic crossings. More recent Concorde is an experience: hugely impressive outside, claustrophobic in (especially queueing to leave). But did David Frost and Joan Collins ever join the Mile-High Club? 7 days; 10am-5pm. Weekends only in winter.

2118
10/R24
ATMOS

✓ ✓ **The Secret Bunker** www.secretbunker.co.uk · 01333 310301 ·
near Crail & Anstruther The nuclear bunker and regional seat of government in the event of nuclear war: a twilight labyrinth beneath a hill in rural Fife so vast, well documented and complete, it's both fascinating and chilling. Few museums are as authentic or as resonant, even down to the claustrophobic canteen with bad food. Makes you wonder what 300 people would have made of it, incarcerated there, what the Cold War was all about and what secrets they are brewing these days for the wars yet to come. Mar-Oct 10am-5pm.

2119
10/Q23
☕

✓ ✓ **Verdant Works** www.scottishmuseums.org.uk · 01382 225282 ·
Dundee West Henderson's Wynd near Westport. Award-winning heritage museum that for once justifies the accolades. The story of jute and the city it made. Immensely effective high-tech and designer presentation of industrial and social history. Excellent for kids. Almost continuous guided tour. Café. 7 days 10am-6pm; winter Wed-Sat till 4.30pm. Every Sun from 11am.

2120
5/E13
☕
ATMOS

✓ ✓ **The Blackhouse Village** www.gerrannan.com · 01851 643416 ·
Gearrannan, Lewis At the end of the road (3km) from A858 the west coast of Lewis, an extraordinary reconstruction of several blackhouses, the traditional thatched dwelling of the Hebrides. One is working Black House Museum (set 1955) with café. Another is a hostel and 4 are self-catering accommodation (1147/HOSTELS). Great walk starts here. Apr-Sep 9.30am-5.30pm. Closed Sun.

2121
6/Q13

✓ ✓ **Wick Heritage Centre** www.caithness.org · 01955 605393 · **Bank Row, Wick** Amazing civic museum run by volunteers. Jam-packed with items about the sea, town and that hard land. Upstairs and downstairs (and from a single wee doorway) stretching halfway along the street. Few places anywhere have so much meticulously gathered that lovingly and loyally portrays and evokes the spirit of a place. The much-used words 'secret gem' are entirely appropriate here. They got a Queen's Award '09 but somebody should give these ladies MBEs or something. Easter-Òct 10am-last entry 3.45pm. Closed Sun.

2122
5/F13
HS
ATMOS

✓ **The Blackhouse at Arnol** www.historic-scotland.gov.uk · 01851 710395 · **Lewis** A857 Barvas road from Stornoway, left at junction for 7km, then right through township for 2km. A blackhouse with earth floor, bed boxes and central peat fire (no chimney hole), occupied by the family and their animals. Remarkably, this house was lived in until the 1960s. Smokists may reflect on that peaty fug. Open all year 9.30am-5.30pm (4.30pm in winter, Oct-Feb). Closed Sun.

2123
10/P25

The Abbot House www.abbothouse.co.uk · Dunfermline Maygate in town centre 'historic area'. Very fine conversion of ancient house showing the importance of this town as a religious and trading centre from this millennium to medieval times. Encapsulates history from Margaret and Bruce to the Beatles. One of the few tourist attractions where 'award-winning' is a reliable indicator of worth. Café and tranquil garden; gate to the graveyard and Abbey. 7 days 10am-5pm. 4pm in winter. Excellent coffee shop by ladies who can cook and bake.

2124
9/H23
ATMOS

Easdale Island Folk Museum www.scottishmuseums.org.uk On Easdale, an island/township reached by a 5-minute (continuous) boat service from Seil 'island' at the end of the B844 (off the A816, 18km south of Oban). Something special about this grassy hamlet of white-washed houses on a rocky outcrop which has a pub, a tearoom and a craft shop, and this museum across the green. The history of the place (a thriving slate industry erased one stormy night in 1881, when the sea drowned the quarry) is brought to life in displays from local contributions. Easter-Sep 11am-5pm.

2125
4/V5
ATMOS

Shetland Museum & Archives www.shetland-museum.org.uk · 01595 695057 · Lerwick Housed in a purpose-built contemporary space developed from what remained of the Lerwick waterfront. 60,000 images bringing the story of these fascinating islands to life. Also the Up-Helly-Aa story (21/FESTIVALS)! Hays Dock Café/Restaurant worth a visit in its own right. 2284x/SHETLAND. 7 days 10am-5.30pm. (12noon-5pm Sun).

2126
6/M13

Strathnaver Museum www.strathnavermuseum.org.uk · 01641 521418 · Bettyhill On north coast 60km west of Thurso in a converted church which is very much part of the whole appalling saga: a graphic account of the Highland clearances told through the history of this fishing village and the Strath that lies behind it whence its dispossessed population came; 2,500 folk were driven from their homes – it's worth going up the valley (from 2km west along the main A836) to see (especially at Achenlochy) the beautiful land they had to leave in 1812 to make way for sheep. Detailed leaflet of Strath to follow by car and foot. Café on roadside for sustenance. Museum: Apr-Oct Mon-Sat 10am-5pm.

2127
7/H18

Applecross Heritage Centre www.applecrossheritage.org.uk Along the strand from the Applecross Inn (1190/GET-AWAY HOTELS) adjacent lovely church built on ancient monastery, a well-designed building and lay-out of the story of this remarkable, end-of-the-world community. Reading room with such comfy chairs! May-Oct 12noon-5pm.

2128
8/T17

The Museum of Scottish Lighthouses Fraserburgh · www.lighthousemuseum.org.uk At Kinnaird Head near the harbour. A top attraction, so signed from all over. Purpose-built and very well done. Something which may appear to be of marginal interest made vital. In praise of the prism and the engineering innovation and skill that allowed Britain once to rule the seas (and the world). A great ambition (to light the coastline) spectacularly realised. *At Scotland's Edge* by Allardyce and Hood is well worth taking home, as is Bella Bathhurst's *The Lighthouse Stevensons*. 10am-5pm (4pm winter, 6pm Jul/Aug).

2129
7/H18

Bright Water Visitor Centre & Gavin Maxwell House 01599 530040 · www.eileanban.org · Eilean Ban, Skye You don't have to be a Maxwell fan, *Ring of Bright Water* reader or otter-watcher to appreciate the remarkable restoration of this fascinating man's last house on the island under the Skye Bridge. Skye is a natural haven and the Stevenson Lighthouse superb. Limited access; approach via the Otter Gate on the bridge. Contact centre for guided tours. Apr-Oct.

2130 **West Highland Museum** www.westhighlandmuseum.org.uk · **Cameron**
9/K21 **Square, Fort William** Off main street in listed building. Good refurbishment yet
retains mood; the setting doesn't overshadow the contents. 7 rooms of Jacobite
memorabilia, archaeology, wildlife, clans, tartans, arms, etc all effectively evoke the
local history. Great oil paintings line the walls, including a drawn battle plan of
Culloden. The anamorphic painting of Charlie isn't so bonny, but a still fascinating
snapshot. Closed Sun except Jul/Aug (2-5pm).

2131 **Mary-Ann's Cottage** www.caithness.org · **Dunnet** On north coast off A836
6/P12 from Thurso to John o' Groats, signed at Dunnet; take the road for Dunnet Head.
Lived in till 1990 by Mary-Ann Calder, 3 generations of crofters are in these stones.
But not nostalgic or heritage heavy, just an old lady's house, the near present and
past. Compare to that other old lady's house 10 minutes up the road (Castle of
Mey; 1764/CASTLES). Open summer 2-4.30pm. Closed Mon.

2132 **Kilmartin House** www.kilmartin.org · **01546 510278** · **near Lochgilphead**
9/H24 North of Lochgilphead on A816. Centre for landscape and archaeology interpretation
☕ – so much to know of the early peoples and Kilmartin Glen is littered with historic
sites. Intelligent, interesting, run by a small independent trust. Excellent organic-
ish café (1405/TEAROOMS) and bookshop without the usual tat. Some nice Celtic
carvings. All year 10am-5.30pm daily (4pm Nov/Dec). Closed Jan/Feb.

2133 **Pictavia** www.pictavia.org.uk · **01356 626241** · **Brechin** South of Brechin on
10/R21 the Forfar road at Brechin Castle. Centre opened summer '99 to give a multimedia
interpretation of our Dark Age ancestors. Sparse on detail, high on kid-orientated
interactivity. Listen to some music, pluck a harp and argue about the Battle of
Dunnichen – was it that important? Gentle parkland beyond, nice for kids. Usual
crap shopping. All year 7 days 9am-5pm (from 10am Sun).

2134 **Cromarty Courthouse Museum** www.cromarty-courthouse.org.uk ·
7/M17 **01381 600418** · **Church Street, Cromarty** Housed in an 18th-century courthouse,
this award-winning museum uses moving, talking models to bring to life a courtroom scene and famous Cromarty figures to paint the varied history of this quite
special little town. 11am-4pm. Closed Fri/Sat. **Hugh Miller's Birthplace** is next
door. Born in 1802 and best known as the father of geology, he was remarkable in
many ways and this tells his singular story. Apr-Sep 1-5pm. Both winter hours vary.

2135 **Summerlee Heritage Park** www.northlan.gov.uk · **01236 638460** ·
10/M26 **Heritage Way, Coatbridge** Follow signs from town centre. Here in the Iron
Town is this tribute to the industry, ingenuity and graft that powered the Industrial
Revolution and made Glasgow great. Anyone with a mechanical bent or an interest
in the social history of the working class will like it; tots and bored teens may not
though there is a great playpark. Tearoom. 7 days, 10am-5pm (winter 10am-4pm).

2136 **Skye Museum of Island Life** www.skyemuseum.co.uk · **Kilmuir** On A855
7/F17 Uig-Staffin road 32km north of Portree. The most authentic of several converted
cottages on Skye where the crofter's life is recreated for the enrichment of ours.
The small thatched township includes agricultural implements and domestic
artefacts, many illustrating an improbable fascination with the royal family. Flora
Macdonald's grave nearby (1837/MONUMENTS). Apr-Oct 9.30am-5pm. Closed Sun.

2137 **Auchendrain** **Inveraray** 8km west of town on A83. A whole township
9/J24 reconstructed to give a very fair impression of both the historical and spatial
relationship between the cottages and their various occupants. Longhouses and
byre dwellings; their furniture and their ghosts. 7 days. Apr-Sep 10am-5pm.

2138 **Inveraray Jail** www.inverarayjail.co.uk · Inveraray 'The story of Scottish
9/J24 crime and punishment' told in award-winning reconstruction of courtroom with
cells, where waxwork miscreants and their taped voices bring local history to life.
Guided Peterhead tours can't be far off. All year, 9.30am-6pm (winter 10am-5pm).

2139 **Arctic Penguin aka Maritime Heritage Centre** www.inveraraypier.com ·
9/J24 Inveraray 'One of the world's last iron sailing ships' moored so you can't miss it
at the loch side in Inveraray. More to it than would seem from the outside; displays on the history of Clydeside (the *Queens Mary* and *Elizabeth* memorabilia, etc),
Highland Clearances, the *Vital Spark*. Lots for kids to get a handle (or hands) on. 7
days 10am till 6pm; 5pm winter.

2140 **Bonawe Ironworks Museum** www.historic-scotland.gov.uk · Taynuilt At
9/J23 its zenith (late 18th-early 19th century), this ironworks was a brutal, fire-breathing
HS monster, as 'black as the Earl of Hell's waistcoat'. But now, all is calm as the gently
sloping grassy sward carries you around from warehouse to foundry and down
onto the shores of Loch Etive to the pier, where the finished product was loaded
on to ships to be taken away for the purpose of empire-building (with cannon-
balls). Apr-Sep daily until 5.30pm.

2141 **Scottish Fisheries Museum** www.scotfishmuseum.org · 01333 310628 ·
10/R24 Anstruther In and around a cobbled courtyard overlooking the old fishing
harbour in this busy East Neuk town. Excellent evocation of traditional industry
still alive (if not kicking). Impressive collection of models and actual vessels
including those moored at adjacent quay. Crail and Pittenweem harbours nearby
for the full picture (and fresh crab/lobster). Open all year 10am-5.30pm, Sun 11am-
5pm (closed 4.30pm in winter). 1365/FISH & CHIPS a must!

2142 **Robert Smail's Printing Works** www.nts.org.uk · 01896 830206 · Main
10/Q27 Street, Innerleithen A traditional printing works till 1986 and still in use. Fasci-
NTS nating vignettes/history. Have a go at hand-setting, then have a go at a Caldwell's
ice cream (1438/ICE CREAM). Apr-Oct, Thu-Mon 12noon-5pm, Sun 1-5pm.

2143 **Myreton Motor Museum** www.myretonmotormuseum.co.uk · 01875
10/Q25 870288 · Aberlady On Drem road, past Luffness Mains. Ideal 'little' museum in
old barn with restored vehicles dating from 1896. Even for the Luddite, engineering
seems an aesthetic here. Dr Finlay's Casebook fans, prepare yourselves. 7 days
11am-4pm; winter 11am-3pm.

2144 **National Museum of Costume** www.nms.ac.uk · New Abbey, near
11/N30 Dumfries Another obsession that became a (national) museum. On 2 floors of
Shambellie House set among spectacular woodlands. Fab frocks etc from every
period. Apr-Oct 10am-5pm. Lovely new gardens nearby; 1532/GARDENS.

2145 **Aberdeen Maritime Museum** www.aagm.co.uk · 01224 337700 · Ship-
8/T19 row, Aberdeen Aberdeen faces the sea; this place tells you the stories. Films,
exhibits, photos and paintings. Decent café. Mon-Sat 10am-5pm, Sun 12-3pm.

2146 **The Scottish Maritime Museum** www.scottishmaritimemuseum.org
10/L25 Over 3 sites: Irvine (01294 278283), Braehead (0141 886 1013) and Dumbarton
(01389 763444). Dumbarton has the ship model experiment tank; Clydebuilt at
Braehead (off the M8 junction 25A) has hands-on engines; Irvine boasts a massive
Victorian engine shed full of the bits that non-engineers never usually see; and
there's the hulk of an old clipper at Irvine harbour. Completely fascinating. Irvine
Easter-Oct, Braehead daily all year. Dumbarton all year Mon-Sat. 10am-4pm.

The Most Interesting Public Galleries

For Edinburgh, see p. 80–84; Glasgow, p. 126–28 and p. 133. ☕ : ***notable** café.*

2147
10/P25
ADM

✓ ✓ **Jupiter Artland** www.jupiterartland.org · 0131 257 4170 · **Wilkieston** West of Edinburgh. Not a public gallery as such but an open-air artland assembled by Robert and Nicky Wilson in the groves and gardens of their home, Bonnington House. In an 'unfolding story', some of the UK's leading artists have been commissioned to produce site-specific work which you discover: Andy Goldsworthy, Anthony Gormley, Anish Kapoor and an enormous landform by Charles Jencks which you pass through when you arrive; and many others. This is art exposure and extraordinary patronage on a grand scale. Best get directions from the website. Allow 1.5 hours on site. Cars must be booked in advance. 7 days 10am-4pm in summer. Check for winter hours.

2148
10/Q23
☕

✓ ✓ **Dundee Contemporary Arts** www.dca.org.uk · 01382 432000 · **Nethergate, Dundee** State-of-contemporary-art gallery (by award-winning architect Richard Murphy) with great café (918/DUNDEE RESTAURANTS), cinema facilities, etc. which transformed the cultural face of Dundee. People actually use it.

2149
8/T19

✓ ✓ **Aberdeen Art Gallery** www.aagm.co.uk · **Schoolhill, Aberdeen** Major gallery with temporary exhibits and eclectic permanent collection from Impressionists to Bellany. Large bequest from local granite merchant Alex Macdonald in 1900 contributes fascinating collection of his contemporaries: Bloomsburys, Scottish, Pre-Raphaelites. Excellent watercolour room. An easy and rewarding gallery to visit. 10am-5pm (Sun 2-5pm). Closed Mon.

2150
10/P23

✓ **The Fergusson Gallery** www.scottishmuseums.org.uk · **Marshall Place, Tay Street, Perth** In distinctive round tower (a former waterworks). The assembled works on two floors of J.D. Fergusson (1874-1961). Though he spent much of his life in France, he had an influence on Scottish art and was preeminent amongst those now called the Colourists. It's a long way from Perth to Antibes 1913 but these pictures are a draught of the warm south. Mon-Sat 10am-5pm.

2151
10/Q24

✓ **Kirkcaldy Museum & Art Gallery** www.scottishmuseums.org.uk Near railway station, but ask for directions (it's easy to get lost). One of the best galleries in central Scotland. Splendid introduction to the history of 19th/20th-century Scottish art. Lots of Colourists/McTaggart/Glasgow Boys. And Sickert to Redpath. And famously the only public collection in Scotland showing Scotland's best-selling artist: one Jack Vettriano who was a Fife lad. Museum ain't bad. Kirkcaldy doesn't get much good press but this and the parks (1546/PARKS) are worth the journey (plus Valente's – 1361/FISH AND CHIPS). 7 days till 5pm.

2152
11/M31
NTS

✓ **Hornel Gallery** www.nts.org.uk · **Kirkcudbright** Hornel's house is a fabulous evocation with a collection of his work and atelier as was. 'Even the Queen was amazed'. Beautiful, atmospheric garden stretches to the river. Apr-Oct 12noon-5pm. Garden all year round. Tearoom only on occasion.

2153
8/R17
☕

✓ **Duff House** www.duffhouse.org.uk · **Banff** Nice walk and easy to find from town. Important outstation of the National Galleries of Scotland in meticulously restored Adam house with interesting history and spacious grounds. Ramsays, Raeburns, portraiture of mixed appeal and an El Greco. Maybe OTT for some but the major local attraction (go further up the Deveron for a pleasant stroll; 2018/WOODLAND WALKS). Nice tearoom. Gallery 11am-4pm (only Thu-Sun in winter).

2154
11/N29
✓ **Sculpture at Glenkiln Reservoir** near Dumfries Take A75 to Castle Douglas and right to Shawshead; into village, right at T-junction, left to Dunscore, immediate left, signed for reservoir. Follow road along loch side and park. Not a gallery at all but greening bronze sculpture scattered in the Galloway Hills 16km southeast of Dumfries. 4 you can see from the road, others you find near the reservoir (but allow 2 hours). Epstein, Moore, Rodin in the great outdoors!

2155
3/Q10
✓ **The Pier Arts Centre** www.pierartscentre.com · 01856 850209 · Stromness, Orkney On main street (1557/COASTAL VILLAGES), a gallery on a pier which could have come lock, stock and canvases from Cornwall. Permanent St Ives-style collection assembled by one Margaret Gardiner: Barbara Hepworth, Ben Nicholson, Paolozzi and others shown in a *simpatico* environment with the sea outside. Important early-20th-century pictures complemented by work of recent notables like Sean Scully and Olafur Eliasson. A rare treat! Mon-Sat 10.30am-5pm.

2156
10/L26
Paisley Art Gallery & Museum www.scottishmuseums.org.uk · 0141 889 3151 · High Street, Paisley Collection of world-famous Paisley shawls and history of weaving. Other exhibitions usually have a local connection and interactive element. Notable Greek Ionic-style building. 10am-5pm, Sun 2-5pm. Closed Mon.

2157
9/F22
☐
Calgary Art In Nature Calgary, Isle of Mull Contemporary artwork and sculpture to be 'found' on a trail through the woods adjacent to the wonderful beach at Calgary Bay on the far west coast of Mull and an exhibition gallery space. The project of Matthew Reade who runs the Calgary Farmhouse Hotel (2246/ISLAND HOTELS), the 1km trail is fun rather than thought provoking, but it's a great idea, nice for kids in one of the best of places.

2158
9/L28
Rozelle House www.south-ayrshire.gov.uk · Ayr In Rozelle Park, the only art in these parts. Exhibitions change monthly (including local artists' work). 4 galleries, and additional 5 rooms featuring the Alexander Goudie collection in Rozelle House; craft shop. Open all year Mon-Sat 10am-5pm, Apr-Oct also Sun 2-5pm.

▬▬ Best Shopping For Scotland

☐ *signifies **notable** café.*

2159
7/N16
☐
✓ **Anta Factory Shop** www.anta.co.uk · 01862 832477 · Fearn Off B9175 from Tain to Nigg ferry, 8km through Hill of Fearn, at disused airfield. Shop with adjacent pottery. Also in Edinburgh and London: Anta is a classy brand. Tartan curtain fabric; rugs, throws and pots. You can commission furniture to be covered in their material. Pottery tour by arrangement. Shop. All year daily 9.30am-5.30pm (Sun 11am-5pm, ring for winter hours). Pottery Mon-Fri only. Nice café shuts 4pm.

2160
7/M16
✓ **Tain Pottery** www.tainpottery.co.uk Off the A9 just south of Tain (opposite side of A9 to road signed for Anta at Fearn; see above). Big working pottery, big stuff and often big, perhaps OTT designs but very popular (they do the National Trust for Scotland). Daily in summer, 10am-5pm. Closed Sat/Sun in winter.

2161
6/L12
✓ **Balnakeil** Durness From Durness and the A836 road, take Balnakeil and Faraid Head road for 2km west. Founded in the 1960s in what one imagines was a haze of hash, this craft village is still home to 'downshifters' and 'creatives'. Paintings, pottery, weaving – silk, glass, wood and jewellery in prefab huts where community members work and hang out (the site was an early-warning station).

Cocoa Mountain (01971 511233) make here their heavenly thin chocolate you get all over the north and have a chocolate bar open all year round. **Loch Croispol Bookshop** (01971 511777) where 2 blokes, Kevin and Simon, have established a browserie par excellence: the shelves surrounding café tables (home-made changing menu) with often notable art on show. It's open all year too. Some businesses seasonal. All open in summer, daily 10am-6 pm (mostly).

2162 ✓ **Highland Stoneware** www.highlandstoneware.com · Lochinver &
6/J14   Mill Street, Ullapool On road to Baddidarach as you enter Lochinver on A837; and on way north beyond Ullapool centre. A large-scale pottery business including a shop/warehouse and open studios that you can walk round (Lochinver is more *engagé*). Similar to the 'ceramica' places you find in the Med, but not as terracotta – rather, painted and heavy-glazed stoneware in set styles. Many broken plates adorn your arrivals. Great selection, pricey, but you may have luck in the Lochinver discount section. Mail-order service. Open all year.

2163 ✓ **Crail Pottery** www.crailpottery.com · Crail At the foot of Rose Wynd,
10/R24   signposted from main street (best to walk). In a tree-shaded Mediterranean courtyard and upstairs attic a cornucopia of brilliant and useful things. Open 9am-5pm (weekends from 10am). Don't miss the harbour nearby, one of the most romantic neuks in the Neuk. New good tearoom nearby (1414/TEAROOMS).

2164 ✓ **MacNaughton's** www.macnaughtonsofpitlochry.com · Station Road,
10/N21   Pitlochry On corner of main street, this the best of many. A vast old-fashioned family-owned outfitter (though not any longer the MacNaughtons) with acres of tartan attire – including obligatory tartan pyjamas and dressing gowns! Make their own cloth, and 9m kilts prepared in 6-8 weeks. This really is the real McCoy. 7 days till 5.30pm (4pm Sun).

2165 ✓ **Kinloch Anderson** www.kinlochanderson.com · Commercial Street,
1/XE1   Leith, Edinburgh A trek from uptown but firmly on the tourist trail and so much better than the High St, ie the tartan-tainted Royal Mile. Experts in Highland dress and all things tartan; they've supplied *everybody*. They design their own tartans, have a good range of men's tweed jackets; even rugs. Mon-Sat 9am-5.30pm.

2166 ✓ **House of Burns** Kirkoswald A major new visitor development in South
11/K28   Ayrshire on the A77 in this strip of village made famous by its Burns characters and the graveyard (1881/GRAVEYARDS). The Costley family have set up shop opposite and it is some shop. Still under development at TGP, it will include retail, a tearoom, a pâtisserie and an ice-cream factory. Souter Johnnie's pub adjacent is a great pub-grub destination (1297/GASTROPUBS). 7 days 9am-5pm, pub till 9pm.

2167 ✓ **Logie Steading** www.logie.co.uk · near Forres In beautiful countryside
8/N17   10km south of Forres signed from A940 Forres-Grantown road. Near pleasant
☕   woodlands and picnic spot (directions: 2005/WOODLAND WALKS) and with lovely walled garden around the big house nearby (Apr-Dec). Much better than your usual crafty courtyard to visit and browse. Highland artists and workshops. Second-hand books, farm shop! Emma Swan's home-baking-with-integrity tearoom. Seems fitting since this estate was built with the fortune made by the guy who invented the digestive biscuit! 1407/TEAROOMS. Mar-Dec, 7 days 10.30am-5pm.

2168 ✓ **Harestanes Countryside Centres** near Jedburgh Off A68 at Ancrum
10/R27   the B6400 to Nisbet. Farm steading complex on Montevoit Estate (1515/GARDENS) with café/exhibition/superior crafts including the excellent **Buy**

Design showing furniture, ceramics and glass. Easter-Oct 10am-5pm. Big event programme. Best tearoom 1km down the road at Woodside (1395/TEAROOMS)

2169 **Octopus Crafts** near Fairlie On A78 Largs to Ardrossan road south of Fairlie.
9/K26 Crafts, wines, cookshop, an excellent restaurant (1339/SEAFOOD RESTAURANTS) and a seafood deli. An all-round roadside experience – the sign says Fencebay Seafood & Crafts. Everything hand-made and/or hand-picked; even wines are well chosen. Good pots. Glass and wood. Choice utensils.

2170 **House of Bruar** www.houseofbruar.com · Pitlochry Courtyard emporia if
10/N21 not euphoria: a shopaholic honey pot on the A9 north of Blair Atholl especially for
☕ those who just missed Pitlochry. Self-service restaurant like a canteen in an old folks' home but food hall has vast range of Scottish cheeses and brands: Mackie's ice cream, MacSween's haggis, etc. Outdoor wear with big labels (Musto, Patagonia), knitwear, golf shop, garden centre, even antiques. They know what you want. This place is always teeming with people. Falls nearby for non-retail therapy (1602/WATERFALLS). 7 days 9am-5pm.

2171 **Brodie Country Fare** www.brodiecountryfare.com · between Nairn &
8/N17 Forres By A96 near Brodie Castle (1761/CASTLES). Not a Scottish shoppie in the
☕ traditional sense, more a drive-in one-stop consumer experience on the taste by-pass. Deli food, a fairly up-market womenswear boutique and every crafty tartana-lia of note. Self-serve restaurant gets as busy as a motorway café and you have to walk through everything else to get there. 7 days till 5.30pm (5pm in winter).

2172 **Falls of Shin Visitor Centre** www.fallsofshin.co.uk · near Lairg Self-serve
7/L17 café/restaurant is notable (1055/BEST HIGHLAND RESTAURANTS) in the visitor centre
☕ and shop across the road from the Falls of Shin on the Achany Glen road 8km south of Lairg (1615/WATERFALLS). Good basic food in an unlikely emporium of all things Harrods (Mohammed al Fayed's estate is here). They come from all over at Christmas for hampers, etc. 9.30am-6pm all year.

2173 **Mortimer's & Ritchie's** Grantown on Spey 3 and 41-45 High St respectively
8/P18 in respectable Speyside holiday town where fishing and shooting gear is in demand. Mortimer's particularly is angling for your custom. Big-name outdoor clothing in all shades of olive. Ritchie's have the guns if you want to kill something. Closed Sun.

2174 **Edinbane Pottery** www.edinbane-pottery.co.uk · Skye 500m off A850
7/F17 Portree (22km) to Dunvegan road. A great working pottery where the various processes are often in progress. Wood-fired and salt-glazed pots of all shapes and for every purpose. Open all year 9am-6pm. 7 days (not weekends winter).

2175 **Skye Silver** www.skyesilver.com · Colbost 10km Dunvegan on B884 to
7/F18 Glendale. Long established and reputable jewellery made and sold in an old Skye schoolhouse in a distant corner; Three Chimneys restaurant nearby (2251/SKYE RESTAURANTS). Well-made, Celtic designs, good gifts. Mar-Oct 7 days, 10am-6pm.

2176 **Kiln Room Pottery & Coffeeshop** Laggan On main A889 route to Fort
7/M20 William and Skye from Dalwhinnie. Simple, usable pottery (though pottery itself
☕ no longer in use) with distinctive warm colouring. Selected knitwear and useful things. Home-made cakes and scones; 1398/COFFEE SHOPS. 10am-5.30pm, 7 days. Hostel out back very inexpensive including comfy lounge with vista and hot tub.

2177 **Skye Batiks** www.skyebatiks.com · Portree Near tourist information centre.
7/G18 Very original Sri Lanka batiks: cotton fabrics of ancient Celtic designs in every shape and size. Mainly hand-made, majorly colourful; a unique souvenir of Skye.

2178 **Achin's Bookshop** www.scotbooks.freeuk.com · **Lochinver** At Inverkirkaig
6/J14 5km from Lochinver on the 'wee mad road' to Achiltibuie (1634/SCENIC ROUTES).
Enduring and unexpected haven of books in the back of beyond providing something to read when you've climbed everything or are unlikely to acquire the incli-
nation. Outdoor wear too and great hats. The path to Kirkaig Falls and Suilven
begins at the gate (see 1850/MONUMENTS). Easter-Oct 7 days; 9.30am-6pm (winter Mon-Sat 10am-5pm). Adjacent café 10am-5pm, summer only.

2179 **Iona Abbey Shop** www.iona.org.uk/abbey · **Iona** Via CalMac ferry from
9/F23 Fionnphort on Mull. Crafts and souvenirs across the way in separate building.
HS Proceeds support a worthy, committed organisation. Christian literature, tapes,
etc, but mostly artefacts from nearby and around Scotland. Celtic crosses much in
evidence, but then this is where they came from! Also, on the way to and from
the abbey, **Columba Steadings** has quality design craftwork of several brands.
Restored farm buildings on the road 200m Abbey. Apr-Oct.

2180 **Borgh Pottery Borve** Lewis On northwest coast of island a wee way from
5/F13 Stornoway (25km north on A857), but no great detour from the road to Callanish
where you are probably going. Alex and Sue Blair's pleasant gallery of hand-
thrown pots with different glazes; domestic and garden wear. Knits. Open all year
9.30pm-6pm. Closed Sun.

2181 **Galloway Lodge Preserves** www.gallowaylodge.co.uk · **Gatehouse of**
11/M30 **Fleet** By the clock tower. Packed with local jams, marmalades, chutneys and
pickles. Scottish pottery by Scotia Ceramics, Highland Stoneware and Dunoon.
Good presents and jam for yourself. 10am-5pm Mon-Sat, and Sun afternoons in
summer. There are other emporia.

2182 **Crafts & Things** near Glencoe Village On A82 between Glencoe village and
9/J21 Ballachulish, overlooking Loch Leven. Eclectic mix, perhaps more things than
☕ crafts. Mind, body and mountain books (and this one) and reasonably priced
knit/outerwear. Good coffee shop doing salads, sandwiches and home baking,
with local artists' work on walls. All-round nice place. All year, daily until 5.30pm.

▬▬▬ Where To Buy Good Scottish Woollies

2183 ✓✓ **Johnston's Cashmere Centre** Elgin Johnston's is, as they say, one
8/P17 of the last of the Mohicans actually making textiles in Scotland and I feel
that I may have undervalued them somewhat in previous editions. They are 'the
only British mill to transform fibre to garment' (yarns spun at their factory in Elgin
and made into garments in the Borders). They stock their own ranges including
couture cashmere, many of which are sold internationally as well as other quality
brands. This extensive mill shop, newer 'home' section, heritage centre and café is
a serious visitor attraction hereabouts. The jumpers, bunnets and cardies are
more classic than cool but they won't fall apart and they ain't made in China.
Lovely garden adjacent the pulsating mill. Mon-Sat 9am-5.30pm, Sun 11am-5pm.
Near the cathedral (1784/RUINS).

2184 ✓ **Judith Glue** www.judithglue.com · 01856 874225 · **Kirkwall, Orkney**
3/Q10 Opposite the cathedral. Distinctive hand-made jumpers, the runic designs are
a real winner. Also the individual Highland and Orkney ceramics and jewellery,
condiments and preserves. Landscape prints of Orkney are by twin sister, Jane.
Mon-Sat 9am-6pm (later in summer), Sun 10am-5.30pm (not Sun in winter).

2185 ✓ **Belinda Robertson** www.belindarobertson.com · 0131 557 8118 · 13a
1/A4 **Dundas Street, Edinburgh** Queen of the commissioned cashmere creation not so much couture as once was. Part of the collection is still made in Hawick. Closed Sun.

2186 **Ragamuffin** www.ragamuffinonline.co.uk · Armadale Pier, Skye On the
7/G19 pier, so one of the first or last things you can do on Skye is rummage through the Ragamuffin store and get a nice knit. Every kind of jumper and some crafts in this Aladdin's cave within a new-build shed; including tweedy things and mad hats. 7 days 9am-6pm.

2187 **Lochcarron Visitor Centre** www.lochcarron.com · Galashiels If you're in
10/R27 Galashiels (or Hawick), which grew up around woollen mills, you might expect to find a good selection of woollens you can't get everywhere else; and bargains. Well, no, but Loch Carron is a big attraction with mill tours, exhibits and an okay mill shop. Vivienne Westwood has been this way and well... Hawick did invent the Y-front.

2188 **Hawick Cashmere** www.hawickcashmere.com · Hawick Factory in
10/R28 Hawick since 1874, with visitor centre beside the river on Duke St. Also shops in Kelso and Edinburgh. 'State-of-the-art colours and designs'. Not only, but mostly cashmere. Mon-Sat 9.30am-5pm; Sun 11am-4pm (in season).

▅ Harris Tweed

Let's face it, many bankers, wankers and fashionistas have loomed large over the looms in recent years. Here is the real tweed you need.

2189 **Joan Maclennan** No 1A, Drinishadder Down the Golden Road (1632/SCENIC
5/E15 ROUTES). Ask for directions or phone 01859 511266 when you can get reception. I don't know, but I've been told, this is where you find the golden fleece.

2190 **Tweeds & Knitwear** www.harristweedandknitwear.co.uk · Tarbert &
5 **Drinishadder** Catherine Campbell's warehouse/garage and shop in Tarbert and croft/shop at 4 Plockropool, Drinishadder 6km south of Tarbert, also on the Golden Road (1632/SCENIC ROUTES) where mum Katie does weaving demos. Bales of tweed in Tarbert with knitwear and clothing at the adjacent shop and in the croft. Closed Sun.

2191 **Luskentyre Harris Tweed** www.luskentyreharristweed.co.uk · No 6,
5/E15 **Luskentyre** 2km off west coast on main road south to Rodel. Donald and Maureen Mackay's place is notable for their bolder-coloured tartan tweed. 9.30am-6pm Closed Sun.

2192 **Lewis Loom Centre** Stornoway Main street, far from Harris but near the
5/F14 tourists. Cloth and clothes. Weaving demo. Closed Sun.

2193 **Harris Tweed Shop** Tarbert Main street small emporium with range of
9/G25 Harris Tweed products. It's near the ferry. Mon-Sat 9.30am-5.30pm.

Not Just Garden Centres, More A Way Of Life

☕ signifies **notable** café. Others may have cafés that have not been recommended.

2194
10/P25
☕
✓✓ **Dougal Philip's New Hopetoun Gardens** near South Queensferry · 01506 834433 · www.newhopetoungardens.co.uk
The mother of all (Scottish) garden centres spread aesthetically among trees with 21 different zones and demonstration gardens (including Oriental and Scottish). Everything you could ever grow or put in a Scottish garden. Acres of accessories; big pots. Orangery tearoom has verdant views and tasty home-made stuff. All year 10am-5.30pm. Tearoom closes 4.30pm.

2195
10/S27
☕
✓✓ **Floors Castle** www.roxburghe.net · Kelso 3km outside town off B6397 St Boswells road (garden centre has separate entrance to main visitors' gate in town). Set amongst lovely old greenhouses within walled gardens some distance from house, it has a showpiece herbaceous border all round. First-class coffee shop, The Terrace (1381/TEAROOMS) and patio. 'Very good roses'. Lovely kids' lawn. Centre is open all year. 10am-5pm. (1830/COUNTRY HOUSES.)

2196
10/P23
☕
✓✓ **Glendoick** www.glendoick.com · 01738 860205 · Glencarse near Perth Take sliproad off the A85, 10km from Perth, in the fertile Carse of the Tay. A large family-owned garden centre long a destination, now more than ever a joy to visit. Well laid out, friendly, informed staff, full of great stuff. Lovely pagoda garden. The (Cox) family have a garden 2km up the road open for snow-drops (Feb) and rhodies and azaleas (weekends in May). Nice coffee shop with home baking, hot meals; big on soups. Good bookshop including Kenneth's own splendid book (see Best Gardens, p. 272). You could spend hours here! 7 days till 5.30pm, 5pm winter.

2197
11/M30
✓ **Cally Gardens** www.callygardens.co.uk · Gatehouse of Fleet An extraordinary assemblage of herbaceous perennials in a gorgeous walled garden. Comprehensive sales online but a must to visit; see 1519/GARDENS.

2198
9/J22
✓ **Kinlochlaich Gardens** www.kinlochlaichgardencentre.co.uk · Appin On main A28 Oban-Fort William road just north of Port Appin turnoff, the West Highlands' largest nursery/garden centre. Set in a large walled garden filled with plants and veg soaking up the climes of the warm Gulf stream. Donald Hutchison and daughter nurture these acres enabling you to reap what they sow. With a huge array of plants on offer it's like visiting a friend's garden and being able to take home your fave bits. Charming cottages and apartments. For the tree-house, book well ahead (01631 730342). 7 days: 9.30am-5.30pm (10.30am Sun). Closed Sun in winter.

2199
7/N19
☕
✓ **Inshriach** www.kincraig.com · 01540 651287 · near Kincraig, near Aviemore On B970 between Kincraig and Inverdruie (which is on the Coylumbridge ski road out of Aviemore), a nursery that puts others in the shade. John and Gunn Borrowman carrying on (and developing) the horticulture of Jack Drake (from 1930s) and John Lawson (1949). Specialising in alpines and bog plants, but with neat beds of all sorts in the grounds (and a wild garden) of the house by the Spey and frames full of perfect specimens, this is a potterer's paradise. Tearoom with famously good cakes and superb bird-viewing gallery (1739/BIRDS). Mar-Oct 7 days 10am-5pm. Closed Wed.

2200
10/R27

✓ **Woodside** near Ancrum On B6400 off A68 opposite Ancrum turnoff just past Harestanes (2168/SHOPPING) and before Monteviot (1515/GARDENS), this is the walled garden of the big hoose that overlooks the Teviot. Beautiful, quiet place with displays and events and organic agenda. They really do care about their plants and yours. Best tearoom around in wooden cabin in the corner: 1395/TEAROOMS. 7 days 10am-5pm.

2201
8/R20

✓ **Raemoir Garden Centre** www.raemoirgardencentre.co.uk · Banchory On A980 off main street 3km north of town. A friendly family-run garden centre and excellent coffee shop though there's an acre of manufactured stuff before you get to anything that grows. Roadside expansion '10. Excellent tearoom (1389/TEAROOMS). 7 days 9am-5.30pm. Tearoom till 5pm.

2202
10/N22

Allium Garden Company 01796 482822 · Ballinluig, near Pitlochry This, the project of Douglas Miller whose family (and he) used to have Jenners in Edinburgh, is literally on the A9 though you have to come off at Ballinlulig and double back following the signs. Developing as a conscientious and connoiseurs' garden centre – products all selected for taste as well as suitability (plants have a money-back guarantee). Suppliers a key factor. Decent caff doing soup, salads and home baking. 7 days. 9.30am-5.30pm. Sun 10am-5pm, caff earlier.

2203
9/J26

Mount Stuart Bute Small garden centre at entrance car park of magnificent Mount Stuart (1823/COUNTRY HOUSES). Plants, robust and good-looking, are from the glorious gardens over by. 1-5pm.

2204
10/R25

Smeaton Nursery & Gardens 01620 860501 · East Linton 2km from village on North Berwick road (signed Smeaton). Up a drive in an old estate is this walled garden going back to early 19th century. Wide range; good for fruit (and other) trees, herbaceous, etc. Nice to wander round, an additional pleasure is the Lake Walk halfway down drive through small gate in woods. 1km stroll round a secret finger lake in magnificent mature woodland (10am-dusk). Mon-Sat 9.30am-4.30pm; Sun 10.30am-4.30pm. Funky tearoom.

2205
10/M26

The Clyde Valley www.clyde-valley.com The lush valley of the mighty Clyde is garden centre central. Best reached say from Glasgow by M74, junction 7, then A72 for Lanark. Between Larkhall and Lanark there's a profusion to choose from and many have sprouted coffee/craft shops. Pick your own fruit in summer and your own picnic spot to eat it. Sandyholm at Crossford is recommended.

Section 12

The Islands

The Magical Islands

2206
7/G18

✓✓ **Raasay** A small car ferry (car useful, but bikes best) from Sconser between Portree and Broadford on Skye takes you to this, the best of places. The distinctive flat top of Dun Caan presides over an island whose history and natural history is Highland Scotland in microcosm. The village with rows of mining-type cottages is 3km from jetty. The 'big house', home to the excellent Outdoor Centre, sadly went on fire in '09 prior to reopening after a major make-over so remains closed at TGP. Let's hope they rise from the ashes. The views from the lawn, or the viewpoint above the house, or better still from Dun Caan with the Cuillin on one side and Torridon on the other, are exceptional (2266/ISLAND WALKS). The island hotel (15 rooms) has a bar but could do with some TLC. There's a ruined castle, a secret rhododendron-lined loch for swimming, seals, otters and eagles. Find *Calum's Road* and read the book. Much to explore but go quietly here. *Regular CalMac ferry from Sconser on Skye.*

2207
9/G25

✓✓ **Jura** www.theisleofjura.co.uk Small regular (car) ferry from Port Askaig on Islay or from Tayvallich takes you ito a different world. Jura is remote, scarcely populated and has an ineffable grandeur indifferent to the demands of tourism. Ideal for wild camping, or there's a serviceable hotel and pub (2250/ISLAND HOTELS) in the only village (Craighouse) 12km from ferry at Feolin. **Antlers** is brilliant (2263/BEST ISLAND RESTAURANTS). Walking guides available at hotel and essential especially for the Paps, the hills that maintain such a powerful hold over the island. Easiest climb is from Three Arch Bridge; allow 6 hours. In May they run up all of them and back to the distillery in 3 hours. The distillery where The Jura comes from is not beautiful but the drink is: tours 01496 820385. **Jura House**'s walled garden is a hidden jewel set above the south coastline (1511/GARDENS). Corryvreckan whirlpool (2276/ISLAND WALKS) is another lure, but you may need a 4-wheel drive to get close enough, and its impressiveness depends upon tides. Barnhill, Orwell's house where he wrote *1984*, isn't open but there are many fascinating side tracks: the wild west coast; around Loch Tarbert; and the long littoral between Craighouse and Lagg. (Also 1579/BEACHES; 1877/GRAVEYARDS.) With one road, no street lamps and over 5000 deer, the sound of silence is everything. *CalMac (01880 730253) 7 days, 5-minute service from Port Askaig. Passenger-only ferry from Tayvallich to Craighouse twice daily Easter to Sep (07768 450000). Bike hire in Craighouse (07092 180747).*

2208
9/F23

✓✓ **Iona** Strewn with daytrippers – not so much a pilgrimage, more an invasion – but Iona still enchants (as it did the Colourists), especially if you can get away to the **Bay at the Back of the Ocean** (1585/BEACHES) or watch the cavalcade from the hill above the Abbey. Or stay: **Argyll Hotel** best (01681 700334; 1185/GET-AWAY HOTELS); **St Columba Hotel** near the Abbey has more rooms and a lovely garden (01681 700304; 2428/MULL) or B&B. Abbey shop isn't bad (2179/SHOPPING). Pilgrimage walks on Tue (10am from St John's Cross). Bike hire from Finlay Ross shop (01681 700357) and Seaview Guest House at Fionnphort (01681 700235) if you're staying in the village. Everything about Iona is benign; even the sun shines here when it's raining on Mull. It is a special place on the planet. *Regular 15-minute CalMac service from Fionnphort till 6pm, earlier in winter (01681 700512).*

2209
9/F24

✓✓ **Colonsay** www.colonsay.org.uk Accessible to daytrippers but time ashore is short so you need to arrange accommodation. The island is a haven of wildlife, flowers and beaches (1568/BEACHES) and a serene and popular stopover. 250 metres from the ferry, the refurbished hotel is congenial and convenient (2239/ISLAND HOTELS). Great bar; self-catering units nearby. Some holiday

cottages and many B&Bs (check Colonsay website), but camping discouraged. Bar meals and supper at the hotel and 'Pantry' at the pier. A wild 18-hole golf course and bookshop (sic) adjacent. Semi-botanical gardens at Colonsay House and fine walks, especially to Oronsay (2270/ISLAND WALKS). Don't miss the house at Shell Beach which sells oysters and honey.
CalMac from Oban (or Islay). Crossing takes just over 2 hours. Times vary.

2210 ✓ ✓ **Eigg** www.isleofeigg.net After changing hands, much to-do and
7/G20 cause célèbre, the islanders seized the time and Eigg is (in-fighting apart) theirs; and of course, ours. A wildlife haven for birds and sealife; otters, eagles and seal colonies. Scot Wildlife Trust warden does weekly walks around the island. Friendly tearoom at pier: home baking, licensed (boat hours only in winter); evening meals on request. Bicycle hire 01687 482432 from the shop. Its owner, the irrepressible Sue Kirk, also does B&B, self-catering (near Laig Bay and the singing sands beach) and has a wee restaurant in her house (01687 482405). Great walk to Sgurr an Eigg – an awesome perch on a summer's day (2277/ISLAND WALKS). The community also has a great events programme. You can camp.
CalMac (from Mallaig) (01687 462403) or better, from Arisaig. Arisaig Marine (01687 450224) every day except Thu in summer. Phone for other timings. No car ferry; but motorbikes possible. Day trips to Rum and Muck.

2211 ✓ ✓ **Rum** www.road-to-the-isles.org.uk The large island in the group
7/F20 south of Skye, off the coast at Mallaig. The CalMac ferry plies between Canna, Eigg, Muck and Rum but not too conveniently and it's not easy to island-hop and make a decent visit (but see below). Rum the most wild and dramatic has an extraordinary time-warp mansion in Kinloch Castle which is mainly a museum (guided tours tie in with boat trips). Hostel rooms (45 beds) contrast to the antique opulence above and below. Rum is run by Scottish Natural Heritage and there are fine trails, climbs, bird-watching spots. 2 simple walks are marked for the 3-hour visitors, but the island reveals its mysteries more slowly. The Doric temple mausoleum to George Bullough, the industrialist whose Highland fantasy the castle was, is a 9km (3 hour) walk across the island to Harris Bay. Sighting the sea eagles (the first to be re-introduced into the UK) may be one of the best things that ever happens to you.
CalMac ferry from Mallaig direct (twice a week) or via Eigg (2 hours 15 minutes). Better from Arisaig (Murdo Grant 01687 450224), summer only (can get 3 hours ashore). Accommodation: 01687 462037 and there is wild camping.

2212 ✓ ✓ **St Kilda** www.nts.org.uk There's nothing quite like St Kilda – any-
5/A15 where. By far the most remote and removed of the islands on this page,
NTS it is an expedition to get there and one of a physical, cultural and spiritual nature. Now accorded World Heritage status and run by NTS, it occupies a special place in the heart and soul of the Scots. The NTS ranger's office on St Kilda can be reached on 01870 604628. Sadly I have never been.
To visit, see p. 303-05, Sealife Cruises, or check www.kilda.org.uk

2213 ✓ **Isle of Tiree** www.isleoftiree.com It is an isle, not just an island – it's
9/E22 flat, it has lovely sand and grass and the weather's usually better than the mainland. A bit of wind does keep away the midges. Lots of outdoor activities: famously, windsurfing, but kayaking, birdwatching and other gentle pursuits. **The Scarinish Hotel** (01879 220308) is friendly, local and loved, there are 3 guest houses, a wee hostel and a campsite. Tiree has a unique character different to the islands on this page. But you may long for trees.
Daily flights from Glasgow (0871 700 2000) & CalMac ferries from Oban (daily in summer, about 4 hours).

2214
9/G26
✓ **Gigha** www.gigha.org.uk Romantic small island off Kintyre coast with classic views of its island neighbours. Easy mainland access (20-minute ferry) contributes to an island atmosphere lacking a feeling of isolation. Like Eigg, Gigha was bought by the islanders so its fragile economy is dependent on your visit. The island is run by a heritage trust. Gardens at **Achamore House** (1520/GARDENS) are a big attraction and a hotel (2240/ISLAND HOTELS) provides comfortable surroundings. Locals are relaxed and friendly. Bike hire at the Boathouse café-bar by the ferry; 07876 506520. 3 B&Bs including exceptional rooms at the big house (01583 505400) and golf (9 holes). Many trails and tracks; ask locally for leaflet. Double Beach, where the Queen once swam off the royal yacht; two crescents of sand on either side of the north end of Eilean Garbh isthmus.
CalMac ferry from Tayinloan on A83, 27km south of Tarbert (Glasgow 165km). One an hour in summer, fewer in winter.

2215
9/F22
✓ **Ulva** Off west coast of Mull. A boat leaves Ulva Ferry on the B8073 26km south of Dervaig. Idyllic wee island with 5 well-marked walks including to the curious basalt columns similar to Staffa, or by causeway to the smaller island of Gometra; plan routes at the Boathouse interpretive centre and tearoom (with Ulva oysters and home-cooked food). 'Sheila's (thatched) Cottage' faithfully restored. No accommodation though camping can be arranged (01688 500264). A charming Telford church has services 4 times a year. Ulva is a perfect day away from the rat race of downtown Tobermory!
All-day 5-minute service (not Sat; Sun summer only) till 5pm. Ferryman (01688 500226).

2216
5/D19
✓ **Eriskay** www.w-isles.gov.uk/eriskay Made famous by the sinking nearby of the SS *Politician* in 1941 and the salvaging of its cargo of whisky, later immortalised by Compton Mackenzie in *Whisky Galore*, this Hebridean gem has all the 'idyllic island' ingredients: perfect beaches (1907/MARY, CHARLIE & BOB), a hill to climb, a pub (called the Politician and telling the story round its walls; it sells decent pub food all day in summer), and the causeway to South Uist (though the road cuts a swathe across the island). Limited B&B and no hotel, but camping is ok if you're discreet. Eriskay and Barra together – the pure island experience. (Also 1860/CHURCHES and 2281/THE OUTER HEBRIDES).
CalMac erry from Barra (Airdmhor) 40 minutes: 5 a day in summer, winter hours vary.

2217
5/C20
NTS
✓ **Mingulay** Deserted mystical island near the southern tip of the Outer Hebrides, the subject of one of the definitive island books, *The Road to Mingulay*. Now easily reached in summer by daily trip from Castlebay on Barra with 1.5-hour journey and 3 hours ashore (ask at tourist information centre or Castlebay Hotel). Last inhabitants left 1912. Ruined village has the poignant air of St Kilda; similar spectacular cliffs on west side with fantastic rock formations, stacks and a huge natural arch, best viewed from boat. Only birds and sheep live here now.

2218
5/F15
The Shiants www.shiantisles.net 3 magical, uninhabited tiny islands off east coast of Harris. Read about them in one of the most detailed accounts (a 'love letter') to any small island ever written: *Sea Room* by Adam Nicolson, the guy who owns them. There's a bothy and it's possible to visit by visiting first his website.

2219
9/H22
Lismore www.isleoflismore.com Sail from Oban (car ferry) or better from Port Appin 5km off the main A828 Oban-Fort William road, 32km north of Oban; there's a seafood bar/restaurant/hotel (1345/SEAFOOD RESTAURANTS) to sit and wait. A road runs down the centre of the island (heritage centre and café a halfway house) but there are many hill and coastal walks; even the near end round Port Ramsay feels away from it all. History, natural history and air. Island bike hire from Mary McDougal (01631 760213) who will deliver to ferry, or Port Appin (01631 730391).

CalMac service from Oban, 4 or 5 times a day (2 on Sun). From Port Appin (32km north of Oban) several per day, 5mins. Last back 8.15pm; 9.45pm Fri & Sat; 6.35pm winter, but check (01631 562125).

2220
9/F22

Staffa For many a must, especially if you're on Mull. The geological phenomenon of Fingal's Cave and Mendelssohn's homage are well known. But it's still impressive. Several boat-trip options, many including the Treshnish Islands. *Trips from Mull (08000 858786). Trips from Iona/Fionnphort (01681 700338 or 01681 700358). Trips from Oban (01631 730686).*

CalMac www.calmac.co.uk · 08705 650000

The Best Skye Hotels

Skye is large and has so many good places that it merits its own hotel and restaurant sections among the islands. See The Best Skye Restaurants, p. 387 and The Best of Skye, p. 390.

2221
7/F18
6 ROOMS
TEL · TV
£85+

✓✓ **The House Over-By at The Three Chimneys** 01470 511258 · www.threechimneys.co.uk At Colbost 7km west of Dunvegan by the B884 to Glendale. When Eddie and Shirley Spear transformed their house over by into the House Over-By, it was the first boutique-style accommodation in the Highlands. Refurbished and more than 10 years later it's still a model of understated luxury in a wild and woolly place. Adjacent or just over-by from their accolade-laden restaurant (in world's top lists) (2251/SKYE RESTAURANTS). Separate dining room for a healthy breakfast transforms into a light conservatory lounge in the evening. Outside the sheep, the sea and the sky.
EAT Obviously!

2222
7/H19
14 ROOMS
TV
NO PETS
£85+

✓ **Kinloch Lodge** www.kinloch-lodge.co.uk · 01471 833333 · **Sleat Peninsula** South of Broadford 5 minutes, new road in Sleat Peninsula, 55km Portree. The ancestral, but not overly imposing home of Lord and Lady Macdonald with newer build house adjacent – adding 4 very well appointed rooms and the Loft (sic) na Dal (after the loch outside) 'super' suite. Spacious, country drawing room. Lady Mac is Claire Macdonald of cookery fame, so her many books are for sale in 'the shop', cookery courses go on through the year though the kitchen is under 'rising star' chef Marcello Tully (all meals in the Lodge itself). A range of Claire Macdonald jams and puds etc is probably in an upmarket supermarket near you. Here at Kinloch you're in the home of the brand (claire-macdonald.com).
EAT At Lady Claire's table. 2252/SKYE RESTAURANTS.

2223
7/H19
12 ROOMS
+ 4 SUITES
TEL · TV
NO PETS
ATMOS
£60-85

✓ **Eilean Iarmain** www.eileaniarmain.co.uk · 01471 833332 · **Isleornsay, Sleat** 60km south of Portree. Tucked into the bay this Gaelic inn with its great pub and good dining provides famously comfortable base in south of the island. Some may find the traditional-value approach a little uncompromising: the hotel still has round-pin plugs, so no appliances, there's no mobile reception and little old tellies that may or may not work. But this place has the indefinable 'it', hasn't changed much and really doesn't have to. Bar is local craic central. 6 rooms in main hotel best value (6 are in house over-by). Also 4 suites in steading – expensive but so nice. Shop and gallery adjacent. You wander down to the quay; you don't want to wander anywhere else.
EAT Especially in the bar but the restaurant is good too.

2224
7/F18
6 ROOMS
TEL · TV
NO PETS
£45-60

✓ **Ullinish Country Lodge** www.theisleofskye.co.uk · 01470 572214 · **near Struan** On west coast 2km from Sligachan-Dunvegan road. Fairly traditional throughout though the bedrooms with big, carved beds, have 'won design awards'. But dinner is the thing here (7.30pm for 8, don't be late): candlelit, contemporary dining well-sourced and beautifully presented. Spectacular location rather than setting, there are views to the Black Cuillin and MacLeod's Tables and walks to die for all around. Johnson and Boswell once stayed at Ullinish. Brian and Pam Howard have put it back on the map. You must eat to stay, first night.
EAT A fair way to drive for dinner, but a new Skye top table.

2225
7/G19
9 ROOMS
TV · TEL
NO PETS
£60-85

✓ **Toravaig House Hotel** www.skyehotel.co.uk · 01471 833231 · **Sleat** On main road south from Broadford to Armadale. Ken Gunn and Anne Gracie's personally run hotel along with Duisdale below, the two great new places to eat and stay on Skye. Small and charming with contemporary refurbished rooms and pleasing Iona Restaurant with unassuming star-chef-in-the-making, Andrew Lipp. As below, you can get on the yacht!

2226
7/G19
17 ROOMS
TEL · TV
£60-85

✓ **Duisdale House** www.duisdale.com · 01471 833202 · **Sleat** Only 4km up the road from Toravaig (above) nearer to Broadford, Ken and Anne's bigger hotel, recently refurbished boutique-style to a high standard (big wallpapers, luxe bathrooms). Hot tub on the garden deck, the gardens themselves quite gorgeous. Graham Campbell the chef here with a growing reputation but I haven't eaten. K&A love to sail and will take you out on the *Solus* most days 10.30am-4.30pm to see the seals, whales and Skye from a different perspective. Then back to a very congenial dry land and excellent staff who look after you.
EAT Either Toravaig or Duisdale – both excellent eats in the south.

2227
7/F18
3 ROOMS
£45-60

✓ **The Spoons** www.thespoonsonskye.com · 01470 532217 · **Skeabost Bridge** 14 miles from Portree. Recently arrived, purpose-built 'luxury B&B' overlooking Loch Snizort. Small but all done beautifully. You'll be lucky to get in. Egyptian cotton, home-made bread, fresh-laid eggs. All rather good really!

2228
7/G18
14 ROOMS
TEL · TV
£45-85

Skeabost Country House Hotel www.oxfordhotelsandinns.com · 01470 532202 · **near Portree** 11km west of Portree on the A850, the Dunvegan road. Venerable Skye chateau with fab interior conserved despite recent chequered history of owners. Now efficiently managed by Oxford Hotels. Conservatory restaurant, original billiard room (and table), loads of public space and some sumptuous bedrooms. Exquisite grounds including the babbling River Snizort (hotel has salmon rights for 8 miles and own ghillie) and a sweet little 9-hole (though can do 18) golf course. The Skeabost is back!

2229
7/G18
19 ROOMS
TEL · TV
£38-60

Bosville Hotel 01478 612846 · **Portree** Refurbished rooms and *the* place to eat in this hotel at the top of the brae heading north from centre on Staffin Rd. Chandlery Restaurant and Bistro (see below); urban standard of comfort and at the heart of Portree.

2230
7/G18
7 ROOMS
TEL · TV

Marmalade www.marmaladehotels.com · 01478 611711 · **Home Farm Road, Portree** Leave from corner of main square up hill away from sea and keep going 1.5km. Unlikely, almost suburban location until you see the view (from gardens and 4 of the 7 rooms). Portree's boutique hotel: rooms above busy bar/restaurant which is popular with locals. Perhaps could do with a freshener (and a new look at the lighting) but friendly staff (and friendly midges if you're out on the lawn in summer). The restaurant is where you go on Skye for a pizza.

2231 **Viewfield House** www.viewfieldhouse.com · 01478 612217 · Portree One
7/G18 of the first hotels you come to in Portree on the road from south (driveway
11 ROOMS opposite gas station); you need look no further. Individual, grand but comfortable,
APR-OCT full of antiques and memorabilia, though not at all stuffy; this is also one of the
TEL best-value hotels on the island. Log fires, Supper available if you want but you
£45-60 don't have to eat in. Hugh Macdonald is your congenial host.

2232 **Cuillin Hills Hotel** www.cuillinhills-hotel-skye.co.uk · 01478 612003 ·
7/G18 Portree On the edge of Portree (off road north to Staffin) near water's edge.
28 ROOMS Secluded mansion house hotel with nice conservatory. Decor: a matter of taste
TV · TEL (you may like leather-studded sofas and draped 4-posters) but in refurbishment
£45-60 and great views from most rooms. Nice walk from garden (2274/ISLAND WALKS).
EAT Dining room with a view is an increasingly popular eating-out place for locals
that non-resident visitors don't know about.

2233 **The Glenview** www.glenviewskye.co.uk · 01470 562248 · By Staffin 25km
7/G17 north of Portree on the A855 Staffin road just north of the Lealt Falls (1605/WATER-
5 ROOMS FALLS). Kirsty and Simon's freshly made rooms, dinner (and family) in this new/old
TEL cosy roadhouse in the north. Simple, nice style and decor and 2-choice, conscien-
£45-60 tiously cooked dinner. You can stop here!

2234 **Flodigarry** www.flodigarry.co.uk · 01470 552203 · Staffin 32km north of
7/G17 Portree. A romantic country house overlooking the sea, with Flora Mac's cottage in
7 ROOMS the grounds. The setting is uniquely special with the Quirang behind (1647/VIEWS)
+ 1 COTT and the silver sea with its sunsets from the terrace. Nice bar serves food and is
FEB-OCT open to non-residents. Dining room and conservatory. Cottage in grounds have the
TEL · TV history (she did live here) and contemporary interiors (and 7 rooms).
£60-85

2235 **Sabhal Mòr Ostaig** www.smo.uhi.ac.uk · 01471 888000 · Sleat Pronounced
7/H19 'Sawal More Ostag'. Part of the Gaelic College off the A851 north of Armadale.
80 ROOMS Excellent inexpensive rooms in modern build overlooking the Sound of Sleat. The
NO KIDS penthouse is spectacular. Breakfast in bright café. Best deal on the island; you
NO PETS could learn Gaelic.
£30 OR LESS

2236 **Broadford Hotel** www.broadfordhotel.co.uk · 01471 822414 · Broadford
7/G19 On left heading north out of Broadford. 'Makeover still in progress at TGP for this
30 ROOMS long-established Skye hotel with a bit of money being spent by the people who
TEL · TV also own the Bosville and Marmalade (above). Decent, not overdone look to new
£45-85 rooms. Busy bar and bistro below.

Greshornish Country House www.greshornishhouse.com · 01470 582266
Report: 1187/GET-AWAY-FROM-IT-ALL.

The Best Island Hotels

This section excludes Skye which has its own hotels listings on p. 382.

2237 5/E16
5 ROOMS
MAR-DEC
DF
£60-85

✓ **Scarista House** South Harris · www.scaristahouse.com · 01859 550238
21km Tarbert, 78km Stornoway. On the west coast famous for its beaches and overlooking one of the best (1573/BEACHES). Tim and Patricia Martin's civilised retreat and home from home. Fixed menu meals in dining rooms overlooking sea. No phones or other intrusions (though TV in the kitchen and WiFi coming); many books. The golf course over the road is exquisite. Check winter opening (probably closed Jan/Feb). Good family hotel but delightfully laid back. Couple of great suites.
EAT A fixed menu but the place to eat in these Hebrides. Open to non-residents.

2238 9/J27
7 ROOMS
EASTER-OCT
TEL · TV
NO KIDS
£60-85

✓ **Kilmichael House** Arran · www.kilmichael.com · 01770 302219 On main road to Brodick Castle/Corrie, take left at bend by golf course. 3km down track to this bucolic haven far (but only minutes) from bustling Brodick. Unapologetically old-style country-house refined, so not great for kids. Rooms in house or garden courtyard – painstaking detail in food, service and surroundings.
EAT The best eats on Arran, no contest. 2262/ISLAND RESTAURANTS.

2239 9/F24
9 ROOMS
MAR-DEC
£45-60

✓ **Colonsay Hotel** Colonsay · www.colonsayestate.co.uk · 01951 200316
Long established but after lapse now fully refurbished: a superb island hotel 100m from the ferry on this island perfectly proportioned for short stays (2209/ISLANDS). The laird (and the wife) and their partners determined to turn this into a contemporary destination hotel. Cool public rooms and buzzy bar (especially Thu quiz nights). Mobiles only work in the garden. Stunning beach 5km. On your bike.

2240 9/G26
11 ROOMS
£30-38

✓ **Achamore House** Gigha · www.achamorehouse.com · 01583 505400
The main house on this small-is-beautiful island (2214/MAGICAL ISLANDS) that's easy to reach from Kintyre. This was the house of James Horlicks (of Horlicks) who made the surrounding fabulous gardens one of Gigha's many attractions (1520/GARDENS). The inimitable Don Dennis runs his mail-order alternative-remedies biz from here but everything about the house, from the large, individual rooms with big, comfy beds to the lawn out front has a soothing, relaxing quality. Not all en-suite but all great value.

2241 9/F26
10 ROOMS
TEL · TV
£45-60

✓ **Port Charlotte Hotel** Islay · www.portcharlottehotel.co.uk · 01496 850360 Epitome perhaps of the comfortable, classy island hotel. Modern, discreet approach to guests, sea swishing below, very much at the heart of this fine whitewashed village (1561/COASTAL VILLAGES). Good whisky choice and good, bistro-style food in dining room; and bar meals. Tourists in summer, hardcore twitchers in winter... us at anytime. Hotel supports local and Scottish artists and music. Jovial owner Grahame Allison is in the Gaelic choir.
EAT All-round best place to dine on Islay. 2259/ISLAND RESTAURANTS.

2242 9/F26
7 ROOMS
+ 2 APTS
TEL · TV
£45-60

✓ **Harbour Inn** Islay · www.harbour-inn.com · 01496 810330 Neil and Carol Scott's island restaurant with rooms is 2 doors up from the harbour in the centre of the main town on lovely, quite lively Islay. Rooms contemporary and comfy, lounge with views and notable restaurant. Bar with malts and bar meals (LO 8.30pm). 2 apartments across the street.

2243 9/F26
11 ROOMS
TEL · TV · DA
£45-60

✓ **Bridgend Inn** Islay · www.bridgend-hotel.com · 01496 810212
Bridgend near Bowmore on the Port Askaig road. Comfortable roadside hostelry, long a fixture on the island and a gathering place for locals and visitors. Bar and dining room.

2244 **9/F26**
5 ROOMS
FEB–OCT, DEC
NO PETS
NO KIDS
£45–60

✓ **An Taigh Osda** Islay · www.antaighosda.co.uk · 01496 850587
Bruichladdich on the road between Bridgend (Bowmore) and Port Charlotte.
Most recent arrival in the good choice of small hotels on Islay (see above) and the
most purposefully boutiqueish. Few but relaxing, quite stylish rooms and notable
restaurant (2260/ISLAND RESTAURANTS). Paul and Joan Graham your amenable
hosts. They're working on the art!

2245 **9/G22**
6 ROOMS
MAR–OCT
TEL · TV
NO PETS
£60–85

✓ **Highland Cottage** Mull · www.highlandcottage.co.uk · 01688 302030
On Breadalbane St opposite the fire station. Traditional Tobermory street
above harbour (from roundabout on road in from Craignure). 6 small, comfy rooms
named after islands (all themed; I'm usually in Nantucket). Their reputation grows
and it's harder to get in but foodies should try harder. All here is small but perfectly formed: relaxed atmosphere with Jo Currie's simply delicious fine dining.
EAT The place to eat on Mull. Fine without fuss. 2282/MULL.

2246 **9/F22**
9 ROOMS
MAR–NOV
£60–85
ATMOS

✓ **Calgary Hotel** Mull · www.calgary.co.uk · 01688 400256 7km south of
Dervany (30 minutes Tobermory) near beautiful Calgary Beach. Roadside
bistro/restaurant (2264/ISLAND RESTAURANTS) with rooms and gallery/ coffeeshop.
Excellent island hospitality – Matthew's furniture in public rooms and 'Art in
Nature' sculpture trail in woods down to the beach. Bohemia on the bay! Get up
early to see the otters (I never have). 2 self-catering suites above gallery.
EAT Informal ambience and good Mod Brit cooking; coolest rooms on the island.

2247 **9/F22**
7 ROOMS
£90 FULL
BOARD
DA

✓ **Coll Hotel** Coll · www.collhotel.com · 01879 230334 Julie and Kevin
Oliphant were surprised in '09 when they won a 'Rising Star' award because
they've been running this hotel for 25 years. Perhaps Coll's time has finally come.
Now I have to admit I've never been here but several correspondents rave and I'm
going to make it soon. It's got a nice garden, a deck and the Gannet Restaurant. 4
rooms have the islands view. Coll is 2.5/3 hours from Oban. Ferries sail all year
round.

2248 **5/C20**
12 ROOMS
TEL · TV
£38–45

Castlebay Hotel Barra · www.castlebayhotel.com · 01871 810223
Prominent position overlooking bay and ferry dock. You see where you're staying
long before you arrive. Old-style holiday hotel at the centre of Barra life. Perhaps
upgrading would spoil its unique charm though the bedrooms are much improved.
Good restaurant and bar meals (2281/OUTER HEBRIDES). Adjacent bar, famed for
craic and car culture, has more than a dash of the Irish (1268/BLOODY GOOD PUBS)
and a busy pool table.

2249 **9/G26**
12 ROOMS
TEL · TV
£38–45

The Gigha Hotel Gigha · www.gigha.org.uk · 01583 505254 A short walk
from the ferry on an island perfectly proportioned for a short visit; easy walking
and cycling. Residents' lounge peaceful with dreamy views to Kintyre. Menu with
local produce, eg Gigha prawns and scallops and especially Laura's halibut (in bar
or dining room). Island life without the remoteness. Also self-catering cottages.
2214/ISLANDS.

2250 **9/G25**
17 ROOMS
£38–45

Jura Hotel Jura · www.jurahotel.co.uk · 01496 820243 Craighouse, 15km
from Islay ferry at Feolin. Serviceable, basic hotel overlooking Small Isles Bay; will
oblige with all walking/exploring requirements. Pub is social hub of island. Rooms
at front may be small, but have the views. Not all en suite.

✓ **Argyll Hotel** Iona · 01681 700334 · **St Columba Hotel** Iona · 01681
700304 1165/SEASIDE INNS, 2282/MULL.

Kildonan Hotel Arran · 01770 820207 2279/ARRAN.

The Best Skye Restaurants

2251 7/F18
£32+

✓✓ **The Three Chimneys** www.threechimneys.co.uk · 01470 511258 · Colbost 7km west of Dunvegan on B884 to Glendale. Shirley and Eddie Spear's classic restaurant in a converted cottage on the edge of the best kind of nowhere, with chef-to-watch Michael Smith on the stoves in the tiny kitchen out back. They shop local for everything (Skye supplies have hugely improved following their example) from lettuce to langoustines. All year. Lunch (except Sun and winter months). Dinner LO 9.30pm. Fantastically good service with a strong kitchen team and gentle island girls out front. It's a long road to Colbost but by the start of your starter you know why you came. They can recommend some B&Bs when their own rooms are (as usual) full. 2221/SKYE HOTELS.

2252 7/H19
£32+

✓ **Kinloch Lodge** www.kinloch-lodge.co.uk · 01471 833333 · Sleat Peninsula In south on Sleat Peninsula, 55km south of Portree signed off the 'main' Sleat road, along a characterful track. Lord and Lady MacDonald's family home/hotel offers a taste of the high life without hauteur; a setting and setup especially appreciated by international visitors, starting with drinks in the drawing room 7.30pm for 8. Lady Claire no longer in the kitchen (what with her 'luxury comestibles' brand rolling out round the country) but chef Marcello Tully making his own mark. This is elegant dining in a lovely room and it all makes you want to stay for one of Claire's cookery courses.

2253 7/G18
£32+/
£15-22

✓ **The Chandlery at The Bosville Hotel** 01478 612846 · Portree Fine dining in Portree winning awards and more importantly, local approval. A la carte and daily menu well thought-out, sourced and presented. But you might do as well to stick with the out-front bistro, Portree's good deal, good food (mainly seafood), drop-in option. Must book for the Chandlery LO 8.30pm. Bistro 9pm.

2254 7/F17
£15-22

✓ **Lochbay Seafood** www.lochbay-seafood-restaurant.co.uk · 01470 592235 · Stein 12km north of Dunvegan off A850. Small; simple fresh seafood in loch-side setting, David and Alison keep it simply divine. Apr-Oct lunch and dinner Tue-Sat. Report: 1337/SEAFOOD RESTAURANTS.

2255 7/G18

✓ **Harbour View** 01478 612069 · Bosville Terrace, Portree On road to Staffin and north Skye with harbour view at least from the door. Local seafood in intimate bistro dining room which doesn't seem to have changed since it was somebody's front room in their cottage. Richard and Clare Smith have built a good local reputation. In summer you may have to put your name down and wait. Easter-Oct lunch and dinner. LO 9.30pm. Closed Mon.

2256 7/G19

Creelers www.creelers.co.uk · 01471 822281 · Broadford Just off A87 road from Kyleakin and bridge to Portree as you come into Broadford. Small cabin seafood restaurant with excellent local reputation. Big on bouillabaisse and surprising wine list. 12noon-10pm.

2257 7/G18

Café Arriba 01478 611830 · Portree Upstairs at the top of the road down to the harbour. A funky, bright, kinda boho caff on Skye with a view of the bay. Some healthy food, some not. Good bread/Green Mountain coffee/vegetarian. Day and evening menus. Does the trick. 7 days. LO 9pm.

2258 7/G18

Caledonian Café Wentworth Street, Portree On the main street. Simple, serviceable caff open long hours in summer for hungry tourists who don't want to cough up loadsa dosh to eat. Hot specials and usual caff fare. Home baking and busy with their home-made ice cream. 7 days 8.30am-9pm.

The Best Restaurants In The Islands

2259 9/F26
£15-32
✓ **Port Charlotte Hotel** Islay · www.portcharlottehotel.co.uk · 01496 850360 Excellent island inn with dining room and bar meals using local produce and as good as anything comparable on the mainland. Chef Ranga Dmamadharon does knock out the occasional curry. Reports: 2241/ISLAND HOTELS.

2260 9/F26
£22-32
✓ **An Taigh Osda** Islay · www.antaighosda.co.uk · 01496 850587 Another decent restaurant down this road in the northwest of the island (Bruichladdich). The ground floor of a seaside mansion, now a smart, contemporary hotel (2244/ISLAND HOTELS). Food likewise. Visitors vie with locals for tables in summer. Lunch and dinner. Closed Nov & Jan.

2261 9/G22
£32+
✓ **The Dining Room @ Highland Cottage** Mull · 01688 302030 · www.highlandcottage.co.uk Jo Currie's down-to-earth fine dining; the Tobermory destination for foodies, a treat for locals. Impeccably sourced. Small, homely: you'd call it a dining room.

2262 9/J27
£22-32
✓ **Kilmichael Hotel** Arran · 01770 302219 3km from seafront road in Brodick, this is the place to go for dinner. Antony Butterworth imaginative in the kitchen with best of local and national produce. Fixed menu, so discuss dos and don'ts ahead. Peacocks in the garden enliven the otherwise classical soundtrack. Report: 2238/ISLAND HOTELS.

2263 9/G25
£22-32
✓ **The Antlers** Jura · www.theantlers.co.uk · 01496 820123 There's not a lot to Craighouse in glorious Jura (well, a hotel and a distillery) but it now has a restaurant that any more populous island would be proud of. Café-bistro by day and bistro-restaurant by night serving great home-made food, especially local seafood in both menus. Well, you just wouldn't go anywhere else. Grahame and Steve have got it covered. BYO. 9.30am-9pm. Closed Mon. Winter hours will vary.

2264 9/F22
ATMOS
£15-22
✓ **Calgary Hotel & Dovecote Restaurant** Mull · 01688 400256 7km from Dervaig on B8073 near Mull's famous beach. Roadside farm setting with inexpensive light, piney bedrooms and a bistro/wine bar restaurant using local produce for Mod Brit cuisine. The Carthouse Gallery/coffeeshop also in summer. A quiet spot for the most ambient meal on Mull. No frills.

2265 5/C20
£22-32
Castlebay Hotel Barra · 01871 810223 A stunning view of a summer's eve. Informal dining room overlooking castle and bay. Best grub on the island though the choice ain't great. Menu to please all sorts. Daily specials best: langoustines, lobster, cockles from the beach by the airport but also comfort-food staples. Puds not home made.

✓ **Argyll Hotel** Iona · 01681 700334 1165/SEASIDE INNS.

✓ **Scarista House** Harris · 01859 550238 2237/ISLAND HOTELS.

✓ **Lochbay Seafood** Skye 12km north of Dunvegan 1137/SEAFOOD.

Creelers Arran · 01770 302810 Edge of Brodick 2279/ARRAN.
Digby Chick Lewis · 01851 700026 2281/OUTER HEBRIDES.
Busta House Shetland · 01806 522506 2284/SHETLAND.

Fantastic Walks In The Islands

For walk codes, see p. 12.

2266 7/G18
10KM · XCIRC
XBIKES
2-B-2

Dun Caan Raasay Still one of my favourite island walks – to the flat top of a magic hill (1732/VIEWS), the one you see from most of the east coast of Skye. Take ferry (2206/MAGICAL ISLANDS), ask for route from Inverarish. Go via old iron mine; looks steep when you get over the ridge, but it's a dawdle. And amazing.

2267 5/E15
12KM RET
XCIRC
XBIKES
2-B-2

The Lost Glen Harris Not visited for '10/11 – hope the directions are still ok. Take B887 west from Tarbert almost to the end (where at Hushinish there's a good beach, maybe a sunset), but go right (was signed Chliostair Power Station) before the big house (1262/HOUSE PARTIES). Park here or further in and walk to dam (3km from road). Take right track round reservoir and left around the upper loch. Over the brim you arrive in a wide, wild glen; an overhang 2km ahead is said to have the steepest angle in Europe. Go quietly; if you don't see deer and eagles here, you're making too much noise on the grass.

2268 9/G23
15/20KM
XCIRC
XBIKES
2-B-2

Carsaig Mull In south of island, 7km from A849 Fionnphort-Craignure road near Pennyghael. 2 walks start at pier: going left towards Lochbuie for a spectacular coastal/woodland walk past Adnunan Stack (7km); or right towards the imposing headland where, under the cliffs, the Nuns' Cave was a shelter for nuns evicted from Iona during the Reformation. Nearby is a quarry whose stone was used to build Iona Abbey and much further on (9km Carsaig), at Malcolm's Point, the extraordinary Carsaig Arches carved by wind and sea.

2269 9/J26
11KM
CIRC
XBIKES

Cock of Arran Lochranza Start and finish at Lochranza Castle following the signs to the magnificent shoreline. Divers and ducks share the littoral with seals. About 1km from where you meet the shore, look for Giant Centipede fossil trail. Further on at opening of wall pace 350 steps and turn left up to Ossian's Cave. Path crosses Fairy Dell Burn and eventually comes out at Lochranza Bay. Allow 4/5 hours and stout boots.

2270 9/F24
12 + 6KM
XCIRC
BIKES
1-A-2

Colonsay 2209/MAGICAL ISLANDS. From hotel or the quay, walk to Colonsay House and its lush, overgrown intermingling of native plants and exotics (8km round trip); or to the priory on Oronsay, the smaller island. 6km to 'the Strand' (you might get a lift with the postman) then cross at low tide, with enough time (at least 2 hours) to walk to the ruins. Allow longer if you want to climb the easy peak of Ben Oronsay. Tide tables at hotel. Nice walk also from Kiloran Beach (1568/BEACHES) to Balnahard Beach – farm track 12km return.

2271 7/F18
30KM
XCIRC
XBIKES

The Trotternish Ridge website.lineone.net/~trotternish/walking.html · Skye The 30km Highland walk which takes in the Quirang and the Old Man of Stoer (see below for both) offers many shorter walks without climbing or scrambling as well as the whole monty (a 2-day hike).

2272 7/G17
5KM
XCIRC
XBIKES
2-B-2

The Old Man Of Stoer Skye The enigmatic basalt finger visible from the Portree-Staffin road (A855). Start from car park on left, 12km from Portree. There's a well-defined path through woodland and then towards the cliffs and a steep climb up the grassy slope to the pinnacle which towers 165ft tall. Great views over Raasay to the mainland. Lots of space and rabbits and birds who make the most of it. It was the location of major environmental art event by notable NVA organisation in summer 2005.

2273 7/G17 **The Quirang** Skye See 1647/VIEWS for directions to start point. The strange
6KM formations have names (eg the Table, the Needle, the Prison) and it's possible to
XCIRC walk round all of them. Start of the path from the car park is easy. At the first
XBIKES saddle, take the second scree slope to the Table, rather than the first. When you
2-B-2 get to the Needle, the path to the right between two giant pinnacles is the easiest
of the 3 options. From the top you can see the Hebrides. This place is
supernatural; anything could happen. So be careful.

2274 7/F18 **Scorrybreac** Skye A much simpler prospect than the above and more quietly
3KM spectacular but mentioned here because anyone could do it; it's only 3km and it's
CIRC more or less in Portree. Head for Cuillin HIlls Hotel off Staffin Rd out of town
XBIKES (2232/SKYE HOTELS). Shoreline path signed just below hotel. Passes 'Black Rock',
1-A-1 where once Bonnie Prince Charlie left for Raasay, and continues round hill. Nice
views back to the bright lights and pink houses of Portree.

2275 3/Q11 **Hoy** Orkney There are innumerable walks on the scattered Orkney Islands; on a
20/25KM good day, head to the north of Hoy for some of the most dramatic coastal scenery
CIRC anywhere. Ferries frequent from Flotta and Houton. Make tracks north or south
MT BIKES from junction near pier and don't miss the landmarks, the bird sanctuaries and the
2-B-2 Old Man himself. See 2045A/COASTAL WALKS.

2276 9/H24 **Corryvreckan** Jura The whirlpool in the Gulf of Corryvreckan is notorious.
6/24KM Between Jura and Scarba; to see it go to far north of Jura. From end of the road at
XCIRC Ardlussa (25km Craighouse, the village), there's a rough track to Lealt then a walk
XBIKES (a local may drive you) of 12km to Kinuachdrach, then a further walk of 3km.
2-C-2 Phenomenon best seen at certain states of tide. There are boat trips from Crinan
and Oban – consult tourist information centres on Jura. Consult at the hotel
(2250/ISLAND HOTELS) and get the walk guide. 2207/MAGICAL ISLANDS.

2277 7/G20 **Sgurr An** Eigg Unmissable treat on Eigg. Take to the big ridge. Not a hard pull;
extraordinary views and island perspective from the top. 2210/MAGICAL ISLANDS.

The Best of Skye

2278 **The Bridge** Unromantic but easy, and free; from Kyle. The **Ferries** Mallaig-
7/H19 Armadale, 30 minutes. Tarbert (Harris)-Uig, 1 hour 35 minutes (CalMac, as Mallaig).
The Best Way to Skye Glenelg-Kylerhea www.skyeferry.co.uk 5-minute sailing. Continuous Easter-Oct . Winter sailings – check tourist information centre.
Community run. See 7/SCOTTISH JOURNEYS.

WHERE TO STAY & EAT
See the separate sections Skye Hotels p. 382–84 and Skye Restaurants, p. 387.

WHAT TO SEE
The Cuillin (2/BIG ATTRACTIONS); **Raasay** (2206/MAGICAL ISLANDS), (2266/ISLAND
WALKS); **The Quirang** (1647/VIEWS), (2273/ISLAND WALKS); **Old Man Of Stoer**
(2272/ISLAND WALKS); **Dunvegan** (1771/CASTLES); **Eas Mor** (1605/WATERFALLS);
Elgol (1654/VIEWS); **Skye Batiks** (2177/SHOPPING); **Skye Museum Of Island
Life** (2136/MUSEUMS); **Flora Macdonald's Grave** (1837/MONUMENTS); **Skye
Silver, Edinbane Pottery** and **Carbost Craft** (2174/2175/SHOPPING); **Fairy
Pools** (1669/PICNICS); **Duirinish** and **Minginish** (2045A/COASTAL WALKS).

Tourist Info 01478 612137 **CalMac** www.calmac.co.uk · 08705 650000

The Best of Arran

2279	**Ferry** Ardrossan-Brodick, 55 minutes. 6 per day Mon-Sat, 4 on Sun.
9/J29	Ardrossan-Glasgow, train or road via A77/A71 1.5 hours.
	Claonaig-Lochranza, 30 minutes. 9 per day (summer only).
	The best way to see Arran is on a bike. Hire: 01770 302868 or 01770 302377.

WHERE TO STAY

7 ROOMS
TEL · TV
NO KIDS/PETS
£60-85

✓ **Kilmichael House** 01770 302219 · **Brodick** Period mansion 3km from the main road and into the glens. Elegant interior and furnishings in house and courtyard rooms. Very discreet hence no groups or kids. Still *the* place to eat on Arran, but book (2238/ISLAND HOTELS). Also has self-catering cottages.

13 ROOMS
£45-60

Glenisle Hotel www.glenislehotel.com · 01770 600559 · **Lamlash** Recently refurbished and rethought hotel in Lamlash looking out to Holy Isle. Local stone, colour and texture in evidence in rooms, especially bar and restaurant. I haven't been at TGP but good things are expected here. Reports, please.

28 ROOMS
+36 IN SPA
TEL · TV
NO PETS
£45-60

Auchrannie House www.auchrannie.co.uk · 01770 302234 · **Brodick** Once an old mansion now expanded into a holiday complex. House has best rooms, eats (Eighteen69 Restaurant) and small pool. But the Spa Resort, like a Holiday Inn in the country, is perfect for families: quite stylish modern rooms, bigger pool and leisure facilities. 'Juice Bar' here means Scottish 'juice'. Upstairs restaurant a bit Glasgow Airport but fits all sizes! There's also 'Brambles'. Plenty indoors for Arran weather but also out: Arran Adventure Centre on hand. Burgeoning timeshares.

17 ROOMS
TV
£45-60

Kildonan Hotel www.kildonanhotel.com · 01770 820207 · **Kildonan** In the south of the island (Brodick 16km) on a beautiful strand overlooking Pladda Island and lighthouse and Ailsa Craig spectral beyond. Great outside terrace (with big stones) for gazing out to sea. Recently refurbished rooms, popular bar with grub and conservatory dining room. Somehow special.

8 ROOMS
APR-OCT TV
£38-45

Burlington www.burlingtonarran.co.uk · 01770 700255 · **Whiting Bay** Possibly the best guest house on the long row of hotels that overlook the bay. The Lamonts are friendly and they've been doing this a long time.

9 ROOMS
EASTER-DEC
TEL · TV
£30-38

Lochranza Hotel www.lochranza.co.uk · 01770 830223 · **Lochranza** Small hotel with tranquil views over bay and 13th-century castle. Basic accommodation but home-spun hospitality. Beer garden with food all day in season. Good malts.

S.Y. Hostel www.syha.org.uk · 0845 293 7373 · **Lochranza** 30km from Brodick. Recently refurbished. 1156/HOSTELS.

WHERE TO EAT

£22-32

✓ **Kilmichael House** www.kilmichael.com · 01770 302219 · **Brodick** (See Where to Stay, above.) Unquestionably the best food on Arran. Fixed menu so discuss ahead. 2262/ISLAND RESTAURANTS.

£15 OR LESS

Brodick Bar & Brasserie **Brodick** Best pub food in Brodick? Yes by common consensus, but no' cheap, as they say. Goes like a fair and can feel like a canteen on summer evenings. Long blackboard menu. Food until 10pm. Off north end of main street by Royal Mail. Bar till 12midnight.

£15-22 **The Wineport** 01770 302101 · **Brodick** On the A841 north of Brodick (5 km) at Cladach just before Brodick Castle beside Arran Brewery and where you come off Goat Fell (1936/HILLS). Newest venture by the family who have the Brodick Bar (above). Lunch and lighter menu during the day, bistro at night. Accessible food in light surroundings. Apr-Sep. Dinner Wed-Sat.

£22-32 **Creelers** www.creelers.co.uk · **01770 302810** · **Brodick** Long-established and most credible seafood on the island. Good kitchen team '09, hopefully will stay 10/11. Owned by the same folk who have Creelers in Edinburgh (211/EDINBURGH SEAFOOD). This is where they have the smokery. See 1340/SEAFOOD RESTAURANTS.

£15 OR LESS **The Pierhead Tavern** 01770 600418 · **Lamlash** Main road. Very serviceable, good-value pub grub with long menu and specials. Home-made chips, even with chicken tikka masala (and rice). Big helpings. The PHT is definitely the people's choice. Lunch and LO 9pm.

£22-32 **Trafalgar** 01770 700396 · **Whiting Bay** On the Shore Rd among many hotels, the Trafalgar for a very long time has been where on Arran you go for your tea, ie dinner. Nothing too fancy, mind, just the Knoners cooking up what we like. An institution, their old-style dining room. Evenings only. You'd better book. LO 8.30pm. Fri/Sat only in winter.

Machrie Golf Course Tearoom 01770 840329 · **Machrie Bay** All the golf courses in Arran seem to have tearooms with ladies who bake. This is on the west coast on the main A841. Good local reputation. 7 days in season (Mar-Oct) 10am-5pm & Mon-Wed 6-8pm.

£15-22 **The Beach Hut** 01770 700738 · **Whiting Bay** Shoreline location with conservatory and contemporary look. Simple, home-made food by the Australian boy. Evenings only. Closed Sun/Mon.

£15-22 **The Lighthouse** 01770 850240 Wholesome menu of great home-made food. The Pattisons here a while now, specialising in local seafood, lamb and beef. Best place on island for sundowners (BYOB) and cappuccinos. Closed Mon. Feb-Nov 10am-4pm & 5pm-9.30pm.

WHAT TO SEE

NT **Brodick Castle** 5km walk or cycle from Brodick. Impressive museum and gardens. Tearoom. Flagship NTS property (1768/CASTLES).

2-A-2 **Goat Fell** 6km/5hr great hill walk starting from the car park at Cladach near castle and Brodick or sea start at Corrie. Free route leaflet at tourist information centre. 1936/HILLS.

1-B-1 **Glenashdale Falls** 4km, but 2-hour forest walk from Glenashdale Bridge at Whiting Bay. Steady, easy climb, sylvan setting. 1603/WATERFALLS.
Corrie The best village 9km north of Brodick. Go by bike. 1566/COASTAL VILLAGES.
Machrie Moor Standing Stones Off main coast road 7km north of Blackwater Foot. Various assemblies of Stones, all part of an ancient landscape. We lay down there.

1-B-2 **Glen Rosa, Glen Sannox** Fine glens: Rosa near Brodick, Sannox 11km north.

Tourist Info 01770 303774 **CalMac** 08705 650000 · www.calmac.co.uk

The Best of Islay & Jura

2280 9/G24	**Ferry** Kennacraig-Port Askaig: 2 hours; Kennacraig-Port Ellen: 2 hours 10 minutes. Port Askaig-Feolin, Jura: (01880 730253) 5 minutes, frequent daily. Passenger ferry from Tayvallich near Crinan Easter-Sep; 077684 50000. **By Air** Flybe (0871 7002000) Glasgow to Port Ellen Airport in south of Islay.

WHERE TO STAY

10 ROOMS TEL · TV £45-60	✓ **Port Charlotte Hotel** www.portcharlottehotel.co.uk · 01496 850360 · **Port Charlotte** Restored Victorian inn and gardens overlooking sea in conservation village. Restful place and views. Good bistro-style menu, the best around. Eat in bar/conservatory or dining room. The Allisons never stop. 2241/ISLAND HOTELS.
7 ROOMS TEL · TV £38-45	✓ **Harbour Inn** www.harbour-inn.com · 01496 810330 · Bowmore Harbourside inn with conservatory lounge, Schooner bar for seafood lunch and less formal supper, and dining room with Modern British menu. Bedrooms vary but all mod and con. Some locals complain of 'attitude'. 2242/ISLAND HOTELS.
5 ROOMS FEB-OCT, DEC NO KIDS/PETS £45-60	✓ **An Taigh Osda** www.antaighosda.co.uk · 01496 850587 · Bruichladdich Stylish, contemporary dreaming and dining in mansion over the road from the sea. The distillery is next door. ('Taigh' is pronounced 'Tie'.)
11 ROOMS TEL · TV £45-60	✓ **Bridgend Inn** www.bridgend-hotel.com · 01496 810212 · Bridgend Middle of island on road from Port Askaig, 4km Bowmore. Roadside inn with good pub meals and surprising number of rooms. A reasonable stopover.
7 ROOMS £90 FULL BOARD DF	✓ **Ardlussa House** Jura · www.ardlussaestate.com · 01496 820323 Hard to be more far-flung than this – the Ardlussa Estate occupies the north of Jura and this lived-in family house is a welcome destination after a single-track journey (28km from Craignure). The Fletchers share their splendid wild backyard with you. George Orwell's house is on their land. B&B but dinner served. Kids run free.
5 ROOMS TV NO KIDS/PETS £45-60	**Kilmeny Farm** www.kilmeny.co.uk · 01496 840668 · near Ballygrant Margaret and Blair Rozga's top-class guest house just off the road south of Port Askaig (the ferry). Huge attention to detail, great home-made food (dinner available Tue and Thu), house-party atmosphere and shared tables. Though small.
5 ROOMS TV · ECO NO KIDS NO C/CARDS £38-45	**Glenmachrie** 01496 302560 · near Port Ellen On A846 between Bowmore and Port Ellen near airport. Same family of Kilmeny owners (above). Here it's Rachel's award-winning farmhouse with everything just so (fluffy bathrobes, toiletries supplied, fruit bowl and a sweet on the pillow). Meals in sister guest house up the road (see below).
6 ROOMS TV NO KIDS/PETS NO C/CARDS £45-60	**Glenegedale House** www.glenegedalehouse.co.uk · 01496 300400 · near Port Ellen The newer venture by Rachel Whyte near Glenmachrie and opposite the airport. It would be hard to find a homelier airport hotel... anywhere! This the more deluxe option, Rachel flits between the two but most likely here: her 5-star B&B. Dinner on request.
16 ROOMS (+15 LODGES) TEL · TV NO PETS £38-45	**The Machrie** www.machrie.com · 01496 302310 · Port Ellen 7km north on A846. Restaurant and bar meals in clubhouse atmosphere. Restaurant in old byre and 15 lodges in the grounds. You'll likely be here for the golf – so you might overlook its rather bleak setting and general ennui. Food, I'm told, is surprisingly good. The great beach (1574/BEACHES) *is* over there.

£38-45 **Lochside Hotel** www.lochsidehotel.co.uk · 01496 810244 · Bowmore
Probably best selection of Islay malts in the world; so great bar and bar meals in
lochside, actually seaside setting. Rooms 50-50. Pub food standard.

15 ROOMS **Jura Hotel** www.jurahotel.co.uk · 01496 820243 · Craighouse The best
£30-38 hotel on the island – well, the only one! But it does what you want. Situated in
front of the distillery by the bay. Front rooms best (not all en suite). There's craic in
the bar. Report: 2250/ISLAND HOTELS.

Camping, Caravan Site www.kintrafarm.co.uk · 01496 302051 · Kintra
Farm Off main road to Port Ellen; take Oa road, follow Kintra signs 7km. Jul-Aug
Grassy strand, coastal walks. 1202/WILD CAMPING.

Islay Youth Hostel www.syha.org.uk · 01496 850385 · Port Charlotte

WHERE TO EAT

✓ **Harbour Inn** Bowmore, **Port Charlotte Hotel** Port Charlotte, **An
Taigh Osda** Bruichladdich. See *Where to Stay*.

£15-22 ✓ **Ardbeg Distillery Café** www.ardbeg.com 5km east of Port Ellen on the
whisky road. Great local reputation for food. Beautiful room. Food home-made
as are those Ardbegs. Most vintages and Ardbeg clothes to boot. All year Mon-Fri
(7 days Jun-Aug) 10am-LO 4pm.

✓ **The Antlers** www.theantlers.co.uk · 01496 820123 · Craighouse, Jura
Middle of the ribbon of village and new '09; instantly popular with locals and
visitors. Bistro by day, restaurant in evening (till 9pm). Local seafood and good
home cooking. Closed Mon. Check winter hours.

Bridgend Inn Bridgend. See *Where to Stay*.

Kilchoman Distillery Café www.kilchomandistillery.com · 01496 850011 ·
Rockside Farm A new distillery in the northwest off the A846 from Bridgend
(8km). First whisky expected '09/10. Meanwhile this caff has much to like, especially the secret-recipe Cullen Skink. Mon-Sat 10am-4pm (not Sat in winter).

WHAT TO SEE
Islay: The Distilleries especially Ardbeg (good café), Laphroaig and Lagavulin
(classic settings), all by Port Ellen; tours by appointment. Bowmore has a regular,
very polished tour (1481/WHISKY); **Museum of Islay, Wildlife Info & Field
Centre** (1757/WILDLIFE): all at Port Charlotte; **American Monument**
(1835/MONUMENTS); **Oa & Loch Gruinart** (1729/BIRDS); **Port Charlotte**
(1861/COASTAL VILLAGES); **Kintra** (2033/COASTAL WALKS); **Finlaggan** The romantic,
sparse ruin on 'island' in Loch Finlaggan: last home of the Lords of the Isles. Off
A846 5km south of Port Askaig, check tourist information centre for opening.

Jura (2207/MAGICAL ISLANDS): **The Paps of Jura**; **Corryvreckan, Barnhill**
(2276/ISLAND WALKS); **Killchianaig, Keils** (1877/GRAVEYARDS); **Lowlandman's
Bay** (1579/BEACHES); **Jura House Walled Garden**; utterly magical (1511/GAR-
DENS); **Jura House** (1254/HOUSEPARTIES).

Tourist Info 01496 810254 **CalMac** 08705 650000

The Best of The Outer Hebrides

2281
5/F14 **Ferries** Ullapool-Stornoway, 2 hours 40 minutes (not Sun).
Oban/Mallaig-Lochboisdale, South Uist and Castlebay, Barra; up to 6.5 hours.
Uig on Skye-Tarbert, Harris (not Sun) or Lochmaddy, North Uist 1 hour 40 minutes.
Also Leverburgh, Harris-Berneray (not Sun) 1 hour.
By Air Flybe (0871 7002000) from Inverness/Glasgow/Edinburgh. Otter to Barra/
Benbecula from Glasgow (1/2 a day).

WHERE TO STAY

✓ **Scarista House** South Harris · www.scaristahouse.com · 01859
550238 20km south of Tarbert. Cosy haven near famous but often deserted
beach; this celebrated retreat offers the real R&R and a lovely dinner. Also self-
catering accommodation. Report: 2237/ISLAND HOTELS.

4 ROOMS
£60-85

✓ **Broad Bay House** Lewis · www.broadbayhouse.co.uk · 01851 820990
11km north of Stornoway on east of island on the sea. Purpose-built with big,
light dining and lounge area and outside deck. Spacious, contemporary rooms with
big TV, iPod docks, etc. Welcome tray includes wine and a stamped postcard to
send home. You'll want to stay a while in this chilled-out back of beyond. Top grub
and a decent wine list. This is a very superior guest house to write home about.

£60-85

✓ **Blue Reef Cottages** South Harris · www.stay-hebrides.com · 01859
550370 1 km from Scarista House (above) and overlooking the same idyllic
beach. I don't usually list self-catering cottages in *StB* but these 2 are exceptional.
For couples only though the study could be another bedroom at a pinch. Stylish,
good facilities, amazing view. Gourmet meals from lady nearby or eat at Scarista
House. 7-day stays. 2-day minimum in winter.

21 ROOMS
£45-60

✓ **Hotel Hebrides** Tarbert, Harris · www.hotel-hebrides.com · 01859
502364 Very contemporary new-build hotel right by the pier where the boat
comes in so convenient and probably just what you want (but the Harris Hotel
nearby is also nice – see below). Opened '09 so I haven't stayed at TGP but both
rooms and restaurant/bar are light, uncluttered modern. I'd say a good base for
Harris trail-finding

7 ROOMS
MAY-SEP
£38-45

✓ **Baile-Na-Cille** Timsgarry, West Lewis · 01851 672241 Near Uig 60km
west of Stornoway. This is about as far away as it gets but guests return again
and again to the Collins' house by the sea. Hospitable hosts allow you the run of
their place – the books, the games room, the tennis court and the most amazing
beach. All home-made grub (bread, ice cream, etc). Great value and especially
good for families. 1126/HOTELS KIDS.

8 ROOMS
TEL · TV
DF
£38-45

✓ **Tigh Dearg (The Red House) Hotel** Lochmaddy, North Uist · 01876
500700 · www.tighdearghotel.co.uk Iain Macleod's personally run, contemporary new-build hotel which, being red, stands out for miles and stands out
also for the level of style and efficiency in these far-flung islands where the
beaches and the sky are immense. 'Leisure Club' includes sauna/steam. Good disabled access and family suite.

Castlebay Hotel Castlebay, Barra · www.castlebay-hotel.co.uk · 01871
810223 Overlooks ferry terminal in the village so superb views. Decent dining,
atmospheric bar. Report: 2248/ISLAND HOTELS; 1268/BLOODY GOOD PUBS.

26 ROOMS	**Royal Hotel** Stornoway, Lewis · www.royalstornoway.co.uk · 01851 702109
TEL · TV	The most central of the 3 main hotels in town, all owned by the same family. HS-1
£38-45	bistro and Boatshed (probably best hotel dining). The **Cabarfeidh** (01851 702604)

The most central of the 3 main hotels in town, all owned by the same family. HS-1 bistro and Boatshed (probably best hotel dining). The **Cabarfeidh** (01851 702604) is the upmarket ie most expensive option – probably the best bedrooms. These hotels are about the only places open in Lewis on Sun. The **Caladh Inn** (pronounced 'Cala') and its caff '11', are possibly best value. 11 has self-service buffet. Best all-round is the Royal.

6 ROOMS
NO PETS
£45-60

Ardhasaig House North Harris · www.ardhasaig.co.uk · 01859 502066
4km north of Tarbert just off A859. Neither this modern-build house nor its locally well-connected chef/proprietor (her family owns everything hereabouts) are especially comfortable to be with but there are redeeming features. Nice location and convenient though the new-build adjacent hasn't helped appreciation of the place. Conservatory and bar are pleasant. Michelin stickers proudly displayed.

22 ROOMS
TEL · TV
NO PETS
£60-85

Harris Hotel Tarbert, Harris · www.harrishotel.com · 01859 502154 In the township near the ferry terminal so good base for travels in North/South Harris. Variety of public rooms and diverse range of bedrooms (view/non-view, refurbished/non-refurbished, standard/superior), some of which are large and very nice. Friendly and well run. Food not a strong point, but adequate in the hotel-like dining room. Both bar and conservatory have better atmosphere.

11 ROOMS
TEL · TV
NO PETS
£38-45

Pollachar Inn South Uist · 01878 700215 South of Lochboisdale near Eriskay causeway (and ferry for Barra; 2216/ISLANDS). An inn at the rocky end of the Uists. Excellent value, good craic and the view/sunset across the sea to Barra. Rooms refurbished to an ok standard. The pub-grub menu uses local produce. LO 8.45pm.

Hostels Simple hostels within hiking distance. 2 in Lewis, 3 in Harris, 1 each in North and South Uist. Am Bothan at Leverburgh is independent and funky. The Blackhouse village in North Lewis is exceptional (1148/HOSTELS).

WHERE TO EAT

£22-32 **Digby Chick** 11 James Street, Stornoway · 01851 700026 Almost 10 years ago, DC set the new contemporary dining standard in Lewis and it still does. Seafood a speciality; a solid local reputation. You can't go wrong here. Mon-Sat, lunch and LO 8.30pm.

£15-22 **The Thai Café** Church Street, Stornoway · 01851 701811 Opposite police station. An unlikely outpost. Though there are palms outside in the rainswept street, you couldn't be further from Phuket. Mrs Panida Macdonald's restaurant an institution here and you may have to book. Great atmosphere and excellent real Thai cuisine. Lunch and LO 11pm. Closed Sun.

£22-32 **Limelite** Francis Street, Stornoway · 01851 700945 At the corner with Keith St. New, contemporary British bistro-restaurant which may give Digby Chick a run for its money. Haven't tried but the word on these Stornoway streets is good. Reports, please. Dinner only. LO 9pm. Closed Sun.

North & West in Lewis 3 further-flung places over the moors from Stornoway that I haven't visited but well you might (reports, please). **Sulair** is up at the Port of Ness; 01851 810222. **Loch Croistean** is towards Uig by Timsgarry; 01851 672772. **The Inn Between** is at Shawbost on the A858 north of Callanish and near the Blackhouse Museum (2122/HERITAGE); 01851 710632. All have growing reputations for home cooking. Opening hours vary. Phone when you can get reception.

Coffee Shops: An Lanntair Gallery Stornoway · www.lanntair.com **& Callanish Visitor Centre** Lewis · www.callananishvisitorcentre.co.uk An Lanntair, an all-embracing arts and cultural centre, is a great rendezvous spot and has a good view of the ferry terminal. Lunch and evening menu. The Callanish caff is far better than most visitor centres. Daytime only (1802/PREHISTORIC SITES). .

Scarista House Harris · www.scaristahouse.com Dinner possible for non-residents. A 20-minutes Tarbert, 45-minutes Stornoway drive for best meal in the Hebrides. Fixed menu. Book. See *Where to Stay*.

Skoon Art Café South Harris · 01859 530268 Near the stunning Golden Road (1632/SCENIC ROUTES) 12km south of Tarbert but best found following the sign off A859 then 4km to Geocrab (pronounced 'jocrab'). Andrew and Emma Craig's café in a gallery (his work on the walls). All done well – interesting soups, great home-baking. Apr-Sept Tue-Sat daytime only; weekends in winter..

First Fruits Tearoom Tarbert, Harris · 01859 502439 Near tourist information centre and ferry to Uig. Home-cooking that hits the spot. Good atmosphere. Wide-ranging menu includes all-day breakfast and fresh OJ. 10am-4pm Apr-Sep.

DA **Orasay Inn** Lochcarnan, South Uist · www.orasayinn.com · 01870 610298 You don't get remoter than this but it's always packed. In summer you may have to book days ahead (or weeks for accommodation) so that says it all. Midway between Lochmaddy and Lochboisdale signed off the spinal A885, go 3km then left at the shrine. Then 500m. No, it ain't easy to find. Conservatory and bar serving good, home-cooked comfort food and fresh seafood: cod, shellfish and 'witches'. Also 9 inexpensive rooms. Open all year, lunch and LO 9pm.

The Anchorage Leverburgh, South Harris · 01859 520225 All-round family restaurant/café/bar at the pierhead where the boat leaves for Berneray and the Uists. But better than your average terminal caff with most stuff home-made and cooked to order. Mar-Sep (weekends in winter) 12noon-9pm. Closed Sun.

Stepping Stones Balvanich, Benbecula · 01870 603377 8 km from main A855. Nondescript building in ex- (though sometimes operational) military air base. Serving the forces and the tourists – it aims to please. 7 days, lunch and LO 9pm (winter hours may vary). Menu changes through day.

The Boatshed at The Royal Hotel Stornoway **& '11' at The Caladh Inn** (see above). Best hotel options (and open Sun).

Langass Lodge North Uist · 01876 580285 Report: 1195/GET-AWAY HOTELS.

Tourist Info 01851 703088 **CalMac** www.calmac.co.uk · 08705 650000

WHAT TO SEE
Eriskay & Mingulay (2216/2217/ISLANDS); **Golden Road** (1632/SCENIC ROUTES); **Beaches** At Port of Ness, Scarista and South Uist (1587/1573/1572/BEACHES); **Dolphins** (1748/DOLPHINS); **Balranald Reserve** (1758/NATURE RESERVES). **Scarista Golf** (2074/GOOD GOLF); **Surfing** (2108/2109/SURFING BEACHES); **St Clement's Church & St Michael's Church** (1859/1860/CHURCHES); **Blackhouse of Arnol** (2122/HERITAGE); **Barpa Lanyass & Callanish Stones** (1817/1802/PREHISTORIC); **Harris Tweed** (p. 375).

2282 **Ferry** Oban-Craignure, 45 minutes. Main route; 6 a day. Lochaline-Fishnish, 15
9/G23 minutes. 9-15 a day. Kilchoan-Tobermory, 35 minutes. 7 a day (Sun in summer
only). Winter sailings – call tourist information centre.

WHERE TO STAY

✓ **Highland Cottage** www.highlandcottage.co.uk · 01688 302030 ·
Breadalbane Street, Tobermory Opposite fire station a street above the
harbour. Like a country house, well... a gorgeous cottage in town. Top spot for
grub. Report: 2245/ISLAND HOTELS.

✓ **Tiroran House** 01681 705232 · **Mull** A treat and a retreat way down in the
southwest of Mull near Iona. Light, comfy house in glorious gardens with
excellent food and flowers. Sea eagles fly over. Report: 1184/GET-AWAY HOTELS.

✓ **Argyll Hotel** www.argyllhoteliona.co.uk · 01681 700334 · **Iona** Near
ferry and on seashore overlooking Mull on road to abbey. Laid-back, cosy
accommodation, home cooking, good vegetarian. Report: 1165/SEASIDE INNS.

5 ROOMS ✓ **Glengorm Castle** www.glengormcastle.co.uk · 01688 302321 · **near**
£60-85 **Tobermory** Minor road on right going north outside town takes you to this
fine castle on a promontory set in an extensive estate which is yours to wander
(excellent walks; they'll give you a map). Fab views over to Ardnamurchan, little
peaks to climb and a natural 'bathing pool'. Luxurious bedrooms in family home –
use the library, complementary bar and grand public spaces. Loads of art, lawn and
gardens. Excellent self-catering cottages on estate. B&B only. Excellent coffee
shop/restaurant over by (1390/COFFEE SHOPS).

✓ **Calgary Hotel** www.calgary.co.uk · 01688 400256 · **Calgary** Near
Dervaig on B8073 near Mull's famous beach. Gallery/coffee shop and good
bistro/restaurant. The laid-back place to stay. Report: 2246/ISLAND HOTELS.

81 ROOMS **Isle of Mull Hotel** www.crerarhotels.com · 0870 9506267 · **Craignure**
TEL · TV Strung-out, low-rise hotel round Craignure Bay near the ferry from Oban (hotel can
£60-85 pick you up), the best of the bigger, proper hotels on Mull. Decent rooms, spa and
pool. Bit of a drive to an alternative restaurant.

16 ROOMS **Tobermory Hotel** 01688 302091 On the waterfront. Creature comforts, great
TV outlook in the middle of the bay. 10 rooms to front. Restaurant ok and others
£38-45 nearby. Very much downtown Tobermory, both hotel and restaurant are probably
better than they have to be – no faint praise intended.

27 ROOMS **St Columba Hotel** www.stcolumba-hotel.co.uk · 01681 700304 · **Iona**
MID MAR-OCT Shares some ownership and ideals of the Argyll (above) and very close on the road
£38-45 and adjacent to the abbey. Larger and more purpose-built than the Argyll, so some
uniformity in rooms. Nice views; extensive lawn and market garden. Relaxing and
just a little religious. Menu has good vegetarian options. Rooms include 9 singles.

S.Y. Hostel In Tobermory main street on bay. Report: 1155/HOSTELS.

Caravan Parks At Fishnish (all facilities, near ferry) Craignure and Fionnphort.

Camping Tobermor on the Dervaig Rd, Craignure (1212/CAMPING WITH KIDS).
Calgary Beach and at Loch Na Keal shore (1200/WILD CAMPING).

WHERE TO EAT

£22-32 ✓ **Highland Cottage** 01688 302030 Only real fine dining on Mull and the local night out so must book. All the niceties. 2261/ISLAND RESTAURANTS.

£15-22 ✓ **Dovecote Restaurant, Calgary Hotel** www.calgary.co.uk · 01688
ATMOS   400256 · Calgary Local produce in a wine-bar setting. Mellow people, art/sculpture in the woods outside. For anyone with a boho/arty bent or kids, this is definitely the coolest dining room on Mull. 2264/ISLAND RESTAURANTS.

✓ **Glengorm Farm Coffeeshop** Excellent daytime eats outside Tobermory. The best casual daytime dining. Report: 1390/TEAROOMS.

£15-22 ✓ **Café Fish** 01688 301253 · Tobermory Macdonald sisters' brilliant caff in the white building at the pier on corner of the bay. Bright upstairs room and terrace on the dock – Johnny's boat moored at the quayside supplies some of their excellent seafood, the rest is meticulously sourced (great mussels from Inverlussa). Home cooking, sensible wine list, nice puds. Lunch and 6-9pm. Closed Jan/Feb

£22-32 **Ninth Wave** www.ninthwaverestaurant.co.uk · 01681 700757 · near Fionnphort A far-flung fine-dining experience in a gorgeous converted croft using local and organic produce. John and Carla Lamont share their passion for good, ecelctic food with you. Everything made here (well, you'd have to), including the chocs. Phone for opening hours and book. No tick coz I haven't been yet.

Mull Pottery www.mullpottery.com · 01688 302592 · Tobermory Mezzanine café above working pottery just outside Tobermory on road south to Craignure. Outside deck. Evening meals (best atmosphere) and usual daytime offerings though all home-baking. Locals do recommend. The ubiquitous teuchter music is on sale downstairs. All year. 7 days. LO 9pm.

£15 OR LESS **Island Bakery** www.islandbakery.co.uk · 01688 302225 · Tobermory Tom and Marjorie Nelson's Main St bakery-deli with quiches, salads and old-fashioned baking. Buy your picnic here. 7 days 8am-5pm. LO 7.45pm (winter weekends only).

£15 OR LESS **The Chip Van aka The Fisherman's Pier** 01688 302390 · Tobermory Tobermory's famous meals-on-wheels under the clock tower on the bay. As fresh as... and usually a queue. All year, 12.30pm-9pm. Closed Sun. (1359/FISH 'N' CHIPS)

WHAT TO SEE

Torosay Castle Walk or train (!) from Craignure. Fabulous gardens and fascinating insight into an endearing family's life. Teashop. (1770/CASTLES.) **Duart Castle** 5km Craignure. Seat of Clan Maclean. Impressive from a distance, homely inside. Good view of clan history and from battlements. Teashop. (1769/CASTLES.) **Eas Fors** Waterfall on Dervaig to Fionnphort road. Very accessible series of cataracts tumbling into the sea (1604/WATERFALLS). **The Mishnish** No mission to Mull complete without a night at the Mish (1265/BLOODY GOOD PUBS). **Ulva & Iona** (many references). **The Treshnish Isles** (Ulva Ferry or Fionnphort). Marvellous trips in summer (1721/BIRDS); walks from **Carsaig Pier** (2268/ISLAND WALKS); or up **Ben More** (1966/MUNROS); **Croig** and **Quinish** in north, by **Dervaig** and **Lochbuie** off the A849 at Strathcoil 9km south of Craignure: these are all serene shorelines to explore. **Aros Park** forest walk, from Tobermory, about 7km round trip.

Tourist Info Craignure · 01680 812377 All year. Tobermory · 01688 302182 **CalMac** www.calmac.co.uk · 08705 650000

2283 **Ferry** Northlink (0845 6000449). Stromness: from Aberdeen – Tue, Thu, Sat, Sun,
3 takes 6 hours; from Scrabster – 2/3 per day, takes 1.5 hours.
John o' Groats to Burwick (01955 611353), 40 minutes, up to 4 a day (May-Sep
only). Pentland Ferries from Gill (near John o' Groats) to St Margaret's Hope (01856
831226) – 3 a day, takes 1 hour.
By Air Flybe (0871 7002000). To Kirkwall: from Aberdeen – 3 daily;
from Edinburgh – 2 daily; from Glasgow – 1 daily; from Inverness – 2 daily;
from Wick – 1 daily (not weekends).

WHERE TO STAY

12 ROOMS **The Lynnfield** www.lynnfieldhotel.co.uk · 01856 872505 · Kirkwall Holm
TEL · TV Rd adjacent to Highland Park (1488/WHISKY) and overlooking the town. Kirkwall's
£45-60 most comfy, sporting '4 Stars' and with good local reputation for food. And
congenial.

8 ROOMS **Foveran Hotel** www.foveranhotel.co.uk · 01856 872389 · St Ola A964
TEL · TV · ECO Orphir road; 5km from Kirkwall. Scandinavian-style, low-rise hotel is a friendly,
NO PETS informal place serveing traditional food using local ingredients; separate vegetarian
£38-45 menu. Great value. Small but comfy and light rooms; garden overlooks Scapa Flow.

13 ROOMS **Merkister Hotel** 01856 771366 · Harray Overlooking loch, north but midway
TEL · TV · ECO between Kirkwall and Stromness. A fave with fishers and twitchers; handy for
£38-45 archaeological sites and possibly the Orkney hotel 'of choice'. Rooms small; good
bar meals.

42 ROOMS **Stromness Hotel** 01856 850298 Orkney's biggest hotel, made over à la mode.
TEL · TV Even has lifts. Central and picturesque. Flattie Bar a wee gem.
£38-45

6 ROOMS **Woodwick House** www.woodwickhouse.co.uk · 01856 751330 · Evie On
£38-45 A966 1km before the village. James Bryan's comfy country house and garden, near
shore with views to Gairsay and Wyre islands. A great retreat. Home cooking, real
fires, local produce and, rare in Orkney, gorgeous, wild, woody grounds. Good
value.

S.Y. Hostels www.syha.org.uk · 01856 850589 · Stromness Excellent
location.
Kirkwall · 01856 872243 The largest.
Other hostels at Hoy, North and South Ronaldsay, Birsay, Sanday.

ECO ✓ **Bis Geos Hostel** www.bisgeos.co.uk · 01857 677420 · Westray Hostel
with 2 self-catering cottages. Traditional features and some luxuries.

✓ **The Barn** www.thebarnwestray.co.uk · 01857 677214 · Westray Near
Pierowall village. 4-star self-catering hostel in renovated stone barn. Great
views.

Peedie Hostel 01856 875477 · Ayre Road, Kirkwall On the front. Private
bedroom (3), sleep 2 or 4, own keys.

Camping/Caravan Kirkwall · 01856 879900 & Stromness · 01856 873535

WHERE TO EAT

3 ROOMS **The Creel Inn & Restaurant With Rooms** www.thecreelinn.co.uk ·
£22-32 01856 831311 · St Margaret's Hope On South Ronaldsay, 20km south of
Kirkwall. In a wild area, an accolade-laden restaurant and long Orkney's finest
though for sale '09 so check for opening hours.

£22-32 **Foveran Hotel** 01856 872389 · St Ola 4km Kirkwall. Excellent views and
decent, locally sourced food. See *Where to Stay.*

£22-32 **Woodwick House** 01856 751330 · Evie Intimate, even romantic dining. Good
cookery rather than cuisine. See *Where to Stay.*

£22-32 **The Lynnfield** 01856 872505 Possibly the best meal in Kirkwall. See *Where to
Stay.*

£15-22 **Kirkwall Hotel** 01856 872232 Long-established central hotel overlooking the
harbour. Popular with locals.

£15-22 **The Hamnavoe Restaurant** 01856 850606 · 35 Graham Place, Stromness
Off main street. Seafood is their speciality, especially lobster. Apr-Oct; Tue-Sun
6.30pm-late. Nov-Mar open weekends only.

£15 OR LESS **Julia's Café & Bistro** 01856 850904 · Stromness Home baking, blackboard
and vegetarian specials. Internet. A favourite with the locals. Gets busy – fill yourself up before the ferry journey! Open all year, 7 days 9am-5pm (from 10am Sun).
Phone for winter opening hours.

The Van Brough of Birsay Bere bannocks (a speciality), home-made soups,
Orkney cheese from a van in the car park at the Brough with spectacular views. 7
days from 11am.

WHAT TO SEE

Skara Brae 25km west of Kirkwall. Amazingly well-preserved underground
labyrinth, a 5,000-year-old village. Report: 1800/PREHISTORIC SITES.

The Old Man of Hoy on Hoy; 30-minute ferry 2 or 3 times a day from
Stromness. 3-hour walk along spectacular coast. See 2275/ISLAND WALKS.

Standing Stones of Stenness, The Ring of Brodgar, Maes Howe Around
18km west of Kirkwall on A965. Strong vibrations. Report: 1801/PREHISTORIC SITES.

Yesnaby Sea Stacks 24km west of Kirkwall. A precarious cliff top at the end of
the world. Report: 1926/ENCHANTING PLACES.

Italian Chapel 8km south of Kirkwall at first causeway. A special act of faith.
Inspirational and moving. Report: 1855/CHURCHES.

Skaill House 01856 841501 · Skara Brae 17th-century 'mansion' built on
Pictish cemetery. Set up as it was in the 1950s; with Captain Cook's crockery in the
dining room looking remarkably unused. Apr-Sep; 7 days 9.30am-6pm (or by
appointment). Tearoom and visitor centre and HS link with Skara are adjacent.

St Magnus Cathedral (1855/CHURCHES); **Stromness** (1557/COASTAL VILLAGES); **The Pier Arts Centre** (2155/INTERESTING GALLERIES); **Tomb of the Eagles** (1807/PREHISTORIC SITES); **Marwick Head** and many of the smaller islands (1703/BIRDS); **Scapa Flow** (1898/BATTLEGROUNDS); **Highland Park Distillery** (1488/WHISKY); **Puffins** (1732/BIRDS).

Craft Trail & Artists' Studio Trail Take in some traditional arts and crafts. Lots of souvenir potential but generally high-quality stuff. The tourist information centre has details and maps.

Many walks. Download walking guides: **www.walkorkney.com**
Tourist Info 01856 872856

The Best of Shetland

2284
4
Ferry Northlink (0845 6000 449). Aberdeen-Lerwick: Mon, Wed, Fri – departs 7pm, 12 hours. Tue, Thu, Sat, Sun – departs 5pm (via Orkney, arrives 11.45pm), 14 hours.
By air Flybe www.flybe.com (0871 7000535). To Sumburgh: from Aberdeen (5 a day, 3 Sat, 3 Sun). From Inverness (2 a day). From Glasgow (1 a day). From Edinburgh (3 a day, 2 a day at weekends).

WHERE TO STAY

5 ROOMS
MAR-OCT
TV
£45-60
✓**Burrastow House** 01595 809307 · **Walls** 40 minutes from Lerwick. Most guides and locals agree this is the place to stay on Shetland. Peaceful Georgian house with views to Island of Vaila. Wonderful home-made/produced food. Full of character with food (set menu; order day before), service and rooms the best on the island.

22 ROOMS
TEL · TV
£38-45
✓**Busta House Hotel** www.bustahouse.com · 01806 522506 Historic country house at Brae just over 30 minutes from Lerwick. Elegant and tranquil. High standards, great malt selection.

30 ROOMS
£38-45
St Magnus Bay Hotel www.stmagnusbayhotel.co.uk · 01806 503372 · Far, far away in the northwest of the mainland 50km from Lerwick on the Hillswick coast, a distinctive, wooden-built (in 1900) hotel. Have to admit I haven't been here but it sounds eminently worth investigating.

17 ROOMS
TEL · TV
NO PETS
£45-60
Kveldsro Hotel www.shetlandhotels.com · 01595 692195 · **Lerwick** Pronounced 'Kel-ro'. Probably best proposition in Lerwick; overlooking harbour. Reasonable standard at a price. Locals do eat here.

6 ROOMS
TEL · TV
£45-60
Westings, The Inn On The Hill www.westings.shetland.co.uk · 01595 840242 · **Whiteness** 12 km from Lerwick. Breathtaking views down Whiteness Voe. Excellent base for exploring. Large selection of real ales. Campsite alongside.

Almara B&B www.almara.shetland.co.uk · 01806 503261 · **Hillswick** We don't usually venture into the world of the B&B in this book but, although we haven't stayed ourselves, couldn't ignore numerous good reports of Mrs Williamson's 4-star establishment. Friendly family home with good food and, they say, nice vibes.

S.Y. Hostel: Islesburgh House www.islesburgh.org.uk · 01595 692114 · Lerwick Beautifully refurbished and very central. A 5-star hostel. Also home of the excellent Islesburgh House Café. Open Apr-Sep.

Camping Bods (fisherman's barns). Cheap sleep in wonderful sea-shore settings. **The Sail Loft** at Voe; **Grieve House** at Whalsay; **Windhouse Lodge** at Mid Yell; **Voe House** at Walls; **Betty Mouat's Cottage** at Dunrossness; **Johnnie Notions** at Eshaness. Remember to take sleeping mats. Check tourist information centre for details: 01595 693434.

WHERE TO EAT

£22-32 ✓**Burrastow House** Walls & **Busta House Hotel** Brae See *Where to Stay*, previous page. The best meals in the islands.

£15 OR LESS ✓**Hays Dock Café Restaurant** www.haysdock.co.uk · 01595 741596 · Lerwick Part of the Shetland Museum & Archive. Contemporary and beautiful space with great views of Lerwick Harbour. Excellent, all-day café, dinner at weekends.

£15 OR LESS **The Spiggie Hotel** www.thespiggiehotel.co.uk · 01950 460409 · Dunrossness 8km Sumburgh Airport, 32km Lerwick. Small, personally run country hotel that is especially good for bar meals.

£22-32 **Monty's Bistro** 01595 696555 · **Mounthooly Street, Lerwick** Up the road from tourist information centre. Renovated building in light Med décor. Best bet in town. Good service; imaginative menu using Shetland's finest seasonal ingredients. Bistro closed Sun/Mon (open Mon evening in season). Lunch and LO 9pm.

£15 OR LESS **The Olive Tree** 01595 697222 · **Lerwick** Nice deli/café/takeaway in the Toll Clock Shopping Centre. Home-made stuff. Daytime only.

£15-22/ **The Maryfield Hotel** 01595 820207 · **Bressay** 5-minute ferry ride from
£22-32 Lerwick to Bressay. Better known for its seafood rather than accommodation, both bar and dining room menus worth a look. LO are for those off the 8pm ferry but book ahead. Don't miss the return ferry.

£15-22 **Da Haaf Restaurant** www.nafc.ac.uk · 01595 880747 · **Scalloway** Part of the North Atlantic Fisheries College, Port Arthur. Basically a canteen but fresh Shetland seafood overlooking the harbour at reasonable prices more than makes up for the plastic trays and fluorescent lights. Daytime only. Closed Sat/Sun.

£15 OR LESS **Osla's Café** www.oslas.co.uk · 01595 696005 · **Commercial Street, Lerwick** Incredibly good value. Cosy and very child-friendly. Art exhibitions on walls. Upstairs La Piazza is a good bet for supper. LO 9pm.

£15 OR LESS **The Peerie Shop Café** www.peerieshopcafe.com · 01595 692816 · **The Esplanade, Lerwick** A local delicacy! 9am-6pm. Closed Sun.

Pub food also recommended at the following:

£15 OR LESS **The Mid Brae Inn** 01806 522634 · **Brae** 32km north of Lerwick. Lunch and supper till 8.45pm (9.30pm weekends), 7 days. Big portions of filling pub grub.

The Pierhead 01806 588332 · **Lower Voe**

WHAT TO SEE

Mousa Broch & Jarlshof See 1804/PREHISTORIC SITES. Also **Clickimin** broch.

Shetland Museum & Archives See 2125/HISTORY & HERITAGE.

Old Scatness 01595 694688 A fascinating, award-winning excavation – site of one of the world's best-preserved Iron Age villages. Ongoing and accessible; climb the tower and witness the unearthing first-hand. Tours, demonstrations and exhibitions. 5 minutes from airport. Open Jul-Aug only.

St Ninian's Isle Bigton 8km north of Sumburgh on West Coast. An island linked by exquisite shell-sand. Hoard of Pictish silver found in 1958 (now in Edinburgh). Beautiful, serene spot.

Scalloway 7km west of Lerwick, a township once the ancient capital of Shetland, dominated by the atmospheric ruins of Scalloway Castle.

Noup Of Noss Isle Of Noss, off Bressay 8km west of Lerwick by frequent ferry and then boat (also direct from Lerwick 01595 692577 or via tourist information centre), May-Sep only. National Nature Reserve with spectacular array of wildlife.

Up-Helly-Aa www.up-helly-aa.org.uk Festival in Lerwick on the last Tue in Jan. Ritual with hundreds of torchbearers and much fire and firewater. Norse, northern and pagan. A wild time can be had.

Sea Races The Boat Race every midsummer from Norway. Part of the largest North Sea international annual yacht race.

Bonhoga Gallery & Weisdale Mill 01595 830400 Former grain mill housing Shetland's first purpose-built gallery. Good café.

Island Trails Historic tours of Lerwick and the islands. Book through tourist information centre (or 01950 422408). Day trips, evening runs or short tours.

Tourist Info 01595 693434

Index

The numbers listed against index entries refer to the page on which the entry appears and not the entry's item number.

A Declaration of Fallibility

Unlike other guides, *Scotland the Best* is thoroughly revised every two years, almost everywhere in it is revisited personally. But we don't have a floorfull of fact checkers ascertaining the accuracy of every item. So if something's wrong and slips through the edit, forgive me, I'm sorry. Please let me know (see below) and I can put it right for next time.

Your Help Needed

Scotland the Best wouldn't be the best if I didn't receive feedback and helpful suggestions from so many people. It is an interactive book because so many of you seem to know what sort of places are likely to fit. With each new edition I believe I get closer to the definitive best guide including everywhere in Scotland that's good. This completeness is because people write to tell me. And I hope very much that they will continue to do so. *Scotland the Best* is supposed to follow the inside track to Scotland and you who live here, or are experiencing it as a visitor, are on it. Send me the word!

This edition it's easier to contact me: the new email address is below but if you want to send an old-fashioned but very welcome letter you can write, too. Please send your comments or suggestions to:

Peter Irvine/*Scotland the Best*
Collins Reference
HarperCollins Publishers
77–85 Fulham Palace Road
London W6 8JB

Or email **stb@lumison.co.uk**

For sharing this information, HarperCollins will be happy to share out good whisky and cheese. A bottle of malt and a drum of Tobermory cheddar will be presented at the launch of the next edition, to the best three suggestions received by 31 August 2011. Recommendations can be for any category or number of categories, and anywhere that you recommend will be included next time if it checks out. Please give reasons for your recommendation and directions if it is hard to find.